Welcome to the 75th Symposium on Molecular Spectroscopy
June 20-24, 2022
Urbana-Champaign, IL

On behalf of the Executive Committee, I extend a heartfelt welcome to all the attendees of the 75th Symposium and welcome you to the University of Illinois at Urbana-Champaign.

The Symposium presents research in fundamental molecular spectroscopy and a wide variety of related fields and applications. The continued vitality and significance of spectroscopy is annually re-affirmed by the number of talks, their variety, and the fact that many are given by students. These presentations are the heart of the meeting and are documented by this Abstract Book. Equally important is the information flowing from informal exchanges and discussions. As organizers, we strive to provide an environment that facilitates both kinds of interactions.

The essence of the meeting lies in the scientific discussions and your personal experiences this week independent of the number of times that you have attended this meeting. It is our sincere hope that you will find this meeting informative and enjoyable both scientifically and personally, whether it is your first or 50th meeting. If we can help to enhance your experience, please do not hesitate to ask the Symposium staff or the Executive Committee.

Josh Vura-Weis
Symposium Chair

SCHEDULE OF TALKS

Monday (M) 1
Tuesday (T) 9
Wednesday (W) 24
Thursday (R) 39
Friday (F) 47

ABSTRACTS

Monday (M) 54
Tuesday (T) 92
Wednesday (W) 160
Thursday (R) 235
Friday (F) 277

AUTHOR INDEX 313

VENUE AND SPONSOR INFORMATION FOLLOWS AUTHOR INDEX

75th INTERNATIONAL SYMPOSIUM ON MOLECULAR SPECTROSCOPY

International Advisory Committee
Gang Feng, Chongqing University
Asuka Fujii, Tohoku University
Etienne Garand, University of Wisconsin-Madison
Marsha Lester, University of Pennsylvania
Helen Leung, Amherst College, Chair
Jinjun Liu, Louisville University
Mike McCarthy, Harvard-Smithsonian Center for Astrophysics
Anne McCoy, University of Washington
Laura McCunn-Jordan, Marshall University
Sonia Melandri, University of Bologna
Stefanie Milam, NASA Goddard
Terry Miller, Ohio State University
Yasuhiro Ohshima, Tokyo Institute of Technology
Brooks Pate, University of Virginia
Anthony Remijan, National Radio Astronomy Observatory
Amanda Ross, University Lyon 1
Maria Sanz, King's College London
Melanie Schnell, Deutsches Elektronen-Synchrotron DESY, Hamburg
Maria Luisa Senent, Instituto de Estructura de la Materia, Spain
Steve Shipman, New College of Florida
Jacob Stewart, Connecticut College
Tim Zwier, Sandia National Laboratories

Executive Committee
Josh Vura-Weis, Chair
Brian DeMarco
Dana Dlott
Gary Eden
Nick Glumac
Martin Gruebele
So Hirata
Leslie Looney
Ben McCall
Dave Woon

Please send correspondence to
Josh Vura-Weis
International Symposium
 on Molecular Spectroscopy
Department of Chemistry
600 S. Mathews Avenue
Urbana IL 61801 USA
e-mail: chair@isms.illinois.edu
http://isms.illinois.edu

Mini-Symposia

BENCHMARKING IN SPECTROSCOPY

Organized by: **Emilio Cocinero** (Universidad del País Vasco), **Gang Feng** (Chongqing University), **Daniel Obenchain** (Georg-August-Universität Göttingen). This will be a forum to compare computational data sets to experimental results, and discuss the quality and methods employed. Invited Speakers: **Taija Fischer** (University of Göttingen), **Brian Esselman** (University of Wisconsin, Madison), **Qian Gou** (Chongqing University), **Lan Cheng** (Johns Hopkins University)

MACHINE LEARNING

Organized by **Kelvin Lee** (MIT), **Daniel Tabor** (Texas A&M University). This mini-symposium will focus on the development and application of the rapidly advancing field of machine learning to spectroscopic problems, with a diverse set of practitioners (experimental and theoretical) and applications. Invited Speakers: **Heather Kulik** (MIT), **Thomas Markland** (Stanford), **Andrés Montoya-Castillo** (University of Colorado Boulder), **Steven Shipman** (New College of Florida), **Andrew White** (University of Rochester)

SPECTROSCOPY MEETS CHEMICAL DYNAMICS

Organized by **David Osborn** (Sandia National Lab), **Krupa Ramasesha** (Sandia National Lab), **Timothy Zwier** (Sandia National Lab). This mini-symposium brings together researchers in the fascinating area at the interface between spectroscopy and dynamics, in which frequency domain and time-domain experimental measurements can work in concert with advances in theory to uncover the unique signatures of dynamical events over a wide range of timescales. Invited Speakers: **Randall Goldsmith** (University of Wisconsin, Madison), **Steve Leone** (UC-Berkeley), **Melanie Reber** (University of Georgia), **Dave Townsend** (Heriot-Watt University)

Picnic (Tuesday)

The Symposium picnic will be held on **Tuesday evening** at Ikenberry Commons. The cost of the picnic is included in your registration (at below cost to students), so that all may attend the event. The **Coblentz Society** is the host for refreshments for one hour.

Sponsorship

We are pleased to acknowledge the many organizations that support the 75th Symposium. Principal funding comes from the **National Radio Astronomy Observatory** (NRAO). We also acknowledge the many efforts and contributions of **The University of Illinois** in hosting the meeting, including financial contributions from the Departments of Chemistry, Electrical and Computer Engineering, and Astronomy.

Our Corporate Sponsors are **Coblentz Society, Elsevier/JMS, Ideal Vacuum Products, Jasco, and Toptica**. Please see the back of this book for their advertisements.

We are also pleased to acknowledge **IOS Press/Biomedical Spectroscopy and Imaging, ACS/The Journal of Physical Chemistry, Light Conversion USA, and Renishaw** as Contributing Sponsors.

Our sponsors will have exhibits at the Symposium and we encourage you to visit their displays.

Rao Prize

The four Rao Prizes for the most outstanding student talks at the 2021 meeting will be presented. The winners are **Parker Crandall** (Technische Universität Berlin); **Nicholas Hölsch** (ETH Zuerich); **Wey-Wey Su** (Stanford University); and **James Thorpe** (University of Florida). The Rao Prize was created by a group of spectroscopists who, as graduate students, benefited from the emphasis on graduate student participation, which has been a unique characteristic of the Symposium. This year three more Rao Prize winners will be selected. The award is administered by a Prize Committee chaired by Jennifer van Wijngaarden (University of Manitoba), and is composed of Dan Obenchain (Georg-August-Universität Göttingen); Brooks Pate (University of Virginia); Maria Sanz (King's College London); Jacob Stewart (Connecticut College); and Tim Zwier, (Sandia National Lab). Any questions or suggestions about the Prize should be addressed to the Committee. Anyone (especially post-docs) willing to serve on a panel of judges should contact Jennifer van Wijngaarden (vanwijng@cc.umanitoba.ca).

Lewis E. Snyder Astrochemistry Award

The Snyder Award winner for the most innovative and unique astrochemical investigation in either observations, theory or laboratory work presented by a graduate student at the 2021 meeting is **Divita Gupta** (Institut de Physique de Rennes). This year one more Snyder Award winner will be selected. The award is administered by Anthony Remijan (NRAO). Anyone (especially post-docs) willing to serve on a panel of judges should email Anthony Remijan (aremijan@nrao.edu).

Miller Prize

The Miller Prize was created in honor of Professor Terry A. Miller, who served as chair of the International Symposium on Molecular Spectroscopy from 1992 to 2013. The Miller Prize for the best presentation given by a recent PhD at the 2021 meeting will be presented. The winner, **Jun Jiang** (Lawrence Livermore National Laboratory) will give a lecture on Thursday. The Miller Prize winner and his or her co-authors will be invited to submit an article to the Journal of Molecular Spectroscopy based on the research in the prize-winning talk. After passing the normal review process, the article will appear in the Journal with a caption identifying the paper with the talk that received the Miller Prize. The award is administered by a Prize Committee chaired by Mike Heaven (Emory University) and comprised Lan Cheng (Johns Hopkins University), Stephen Cooke (Purchase College, SUNY), Jinjun Liu (University of Louisville), Edwin Sibert (University of Wisconsin), Cristina Puzzarini (University of Bologna), Susanna Widucs-Weaver (University of Wisconsin, Madison) and Lucy Ziurys (University of Arizona). Any questions or suggestions about the Prize should be addressed to the Committee. Anyone willing to serve on a panel of judges should contact Mike Heaven (mheaven@emory.edu).

Jon T. Hougen Memorial Award

The Hougen Award was created in honor of Jon Hougen, to support the travel expenses of an exceptional young international spectroscopist who would otherwise be unable to attend the ISMS. The 2022 winners are **Lorrie Jacob** (University of Cambridge) and **Kenneth Koziol** (RWTH Aachen University) who will give talks in the WH and FB sessions, respectively. The Hougen award is administered by a Prize Committee consisting of Masaaki Baba (Kyoto University), Malgorzata Biczysko (Shanghai University), Anthony Remijan (NRAO), and Maria Sanz (King's College London).

Information

ACCOMMODATIONS

Check-In - Off hours check-in for dormitory accommodations is located in **Nugent Hall,** 207 E Gregory Drive and will be staffed 24/7. **On Sunday (only), check-in will be at Bousfield Hall, 1214 South First Street, from noon until ~10 PM.**

Check-Out - Off hours check-out for dormitory accommodations is located in **Nugent Hall,** 207 E Gregory Drive and will be staffed 24/7. **On Friday (only), check-out will be at Bousfield Hall, 1214 South First Street, from 7:00 AM – 1:30 PM.**

Aside from check-in on Sunday and check-out on Friday, the desk at Bousfield will be unstaffed.

PARKING

Parking permits are for lot E14 (map @ end of book). Purchase parking as part of your check-in at the dorm. You may purchase meter hang-tags for parking near the meeting rooms at the registration desk.

REGISTRATION

The registration desk is located in the Chemistry Library in Noyes Lab, and is open on Sunday from 4:00-6:00 PM, and Monday through Friday from 8:00 AM-4:30 PM. Refreshments will be available from 8:00 AM-4:30 PM. **It is possible that registration will be relocated nearby. Check for signs.**

CHEMISTRY LIBRARY

The Chemistry Library will be the home for our exhibitor space (plus coffee and donuts) again this year. The library has a few small conference rooms, and comfy chairs (and books!).

READY ROOM/STATION

We will have 2 desks in the Library with computers that you can use to test your powerpoint presentation. If you have any problems, the staff at the "Ready Station" (front counter in the library) can assist you.

INTERNET ACCESS/Wi-Fi

Each attendee will receive a login and password to access campus WiFi (SSID: IllinoisNet) as a guest. This access should work in most locations through campus. Please read the Internet Acceptable Use Policy below.

VIDEO UPLOAD

You must upload your video presentation **BEFORE MONDAY, JUNE 13th** on our web site. All files will then be available on the website for our virtual attendees to view.

PRESENTATION UPLOAD INFORMATION & AUDIO/VIDEO

Each session room is equipped with a laptop computer, onto which presentation files will be pre-loaded by Symposium staff. To submit your presentation file, you must go to the **Manage Presentations** link on our web site and follow the instructions. All files must be submitted by **11:59 PM CDT THE DAY**

BEFORE your presentation session. All submitted files will be loaded onto the presentation computer one half-hour prior to the beginning of the session.

ACKNOWLEDGMENTS

The Symposium Chair wishes to acknowledge the hard work of numerous people who made this meeting possible. First and foremost is the Symposium Coordinator Birgit McCall, who has smoothly and single-handedly taken care of almost all of the electronic and logistical aspects of the meeting. Second are our symposium assistants, Grant Barton, Lauren Boedicker, John Henry Burke, Kavita Desai, Conner Dykstra, Amanda Hungerford, Justin Malme, Brandon Rasmussen, Thomas Reboli, Angela Roesler, Juniper Shapiro, Laura Smith, Rachel Wallick, and Alison Marie Wallum, who have handled innumerable important details to ensure the sessions and exhibitions go well. I also thank Outgoing Chair Ben McCall for his guidance and help in my transition to Chair. I wish to acknowledge the hospitality of the Chemistry Department and the School of Chemical Sciences (as well as the School of Molecular and Cell Biology) in tolerating our takeover of their buildings.

LIABILITY

The Symposium fees DO NOT include provisions for the insurance of participants against personal injuries, sickness, theft, or property damage. Participants and companions are advised to obtain whatever insurance they consider necessary. The Symposium organizing committee, its sponsors, and individual committee members DO NOT assume any responsibility for loss, injury, sickness, or damages to persons or belongings, however caused. The statements and opinions stated during oral presentations or in written abstracts are solely the author's responsibilities and do not necessarily reflect the opinions of the organizers.

INTERNET ACCEPTABLE USE POLICY

Each attendee will receive a login and password to access campus WiFi (SSID: IllinoisNet) as a guest. Guest accounts are intended to support a broad range of communications. Professional and appropriate etiquette is required. Anonymous access and posting through guest accounts is forbidden. All users must accept that their identity may be associated with any content they provide while using the service. By accessing the campus WiFi network, you expressly acknowledge and agree to the following:

Use of the guest account service is at your sole risk and the entire risk as to satisfactory quality and performance is with you. You agree not to use the guest account intentionally or unintentionally to violate any applicable local, state, national or international law, including, but not limited to, any regulations having the force of law. To the extent not prohibited by law, in no event shall the university be liable for personal injury, or any incidental, special, indirect or consequential damages whatsoever, including, without limitation, damages for loss of profits, loss of data, business interruption or any other commercial damages or losses, arising out of or related to your use or inability to use the guest account, however caused, regardless of the theory of liability (contract, tort or otherwise) and even if the university has been advised of the possibility of such damages. The use of the guest account is subject, but not limited to, all University policies and regulations detailed at the Campus Administrative Manual (http://www.cam.illinois.edu). See the University's Web Privacy Notice (http://www.vpaa.uillinois.edu/policies/web_privacy.cfm) for all applicable laws and policies.

MA. Plenary
Monday, June 20, 2022 – 8:30 AM
Room: Foellinger Auditorium

Chair: Cathy Murphy, University of Illinois at Urbana-Champaign, Urbana, IL, USA

Welcome   8:30
Timothy Killeen, President
University of Illinois

MA01   8:41 – 9:21
INTEGRATING CRYOGENIC ION CHEMISTRY AND OPTICAL SPECTROSCOPY: CAPTURING THE MOLECULAR LEVEL MECHANICS DRIVING BULK CHEMICAL BEHAVIORS FROM CATALYSIS TO THE SPECTRAL DYNAMICS OF WATER, Mark Johnson

MA02   9:26 – 10:06
CHEMISTRY IN THE ULTRACOLD REGIME: PRECISION MOLECULAR ASSEMBLY AND TEST OF STATISTICAL REACTION DYNAMICS, Kang-Kuen Ni

Intermission

FLYGARE AWARDS   10:36
Introduction by Yunjie Xu, University of Alberta

MA03   10:45 – 11:00
VIBRATIONAL SPECTRAL SIGNATURES AND DYNAMICS OF STRONG INTRAMOLECULAR H-BONDS INVESTIGATED WITH GAS-PHASE ION AND SOLUTION-PHASE ULTRAFAST INFRARED SPECTROSCOPIES, Joseph Fournier

MA04   11:05 – 11:20
NEW FRONTIERS IN COSMIC CARBON CHEMISTRY, Brett A. McGuire

MA05   11:25 – 11:40
PROBLEMS, PROBLEMS, PROBLEMS: THE LONG JOURNEY OF PHENYL ACETATE, Lynn Ferres, Wolfgang Stahl, Luca Evangelisti, Assimo Maris, Sonia Melandri, Walther Caminati, Ha Vinh Lam Nguyen

MA06   11:45 – 12:25
SPECTROSCOPIC STUDIES OF CHIRALITY, Anne Zehnacker-Rentien

MH. Mini-symposium: Spectroscopy meets Chemical Dynamics
Monday, June 20, 2022 – 1:45 PM
Room: 100 Noyes Laboratory

Chair: Stephen R. Leone, University of California, Berkeley, Berkeley, CA, USA

MH01 *Journal of Molecular Spectroscopy Review Lecture* 1:45 – 2:15
MAPPING EXTENDED REACTION COORDINATES IN PHOTOCHEMICAL DYNAMICS, Dave Townsend

MH02 2:21 – 2:36
FULLY ISOMER-RESOLVED SPECTROSCOPY AND ULTRAFAST DYNAMICS, Grite L. Abma, Daniel Horke

MH03 2:39 – 2:54
ABSOLUTE-PHASE-RESOLVED STRONG FIELD IONIZATION, Yasashri Ranganath Ranathunga, Duke A. Debrah, Gabriel A. Stewart, Suk Kyoung Lee, Wen Li

MH04 2:57 – 3:12
ALL-OPTICAL THREE-DIMENSIONAL ELECTRON MOMENTUM IMAGING, Emmanuel Ayorinde Orunesajo, Gihan Basnayake, Yasashri Ranganath Ranathunga, Gabriel A. Stewart

Intermission

MH05 3:54 – 4:09
PROBING THE VIBRATIONAL WAVE PACKET DYNAMICS ON THE ELECTRONIC GROUND STATE OF NEUTRAL SILVER TETRAMER: VIBRATIONAL FREQUENCIES, ANHARMONICITIES AND ANISOTROPY, Jiaye Jin, Max Grellmann, Knut R. Asmis

MH06 4:12 – 4:27
PHOTOFRAGMENTATION PATHWAYS OF N-BUTYL BROMIDE, Lauren F Heald, Scott G Sayres

MH07 4:30 – 4:45
OBSERVATION OF RESONANCES IN THE F+NH$_3$ REACTION VIA TRANSITION-STATE SPECTROSCOPY, Mark C Babin, Martin DeWitt, Jascha Lau, Hongwei Song, Hua Guo, Daniel Neumark

MH08 4:48 – 5:03
TRACKING THE PHOTOIONIZATION OF ANILINE IN WATER: THE ROLE OF $\pi\sigma^*$ STATES, Raúl Montero, Iker Lamas, Asier Longarte

MH09 5:06 – 5:21
PULSE INDUCED DARK STATE OF ACETYLENE, Antoine Aerts, Pascal Kockaert, Simon Pierre Gorza, Jean Vander Auwera, Nathalie Vaeck

MH10 5:24 – 5:39
A PHASE DIAGRAM FOR ENERGY FLOW-LIMITED REACTIVITY, Chenghao Zhang, Edwin Sibert, Martin Gruebele

MI. Structure determination
Monday, June 20, 2022 – 1:45 PM
Room: 116 Roger Adams Lab

Chair: M. Eugenia Sanz, King's College London, London, United Kingdom

MI01   1:45 – 2:00
Q| R: QUANTUM-BASED REFINEMENT OF BIOMACROMOLECULES, Malgorzata Biczysko, Yanting Xu, Nigel W Moriarty, Holger Kruse, Mark P Waller, Pavel V Afonine

MI02   2:03 – 2:18
THE NICOTINIC-AGONIST CYTISINE: THE ROLE OF THE NH···N INTERACTION , Raúl Aguado, Santiago Mata, Miguel Sanz-Novo, Elena R. Alonso, Iker León, José L. Alonso

MI03   2:21 – 2:36
WETTING FERROCENE AS A WAY TO INVESTIGATE ITS GAS PHASE STRUCTURE BY ROTATIONAL SPECTROSCOPY, Susana Blanco, Andres Verde, Juan Carlos Lopez, Manuel Yáñez, Ibon Alkorta

MI04   2:39 – 2:54
THE SHAPE OF PROGESTERONE, Elena R. Alonso, Aran Insausti, Lucie Kolesniková, Iker León, José L. Alonso

MI06   3:15 – 3:30
UNDERSTANDING THE SHAPE OF β-D-ALLOSE: A LASER ABLATION ROTATIONAL STUDY., Gabriela Juárez, Santiago Mata, José L. Alonso, Elena R. Alonso, Iker León

Intermission

MI07   4:12 – 4:27
THE PRECISE EQUILIBRIUM STRUCTURE DETERMINATION OF CHLOROBENZENE (C_6H_5Cl) BY ROTATIONAL SPECTROSCOPY, Natalie A. Schuler, P. Matisha Dorman, Brian J. Esselman, Maria Zdanovskaia, Bryan Changala, John F. Stanton, Michael C McCarthy, R. Claude Woods, Robert J. McMahon

MI08   4:30 – 4:45
HIGH ACCURACY MOLECULAR STRUCTURES, Nitai Prasad Sahoo, John F. Stanton

MI09   4:48 – 5:03
MICROWAVE SPECTROSCOPY AND STRUCTURE DETERMINATION OF ORGANOSILICON COMPOUNDS: A CELEBRATION OF A DECADE OF COLLABORATION, Nathan A. Seifert, Thomas M. C. McFadden, Gamil A Guirgis, Nicole Moon, Amanda Duerden, G. S. Grubbs II

MI10   5:06 – 5:21
CONFORMATIONAL ANALYSIS OF CYCLOBUTANECARBOXYLIC ACID , Karla V. Salazar, Joshua E. Isert, Nicole Moon, G. S. Grubbs II, Zunwu Zhou, Stephen G. Kukolich, Michael J. Carrillo, Shervin Fatehi, Wei Lin

MI11   5:24 – 5:39
A ROTATIONAL STUDY OF 6-APA , Sergio Mato, Santiago Mata, Elena R. Alonso, José L. Alonso, Iker León

MJ. Comparing theory and experiment
Monday, June 20, 2022 – 1:45 PM
Room: B102 Chemical and Life Sciences

Chair: Edwin Sibert, University of Wisconsin–Madison, Madison, WI, USA

MJ01   1:45 – 2:00
A FLEXIBLE APPROACH TO VIBRATIONAL PERTURBATION THEORY, Mark A. Boyer, Anne B McCoy

MJ02   2:03 – 2:18
UNDERSTANDING $X^- \cdots HOCl$ (X=Cl, Br, I) THROUGH VIBRATIONAL PERTURBATION THEORY, Mark A. Boyer, Coire F Gavin-Hanner, Anne B McCoy

MJ03   2:21 – 2:36
VIBRONIC COUPLING MECHANISMS IN THE NITRATE RADICAL, John F. Stanton

MJ04   2:39 – 2:54
SUB TWENTY WAVENUMBER COMPUTATIONAL PREDICTION OF MOLECULAR BOND ENERGIES AND THE INTRIGUING BDE OF F_2, James H. Thorpe, Josie L. Kilburn, David Feller, Bryan Changala, David H. Bross, Branko Ruscic, John F. Stanton

MJ05   2:57 – 3:12
ON THE USEFULNESS OF ELECTRON PROPAGATOR METHODS FOR A RELIABLE COMPUTATION OF EXPERIMENTAL OBSERVABLES, Lorenzo Paoloni

MJ06   3:15 – 3:30
EXTENSIONS TO GUIDED DIFFUSION MONTE CARLO FOR EXCITED STATES, Jacob M Finney, Anne B McCoy

Intermission

MJ07   4:12 – 4:27
DIRECT ELUCIDATION OF THE REASON FOR ALMOST THE SAME BOND LENGTHS FOR THE C–H AND C–D BONDS IN C_6H_6 AND C_6D_6: A PATH INTEGRAL MOLECULAR DYNAMICS STUDY, Taro Udagawa, Hikaru Tanaka, Kazuaki Kuwahata, Masaaki Baba, Tsuneo Hirano, Umpei Nagashima, Masanori Tachikawa

MJ08   4:30 – 4:45
RELATIVISTIC COUPLED-CLUSTER CALCULATIONS OF CHLORINE L-EDGE SPECTRUM OF CH_2ICL, Zhe Lin, Xuechen Zheng, Chaoqun Zhang, Lan Cheng

MJ09   4:48 – 5:03
HIGH-RESOLUTION LASER SPECTROSCOPY OF THE RYDBERG STARK MANIFOLD IN H_2, Nicolas Hölsch, Ioana Doran, Frédéric Merkt

MJ10   5:06 – 5:21
INTERPLAY OF ELECTRONIC CORRELATIONS AND ELECTRIC-QUADRUPOLE TRANSITIONS IN THE ISOLATED-CORE EXCITATION OF Sr BELOW THE $Sr^+(5g)$ THRESHOLD, Matthieu Génévriez, Ulli Eichmann

MJ11   5:24 – 5:39
INFRARED PHOTODISSOCIATION SPECTROSCOPY OF PLATINUM-CATION ACETYLENE COMPLEXES, Anna G Batchelor, Joshua H Marks, Timothy B Ward, Michael A Duncan

MK. Mini-symposium: Machine Learning
Monday, June 20, 2022 – 1:45 PM
Room: 217 Noyes Laboratory

Chair: Daniel P. Tabor, Texas A&M University, College Station, TX, USA

MK01   *INVITED TALK*   1:45 – 2:15
ELUCIDATING, ANALYZING, AND DESIGNING SPECTROSCOPIES: LEVERAGING THEORY AND CHEMICAL INTUITION TO GET THE MOST OUT OF MACHINE LEARNING, Thomas E Markland

MK02   2:21 – 2:36
LOW-FREQUENCY INFRARED SPECTRUM OF LIQUID WATER FROM MACHINE-LEARNING BASED PARTIAL ATOMIC CHARGES, Bowen Han, Christine M Isborn, Liang Shi

MK03   2:39 – 2:54
MULTI-FIDELITY DEEP LEARNING AND ACTIVE LEARNING FOR MOLECULAR OPTICAL PROPERTIES, Kevin P. Greenman, William H. Green, Rafael Gómez-Bombarelli

MK04   2:57 – 3:12
MULTIVARIATE ANALYSIS OF MOLECULAR SPECTROSCOPY DATA FOR COVID-19 DETECTION, Qizhong Liang, Ya-Chu Chan, Jutta Toscano, Kristen K. Bjorkman, Leslie A. Leinwand, Roy Parker, David J. Nesbitt, Jun Ye

Intermission

MK05   *INVITED TALK*   3:54 – 4:24
CAPTURING, PREDICTING, AND UNDERSTANDING OPTICAL SIGNALS: HARNESSING MACHINE LEARNING TO TACKLE ENERGY DISSIPATION IN THE CONDENSED PHASE, Andres Montoya-Castillo

MK06   4:30 – 4:45
SYMMETRY-CONSTRAINED MOLECULAR DYNAMICS, Andrew White, Sam Cox

MK07   4:48 – 5:03
ACCELERATING MANY-BODY EXPANSION THEORY THROUGH GRAPH CONVOLUTIONAL NETWORKS, Yili Shen, Chengwei Ju, Jun Yi, Zhou Lin, Hui Guan

ML. Small molecules
Monday, June 20, 2022 – 1:45 PM
Room: 1024 Chemistry Annex

Chair: Leah C O'Brien, Southern Illinois University, Edwardsville, IL, USA

ML01   1:45 – 2:00
CALCIUM MONOXIDE FORMATION IN LASER PLASMA STUDIED BY EMISSION AND FLUORESCENCE SPECTROSCOPY, Aleksandr Zakuskin, Babken Beglaryan, Andrey Popov, Timur A. Labutin

ML02   2:03 – 2:18
IN SEARCH OF EQUILIBRIUM IN LASER-PRODUCED CLOUD: ROLE OF PRESSURE, CHEMICAL QUENCHING, AND PLASMA EXPANSION, Timur A. Labutin, Aleksandr Zakuskin, Sergey Zaytsev, Andrey Popov, Vladislav E. Chernov, Alexey A. Berezhnoy, Ekaterina A. Bormotova, Andrey Stolyarov

ML03   2:21 – 2:36
TWO COLOR FORMALDEHYDE PLIF THERMOMETRY USING A BURST MODE LASER, Xunchen Liu

ML04   2:39 – 2:54
FLASH PYROLYSIS MECHANISM OF TRIMETHYLCHLOROSILANE BY FLASH PYROLYSIS VACUUM ULTRAVIOLET PHOTOIONIZATION TIME-OF-FLIGHT MASS SPECTROMETRY., Kuanliang Shao, Jonah Brunson, Yi Tian, Jingsong Zhang

ML05   2:57 – 3:12
ULTRAVIOLET SPECTROSCOPY OF SUBCRITICAL AND SUPERCRITICAL ETHANOL, Timothy W Marin, Ireneusz Janik

Intermission

ML06   3:54 – 4:09
COLLISIONAL RELAXATION OF LOW-FREQUENCY VIBRATIONAL MODES OF SMALL MOLECULES IN A PULSED SEEDED SUPERSONIC JET, Piyush Mishra, Alexander W Hull, Timothy J Barnum, Stephen L Coy, Robert W Field

ML07   4:12 – 4:27
ROTATIONAL LEVEL INTERVALS IN HD FROM CRYO-COOLED SUB-DOPPLER ROVIBRATIONAL SPECTROSCOPY, Meissa Diouf, Frank M.J. Cozijn, Edcel John Salumbides, Wim Ubachs

ML08   4:30 – 4:45
QUANTIFYING EMISSION OF NIR-I AND NIR-II DYES VIA FLUORESCENCE QUANTUM YIELD, David D.N. Ndaleh, Cameron L Smith, Mahesh Loku Yaddehige, Abdul Kalam Shaik, Davita Watkins, Nathan I Hammer, Jared Delcamp

ML09   4:48 – 5:03
FLUORESCENCE AND QUANTUM YIELD STUDIES OF NEW SWIR EMITTING RHODINDOLIZINE DYES, Abdul Kalam Shaik, Satadru Chatterjee, Kalpani Hirunika Wijesinghe, David D.N. Ndaleh, Amal Dass, Jared Delcamp, Nathan I Hammer

ML10   5:06 – 5:21
HIGHLY SELECTIVE GAS ANALYZER BASED ON MOLECULAR ROTATIONAL RESONANCE SPECTROSCOPY FOR SO_2 MONITORING IN AMBIENT AIR , Md Abrar Jamil, Sylvestre Twagirayezu, Justin L. Neill

ML11   5:24 – 5:39
SENSITIVITY TO VARIATION OF FUNDAMENTAL CONSTANTS FROM FREQUENCY MEASUREMENTS OF ACETYLENE REFERENCE TRANSITIONS, Florin Lucian Constantin

MM. Cold and ultracold molecules
Monday, June 20, 2022 – 1:45 PM
Room: 124 Burrill Hall

Chair: Mitsunori Araki, Tokyo University of Science, Shinjuku-ku, Tokyo, Japan

MM01   1:45 – 2:00
ELECTRONIC SPECTROSCOPY AND PHOTOIONIZATION OF LiBe, Thomas D. Persinger, Jiande Han, Michael Heaven

MM02   2:03 – 2:18
FLUORESCENCE SPECTROSCOPY DETECTION OF THE $4f^{-1}$ STATES OF YbF, Thomas D. Persinger, Jiande Han, Timothy Steimle, Michael Heaven

MM03   2:21 – 2:36
SINGLET-TRIPLET DOORWAY STATES OF ALUMINUM MONOFLUORIDE, Nicole Walter, Johannes Seifert, Stefan Truppe, Christian Schewe, Boris Sartakov, Gerard Meijer

MM04   2:39 – 2:54
FUNCTIONALIZED AROMATIC MOLECULES FOR LASER COOLING AND TRAPPING, Benjamin Augenbraun, Sean Burchesky, Guo-Zhu Zhu, Debayan Mitra, Claire E Dickerson, Guanming Lao, Zack Lasner, Anastassia Alexandrova, Wesley Campbell, Justin Caram, Eric Hudson, John M. Doyle

MM05   2:57 – 3:12
LASER SPECTROSCOPY OF BUFFER-GAS-COOLED POLYATOMIC MOLECULES, Yuiki Takahashi, Masaaki Baba, Katsunari Enomoto, Kana Iwakuni, Susumu Kuma, Ayami Hiramoto, Reo Tobaru, Yuki Miyamoto

Intermission

MM06   3:54 – 4:09
CRYOGENIC ION SPECTROSCOPY OF TRANSITION METAL-EDTA COMPLEXES: ION-DEPENDENT SPECTRAL AND STRUCTURAL SHIFTS, Madison M. Foreman, J. Mathias Weber

MM07   4:12 – 4:27
DEVELOPMENT OF A SUPERSONIC EXPENSION SOURCE FOR HIGH-RESOLUTION INFRARED SPECTROSCOPY OF ISOPRENE, Katarina Reyna, Binh Nguyet Vo, Sebastian Guerrero, Jacob Stewart

MM08   4:30 – 4:45
INTERSTELLAR PEPTIDE BOND FORMATION BY ACETALDEHYDE AND AMMONIA IN ANALOG ICE, Joshua H Marks, Jia Wang, André K. Eckhardt, N. Fabian Kleimeier, Andrew Martin Turner, Ralf Ingo Kaiser

MM09   4:48 – 5:03
THE COMPLEXES OF HYDROXYLAMINE VIA VIBRATIONAL AND ROTATIONAL SPECTROSCOPY, Xiaolong Li, Dingding Lv, Weixing Li, Mingfei Zhou

MM10   *Post-Deadline Abstract*   5:06 – 5:21
REACTION OF ELECTRONS TRAPPED IN CRYOGENIC MATRICES WITH BENZOPHENONE, Ankit Somani, Wolfram Sander

MN. Astronomy
Monday, June 20, 2022 – 1:45 PM
Room: 274 Medical Sciences Building

Chair: L. Margulès, Universite de Lille, Villeneuve de Ascq, France

MN01 1:45 – 2:00
NOEMA OBSERVATIONS OF COMPLEX ORGANIC CHEMISTRY IN THE W3 STAR-FORMING REGION, Will E. Thompson, Susanna L. Widicus Weaver, Dariusz Lis

MN02 2:03 – 2:18
A MACHINE LEARNING APPROACH TO CHARACTERIZING THE CHEMICAL INVENTORY OF ORION-KL, Haley N. Scolati, Joshua Carder, Eric Herbst, Brett A. McGuire, Kelvin Lee

MN03 2:21 – 2:36
USING HCO$^+$ LINE (& ITS ISOMERS) AS AN ASTROCHEMICAL TOOL TO PROBE THE STRUCTURE OF CLASS 0/I PROTOSTARS, Mihika Rao, Anthony Remijan, Adele Plunkett

MN04 2:39 – 2:54
MAGNETIC FIELD STRENGTH LIMITS IN A PROTOPLANETARY DISK FROM MULTI-WAVELENGTH ZEEMAN OBSERVATIONS, Rachel E. Harrison, Leslie Looney, Aassik Pazhani, Zhi-Yun Li, Haifeng Yang, Ian Stephens, Richard Teague, Richard Crutcher, Crystal L. Brogan, Erin Guilfoil Cox

MN05 2:57 – 3:12
DETECTION OF $c-C_3H_2$, NO, and CH_3CN TOWARDS MOLECULAR CLOUDS AT THE EDGE OF THE GALAXY, Lilia Koelemay, Lucy M. Ziurys

MN06 3:15 – 3:30
MOLECULAR LINE OBSERVATIONS IN TWO DUSTY STAR FORMING GALAXIES AT Z=6.9, Sreevani Jarugula

Intermission

MN07 4:12 – 4:27
HIGH-RESOLUTION MID-IR OBSERVATIONS OF SiO AND THE SEARCH FOR TiO IN THE CIRCUMSTELLAR ENVELOPE OF THE VARIABLE STAR χ Cyg, Guido W. Fuchs, Eileen Döring, Daniel Witsch, Thomas Giesen, John H. Lacy, Rohini S Giles, Thomas K Greathouse

MN08 4:30 – 4:45
EXAMINING ANOMALOUS PHOTOCHEMISTRY IN THE DENSE INNER WIND OF IRC+10216 THROUGH ALMA OBSERVATIONS OF HC_3N, Mark A. Siebert, Marie Van de Sande, Thomas J. Millar, Anthony Remijan

MN09 4:48 – 5:03
ALMA REVEALS THE MOLECULAR OUTFLOWS IN THE ENVELOPE OF HYPERGIANT VY CANIS MAJORIS, Ambesh Pratik Singh, Anita M Richards, Roberta M. Humphreys, Lucy M. Ziurys

MN10 5:06 – 5:21
REEXAMINING THE CHEMISTRY IN PROTOPLANETARY NEBULAE: M1-92, COTTON CANDY NEBULA, AND IRAS22036, Katherine R. Gold, Deborah Schmidt, Lucy M. Ziurys

MN11 5:24 – 5:39
AN ABSORPTION SURVEY OF C_3H^+ AND C_4H IN DIFFUSE CLOUDS TOWARD GALACTIC CONTINUUM REGIONS, Harshal Gupta, Kelvin Lee, Maryvonne Gerin, Michael C McCarthy

TA. Mini-symposium: Spectroscopy meets Chemical Dynamics
Tuesday, June 21, 2022 – 8:30 AM
Room: 100 Noyes Laboratory

Chair: Nathanael M. Kidwell, The College of William and Mary, Williamsburg, VA, USA

TA01   *INVITED TALK*   8:30 – 9:00
X-RAY MOLECULAR SPECTROSCOPIC DYNAMICS, Stephen R. Leone

TA02   9:06 – 9:21
ULTRAFAST XUV MAGNETIC CIRCULAR DICHROISM: OBSERVING SPIN TRANSPORT AT INTERFACES, Robert Baker, Martin Schultze, Harshad Gajapathy, Savini Sandunika Bandaranayake, Emily B Hruska, Stephen Londo

TA03   9:24 – 9:39
ULTRAFAST ELECTRON TRANSFER AND SPIN FLIP IN A HETEROBIMETALLIC COMPLEX, John H Burke, Josh Vura-Weis

TA04   9:42 – 9:57
MONITORING VALENCE-ELECTRON DYNAMICS IN MOLECULES WITH ULTRAFAST X-RAY DIFFRACTION, Haiwang Yong, Stefano M. Cavaletto, Shaul Mukamel

TA05   10:00 – 10:15
ULTRAFAST DYNAMICS OF TWO- AND THREE-BODY DISSOCIATION CAPTURED BY CORE-TO-VALENCE TRANSIENT ABSORPTION SPECTROSCOPY, Jan Tross, Neil C. Cole-Filipiak, Paul Schrader, Laura M McCaslin, Krupa Ramasesha

TA06   10:18 – 10:33
MAPPING COMPLEX PHOTOCHEMICAL REACTIONS USING FEMTOSECOND UV-PUMP XUV-PROBE PHOTO-ELECTRON SPECTROSCOPY, Daniel Horke, Grite L. Abma

Intermission

TA07   11:15 – 11:30
ELECTRON LOCALIZATION IN MOLECULES INTERACTING WITH INTENSE LASER PULSES, Agnieszka Jaron, Lauren Bauerle

TA08   11:33 – 11:48
PROBING SPATIAL EVOLUTION OF ULTRAFAST ELECTRONIC WAVEPACKETS WITH TWO-ELECTRON ANGULAR STREAKING, Gabriel A. Stewart, Duke A. Debrah, Gihan Basnayake, Suk Kyoung Lee, Wen Li

TA09   11:51 – 12:06
SIMULATING PHOTOEXCITATION WITH A LASER PULSE BEYOND THE PERTURBATIVE LIMIT, Diptesh Dey, Graham Worth

TA10   12:09 – 12:24
IMAGING THE REACTIVE RADICAL-CATION COMPLEX IN THE IONIZED LIQUID WATER, Ming-Fu Lin

TB. Mini-symposium: Benchmarking in Spectroscopy
Tuesday, June 21, 2022 – 8:30 AM
Room: 116 Roger Adams Lab

Chair: L. H. Coudert, Université Paris-Saclay, CNRS, Orsay, France

TB01   *INVITED TALK*   8:30–9:00
EXTENDING ACCURATE QUANTUM CHEMISTRY TO HEAVY ELEMENTS, Xuechen Zheng, Chaoqun Zhang, Lan Cheng

TB02   9:06–9:21
ELECTRONIC STRUCTURE OF RuO, Yao Yu, Lei Zhang, Xinwen Ma, Jie Yang

TB04   9:42–9:57
ACCURATE PREDICTION OF EQUILIBRIUM STRUCTURE FOR HEAVY ELEMENT CONTAINING MOLECULES, Chaoqun Zhang, Lan Cheng

TB05   10:00–10:15
LaO LINE LIST FOR THE $B^2\Sigma^+$- $X^2\Sigma^+$ BAND SYSTEM, Peter F. Bernath, Randika Dodangodage, Jacques Liévin

Intermission

TB06   10:57–11:12
PREDICTION AND INTERPRETATION OF TRANSITION METAL X-RAY SPECTRA USING REAL-TIME TIME-DEPENDENT DENSITY FUNCTIONAL THEORY, Jun Yi, Zhou Lin, Ying Zhu

TB07   11:15–11:30
SIMPLIFIED LR-TDDFT/ZORA APPROACH FOR GENERATING SPIN-ORBIT COUPLINGS FOR X-RAY ABSORPTION SPECTRA, Sarah Pak, Daniel R. Nascimento

TB08   11:33–11:48
VIBRONIC ANALYSIS OF MOLECULES WITH QUASI-DEGENERATE ELECTRONIC STATES, Ketan Sharma, Terry A. Miller, Jinjun Liu

TB09   11:51–12:06
ELECTRONIC SPECTROSCOPY OF THE $\tilde{A} - \tilde{X}$ TRANSITIONS OF JET-COOLED CALCIUM MONOALKOXIDE RADICALS: SPIN-VIBRONIC STRUCTURE OF NONLINEAR MOLECULES AS CANDIDATES FOR DIRECT LASER COOLING, Anam C. Paul, Hamzeh Telfah, Ketan Sharma, S M Shah Riyadh, Terry A. Miller, Jinjun Liu

TB10   12:09–12:24
ALKALI DIATOMICS: ASYMPTOTIC LONG RANGE BEHAVIOR OF ELECTRONIC MATRIX ELEMENTS BASED ON AB INITIO CALCULATIONS, Ekaterina A. Bormotova, Andrey Stolyarov

TB11   12:27–12:42
RELATIVISTIC DELTA-COUPLED-CLUSTER CALCULATIONS OF K-EDGE CORE-IONIZATION ENERGIES FOR THIRD-ROW ELEMENTS, Xuechen Zheng, Chaoqun Zhang, Lan Cheng

TC. Linelists
Tuesday, June 21, 2022 – 8:30 AM
Room: B102 Chemical and Life Sciences

Chair: Holger S. P. Müller, Universität zu Köln, Köln, NRW, Germany

TC01   8:30 – 8:45
HIGH-ACCURACY LINE LISTS OF METHANE AND FORMALDEHYDE BETWEEN 1240 AND 1380 cm^{-1} FROM FOURIER-TRANSFORM OPTICAL FREQUENCY COMB SPECTROSCOPY, Matthias Germann, Adrian Hjältén, Isak Silander, Aleksandra Foltynowicz, Vincent Boudon, Cyril Richard, Karol Krzempek, Arkadiusz Hudzikowski, Aleksander Gluszek, Grzegorz Soboń

TC02   8:48 – 9:03
IMPROVED CO_2 IR LINE LIST FOR 1500K - 3000K, Xinchuan Huang, David Schwenke, Richard S Freedman, Timothy J. Lee

TC03   9:06 – 9:21
AMES-1 296K IR LINE LISTS FOR CS_2 ISOTOPOLOGUES, Xinchuan Huang, David Schwenke, Timothy J. Lee

TC04   9:24 – 9:39
AMES-1 296K IR LINE LISTS FOR OCS ISOTOPOLOGUES, Xinchuan Huang, David Schwenke, Timothy J. Lee

TC05   9:42 – 9:57
AMES-1 296K IR LINE LISTS FOR N_2O ISOTOPOLOGUES, Xinchuan Huang, David Schwenke, Timothy J. Lee

Intermission

TC06   10:39 – 10:54
ROVIBRONIC INFRARED AND VISIBLE LINE LIST FOR O_2, Wilfrid Somogyi, Sergei N. Yurchenko, Gap-Sue Kim

TC07   10:57 – 11:12
EXOMOL ROVIBRONIC LINE LIST AND TEMPERATURE DEPENDENT PHOTODISSOCIATION CROSS SECTION CALCULATIONS FOR OH FROM *AB INITIO* ELECTRONIC STRUCTURE CALCULATIONS, Georgi B Mitev, Jonathan Tennyson, Sergei N. Yurchenko

TC08   11:15 – 11:30
HIGH LEVEL AB INITIO STUDY OF THE ROVIBRONIC SPECTRUM OF SULFUR MONOXIDE (SO): DIABATIC REPRESENTATION, Ryan Brady, Gap-Sue Kim, Wilfrid Somogyi, Sergei N. Yurchenko, Jonathan Tennyson

TC09   11:33 – 11:48
VISIBLE OPACITY OF M DWARFS AND HOT JUPITERS: THE TiO $B^3\Pi$- $X^3\Delta$ BAND SYSTEM, William D Cameron, Peter F. Bernath

TC10   11:51 – 12:06
RECENT UPDATES TO THE HITEMP DATABASE, Robert J. Hargreaves, Iouli E Gordon, Xinchuan Huang, Eamon K Conway, Laurence S. Rothman

TC11   12:09 – 12:24
A DIGITAL TELLURIUM ATLAS FOR SPECTRAL CALIBRATION, 19000 – 24000 cm^{-1}, Joseph M. Cardon, Tony Smith, Dennis Clouthier, Amanda J. Ross

TC12   12:27 – 12:42
LINE LISTS FOR $X^3\Sigma^-$ AND $a^1\Delta$ VIBRATION-ROTATION BANDS OF SO, Peter F. Bernath, Ryan Johnson, Jacques Liévin

TD. Rotational structure/frequencies
Tuesday, June 21, 2022 – 8:30 AM
Room: 217 Noyes Laboratory

Chair: Kyle N. Crabtree, University of California, Davis, CA, USA

TD01   8:30 – 8:45
MICROWAVE SPECTROSCOPY OF ISOTHIAZOLE, Hoga Furukawa, Kaori Kobayashi, Maria Zdanovskaia, Brian J. Esselman, R. Claude Woods, Robert J. McMahon

TD02   8:48 – 9:03
EXTENDED LABORATORY INVESTIGATION OF THE PURE ROTATIONAL SPECTRUM OF THE CH_2CN RADICAL IN THE (SUB-)MILLIMETER REGION (79-860 GHz), Olivia Chitarra, Thomas Sandow Hearne, Olivier Pirali, Marie-Aline Martin-Drumel

TD03   9:06 – 9:21
ELECTRICAL DISCHARGE OF NITROGEN CONTAINING MOLECULES: A DETAILED STUDY OF THE DISCHARGE PRODUCTS OF PYRROLE AND PYRIDINE, Eva Gougoula, Donatella Loru, Gayatri Batra, Melanie Schnell

TD04   9:24 – 9:39
ACCURATE SPECTROSCOPIC CHARACTERIZATION OF UNSATURATED CARBON-CHAINS OF ASTROCHEMICAL IMPORTANCE, Alessio Melli, Silvia Alessandrini, Vincenzo Barone, Mattia Melosso, Ningjing Jiang, Luca Dore, Cristina Puzzarini, Luca Bizzocchi, J.-C. Guillemin

TD05   9:42 – 9:57
SPECTROSCOPIC AND COMPUTATIONAL CHARACTERIZATION OF 2-AZA-1,3-BUTADIENE, A MOLECULE OF ASTROCHEMICAL SIGNIFICANCE , Ningjing Jiang, Mattia Melosso, Luca Bizzocchi, Silvia Alessandrini, J.-C. Guillemin, Luca Dore, Cristina Puzzarini

Intermission

TD06   10:39 – 10:54
THE MILLIMETER/SUBMILLIMETER SPECTRUM OF 3-HYDROXYPROPANAMIDE, Colton Moore, Hayley Bunn, Chase P Schultz, Susanna L. Widicus Weaver

TD07   10:57 – 11:12
ANALYSIS OF THE HIGH RESOLUTION ROTATIONAL SPECTRUM OF 2-CHLOROETHANOL, Hayley Bunn, Brian J. Esselman, Andi Wright, Steven Shipman, Susanna L. Widicus Weaver

TD08   11:15 – 11:30
FOURIER TRANSFORM MICROWAVE SPECTRA OF *cis*-3-HEXENAL, *trans*-3-HEXENAL, *cis*-2-HEXENAL AND *trans*-2-HEXENAL: STRUCTURAL ISOMERS AND ISOMERIZATION, Ryoto Ozawa, Nobuhiko Kuze, Yoshiyuki Kawashima

TD09   11:33 – 11:48
DECIPHERING THE COMPLETE NUCLEAR QUADRUPOLE COUPLING TENSOR OF IODINE WITH THE ROTATIONAL SPECTRUM OF 2-IODOETHANOL, Michael J. Carrillo, Lindsey Ann Speare, Dinesh Marasinghe, Michael Tubergen

TD10   11:51 – 12:06
CENTIMETER-WAVE SPECTROSCOPY OF SEVERAL NEW SILICON-BEARING CARBON CHAINS, Michael C McCarthy, Bryan Changala, Brandon Carroll

TD11   12:09 – 12:24
A HIGH SPEED FITTING PROGRAM FOR ROTATIONAL SPECTROSCOPY, Brandon Carroll, Michael C McCarthy

TE. Chirality and stereochemistry
Tuesday, June 21, 2022 – 8:30 AM
Room: 1024 Chemistry Annex

Chair: Ha Vinh Lam Nguyen, Université Paris-Est Créteil, Créteil, France

TE01 8:30 – 8:45
HIGH RESOLUTION INFRARED SPECTROSCOPY OF AZIRIDINE-2-CARBONITRILE ($C_3H_4N_2$), Karen Keppler, Sieghard Albert, Carine Manca Tanner, Martin Quack, Jürgen Stohner

TE02 8:48 – 9:03
TRANSIENT CHIRALITY AND MICROSOLVATION IN p-ETHYLPHENOL, Juan Carlos Lopez, Fernando Gonzalez, Alberto Macario, Susana Blanco

TE03 9:06 – 9:21
THE MICROWAVE SPECTRA AND MOLECULAR STRUCTURES OF THE CHIRAL AND ACHIRAL ROTAMERS OF 2,3,3-TRIFLUOROPROPENE AND THEIR GAS PHASE HETERODIMERS WITH THE ARGON ATOM, Helen O. Leung, Mark D. Marshall, Taha Ahmad, David W. Borden, Caitlin Hoffman, Navie Kim

TE04 9:24 – 9:39
HIGH PRECISION SPECTROSCOPY AND CONTROLLED DIMER FORMATION IN A CRYOGENIC ENVIRONMENT, David Patterson, Greta Koumarianou, Lincoln Satterthwaite, Daniel Sorensen

TE05 9:42 – 9:57
BROADBAND MICROWAVE 3-WAVE MIXING: ASSIGNMENT-FREE CHIRALITY DETECTION IN UNKNOWN SAMPLES, Greta Koumarianou, Irene Wang, Lincoln Satterthwaite, David Patterson

Intermission

TE06 10:39 – 10:54
THE MICROWAVE SPECTRA AND MOLECULAR STRUCTURES OF THE CHIRAL TAGGING CANDIDATE *CIS*-1,3,3,3-TETRAFLUORO-1,2-EPOXYPROPANE AND ITS GAS PHASE HETERODIMER WITH THE ARGON ATOM, Jonah R. Horowitz, Helen O. Leung, Mark D. Marshall

TE07 10:57 – 11:12
THE MICROWAVE SPECTRA AND MOLECULAR STRUCTURES OF *CIS*- and *TRANS*-1,1,1-TRIFLUORO-2,3-EPOXYBUTANE, Mark D. Marshall, Helen O. Leung, Caitlin Knight

TE08 11:15 – 11:30
ENHANCED ENANTIOMER-SELECTIVE POPULATION ENRICHMENT USING MICROWAVE SPECTROSCOPY WITH RAPID ADIABATIC PASSAGE, Freya E. L. Berggötz, Himanshi Singh, Wenhao Sun, Cristobal Perez, Melanie Schnell

TE09 11:33 – 11:48
INSIGHT INTO CHIRAL RAMAN SIGNALS UNDER RESONANCE CONDITION., Guojie Li, Yunjie Xu

TE10 11:51 – 12:06
ANISOTROPIC CIRCULAR DICHROISM SPECTROSCOPY OF JET-COOLED CHIRAL MOLECULES, Changseop Jeong, Nam Joon Kim

TF. Comparing theory and experiment
Tuesday, June 21, 2022 – 8:30 AM
Room: 124 Burrill Hall

Chair: Rebecca A. Peebles, Eastern Illinois University, Charleston, IL, USA

TF01   8:30 – 8:45
THE INTRIGUING $F_{bc}(P_bP_c + P_cP_b)$ TERM IN THE INTERACTION HAMILTONIAN FOR TUNNELING BETWEEN EQUIVALENT GAUCHE CONFORMERS , Peter Groner

TF02   8:48 – 9:03
A LOCAL MODE STUDY OF PSEUDOROTATIONAL EFFECTS IN THE INFRARED SPECTRA OF THE SCISSOR AND CH STRETCH VIBRATIONS OF CYCLOPENTANE, Edwin Sibert, Peter F. Bernath

TF03   9:06 – 9:21
ROTATIONAL AND PHOTOELECTRON SPECTROSCOPIES MEET QUANTUM CHEMISTRY: N,N-DIETHYLHYDROXYLAMINE, Giovanna Salvitti, Assimo Maris, Sonia Melandri, Luca Evangelisti, Fabrizia Negri, Marcello Coreno, Alessandra Ciavardini, Hanan Sa'adeh

TF04   9:24 – 9:39
CONFORMATIONAL EQUILIBRIUM OF THE CHALCOGEN-BRIDGED COMPOUNDS ALLYL ETHYL ETHER AND ALLYL ETHYL SULFIDE REVEALED BY MICROWAVE SPECTROSCOPY AND COMPUTATIONAL CHEMISTRY, TAMANNA POONIA, Jennifer van Wijngaarden

TF05   9:42 – 9:57
MILLIMETER-WAVE SPECTRUM OF THE LOWEST ENERGY, VIBRATIONALLY EXCITED COUPLED DYAD OF S-TRANS-Z-1-CYANO-1,3-BUTADIENE, P. Matisha Dorman, Brian J. Esselman, Robert J. McMahon, R. Claude Woods

TF06   10:00 – 10:15
THE ROTATIONAL SPECTRA OF 2-CYANOPYRIMIDINE ($C_5H_3N_3$) AND 2-CYANOPYRAZINE ($C_5H_3N_3$): VIBRATIONAL GROUND STATES AND DYAD OF LOWEST-ENERGY VIBRATIONALLY EXCITED STATES, Houston H. Smith, Brian J. Esselman, Maria Zdanovskaia, R. Claude Woods, Robert J. McMahon

Intermission

TF07   10:57 – 11:12
HYDROXYL GROUPS TORSIONAL MOTION IN CATECHOL MOLECULE., Darya Kisuryna, Alex Malevich, Aryna Khrapunova, Uladzimir Sapeshka, George Pitsevich

TF08   11:15 – 11:30
ORIGINS OF THE INTENSITY OF THE STRETCH-BEND COMBINATION TRANSITION IN WATER CLUSTERS AND IMPLICATIONS FOR CHARACTERIZING HYDROGEN BONDING, Rachel M. Huchmala, Anne B McCoy

TF09   11:33 – 11:48
SPECTROSCOPY AND BRAIN CHEMISTRY Of SEROTONIN AND DOPAMINE CONFORMERS , Vipin Bahadur Singh

TF10   11:51 – 12:06
TORSIONAL POTENTIALS, BARRIER TO INTERNAL ROTATION, MOLECULAR STRUCTURE, VIBRATIONAL PROPERTIES, NLO BEHAVIOUR AND NBO CHARACTERISTICS OF 2-(PHENYLSULFONYL)VINYLBENZENE AND 2-(TOSYL)VINYLBENZENE EMPLOYING FT-IR, FT RAMAN SPECTRAL TECHNIQUES AND DFT APPROACH, K Srishailam, Balakrishna Aegurla, Byru Venkatram Reddy, G. Ramana Rao

TF11   12:09 – 12:24
THEORETICAL AND EXPERIMENTAL ROTATIONAL SPECTROSCOPIC STUDIES OF SUBSTITUTED BENZOIC ACID HETERODIMERS, Mohamad H. Al-Jabiri, Mihael Eraković, Aran Insausti, Marko Cvitaš, Wolfgang Jäger

TG. Vibrational structure/frequencies
Tuesday, June 21, 2022 – 8:30 AM
Room: 274 Medical Sciences Building

Chair: Stephen J. Daunt, University of Tennessee, Knoxville, TN, USA

TG01   8:30 – 8:45
IS IT POSSIBLE TO IMPROVE THEORETICAL PREDICTION OF THE FREQUENCIES OF THE TORSIONAL VIBRATIONS BY ACCOUNTING ZPVE? TESTING MOST SIMPLE MOLECULES, George Pitsevich, Alex Malevich, Aryna Khrapunova, Uladzimir Sapeshka, Darya Kisuryna

TG02   8:48 – 9:03
FIRST HIGH-RESOLUTION STUDY OF VIBRATIONALLY EXCITED STATES ν_{17} AND ν_{12} OF PROPYLENE OXIDE, Karel Vávra, Eileen Döring, Jan Jakob, Guido W. Fuchs, Pascal Stahl, Arne Vereijken, Marcel Schlesag, Thomas Giesen

TG03   9:06 – 9:21
CHARACTERIZATION OF 4-PYRONE PYROLYSIS PRODUCTS VIA MATRIX-ISOLATION FT-IR, Khaled Aley El-Shazly, Heather Legg, Kathryn Narkin, Elizabeth Renee Sparks, Laura R. McCunn

TG04   9:24 – 9:39
WEAKLY-BOUND COMPLEX FORMATION BETWEEN HCN AND CH_3Cl: A MATRIX-ISOLATION AND COMPUTATIONAL STUDY, Emily K Hockey, Korina Vlahos, Thomas Howard, Jessica Palko, Leah G Dodson

TG05   9:42 – 9:57
GAS-PHASE CH-OVERTONE BAND SPECTRA OF METHYL ACETATE AND ETHYL ACETATE VIA INCOHERENT BROAD-BAND CAVITY-ENHANCED ABSORPTION SPECTROSCOPY, Takeru Sato, Mitsunori Araki, Takahiro Oyama, Shoma Hoshino, Koichi Tsukiyama

TG06   10:00 – 10:15
SUPERSONIC JET CAVITY RING DOWN SPECTROSCOPY OF MOLECULES IN THE MID INFRARED, Fabian Peterß, Guido W. Fuchs

Intermission

TG07   10:57 – 11:12
UNRAVELING HYDROGEN-BONDING INTERACTION, FERMI RESONANCES AND SOFT-MODE COUPLING IN PHENOL-BENZIMIDAZOLE PROTON-COUPLED ELECTRON TRANSFER MODEL COMPLEXES WITH CRYOGENIC ION VIBRATIONAL SPECTROSCOPY, Liangyi Chen, Joseph Fournier

TG08   11:15 – 11:30
STRUCTURAL DEFORMATION OF 4-BENZOYLBENZOATE UPON COMPLEXATION WITH METAL IONS AND SOLVENT UTILIZING MASS-SELECTED CRYOGENIC IR, Anna Gabriella del Rosario Rullán Buxó, Evan H Perez, Joseph P. Messinger, Sean Coleman Edington, Fabian Menges, Mark Johnson

TG09   11:33 – 11:48
CRYOGENIC IR SPECTROSCOPY OF CARBANION INTERMEDIATES: CIRCUMAMBULATORY REARRANGEMENT FOLLOWING DECARBOXYLATION OF BENZOIC ACID DERIVATIVES, Olivia Moss, Joseph P. Messinger, Evan H Perez, Anna Gabriella del Rosario Rullán Buxó, Tim Schleif, Kim Greis, Mark Johnson

TG10   11:51 – 12:06
PROTON, HYDRIDE, OR NEITHER? THE IDENTITY OF H IN THE $Au_9(PPh_3)_8H^{2+}$ CLUSTER, Hanna Morales Hernandez, Jonathan Wood Fagan, Christopher J. Johnson

TG11   12:09 – 12:24
INFRARED SPECTROSCOPY OF CARBOCATIONS UPON ELECTRON IONIZATION OF ETHYLENE IN HELIUM NANODROPLETS, Swetha Erukala, Alexandra J Feinberg, Amandeep Singh, Andrey Vilesov

TH. Mini-symposium: Spectroscopy meets Chemical Dynamics
Tuesday, June 21, 2022 – 1:30 PM
Room: 100 Noyes Laboratory

Chair: Bryan Changala, Ctr for Astrophysics/Harvard & Smithsonian, Cambridge, MA, USA

TH01 *INVITED TALK* 1:30 – 2:00
ULTRAFAST SPECTROSCOPY WITH FREQUENCY COMBS: ENABLING NEW MEASUREMENTS OF DILUTE SPECIES IN MOLECULAR BEAMS, Nicholas D. Cooper, Walker M. Jones, Todd Eliason, Melanie A.R. Reber

TH02 2:06 – 2:21
REAL-TIME TRACKING OF COHERENT VIBRATIONAL MOTION IN GROUND AND EXCITED ELECTRONIC STATES, Shaina Dhamija, Garima Bhutani, Ajay Jayachandran, Arijit K De

TH03 2:24 – 2:39
PHOTOPHYSICS OF Ni^{II} PYRIDINOPHANE PHOTOCATALYSTS USED FOR C-O CROSS-COUPLING REACTIONS PROBED VIA FEMTOSECOND OPTICAL ABSORPTION SPECTROSOCPY, Rachel Wallick, Josh Vura-Weis, Renske van der Veen

TH04 2:42 – 2:57
ULTRAFAST VIBRATIONAL DYNAMICS OF THE INTRAMOLECULAR H-BOND IN ACETYLACETONE INVESTIGATED WITH 2D IR SPECTROSCOPY, Jessika L.S. Dean, Joseph Fournier

TH05 3:00 – 3:15
RAPID FREQUENCY-COMB INFRARED SPECTROSCOPY WITH CROSS-DISPERSED SPECTROMETERS, D. Michelle Bailey, Joseph T. Hodges, Adam J. Fleisher

Intermission

TH06 3:39 – 3:54
SIMULATING FRANCK-CONDON SPECTRA WITH IMAGINARY-FREQUENCY VIBRATIONS, Bryan Changala, Nadav Genossar, Joshua H Baraban

TH07 3:57 – 4:12
PROTON TRANSFER AND INTERSYSTEM CROSSING IN 2-NITROPHENOL PROBED BY GAS-PHASE TRANSIENT ABSORPTION SPECTROSCOPY, Myles C Silfies, Arshad Mehmood, Grzegorz Kowzan, Benjamin G Levine, Thomas K Allison

TH08 4:15 – 4:30
SOLVENT DRIVEN COHERENT POPULATION TRANSFER IN TRYPTOPHAN, Vishal K. Jaiswal, Marziogiuseppe Gentile, Irene Conti, Artur Nenov, Marco Garavelli, Piotr Kabaciński, Rocio Borrego-Varillas, Giulio Cerullo

TH09 4:33 – 4:48
TWO-DIMENSIONAL TRANSIENT UV INVESTIGATION OF REDUCED FLAVINS, Eric Yokie, Arkaprabha Konar

TI. Mini-symposium: Benchmarking in Spectroscopy
Tuesday, June 21, 2022 – 1:30 PM
Room: 116 Roger Adams Lab

Chair: Eva Gougoula, Deutsches Elektronen-Synchrotron DESY, Hamburg, Germany

TI01   1:30 – 1:45
THE "LEGO BRICK" APPROACH AT WORK: A COST-EFFECTIVE STRATEGY FOR PREDICTING ACCURATE ROTATIONAL CONSTANTS, Hexu Ye, Silvia Alessandrini, Mattia Melosso, Cristina Puzzarini

TI02   1:48 – 2:03
CONCENTRATION DETERMINATIONS FOR REACTIVE CHEMICAL INTERMEDIATES USING EMPIRICALLY DETERMINED AND THEORETICALLY CALCULATED TRANSITION PROBABILITIES, Ian Jones, Jonathan Swift Bersson, Jinjun Liu, Ketan Sharma, Terry A. Miller, John F. Stanton

TI03   2:06 – 2:21
AMINO ACIDS AND PEPTIDES (AAP) STRUCTURES, ENERGETICS AND SPECTROSCOPY (SES) DATABASE, Malgorzata Biczysko

TI04   2:24 – 2:39
COMPUTATIONAL STUDIES OF MGC$_4$H ISOMERS, Aland Sinjari, TARUN ROY, SUBHAS GHOSAL, Venkatesan S. Thimmakondu

TI05   2:42 – 2:57
ULTRAHIGH FINESSE CAVITY-ENHANCED SPECTROSCOPY OF DEUTERIUM MOLECULE FOR QED TESTS, Mikołaj Zaborowski, Michał Słowiński, Kamil Stankiewicz, Franck Thibault, Agata Cygan, Hubert Jóźwiak, Grzegorz Kowzan, Piotr Maslowski, Akiko Nishiyama, Nikodem Stolarczyk, Szymon Wojtewicz, Roman Ciurylo, Daniel Lisak, Piotr Wcislo

Intermission

TI06   3:21 – 3:36
RESONANT INELASTIC X-RAY SCATTERING CALCULATIONS OF Ru COMPLEXES WITHIN A SIMPLIFIED TIME-DEPENDENT DENSITY FUNCTIONAL THEORY FRAMEWORK, Daniel R. Nascimento

TI07   3:39 – 3:54
DECONVOLUTING VIBRATIONAL PROBE RESPONSES USING CRYOGENIC ION INFRARED SPECTROSCOPY, Ahmed Mohamed, Sean Coleman Edington, Mark Johnson

TI08   3:57 – 4:12
QUARANTINED CC-STRETCHED FORMIC ACID: MOLECULAR WORK-OUT IN (SELF) ISOLATION, Katharina A. E. Meyer, Arman Nejad

TI09   4:15 – 4:30
THE FORMIC ACID MONOMER: EXTENSION OF THE VIBRATIONAL DATABASE AND RIGOROUS ELECTRONIC AND NUCLEAR VIBRATIONAL STRUCTURE BENCHMARKS, Arman Nejad, Edwin Sibert, Martin A. Suhm

TJ. Photodissociation and photochemistry
Tuesday, June 21, 2022 – 1:30 PM
Room: B102 Chemical and Life Sciences

Chair: Fleming Crim, The University of Wisconsin, Madison, WI, USA

TJ01   1:30 – 1:45
RESONANCE ENHANCED PHOTODISSOCIATION SPECTROSCOPY OF AuAg+ REVEALS ISOTOPIC DEPENDANCE ON PHOTODISSOCIATION, Samuel Jack Palmer Marlton, Chang Liu, Patrick Watkins, Jack T Buntine, Evan Bieske

TJ02   1:48 – 2:03
PHOTODISSOCIATION SPECTRUM OF $Au_2^+N_2$, Nima-Noah Nahvi, Marko Förstel, Kai Pollow, Taarna Studemund, Otto Dopfer

TJ03   2:06 – 2:21
GAS-PHASE ELECTRONIC SPECTROSCOPY OF C_6^+, Jason E. Colley, Dylan S. Orr, Michael A Duncan

TJ04   2:24 – 2:39
$Si_2O_2^+$ - PHOTODISSOCIATION AND OPTICAL ABSORPTION PROPERTIES, Taarna Studemund, Marko Förstel, Kai Pollow, Emil Mickein, Otto Dopfer

Intermission

TJ05   3:03 – 3:18
SPECTROSCOPIC STUDIES OF π-BACKDONATING EARLY TRANSITION METAL AND MONOVALENT LANTHANIDE DIBORIDES, Dakota M. Merriles, Kimberly H. Tomchak, Christopher Nielson, Michael D. Morse

TJ06   3:21 – 3:36
BOND DISSOCIATION ENERGIES AND IONIZATION ENERGIES OF RHENIUM CONTAINING SMALL MOLECULES, Kimberly H. Tomchak, Erick Tieu, Thomas T. Kawagoe, Jordan Derbidge, Keith T. Clark, Michael D. Morse

TJ07   3:39 – 3:54
ULTRAFAST CARRIER DYNAMICS IN QUANTUM DOT SENSITIZED ZnO, Conner Dykstra, Thomas Rossi, Renske van der Veen, Josh Vura-Weis

TJ08   3:57 – 4:12
PHOTOCHEMISTRY OF CYANOMETHYLENE CYCLOPROPANE (C_5H_5N) IN A LOW TEMPERATURE RARE GAS MATRIX, Samuel A. Wood, Samuel M. Kougias, Brian J. Esselman, R. Claude Woods, Robert J. McMahon

TJ09   4:15 – 4:30
UV PHOTOLYSIS STUDY OF *PARA*-AMINOBENZOIC ACID USING PARAHYDROGEN MATRIX ISOLATED SPECTROSCOPY, Alexandra McKinnon, Brendan Moore, Pavle Djuricanin, Takamasa Momose

TJ10   4:33 – 4:48
UV PHOTOLYSIS OF AMINO ACIDS IN A SOLID PARAHYDROGEN MATRIX, Brendan Moore, Shin Yi Toh, Termeh Bashiri, Kyle Mahoney, Alexandra McKinnon, Mei Fei Zeng, Ying-Tung Angel Wong, Pavle Djuricanin, Takamasa Momose

TK. Mini-symposium: Machine Learning
Tuesday, June 21, 2022 – 1:30 PM
Room: 217 Noyes Laboratory

Chair: Andrew White, University of Rochester, Rochester, NY, USA

TK01 *INVITED TALK* 1:30 – 2:00
AN OVERVIEW OF MACHINE LEARNING IN ROTATIONAL SPECTROSCOPY, Steven Shipman

TK02 2:06 – 2:21
DEVELOPMENT OF HIGH-SPEED AB INITIO CCSD(T) LEVEL NEURAL NETWORK POTENTIAL ENERGY SURFACES FOR DIFFUSION MONTE CARLO , Fenris Lu, Anne B McCoy

TK03 2:24 – 2:39
DIFFUSION MONTE CARLO STUDY OF $C_2H_5^+$ USING AN AB INITIO POTENTIAL ENERGY SURFACE , Pattarapon Moonkaen, Fenris Lu, Anne B McCoy

Intermission

TK04 *INVITED TALK* 3:03 – 3:33
PUTTING DENSITY FUNCTIONAL THEORY TO THE TEST WITH MACHINE LEARNING, Heather J Kulik

TK05 3:39 – 3:54
PARTITION FUNCTION ESTIMATION FROM INCOMPLETE SPECTROSCOPIC GRAPHS, Kelvin Lee, Kyle N. Crabtree

TK06 3:57 – 4:12
ACCURATE PHOTOPHYSICS OF ORGANIC RADICALS FROM MACHINE LEARNED RANGE-SEPARATED FUNCTIONALS, Chengwei Ju, Yili Shen, Aaron Tian, Ethan French, Hongshan Bi, Zhou Lin

TL. Theory and Computation
Tuesday, June 21, 2022 – 1:30 PM
Room: 1024 Chemistry Annex

Chair: János Sarka, Texas Tech University, Lubbock, TX, USA

TL01   1:30 – 1:45
CALCULATIONS OF ACTINIDE- AND LANTHANIDE-CONTAINING SMALL MOLECULES USING SPINOR-BASED RELATIVISTIC COUPLED-CLUSTER METHODS, Tianxiang Chen, Chaoqun Zhang, Lan Cheng

TL02   1:48 – 2:03
THEORETICAL INVESTIGATION OF THE X-RAY STARK EFFECT IN SMALL MOLECULES, Catherine Wright, Avdhoot Datar, Devin A. Matthews

TL03   2:06 – 2:21
AB INITIO INVESTIGATION OF INTRAMOLECULAR CHARGE TRANSFER IN DMABN BY CALCULATION OF TRANSIENT X-RAY ABSORPTION FEATURES, Avdhoot Datar, Saisrinivas Gudivada, Devin A. Matthews

TL04   2:24 – 2:39
ENHANCING THERMALLY ACTIVATED DELAYED FLUORESCENCE THROUGH STRUCTURAL AND ENERGETIC FLEXIBILITY: THEORETICAL STUDIES , Dieaa H Alhmoud, Zhou Lin

TL05   2:42 – 2:57
AB INITIO MODELING OF ULTRAFAST NONLINEAR OPTICAL SIGNALS IN MOLECULAR SYSTEMS INVOLVING ELECTRONIC TRANSITIONS, Richard Thurston, Thorsten Weber, Liang Z. Tan, Daniel S. Slaughter

Intermission

TL06   3:21 – 3:36
VIBRATIONALLY UNUSUAL BEHAVIORS PREDICTED FOR $(XeHXe)^+$: COMPUTATIONAL MOLECULAR SPECTROSCOPY STUDY, Tsuneo Hirano, Umpei Nagashima, Masaaki Baba

TL07   3:39 – 3:54
FINE AND HYPERFINE RESOLVED EMPIRICAL ENERGY LEVELS OF VANADIUM OXIDE (VO), Charles A Bowesman, Scott Hopkins, Sergei N. Yurchenko, Jonathan Tennyson

TL08   3:57 – 4:12
USING ASIMUT-ALVL TO MODEL THE VIS-NIR SPECTRUM OF JUPITER'S ATMOSPHERE, Miriam E. Cisneros-González, Manuel López-Puertas, Justin Erwin, Ann Carine Vandaele, Clément Lauzin, Séverine Robert

TL09   4:15 – 4:30
THE GPU ACCELERATED ABSORPTION SIMULATION (GAAS) PLATFORM, Charlie Scott Callahan, Sean Coburn, Gregory B Rieker

TL10   4:33 – 4:48
QUANTUM SCRAMBLING IN MOLECULES, Chenghao Zhang, Martin Gruebele, Peter Guy Wolynes

TM. Clusters/Complexes
Tuesday, June 21, 2022 – 1:30 PM
Room: 124 Burrill Hall

Chair: G. S. Grubbs II, Missouri University of Science and Technology, Rolla, MO, USA

TM01   1:30 – 1:45
PURE ROTATIONAL SPECTROSCOPY OF RARE GAS DIMERS BASED ON ROTATIONAL WAVE PACKET IMAGING, Kenta Mizuse, Yuya Tobata, Urara Sato, Yasuhiro Ohshima

TM02   1:48 – 2:03
PARTIAL PROTON TRANSFER IN THE TRIFLUOROACETIC ACID - TRIMETHYLAMINE COMPLEX, Aaron J Reynolds, Nathan Love, Kenneth R. Leopold

TM03   2:06 – 2:21
ALTERNATING 1-PHENYL-2,2,2-TRIFLUOROETHANOL CONFORMATIONAL LANDSCAPE WITH THE ADDITION OF ONE WATER: TUNNELLING AND LARGE AMPLITUDE MOTIONS, Colton Carlson, Daniel Mason, Qian Yang, Nathan A. Seifert, Yunjie Xu

TM04   2:24 – 2:39
CONFORMATIONAL BEHAVIOUR OF m-ANISALDEHYDE AND ITS MICROSOLVATES, Andres Verde, Juan Carlos Lopez, Susana Blanco

Intermission

TM06   3:21 – 3:36
POINT MUTATION CHANGES VIBRATIONAL COUPLING IN LEPIDIUM VIRGINICUM WATER SOLUBLE CHLOROPHYLL BINDING PROTEIN, Galina Grechishnikova, Amit Srivastava, Safa Ahad, Mike Earl Reppert, Libai Huang

TM07   3:39 – 3:54
STABILITY OF NEUTRAL MANGANESE OXIDE CLUSTERS, Chase H Rotteger, Shaun Sutton, Scott G Sayres

TM08   3:57 – 4:12
EXCITED STATE PHOTODYNAMICS OF SUB-NANOMETER METAL OXIDE CLUSTERS, Scott G Sayres

TM09   4:15 – 4:30
THE MILLIMETER-WAVE SPECTRUM OF THE WEAKLY BOUND ARGON-METHANOL CLUSTER, Connor J. Wright, Kevin Roenitz, Jonathan Rebelsky, Anna Kay Gerosolina, Morgan Giese, Steven Shipman, Susanna L. Widicus Weaver

TN. Radicals
Tuesday, June 21, 2022 – 1:30 PM
Room: 274 Medical Sciences Building

Chair: Ugo Jacovella, CNRS, Université Paris-Saclay, Orsay, France

TN01   1:30 – 1:45
HIGH-RESOLUTION INFRARED SPECTROSCOPY OF GAS-PHASE CYCLOBUTYL RADICAL IN THE α-CH STRETCH REGION: STRUCTURAL AND DYNAMICAL INSIGHTS, Ya-Chu Chan, David Nesbitt

TN02   1:48 – 2:03
EXTENDING PURE ROTATIONAL MEASUREMENTS OF THE CH_3O RADICAL TOWARD THE TERAHERTZ DOMAIN, Marie-Aline Martin-Drumel, Olivia Chitarra, Jean-Thibaut Spaniol, Thomas Sandow Hearne, Olivier Pirali, J.-C. Loison

TN03   2:06 – 2:21
THE MICROWAVE SPECTRUM OF THE DIFLUOROCYANOMETHYL RADICAL, $\dot{C}F_2CN$, Lu Kang, Ha Vinh Lam Nguyen, Christopher Falls, Alexander Seys, Wallace C. Pringle, Thomas A. Blake, Stewart E. Novick, S. A. Cooke

TN04   2:24 – 2:39
IMPROVEMENTS TO NEW PROGRAM FOR SPIN-TORSION-ROTATION & THE METHYL-PHENOXYL RADICALS, J. H. Westerfield, Blair Welsh, Timothy S. Zwier, Kyle N. Crabtree

TN05   2:42 – 2:57
PRODUCT-SPECIFIC REACTION KINETICS OF CN WITH PROPENE PROBED BY CHIRPED-PULSE FOURIER TRANSFORM MILLIMETER WAVE SPECTROSCOPY, Divita Gupta, Brian M Hays, Myriam Drissi, Theo Guillaume, Omar Abdelkader Khedaoui, Ilsa Rose Cooke, Ian R. Sims

TN06   3:00 – 3:15
EXAMINING METHYLAMINE DISSOCIATION PRODUCTS USING THEORY AND ROTATIONAL SPECTROSCOPY: THE CH_2NH_2 RADICAL, Connor J. Wright, Jonathan Rebelsky, Anna Kay Gerosolina, John F. Stanton, Susanna L. Widicus Weaver

Intermission

TN07   3:39 – 3:54
PRODUCTION OF •CH_2NH_2 AND CH_2NH IN THE REACTIONS OF METHYLAMINE (CH_3NH_2) WITH •H OR •OH IN SOLID p-H_2 AND ITS IMPLICATION IN ASTROCHEMISTRY, Prasad Ramesh Joshi, Yuan-Pern Lee

TN08   3:57 – 4:12
ORIENTATION DYNAMICS OF CH_3, CH_4, AND CD_4 QUANTUM ROTORS IN SOLID METHANES AT CRYOGENIC TEMPERATURES, Yurij Dmitriev

TN09   4:15 – 4:30
FORMATION REACTION MECHANISM AND INFRARED SPECTRA OF CRIEGEE INTERMEDIATE ANTI-TRANS-METHACROLEIN OXIDE [$CH_2C(CH_3)CHOO$] AND ITS ASSOCIATED PRECURSOR AND ADDUCT RADICALS, Yuan-Pern Lee, Jia-Rong Cai, Jung-Hsuan Su, Chen-An Chung

TN10   4:33 – 4:48
STUDY OF THE KINETICS AND PRODUCT YIELDS FOR THE REACTION OF CRIEGEE INTERMEDIATE CH_2OO WITH HNO_3 USING MID-INFRARED TIME-RESOLVED DUAL-COMB SPECTROSCOPY, Pei-Ling Luo

TO. Plenary Special Session
Tuesday, June 21, 2022 – 5:15 PM
Room: 2025A/B/C Ikenberry Commons

Chair: Helen O. Leung, Amherst College, Amherst, MA, USA

TO01   **5:20 – 5:55**
SPECTROSCOPY TODAY: THE URGENT NEED FOR SCIENCE AND INNOVATION TO SAVE THIS WARMING PLANET, Geraldine Richmond

TO02   **6:00 – 6:35**
ISMS AND NSF: SOME HISTORY AND A LOOK FORWARD, Fleming Crim

WA. Mini-symposium: Spectroscopy meets Chemical Dynamics
Wednesday, June 22, 2022 – 8:30 AM
Room: 100 Noyes Laboratory

Chair: Melanie A.R. Reber, University of Georgia, Athens, GA, USA

WA01   *INVITED TALK*   **8:30 – 9:00**
MICROBUBBLE RESONATORS FOR FUN AND PROFIT, Randall Goldsmith

WA02   **9:06 – 9:21**
PHOTOELECTRON SPECTROSCOPIC STUDY ON DIPOLE-BOUND STATES: INTRAMOLECULAR ELECTRIC FIELD INDUCED ELECTRONIC CORRELATION, Daofu Yuan, Yue-Rou Zhang, Lai-Sheng Wang

WA03   **9:24 – 9:39**
SINGLE-CONFORMATION SPECTROSCOPY AND DYNAMICS ON MULTIPLE POTENTIAL ENERGY SURFACES: FLEXIBLE NITROGEN-HETEROCYCLE CHROMOPHORES AND COMPLEXES IN AEROSOLS, Nathanael M. Kidwell

WA04   **9:42 – 9:57**
DEVELOPMENT OF STRUCTURAL COMPLEXITY IN BARE AND HYDROGENATED CARBON CLUSTERS, Samuel Jack Palmer Marlton, Jack T Buntine, Chang Liu, Patrick Watkins, Evan Bieske

WA05   **10:00 – 10:15**
POLYCYCLIC AROMATIC HYDROCARBON GROWTH IN A PLASMA REVEALED BY IR-UV ACTION SPECTROSCOPY, Alexander Karel Lemmens, Daniel Rap, Sandra Brünken, Wybren Jan Buma, Anouk Rijs

Intermission

WA06   **10:57 – 11:12**
CONFORMATION-SPECIFIC INSIGHTS INTO THE CHEMICAL DYNAMICS OF NO:CH_4 MOLECULAR COMPLEXES, John Patrick Davis, Nathanael M. Kidwell

WA07   **11:15 – 11:30**
DFT INVESTIGATION ABOUT ELECTRONIC AND VIBRATIONAL PROPERTIES OF CHROMONE SCHIFF BASE LIGANDS WITH METAL COMPLEXES, SQM ANALYSIS, Berna Catikkas

WA09   **11:51 – 12:06**
IR INDUCED ISOMERIZATION AND ITS BACKWARD REACTION OF COLD PHENOL-METHANOL CLUSTER CATIONS, Masayoshi Ozeki, Masataka Orito, Hikaru Sato, Kenta Mizuse, Haruki Ishikawa

WB. Mini-symposium: Benchmarking in Spectroscopy
Wednesday, June 22, 2022 – 8:30 AM
Room: 116 Roger Adams Lab

Chair: Juan Carlos Lopez, Universidad de Valladolid, Valladolid, Spain

WB01   ***INVITED TALK***   8:30 – 9:00
A NEW STANDARD OF AGREEMENT OF SEMI-EXPERIMENTAL EQUILIBRIUM (r_e^{SE}) AND COMPUTED EQUILIBRIUM (r_e) STRUCTURES, Brian J. Esselman

WB02   9:06 – 9:21
THE PREFERRED CONFORMATION AND NON-COVALENT INTERACTIONS OF THE METHYL ALLYL DISULFIDE-FORMALDEHYDE COMPLEX REVEALED BY ROTATIONAL SPECTROSCOPY, Zhen Wang, Yuago Xu, Gang Feng

WB03   9:24 – 9:39
MILLIMETER/SUBMILLIMETER SPECTRUM AND PRECISE EQUILIBRIUM STRUCTURE OF 1H-1,2,4-TRIAZOLE, Hayley Bunn, Brian J. Esselman, Samuel M. Kougias, John F. Stanton, R. Claude Woods, Robert J. McMahon, Susanna L. Widicus Weaver

WB04   9:42 – 9:57
ON THE NATURE OF THE INTERACTION OF CO WITH PERFLURINATED AROMATICS: NEW INSIGHTS FROM THE EXPERIMENTA DATA AND THEORETICAL STUDY, Luca Evangelisti, Assimo Maris, Camilla Calabrese, Imanol Usabiaga, Weixing Li, Giovanni Bistoni, Sonia Melandri

WB05   10:00 – 10:15
ROTATIONAL SPECTROSCOPIC STUDY OF MICROSOLVATED CLUSTERS OF 1- AND 2-NITRONAPHTHALENE, Shefali Saxena, M. Eugenia Sanz

Intermission

WB06   10:57 – 11:12
SUB-PERMILLE MEASUREMENTS AND CALCULATIONS OF 3-0 BAND CO LINE INTENSITIES, Zachary Reed, Katarzyna Bielska, Aleksandra A. Kyuberis, Gang Li, Agata Cygan, Roman Ciurylo, Daniel Lisak, Erin M. Adkins, Joseph T. Hodges, Lorenzo Lodi, Nikolay F. Zobov, Volker Ebert, Jonathan Tennyson, Oleg L. Polyansky

WB07   11:15 – 11:30
QUANTUM CHEMICAL INVESTIGATION OF INTRAMOLECULAR HYDROGEN BONDS IN OXYGENATED AROMATIC MOLECULES: INFLUENCE OF RING SIZE, DONOR/ACCEPTOR GROUPS AND SUBSTITUTANTS, Jonas Bruckhuisen, Cecilia Gomez-Pech, Guillaume Dhont, Arnaud Cuisset, Malgorzata Olejniczak, Manuel Goubet, Valérie Vallet

WB08   11:33 – 11:48
INFRARED PREDISSOCIATION SPECTROSCOPY OF PROTONATED METHYL CYANIDE, Aravindh Nivas Marimuthu, Frank Huis in't Veld, Sven Thorwirth, Britta Redlich, Sandra Brünken

WB09   11:51 – 12:06
AUTOMATED SEARCH ALGORITHMS FOR STRUCTURAL ISOMERISM: THE PROS AND CONS, Venkatesan S. Thimmakondu

WC. Electronic structure, potential energy surfaces
Wednesday, June 22, 2022 – 8:30 AM
Room: B102 Chemical and Life Sciences

Chair: Lan Cheng, The Johns Hopkins University, Lutherville Timonium, MD, USA

WC01   8:30 – 8:45
ROTATIONAL ANALYSIS OF HIGH RESOLUTION LASER EXCITATION AND DISPERSED FLUORESCENCE SPECTRA FROM THE $B^1\Sigma^+ - A^1\Pi$, $B^1\Sigma^+ - X^1\Sigma^+$, AND $B^1\Sigma^+ - a^3\Pi_1$ SYSTEMS OF MgS., Nicholas Caron, Bradley Guislain, Dennis W. Tokaryk, Allan G. Adam

WC02   8:48 – 9:03
EXTENSION OF AN ATOMIC-IONS-IN-MOLECULE ELECTRONIC STRUCTURE MODEL FROM CALCIUM MONOXIDE TO SCANDIUM MONOXIDE, Robert W Field, Sanjay G. Nakhate

WC03   9:06 – 9:21
ELECTRONIC STRUCTURE OF THE GROUND AND EXCITED STATES OF EUROPIUM OXIDE (EuO), Bradley Welch, Nuno M. S. Almeida, Angela K. Wilson

WC04   9:24 – 9:39
MULTIREFERENCE CALCULATIONS ON THE GROUND AND EXCITED STATES AND DISSOCIATION ENERGIES OF LrF AND LrO, Nuno M. S. Almeida, Sasha C. North, Timothé R. L. Melin, Angela K. Wilson

WC05   9:42 – 9:57
SPECTROSCOPIC CHARACTERIZATION OF THE [H, P, S, O] MOLECULAR SYSTEM AND CHEMICAL INSIGHTS INTO THE NON-DETECTION OF PHOSPHORUS- AND SULFUR-BEARING DIATOMIC MOLECULES PS AND PH, Vincent J. Esposito, Jacqueline M. Friskey, Tarek Trabelsi, Joseph S Francisco

Intermission

WC06   10:39 – 10:54
COMPUTATIONAL AND SPECTROSCOPIC STUDIES OF NITROGEN-CONTAINING DIPOLE BOUND ANIONS, Nicholas A. Kruse, Nathan I Hammer

WC07   10:57 – 11:12
LOW AND HIGH-RESOLUTION LASER-INDUCED FLUORESCENCE (LIF) of JET-COOLED NdO, Joel R Schmitz, Arianna Rodriguez, Timothy Steimle, Michael Heaven

WC08   11:15 – 11:30
PHOTOPHYSICS OF A RIGID MACROCYCLE Fe^{II} COMPLEX WITH A NANOSECOND LIFETIME MLCT EXCITED STATE, Justin Thomas Malme, Ryan T Ash, Reese Clendening, Josh Vura-Weis, Tong Ren

WC09   11:33 – 11:48
MECHANISM AND KINETICS OF THE REACTION OF CRIEGEE INTERMEDIATE CH_2OO WITH ACETIC ACID STUDIED WITH A STEP-SCAN FOURIER-TRANSFORM IR SPECTROMETER, Bedabyas Behera, Kaito Takahashi, Yuan-Pern Lee

WC10   11:51 – 12:06
A MICROWAVE AND COMPUTATIONAL STUDY OF PIVALIC SULFURIC ANHYDRIDE AND THE PIVALIC ACID MONOMER: MECHANISTIC INSIGHTS INTO THE RCOOH + SO_3 REACTION, Nathan Love, Kenneth R. Leopold

WC11   12:09 – 12:24
INVESTIGATING STRUCTURE AND REACTIVITY RELATIONSHIPS OF NITROGEN-CONTAINING RADICALS WITH COMPUTATIONAL CHEMISTRY AND PHOTOIONIZATION MASS SPECTROMETRY, Sommer L. Johansen, Judit Zador, Leonid Sheps

WD. Clusters/Complexes
Wednesday, June 22, 2022 – 8:30 AM
Room: 217 Noyes Laboratory

Chair: Josh Vura-Weis, University of Illinois at Urbana-Champaign, Urbana, IL, USA

WD01   8:30 – 8:45
MAPPING ELECTRONIC RELAXATION DYNAMICS IN METAL NANOCLUSTERS USING POLARIZATION-SELECTIVE TWO-DIMENSIONAL ELECTRONIC SPECTROSCOPY, William R. Jeffries, Kenneth L. Knappenberger, Jr.

WD02   8:48 – 9:03
PHOTOELECTRON SPECTROSCOPY OF THE BERYLLIUM PENTAMER ANION, Noah B Jaffe, David Archie Stewart, John F. Stanton, Michael Heaven

WD03   9:06 – 9:21
A SPECTROSCOPIC INVESTIGATION OF THE EFFECTS OF SPIN STRAIN ON LN_3O^- CLUSTERS, Caleb D Huizenga, Caroline Chick Jarrold, Shivangi Vaish

WD04   9:24 – 9:39
ZINC OXIDE ELECTRONIC STRUCTURE STUDY USING PES, Shivangi Vaish, Caroline Chick Jarrold

WD05   9:42 – 9:57
SPECTROSCOPIC STUDY OF THE N_2-H_2O COMPLEX IN THE 2 OH STRETCHING REGIONS, Robin Glorieux, Alexandr Bogomolov, Brian M Hays, Thomas Vanfleteren, Michel Herman, Nasser Moazzen-Ahmadi, Clément Lauzin

WD06   10:00 – 10:15
WEAKLY BOUND CLUSTERS OF ATMOSPHERIC MOLECULES: INFRARED SPECTRA AND STRUCTURAL CALCULATIONS OF $(CO_2)_n$-$(CO)_m$-$(N_2)_p$, $(n,m,p) = (2,1,0), (2,0,1), (1,2,0), (1,0,2), (1,1,1), (1,3,0), (1,0,3), (1,2,1), (1,1,2)$, A. J. Barclay, A.R.W. McKellar, Andrea Pietropolli Charmet, Nasser Moazzen-Ahmadi

Intermission

WD07   10:57 – 11:12
MATRIX ISOLATION FTIR ANALYSIS OF WEAKLY-BOUND COMPLEXES OF WATER WITH γ-LACTONES, Annabelle N Carney, Kenneth C Mogauro, Emily M Weaver, Josh Newby

WD08   11:15 – 11:30
VIBRATIONAL SPECTROSCOPY OF BENZONITRILE–(WATER)$_{1-2}$ CLUSTERS IN HELIUM DROPLETS, Jai Khatri, Tarun Kumar Roy, Kuntal Chatterjee, Gerhard Schwaab, Martina Havenith

WD09   11:33 – 11:48
MICROSOLVATION AND PHOTODYNAMICS IN FORMIC ACID-WATER CLUSTERS, Shaun Sutton, Chase H Rotteger, tarakeshwar pilarisetty, Dane Miller, Scott G Sayres

WD10   11:51 – 12:06
THE 2OH OVERTONE SPECTRUM OF H_2O-CO_2 VAN DER WAALS COMPLEX: SEARCH FOR INTERMOLECULAR MODES EXCITATION AND LARGER COMPLEXES, Brian M Hays, Robin Glorieux, Michel Herman, Clément Lauzin

WE. Coblentz Special Session
Wednesday, June 22, 2022 – 8:30 AM
Room: 1024 Chemistry Annex

Chair: Zachary Schultz, The Ohio State University, Columbus, OH, USA

WE01   8:30 – 8:45
UNDERSTANDING THE SURFACE ENHANCED RAMAN SPECTROSCOPY (SERS) SIGNALS OF AMINO ACIDS, PEPTIDES, AND PROTEINS FOR BIOSENSING APPLICATIONS, Taylor Payne, Zachary Schultz

WE02   8:48 – 9:03
APTAMER BASED MICROPARTICLES IMMUNOASSAY METHOD FOR CA125 DETECTION USING RAMAN SPECTROSCOPY, Robinson Karunanithy, Torrey E. Holland, P Sivakumar

WE03   9:06 – 9:21
CELL PHASE IDENTIFICATION IN A THREE-DIMENSIONAL TUMOR CELL CULTURE MODEL BY FOURIER TRANSFORM INFRARED (FT-IR) SPECTROSCOPIC IMAGING, Pei-Hsuan Hsieh, Rohit Bhargava

WE04   9:24 – 9:39
LABEL-FREE AUTOFLUORESCENCE-DETECTED MID-IR PHOTOTHERMAL MICROSCOPY, Aleksandr Razumtcev, Garth Simpson

WE05   9:42 – 9:57
A WIDE-FIELD IMAGING APPROACH FOR SIMULTANEOUS SUPER-RESOLUTION SURFACE-ENHANCED RAMAN SCATTERING IMAGING AND SPECTROSCOPY, Deben Shoup, Zachary Schultz

WE06   10:00 – 10:15
ISOLATING THE INTRINSIC SPECTRAL RESPONSES OF VIBRATIONAL PROBES: BENCHMARKS FOR REPORTERS OF CONDENSED PHASE AND BIOLOGICAL PROCESSES, Sean Coleman Edington, Ahmed Mohamed, Mark Johnson

Intermission

WE07   10:57 – 11:12
HIGH-THROUGHPUT MICROPLASTIC MONITORING IN MICROFLUIDICS BY RAPID COHERENT RAMAN SCATTERING SPECTROSCOPY, Minjian Lu, Yujia Zhang, Yan LI, Haoyun Wei

WE08   11:15 – 11:30
UNDERSTANDING POLARIZATION EFFECTS ON ABSORPTION SPECTRA MEASURED USING A QUANTUM CASCADE LASER-BASED SPECTROMETER, Ruo-Jing Ho, Yamuna Dilip Phal, Rohit Bhargava

WE09   11:33 – 11:48
DETECTION OF MEDICAL INHALER USE VIA TERAHERTZ SPECTROSCOPY, Daniel J Tyree, Ivan Medvedev, Steve S Kim, Michael C Brothers

WE10   11:51 – 12:06
A PHOTONIC GAS SENSOR FOR THE MID-INFRARED, Travis A Gartner, Nasser Moazzen-Ahmadi, A. J. Barclay

WE11   12:09 – 12:24
THE IMPACT OF PLASMONICALLY GENERATED HOT-CARRIERS ON SERS ANALYSIS, Chelsea M. Zoltowski, Zachary Schultz

WF. Large amplitude motions, internal rotation
Wednesday, June 22, 2022 – 8:30 AM
Room: 124 Burrill Hall

Chair: Mark D. Marshall, Amherst College, Amherst, MA, USA

WF01   8:30 – 8:45
A GLOBAL RAM METHOD FOR FITTING ASYMMETRIC TOPS WITH ONE METHYL INTERNAL ROTOR AND TWO ^{14}N NUCLEI: APPLICATION OF THE BELGI-2N CODE TO THE MICROWAVE SPECTRA OF THE METHYLIMIDAZOLE ISOMERS., Ha Vinh Lam Nguyen, Isabelle Kleiner, Martin SCHWELL, Eva Gougoula, Nick Walker

WF02   8:48 – 9:03
A GLOBAL RAM METHOD FOR FITTING INFRARED AND FAR-INFRARED DATA FOR SMALL VOLATILE ORGANIC COUMPOUNDS: APPLICATION TO TOLUENE, V. Ilyushin, Isabelle Kleiner, SELLITTO Pasquale, F. Kwabia Tchana, Pierre Asselin, Pascale Soulard, Olivier Pirali, Manuel Goubet, Robert Georges

WF03   9:06 – 9:21
AN OH IN FLUORINE'S CLOTHING - THE CURIOUS ROTATIONAL SPECTROSCOPY OF PERFLUOROPHENOL, Blair Welsh, Amanda Dewyer, Angie Zhang, Kendrew Au, Nils Hansen, Timothy S. Zwier

WF04   9:24 – 9:39
MICROWAVE SPECTRA OF DINITROTOLUENE ISOMERS: A NEW STEP TOWARDS THE DETECTION OF EXPLOSIVE VAPORS , Mhamad Chrayteh, Pascal Dréan, Manuel Goubet, Anthony Roucou, Arnaud Cuisset

WF05   9:42 – 9:57
CONFORMATIONAL ANALYSIS OF VALINE METHYL ESTER BY MICROWAVE SPECTROSCOPY, Dinesh Marasinghe, Michael Tubergen

Intermission

WF06   10:39 – 10:54
ROTATIONAL SPECTRUM OF ACETOIN (CH$_3$COCH(OH)CH$_3$), Jonathan Rebelsky, Chase P Schultz, Steven Shipman, Susanna L. Widicus Weaver

WF07   10:57 – 11:12
ON THE CHOICE OF HAMILTONIAN REDUCTION AND REPRESENTATION FOR THE ROTATIONAL SPECTRUM OF 1,1-DIFLUOROACETONE RECORDED UP TO 640 GHz, S. A. Cooke, Peter R. Franke, Peter Groner, L. Margulès, R. A. Motiyenko

WF08   11:15 – 11:30
THE FAR-INFRARED SPECTRA OF CYCLOPROPYLAMINE, Yue Liang, Brant E. Billinghurst, Bowen Liu, Ziqiu Chen

WF09   11:33 – 11:48
LINE POSITION AND LINE INTENSITY ANALYSES OF H$_2^{18}$O UP TO THE FIRST TRIAD AND $J = 20^a$, L. H. Coudert, Georg Ch. Mellau, Semen Mikhailenko, Alain Campargue

WF10   11:51 – 12:06
HIGH-RESOLUTION LASER SPECTROSCOPY OF THE $S_1 \leftarrow S_0$ TRANSITION OF ACETALDEHYDE, Kosuke Nakajima, Shunji Kasahara, Akira Shimizu, Rin Taniguchi, Masaaki Baba

WF11   12:09 – 12:24
ROTATIONAL SPECTROSCOPY OF n-PROPANOL: Aa AND Ag CONFORMERS, Oliver Zingsheim, Holger S. P. Müller, Bettina Heyne, Mariyam Fatima, Luis Bonah, Arnaud Belloche, Frank Lewen, Stephan Schlemmer

WG. Ions
Wednesday, June 22, 2022 – 8:30 AM
Room: 274 Medical Sciences Building

Chair: Harshal Gupta, National Science Foundation, Alexandria, VA, USA

WG01   8:30 – 8:45
OPTICAL SPECTRUM OF Si_2^+, Emil Mickein, Taarna Studemund, Kai Pollow, Sophie Verhoeven, Marko Förstel, Otto Dopfer

WG02   8:48 – 9:03
INTERESTING BEHAVIOR OF THE $Si_3O_2^+$ SILICON OXIDE CLUSTER CATION, Kai Pollow, Taarna Studemund, Emil Mickein, Marko Förstel, Otto Dopfer

WG03   9:06 – 9:21
ON THE SPECTROSCOPY OF ACYLIUM IONS: INFRARED ACTION SPECTROSCOPIC DETECTION OF $NCCO^+$, Oskar Asvany, Marcel Bast, Stephan Schlemmer, Sven Thorwirth

WG04   9:24 – 9:39
HIGH-RESOLUTION SPECTROSCOPY OF $MgKr^+$ IN ITS GROUND AND LOW-LYING ELECTRONICALLY EXCITED STATES, Carla Kreis, Matthieu Génévriez, Frédéric Merkt

WG05   9:42 – 9:57
RO-VIBRATIONAL SPECTROSCOPY OF LINEAR C_3H^+, Philipp C Schmid, Thomas Salomon, Sven Thorwirth, Oskar Asvany, Stephan Schlemmer

WG06   10:00 – 10:15
GAS-PHASE CHARGE TRANSFER ELECTRONIC SPECTROSCOPY OF AG+-BENZENE COMPLEX, Dylan S. Orr, Jason E. Colley, Michael A Duncan

Intermission

WG07   10:57 – 11:12
HIGH-RESOLUTION INFRARED SPECTRA OF THE OH-STRETCHING BANDS OF PROTONATED WATER DIMER, $H_5O_2^+$, Thomas Salomon, Oskar Asvany, Charles R. Markus, Stephan Schlemmer

WG08   11:15 – 11:30
PROBING THE DEGREE OF NITROGEN ACTIVATION BY TRIDENTATE COPPER(I) COMPLEXES USING CIVP SPECTROSCOPY, Alexandra Tsybizova, Vladimir Gorbachev, Peter Chen

WG09   11:33 – 11:48
ANIONIC REARRANGEMENTS FOLLOWING DECARBOXYLATION OF BENZOPHENONE DERIVATIVES WITH CRYOGENIC IR SPECTROSCOPY, Joseph P. Messinger, Evan H Perez, Anna Gabriella del Rosario Rullán Buxó, Tim Schleif, Olivia Moss, Kim Greis, Mark Johnson

WG10   11:51 – 12:06
CARBOXYLATE STRETCHING MODES ARE STRUCTURAL PROBES FOR ION-DEPENDENT BINDING PROPERTIES IN ALKALI EARTH METAL-EDTA COMPLEXES, Madison M. Foreman, J. Mathias Weber

WG11   *Post-Deadline Abstract*   12:09 – 12:24
FIRST LABORATORY DETECTION OF $N^{13}CO^-$ AND SEMIEXPERIMENTAL EQUILIBRIUM STRUCTURE OF THE NCO^- ANION, Luca Dore, Luca Bizzocchi, Valerio Lattanzi, Mattia Melosso, Filippo Tamassia, Michael C McCarthy

WLUN. Plenary Panel Discussion
Wednesday, June 22, 2022 – 12:35 PM
Room: Ballroom Illini Union

Chair: Anthony Remijan, NRAO, Charlottesville, VA, USA

WLUN01 12:35 – 1:30
A PERSONAL VIEW OF THE ISMS, Terry A. Miller

WLUN02 12:35 – 1:30
THANK YOU ISMS!, Takeshi Oka

WLUN03 12:35 – 1:30
MY ISMS, Yasuki Endo

WH. Mini-symposium: Spectroscopy meets Chemical Dynamics
Wednesday, June 22, 2022 – 1:45 PM
Room: 100 Noyes Laboratory

Chair: Krupa Ramasesha, Sandia National Laboratories, Livermore, CA, USA

WH01   1:45 – 2:00
PHOTODISSOCIATION AND VELOCITY-MAP IMAGING OF CARBON CLUSTER CATIONS, Nathan John Dynak, Brandon M. Rittgers, Jason E. Colley, Douglas J. Kellar, Michael A Duncan

WH02   2:03 – 2:18
PHOTODISSOCIATION DYNAMICS OF CH_2OO ON MULTIPLE POTENTIAL ENERGY SURFACES: EXPERIMENT AND THEORY , Vincent J. Esposito, Tianlin Liu, Guanghan Wang, Adriana Caracciolo, Michael F. Vansco, Ernest Antwi, Olivia Werba, Sarah A. Bush, Rachel E. Bush, Barbara Marchetti, Tolga N. V. Karsili, Marsha Lester

WH03   2:21 – 2:36
OZONE PHOTODISSOCIATION IN THE SINGLET CHANNEL AT 226 NM, Megan Aardema, George McBane, Simon North

WH04   2:39 – 2:54
RAPID ALLYLIC 1,6 H-ATOM TRANSFER IN A CRIEGEE INTERMEDIATE WITH UNSATURATED SUBSTITUENTS, Anne S Hansen, Yujie Qian, Stephen J. Klippenstein, Marsha Lester

WH05   2:57 – 3:12
THE VIBRATIONAL PREDISSOCIATION OF THE Ã STATE OF THE C_3Ar VAN DER WAALS COMPLEX WITH VIBRATIONAL ENERGIES OF 1558-1660 cm^{-1}, Sheng-Chang Hsiao, Yen-Chu Hsu

WH06   3:15 – 3:30
THE VIBRATIONAL PREDISSOCIATION AND INTRAMOLECULAR VIBRATIONAL REDISTRIBUTION OF THE Ã STATE OF THE C_3Ar VAN DER WAALS COMPLEX, Sheng-Chang Hsiao, Yen-Chu Hsu

Intermission

WH07   4:12 – 4:27
DETECTION OF NASCENT PRODUCTS FROM THE PHOTOLYSIS OF ACRYLONITRILE VIA TIME-RESOLVED MILLIMETER WAVE SPECTROSCOPY, Nathan A. Seifert, Kirill Prozument

WH08   4:30 – 4:45
EXOMOLHD: RECENT PROGRESSES ON PHOTODISSOCIATION OF SMALL MOLECULES, Marco Pezzella, Jonathan Tennyson, Sergei N. Yurchenko

WH09   4:48 – 5:03
CO FORMATION FROM ACETONE PHOTOLYSIS: THE ROAMING PATHWAY, Lorrie S. D. Jacob, Kelvin Lee, Timothy Schmidt, Klaas Nauta, Scott Kable

WH10   5:06 – 5:21
SPECTROSCOPY AND PREDISSOCIATION DYNAMICS OF SH RADICALS VIA THE $A^2\Sigma^+$ STATE, Yuan Qin, Xianfeng Zheng, Yu Song, Ge Sun, Jingsong Zhang

WH11   5:24 – 5:39
VELOCITY MAP IMAGING OF GOLD ION - LIGAND COMPLEXES, Brandon M. Rittgers, Michael A Duncan

WI. Mini-symposium: Benchmarking in Spectroscopy
Wednesday, June 22, 2022 – 1:45 PM
Room: 116 Roger Adams Lab

Chair: Cristina Puzzarini, University of Bologna, Bologna, Italy

WI01   1:45 – 2:00
NON-ADIABATIC COUPLING IN NO@C_{60}: PREDICTION OF A RENNER-TELLER LIKE EFFECT FOR SPHERICALLY ENCAPSULATED DIATOMIC MOLECULES, Andreas W. Hauser, Johann V. Pototschnig

WI02   2:03 – 2:18
USING HIGH-RESOLUTION PHOTOELECTRON IMAGING TO PROBE THE SPECTROSCOPY OF CRYOGENICALLY COOLED AZOLIDE MOLECULES, Yue-Rou Zhang, Daofu Yuan, Lai-Sheng Wang

WI03   2:21 – 2:36
CAN LONDON DISPERSION OVERRIDE CATION- π INTERACTIONS?, Vladimir Gorbachev, Alexandra Tsybizova, Larisa Miloglyadova, Peter Chen

WI04   2:39 – 2:54
ELECTRONIC SPECTROSCOPY OF THE PREVIOUSLY UNKNOWN PALLADIUM MONOSULFIDE (PdS) RADICAL, Lei Zhang, Yao Yu, Xinwen Ma, Jie Yang

WI05   2:57 – 3:12
NEW METHODS FOR CORE-HOLE SPECTROSCOPY BASED ON COUPLED CLUSTER, Megan Simons, Devin A. Matthews

WI06   3:15 – 3:30
GENERALIZED OSCILLATOR STRENGTH OF THE INNER SHELL EXCITATION OF NITROGEN STUDIED BY NONRESONANT INELASTIC X-RAY SCATTERING, LiHan Wang

Intermission

WI07   4:12 – 4:27
FESCHBACH RESONANCE IN TETRACENE RADICAL ANION: THE SECRET TO A LONG LIFETIME OF NEGATIVITY, Cole R Sagan, Etienne Garand

WI08   4:30 – 4:45
FLUORESCENCE-DETECTED MID-INFRARED PHOTOTHERMAL MICROSCOPY, Minghe Li, Aleksandr Razumtcev, Garth Simpson

WI09   4:48 – 5:03
THE COUPLED-CHANNEL DEPERTURBATION ANALYSIS OF THE A~B~X STATES MANIFOLD OF CN WITH ALMOST SPECTROSCOPIC ACCURACY, Vera Terashkevich, Elena Alexandrovna Pazyuk, Andrey Stolyarov

WI10   5:06 – 5:21
CAVITY RING-DOWN SPECTROSCOPY OF WATER VAPOR IN THE NEAR-UV REGION, Q.-Y. Yang, Y. Tan, Shui-Ming Hu, Eamon K Conway, Iouli E Gordon

WI11   5:24 – 5:39
IN SITU SPECTROSCOPIC DIAGNOSTIC OF SHOCK INDUCED DECOMPOSITION OF C_{60}, Shubhadip Chakraborty, Sergei N. Yurchenko, Robert Georges, Vijayanand Chandrasekaran, V Jayaram, Elangannan Arunan, Ludovic Biennier

WJ. Instrument/Technique Demonstration

Wednesday, June 22, 2022 – 1:45 PM
Room: B102 Chemical and Life Sciences

Chair: Deacon J Nemchick, Jet Propulsion Laboratory, Pasadena, CA, USA

WJ01   1:45 – 2:00
INFRARED HIGH RESOLUTION COHERENT 2D SPECTROSCOPY, DeAunna A Daniels, Thresa Wells, Peter Chen

WJ02   2:03 – 2:18
A NEW FEMTOSECOND XUV SOURCE AT THE UNIVERSITY OF WISCONSIN, Ryan T Ash, Zain Abhari, Uwe Bergmann

WJ03   2:21 – 2:36
DEVELOPMENT OF A CRYOGENIC, MASS SELECTIVE, MULTI-REACTION TRAP ION SPECTROMETER, Gina Roesch, Etienne Garand

WJ04   2:39 – 2:54
DEMONSTRATION OF CRESU-REMPI FOR REACTION KINETIC MEASUREMENTS IN THE GAS-PHASE, Ranil Gurusinghe, Nureshan Dias, Jinxin Lang, Matthew L Edlin, Arthur Suits

WJ05   2:57 – 3:12
TOWARDS THE RESOLUTION LIMIT OF PFI-ZEKE PHOTOELECTRON SPECTROSCOPY, Holger Herburger, Vincent Wirth, Urs Hollenstein, Frédéric Merkt

Intermission

WJ06   3:54 – 4:09
MID-INFRARED CW OPTICAL PARAMETRIC OSCILLATOR PUMPED BY AN ELECTRO-OPTIC FREQUENCY COMB, Matthew J. Cich, Adam Heiniger, David B. Foote, Walter Hurlbut, Chris Haimberger, David A. Long

WJ07   4:12 – 4:27
CAVITY RING-DOWN SPECTROSCOPY WITH INTERBAND CASCADE OPTICAL FREQUENCY COMBS, TzuLing Chen, Charles R. Markus, Douglas Ober, Lukasz A. Sterczewski, Chadwick L Canedy, Igor Vurgaftman, Clifford Frez, Jerry R Meyer, Mahmood Bagheri, Mitchio Okumura

WJ08   4:30 – 4:45
MID-INFRARED SPECTROSCOPY OF TRANSIENT SPECIES USING A CHIP-SCALE MID-INFRARED OPTICAL FREQUENCY COMB, Charles R. Markus, TzuLing Chen, Douglas Ober, Lukasz A. Sterczewski, Chadwick L Canedy, Igor Vurgaftman, Clifford Frez, Jerry R Meyer, Mahmood Bagheri, Mitchio Okumura

WJ09   4:48 – 5:03
HIGH-SPEED, HIGH-RESOLUTION, BROADBAND DUAL-COMB SPECTROMETER FROM 3-5 μm, Scott C Egbert, Peter Chang, Scott Diddams, Gregory B Rieker, Nazanin Hoghooghi

WJ10   5:06 – 5:21
RAPID DUAL-COMB COHERENT RAMAN SPECTROSCOPY IN THE HIGH-WAVENUMBER REGION, Yujia Zhang, Minjian Lu, Yan LI, Haoyun Wei

WJ11   5:24 – 5:39
ABSOLUTE FREQUENCY SCALE FOR HIGH-RESOLUTION QUANTUM CASCADE LASER DUAL-COMB SPECTROMETER, Michele Gianella, Kenichi Komagata, Simon Vogel, Jérôme Faist, Thomas Südmeyer, Lukas Emmenegger

WK. Mini-symposium: Machine Learning
Wednesday, June 22, 2022 – 1:45 PM
Room: 217 Noyes Laboratory

Chair: Daniel R. Nascimento, The University of Memphis, Memphis, TN, USA

WK01   *INVITED TALK*   1:45 – 2:15
INTERPRETABLE DEEP LEARNING FOR MOLECULES AND MATERIALS, Andrew White

WK02   2:18 – 2:33
SUPERVISED LEARNING FOR SELECTIVE MULTI-SPECIES QUANTIFICATION FROM NOISY INFRARED SPECTROSCOPY DATA, Emad Al ibrahim, Aamir Farooq

WK03   2:36 – 2:51
COMPUTATIONAL OPTIMAL TRANSPORT FOR MOLECULAR SPECTRA, Nathan A. Seifert, Kirill Prozument, Michael J. Davis

Intermission

WK04   3:33 – 3:48
INVERSE INFRARED SPECTROSCOPY WITH BAYESIAN METHODS, Jezrielle R. Annis, Daniel P. Tabor

WK05   3:51 – 4:06
SEQUENCE-TO-SEQUENCE LEARNING FOR MOLECULAR STRUCTURE DERIVATION FROM INFRARED SPECTRA, Ethan French, Zhou Lin

WK06   4:09 – 4:24
GAS-PHASE INFRARED SPECTRA ANALYSIS VIA DEEP NEURAL NETWORKS, Abigail A Enders, Nicole North, Heather C. Allen

WK07   4:27 – 4:42
COMPARISON OF EXPERIMENTAL AND SIMULATED RAMAN SPECTRA THROUGH REVERSE SELF MODELING CURVE RESOLUTION FOR REGRESSION-BASED MACHINE LEARNING, Nicole North, Abigail A Enders, Heather C. Allen

WL. Conformers and isomers
Wednesday, June 22, 2022 – 1:45 PM
Room: 1024 Chemistry Annex

Chair: Isabelle Kleiner, CNRS, UPEC et Université de Paris, Créteil, France

WL01   1:45 – 2:00
FOURIER TRANSFORM MICROWAVE SPECTRA OF 1-PENTANETHIOL-*d*, Nobuhiko Kuze, Yoshiyuki Kawashima

WL02   2:03 – 2:18
MICROWAVE SPECTRUM OF ACETIC DIFLUOROACETIC ANHYDRIDE, Kaitlyn Belmont, Nathan Love, Kenneth R. Leopold

WL03   2:21 – 2:36
FLUORINATION AND DEOXYGENATION AS CHEMICAL TOOLS TO STUDY THE CONFORMATIONAL PREFERENCES OF HEXOPYRANOSES: A JOURNEY FROM GAS PHASE TO SOLUTION, Elena R. Alonso, Aran Insausti, Camilla Calabrese, Francisco J. Basterretxea, Francisco Corzana, Omar Boutureira, Emilio J. Cocinero

WL04   2:39 – 2:54
UNVEILING THE EIGHT FORMS OF CAFFEIC ACID, Gabriela Juárez, Miguel Sanz-Novo, Elena R. Alonso, Iker León, Santiago Mata, José L. Alonso

WL05   2:57 – 3:12
THE MICROWAVE SPECTRUM OF PIPERONAL: DESIGNING AND TESTING A NEW HEATED NOZZLE ASSEMBLY, Brayden Carty, Galen Sedo, Amanda Duerden, Joshua E. Isert, Nicole Moon, G. S. Grubbs II

WL06   3:15 – 3:30
THE JET-COOLED ROTATIONAL SPECTRUM OF N,N'-BIS(HYDROXYMETHYL)UREA AND ITS PHOTO-FRAGMENTED SPECIES, Lucie Kolesniková, Santiago Mata, Iker León, Elena R. Alonso, José L. Alonso

Intermission

WL07   4:12 – 4:27
ROTAMERS OF METHANEDIOL: COMPOSITE AB INITIO PREDICTIONS OF FUNDAMENTAL FREQUENCIES AND ROVIBRATIONAL CONSTANTS, Peter R. Franke, John F. Stanton

WL08   4:30 – 4:45
CONFORMATIONAL DIVERSITY OF NON-AROMATIC HETEROCYCLIC MOLECULAR COMPOUNDS AS STUDIED BY MEANS OF MATRIX ISOLATION INFRARED SPECTROSCOPY, Joanna Stocka, Rasa Platakyte, Justinas Ceponkus, Jogile Macyte, Daniel Vincent Hickman, Theodore Jacob Carrigan-Broda, Pawel Rodziewicz, Gamil A Guirgis, Valdas Sablinskas

WL09   4:48 – 5:03
STRUCTURAL ELUCIDATION OF IONS USING CHEMICAL REACTIONS, Ugo Jacovella, Corentin Rossi, Claire Romanzin, Christian Alcaraz, Roland Thissen

WL10   5:06 – 5:21
VISUALIZING ELECTRON DYNAMICS FOR A PHOTOISOMERIZATION REACTION, Lauren Bauerle, Agnieszka Jaron

WL11   5:24 – 5:39
STRUCTURE AND SPECTRA OF A COMPLEX BIOCHROMOPHORE - DEPROTONATED BILIVERDIN IX, Wyatt Zagorec-Marks, Leah G Dodson, Erik K. Schneider, Patrick Weis, Manfred M Kappes, J. Mathias Weber

WM. Non-covalent interactions
Wednesday, June 22, 2022 – 1:45 PM
Room: 124 Burrill Hall

Chair: Steven Shipman, New College of Florida, Sarasota, FL, USA

WM01   1:45 – 2:00
HELIUM NANODROPLET ISOLATION SPECTROSCOPY OF METHANOL AND METHANOL-WATER CLUSTERS IN THE SYMMETRIC METHYL STRETCHING BAND, Maameyaa Asiamah, Paul Raston

WM02   2:03 – 2:18
CHARACTERISATION OF THE STRUCTURE OF THE HYDROGEN-BONDED COMPLEX, THIAZOLE...$(H_2O)_2$, BY FOURIER-TRANSFORM MICROWAVE SPECTROSCOPY, Charlotte Nicole Cummings, Eva Gougoula, Yuago Xu, Gang Feng, Nick Walker

WM03   2:21 – 2:36
MULTIPLE WATER CONFIGURATIONS IN FENCHONE···$(H_2O)_{1-6}$ HYDRATES REVEALED BY ROTATIONAL SPECTROSCOPY, Ecaterina Burevschi, Mhamad Chrayteh, Donatella Loru, Pascal Dréan, M. Eugenia Sanz

WM04   2:39 – 2:54
TOWARDS UNDERSTANDING THE SOLVENT-ROLE IN THE CATALYSIS OF THE BIOMASS-MOLECULE 6-AMYL-α-PYRONE USING MICROWAVE SPECTROSCOPY, Himanshi Singh, Mariyam Fatima, Md. Ali Haider, Melanie Schnell

WM05   2:57 – 3:12
A NOVEL STRUCTURE FOR THE GAS PHASE HETERODIMER FORMED BETWEEN (Z)-1-CHLORO-3,3,3-TRIFLUOROPROPENE AND ACETYLENE, Seohyun (Cece) Hong, Mark D. Marshall, Helen O. Leung

WM06   3:15 – 3:30
AN INTERNAL AFFAIR: THE INFLUENCE OF INTRAMOLECULAR HYDROGEN BONDING ON THE STRUCTURE OF METAL-ION-PEPTIDE COMPLEXES , Katharina A. E. Meyer, Kathleen Ann Nickson, Etienne Garand

Intermission

WM07   4:12 – 4:27
MOLECULAR RECOGNITION IN OLFACTION: INTERACTIONS OF THE ODORANT CARVONE WITH ETHANOL , S. Indira Murugachandran, Donatella Loru, Isabel Peña, M. Eugenia Sanz

WM08   4:30 – 4:45
EXAMINING INTERMOLECULAR INTERACTIONS BETWEEN HYDROCARBONS AND WATER: A BROADBAND ROTATIONAL SPECTROSCOPIC STUDY OF THE α-PINENE – WATER COMPLEX , Arsh Singh Hazrah, Mohamad H. Al-Jabiri, Wolfgang Jäger

WM09   4:48 – 5:03
THE 3-METHYLCATECHOL-$(H_2O)_{N=1-4}$ COMPLEXES: STUDYING MICROSOLVATION USING BROADBAND ROTATIONAL SPECTROSCOPY , Arsh Singh Hazrah, Aran Insausti, Mohamad H. Al-Jabiri, Jiarui Ma, Yunjie Xu, Wolfgang Jäger

WM10   5:06 – 5:21
INTERMOLECULAR FREQUENCIES OF N_2O–KR AND SYMMETRY BREAKING OF THE N_2O BENDING MODE IN THE PRESENCE OF A RARE GAS, Chris Gergess, M. Dehghany, K. H. Michaelian, A.R.W. McKellar, Nasser Moazzen-Ahmadi

WM11   5:24 – 5:39
AB INITIO INVESTIGATIONS ON THE TRIMERS CONTAINING HC_3N IN COMBINATION WITH H_2C_2 AND/OR HCN , Andrea Pietropolli Charmet

WN. Astronomy
Wednesday, June 22, 2022 – 1:45 PM
Room: 274 Medical Sciences Building

Chair: Brett A. McGuire, Massachusetts Institute of Technology, Cambridge, MA, USA

WN01   1:45 – 2:00
SUBMILLIMETER WAVE STUDY OF NITROSOMETHANE (CH_3NO), L. Margulès, Luyao Zou, R. A. Motiyenko, J.-C. Guillemin

WN02   2:03 – 2:18
MILLIMETER AND SUB-MILLIMETER SPECTROSCOPY OF DOUBLY DEUTERATED ACETALDEHYDE (CD_2HCHO), Judit Ferrer Asensio, Silvia Spezzano, Christian Endres, Valerio Lattanzi, L. H. Coudert, Paola Caselli

WN03   2:21 – 2:36
THE ROTATION-TUNNELING SPECTRUM OF DIMETHYLAMINE, $(CH_3)_2NH$, Holger S. P. Müller, Frank Lewen, Stephan Schlemmer

WN04   2:39 – 2:54
RE-INVESTIGATION OF THE CYANOACETALDEHYDE ($NCCH_2CHO$) ROTATIONAL SPECTRUM, L. Margulès, Luyao Zou, R. A. Motiyenko, J.-C. Guillemin

WN05   2:57 – 3:12
ROTATIONAL SPECTRUM OF CD_3OD: NEW MEASUREMENTS AND ASSIGNMENTS IN THE $v_t = 0, 1$ and 2 TORSIONAL STATES, V. Ilyushin, R. Porohovoi, E. A. Alekseev, Olga Dorovskaya, Holger S. P. Müller, Frank Lewen, Stephan Schlemmer, Christof Maul, Ronald M. Lees

WN06   3:15 – 3:30
LABORATORY MEASUREMENT OF MILLIMETER-WAVE TRANSITIONS OF $^{13}CH_2DOH$ FOR ASTRONOMICAL USE, Takahiro Oyama, Yuki Ohno, Akemi Tamanai, Shaoshan Zeng, Yoshimasa Watanabe, Riouhei Nakatani, takeshi sakai, Nami Sakai

Intermission

WN07   4:12 – 4:27
MILLIMETER-WAVE SPECTRUM OF 2-PROPANIMINE AND ITS SEARCH IN THE INTERSTELLAR MEDIUM, Luyao Zou, L. Margulès, R. A. Motiyenko, J.-C. Guillemin, Arnaud Belloche, Jes Jorgensen

WN08   4:30 – 4:45
MILLIMETER AND SUBMILLIMETER SPECTROSCOPY OF ISOBUTENE, Mariyam Fatima, Oliver Zingsheim, Holger S. P. Müller, Dirk Hoppen, Stephan Schlemmer

WN09   4:48 – 5:03
EXTENSION OF THE MILLIMETER AND SUBMILLIMETER SPECTRUM OF GLYCOLIC ACID: ROTATIONAL SPECTROSCOPIC STUDY OF A POTENTIAL PREBIOTIC INTERSTELLAR MOLECULE, Chase P Schultz, Hayley Bunn, Susanna L. Widicus Weaver

WN10   5:06 – 5:21
THE MILLIMETER WAVE SPECTRA OF VINYL ISOCYANATE AND VINYL KETENE, CANDIDATES FOR ASTRONOMICAL OBSERVATIONS, Lucie Kolesniková, Jan Koucký, Karel Vávra, Kateřina Luková, Tereza Uhlíková, Patrik Kania, J.-C. Guillemin, Stepan Urban

WN11   5:24 – 5:39
ROTATIONAL SPECTROSCOPY AND INTERSTELLAR SEARCH FOR N- AND I-BUTYRALDEHYDE, Miguel Sanz-Novo, José L. Alonso, Arnaud Belloche, Karl M. Menten, Victor Manuel Rivilla, Lucas Rodríguez-Almeida, Izaskun Jiménez-Serra, Jesús Martín-Pintado, Robin T. Garrod, Pilar Redondo, Carmen Barrientos, Juan Carlos Valle, Lucie Kolesniková, Holger S. P. Müller

RA. Plenary
Thursday, June 23, 2022 – 8:30 AM
Room: Foellinger Auditorium

Chair: Anne B McCoy, University of Washington, Seattle, WA, USA

RA01   8:30 – 9:10
SPECTROSCOPY OF METAL AND PHOSPHORUS BEARING MOLECULES: A WINDOW ON THE UNIVERSE, Lucy M. Ziurys

RA02   9:15 – 9:55
THEORETICAL DESCRIPTIONS OF THE FUNDAMENTALS OF CH, NH AND OH STRETCH VIBRATIONS WITH SIMPLE MODELS THAT INCLUDE ANHARMONIC EFFECTS, Edwin Sibert

Intermission

JON T. HOUGEN MEMORIAL AWARDS   10:30
Introduction of Award by Isabelle Kleiner, CNRS, UPEC et Universite de Paris, Creteil, France

2022 Jon T. Hougen Memorial Award Winners
Kenneth Koziol, RWTH Aachen University
Lorrie Jacob, University of Cambridge

SNYDER AWARD   10:35
Presentation of Award by Anthony Remijan, NRAO

2021 Snyder Award Winner
Divita Gupta, Institut de Physique de Rennes

RAO AWARDS   10:40
Presentation of Awards by Timothy Zwier, Sandia National Laboratories

2021 Rao Award Winners
Parker Crandall, Technische Universität Berlin
Nicholas Hölsch, ETH Zuerich
Wey-Wey Su, Stanford University
James Thorpe, University of Florida

MILLER PRIZE   10:50
Introduction by Michael Heaven, Emory University

RA03   *Miller Prize Lecture*   10:55 – 11:10
DIABATIC VALENCE-HOLE STATES IN THE C_2 MOLECULE: "PUTTING HUMPTY DUMPTY TOGETHER AGAIN", Jun Jiang, Hong-Zhou Ye, Klaas Nauta, Troy Van Voorhis, Timothy Schmidt, Robert W Field

COBLENTZ AWARD   11:15
Presentation of Award by Zac Schultz, Coblentz Society

RA04   *Coblentz Society Award Lecture*   11:20 – 12:00
ADVANCING DYNAMIC METHODS FOR COMPUTATIONAL SPECTROSCOPY IN THE GAS AND CONDENSED PHASE, Sandra Luber

RH. Mini-symposium: Spectroscopy meets Chemical Dynamics
Thursday, June 23, 2022 – 1:45 PM
Room: 100 Noyes Laboratory

Chair: Timothy S. Zwier, Sandia National Laboratories, Livermore, CA, USA

RH01   1:45 – 2:00
A DFT STUDY: SPECTROSCOPIC ANALYSIS OF SCHIFF BASE LIGAND WITH FE(II) COMPLEX, Berna Catikkas

RH02   2:03 – 2:18
HIGH-RESOLUTION LASER SPECTROSCOPIC STUDIES OF UROCANIC ACID AND DERIVATIVES: TOWARDS NOVEL NATURE-INSPIRED SUNSCREENS, Jiayun Fan, Laura Finazzi, Alexander Karel Lemmens, Wybren Jan Buma

RH03   2:21 – 2:36
HIGH-RESOLUTION LASER SPECTROSCOPIC STUDIES OF CINNAMATE-BASED MOLECULAR HEATERS, I. Romanov, Y. Boeije, Wybren Jan Buma, Josene Maria Toldo, Mariana Telles do Casal, Mario Barbatti

RH04   2:39 – 2:54
HYPERFINE EXCITATION OF $HC^{17}O^+$ WITH p-H_2 COLLISIONS, Francesca Tonolo, Luca Bizzocchi, François Lique, Mattia Melosso, Vincenzo Barone, Cristina Puzzarini

RH05   2:57 – 3:12
EXTENDED PREDICTION OF CAF ELECTRONIC STATES: ENERGIES, MULTIPOLE MOMENTS, AND A SHAPE RESONANCE STATE, Stephen L Coy, Timothy J Barnum, Robert W Field, John F. Stanton

Intermission

RH06   3:54 – 4:09
STATE-RESOLVED MODELING FOR THE ENERGY TRANSFER PROCESSES IN LASER-INDUCED FLUORESCENCE OF DIATOMIC MOLECULES, Shengkai Wang

RH07   4:12 – 4:27
PRESSURE AND TEMPERATURE DEPENDENCE OF ABSORPTION CROSS-SECTION OF HCN IN THE LONG-WAVE MID-INFRARED REGION, Ali Elkhazraji, Mohammad Adil, Mhanna Mhanna, Nawaf Abualsaud, Ahmed Ayidh Alsulami, Mohammad Khaled Shakfa, Marco Marangoni, Binod Giri, Aamir Farooq

RH08   4:30 – 4:45
HITTING THE TRIFECTA: HOW TO SIMULTANEOUSLY PUSH THE LIMITS OF SCHRÖDINGER SOLUTION WITH RESPECT TO SYSTEM SIZE, CONVERGENCE ACCURACY, AND NUMBER OF COMPUTED STATES, János Sarka, Bill Poirier

RH09   4:48 – 5:03
ANALOG QUANTUM SIMULATION OF MOLECULAR DYNAMICS AND SPECTROSCOPIC OBSERVABLES, Ryan J MacDonell, Ivan Kassal

RH10   5:06 – 5:21
MEASUREMENTS OF HIGH-TEMPERATURE ABSORPTION SPECTRA OF DIMETHYL ETHER AND DIETHYL ETHER BETWEEN 950 AND 1190 cm^{-1} AND THEIR DIRECT PYROLYSIS STUDY IN A SHOCK TUBE, Mohammad Adil, Binod Giri, Aamir Farooq

RH11   5:24 – 5:39
MECHANISTIC STUDY OF PHOTOCHEMICAL [2+2] CYCLOADDITION BETWEEN 1,5-CYCLOOCTADIENE AND MALEIC ANHYDRIDE, Jun Yi, Zhou Lin, Junpeng Wang

RI. Mini-symposium: Benchmarking in Spectroscopy
Thursday, June 23, 2022 – 1:45 PM
Room: 116 Roger Adams Lab

Chair: Daniel A. Obenchain, Georg-August-Universität Göttingen, Göttingen, Germany

RI01　　　　　　　　　　　　　　　*INVITED TALK*　　　　　　　　　　　　　　　1:45 – 2:15
THE HyDRA BLIND CHALLENGE: INVITING THEORY TO PREDICT UNKNOWN VIBRATIONAL SPECTROSCOPY DATA, Taija L. Fischer, Maragrethe Bödecker, Sophie M. Schweer, Anne Zehnacker-Rentien, Ricardo A Mata, Martin A. Suhm

RI02　　　　　　　　　　　　　　　　　　　　　　　　　　　　　　　　　　　　　　2:21 – 2:36
NEW JET-COOLED VIBRATIONAL SPECTROSCOPIC BENCHMARK DATA OF THE CYCLIC DIMER AND TRIMER OF FORMIC ACID, Arman Nejad, Katharina A. E. Meyer, Martin A. Suhm

RI03　　　　　　　　　　　　　　　　　　　　　　　　　　　　　　　　　　　　　　2:39 – 2:54
A VIBRATIONAL ACTION SPECTROSCOPIC STUDY OF THE RENNER-TELLER AND SPIN-ORBIT AFFECTED CYANOACETYLENE RADICAL CATION HC_3N^+ ($^2\Pi$), Kim Steenbakkers, Aravindh Nivas Marimuthu, Gerrit Groenenboom, Britta Redlich, Sandra Brünken

RI04　　　　　　　　　　　　　　　　　　　　　　　　　　　　　　　　　　　　　　2:57 – 3:12
MODEL CHEMISTRY RECOMMENDATIONS FOR HARMONIC FREQUENCY CALCULATIONS: A BENCHMARK STUDY, Juan C. Zapata Trujillo, Laura K McKemmish

RI05　　　　　　　　　　　　　　　　　　　　　　　　　　　　　　　　　　　　　　3:15 – 3:30
NON-LTE INFRARED SPECTRUM OF JET-COOLED NAPHTHALENE, Shubhadip Chakraborty, Giacomo Mulas, Olivier Pirali, Pascale Soulard, Pierre Asselin, Manuel Goubet, Ludovic Biennier, Robert Georges

Intermission

RI06　　　　　　　　　　　　　　　　　　　　　　　　　　　　　　　　　　　　　　4:12 – 4:27
PROBING HALOGEN BONDING INTERACTIONS BETWEEN HEPTAFLUORO-2-IODOPROPANE AND THREE AZABENZENES WITH RAMAN SPECTROSCOPY AND DENSTIY FUNCTIONAL THEORY, Ethan Chase Lambert, Ashley E. Williams, Ryan C. Fortenberry, Nathan I Hammer

RI07　　　　　　　　　　　　　　　　　　　　　　　　　　　　　　　　　　　　　　4:30 – 4:45
VIBRATIONAL CHARACTERIZATION OF HEMI-BONDED HALIDE-THIOCYANATE DIMER RADICAL ANIONS $(XSCN)^{.-}$ IN WATER , Ireneusz Janik, Susmita Bhattacharya

RI08　　　　　　　　　　　　　　　　　　　　　　　　　　　　　　　　　　　　　　4:48 – 5:03
THE HIGHER TORSIONAL STATES OF METHYLAMINE - PRELIMINARY ANALYSIS , Iwona Gulaczyk, Marek Kreglewski

RI09　　　　　　　　　　　　　　　　　　　　　　　　　　　　　　　　　　　　　　5:06 – 5:21
COMPLETION OF THE FIRST SOLVATION SHELL OF CARBON DIOXIDE IN ARGON: ROTATIONALLY RESOLVED INFRARED SPECTRA OF CO_2-AR_{15} AND CO_2-AR_{17}, A. J. Barclay, A.R.W. McKellar, Nasser Moazzen-Ahmadi

RI10　　　　　　　　　　　　　　　　　　　　　　　　　　　　　　　　　　　　　　5:24 – 5:39
HIGH RESOLUTION INFRARED SPECTROSCOPY OF DIBORANE DISPERSED IN SOLID PARAHYDROGEN, Aaron I. Strom, Ibrahim Muddasser, David T. Anderson

RI11　　　　　　　　　　　　　　　　　　　　　　　　　　　　　　　　　　　　　　5:42 – 5:57
TRIHYBRID LINE LIST CONSTRUCTION FOR NH AND ZrO, Armando N. Perri, Laura K McKemmish

RJ. Instrument/Technique Demonstration
Thursday, June 23, 2022 – 1:45 PM
Room: B102 Chemical and Life Sciences

Chair: Jacob Stewart, Connecticut College, New London, CT, USA

RJ01   1:45 – 2:00
PROGRESS ON SHOCKGAS-IR: MEASUREMENTS OF METHYL FORMATE AT ELEVATED TEMPERATURES, Wey-Wey Su, Yiming Ding, Christopher L Strand, Ronald K Hanson

RJ02   2:03 – 2:18
CO2 COLLISIONAL BROADENING OF THE 557 GHz WATER ABSORPTION FEATURE PROFILED WITH A DIFFERENTIAL ABSORPTION RADAR PLATFORM, Ken Cooper, Deacon J Nemchick, Omkar Pradhan, Robert Dengler, Raquel Rodriquez Monje, Brian Drouin, Jose Siles, Leslie Tamppari

RJ03   2:21 – 2:36
ROOM-TEMPERATURE QUANTIFICATION OF $^{14}CO_2$ BELOW THE NATURAL ABUNDANCE WITH TWO-COLOR, CAVITY RINGDOWN SPECTROSCOPY, Jun Jiang, A. Daniel McCartt

RJ04   2:39 – 2:54
SELECTIVE PRODUCTION OF HCN MONOMER AND EVIDENCE FOR GAS-PHASE DIMERIZATION, Thomas Howard, Emily K Hockey, Darya Kisuryna, Jessica Palko, Leah G Dodson

RJ05   2:57 – 3:12
INSTRUMENT DESIGN AND PREPARATION OF *PARA*-HYDROGEN FOR MATRIX EXPERIMENTS, Korina Vlahos, Emily K Hockey, Leah G Dodson

RJ06   3:15 – 3:30
W BAND CHIRPED-PULSE: THE BEAUTY OF COHERENT SPECTROSCOPY, Bettina Heyne, Marius Hermanns, Nadine Wehres, Stephan Schlemmer

Intermission

RJ07   4:12 – 4:27
LLWP – UPDATES ON A NEW LOOMIS-WOOD SOFTWARE AT THE EXAMPLE OF ACETONE-$^{13}C_1$, Luis Bonah, Oliver Zingsheim, Holger S. P. Müller, Sven Thorwirth, J.-C. Guillemin, Frank Lewen, Stephan Schlemmer

RJ08   4:30 – 4:45
DUAL BAND MINIATURIZED SEMI-CONFOCAL FABRY-PEROT SPECTROMETERS FOR H2O AND HDO MILLIMETER-WAVE SENSING, Deacon J Nemchick, Adrian Tang, Brian Drouin, Ananda Q. Nole, Neda Khiabani, Chung-Tse Michael Wu, Maria Alonso, M.-C. Frank Chang

RJ09   4:48 – 5:03
DEVELOPMENT OF A MM-WAVE ULTRA-SENSITIVE SPECTROMETER FOR THE DETECTION OF SEMI-VOLATILE ORGANIC VAPORS , Mhamad Chrayteh, Fabien Simon, Coralie Elmaleh, Francis Hindle, Gaël Mouret, Arnaud Cuisset

RJ10   5:06 – 5:21
INTERFERENCE BETWEEN THE $5d_{5/2} - 5p_{3/2}$ AND $5p_{3/2} - 5s_{1/2}$ COHERENCES (386.4 AND 384.1 THz) IN Rb OBSERVED BY ULTRAFAST FOUR-WAVE MIXING SPECTROSCOPY , Thomas Reboli, J. Gary Eden

RK. Metal containing
Thursday, June 23, 2022 – 1:45 PM
Room: 217 Noyes Laboratory

Chair: Michael Heaven, Emory University, Atlanta, GA, USA

RK01   1:45 – 2:00
SPECTROSCOPIC CHARACTERIZATION OF REACTIVE INTERMEDIATES IN VARIOUS METAL CATALYSTS, Kathleen Ann Nickson, Etienne Garand

RK02   2:03 – 2:18
THE PURE ROTATIONAL SPECTRUM OF MgCl IN THE $(2)^2\Pi_i$ EXCITED STATE, Tyler J Herman, Parker Crowther, Lucy M. Ziurys

RK03   2:21 – 2:36
METAL IDENTITY AND PRODUCT BINDING TUNE STRUCTURE AND CHARGE DISTRIBUTION: INFRARED SPECTRA OF CATALYTICALLY RELEVANT METAL BIPYRIDINE COMPLEXES, Madison M. Foreman, Wyatt Zagorec-Marks, J. Mathias Weber

RK04   2:39 – 2:54
HIGH RESOLUTION LASER SPECTROSCOPY OF THE [16.0]5 - $X^5\Delta_4$ ELECTRONIC SYSTEM OF RUTHENIUM MONOXIDE, Allan G. Adam, Geoffrey M. Chenard, Colan Linton, Dennis W. Tokaryk

RK05   2:57 – 3:12
OBSERVATIONS OF THE ZEEMAN/PASCHEN-BACK EFFECT IN THE A-X SYSTEM OF CrH, Patrick Crozet, Jérôme Morville, Amanda J. Ross, Julien Morin

Intermission

RK06   3:54 – 4:09
TERAHERTZ SPECTROSCOPY OF CaH, Shota Suzuki, Tatsuki Sumi, Fusakazu Matsushima, Kaori Kobayashi, Yoshiki Moriwaki, Hiroyuki Ozeki

RK07   4:12 – 4:27
ANALYSIS OF THE $A\ ^4\Pi_r - X\ ^4\Sigma^-$ ELECTRONIC TRANSITION OF MOLYBDENUM NITRIDE (MoN), Leah C O'Brien, Gabriel A Hotz, Kristin N Bales, Jack C Harms, James J O'Brien, Nyla S Woods, Wenli Zou

RK08   4:30 – 4:45
MASS-INDEPENDENT ROTATIONAL AND DEPERTURBATION ANALYSIS OF THE [15.30]1 AND [14.26]0^+ ELECTRONIC STATES OF TUNGSTEN SULFIDE (WS), Kristin N Bales, Jack C Harms, James J O'Brien, Leah C O'Brien

RK10   5:06 – 5:21
LOW- AND HIGH-RESOLUTION LASER-INDUCED FLUORESCENCE (LIF) OF JET-COOLED SmO, Joel R Schmitz, Arianna Rodriguez, Timothy Steimle, Michael Heaven

RL. Structure determination
Thursday, June 23, 2022 – 1:45 PM
Room: 1024 Chemistry Annex

Chair: Nathan A. Seifert, University of New Haven, New Haven, CT, USA

RL01 1:45 – 2:00
THE ROTATIONAL SPECTRUM OF SULFANILAMIDE AND ITS HYDRATED CLUSTER , Sergio Mato, Raúl Aguado, José L. Alonso, Iker León

RL02 2:03 – 2:18
THE ROTATIONAL SPECTRUM OF NONAFLUORO-TERT-BUTYL ALCOHOL, Joshua E. Isert, Zayra Leticia Gonzalez, Karla V. Salazar, Diego Rodriguez, Nicole Moon, Wei Lin, G. S. Grubbs II

RL03 2:21 – 2:36
INTERNAL ROTATION ANALYSIS AND STRUCTURAL DETERMINATION OF R-CARVONE, Nicole Moon, G. S. Grubbs II

RL04 2:39 – 2:54
ROTATIONAL SPECTRUM AND CONFORMATIONAL ANALYSIS OF PERILLARTINE: INSIGHTS INTO THE STRUCTURE-SWEETNESS RELATIONSHIP , Gabriela Juárez, Miguel Sanz-Novo, José L. Alonso, Elena R. Alonso, Iker León

RL05 2:57 – 3:12
HIGH-RESOLUTION LASER SPECTROSCOPY OF $S_1 \leftarrow S_0$ TRANSITION OF TRANS-STILBENE : NONPLANAR STRUCTURE IN THE GROUND STATE , Akira Shimizu, Kosuke Nakajima, Shunji Kasahara, Masatoshi Misono, Masaaki Baba

RL06 3:15 – 3:30
PROPANE ISOTOPOLOGUES: HIGH RESOLUTION FAR-IR SYNCHROTRON SPECTRA OF PROPANE-D7 (CD3-CDH-CD3) AND PROPANE-D5 (CH3-CD2-CD3), Stephen J. Daunt, Colin Western, Brant E. Billinghurst, Jianbao Zhao, Robert Grzywacz

RL07 3:33 – 3:48
SEMI-EXPERIMENTAL EQUILIBRIUM STRUCTURE OF METHACRYLONITRILE (C_4H_5N), Houston H. Smith, Samuel M. Kougias, Danny J Lee, Brian J. Esselman, Bryan Changala, Michael C McCarthy, R. Claude Woods, Robert J. McMahon

Intermission

RL08 4:30 – 4:45
SPECTROSCOPIC CONSTANTS AND POTENTIAL FUNCTIONS FOR THE $A^3\Pi_1$ AND $X^1\Sigma^+$ STATES OF IBr BY USING MERGED DATA OF STARK SPECTROSCOPY, Nobuo Nishimiya, Tokio Yukiya, Katsuki Nomura, Masao Suzuki

RL09 4:48 – 5:03
THE CONFORMATIONAL PANORAMA OF D-PENICILLAMINE: A LASER ABLATION ROTATIONAL STUDY. , Diego Herreras, Elena R. Alonso, Iker León, José L. Alonso

RL10 5:06 – 5:21
STRUCTURE AND DYNAMICS OF HHe_3^+: THE EMERGENCE OF LARGE-SCALE NUCLEAR DELOCALIZATION, Irén Simkó, Csaba Fábri, Attila Császár, Fabien Brieuc, Christoph Schran, Dominik Marx, Oskar Asvany, Stephan Schlemmer

RL11 *Post-Deadline Abstract* 5:24 – 5:39
MID-INFRARED DOPPLER-FREE SATURATION ABSORPTION SPECTROSCOPY OF METHANE FOR FUTURE CAVITY-ENHANCED DOUBLE-RESONANCE SPECTROSCOPY INVESTIGATING ITS HIGH POLYADS., S M Shah Riyadh, Hamzeh Telfah, Md Touhidul Islam, Jinjun Liu

RL12 5:42 – 5:57
HIGH-RESOLUTION LASER SPECTROSCOPY AND THE ZEEMAN EFFECT: DIBENZOTHIOPHENE, Naofumi Nakayama, Masaaki Baba

RM. Fundamental physics
Thursday, June 23, 2022 – 1:45 PM
Room: 124 Burrill Hall

Chair: Terry A. Miller, The Ohio State University, Columbus, OH, USA

RM01   1:45 – 2:00
ROTATIONAL CLOSURE IN LASER-COOLING NONLINEAR MOLECULES, Jinjun Liu

RM02   2:03 – 2:18
A NEW UNDERSTANDING OF LAMBDA DOUBLING, Robert J Gordon, Robert W Field

RM03   2:21 – 2:36
TOWARDS A GLOBAL EIGHT-STATE FIT OF THE ROTATIONAL AND VIBRATIONAL SPECTRA OF HN_3, R. Claude Woods, Brent K. Amberger, Brant E. Billinghurst, Brian J. Esselman, Patrik Kania, Zbigniew Kisiel, Robert J. McMahon, Vanessa L. Orr, Andrew N. Owen, Houston H. Smith, Stepan Urban, Karel Vávra, Samuel A. Wood

RM05   2:57 – 3:12
A SCALE QUANTIFYING THE STRENGTH OF INTRAMOLECULAR HYDROGEN BONDS FROM IR SPECTROSCOPY, Garrett D Santis, Sotiris Xantheas

RM06   3:15 – 3:30
PUSHING MULTIPHOTON RESONANT IONIZATION OF ARGON TO LOW-INTENSITY REGIEM, Xuan Yu, Na Wang, Jianting Lei, Bennaceur Najjari, Shaofeng Zhang, Xinwen Ma

Intermission

RM07   4:12 – 4:27
PRECISION MEASUREMENT WITH CAVITY-ENHANCED BUFFER-GAS COOLED MICROWAVE SPECTROSCOPY, Lincoln Satterthwaite, Greta Koumarianou, Daniel Sorensen, David Patterson

RM08   4:30 – 4:45
PRECISION SPECTROSCOPY STUDIES OF RADIOACTIVE MOLECULES FOR FUNDAMENTAL PHYSICS, Silviu-Marian Udrescu, Shane Wilkins, Ronald Fernando Garcia Ruiz, Alex Brinson, Adam Vernon, Alexander A. Breier, Thomas Giesen, Robert Berger, Konstantin Gaul, Carsten Zulch, Bran van den Borne, Thomas Cocolios, Ruben Degroote, Anais Dorne, Sarina Geldhof, Louis Lalanne, Gerda Neyens, Kieran Flanagan, Holly Perrett, Jordan Reilly, Julius Wessolek, Michail Athanasakis-Kaklamanakis, Mia Au, Katherina Chrysalidis, Agota Koszorus, Sebastian Rothe, Timur A. Isaev, Ivana Belosevic, Serge Franchoo, Sonja Kujanpaa, Miranda Nichols, Xiaofei Yang

RM09   4:48 – 5:03
CAVITY ENHANCED MICROWAVE SPECTROSCOPY IN A BUFFER GAS CELL, Daniel Sorensen, Lincoln Satterthwaite, Greta Koumarianou, David Patterson

RM10   5:06 – 5:21
A COMBINED mm-WAVE AND FAR-INFRARED STUDY OF PYRAZOLE, Dennis W. Tokaryk, Brian J. Esselman, R. Claude Woods, Robert J. McMahon, Jeff Crouse, Doyeon Kim

RM11   5:24 – 5:39
COMBINED MILLIMETER WAVE AND FTIR SPECTRA OF DN_3, R. Claude Woods, Brent K. Amberger, Brant E. Billinghurst, Brian J. Esselman, Patrik Kania, Zbigniew Kisiel, Robert J. McMahon, Vanessa L. Orr, Andrew N. Owen, Houston H. Smith, Stepan Urban, Karel Vávra, Samuel A. Wood

RN. Astronomy
Thursday, June 23, 2022 – 1:45 PM
Room: 274 Medical Sciences Building

Chair: Gustavo A. Cruz-Diaz, University of Wisconsin-Madison, Madison, WI, USA

RN01   1:45 – 2:00
LILLE SPECTROSCOPIC DATABASE FOR ASTROPHYSICALLY AND ATMOSPHERICALLY RELEVANT MOLECULES, R. A. Motiyenko, L. Margulès

RN02   2:03 – 2:18
A NEW APPROACH FOR AUTOMATED ANALYSIS OF HIGH-RESOLUTION MOLECULAR LINE SURVEYS, Samer El-Abd, Crystal L. Brogan, Todd R. Hunter, Kelvin Lee, Brett A. McGuire

RN03   2:21 – 2:36
REFERENCE DATA FOR AMMONIA SPECTRA IN THE 3900-6300 CM^{-1} RANGE, Peter Čermák, Patrice Cacciani, Jean Cosleou, Alain Campargue, Serge Béguier, Jean Vander Auwera, Ondřej Votava, Jozef Rakovský

RN04   2:39 – 2:54
FORBIDDEN ROTATIONAL TRANSITIONS AND ASTROPHYSICS, Takeshi Oka

RN05   2:57 – 3:12
EXPERIMENTAL INSIGHTS INTO THE FORMATION OF INTERSTELLAR FULLERENES AND CARBON NANOTUBES, Jacob Bernal, Thomas J. Zega, Lucy M. Ziurys

Intermission

RN06   3:54 – 4:09
PREBIOTIC MOLECULES IN INTERSTELLAR SPACE: THE ROLE OF ROTATIONAL SPECTROSCOPY AND QUANTUM-CHEMICAL CALCULATIONS, Cristina Puzzarini, Mattia Melosso, Luca Bizzocchi, Silvia Alessandrini

RN07   4:12 – 4:27
MULTI-WAVELENGTH INVESTIGATION ON NEW MOLECULAR MASERS TOWARD THE GALACTIC CENTER, Ci Xue, Alexandre Faure, Emmanuel Momjian, Anthony Remijan, Todd R. Hunter, Brett A. McGuire

RN08   4:30 – 4:45
ASSESSING 27 MOLECULES FOR SENSITIVITY TO PROTON-TO-ELECTRON MASS VARIATION: STRENGTHS AND LIMITATIONS OF A HIGH-THROUGHPUT APPROACH, Anna-Maree Syme, Laura K McKemmish

RN09   4:48 – 5:03
THE OPTICAL SPECTRUM OF THE DIAMANTANE RADICAL CATION, Parker B. Crandall, Robert G. Radloff, Marko Förstel, Otto Dopfer

RN10   5:06 – 5:21
CS ABSORPTION AT 140 NM IN SPECTRA ACQUIRED WITH THE HUBBLE SPACE TELESCOPE, Steven Federman, Adam Ritchey, Kyle N. Crabtree, Zhongxing Xu, William M. Jackson

RN11   5:24 – 5:39
CAVITY RING DOWN SPECTROSCOPY OF INTERSTELLAR PAHS AND PAH-RELATED ANALOGS - ASTRONOMICAL APPLICATIONS, Salma Bejaoui, Farid Salama

FA. Mini-symposium: Spectroscopy meets Chemical Dynamics
Friday, June 24, 2022 – 8:30 AM
Room: 100 Noyes Laboratory

Chair: Ryan T Ash, University of Wisconsin Madison, Madison, WI, USA

FA01   8:30 – 8:45
MULTICHANNEL RADICAL-RADICAL REACTION DYNAMICS OF NO + PROPARGYL PROBED BY ROTATIONAL SPECTROSCOPY, Nureshan Dias, Ranil Gurusinghe, Arthur Suits

FA02   8:48 – 9:03
DYNAMICS AND KINETICS STUDIED BY CHIRPED PULSE MICROWAVE SPECTROSCOPY IN COLD UNIFORM SUPERSONIC FLOWS , Alberto Macario, Myriam Drissi, Omar Abdelkader Khedaoui, Theo Guillaume, Brian M Hays, Divita Gupta, Ilsa Rose Cooke, Ian R. Sims

FA03   9:06 – 9:21
BRANCHING RATIO MEASUREMENTS FOR THE $O(^3P)$ + PROPENE REACTION USING CHIRPED PULSE MICROWAVE SPECTROSCOPY AT LOW TEMPERATURE, Myriam Drissi, Alberto Macario, Omar Abdelkader Khedaoui, Brian M Hays, Divita Gupta, Theo Guillaume, Ilsa Rose Cooke, Ian R. Sims

FA04   9:24 – 9:39
CONFORMER SELECTED DIMER FORMATION IN A CRYOGENIC BUFFER GAS CELL, Lincoln Satterthwaite, Greta Koumarianou, David Patterson

FA05   9:42 – 9:57
ROTATIONAL SPECTROSCOPY OF CHEMICAL REACTIONS IN A CRYOGENIC BUFFER GAS CELL, Brandon Carroll, Bryan Changala, Michael C McCarthy

FA06   10:00 – 10:15
UV PHOTOFRAGMENT SPECTROSCOPY AND ELECTRONIC ENERGY TRANSFER ON A PEPTIDE SCAFFOLD: THE CASE OF NEAR-DEGENERATE UV CHROMOPHORES, Casey Daniel Foley, Etienne Chollet, Matthew A. Kubasik, Timothy S. Zwier

Intermission

FA07   10:57 – 11:12
STRUCTURE AND DYNAMICS OF THE WEAKLY BOUND TRIMER $(H_2S)_2(H_2O)$ OBSERVED USING ROTATIONAL SPECTROSCOPY, Arijit Das, Eva Gougoula, Nick Walker, Elangannan Arunan

FA08   11:15 – 11:30
EVIDENCE OF NITROGEN AS ACCEPTOR IN NITROMETHANE-FORMALDEHYDE HETERODIMERS CHARACTERIZED USING MATRIX ISOLATION INFRARED SPECTROSCOPY AND COMPUTATIONAL METHODS, NANDALAL MAHAPATRA, S Chandra, Nagarajan Ramanathan, K Sundararajan

FA09   11:33 – 11:48
OXYGEN ATOM DIFFUSION BY QUANTUM TUNNELING IN SOLID PARAHYDROGEN: A NEW TOOL TO STUDY LOW TEMPERATURE SOLID STATE REACTIONS, Ibrahim Muddasser, David T. Anderson

FA10   11:51 – 12:06
USING THE METROPOLIS MONTE CARLO METHOD TO EXTRACT REACTION KINETICS FROM EQUILIBRIUM DISTRIBUTIONS OF STATES, Sergei F. Chekmarev

FB. Mini-symposium: Benchmarking in Spectroscopy
Friday, June 24, 2022 – 8:30 AM
Room: 116 Roger Adams Lab

Chair: Brian J. Esselman, The University of Wisconsin, Madison, Madison, WI, USA

FB01   *INVITED TALK*   8:30 – 9:00
ROTATIONAL SPECTROSCOPIC BENCHMARK FOR π INTERATION, Hao Wang, Yang Zheng, Juan Wang, Walther Caminati, Jens-Uwe Grabow, Julien Bloino, Cristina Puzzarini, Vincenzo Barone, Junha Chen, Qian Gou

FB02   9:06 – 9:21
FIRST OBSERVATIONS OF THE HONO · H_2O COMPLEX WITH MICROWAVE SPECTROSCOPY, Kenneth J. Koziol, Ha Vinh Lam Nguyen, Safa Khemissi, Martin SCHWELL, Isabelle Kleiner, Tarek Trabelsi, Joseph S Francisco

FB03   9:24 – 9:39
INSTRUMENT DEVELOPMENT FOR CHIRPED PULSE FOURIER-TRANSFORM MICROWAVE SPECTROSCOPY OF ALCOHOL:WATER CLUSTERS, S E Dutton, Geoffrey Blake

FB04   9:42 – 9:57
MULTIDIMENSIONAL TUNNELING IN 2-NITROTOLUENE[a], Anthony Roucou, Arnaud Cuisset, Manuel Goubet, L. H. Coudert

FB05   10:00 – 10:15
DOUBLE-PROTON TRANSFER OVER A PHENYL RING REVEALED BY CP-FTMW SPECTROSCOPY, Weixing Li, Denis Tikhonov, Melanie Schnell, Walther Caminati, Dingding Lv, Guanjun Wang, Mingfei Zhou

Intermission

FB06   10:57 – 11:12
BRIDGING THE GAP: ROTATIONAL STUDY OF H_2 IN COMPLEXES WITH SMALL AROMATIC MOLECULES, Robin Dohmen, Melanie Schnell, Pablo Pinacho, Daniel A. Obenchain

FB07   11:15 – 11:30
STRONG ORTHO/PARA EFFECTS IN THE VIBRATIONAL SPECTRA OF Cl-H2 and CN-H2, Franziska Dahlmann, Pavol Jusko, Miguel Lara-Moreno, Christine Lochmann, Aravindh Nivas Marimuthu, Philippe Halvick, Robert Wild, Tim Michaelsen, Stephan Schlemmer, Thierry Stoecklin, Sandra Brünken, Roland Wester

FB08   11:33 – 11:48
ACCURATE EXPERIMENTAL VALIDATION OF AB INITIO QUANTUM SCATTERING CALCULATIONS USING THE SPECTRA OF He-PERTURBED H_2, Michał Słowiński, Hubert Jóźwiak, Maciej Grzegorz Gancewski, Kamil Stankiewicz, Nikodem Stolarczyk, Piotr Żuchowski, Roman Ciurylo, Piotr Wcislo, Yan Tan, Jin Wang, An-Wen Liu, Shui-Ming Hu, Samir Kassi, Alain Campargue, Konrad Patkowski, Franck Thibault

FB09   11:51 – 12:06
INVESTIGATION OF COLLISIONAL EFFECTS IN MOLECULAR SPECTRA - COMPREHENSIVE DATASET OF LINE-SHAPE PARAMETERS FROM AB INITIO CALCULATIONS FOR He-PERTURBED HD, Kamil Stankiewicz, Hubert Jóźwiak, Nikodem Stolarczyk, Maciej Grzegorz Gancewski, Piotr Wcislo, Franck Thibault

FB10   12:09 – 12:24
PRECISION SPECTROSCOPY OF HD, Qian-Hao Liu, Cunfeng Cheng, Shui-Ming Hu

FC. Atmospheric science
Friday, June 24, 2022 – 8:30 AM
Room: B102 Chemical and Life Sciences

Chair: Steven Federman, University of Toledo, Toledo, OH, USA

FC01   8:30 – 8:45
ROTATIONAL STUDY OF ATMOSPHERIC VOCS USING THE NEW CP-FTMW SPECTROMETER OF LILLE, Elias M. Neeman, Noureddin OSSEIRAN, Manuel Goubet, Pascal Dréan, Therese R. Huet

FC02   8:48 – 9:03
THE WATER VAPOUR SELF- AND FOREIGN CONTINUUM ABSORPTION AT ROOM TEMPERATURE IN THE 1.25 μm window , Aleksandra Koroleva, Samir Kassi, Didier Mondelain, Alain Campargue

FC03   9:06 – 9:21
WILDFIRE SMOKE DESTROYS STRATOSPHERIC OZONE, Peter F. Bernath, Chris Boone, Jeff Crouse

FC04   9:24 – 9:39
STRATOSPHERIC AEROSOL COMPOSITION OBSERVED BY THE ATMOSPHERIC CHEMISTRY EXPERIMENT FOLLOWING THE 2019 RAIKOKE ERUPTION, Chris Boone, Peter F. Bernath, Keith LaBelle, Jeff Crouse

FC05   9:42 – 9:57
ATLAS OF ACE SPECTRA OF CLOUDS AND AEROSOLS, Jason J Sorensen, Peter F. Bernath, Mike Lecours, Chris Boone, Ryan Johnson, Keith LaBelle

FC06   10:00 – 10:15
LOW-PRESSURE YIELDS OF STABILIZED CRIEGEE INTERMEDIATES PRODUCED FROM OZONOLYSIS OF A SERIES OF ALKENES, Lei Yang, Mixtli Campos-Pineda, Jingsong Zhang

Intermission

FC07   10:57 – 11:12
REACTION MECHANISM AND KINETICS OF THE GAS PHASE REACTIONS OF METHANE SULFONAMIDE WITH Cl RADICALS AND THE FATE OF $CH_2S(=O)_2NH_2$ RADICAL, Parandaman Arathala, Rabi A. Musah

FC08   11:15 – 11:30
FIRST ANALYSIS OF THE ν_1 BAND OF HNO_3 AT 3551.766 CM^{-1} , Agnes Perrin, Laurent Manceron, raymond armante, P. Roy, F. Kwabia Tchana, Geoffrey C. Toon

FC09   11:33 – 11:48
MILLIMETER-WAVE SPECTROSCOPY OF METHYLFURAN ISOMERS: LOCAL vs GLOBAL TREATMENT OF THE INTERNAL ROTATION, Jonas Bruckhuisen, SATHAPANA CHAWANANON, Pierre Asselin, Isabelle Kleiner, Anthony Roucou, Guillaume Dhont, Colwyn Bracquart, Arnaud Cuisset

FC10   11:51 – 12:06
AB INITIO STUDY OF THE EXCITED STATES OF O_2, Gap-Sue Kim, Wilfrid Somogyi, Sergei N. Yurchenko

FC11   12:09 – 12:24
INFRARED SPECTROSCOPIC AND QUANTUM CHEMICAL EXPLORATION OF AMMONIUM IODATE CLUSTERS, Nicoline C. Frederiks, Danika Lee Heaney, John J. Kreinbihl, Christopher J. Johnson

FD. Clusters/Complexes
Friday, June 24, 2022 – 8:30 AM
Room: 217 Noyes Laboratory

Chair: Joseph Fournier, Washington University in St. Louis, St. Louis, MO, USA

FD01   8:30 – 8:45
CHARACTERIZATION OF ALCOHOL:WATER TETRAMERS AND PENTAMERS VIA CHIRPED PULSE FOURIER-TRANSFORM MICROWAVE SPECTROSCOPY, S E Dutton, Geoffrey Blake

FD02   8:48 – 9:03
INTERPLAY OF INTERMOLECULAR INTERACTIONS: COMPLEXES OF 2-DECALONE WITH WATER, BENZENE, AND PHENOL, Swantje V. M. Caliebe, Pablo Pinacho, Melanie Schnell

FD03   9:06 – 9:21
MOLECULAR STRUCTURES OF DIFLUOROBENZALDEHYDES AND THEIR HYDRATED COMPLEXES CHARACTERIZED BY CP-FTMW SPECTROSCOPY, Dingding Lv, Weixing Li, Xiaolong Li, Guanjun Wang, Mingfei Zhou

FD04   9:24 – 9:39
ANALYSIS OF THE MICROWAVE SPECTRUM, STRUCTURE AND INTERNAL ROTATION OF THE CH_3 GROUP IN N-METHYLIMIDAZOLE...H_2O AND 2-METHYLIMIDAZOLE...H_2O COMPLEXES, Charlotte Nicole Cummings, Eva Gougoula, Chris Medcraft, Juliane Heitkämper, Nick Walker

FD05   9:42 – 9:57
GEOMETRIES AND CONFORMATIONAL CONVERSION OF THE BINARY 3,3,3-TRIFLUOROPROPANOL CONFORMERS: ROTATIONAL SPECTRA AND DFT CALCULATIONS, Alex Neilson Mort, FAN XIE, Yunjie Xu

Intermission

FD06   10:39 – 10:54
MICROWAVE SPECTROSCOPY OF TERPENOIDS NON-COVALENTLY BONDED TO HYDROGEN SULFIDE, Noureddin OSSEIRAN, Elias M. Neeman, Manuel Goubet, Pascal Dréan, Therese R. Huet

FD07   10:57 – 11:12
STRUCTURE AND NON-COVALENT INTERACTIONS OF THE BENZOFURAN-DIETHYL DISULFIDE COMPLEX CHARACTERIZED BY ROTATIONAL SPECTROSCOPY, Yuago Xu, Wenqin Li, Rizalina Tama Saragi, Alberto Lesarri, Gang Feng

FD08   11:15 – 11:30
MODELING CO_2 MICROSOLVATION: MICROWAVE SPECTROSCOPIC STUDIES OF DIFLUOROETHYLENE (DFE)/CO_2 CLUSTERS, $(DFE)_1(CO_2)_x$, FOR A TRIMER, TETRAMER, AND PENTAMER, Hannah Fino, Tulana Ariyaratne, Prashansa Kannangara, Rebecca A. Peebles, Sean A. Peebles, Channing West, Brooks Pate

FD09   11:33 – 11:48
REINVESTIGATION OF THE MICROWAVE SPECTRUM OF THE O_2-H_2O VAN DER WAALS COMPLEX, W. H. Rice IV, Caitlyn Saiz, Amanda Duerden, Frank E Marshall, G. S. Grubbs II

FD10   11:51 – 12:06
MICROSOLVATION COMPLEXES OF α-METHOXY PHENYLACETIC ACID STUDIED BY MICROWAVE SPECTROSCOPY, Himanshi Singh, Pablo Pinacho, Melanie Schnell

FE. Lineshapes, collisional effects
Friday, June 24, 2022 – 8:30 AM
Room: 1024 Chemistry Annex

Chair: Wei Lin, The University of Texas Rio Grande Valley, Brownsville, TX, USA

FE01   8:30–8:45
A QUANTUM CASCADE LASER DUAL-COMB SPECTROMETER IN STEP-SWEEP MODE FOR HIGH-RESOLUTION MOLECULAR SPECTROSCOPY, Markus Mangold, Pitt Allmendinger, Jakob Hayden, Andreas Hugi, Olivier Browet, Jean Clément, Bastien Vispoel, Muriel Lepère

FE02   8:48–9:03
A SPECTROSCOPIC PRESSURE SENSOR TARGETING ATOMIC POTASSIUM FOR HYPERSONIC FACILITIES, Tal Schwartz, Joshua A Vandervort, Sean Clees, Christopher L Strand, Ronald K Hanson

FE03   9:06–9:21
LEAST SQUARES FIT OF LINE PROFILES IN TRANSMITTANCE AND ABSORBANCE SPECTRA WITH DETECTOR OR SOURCE NOISE, Hiroyuki Sasada

FE04   9:24–9:39
MEASUREMENT OF COLLISIONAL SELF-BROADENING AT LOW-TEMPERATURES USING SUB-DOPPLER SPECTROSCOPY, Brian Drouin, Deacon J Nemchick, Timothy J. Crawford, Paul Von Allmen, Dariusz Lis

FE05   9:42–9:57
APPLICATION OF THEORETICAL CONSTRAINTS TO MODEL THE MEASURED TEMPERATURE AND WAVELENGTH DEPENDENCE OF COLLISION-INDUCED ABSORPTION IN THE 0.76 μm AND 1.27 μm O_2 BANDS, Erin M. Adkins, Helene Fleurbaey, Tijs Karman, David A. Long, Alain Campargue, Didier Mondelain, Joseph T. Hodges

FE06   10:00–10:15
CHARACTERIZATION OF THE H_2O+CO_2 CONTINUUM ABSORPTION WITHIN THE INFRARED TRANSPARENCY WINDOWS FOR PLANETARY APPLICATIONS, Helene Fleurbaey, Didier Mondelain, Jean-Michel Hartmann, Wissam Fakhardji, Alain Campargue

Intermission

FE08   11:15–11:30
LINE MIXING STUDY OF CARBON MONOXIDE BROADENED BY NITROGEN, HELIUM, AND HYDROGEN, Wey-Wey Su, Yiming Ding, Christopher L Strand, Ronald K Hanson

FE09   11:33–11:48
FT-IR MEASUREMENTS OF CROSSSECTIONS FOR TRANS-2-BUTENE IN THE 7-15 μM REGION AT 160-297 K FOR TITAN'S ATMOSPHERE, Brendan Steffens, Keeyoon Sung, Michael Malaska, Rosaly M Lopes, Conor A Nixon

FE10   11:51–12:06
POTASSIUM LINESHAPE STUDY WITH COLLISIONAL PARTNERS OF NITROGEN, HELIUM, AND HYDROGEN, Joshua A Vandervort, Yiming Ding, Richard S Freedman, Mark S Marley, Christopher L Strand, Ronald K Hanson

FE11   12:09–12:24
FILLING A CRITICAL GAP IN THE PRESSURE-BROADENING DATA NEEDED FOR MODELING SUPER-EARTHS AND NEPTUNIAN ATMOSPHERES, Ehsan Gharib-Nezhad, Natasha E Batalha, Robert R. Gamache, Richard S Freedman

FF. Spectroscopy as an analytical tool
Friday, June 24, 2022 – 8:30 AM
Room: 124 Burrill Hall

Chair: R. A. Motiyenko, Université de Lille, Villeneuve d'Ascq, France

FF01 8:30 – 8:45
FLUORESCENCE EXCITATION, EMISSION, AND SYNCHRONOUS SPECTRA AT LOW TEMPERATURES, Carlos Manzanares, Suresh Sunuwar

FF02 8:48 – 9:03
NEAR INFRARED SPECTROSCOPY AS EFFICIENT ANALYTICAL TOOL IN PLASTIC ADDITIVES INDUSTRY., Emanuele Pizzano, Assimo Maris, Marzia Mazzacurati

FF03 9:06 – 9:21
ANALYSIS OF TINNEVELLY SENNA LEAVES HERBAL MEDICINE USING LASER-INDUCED BREAKDOWN SPECTROSCOPY AND ITS ANTI-CANCEROUS & ANTIBACTERIAL EFFICACY STUDIES, Mohammed A Gondal, R. K. Aldakheel, M A. Almessiere

FF04 9:24 – 9:39
IDENTIFICATION OF CHLOROBENZENE IN MIXTURES WITH THE SUGGESTED PRECURSORS BENZENE, BENZOIC ACID, PHTHALIC ACID, AND MELLITIC ACID IN MARS SAMPLES, Suresh Sunuwar, Carlos Manzanares

FF05 9:42 – 9:57
SYNCHROTRON-BASED ATTENUATED TOTAL REFLECTION INFRARED SPECTROSCOPY OF ARTIFICIAL GASOLINE BLEND, Joshua G Smith, Sylvestre Twagirayezu, Brant E. Billinghurst, Jianbao Zhao

Intermission

FF06 10:39 – 10:54
PYROLYSIS REACTIONS OF OXOLAN-3-ONE STUDIED VIA MATRIX-ISOLATION FTIR, Heather Legg, Kathryn Narkin, Khaled Aley El-Shazly, Elizabeth Renee Sparks, Xinli Song, Carol Parish, Laura R. McCunn

FF07 10:57 – 11:12
ANALYSIS OF THE METHANE CH STRETCH OVERTONE USING INFRARED HIGH RESOLUTION COHERENT TWO DIMENSIONAL SPECTROSCOPY, DeAunna A Daniels, Thresa Wells, Peter Chen

FF08 11:15 – 11:30
STIMULATED RAMAN SCATTERING IN KXe: A NOVEL SPECTROSCOPIC TOOL, Kavita V. Desai, Andrey E. Mironov, J. Gary Eden

FF09 11:33 – 11:48
SATURATED ABSORPTION SPECTROSCOPY AND TWO-PHOTON CAVITY RING-DOWN ABSORPTION SPECTROSCOPY FOR TRACE GAS DETECTION OF NITROUS OXIDE, Madeline Memovich, Kevin Lehmann

FF10 *Post-Deadline Abstract* 11:51 – 12:06
PROBING PLASMON-INDUCED TEMPERATURES IN FLUOROPHORE-PLASMONIC SYSTEMS USING RAMAN THERMOMETRY., Gerrit Christenson, Ziwei Yu, Renee R. Frontiera

FF11 12:09 – 12:24
SPECTROSCOPY AND THE ETIOLOGY OF CATARACT AND DRY EYE, Douglas Borchman

FG. Astronomy
Friday, June 24, 2022 – 8:30 AM
Room: 274 Medical Sciences Building

Chair: Anthony Remijan, NRAO, Charlottesville, VA, USA

FG01 8:30 – 8:45
ROTATIONAL SPECTROSCOPY AS A TOOL FOR STRUCTURE-SPECIFIC IDENTIFICATION OF PRODUCTS OF UV-PHOTOLYZED COSMIC ICE ANALOGUES, Olivia H. Wilkins, Katarina Yocum, Stefanie N Milam, Perry A. Gerakines, Will E. Thompson, Gustavo A. Cruz-Diaz, Susanna L. Widicus Weaver

FG02 8:48 – 9:03
RATIO OF OTHO/PARA-FORMALDEHYDE SUBLIMATED FROM ENERGETICALLY PROCESSED INTERSTELLAR ICE ANALOGS, Katarina Yocum, Olivia H. Wilkins, Stefanie N Milam, Perry A. Gerakines

FG03 9:06 – 9:21
THE SEARCH FOR COMPLEX ORGANIC MOLECULES DESORBING FROM INTERSTELLAR ICE ANALOGS: PRESENTING SubLIME2, Gustavo A. Cruz-Diaz, Will E. Thompson, Collette C Sarver, Catherine E Walker, Perry A. Gerakines, Stefanie N Milam, Susanna L. Widicus Weaver

FG04 9:24 – 9:39
ICE-SURFACE CHEMISTRY OF MgNC AND OTHER METAL-CONTAINING COMPOUNDS, David E. Woon

FG05 9:42 – 9:57
SPECTROSCOPY AND ASTROCHEMISTRY OF THE CN-TAGGED CYCLIC HYDROCARBONS CYANOCYCLOPENTADIENE AND CYANOINDENE, Bryan Changala, Kelvin Lee, Ryan A Loomis, Andrew M Burkhardt, Ci Xue, Ilsa Rose Cooke, Martin Cordiner, Steven B Charnley, Michael C McCarthy, Brett A. McGuire

Intermission

FG06 10:39 – 10:54
BROADBAND ROTATIONAL SPECTROSCOPY OF 2,4,6-CYCLOHEPTATRIENE-1-CARBONITRILE: A POTENTIAL INTERSTELLAR MOLECULE, Laura Pille, Gayatri Batra, Benjamin E Arenas, Donatella Loru, Melanie Schnell

FG07 10:57 – 11:12
THE SOLEIL VIEW ON PROTOTYPICAL ORGANIC NITRILES: THE ^{13}C SPECIES OF ETHYL CYANIDE, Christian Endres, Marie-Aline Martin-Drumel, Olivier Pirali, J.-C. Guillemin, Oliver Zingsheim, Luis Bonah, Michael C McCarthy, Paola Caselli, Stephan Schlemmer, Sven Thorwirth

FG08 11:15 – 11:30
PROTONATED ETHYL CYANIDE: QUANTUM CHEMISTRY AND ROTATIONAL SPECTROSCOPY, Harshal Gupta, Kelvin Lee, Sven Thorwirth, Oskar Asvany, Stephan Schlemmer, Michael C McCarthy

FG09 11:33 – 11:48
LABORATORY SPECTROSCOPY OF $A^2\Sigma^+$–$X^2\Pi_{3/2}$ ELECTRONIC TRANSITION OF ICN$^+$ TO ESTIMATE PROFILES OF INTERSTELLAR ABSORPTION LINES BY HALOGEN CYANIDE CATIONS, Takumi Ito, Mitsunori Araki, Shoma Hoshino, Koichi Tsukiyama

FG10 11:51 – 12:06
JET-COOLED MID-INFRARED LASER SPECTROSCOPY OF CENTROSYMMETRIC TWO-RING PAHS, Pierre Asselin, SATHAPANA CHAWANANON, Manuel Goubet, Olivier Pirali

FG11 12:09 – 12:24
HIGH-RESOLUTION INFRARED SPECTRUM OF THE DIATOMIC VANADIUM OXIDE , Eileen Döring, Luisa Blum, Alexander A. Breier, Thomas Giesen, Guido W. Fuchs

MA. Plenary
Monday, June 20, 2022 – 8:30 AM
Room: Foellinger Auditorium

Chair: Cathy Murphy, University of Illinois at Urbana-Champaign, Urbana, IL, USA

Welcome 8:30
Timothy Killeen, President
University of Illinois

MA01 8:41 – 9:21

INTEGRATING CRYOGENIC ION CHEMISTRY AND OPTICAL SPECTROSCOPY: CAPTURING THE MOLECULAR LEVEL MECHANICS DRIVING BULK CHEMICAL BEHAVIORS FROM CATALYSIS TO THE SPECTRAL DYNAMICS OF WATER

MARK JOHNSON, *Department of Chemistry, Yale University, New Haven, CT, USA.*

The coupling between ambient ionization sources, developed for mass spectrometric analysis of biomolecules, and cryogenic ion processing, originally designed to study interstellar chemistry, creates a new and general way to capture transient chemical species and elucidate their structures with optical spectroscopies. Advances in non-linear optics over the past decade allow single-investigator, table top lasers to access radiation from 550 cm-1 in the infrared to the vacuum ultraviolet. When spectra are acquired using predissociation of weakly bound rare gas "tags," the resulting patterns are directly equivalent to absorption spectra of target ions at temperatures below 10 K, and quenched close to their global minimum energy geometries. Taken together, what emerges is a new and powerful structural capability that augments the traditional tools available in high resolution mass spectrometry. Currently, these methods are being exploited to monitor chemical and physical processes in assemblies with well-defined temperatures and compositions. Recent applications, ranging from the mechanisms of small molecule activation by homogeneous catalysts to the microscopic mechanics underlying the ultrafast spectral diffusion in water, emphasize the generality and utility of the methods in contemporary chemistry.

MA02 9:26 – 10:06

CHEMISTRY IN THE ULTRACOLD REGIME: PRECISION MOLECULAR ASSEMBLY AND TEST OF STATISTICAL REACTION DYNAMICS

KANG-KUEN NI, *Department of Chemistry and Chemical Biology, Harvard University, Cambridge, MA, USA.*

Advances in quantum manipulation of molecules bring unique opportunities, including the use of molecules to search for new physics, harnessing molecular resources for quantum engineering, and exploring chemical reactions in the ultralow temperature regime. In this talk, I will focus on the latter two topics. First, I will introduce our effort on building single ultracold molecules with full internal and motional state control in optical tweezers for future quantum simulators and computers. This work allows us to go beyond the usual paradigm of chemical reactions that proceed via stochastic encounters between reactants, to a single, controlled reaction of exactly two atoms. Second, I will present our work giving a detailed microscopic picture of molecules transforming from one species to another. We develop full quantum state mapping of chemical reaction product-pairs from single events, which we use to precisely benchmark statistical theory.

Intermission

FLYGARE AWARDS 10:36
Introduction by Yunjie Xu, University of Alberta

MA03　　10:45 – 11:00
VIBRATIONAL SPECTRAL SIGNATURES AND DYNAMICS OF STRONG INTRAMOLECULAR H-BONDS INVESTIGATED WITH GAS-PHASE ION AND SOLUTION-PHASE ULTRAFAST INFRARED SPECTROSCOPIES

JOSEPH FOURNIER, *Department of Chemistry, Washington University, St. Louis, MO, USA.*

Strong H-bonding interactions often manifest in extremely broad shared proton stretch vibrational transitions and exhibit ultrafast relaxation dynamics which have made the study of strongly H-bonded systems challenging both experimentally and computationally. Here, we report on the characterization of vibrational signatures and dynamics of strong, neutral intramolecular O-H H-bonds in several model systems by complementing frequency-resolved cryogenic ion vibrational spectroscopy on isolated gas-phase species with ultrafast solution-phase transient and 2D IR spectroscopies. The gas-phase experiments reveal the complex interplay between stretch-bend Fermi resonance interactions and coupling of the proton stretch to H-bond soft-mode vibrations. The nonlinear ultrafast experiments directly reveal the high degree of anharmonic mode mixing and coupling between the OH stretch, OH bend, fingerprint modes, and soft modes and show rapid intramolecular population relaxation dynamics. Significant isotopic dependence in polarization anisotropy dynamics suggest key differences in proton vs. deuteron transfer dynamics in the vibrationally excited systems. Time permitting, the initial steps towards combining ultrafast IR spectroscopies with cryogenic ion techniques for the acquisition of multidimensional and time-resolved spectra of isolated ion ensembles will be discussed.

MA04　　11:05 – 11:20
NEW FRONTIERS IN COSMIC CARBON CHEMISTRY

BRETT A. McGUIRE, *Department of Chemistry, Massachusetts Institute of Technology, Cambridge, MA, USA.*

The last four years have seen a massive explosion in the spectroscopic detection and characterization of large carbon-containing molecules in the interstellar medium, including the first detections of individual polycyclic aromatic hydrocarbon (PAH) molecules. The detections of PAHs and other carbon rings in the cold, dark starless cloud TMC-1 by the GOTHAM and QUIJOTE projects has opened new frontiers for the exploration of this massive reservoir of as much as 25% of interstellar carbon. In this talk, I will highlight the GOTHAM collaboration's pioneering work in laboratory (rotational) spectroscopy, radio-astronomical observational spectroscopy, astrochemical modeling, and machine learning all working together to unravel the chemistry and physics underlying these new discoveries.

MA05　　11:25 – 11:40
PROBLEMS, PROBLEMS, PROBLEMS: THE LONG JOURNEY OF PHENYL ACETATE

LYNN FERRES, WOLFGANG STAHL[a], *Institute for Physical Chemistry, RWTH Aachen University, Aachen, Germany*; LUCA EVANGELISTI, ASSIMO MARIS, SONIA MELANDRI, WALTHER CAMINATI, *Dipartimento di Chimica G. Ciamician, Università di Bologna, Bologna, Italy*; HA VINH LAM NGUYEN, *Université Paris-Est Créteil et Université de Paris, Laboratoire Interuniversitaire des systèmes atmosphériques (LISA), CNRS UMR7583, Creteil, France.*

The rotational spectrum of phenyl acetate, $CH_3COOC_6H_5$, was measured using a free jet absorption millimeterwave spectrometer in the range from 60 to 78 GHz and two pulsed jet Fourier transform microwave spectrometers covering a total frequency range from 2 to 26.5 GHz. The features of two coupled large amplitude motions, the methyl group internal rotation and the skeletal torsion tunneling of the CH_3CO group with respect to the phenyl ring C_6H_5 (tilted of about $70°$), characterize the spectrum. The vibrational ground state splits into four widely spaced sublevels, labeled as A0, E0, A1, and E1, each of them with its set of rotational transitions, and with additional interstate transitions. A global fit of the line frequencies of the four sublevels leads to the determination of 40 spectroscopic parameters, including the $\Delta E_{A0/A1}$ and $\Delta E_{E0/E1}$ vibrational splittings of about 36.4 GHz and 34.0 GHz, respectively. These parameters were used to deduce the V_3 barrier to methyl internal rotation (about 136 cm^{-1}) and the skeletal torsion B_2 barrier to orthogonality of the two planes (about 68 cm^{-1}).

---
[a]Deceased.

MA06 11:45 – 12:25

SPECTROSCOPIC STUDIES OF CHIRALITY

<u>ANNE ZEHNACKER-RENTIEN</u>, *Institut des Sciences Moléculaires d'Orsay, Université Paris Saclay, CNRS, Orsay, France*.

Chirality is pervasive in Nature and describes the property of an object not to be superimposable on its mirror image. To differentiate between the two mirror images of a chiral molecule, called enantiomers, one must probe them with a probe that is itself chiral. The probe can be of chemical nature, for example another chiral molecule, or of physical nature, for example a chiral light. I will give examples of these two approaches. I will describe how laser spectroscopy at low temperature sheds light on the structural differences between the homochiral and heterochiral complexes of chiral biomolecules, such as amino acids or sugars.[a] [b] Then I will illustrate the sensitivity of chiroptical spectroscopy to conformational isomerism and molecular interactions on the example of 1-indanol studied by Vibrational Circular Dichroism (VCD) in the condensed phase [c] and PhotoElectron Circular Dichroism (PECD) under jet-cooled conditions.

---

[a] Hirata, K.; Mori, Y.; Ishiuchi, S. I.; Fujii, M.; Zehnacker, A. Physical Chemistry Chemical Physics 2020, 22 (43), 24887-24894

[b] Tamura, M.; Sekiguchi, T.; Ishiuchi, S.-I.; Zehnacker-Rentien, A.; Fujii, M. The Journal of Physical Chemistry Letters 2019, (10), 2470-2474

[c] Le Barbu-Debus, K.; Scherrer, A.; Bouchet, A.; Sebastiani, D.; Vuilleumier, R.; Zehnacker, A. Physical Chemistry Chemical Physics 2018, 20 (21), 14635-14646

MH. Mini-symposium: Spectroscopy meets Chemical Dynamics
Monday, June 20, 2022 – 1:45 PM
Room: 100 Noyes Laboratory

Chair: Stephen R. Leone, University of California, Berkeley, Berkeley, CA, USA

MH01   *Journal of Molecular Spectroscopy Review Lecture*   1:45 – 2:15

MAPPING EXTENDED REACTION COORDINATES IN PHOTOCHEMICAL DYNAMICS

<u>DAVE TOWNSEND</u>, *Institute of Photonics and Quantum Sciences, Heriot-Watt University, Edinburgh, United Kingdom.*

Modern laser sources facilitate a wide range of experimental strategies for interrogating the complex non-adiabatic dynamics operating in the excited states of molecules. Developing detailed insight into such processes is vital in understanding various fundamental processes of biological, environmental, and technological significance. Measurements may be broadly separated into frequency- and time-resolved variants, with a combination of different approaches (with different associated observables) typically being required to reveal a complete mechanistic picture. In the former category, quantum state-resolved information may often be obtained using narrow linewidth lasers. This provides detailed information relating to the starting point on the photochemical reaction coordinate (via the absorption spectrum) and the asymptotic endpoints (i.e. the photoproducts). No direct observation of the intermediate pathways connecting these two limits is generally possible, though, due to the inherently long temporal duration of the laser pulses relative to the typical timescales of non-adiabatic energy redistribution processes. It is therefore desirable to obtain complementary information that monitors real-time evolution along the reaction coordinate as excited state population traverses the potential energy landscape. This may be achieved in time-resolved pump-probe experiments conducted using laser pulses with temporal durations comparable to the ultrafast (i.e. sub-picosecond) timescales of vibrational motion. The use of valence state photoionization for the probe step is a commonly employed methodology and has proved highly instructive in revealing subtle mechanistic details of key energy redistribution pathways operating in a wide range of molecular systems. One common limitation in such measurements, however, is the restricted "view" along the reaction coordinate(s) connecting the initially prepared excited states to various photoproducts. Guided by examples drawn from our own recent work using time-resolved photoelectron imaging, this talk will discuss such issues in detail and highlight some new directions that potentially help overcome them – with particular emphasis placed on the advantages of projecting as deeply as possible into the ionization continuum. The role of complementary measurements using other spectroscopic techniques and the importance of high-level supporting theory to guide data interpretation will also be reinforced.

MH02   2:21 – 2:36

FULLY ISOMER-RESOLVED SPECTROSCOPY AND ULTRAFAST DYNAMICS

<u>GRITE L. ABMA</u>, DANIEL HORKE, *Institute for Molecules and Materials (IMM), Radboud University Nijmegen, Nijmegen, Netherlands.*

In gas-phase experiments using molecular beams, formation of many isomers cannot be prevented and their presence significantly complicates assignment of spectral lines. Current isomer-resolved spectroscopy techniques make use of elaborate double-resonance schemes, requiring at least two fully tuneable laser sources. We present here an alternative approach that utilises electrostatic deflection to spatial separate isomers and create isomer-pure molecular beams. This adds isomer resolution to conventional single-color REMPI spectroscopy, which we demonstrate here for the *syn* and *anti* conformers of 3-aminophenol, as shown in Figure 1. This approach furthermore makes the assignment of all transitions to an isomer trivial, without any additional *a priori* information.

This approach can add isomer resolution to any molecular beam based spectroscopy experiment. We show here also the first application of this methodology to study ultrafast dynamics and present the first results of fully isomer-resolved dynamics. In particular, we show that the *syn* and *anti* conformers of 2-chlorophenol exhibit very different relaxation dynamics following UV excitation, highlighting the influence of a single hydrogen bond on the underlying ultrafast relaxation processes. Our approach is generally applicable to all isomers that exhibit a difference in dipole moment and will, for example, allow the study of tautomer-resolved dynamics in biomolecules.

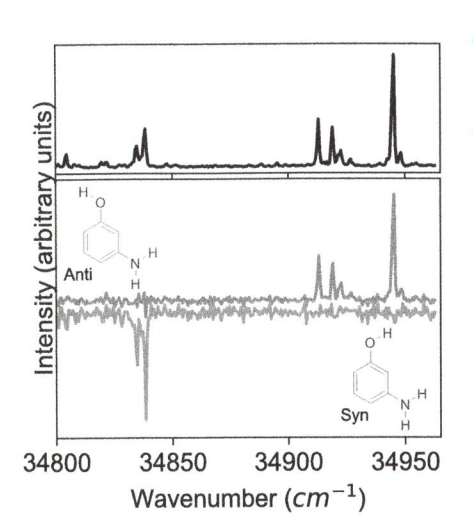

Figure 1: Single-color REMPI spectra of 3-Aminophenol. Top - conventional molecular beam. Bottom - spectra in fully conformer-separated beam.

MH03
ABSOLUTE-PHASE-RESOLVED STRONG FIELD IONIZATION

2:39 – 2:54

YASASHRI RANGANATH RANATHUNGA, *Chemistry Department, Wayne State University, Detroit, MI, USA*; DUKE A. DEBRAH, *Chemistry, Wayne State University, Detroit, MI, USA*; GABRIEL A. STEWART, *Chemistry, Wayne State University, Detroit,, MI, USA*; SUK KYOUNG LEE, *Chemistry Department, Wayne State University, Detroit, MI, USA*; WEN LI, *Department of Chemistry, Wayne State University, Detroit, MI, USA*.

Many important physical processes such as non-linear optics and coherent control are highly sensitive to the absolute carrier-envelop-phase (CEP) of driving ultrashort laser pulses. A significant amount of previous theory work has been carried out to study the effect of the absolute CEP on strong-field ionization and related phenomena such as high harmonic generation (HHG) and nonsequential double ionization (NSDI). This makes the measurement of absolute CEP in the photoionization process immensely important in attosecond and strong-field physics. Even though relative CEPs can be measured with a few existing methods, the estimate of the absolute CEP has not been straightforward and has always required theoretical inputs. Recently, we have developed an in-situ method for measuring the absolute CEP of elliptical polarized few-cycle pulse without the assistance of theoretical modelings. Here we will show that the absolute CEP of linear polarized light can also be measured with a similar method. This capability enables the measurement of absolute-phase-resolved strong field ionization for the first time. We are able to compare the experimental results directly with those obtained with numerical solutions of time-dependent Schrodinger equations (TDSE). Preliminary results suggest the TDSE method might have issues in modeling strong field multi-electron dynamics, which have been routinely carried out to help understand the dynamics or calibrate CEP measurement. This failure could be due to the employed single active electron approximation and warrants further investigation. The results of this study will provide theorists with a clear standard for studying strong-field ionization processes in atoms and molecules and will lead to independent experimental measurements of the absolute phase.

MH04
ALL-OPTICAL THREE-DIMENSIONAL ELECTRON MOMENTUM IMAGING

2:57 – 3:12

EMMANUEL AYORINDE ORUNESAJO, *Chemistry Department, Wayne State University, Detroit, MI, USA*; GIHAN BASNAYAKE, *Chemistry, Wayne State University, Detroit,, MI, USA*; YASASHRI RANGANATH RANATHUNGA, *Chemistry Department, Wayne State University, Detroit, MI, USA*; GABRIEL A. STEWART, *Chemistry, Wayne State University, Detroit,, MI, USA*.

To achieve an efficient 3-D imaging detection of electrons/ions in coincidence, a conventional 2D imaging detector (MCP/phosphor screen) and a fast frame camera are used in the 3D velocity map imaging (VMI) technique[1, 2] . However, it is still difficult to obtain two separate TOF events for two electrons using a conventional MCP detector coupled with a photomultiplier tube (PMT). This is because the phosphor screen is usually made of P47 phosphor which has longer decay time and thus not good to achieve high temporal resolution. Furthermore, due to the very short time separation interval between two electrons, it is imperative to use different phosphor/scintillator for improved 3D electron momentum imaging. Herein, we demonstrate that a scintillator screen coated with poly-para-phenylene laser dye (Exalite 404) can be used to achieve a greatly improved TOF resolution, which is sufficienct for 3D electron imaging.. A silicon photomultiplier tube (si-PMT) is also adopted to suppress the ringing in electric signals, typically associated with MCP pick-off.. The shorter emission lifetime of the poly-paraphenylene dye compared to the conventional P47 phosphor helps achieve an unprecedented dead time (0.48 ns). This has greatly enhanced the multi-hit capability of the 3D VMI technique in detecting two or more electrons in coincidence.

Intermission

MH05   3:54 – 4:09

PROBING THE VIBRATIONAL WAVE PACKET DYNAMICS ON THE ELECTRONIC GROUND STATE OF NEUTRAL SILVER TETRAMER: VIBRATIONAL FREQUENCIES, ANHARMONICITIES AND ANISOTROPY

<u>JIAYE JIN</u>, MAX GRELLMANN, KNUT R. ASMIS, *Wilhelm-Ostwald-Institut für Physikalische und Theoretische Chemie, Universität Leipzig, Leipzig, Germany.*

Small silver clusters possess remarkable luminescence and photoelectric properties, making them subject of current research.[a] However, obtaining vibrations on small, neutral silver clusters remain challenging, due to difficulties in mass-selecting neutral clusters and a lack of easily accessible and widely wavelength-tunable far infrared light sources.

Here, we report our study on experimentally probing the vibrational wave packet dynamics on the ground state potential energy surface of the neutral silver tetramer Ag_4, a benchmark system for small neutral metal clusters, and unambiguously assign its structure. We combine femtosecond pump-probe spectroscopy employing the NeNePo (negative-neutral-positive) excitation scheme[b] with a cryogenic ion-trap tandem mass spectrometer. A linear polarized ultrafast pump pulse (∼40 fs, tunable center wavelength from 700 nm - 820 nm) is used to selectively prepare a coherent wave packet by photodetachment from thermalized (20 - 300 K) Ag_4^- anions. The wave packet dynamics on the electronic ground state are then probed using a second polarized ultrafast pulse (∼50 fs, centered at 400 nm), which ionizes Ag_4 in a two-photon process. The mass-selected cation yield as a function of the delay time (0 - 60 ps) between the two laser pulses yields the fs-NeNePo spectrum. Frequency analysis with a resolution down to about 0.5 cm^{-1} by using Fourier transform of transient traces reveal one prime frequency band (109.5 ± 0.4 cm^{-1}) in all conditions and four bands at 32 cm^{-1}, 78 cm^{-1}, 186 cm^{-1} and 295 cm^{-1} dependent on pump wavelengths and temperatures. These frequencies are consists with predicted fundamental vibration frequencies (ν_1, ν_2, ν_5 and ν_6) and one combination ($\nu_1 + \nu_2$) for rhombic D_{2h} geometry of Ag_4. The rephrasing period of the wave packet allows determining vibrational anharmonicities. A strong dependence of the NeNePo cation signal on the polarization of ultrafast pulses is observed, revealing information on the anisotropy of the partial waves involved in the photodetachment process.

---

[a]Grandjean, D. et al. Science 2018, 361, 686–690.
[b]Wolf, S. et al., Phys. Rev.Lett. 74(21), 4177; Hess, H. et al., Eur. Phys. J. D, 16(1), 145-149.

MH06   4:12 – 4:27

PHOTOFRAGMENTATION PATHWAYS OF N-BUTYL BROMIDE

<u>LAUREN F HEALD</u>, SCOTT G SAYRES, *School of Molecular Sciences and Biodesign Center for Applied Structural Discovery, Arizona State University, Tempe, AZ, USA.*

Dissociation of organic halides has been use for studying ultrafast processes over the last three decades given their relative simplicity and the significance in atmospheric chemistry. Specifically, photofragmentation of alkyl bromides with UV light has attracted substantial attention because of the ozone depletion potential of Br atoms. This presentation summarizes our recent results on the ultrafast photodissociation mechanisms of n-butyl bromide resolved using femtosecond time-resolved mass spectrometry. Multiple dissociative pathways occur upon photo excitation of n-butyl bromide include C-Br scission, C-C dissociation, and hydrogen elimination leading to unsaturated carbon bonds. The dissociative A state is accessed via two UV photon adsorption of two UV pump photons. This state undergoes direct dissociation of the C-Br bond within 160 fs. Three photon excitation reaches the n-5p Rydberg state, where several competing fragmentation pathways are monitored. The fastest relaxations occur in states which are highly excited and have C-H dissociation leading to double and triple C-C bond formation with lifetimes of 500 fs. Dissociation on the ion-pair state occurs within 10 ps to produce the butyl radical. Additionally, β elimination of HBr from the parent molecule occurs within 4 ps. The depopulation of the 5p Rydberg state through internal conversion activates vibrations along the carbon backbone and produces an the intermediate (bromopropyl radical) within 600 fs. The bromopropyl radical undergoes a concerted ring-closure and Br elimination into highly stable cyclopropane within 7.5 ps. The reaction pathways and potential energy curves were identified with the aid of density functional theory calculations. These results elucidate the elementary steps and mechanism which are fundamental in atmospheric chemistry and provide insight into how electronic photoexcitation is dissipated into the vibrational motions of the carbon backbone of simple hydrocarbons.

MH07   4:30 – 4:45
OBSERVATION OF RESONANCES IN THE F+NH$_3$ REACTION VIA TRANSITION-STATE SPECTROSCOPY

MARK C BABIN, *Department of Chemistry and Chemical Biology, Harvard University, Cambridge, MA, USA*; MARTIN DeWITT, *Chemistry, University of California, Berkeley, Berkeley, CA, USA*; JASCHA LAU, *Department of Chemistry, University of California, Berkeley, Berkeley, CA, USA*; HONGWEI SONG, *Wuhan Institute of Physics and Mathematics, Chinese Academy of Sciences, Wuhan, China*; HUA GUO, *Department of Chemistry and Chemical Biology, University of New Mexico, Albuquerque, NM, USA*; DANIEL NEUMARK, *Department of Chemistry, The University of California, Berkeley, CA, USA*.

Transition state spectroscopy experiments, based on negative-ion photodechament, allow for the direct probing of the vibrational structure and metastable resonances that are characteristic of the neutral reactive surface. Here, we study the four-atom F + NH$_3$ → HF + NH$_2$ reaction using slow photoelectron velocity-map imaging spectroscopy of cryogenically cooled NH$_3$F$^-$ anions. The resulting spectra reveal features associated with a manifold of vibrational Feshbach resonances in the post-transition state product well of this reactive surface. Beyond this, the spectra contain structure reporting on reactive resonances in the pre-transition state reaction complex well. Quantum dynamical calculations performed on a full-dimensional potential surface show excellent agreement with the experimental results, allowing for the assignment of spectral structure and demonstrating that key dynamics of this bimolecular reaction are well described by this theoretical framework.

MH08   4:48 – 5:03
TRACKING THE PHOTOIONIZATION OF ANILINE IN WATER: THE ROLE OF $\pi\sigma^*$ STATES

RAÚL MONTERO, *SGIker Laser Facility, Universidad del País Vasco (UPV/EHU), Bilbao, Spain*; IKER LAMAS, ASIER LONGARTE, *Physical Chemistry, Universidad del País Vasco (UPV/EHU), Bilbao, Spain*.

The dynamics of aniline in water, after excitation along its lowest energy absorption (267 nm), has been investigated, from the femto (fs) to the nanoseconds (ns) scale, by pump-probe broadband transient absorption (TA) methods. The complex prompt TA spectrum, which evolves over the fs to ns scales, is analyzed by using a pump-repump-probe scheme that permits to interrogate the nature of the contributing species. The results permit us to identify, in addition to the long-living $\pi\pi^*$ state responsible of the fluorescence, the formation of a charge transfer to solvent state (CTTS) that will autoionize to form the fully solvated cation and electron. The nature of this CTTS state is discussed in terms of the 3s/$\pi\sigma^*$ state characterized in the gas phase[a] and the specific water-solute interactions established.

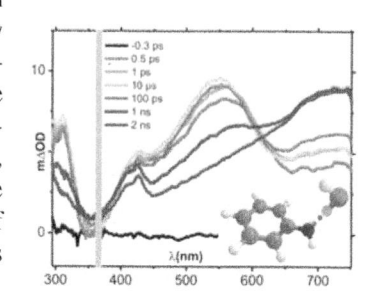

[a]J. O. F. Thompson *et al. J. Chem. Phys.* **142**, 114309 (2015); doi:10.1063/1.4914330

MH09   5:06 – 5:21
PULSE INDUCED DARK STATE OF ACETYLENE

ANTOINE AERTS, *SQUARES, Université Libre de Bruxelles, Brussels, Belgium*; PASCAL KOCKAERT, SIMON PIERRE GORZA, *OPERA Photonique, Université libre de Bruxelles, Brussels, Belgium*; JEAN VANDER AUWERA, NATHALIE VAECK, *SQUARES, Université Libre de Bruxelles, Brussels, Belgium*.

We simulate laser-induced dynamics in acetylene (C$_2$H$_2$) using fully-experimental structural parameters. The rotation-vibration energy structure, including anharmonicities, is defined by the global spectroscopic Hamiltonian for the ground electronic state of C$_2$H$_2$ built from the extensive high resolution spectroscopy studies on the molecule, transition dipole moments from intensities, and effects of the (inelastic) collisions are parametrized from line broadenings using the relaxation matrix [J. Chem. Phys. **154**, 144308 (2021)]. The approach, based on an effective Hamiltonian outperforms today's *ab initio* computations both in terms of accuracy and computational cost, however, is limited to a few small molecules. With such accuracy, the Hamiltonian permits to study the inside machinery of theoretical pulse shaping [J. Chem. Phys. **156**, 084302 (2022)] for laser quantum control. With an adequate pulse shaping technique (in mid-IR) based on "super-Gaussian" pulses, we show a realistic and performant path to the population of a "dark" ro-vibrational state in C$_2$H$_2$.

MH10

A PHASE DIAGRAM FOR ENERGY FLOW-LIMITED REACTIVITY

CHENGHAO ZHANG, *Department of Physics, University of Illinois at Urbana-Champaign, Urbana, IL, USA*; EDWIN SIBERT, *Department of Chemistry, University of Wisconsin–Madison, Madison, WI, USA*; MARTIN GRUEBELE, *Department of Chemistry, University of Illinois at Urbana-Champaign, Urbana, IL, USA*.

Intramolecular vibrational redistributionis often assumed in Rice–Ramsperger–Kassel–Marcus and other rate calculations. In contrast, experimental spectroscopy, computational results, and models based on Anderson localization have shown that ergodicity is achieved rather slowly during molecular energy flow and the statistical assumption might easily fail due to quantum localization.

Here, we develop a simple model for the interplay of IVR and energy transfer and simulate the model with near-exact quantum dynamics for 10-degree of freedom system. We find that there is a rather sharp "phase transition" as a function of molecular anharmonicity "a" between a region of facile energy transfer and a region limited by IVR with incomplete accessibility of the state space. The very narrow transition range of the order parameter "a" happens to lie right in the middle of the range expected for molecular vibrations, thus demonstrating that reactive energy transfer dynamics occurs not far from the localization boundary, with implications for controllability of reactions.

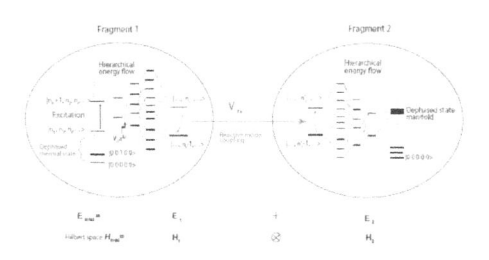

This work is published on JCP: doi: 10.1063/5.0043665

MI. Structure determination

Monday, June 20, 2022 – 1:45 PM

Room: 116 Roger Adams Lab

Chair: M. Eugenia Sanz, King's College London, London, United Kingdom

MI01   1:45 – 2:00

Q| R: QUANTUM-BASED REFINEMENT OF BIOMACROMOLECULES

MALGORZATA BICZYSKO, YANTING XU, *International Centre for Quantum and Molecular Structures, Shanghai University, Shanghai, China*; NIGEL W MORIARTY, *Molecular Biophysics and Integrated Bioimaging Division, Lawrence Berkeley National Laboratory, Berkeley, CA, USA*; HOLGER KRUSE, *Institute of Biophysics, Czech Academy of Sciences, Brno, Czech Republic*; MARK P WALLER, *Pending AI Pty Ltd, iAccelerate, North Wollongong, Australia*; PAVEL V AFONINE, *Molecular Biophysics and Integrated Bioimaging Division, Lawrence Berkeley National Laboratory, Berkeley, CA, USA.*

Protein structure determination is largely reliant on crystallography (X-ray, neutron or electron), electron cryo-microscopy (Cryo-EM) or NMR experiments. Refinement is the final step in obtaining accurate three-dimensional atomic model based on experimental data. Since the quality of the data (e.g., resolution) is rarely sufficient to utilize these data alone, this step has traditionally relied on parameterized libraries that describe stereochemistry of the molecules in question. The libraries used in major refinement packages do not describe unusual local arrangements of protein residues in Ramachandran space, novel ligands, or non-covalent interactions such as π stacking, halogen, hydrogen or salt bridges.

The methods we are developing in the Q| R project [1-4], which is our next generation open-source software package (http://github.com/qrefine), combine experimental data with chemical restraints derived from quantum-chemical methods. These procedures allow at present quantum refinement of proteins based on both X-ray crystallography or Cryo-EM experiments. Quantum refinement has shown to significantly improve model geometry, considering both the overall aspects of model and model-to-data fit statistics, as well as specific detailed structural features, in particular the hydrogen bonding.

[1] M. Zheng, J. R. Reimers, M. P. Waller, P. V. Afonine, Acta Cryst. D 73, 45 (2017)

[2] M. Zheng, N. W. Moriarty, Y. Xu, J. R. Reimers, P. V. Afonine, M. P. Waller, Acta Cryst. D 73, 1020 (2017)

[3] M. Zheng, M. Biczysko, Y. Xu, N. W. Moriarty, H. Kruse, A. Urzhumtsev, M. P. Waller, P. V. Afonine, Acta Cryst. D 76, 41-50 (2020)

[4] L. Wang, H. Kruse, O. V. Sobolev, N. W. Moriarty, M. P. Waller, P. V. Afonine, M. Biczysko, Acta Cryst. D 76, 1184–1191 (2020)

MI02   2:03 – 2:18

THE NICOTINIC-AGONIST CYTISINE: THE ROLE OF THE NH···N INTERACTION [a]

RAÚL AGUADO, SANTIAGO MATA, MIGUEL SANZ-NOVO, ELENA R. ALONSO, IKER LEÓN, JOSÉ L. ALONSO, *Grupo de Espectroscopia Molecular, Lab. de Espectroscopia y Bioespectroscopia, Unidad Asociada CSIC, Universidad de Valladolid, Valladolid, Spain.*

In this work, we present a comprehensive structural study of cytisine, a potent nicotinic agonist, for which we aim to clarify its bioactivity using high-resolution rotational spectroscopy. In a first step, we used our chirped-pulse spectrometer to characterize two different conformers presenting axial and equatorial arrangements of the piperidine NH group. In sight of the crucial role of the environment of the heteroatoms in cytisine molecule for docking the nicotinic receptor, we used a cavity-based technique to resolve the ^{14}N quadrupole hyperfine structure in a second step. It has allowed us to obtain a detailed structural description of the molecule, clarifying the disposition of the piperidine NH group and further revealing an exotic intramolecular NH···N interaction. This intramolecularity justifies the over-stabilization of the axial conformer over the equatorial form and demonstrates the positive action of this alkaloid on the nicotinic receptor.

[a] ACKNOWLEDGMENTS: THE AUTHORS THANKS THE FINANCIAL FUNDINGS FROM MINISTERIO DE CIENCIA E INNOVACIÓN (GRANTS PID2019-111396GB-I00) AND JUNTA DE CASTILLA Y LEÓN (GRANTS VA244P20).

MI03 2:21–2:36

WETTING FERROCENE AS A WAY TO INVESTIGATE ITS GAS PHASE STRUCTURE BY ROTATIONAL SPECTROSCOPY

<u>SUSANA BLANCO</u>, ANDRES VERDE, JUAN CARLOS LOPEZ, *Departamento de Química Física y Química Inorgánica - I.U. CINQUIMA, Universidad de Valladolid, Valladolid, Spain*; MANUEL YÁÑEZ, *Departamento de Quimica, Universidad Autonoma de Madrid, Madrid, Spain*; IBON ALKORTA, *Instituto de Quimica Medica, IQM-CSIC, Madrid, Spain*.

In ferrocene (Fe(C_5H_5)$_2$), the first discovered metallocene, iron is sandwiched between two cyclopentadienyl rings in an eclipsed configuration. Ferrocene is an orange solid that sublimates easily and is stable at high temperatures. Due to its symmetry (D_{5h}) this compound does not have a dipole moment, so it is not active in the microwave region and consequently, its gas phase structure is not accessible through microwave spectroscopy. However, as it has been shown for triacetone triperoxide [1], its complexation with water makes it possible. In this work, we have done a combined theoretical and experimental work to observe and analyze the microwave spectrum of ferrocene – H_2O. The theoretical computations predict two possible low-energy structures of the complex. In one form, water lies in the σ_h plane of ferrocene. In the other form, water is close to the C_5 axis of ferrocene on top of one of the cyclopentadienyl rings. Both forms have been observed. The most intense spectrum is that of a symmetric top with satellite patterns consistent with the effects of the free rotation of water. The rotational constant B determined for this spectrum is close to that predicted for the second axial form so that we can conclude that water is located along the C_5 axis and freely rotating around it. This motion averages the ferrocene – H_2O structure to that of a symmetric top. Different isotopic species have been detected, including ^{54}Fe and ^{13}C in their natural abundances, which have made it possible to determine the structure of the heavy atom skeleton of ferrocene and the axial location of water. A second weaker rotamer with an asymmetric top spectrum has rotational constants very close to those predicted for the other ferrocene-water conformer. Experimental and theoretical work is still in progress.

1. Blanco, S.; Macario, A.; Garcia-Calvo, J.; Revilla-Cuesta, A.; Torroba, T.; Lopez, J.C.; Microwave Detection of Wet Triacetone Triperoxide (TATP: Non-Covalent Forces and Water Dynamics. Chem. Eur. J. 2021, 27, 1680–1687.

MI04 2:39–2:54

THE SHAPE OF PROGESTERONE

ELENA R. ALONSO, *Grupo de Espectroscopia Molecular, Lab. de Espectroscopia y Bioespectroscopia, Unidad Asociada CSIC, Universidad de Valladolid, Valladolid, Spain*; ARAN INSAUSTI, *Departamento de Química Física, Universidad del País Vasco (UPV-EHU), Bilbao, Spain*; <u>LUCIE KOLESNIKOVÁ</u>, *Department of Analytical Chemistry, University of Chemistry and Technology, Prague, Prague, Czech Republic*; IKER LEÓN, JOSÉ L. ALONSO, *Grupo de Espectroscopia Molecular, Lab. de Espectroscopia y Bioespectroscopia, Unidad Asociada CSIC, Universidad de Valladolid, Valladolid, Spain*.

Solid samples of progesterone (m.p. 126°C), one of the essential hormones, have been vaporized by laser ablation and probed in a supersonic expansion using a broadband Fourier transform microwave spectroscopy. The analysis of around 150 rotational transitions revealed the existence of a single conformation. Like for the related testosterone[a], progesterone adopts an extended configuration which is the most stable form predicted by quantum-chemical calculations. Due to the methyl group internal rotation, *A–E* splittings have been observed and allowed for the precise determination of the barrier height. The considerable molecular size of progesterone, one of the largest ever attempted solid, illustrates the potential of the LA-CP-FTMW[b] technique in structural chemistry.

Acknowledgments: The authors thank the financial fundings from Ministerio de Ciencia e Innovacion (PID2019-111396GB-I00) and Junta de Castilla y León (VA077U16 and VA244P20).

---
[a] I. León, E. R. Alonso, S. Mata, and J. L. Alonso, *J. Phys. Chem. Lett.* 2021, 12, 6983-6987.
[b] E. R. Alonso, I. León, J. L. Alonso, Intra- and Intermolecular Interactions between non-covalently Bonded Species. Elsevier, 2021, 93-141.

MI06 3:15 – 3:30

UNDERSTANDING THE SHAPE OF β-D-ALLOSE: A LASER ABLATION ROTATIONAL STUDY[a].

GABRIELA JUÁREZ[b], SANTIAGO MATA, JOSÉ L. ALONSO, ELENA R. ALONSO, IKER LEÓN, *Grupo de Espectroscopia Molecular, Lab. de Espectroscopia y Bioespectroscopia, Unidad Asociada CSIC, Universidad de Valladolid, Valladolid, Spain.*

Allose, an aldohexose sugar, is a rare monosaccharide. It differs from the archetypal glucose in the hydroxyl group at the C3 position. However, this slight variation seems to be decisive in its natural abundance, as well as its biological role. Because of the structure-property relationship and to shed light on the effects of epimerization, we have brought β-D-allose into the gas phase using laser ablation techniques, and its conformational panorama has been characterized using chirped-pulse Fourier transform microwave (LA-CP-FTMW) spectroscopy. Three conformers have been unequivocally identified based on the spectroscopic rotational parameters. All the detected conformers exhibit a counter-clockwise arrangement (cc) network formed by an intramolecular hydrogen bond similar to what is observed in β-D-glucose. In opposition, we found that the intramolecular hydrogen bonds in β-D-allose are stronger than in β-D-glucose, which could have drastic biological implications.

[a]ACKNOWLEDGMENTS: THIS RESEARCH WAS FUNDED BY MINISTERIO DE CIENCIA E INNOVACIÓN, GRANT NUMBER PID2019-111396GB-I00, AND BY JUNTA DE CASTILLA Y LEÓN, GRANT NUMBER VA244P20

[b]G.J.L. ACKNOWLEDGES FUNDING FROM THE SPANISH "MINISTERIO DE CIENCIA, INNOVACIÓN Y UNIVERSIDADES" UNDER PREDOCTORAL FPI GRANT (BES-2017-082173).

Intermission

MI07 4:12 – 4:27

THE PRECISE EQUILIBRIUM STRUCTURE DETERMINATION OF CHLOROBENZENE (C_6H_5Cl) BY ROTATIONAL SPECTROSCOPY

NATALIE A. SCHULER, P. MATISHA DORMAN, BRIAN J. ESSELMAN, MARIA ZDANOVSKAIA, *Department of Chemistry, University of Wisconsin-Madison, Madison, WI, USA*; BRYAN CHANGALA, *Atomic and Molecular Physics, Harvard-Smithsonian Center for Astrophysics, Cambridge, MA, USA*; JOHN F. STANTON, *Quantum Theory Project, University of Florida, Gainesville, FL, USA*; MICHAEL C McCARTHY, *Atomic and Molecular Physics, Harvard-Smithsonian Center for Astrophysics, Cambridge, MA, USA*; R. CLAUDE WOODS, ROBERT J. McMAHON, *Department of Chemistry, University of Wisconsin-Madison, Madison, WI, USA.*

The rotational spectra of over 30 isotopologues of chlorobenzene (C_6H_5Cl, C_{2v}) have been collected over portions of the 2 – 360 GHz frequency region. The transitions of these isotopologues were least-squares fit to complete sextic Hamiltonians with the support of computationally predicted spectroscopic constants. The resultant rotational constants of all available isotopologues, alongside high-level computational corrections for vibration-rotation interaction and electron-mass distribution, were used to determine a highly precise semi-experimental equilibrium (r_e^{SE}) structure of chlorobenzene. Finally, advanced quantum mechanical calculations were performed at the CCSD(T)/cc-pCV5Z level to compare to the experimental results. Analysis of the chlorobenzene r_e^{SE} structure will provide insight into the limitations of molecular structure determination when some atoms lie close to (or directly on) principal axes, a difficulty observed in previous molecular structure determinations.

MI08   4:30 – 4:45

HIGH ACCURACY MOLECULAR STRUCTURES

NITAI PRASAD SAHOO, JOHN F. STANTON, *Quantum Theory Project, University of Florida, Gainesville, FL, USA.*

Molecular structures determine spectroscopic parameters that allow molecular identification and reveal qualitative information about bonding and energetics. Over the years, a number of distinct operational definitions of molecular structure (bond lengths and bond angles) have emerged and some confusion often exists when theoreticians and experimentalists debate "a bond length". Here I briefly review the practical value of accurate molecular structures and survey existing experimental and theoretical methods for determining them. I place particular emphasis on the Kraitchman r_s substitution structure, the computationally obtained r_e structure and the semi-experimental r_e^{SE} structure. Ultimately, the most satisfactory method for determining very high-accuracy structures today is a mixed experimental-theoretical approach that uses data from microwave spectroscopy and quantum-chemical calculations. After discussing that, I talk in detail about a different approach to obtaining Kraitchman substitution structures that we have recently employed.

MI09   4:48 – 5:03

MICROWAVE SPECTROSCOPY AND STRUCTURE DETERMINATION OF ORGANOSILICON COMPOUNDS: A CELEBRATION OF A DECADE OF COLLABORATION

NATHAN A. SEIFERT, *Department of Chemistry, University of New Haven, West Haven, CT, USA*; THOMAS M. C. McFADDEN, GAMIL A GUIRGIS, *Department of Chemistry and Biochemistry, College of Charleston, Charleston, SC, USA*; NICOLE MOON, AMANDA DUERDEN, G. S. GRUBBS II, *Department of Chemistry, Missouri University of Science and Technology, Rolla, MO, USA.*

In this reflective presentation, we will discuss a fruitful, decade long collaboration between the speaker and Prof. Gamil Guirgis at the College of Charleston[a] and Gamil's now distinct contributions to organosilicon chemistry. In particular, we will focus on Gamil's facilitation of undergraduate students and young scientists in their study of the chemical and spectroscopic properties of these molecules, as well as his use of microwave and infrared spectroscopy (and spectroscopists!) as essential methods for chemical analysis.

Our discussion will primarily focus on recent microwave studies, such as silylcyclohex-2-ene, 1,1-difluorosilylcyclohex-2-ene and cyclopentylsilane, whose spectra were recently acquired in the Grubbs lab at Missouri S&T. However, given the timely nature of celebrating a decade of collaboration between Gamil and the speaker, we will highlight the history and past results of Gamil's collaborations with microwave spectroscopists in the past decade, which stretches across multiple laboratories and research groups, many of which have been featured at ISMS in past years.[b]

Finally, we use this story as motivation to discuss the collaborative interface between the "spectroscopist" with the "chemist". As microwave spectroscopy continues to climb up the formidable but traversable mountain towards mainstream chemical applicability, Gamil's work with microwave spectroscopists offers a unique and compelling example of how microwave spectroscopy and spectroscopists can provide (and have provided) essential services for those interested in chemical synthesis.

---

[a] N. A. Seifert; G. A. Guirgis; B. H. Pate, *J. Mol. Struct* **2012**, *1023*, 222.

[b] Examples include: T. M. C. McFadden; N. Moon; F. E. Marshall, *et al.*, *Phys. Chem. Chem. Phys* **2022**, *24*, 2454; G. A. Guirgis; J. S. Overby; M. H. Palmer, *et al.*, *J. Phys. Chem. A* **2012**, *116*, 7822; G. A. Guirgis; R. E. Sonstrom; A. J. Clark, *et al.*, *J. Phys. Chem. A* **2019**, *123*, 4389.

MI10   5:06–5:21

CONFORMATIONAL ANALYSIS OF CYCLOBUTANECARBOXYLIC ACID

KARLA V. SALAZAR, *Department of Chemistry, University of Texas Rio Grande Valley, Brownsville, TX, USA*; JOSHUA E. ISERT, NICOLE MOON, G. S. GRUBBS II, *Department of Chemistry, Missouri University of Science and Technology, Rolla, MO, USA*; ZUNWU ZHOU, STEPHEN G. KUKOLICH, *Department of Chemistry and Biochemistry, University of Arizona, Tucson, AZ, USA*; MICHAEL J. CARRILLO, SHERVIN FATEHI, WEI LIN, *Department of Chemistry, University of Texas Rio Grande Valley, Brownsville, TX, USA*.

There has been continued interest in the structure of substituted cyclobutanes. In this work, we measured the rotational spectrum of cyclobutanecarboxylicacid (CBCA) for the first time using a chirp-pulse and a cavity-based Fourier transform microwave spectrometers. To aid in our analysis of the spectrum, we performed potential energy surface scans at B3LYP/ aug-cc-pVTZ level in the ring–COOH dihedral angle of both equatorially- and axially-substituted CBCA. These scans revealed a unique local minimum and a shallow, symmetrical double-well at the global minimum, implying the existence of four distinct stable (yet facilely interconvertible) conformers. We re-optimized these conformers using both density functional theory and second-order Møller–Plesset perturbation theory with the aug-cc-pVTZ basis set and computed their relative energies, dipole moments, and rotational constants. We will present and discuss the corresponding assignments of features in the rotational spectrum.

MI11   5:24–5:39

A ROTATIONAL STUDY OF 6-APA [a]

SERGIO MATO, SANTIAGO MATA, ELENA R. ALONSO, JOSÉ L. ALONSO, IKER LEÓN, *Grupo de Espectroscopia Molecular, Lab. de Espectroscopia y Bioespectroscopia, Unidad Asociada CSIC, Universidad de Valladolid, Valladolid, Spain*.

6-Aminopenicillanic acid (6-APA) is one of the essential intermediates in synthesizing semisynthetic and naturally occurring penicillins. We have transferred 6-APA into the gas phase using laser ablation techniques and characterized its conformational panorama using chirped-pulse Fourier transform microwave (LA-CP-FTMW) spectroscopy. The spectroscopic parameters derived from the spectrum analysis conclusively identify the existence of four conformers of 6-APA. The 14N nuclear quadrupole coupling constants have been analyzed, allowing an accurate structural determination. The observed structures correlate nicely with the biological function of 6-APA.

[a] Acknowledgments: THIS RESEARCH WAS FUNDED BY MINISTERIO DE CIENCIA E INNOVACIÓN, GRANT NUMBER PID2019-111396GB-I00, AND JUNTA DE CASTILLA Y LEÓN, GRANT NUMBER VA244P20. S.M. THANKS CONSEJO SOCIAL FROM UNIVERSIDAD DE VALLADOLID FOR AN UNDERGRADUATE FELLOWSHIP

MJ. Comparing theory and experiment

Monday, June 20, 2022 – 1:45 PM

Room: B102 Chemical and Life Sciences

Chair: Edwin Sibert, University of Wisconsin–Madison, Madison, WI, USA

MJ01   1:45 – 2:00

A FLEXIBLE APPROACH TO VIBRATIONAL PERTURBATION THEORY

<u>MARK A. BOYER</u>, ANNE B McCOY, *Department of Chemistry, University of Washington, Seattle, WA, USA.*

Vibrational perturbation theory is a commonly-used method for obtaining anharmonic corrections to harmonic zero-order wave functions and energies. Traditional approaches use analytic expressions for second order corrections derived from the Watson Hamiltonian expressed in normal modes constructed from displacements of Cartesian coordinates. Given that in the absence of resonances internal and Cartesian coordinates provide identical corrections to the energies and other properties, Cartesian coordinates provide a convenient choice. However, when the Hamiltonian is expressed in Cartesian coordinates, the corrections to the energies result from large cancellations of positive and negative contributions from cubic and quartic terms in the expansion of the Hamiltonian. In internal coordinates the amount of cancellation is significantly smaller.

We present a recently-developed implementation of perturbation theory that allows for flexibility in coordinate choice, order of correction, and handling of degeneracies.[1] This approach is straightforward and provides a route to obtain insights into the origins of spectral intensities among other applications. We apply this method to a fully *ab initio* potential energy surfaces for several polyatomic molecules as well as model systems.

Boyer, M. A. and McCoy, A. B. *J. Chem. Phys.* 156, 054107 **2022**; https://doi.org/10.1063/5.0080892

MJ02   2:03 – 2:18

UNDERSTANDING $X^- \cdots HOCl$ (X=Cl, Br, I) THROUGH VIBRATIONAL PERTURBATION THEORY

MARK A. BOYER, COIRE F GAVIN-HANNER, <u>ANNE B McCOY</u>, *Department of Chemistry, University of Washington, Seattle, WA, USA.*

Complexes of halide ions (Cl, Br and I) with water have provided a set of systems that allow us to explore spectral signatures of hydrogen bonding and how the frequencies and intensities map onto the strength of the hydrogen bond interactions. By substituting HOCl for HOD, we are able to further explore how the acidity of the hydrogen bonding partner is reflected in the spectroscopy. Building off of prior studies of $X^- \cdots H_2O$[1] it is possible to provide tentative assignments for only a subset of the features of interest. Through vibrational perturbation theory (VPT), we can obtain a more complete assignment of the vibrational spectrum of $X^- \cdots HOCl$ from 1200-4000 cm^{-1}. Applying VPT to these systems requires a flexible approach, where resonances are handled appropriately and state energies are tuned to correct for overbinding of the hydrogen to the halide ion at the MP2/aug-cc-pVTZ level of theory/basis used for this study. After including these corrections, the calculated spectra are in very good agreement with experimental spectra. This flexibility also allows for the interpretation of the origin of spectral intensity, making it possible to determine whether a transition obtains intensity through higher order terms in the expansion of the dipole moment (electrical anharmonicity), higher order terms in the expansion of the potential surface (mechanical anharmonicity), or state mixing through through couplings of nearly degenerate zero-order states. The $X^- \cdots HOCl$ systems also provide the opportunity to explore spectral implications of halogen bonding and vibrational perturbation theory is applied to the differentiation of contributions to the spectra from the halogen- and hydrogen-bonded isomers of $ClHOI^-$.

Horvath, S. *et al. J. Phys. Chem. A* 114, 3, 1556–1568 **2010**; https://doi.org/10.1021/jp9088782

MJ03

VIBRONIC COUPLING MECHANISMS IN THE NITRATE RADICAL

<u>JOHN F. STANTON</u>, *Quantum Theory Project, University of Florida, Gainesville, FL, USA.*

An argument can be made that the nitrate radical (NO$_3$) is the most complicated tetraatomic molecule in nature, an assertion that becomes undoubtedly correct when its quantum mechanical complexity is convolved with its environmental importance. The three lowest electronic states of this molecule ($X^2A'_2$, A^2E'' and B^2E') are separated by less than 2 eV, and considerable vibronic mixing between these states leads to the complicated spectral patterns observed experimentally for NO$_3$. This talk reviews the various (qualitative) coupling mechanisms responsible for the abundance of various Franck-Condon forbidden features in electronic spectra of this species, with particular emphasis given to: photodetachment of the (well-behaved) nitrate anion; the $A-X$ absorption spectrum; and the $B-X$ absorption and dispersed fluorescence spectra. Apart from the A-X absorption spectrum, all of the above can be qualitatively reproduced by an extremely simple vibronic Hamiltonian, and semi-quantitative agreement is achieved with a more elaborate but conceptually identical form. As time permits, a progress report will be given on the interpretation of the $A-X$ spectrum, some features of which remain poorly understood.

MJ04

SUB TWENTY WAVENUMBER COMPUTATIONAL PREDICTION OF MOLECULAR BOND ENERGIES AND THE INTRIGUING BDE OF F$_2$

<u>JAMES H. THORPE</u>, *Quantum Theory Project, University of Florida, Gainesville, FL, USA*; JOSIE L. KILBURN, *Department of Chemistry, University of Florida, Gainesville, FL, USA*; DAVID FELLER, *Department of Chemistry, Washington State University, Pullman, WA, USA*; BRYAN CHANGALA, *Atomic and Molecular Physics, Harvard-Smithsonian Center for Astrophysics, Cambridge, MA, USA*; DAVID H. BROSS, BRANKO RUSCIC, *Chemical Sciences and Engineering Division, Argonne National Laboratory, Lemont, IL, USA*; JOHN F. STANTON, *Quantum Theory Project, University of Florida, Gainesville, FL, USA.*

The determination of molecular bond dissociation energies (BDE) is a fundamental pursuit of chemistry. This is an area where computational approaches have proved useful, especially when addressing molecules or environments that are difficult to study in the lab. High-accuracy composite methods can typically compute bond-energies to within one kJ mol^{-1} via a series of additive energy increments, with corrections for relativistic effects, the vibrational zero-point energy, and the Born-Oppenheimer approximation.

Recently, the present authors explored an extension to the HEAT composite method, currently named KS-HEAT, which routinely reproduces the Active Thermochemical Tables (ATcT) total-atomization energies of small molecules to within 20 cm^{-1}. F$_2$, however, differs from the ATcT value by nearly 30 cm^{-1}. While fluorine-containing species are historically challenging to model, disagreement of this magnitude is surprising given the considerable level of theory and size of basis sets employed here.

To confound the issue, while the BDE predicted by KS-HEAT agrees closely with the combined ZEKE and IPP study of Yang *et al.* and the computational work of Csontos *et al.*, a recent CIPP study by Matthíasson *et al.* and the FPD value calculated by Feller *et al.* agree with the current ATcT assignment. As the BDE of F$_2$ influences the ATcT enthalpies of formation of all fluorine containing molecules, this is an important quantity to get "right". The details of these calculations are presented, and the BDE of F$_2$ is discussed.

MJ05   2:57 – 3:12

ON THE USEFULNESS OF ELECTRON PROPAGATOR METHODS FOR A RELIABLE COMPUTATION OF EXPERIMENTAL OBSERVABLES

<u>LORENZO PAOLONI</u>, *Dipartimento di Fisica e Astronomia, Università degli studi di Padova, Padova, Italy*.

Electron propagator methods (EPMs) are well known in the physical-chemical community as a useful tool for the identification of signals observed in ultraviolet photoelectron spectra (UPS) of isolated organic molecules. However, to completely reproduce an experimental UPS the vibrational signature associated to each electronic signal of interest should be computed.

In the first part of this contribution, the implementation of a simple protocol for the simulation of vibrationally resolved UPS is briefly described and its application to the calculation of the spectra of seven semi-rigid organic molecules is proposed.[a,b]

Chemical community is particularly interested in processes that occur in solutions, and therefore the energy which is needed to remove (or to add) an electron from a molecular system is often measured by means of electrochemical techniques. As a consequence, in this case the experimental observables of interest are oxidation and reduction potentials, which differ from the ionization potentials and the electron affinities computed with EPMs.

In the second part of this contribution, experimental redox potentials of 12 organic dyes are compared with ionization potentials and electron affinities computed through EPMs. Differences between computed and observed values are rationalised in terms of polarization and solvation effects, and the estimation of redox potentials through the employment of suitable corrections to the values calculated with EPMs is discussed.

---

[a] A. Baiardi, L. Paoloni, V. Barone, V. G. Zakrzewski, J. V. Ortiz, *J. Chem. Theory Comput.*, **2017**, 13, 3120-3135.
[b] L. Paoloni, M. Fusè, A. Baiardi, V. Barone, *J. Chem. Theory Comput.*, **2020**, 16, 5218-5226.

MJ06   3:15 – 3:30

EXTENSIONS TO GUIDED DIFFUSION MONTE CARLO FOR EXCITED STATES

<u>JACOB M FINNEY</u>, ANNE B McCOY, *Department of Chemistry, University of Washington, Seattle, WA, USA*.

Diffusion Monte Carlo (DMC) is a stochastic method that is used to obtain the ground state energy and ground state wave function of a system of interest. DMC requires a potential energy surface (PES) that describes all degrees of freedom of the system. We have found that the use of guiding functions, functions that describe some of the vibrational degrees of freedom within the system, allow improved sampling of the ground state wave function if the guiding function is chosen carefully.[a,b] While this enables us to used DMC to study larger systems, to obtain spectra we will also need to calculate the excited state energies and matrix elements of the dipole moment operator involving the ground and excited state wave functions. In this work we explore the use of excited state guiding functions for the evaluation of vibrationally excited states. Specifically, we combine the approaches taken from previous work using ground state guided DMC simulations and fixed-node approaches, which we have used to obtain excited state wave functions from unguided DMC calculations. This approach has been applied to studies of OH stretching vibrations in H_2O and $H_3O_2^-$, where comparisons to previous studies can be made. Various approaches for obtaining the intensities from the ground and excited state DMC wave functions are explored.[c]

---

[a] Lee, V. G. M. and McCoy, A.B., *J. Phys. Chem. A* (2019), **123**, 37, 8063-8070.
[b] Finney, J. M., DiRisio, R. J., McCoy, A.B., *J. Phys. Chem. A* (2020), **124**, 45, 9567-9577
[c] Barnett, R. N., Reynolds, P. J., Lester Jr., W. A., *J. Chem. Phys.* (1992), **96**, 2141-2154

Intermission

MJ07   4:12–4:27
DIRECT ELUCIDATION OF THE REASON FOR ALMOST THE SAME BOND LENGTHS FOR THE C–H AND C–D BONDS IN C_6H_6 AND C_6D_6: A PATH INTEGRAL MOLECULAR DYNAMICS STUDY

<u>TARO UDAGAWA</u>, HIKARU TANAKA, *Department of Chemistry and Biomolecular Science, Gifu University, Gifu, Japan*; KAZUAKI KUWAHATA, *Graduate school of Nanobioscience, Yokohama City University, Yokohama, Japan*; MASAAKI BABA, *Molecular Photoscience Research Center, Kobe University, Kobe, Japan*; TSUNEO HIRANO, *Department of Chemistry, Ochanomizu University, Tokyo, Japan*; UMPEI NAGASHIMA, MASANORI TACHIKAWA, *Graduate school of Nanobioscience, Yokohama City University, Yokohama, Japan*.

Recently, Baba group found that ro-vibrationally averaged bond lengths of C–H and C–D are observed as being almost identical ($r_{0,\text{eff}}$(C–H) $\cong r_{0,\text{eff}}$(C–D)) for planar aromatic hydrocarbons from high-resolution laser spectroscopy.[a] Quite recently, the reason of the same $r_{0,\text{eff}}$(C–H) and $r_{0,\text{eff}}$(C–D) bond lengths has been brilliantly unveiled by Hirano et al. by high-level *ab initio* molecular orbital calculations.[b] They revealed that the experimental bond lengths derived from effective rotational constants are "not" the ro-vibrationally averaged bond lengths but their projected lengths on the principle axis.

In this study, we have carried out the path integral molecular dynamics (PIMD) simulations for C_6H_6 and C_6D_6 to directly estimate the distribution of the C–H and C–D bond lengths projected onto the principle axis. Our PIMD simulation strongly supports the previous explanation by Hirano et al.[a] for the experimentally observed fact ($r_{0,\text{eff}}$(C–H) $\cong r_{0,\text{eff}}$(C–D)) in C_6H_6 and C_6D_6.

---
[a]S. Kunishige, T. Katori, M. Baba, et al., J. Chem. Phys. **143**, 244302 (2015).
[b]T. Hirano, U. Nagashima, M. Baba, J. Mol. Struct. **1243**, 130537 (2021).

MJ08   4:30–4:45
RELATIVISTIC COUPLED-CLUSTER CALCULATIONS OF CHLORINE L-EDGE SPECTRUM OF CH_2ICL

<u>ZHE LIN</u>, XUECHEN ZHENG, CHAOQUN ZHANG, LAN CHENG, *Department of Chemistry, Johns Hopkins University, Baltimore, MD, USA*.

We present a computational study of x-ray absorption spectra for CH_3Cl and CH_2ICl using relativistic equation-of-motion coupled-cluster methods with spin-orbit coupling. The 1:1 ratio of the peak intensities for the chlorine L_3 edge and L_2 edge in the experimental x-ray absorption spectrum of CH_2ICl [1] shows an interesting deviation from the ratio of 2:1 between $2p_{3/2}$ and $2p_{1/2}$ electrons. Here we study the origin of this phenomenon using high-accuracy *ab initio* calculations. Our computational results explain the relation between this anomaly in intensities and "multiplet effects" [2].

Reference:
[1] Z. Yang, K. Schnorr, A. Bhattacherjee, P.-L. Lefebvre, M. Epshtein, T. Xue, J.F. Stanton, and S.R. Leone, J. Am. Chem. Soc. **140**, 13360 (2018).
[2] F. de Groot, Coordination Chemistry Reviews **249**, 31 (2005).

MJ09   4:48 – 5:03

HIGH-RESOLUTION LASER SPECTROSCOPY OF THE RYDBERG STARK MANIFOLD IN H_2

<u>NICOLAS HÖLSCH</u>, IOANA DORAN, FRÉDÉRIC MERKT, *Laboratorium für Physikalische Chemie, ETH Zurich, Zurich, Switzerland.*

From the precise measurement of the ionization energy of H_2 its dissociation energy can be determined[a], which serves as a benchmark quantity for QED calculations[b]. The most precise determinations of the ionization energies of molecular hydrogen currently rely on the extrapolation of Rydberg series using multichannel quantum-defect theory (MQDT)[c].

Nonpenetrating high-ℓ states offer significant advantages for these extrapolations: they have small quantum defects and are much less perturbed by channel interactions than low-ℓ states. Their high polarisabilities are a disadvantage in zero-field measurements, but can be exploited to our advantage in Stark measurements. We show that the combination of a 3-photon excitation scheme with application of relatively weak electric fields (10 - 250 mV/cm) provides easy optical access to the linear Stark manifolds associated with near-degenerate high-ℓ states. We perform spectroscopy of the high-Rydberg Stark manifold with both continuous-wave millimeter-wave and near-infrared (NIR) radiation.

The manifold states are desirable as spectroscopic targets because their positions are less sensitive to errors in the quantum defects, a limiting factor in the determination of ionization energies by Rydberg series extrapolation. Extrapolating the linear Stark manifold to zero field yields accurate values of the zero-quantum-defect positions, given by $-\mathcal{R}_{H_2}/n^2$ relative to the ionization thresholds. These positions constitute references for the respective $\ell = 3$ states and provide an assessment of multichannel-quantum-defect-theory calculations at a precision on the order of 100 kHz.

We show that this method can contribute to a one-order-of-magnitude improvement in the determination of ionization energies in molecular hydrogen and that, by using narrow-band NIR laser light, it can be extended beyond the ground state of para-H_2^+.

---

[a] N. Hölsch, M. Beyer, E.J. Salumbides, K.S.E. Eikema, W. Ubachs, Ch. Jungen, and F. Merkt, Phys. Rev. Lett., 122(10), 103003 (2019)
[b] M. Puchalski, J. Komasa, P. Czachorowski, and K. Pachucki, Phys. Rev. Lett., 122(10), 103003 (2019)
[c] D. Sprecher, Ch. Jungen and F. Merkt, J. Chem. Phys. 140, 104303:1-18 (2014)

MJ10   5:06 – 5:21

INTERPLAY OF ELECTRONIC CORRELATIONS AND ELECTRIC-QUADRUPOLE TRANSITIONS IN THE ISOLATED-CORE EXCITATION OF Sr BELOW THE $Sr^+(5g)$ THRESHOLD

<u>MATTHIEU GÉNÉVRIEZ</u>, *Institute of Condensed Matter and Nanosciences (IMCN), Université catholique de Louvain, Louvain-la-Neuve, Belgium*; ULLI EICHMANN, *Department B2, Max-Born-Institute, Berlin, Germany.*

Atoms and molecules in a Rydberg state with a large principal or orbital-angular-momentum quantum number ($n \geq 100$ or $l \geq 10$) have an ion core that, to a good approximation, is isolated from the Rydberg electron and behaves as the bare ion. Properties of cations, such as their rovibronic structure, can thus be spectroscopically determined by studying the ion core within the orbit of a Rydberg electron. This led to the development of the isolated-core-excitation (ICE) technique [1] and isolated-core multiphoton Rydberg dissociation spectroscopy [2]. Until now, the photoexcitation of the ion core relied on electric-dipole transitions. We report the first observation of an electric-*quadrupole* ICE transition observed in the Sr atom and attributed to the one-photon excitation of the ion core from the $Sr^+(5d_{5/2})$ state to the $Sr^+(5g_{7/2,9/2})$ states.

Photoexcitation spectra from $Sr(5d_{5/2}nl)$ states ($n = 16 - 21$, $l = 12$), located high in energy in the Sr^+ continuum, to an energy region between the $Sr^+(5f)$ and $Sr^+(5g)$ ionization thresholds were studied in a joint experimental and theoretical investigation. They show series of lines attributed to $Sr(5gn''l'')$ states, which cannot be reached by electric-dipole ICE from $Sr(5d_{5/2}nl)$ states. We have identified two mechanisms responsible for these lines: (i) the direct electric-quadrupole excitation from $Sr(5d_{5/2}nl)$ to $Sr(5gn'l)$ states, and (ii) the electric-dipole excitation to the weak $Sr(5fnl)$ component of the $Sr(5gn'l')$ states, this mixing being caused by the Coulomb interaction between the two excited electrons. The two excitation mechanisms can be unambiguously identified because they lead to spectra with different line-intensity distributions. A detailed analysis of the spectra is under way.

[1] W. E. Cooke, T. F. Gallagher, S. A. Edelstein and R. M. Hill, *Phys. Rev. Lett.* **40**, 178 (1978)
[2] M. Génévriez, D. Wehrli and F. Merkt, *Mol. Phys.* **118**, e1703051 (2020)

MJ11

INFRARED PHOTODISSOCIATION SPECTROSCOPY OF PLATINUM-CATION ACETYLENE COMPLEXES

<u>ANNA G BATCHELOR</u>, *Department of Chemistry, University of Georgia, Athens, GA, USA*; JOSHUA H MARKS, *W. M. Keck Research Laboratory in Astrochemistry, University of Hawaii at Manoa, Honolulu, HI, USA*; TIMOTHY B WARD, MICHAEL A DUNCAN, *Department of Chemistry, University of Georgia, Athens, GA, USA*.

$Pt^+(C_2H_2)_n$ (n = 1 – 9) complexes are studied with tunable infrared laser photodissociation spectroscopy. These complexes are produced with laser vaporization of a platinum rod in a pulsed supersonic expansion of argon seeded with acetylene. Argon-tagged and tag-free complexes are then mass-selected in a specially made reflectron time-of-flight mass spectrometer, and their spectra are measured in the C – H stretching region (2800 – 3400 cm^{-1}) with infrared laser photodissociation spectroscopy. A coordination number of three acetylenes is found for platinum-cation. The experimental spectra are assigned using B3LYP/DEF2TZVP with an effective core potential on platinum. Peaks for the asymmetric and normally forbidden symmetric stretch of acetylene are red shifted from free acetylene molecules. The presence of cation – pi complexes and reacted structures is investigated by comparing experiment to theory.

MK. Mini-symposium: Machine Learning
Monday, June 20, 2022 – 1:45 PM
Room: 217 Noyes Laboratory

Chair: Daniel P. Tabor, Texas A&M University, College Station, TX, USA

MK01   *INVITED TALK*   1:45 – 2:15

ELUCIDATING, ANALYZING, AND DESIGNING SPECTROSCOPIES: LEVERAGING THEORY AND CHEMICAL INTUITION TO GET THE MOST OUT OF MACHINE LEARNING

THOMAS E MARKLAND, *Department of Chemistry, Stanford University, Stanford, CA, USA.*

Advances in machine learning are pushing the forefront of what can be simulated and understood about the nature of chemical systems, offering intriguing possibilities for developing new chemical insights in spectroscopies ranging from NMR, to multidimensional electronic spectroscopies, and the recently introduced impulsive nuclear x-ray scattering. In this talk I will present our latest developments showing how machine learning's potential to simulate, analyze and design spectroscopic experiments can be maximized by building chemical intuition and theoretical insights into the underlying frameworks.

MK02   2:21 – 2:36

LOW-FREQUENCY INFRARED SPECTRUM OF LIQUID WATER FROM MACHINE-LEARNING BASED PARTIAL ATOMIC CHARGES

BOWEN HAN, CHRISTINE M ISBORN, LIANG SHI, *Department of Chemistry and Biochemistry, University of California, Merced, Merced, CA, USA.*

Modeling water in condensed phases is an indispensable part of modern water research and rigid non-polarizable water models, such as TIP4P/2005, have been very popular in molecular simulations due to their high efficiency. Although these water models can reproduce many properties of water, they fail in predicting the dielectric properties of water, such as the dielectric constant and low-frequency infrared spectra. We propose to improve these models by re-assigning the partial atomic charges of water molecules according to their local environment using a machine-learning (ML) model that is trained on quantum chemical data. With the ML-based charges, the calculated low-frequency infrared spectrum of liquid water is in good agreement with experiment, showing a peak at about 200 cm^{-1}, which non-polarizable water models fail to reproduce. The effects of charge redistributions in liquid water and their dependence on the choice of the density functional are also discussed.

MK03   2:39 – 2:54

MULTI-FIDELITY DEEP LEARNING AND ACTIVE LEARNING FOR MOLECULAR OPTICAL PROPERTIES

KEVIN P. GREENMAN, WILLIAM H. GREEN, *Department of Chemical Engineering, Massachusetts Institute of Technology, Cambridge, MA, USA*; RAFAEL GÓMEZ-BOMBARELLI, *Department of Materials Science and Engineering, Massachusetts Institute of Technology, Cambridge, MA, USA.*

A variety of physics-based and statistical methods have been developed to guide molecular design based on optical properties. Each method has a trade-off between cost, accuracy, and generalizability. While methods such as time-dependent density functional theory (TD-DFT) are often generalizable across chemical space due to their foundations in physics, they are relatively slow and are less suitable for screening large libraries of molecules. Statistical or machine learning methods are fast, but their performance is highly dependent on the choice of training data and representation. This makes them useful for design within chemical families that already have large datasets available, but less useful for de novo design tasks that explore new parts of chemical space. We propose a new deep learning method that leverages a combination of low fidelity (TD-DFT) and high fidelity (experimental) data sets to predict molecular optical properties with improved accuracy and generalizability over existing statistical methods. We also illustrate the importance of non-random data splitting strategies to assess generalizability of predictions for spectra in condensed phase. Finally, we demonstrate the use of active learning for model improvement by gathering new experimental data in regions of high prediction uncertainty.

MK04 2:57 – 3:12

MULTIVARIATE ANALYSIS OF MOLECULAR SPECTROSCOPY DATA FOR COVID-19 DETECTION

QIZHONG LIANG, YA-CHU CHAN, JUTTA TOSCANO, *JILA and NIST, University of Colorado, Boulder, CO, USA*; KRISTEN K. BJORKMAN, LESLIE A. LEINWAND, ROY PARKER, *BioFrontiers Institute, University of Colorado Boulder, Boulder, CO, USA*; DAVID J. NESBITT, JUN YE, *JILA and NIST, University of Colorado, Boulder, CO, USA*.

In exhaled human breath, there exist hundreds of sparse molecular species and many contain rich information about various health conditions or diseases. When associated with a specific medical response, a co-variation in concentrations for multiple molecular species can occur, thereby facilitating diagnosis. A recent technological improvement to the cavity-enhanced frequency comb spectroscopy (CE-DFCS) has enabled broadband molecular spectra to be collected at the parts-per-trillion detection sensitivity [a], allowing unambiguous and objective detection of multiple molecular species in a simultaneous manner. Here, we show how the breath spectroscopy data collected by CE-DFCS can realize non-invasive medical diagnostics [b]. The key to such realization comes from the use of supervised machine learning to process the comb spectroscopy data in parallel with extreme-dimensional data channel inputs. Using a total of 170 individual breath samples, we report cross-validated results with excellent discrimination capability for COVID-19. At the same time, significant differences are identified for several other personal attributes, including smoking, abdominal pain, and biological sex difference. Our demonstrated approach can be extended immediately to investigate the diagnostic potential for a number of other disease states, including breast cancer, asthma, and intestinal problems. We discuss how further development in machine learning and frequency comb-based breath analysis can benefit significantly from enriching the absorption database to include more molecular species.

[a] Q. liang, et al., "Ultrasensitive multispecies spectroscopic breath analysis for real-time health monitoring and diagnostics," PNAS 118(40) (2021).
[b] Q. liang, et al., "Frequency comb and machine learning-based breath analysis for COVID-19 classification," arXiv:2202.02321 (2022).

Intermission

MK05 *INVITED TALK* 3:54 – 4:24

CAPTURING, PREDICTING, AND UNDERSTANDING OPTICAL SIGNALS: HARNESSING MACHINE LEARNING TO TACKLE ENERGY DISSIPATION IN THE CONDENSED PHASE

ANDRES MONTOYA-CASTILLO, *Department of Chemistry, University of Colorado, Boulder, CO, USA*.

While optical spectroscopies provide an essential and ever-expanding toolbox for probing and elucidating how materials absorb, transport, and dissipate energy, accurately predicting their signals remains a formidable challenge to theory. By drastically expanding our ability accurately and efficiently simulate complex systems and their dynamics, machine learning techniques are opening fascinating possibilities for the simulation and analysis of various spectroscopies. In this talk, I will focus on our latest advances showing how one can exploit chemical intuition to combine machine learning techniques with robust theoretical frameworks to faithfully capture and interpret energy transport pathways encoded in optical signals.

MK06
SYMMETRY-CONSTRAINED MOLECULAR DYNAMICS

4:30 – 4:45

<u>ANDREW WHITE</u>, SAM COX, *Chemical Engineering, University of Rochester, Rochester, NY, USA.*

Molecular dynamics is a popular tool for molecular structure prediction, but the application into crystal structures has been limited by the inability to treat point group symmetries. For this reason, many space groups are inaccessible in typical molecular dynamics, though the inaccessible space groups are often desirable. We propose symmetry-constrained molecular dynamics as a new approach to address these space groups. This method allows all point group symmetries to be accessible in molecular dynamics simulations. Because there is a small number of possible space groups, these can be enumerated, as shown in this work. Spectroscopy and molecular dynamics are mutually beneficial techniques to understand systems more fully, and spectroscopy has deep roots in symmetry, as symmetries give insight into chemical shift prediction, for molecules and crystals. Therefore, this work bridges the gap between spectroscopy and structure prediction by molecular dynamics.

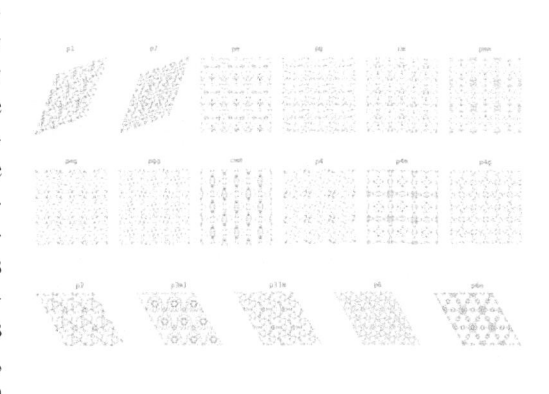

MK07
ACCELERATING MANY-BODY EXPANSION THEORY THROUGH GRAPH CONVOLUTIONAL NETWORKS

4:48 – 5:03

<u>YILI SHEN</u>, *College of Software Engineering, Tongji University, Shanghai, China*; CHENGWEI JU, *Pritzker School of Molecular Engineering, The University of Chicago, Chicago, IL, USA*; JUN YI, ZHOU LIN, *Department of Chemistry, University of Massachusetts, Amherst, MA, USA*; HUI GUAN, *College of Information and Computer Sciences, University of Massachusetts, Amherst, MA, USA.*

First-principles quantum mechanical modeling can potentially interpret and predict experimentally measurable properties of large molecules or systems, such as energies, provided that the difficulty in balancing its computational efficiency and accuracy is overcome. Many-body expansion theory (MBET) has been developed to resolve this issue: it approximates the total energy of a large system through a truncated expansion of one-, two-, ..., n-body energies, but it still suffers from a computational bottleneck, expensive first-principles evaluations of all many-body energies. In the present study, we integrated the graph convolutional network (GCN), a state-of-the-art machine learning (ML) algorithm, into the existing first-principles workflow, and developed a novel scheme referred to as GCN-MBET. Operationally, we evaluated all one-body energies using conventional first-principle quantum mechanics, but obtained many-body energies based on their relationships with effortless molecular descriptors established by GCN. As the initial stage of the study, we provided a proof-of-concept of our GCN-MBET model using two- and three-body energies from representative van der Waals or hydrogen-bonded molecular aggregates, including the water cluster, the phenol cluster, and water–phenol mixture. Given sufficient configurational diversity in the training set, we successfully reproduced first-principles two- and three-body energies in the test set to the chemical accuracy (< 1 kcal/mol), but at a fractional computational cost ($\simeq 1$ %). Our results indicated that GCN-MBET provides a promising unique and powerful tool to unlock the potential of first-principles quantum mechanical modeling of large molecules or systems.

ML. Small molecules

Monday, June 20, 2022 – 1:45 PM

Room: 1024 Chemistry Annex

Chair: Leah C O'Brien, Southern Illinois University, Edwardsville, IL, USA

ML01   1:45 – 2:00

CALCIUM MONOXIDE FORMATION IN LASER PLASMA STUDIED BY EMISSION AND FLUORESCENCE SPECTROSCOPY

<u>ALEKSANDR ZAKUSKIN</u>, BABKEN BEGLARYAN, ANDREY POPOV, TIMUR A. LABUTIN, *Department of Chemistry, Lomonosov Moscow State University, Moscow, Russia.*

Laser-induced plasma is a universal plasma source for spectral diagnostics of processes under extreme conditions. Due to possibility to freely vary laser energy, ambient pressure, compositions of the ablation target and surrounding environment plasma parameters can also be varied within a wide range. Typical temperatures (0.2-4 eV) and electron number densities (10^{15}-10^{19} cm^{-3}) allow observation of both atomic emission and emission of small, predominantly diatomic, molecules. In spite of spatial inhomogeneity of laser plasma, its certain symmetry opens up space for spatially resolved studies. Laser-induced fluorescence in plasma appears to be one of the most promising tools for spatially resolved plasma diagnostics. All these unique properties of laser plasma, combined with research interest in combustion processes during the meteor events in the Earth's atmosphere, led us to the study of Ca and CaO distribution in laser plasma under low ambient pressure.

We measured emission spectra of atomic calcium and calcium monoxide varying delay after laser pulse and ambient pressure from 0.16 Torr to atmospheric. Plasma temperature and electron number density were calculated where possible. By comparison of experimental spectra and spectra of Benešov bolide at different heights we showed that the emitting bolide wake is formed under 7-10 times higher pressure than the one at the corresponding altitude. The obtained data lead us to suggestion that the formation of CaO in plasma occurs primarily using oxygen from atmosphere. Therefore, abundance of CaO should have a strong dependency on the pressure of the surrounding media.

Also, we performed plasma elemental imaging (resolution of 200μm along each of 2 axes) by the means of Ca and CaO fluorescence in laser plasma. Ca atomic lines Ca I 428.30 nm and Ca I 430.52 nm and bands of CaO red system were used for this purpose. The estimated spatial distribution of Ca atoms and CaO molecules in laser plasma proves our suggestion that CaO is formed both in laser plasma and in the meteor wake primarily using oxygen from ambient air on the periphery of the cloud and this process almost does not involve oxygen from the ablated material ($CaCO_3$).

This work was supported by the Russian Science Foundation (grant 18-13-00269-П)

ML02 2:03 – 2:18

IN SEARCH OF EQUILIBRIUM IN LASER-PRODUCED CLOUD: ROLE OF PRESSURE, CHEMICAL QUENCHING, AND PLASMA EXPANSION

TIMUR A. LABUTIN, ALEKSANDR ZAKUSKIN, SERGEY ZAYTSEV, ANDREY POPOV, *Department of Chemistry, Lomonosov Moscow State University, Moscow, Russia*; VLADISLAV E. CHERNOV, *Physics, Voronezh State University, Voronezh, Russia*; ALEXEY A. BEREZHNOY, *Sternberg Astronomical Institute, Lomonosov Moscow State University, Moscow, Russia*; EKATERINA A. BORMOTOVA, *Department of Chemistry, Moscow State University, Moscow, Russia*; ANDREY STOLYAROV, *Department of Chemistry, Lomonosov Moscow State University, Moscow, Russia.*

The properties of laser plasma vary significantly depending on the pressure and composition of the environment, thus it a promising emission source to imitate of radiation from various objects in atmosphere (meteor wake, airglow) and in outer space. We aimed to register spectra of FeO and CaO bands in laser plasma as close as possible to the ones observed during the Benešov bolide event to reconstruct the composition and behavior of meteor wake.

We fit synthetic spectra of spontaneous vatying temperatures in the region of 1000-8000 K for the infrared system of CaO molecules to those measured in laser-induced plasma. It was found that the excitation (atomic species), vibrational and rotational temperatures of the experimental spectra indicate the absence of local thermodynamic equilibrium (LTE) and does not coincide with each other. The atomic excitation temperature are close to 10000 , vibrational temperature varies in the range of 3500–5000 K, while the rotational temperature is noticeably lower than 2000–3000 K. Moreover, the specific values of rotational temperatures vary greatly from band to band. We also found the valuable deviation of lines wavelengths and transition probabilities between model spectra based on EXOMOL data.

Calculations of the chemical composition of laser-produced clouds formed by laser heating of Fe and $CaCO_3$ targets were performed. Timescales of main reactions with participation of Fe- and Ca- containing species were calculated using rate constants of the reactions. Results of calculations of equilibrium composition of laser-produced and impact-produced clouds are presented. Quenching conditions of chemical reactions in laser-produced and impact-produced clouds are found.

This work was supported by the Russian Science Foundation (grant 18-13-00269-П).

ML03 2:21 – 2:36

TWO COLOR FORMALDEHYDE PLIF THERMOMETRY USING A BURST MODE LASER

XUNCHEN LIU[a], *School of Mechanical Engineering, Shanghai Jiao Tong University, Shanghai, China.*

Two color planar laser induced fluorescence (PLIF) is a robust combustion diagnostics technique to flame temperature field. Widely used OH-PLIF can measure the high temperature post flame front zone, but cannot accurately measure the intermediate temperature pre-flame front region where OH radical concentration is low. Here, the rotational resolved absorption cross section of formaldehyde in this region was analyzed and two peaks at 28183.5 cm^{-1} and 28184.5 cm^{-1} were selected as the line pair to determine flame temperature. The wavelength region can be easily accessed using the 3rd harmonics of Nd:YAG lasers at 355 nm. We demonstrate 20 kHz two dimensional flame temperature field measurement of a laminar coflow diffusion flame, a free jet flame and a reacting jet in hot crossflow using a wavelength-switching injection seeding burst mode laser and a single high speed camera.

---
[a]current address: School of Aeronautics and Astronautics, Shanghai Jiao Tong University

ML04
FLASH PYROLYSIS MECHANISM OF TRIMETHYLCHLOROSILANE BY FLASH PYROLYSIS VACUUM ULTRAVIOLET PHOTOIONIZATION TIME-OF-FLIGHT MASS SPECTROMETRY.

KUANLIANG SHAO, *Department of Chemistry, University of California, Riverside, Riverside, CA, USA*; JONAH BRUNSON, *Department of Molecular, Cell and Systems Biology, University of California, Riverside, Riverside, CA, USA*; YI TIAN, *Department of Chemistry, Stony Brook University, New York, NY, USA*; JING-SONG ZHANG, *Department of Chemistry, University of California, Riverside, Riverside, CA, USA*.

The thermal decomposition mechanism of trimethylchlorosilane at temperatures up to 1400 K was investigated using flash pyrolysis microreactor coupled with vacuum ultraviolet (118.2 nm) photoionization time-of-flight mass spectrometry. The main initiation reaction of the parent molecule was identified to be molecular elimination producing HCl and $Me_2Si = CH_2$. Other initiation pathways such as chlorine-atom loss, methyl radical loss, and methane elimination were also observed. Density function theory (DFT) calculations at UB3LYP/6-311++G(d,p) level of theory, with Grimme's empirical dispersion correction GD3, were performed to study the energetics of the possible initiation pathways. The theoretical calculations revealed that the HCl elimination channel via a van der Waals intermediate was the most energetically favored pathway among all initiation channels, in agreement with the experimental observations. Some secondary reactions of the initial products were identified, and their possible mechanisms were proposed.

ML05
ULTRAVIOLET SPECTROSCOPY OF SUBCRITICAL AND SUPERCRITICAL ETHANOL

TIMOTHY W MARIN, *Physical Science, Benedictine University, Lisle, IL, USA*; IRENEUSZ JANIK, *Radiation Laboratory, University of Notre Dame, Notre Dame, IN, USA*.

Vacuum ultraviolet spectroscopy was used to investigate the lowest-lying electronic state band edge of subcritical ethanol as a function of temperature from 25-200 °C, and for supercritical ethanol as a function of density at 250 °C. For subcritical ethanol, the band edge is observed to red shift with increasing temperature. Supercritical spectra clearly demonstrate a gradual transition from gas-phase to liquid-phase behavior with increasing density, as evidenced by a gradual blue shift and loss of spectral detail. We discuss both effects regarding the extent of hydrogen bonding in the system and Rydbergization effects, similar to those observed for subcritical and supercritical water.

Intermission

ML06 3:54 – 4:09

COLLISIONAL RELAXATION OF LOW-FREQUENCY VIBRATIONAL MODES OF SMALL MOLECULES IN A PULSED SEEDED SUPERSONIC JET

PIYUSH MISHRA, ALEXANDER W HULL, TIMOTHY J BARNUM, STEPHEN L COY, ROBERT W FIELD, *Department of Chemistry, MIT, Cambridge, MA, USA*.

Vibrational energy transfer is a fundamental process in molecules which is closely related to chemical reactivity. Supersonic jet expansions have been an important tool in spectroscopy and chemical physics. These expansions are used to produce cold molecules under collision-free conditions. Among the various degrees of freedom that are collisionally relaxed, our focus is on vibrationally inelastic collisions between the analyte molecule and the carrier gas. A chirped-pulse Fourier-transform millimeter wave spectrometer (CP-FTmmW) is employed to observe vibrational relaxation (VR) of low-frequency vibrational modes in small molecules SO_2, CHF_3, CH_3CN and a medium sized molecule CH_2CHCN. Systematic study of several supersonic expansion parameters extracts empirical relationships between VR and collision conditions. This includes a study of VR in molecules seeded in helium considering different valve types (Even-Lavie valve vs. General Valve), instrumental parameters (nozzle temperature, stagnation pressure, orifice dimensions), and variation of the seeded molecule concentration. The identity of the collision partner is explored using several carrier gases (neon, argon, nitrogen, and hydrogen) and comparing the observed VR with that of helium. A universal inverse-linear relationship between the extent of VR and the frequency of the vibrational mode has been revealed by the experiments using helium. This was strikingly different from what was observed for other choices of carrier gases, where mode-specific VR was observed. For CH_3CN (which has a degenerate bending mode, $2\nu_8^{0,2}$), efficient *l*-relaxation was observed. Separate use of two complementary laser-based techniques, laser induced fluorescence and millimeter wave optical double resonance, led to characterization of the velocity slip effect, the onset of clustering, and effects of Van der Waals bonding, studied as analyte concentrations were increased. Apart from demonstrating the power of a multiplexed form of rotationally resolved spectroscopy (CP-FTmmW), a 'roadmap' is generated to aid the design of future experiments by tailoring the choices of supersonic conditions. Empirical and intuitive approximate models are assembled that will aid in understanding vibrationally inelastic scattering and VR across a wide range of expansion parameters.

ML07 4:12 – 4:27

ROTATIONAL LEVEL INTERVALS IN HD FROM CRYO-COOLED SUB-DOPPLER ROVIBRATIONAL SPECTROSCOPY

MEISSA DIOUF, FRANK M.J. COZIJN, EDCEL JOHN SALUMBIDES, WIM UBACHS, *Department of Physics and Astronomy, VU University, Amsterdam, Netherlands*.

The spectroscopic investigation of the hydrogen molecule and its isotopologues has played a crucial role in the advancement of quantum mechanics in the molecular domain. Particularly, highly accurate measurements of rovibrational transitions allow for various tests of fundamental physics including searches for physics beyond the Standard Model[a].

Recent Doppler-free measurements performed at room temperature[b,c,d], in the (2,0) overtone band of the hydrogen deuteride molecule spurred a stimulating debate on the interpretation of the spectra which significantly differ from typical Lamb-dips. New measurements were performed in a cryogenically cooled cavity with the hope of resolving the underlying hyperfine structure. However the resulted spectra observed shared the same unusual lineshapes which still hinder the extraction of the absolute rovibrational positions. With the goal of extracting the rotational interval with a better accuracy, pairs of P and R transitions were considered. This leads to accurate values for rotational energy intervals and to a precise test of molecular QED theory[e].

---

[a] W. Ubachs, J.C.J. Koelemeij, K.S.E. Eikema, E.J. Salumbides, J. Mol. Spectr. 320, 1-12 (2016)
[b] F.M.J. Cozijn, P. Dupre, K.S.E. Eikema, E.J. Salumbides, W. Ubachs,, Phys. Rev. Lett. 120, 153002 (2018)
[c] M.L. Diouf , F.M.J. Cozijn, B. Darquie, E.J. Salumbides, W. Ubachs, Opt. Lett. 44, 4733 (2019)
[d] M.L. Diouf, F.M.J. Cozijn, K.F. Lai, E.J. Salumbides, W. Ubachs , Phys. Rev. Res. 2, 023209 (2020)
[e] P. Czachorowski, M. Puchalski, J. Komasa, K. Pachucki, Phys. Rev. A 98, 052506 (2018)

ML08 4:30 – 4:45

QUANTIFYING EMISSION OF NIR-I AND NIR-II DYES VIA FLUORESCENCE QUANTUM YIELD

DAVID D.N. NDALEH, CAMERON L SMITH, MAHESH LOKU YADDEHIGE, ABDUL KALAM SHAIK, DAVITA WATKINS, NATHAN I HAMMER, *Chemistry and Biochemistry, University of Mississippi, Oxford, MS, USA*; JARED DELCAMP, *Chemistry, University of Mississippi, Oxford, MS, USA*.

Fluorescence Quantum Yield allows scientists to both quantify spectroscopic properties of dyes and compare to literature references. With the growing interest in NIR-emissive dyes for biological imaging, it is of great importance to reliably measure the fluorescent quantum yield of these novel dyes. Using a broadband excitation source and liquid nitrogen cooled InGaAs detector, steady state emission of four novel pentamethine indolizine cyanine dyes synthesized with N,N-dimethylaniline-based substituents on the indolizine periphery at varied substitutions sites is recorded.

ML09 4:48 – 5:03

FLUORESCENCE AND QUANTUM YIELD STUDIES OF NEW SWIR EMITTING RHODINDOLIZINE DYES

ABDUL KALAM SHAIK, SATADRU CHATTERJEE, KALPANI HIRUNIKA WIJESINGHE, DAVID D.N. NDALEH, AMAL DASS, *Chemistry and Biochemistry, University of Mississippi, Oxford, MS, USA*; JARED DELCAMP, *Chemistry, University of Mississippi, Oxford, MS, USA*; NATHAN I HAMMER, *Chemistry and Biochemistry, University of Mississippi, Oxford, MS, USA*.

The design and characterization of organic dyes emitting in the near infrared (NIR) and short-wave infrared (SWIR) regions are of a great interest to the research community for several applications including bio-imaging. These abstract reports the results of photo-physical studies of a set of four newly-designed and synthesized SWIR emissive RhodIndolizine dyes. All the dyes were found to absorb and emit well within the SWIR domain (reaching emission maximum up to 1256 nm) with an onset beyond 1400 nm and Stokes shifts varying between 140-170 nm. The quantum yields of these dyes were estimated relative to the emission standard of IR1061 with a quantum yield of 0.0059 or 0.59% in dichloromethane. Further, nanoencapsulation studies in a water-soluble surfactant demonstrate their efficiency towards biological imaging.

ML10 5:06 – 5:21

HIGHLY SELECTIVE GAS ANALYZER BASED ON MOLECULAR ROTATIONAL RESONANCE SPECTROSCOPY FOR SO_2 MONITORING IN AMBIENT AIR

MD ABRAR JAMIL, SYLVESTRE TWAGIRAYEZU, *Chemistry and Biochemistry, Lamar University, Beaumont, TX, USA*; JUSTIN L. NEILL, *BrightSpec Labs, BrightSpec, Inc., Charlottesville, VA, USA*.

As part of the efforts to determine the applications of molecular rotational resonance (MRR) technique to SO_2 monitoring in ambient air, a K-band MRR analyzer has been employed to record the MRR signature of multiple synthetic air samples containing SO_2 pollutant as well as that of standard SO_2 samples. The observed MRR features reveal a rich rotational pattern due to MRR's sensitivity. The interfering matrix (i.e., air moisture), which typically challenges other conventional techniques, showed no impact on MRR signatures of SO_2. The validity of MRR for SO_2 monitoring has been examined by measuring MRR signal response of a set of standard SO_2 samples over a range of sampling pressures (5-15). The obtained linear correlations allowed the determination of recovery percentage (97-100%) and low detection limit of better than $1mg/m^3$. Work to improve this analytical procedure is underway and will be reported in this talk.

ML11

SENSITIVITY TO VARIATION OF FUNDAMENTAL CONSTANTS FROM FREQUENCY MEASUREMENTS OF ACETYLENE REFERENCE TRANSITIONS

FLORIN LUCIAN CONSTANTIN, *Laboratoire PhLAM, UMR 8523 CNRS - Université Lille 1, Villeneuve d'Ascq, France.*

Space-time variations of fundamental constants that are assumed in theories beyond the Standard Model may be investigated by precision molecular spectroscopy. The molecular energy levels are intrinsically sensitive to a variation of the proton-to-electron mass ratio μ and the transitions between closely-spaced energy levels display an enhanced sensitivity[a]. The lasers stabilized to isotopic acetylene lines probed by saturated absorption spectroscopy provided secondary frequency references in the 1.5 μm spectral region. The acetylene optical clock enables now access to fractional frequency stability of 3×10^{-13} at one second in a compact and robust setup that ensures optical frequency referencing with drifts lower than 1 Hz/day, as it is indicated in ref.[b]. This contribution discusses the potential in constraining time variation of μ from precision spectroscopy of $^{12}C_2H_2$ transitions pertaining to the $\nu_1+\nu_3$ and $\nu_1+\nu_2+\nu_4+\nu_5$ combination bands[c]. The acetylene energy levels are modeled with a state-of-the-art Hamiltonian that takes into account different rovibrational interactions and the sensitivities of the reference acetylene transitions are calculated. The frequency splittings between near resonant transitions, that may arise from the cancellation of the rotational intervals with frequency shifts associated to the origins of the vibrational bands, the anharmonicity, and the rovibrational interactions, display sensitivity coefficients up to $\pm 10^3$ level. The systematic frequency shifts are conservatively evaluated for intracavity spectroscopy setups. The constraint to the time variation of μ derived from absolute frequency measurements of acetylene optical clocks is estimated at the 10^{-13}/yr level.

---

[a] V.V. Flambaum and M.G. Kozlov, Phys. Rev. Lett. 99, 150801 (2007).
[b] T. Talvard *et al*, Optics Express 25, 2259-2269 (2017).
[c] F.L. Constantin, Vibrational Spectroscopy 85, 228-234 (2016).

MM. Cold and ultracold molecules

Monday, June 20, 2022 – 1:45 PM

Room: 124 Burrill Hall

Chair: Mitsunori Araki, Tokyo University of Science, Shinjuku-ku, Tokyo, Japan

MM01   1:45 – 2:00
ELECTRONIC SPECTROSCOPY AND PHOTOIONIZATION OF LiBe

THOMAS D. PERSINGER, JIANDE HAN, MICHAEL HEAVEN, *Department of Chemistry, Emory University, Atlanta, GA, USA.*

Heterodimers consisting of an alkaline and alkaline-earth metal, such as LiBe are plausible candidates for laser cooling experiments. Once cooled, the unpaired electron on the lithium allows LiBe to be manipulated by both magnetic and electric fields. The electronic structure calculations of You et. al[1] predicted that the $2^2\Sigma^+$ transition is very diagonal, with a 0-0 band Franck-Condon factor of 0.998. Prior to the present study, only the $2^2\Pi$ - $X^2\Sigma^+$ bands (labeled as the C-X system in earlier literature)[2] had been observed between 19,200 – 20,600 cm^{-1}. We have subsequently extended the spectroscopic characterization of LiBe and recorded the first experimental data for LiBe$^+$. Included in this work are the first observations of the $1^2\Pi$, $2^2\Sigma^+$, $3^2\Sigma^+$, and $4^2\Pi$ states of LiBe, and the $X^1\Sigma^+$ ground state of LiBe$^+$. Data for the $2^2\Sigma^+$ - $X^2\Sigma^+$ transition confirmed the theoretical prediction that LiBe is a promising candidate for laser cooling.

1. You, Y.; Yang, C.L.; Wang, M.S.; Ma, X.G.; Lui, W.W. Theoretical investigations of the laser cooling of a LiBe molecule. Phys. Rev. A. At., Mol., Opt. Phys. 92 (3-A), 032502 (2015).
2. Schlachta, R.; Fischer, L.; Rosmus, P.; Bondybey, V.E. The simplest heteronuclear metal cluster lithium-berllium (LiBe). Chem. Phys. Lett. 170 (5-6), 485-91 (1990).

MM02   2:03 – 2:18
FLUORESCENCE SPECTROSCOPY DETECTION OF THE 4f^{-1} STATES OF YbF

THOMAS D. PERSINGER, JIANDE HAN, *Department of Chemistry, Emory University, Atlanta, GA, USA*; TIMOTHY STEIMLE, *School of Molecular Sciences, Arizona State University, Tempe, AZ, USA*; MICHAEL HEAVEN, *Department of Chemistry, Emory University, Atlanta, GA, USA.*

A measurement of the electron electric dipole moment (eEDM) might be achieved using ytterbium fluoride (YbF) under ultra-cold conditions. One-dimensional laser cooling using the $A^2\Pi_{1/2}$ - $X^2\Sigma^+$ transition of YbF has been demonstrated, but it appears that laser cooling by means of this transition may be limited by radiative loss of population from the cooling cycle. YbF has low-energy states that arise from the Yb$^+$(4f^{13}6s)F$^-$ configuration (labeled in previous papers as 4f^{-1} states). Recent theoretical calculations[1] predict that radiative decay from $A^2\Pi_{1/2}$ to the 4f^{-1} states occurs with a branching fraction of approximately 5x10^{-4}, which may explain why attempts to achieve 3-dimensional cooling have not been successful to date. In the present study we have used dispersed laser induced fluorescence spectroscopy to the observe the lowest energy 4f^{-1} states. These measurements were carried out using excitation of previously unobserved YbF transitions in the near UV spectral range. The 4f^{-1} Ω = 1/2 and 3/2 states were found at energies of 8470 and 9070 cm^{-1} above the ground state. The results are in excellent agreement with the calculations, bolstering confidence in the predicted electric transition dipole moments of Ref. 1.

1. Zhang, C.; Zhang C.; Cheng, L.; Steimle T. C.; Tarbutt M. R., Inner-shell excitation in the YbF molecule and its impact on laser cooling. Accepted for publication, J. Mol. Spec. (2022) and arXiv.org, e-Print Archive, Physics (2022), 1-11

MM03   2:21 – 2:36
SINGLET-TRIPLET DOORWAY STATES OF ALUMINUM MONOFLUORIDE

NICOLE WALTER, JOHANNES SEIFERT, STEFAN TRUPPE, CHRISTIAN SCHEWE, *Department of Molecular Physics, Fritz-Haber-Institut der Max-Planck-Gesellschaft, Berlin, Germany*; BORIS SARTAKOV, *Prokhorov General Physics Institute, Russian Academy of Sciences, Moscow, Russia*; GERARD MEIJER, *Department of Molecular Physics, Fritz-Haber-Institut der Max-Planck-Gesellschaft, Berlin, Germany*.

Aluminum monofluoride (AlF) possesses highly favorable properties for laser cooling, both via the $A^1\Pi$ and $a^3\Pi$ states. Determining efficient pathways between the singlet and the triplet manifold of electronic states will be advantageous for future experiments at ultralow temperatures. The lowest rotational levels of the $A^1\Pi, v = 6$ and $b^3\Sigma^+, v = 5$ states of AlF are nearly iso-energetic and interact via spin-orbit coupling. These levels thus have a strongly mixed spin-character and provide a singlet-triplet doorway. We present a hyperfine resolved spectroscopic study of the $A^1\Pi, v = 6 // b^3\Sigma^+, v = 5$ perturbed system in a jet-cooled, pulsed molecular beam. From a fit to the observed energies of the hyperfine levels, the fine and hyperfine structure parameters of the coupled states, their relative energies as well as the spin-orbit interaction parameter are determined. The radiative lifetimes of selected hyperfine levels are experimentally determined using time-delayed ionization, Lamb dip spectroscopy and accurate measurements of the transition lineshapes. The measured lifetimes range between 2 ns and 200 ns, determined by the degree of singlet-triplet mixing for each level.

MM04   2:39 – 2:54
FUNCTIONALIZED AROMATIC MOLECULES FOR LASER COOLING AND TRAPPING

BENJAMIN AUGENBRAUN, SEAN BURCHESKY, *Department of Physics, Harvard University, Cambridge, MA, USA*; GUO-ZHU ZHU, *Department of Physics, University of California, Los Angeles, Los Angeles, CA, USA*; DEBAYAN MITRA, *Department of Physics, Harvard University, Cambridge, MA, USA*; CLAIRE E DICKERSON, *Department of Chemistry and Biochemistry, University of California, Los Angeles, Los Angeles, CA, USA*; GUANMING LAO, *Department of Physics, University of California, Los Angeles, Los Angeles, CA, USA*; ZACK LASNER, *Department of Physics, Harvard University, Cambridge, MA, USA*; ANASTASSIA ALEXANDROVA, *Department of Chemistry and Biochemistry, University of California, Los Angeles, Los Angeles, CA, USA*; WESLEY CAMPBELL, *Department of Physics, University of California, Los Angeles, Los Angeles, CA, USA*; JUSTIN CARAM, *Department of Chemistry and Biochemistry, University of California, Los Angeles, Los Angeles, CA, USA*; ERIC HUDSON, *Department of Physics, University of California, Los Angeles, Los Angeles, CA, USA*; JOHN M. DOYLE, *Department of Physics, Harvard University, Cambridge, MA, USA*.

Rapid and repeated scattering of laser photons ("optical cycling") underlies many uses of atoms and small molecules for quantum science and measurement. Larger polyatomic molecules are also appealing targets, partly because these species may be decorated with functional groups offering unique scientific opportunities. In this talk, we discuss a large class of aromatic molecules that can be functionalized with an alkaline-earth metal atom to enable optical cycling. We describe the gas-phase production of Ca- and Sr-bearing derivatives of phenyl (Ph) and naphthyl radicals and, using dispersed fluorescence spectroscopy, we show that these molecules contain multiple electronic transitions suitable for optical cycling and laser cooling. We present high-resolution laser excitation spectra for molecules such as fluorinated-CaOPh and SrOPh and compare these to the well-known alkaline-earth monoalkoxides and monoamides. These data inform ongoing work to laser cool and magneto-optically trap a functionalized aromatic molecule.

MM05 2:57 – 3:12

LASER SPECTROSCOPY OF BUFFER-GAS-COOLED POLYATOMIC MOLECULES

YUIKI TAKAHASHI, *Physics, Mathematics and Astronomy, Caltech, Pasadena, CA, USA*; MASAAKI BABA, *Division of Chemistry, Graduate School of Science, Kyoto University, Kyoto, Japan*; KATSUNARI ENOMOTO, *Department of Physics, University of Toyama, Toyama, Japan*; KANA IWAKUNI, *Institute for Laser Science, The University of Electro-Communications, Chofu-shi, Japan*; SUSUMU KUMA, *Atomic, Molecular and Optical Physics Laboratory, RIKEN, Saitama, Japan*; AYAMI HIRAMOTO, REO TOBARU, YUKI MIYAMOTO, *Research Institute for Interdisciplinary Science, Okayama University, Okayama, Japan.*

Buffer gas cooling has emerged as a powerful tool in the study of cold and ultracold molecules. We have demonstrated buffer gas cooling and CW laser absorption spectroscopy on two species: Calcium monohydroxide radical (CaOH) and Phthalocyanine ($C_{32}H_{18}N_8$). CaOH has gained an increasing attention from astrophysics community due to its expected presence in the atmospheres of cool stars and rocky exoplanets. 3D Magneto-Optical trapping and subsequent sub-Doppler cooling of buffer-gas-cooled CaOH has also recently been reported [1]. Phthalocyanine, on the other hand, is much larger and more complex molecule than CaOH, possessing extremely rich rotational and vibrational structure. For both species, significant rotational cooling has been observed inside the ∼5 K Helium buffer gas cell with estimated rotational temperature of ∼10 K. This is promising, especially for large molecules with spectral congestion, to move molecular population into fewer lines, enhance signals, and drastically simplify spectrum. In this talk, we will present these results and analyses, including the latest data.

[1] N. B. Vilas, C. Hallas, L. Anderegg, P. Robichaud, A. Winnicki, D. Mitra, and J. M. Doyle (2021). arXiv:2112.08349

Intermission

MM06 3:54 – 4:09

CRYOGENIC ION SPECTROSCOPY OF TRANSITION METAL-EDTA COMPLEXES: ION-DEPENDENT SPECTRAL AND STRUCTURAL SHIFTS

MADISON M. FOREMAN, J. MATHIAS WEBER, *JILA and Department of Chemistry, University of Colorado, Boulder, CO, USA.*

Ethylenediaminetetraacetic acid (EDTA) is a useful model system for studying the ubiquitous divalent ion-carboxylate interactions in protein binding pockets.[a,b] EDTA can chelate most metal cations by forming up to six bonds with its four carboxyl groups and two nitrogen atoms, resulting in water-soluble complexes that are biologically relevant.

Here, we present cryogenic gas-phase infrared spectra of a series of transition metal-EDTA complexes of the form $[M(II)\cdot EDTA]^{2-}$ and assign spectral features using density functional theory calculations. The vibrational spectra inform us of the structure of and intermolecular forces in each complex, revealing the binding geometry of the metal ion within the EDTA binding pocket and its response to changes in ionic radius and electron configuration. The positions of carboxylate vibrational bands depend on the identity of the bound metal, displaying a clear spectral response to changes in binding properties.

[a] S. C. Edington, C. R. Baiz, J. Phys. Chem. A 122 (2018) 6585-6592
[b] Q. Yuan, X. T. Kong, G. L. Hou, L. Jiang, X. B. Wang, Faraday Discuss. 217 (2019) 383

MM07 4:12 – 4:27
DEVELOPMENT OF A SUPERSONIC EXPENSION SOURCE FOR HIGH-RESOLUTION INFRARED SPECTROSCOPY OF ISOPRENE

<u>KATARINA REYNA</u>, BINH NGUYET VO, SEBASTIAN GUERRERO, JACOB STEWART, *Department of Chemistry, Connecticut College, New London, CT, USA.*

Isoprene (C_5H_8) is a biogenic volatile organic compound (BVOC) found abundantly in our atmosphere. It is produced by plants and reacts in the atmosphere which leads to the production of aerosols and ozone. Previous spectra taken by our group have shown that, at room temperature, the infrared spectrum of isoprene is congested and difficult to assign, in part due to hot bands. We are currently building a supersonic expansion source that will allow us to cool the isoprene sample to a temperature of around 20 - 30 K. Lowering the temperature of the gas will eliminate hot bands and produce much clearer, less congested spectra. This will allow for a better understanding of isoprene's fundamental properties through spectral analysis. During this talk we will discuss the progress of the experiment and present preliminary spectra if available.

MM08 4:30 – 4:45
INTERSTELLAR PEPTIDE BOND FORMATION BY ACETALDEHYDE AND AMMONIA IN ANALOG ICE

<u>JOSHUA H MARKS</u>, JIA WANG, *Department of Chemistry, University of Hawaii at Manoa, Honolulu, HI, USA*; ANDRÉ K. ECKHARDT, *Department of Chemistry, Massachusetts Institute of Technology, Cambridge, MA, USA*; N. FABIAN KLEIMEIER, ANDREW MARTIN TURNER, RALF INGO KAISER, *Department of Chemistry, University of Hawaii at Manoa, Honolulu, HI, USA.*

Observation of complex organic molecules containing peptide bonds such as acetamide and propionamide in the interstellar medium raises the prospect of amino acid formation. Reactions of interstellar ice analogs containing acetaldehyde and ammonia were investigated to better understand the reactivity of oxygen-containing organic molecules with ammonia. These ices were submitted to energetic electron irradiation to simulate the effects of secondary electrons generated by galactic cosmic rays. Photoionization mass spectrometry was used to detect reaction products, while four-wave mixing provided tunable vacuum UV light for single photon ionization. Isotopically labeled acetaldehyde was employed to verify the formula of the observed reaction products. Electronic structure calculations at the CCSD(T)/CBS level predicted the adiabatic ionization energy of all plausible isomers. The differences between the ionization energies of the C_2H_5NO reaction products were used to identify the isomers present. The amino radical, NH_2, was found to bind to the acetaldehyde radical at either carbon. This resulted in the formation of 1-aminoacetaldehyde ($CH_3C(O)NH_2$), better known as acetamide, and 2-aminoacetaldehyde (NH_2CH_2CHO). Furthermore, with sufficient irradiation, high energy tautomers of both 1- and 2-aminoacetaldehyde were found to form. Both 1-aminoethenol ($CH_2C(OH)NH_2$) and 2-aminoethenol ($OHCHCHNH_2$) were identified by measurement of their photoionization efficiency spectra.

MM09 4:48 – 5:03
THE COMPLEXES OF HYDROXYLAMINE VIA VIBRATIONAL AND ROTATIONAL SPECTROSCOPY

<u>XIAOLONG LI</u>, DINGDING LV, *Department of Chemistry, Fudan University, Shanghai, China*; WEIXING LI, MINGFEI ZHOU, *Fudan University, Department of Chemistry, Shanghai, China.*

Although hydroxylamine is detected in the interstellar medium, there is a fewer study about its complexes and photochemistry. Herein, we study the photodissociation of hydroxylamine using cryogenic matrix-isolation spectroscopy.Furthermore, the reactions of hydroxyylmaine in CO and CO2 ice are investigated via cryogenic matrix-isolation. As a consequence, the organic molecules form in the matrix cage. The complexes between hydroxylamine and aromatics are also studied by rotational spectroscopy in 2-8 GHz. The structures of observed isomers are determined by their rotational constants.

MM10 — Post-Deadline Abstract

REACTION OF ELECTRONS TRAPPED IN CRYOGENIC MATRICES WITH BENZOPHENONE

<u>ANKIT SOMANI</u>, WOLFRAM SANDER, *Organische Chemie II, Ruhr-Universität Bochum, Bochum, Germany.*

Electron transfer reactions are among the most elementary chemical reactions, which play a fundamental role in organic synthesis, electrochemical processes, and biochemical reactions. In our study, we used sodium as a source of electrons and probed the formation of benzophenone radical anion **2** in an argon and low density amorphous (LDA) water ice matrices using matrix isolation technique.

In solid argon, mixture of sodium vapors and benzophenone **1** was co-deposited and after irradiating the matrix with the visible light, electron transfer takes place from sodium to **1** under the formation of radical anion **2**. In LDA water ice, hydrated electrons are produced after co-deposition of water with sodium. The hydrated electrons react with benzophenone without photochemical activation and resulted in radical anion **2**. However, the photoexcitation of radical anion **2** yielded back benzophenone **1** after losing an electron to the matrix.[1]

Reference:
[1] A. Somani, W. Sander, *J. P. Org. Chem.* **2022**, e4335.

MN. Astronomy

Monday, June 20, 2022 – 1:45 PM

Room: 274 Medical Sciences Building

Chair: L. Margulès, Universite de Lille, Villeneuve de Ascq, France

MN01   1:45 – 2:00

NOEMA OBSERVATIONS OF COMPLEX ORGANIC CHEMISTRY IN THE W3 STAR-FORMING REGION

WILL E. THOMPSON, *Department of Chemistry, University of Wisconsin-Madison, Madison, WI, USA*; SUSANNA L. WIDICUS WEAVER, *Chemistry and Astronomy, University of Wisconsin-Madison, Madison, WI, USA*; DARIUSZ LIS, *Jet Propulsion Laboratory, California Institute of Technology, Pasadena, CA, USA*.

The process of star formation provides a rich environment for complex interstellar chemistry to occur. We are able to probe the physical and chemical processes of star and planet forming regions in detail using high resolution millimeter wave interferometry. We have used the Northern Extended Millimeter Array (NOEMA) to conduct observations of complex organic molecules (COMs) within the W3 star forming region at selected frequencies in the λ=2 mm band. W3 is a binary system with two high-mass hot cores centered on masers, W3(OH) and W3(H2O). The two cores display different chemistry despite being formed from the same interstellar cloud. This difference in chemistry may arise either because of a difference in source age, or because of different physical conditions within the sources. Interferometric observations of molecules in this region allow us to disentangle the spatial distribution of COMs and investigate the drivers of chemical differentiation between the two star-forming cores. Our results show the chemical morphology of prebiotically relevant molecules such as methanol, methyl formate, methyl cyanide, and formaldehyde, as well as kinematics and temperature distributions within the W3 complex. We will report on these findings and discuss the results in the context of interstellar prebiotic chemistry.

MN02   2:03 – 2:18

A MACHINE LEARNING APPROACH TO CHARACTERIZING THE CHEMICAL INVENTORY OF ORION-KL

HALEY N. SCOLATI, JOSHUA CARDER, *Department of Chemistry, University of Virginia, Charlottesville, VA, USA*; ERIC HERBST, *Department of Chemistry, The University of Virginia, Charlottesville, VA, USA*; BRETT A. McGUIRE, *Department of Chemistry, Massachusetts Institute of Technology, Cambridge, MA, USA*; KELVIN LEE, *Accelerated Computing Systems and Graphics, Intel Corporation, Hillsboro, OR, USA*.

The interplay of the chemistry and physics that exists within astrochemically relevant sources can only be fully appreciated if we can gain a holistic understanding of their chemical inventories. Previous work by Lee et al. demonstrated the capabilities of simple regression models to reproduce the abundances of the chemical inventory of TMC-1, as well as provide predictions for the abundances of new candidate molecules. It remains to be seen, however, to what degree TMC-1 is a "unicorn" in astrochemistry, where the simplicity of its chemistry and physics readily facilitates characterization with simple machine learning models. Here we present an extension in chemical and physical complexity to an extensively studied hot star forming region, Orion-KL. Unlike TMC-1, the Orion-KL nebula is composed of several structurally distinct environments that differ chemically and kinematically, wherein abundances of molecules between components can have non-linear correlations that can cause the unexpected appearance or even the lack of unlikely species in various environments. A proof-of-concept study was performed to assess if similar regression models could accurately reproduce the abundances from the XCLASS chemical inventory obtained by the Herschel spectral survey. A new self-referencing embedded string (SELFIES) molecular embedder was adopted to account for vibrationally excited states and isotopologues. This additional complexity is considered with a hierarchical classification algorithm to indicate any relationships between environments with respect to the present species. Alongside the promising performance of our regression and classifier models, we attempted to fully capture the complexity of Orion-KL with increased efficiency using a neural network. The results of the classical models and neural network, as well as a discussion of their construction and performance, will be presented.

MN03   2:21 – 2:36
USING HCO$^+$ LINE (& ITS ISOMERS) AS AN ASTROCHEMICAL TOOL TO PROBE THE STRUCTURE OF CLASS 0/I PROTOSTARS

MIHIKA RAO, *Department of Astronomy, University of Virginia, Charlottesville, VA, USA*; ANTHONY REMIJAN, *NAASC, National Radio Astronomy Observatory, Charlottesville, VA, USA*; ADELE PLUNKETT, *NAASC, NRAO, Charlottesville, VA, USA.*

The chemistry of Class 0/I protostars have become increasingly important due to the mounting evidence of their impact on the chemical composition of future nascent planetary systems. Prior observations of molecular outflows, which are an energetic mass-ejection phenomenon associated with early stages of stellar evolution, have revealed that not only do these harsh environments contain a surprising array of complex molecules, but they also show highly-localized spatio-chemical differentiation. Because the velocities of these jets are relatively well-constrained based on mm-wave observations, it is possible to associate distance within the outflow with temporal evolution of chemistry. As well, the collimated nature of the outflows provides a relatively compact region in which comparisons can be made between outflow, shocked walls, and background ambient gas in a variety of density and temperature conditions as the chemistry evolves. We use Atacama Large Millimeter Array (ALMA) spectral line observations in the range of 300-360 GHz of HCO$^+$ line and its isomers in five outflows in the southern hemisphere of widely-varying ages, velocities, and chemical conditions to elucidate the underlying links between physical conditions, outflow properties, and chemical evolution in these important pre-stellar environments.

MN04   2:39 – 2:54
MAGNETIC FIELD STRENGTH LIMITS IN A PROTOPLANETARY DISK FROM MULTI-WAVELENGTH ZEEMAN OBSERVATIONS

RACHEL E. HARRISON, *Astronomy, University of Illinois at Urbana-Champaign, Urbana, IL, USA*; LESLIE LOONEY, AASSIK PAZHANI, *Department of Astronomy, University of Illinois at Urbana-Champaign, Urbana, IL, USA*; ZHI-YUN LI, *Department of Astronomy, The University of Virginia, Charlottesville, VA, USA*; HAIFENG YANG, *Institute for Advanced Study, Tsinghua University, Beijing, China*; IAN STEPHENS, *Department of Earth, Environment, and Physics, Worcester State University, Worcester, MA, USA*; RICHARD TEAGUE, *Radio and Geoastronomy Division, Harvard-Smithsonian Center for Astrophysics, Cambridge, MA, USA*; RICHARD CRUTCHER, *Department of Astronomy, University of Illinois at Urbana-Champaign, Urbana, IL, USA*; CRYSTAL L. BROGAN, *NAASC, National Radio Astronomy Observatory, Charlottesville, VA, USA*; ERIN GUILFOIL COX, *Center for Interdisciplinary Exploration and Research in Astrophysics (CIERA), Northwestern University, Evanston, IL, USA.*

Magnetic fields likely play a critical role in the accretion of material from protoplanetary disks onto protostars by providing a mechanism of angular momentum transport, particularly through magnetic disk winds. Constraining magnetic field strengths in protoplanetary disks is therefore necessary to test theories of magnetically-driven accretion. Zeeman splitting observations offer a way to directly measure or set upper limits on magnetic field strengths. We present the results of Zeeman splitting observations of several hyperfine lines of the CN(2-1) and CN(1-0) transitions in the Class II protoplanetary disk V4046 Sgr. We also present observations of the linear continuum dust polarization in this source and discuss their implications for the disk's dust population.

MN05   2:57 – 3:12
DETECTION OF $c - C_3H_2$, NO, and CH_3CN TOWARDS MOLECULAR CLOUDS AT THE EDGE OF THE GALAXY

LILIA KOELEMAY, *Department of Chemistry and Biochemistry, University of Arizona, Tucson, AZ, USA*; LUCY M. ZIURYS, *Dept. of Astronomy, Dept. of Chemistry, Arizona Radio Observatory, The University of Arizona, Tucson, AZ, USA.*

In previous studies, we detected methanol in molecular clouds towards the edge of the Milky Way galaxy using the Arizona Radio Observatory (ARO) 12m. These observations implied that the Galactic Habitable Zone (GHZ) may extend beyond 20 kpc from the Galactic Center. As a continuation of this study, we have searched for other organic molecules towards these same edge clouds. We have current detections of $c - C_3H_2$, NO, and CH_3CN towards WB89-640, WB89-380, and 19423+2541, among other sources. These molecules appear to show no decrease in abundance with respect to galactic radius despite the decrease in metallicity. Clearly organic chemistry is active towards the edge of our galaxy. The detection of these organic molecules show that the universe is far more molecular in nature than previously thought.

MN06 3:15 – 3:30

MOLECULAR LINE OBSERVATIONS IN TWO DUSTY STAR FORMING GALAXIES AT Z=6.9

SREEVANI JARUGULA, *Department of Astronomy, University of Illinois at Urbana-Champaign, Urbana, IL, USA.*

SPT0311-58 is a pair of dusty star-forming galaxies (West and East) at z=6.9, less than 800 Myr after the Big Bang. It is the most massive infrared luminous galaxy pair discovered in the Epoch of Reionization (EoR). In this talk, I will present the analysis of the molecular emission lines in this source, observed with ALMA at 0.3" - 0.5" corresponding to 1.6 - 2.7 kpc. We analyzed CO(6-5), CO(7-6), CO(10-9), [CI](2-1), and H2O(211-202) molecular lines and dust continuum emission using non-local thermodynamic equilibrium (non-LTE) radiative transfer models. We find that the CO spectral line energy distribution and brightness temperature ratios in West and East are typical of high-redshift sub-millimeter galaxies (SMGs). The CO-to-H2 conversion factor and the gas depletion time scales estimated from the model are consistent with the other high-redshift SMGs within the uncertainties. Based on the energy budget calculations, we find that turbulence driven mechanical heating and energy from stellar winds and supernovae contribute significantly to the overall CO line excitation in the dense molecular region. This is the most detailed study of molecular gas content of a galaxy in the EoR to-date, with the most distant detection of H2O in the literature.

Intermission

MN07 4:12 – 4:27

HIGH-RESOLUTION MID-IR OBSERVATIONS OF SiO AND THE SEARCH FOR TiO IN THE CIRCUMSTELLAR ENVELOPE OF THE VARIABLE STAR χ Cyg

GUIDO W. FUCHS, *Institute of Physics, University Kassel, Kassel, Germany*; EILEEN DÖRING, DANIEL WITSCH, *Institute of Physics, University of Kassel, Kassel, Germany*; THOMAS GIESEN, *Institute of Physics, University Kassel, Kassel, Germany*; JOHN H. LACY, *Department of Astronomy, The University of Texas at Austin, Austin, TX, USA*; ROHINI S GILES, THOMAS K GREATHOUSE, *Space Science Department, Southwest Research Institute, San Antonio, TX, USA.*

The Mira-type variable χ Cyg is an old S-type asymptotic giant branch (AGB) star that expels large amounts of material into space. This material forms dust and small to intermediate sized molecules - especially molecules composed of refractory materials. It is assumed that molecules like TiO and other small metal oxides that are formed in the expanding stellar envelope play a key role in the darkening process during the stellar pulsation. At temperatures around 1000 K the maximum radiation is shifted to the mid-infrared region, where laboratory spectroscopic data of small metal oxide molecules are sparse. To overcome the lack of data we have recently studied the molecules TiO, Al_2O and VO in the Kassel laboratory for astrophysics at high spectral resolution in the mid-infrared (IR) region. In addition, new observations using the TEXES spectrograph on the NASA Infrared Telescope Facility (IRTF) have been performed to investigate this star at high spectral resolution around 8.3 and 10 μm, i.e., at wavelengths were SiO, TiO, and VO have strong vibrational bands. We performed spectral and line shape analysis of SiO to study the dynamical behavior of the molecular layer surrounding the star. Preliminary results concerning TiO in χ Cyg will be presented.

MN08   4:30–4:45

EXAMINING ANOMALOUS PHOTOCHEMISTRY IN THE DENSE INNER WIND OF IRC+10216 THROUGH ALMA OBSERVATIONS OF HC$_3$N

MARK A. SIEBERT, *Department of Astronomy, University of Virginia, Charlottesville, VA, USA*; MARIE VAN DE SANDE, *School of Physics and Astronomy, University of Leeds, Leeds, UK*; THOMAS J. MILLAR, *School of Mathematics and Physics, Queen's University Belfast, Belfast, United Kingdom*; ANTHONY REMIJAN, *NAASC, National Radio Astronomy Observatory, Charlottesville, VA, USA.*

In recent years, many questions have arisen regarding the chemistry of CN-bearing molecules in the carbon-rich winds of evolved stars. To address them, it is imperative to constrain the distributions of such species through high angular resolution interferometric observations of multiple rotational transitions. To that end, we used several archival ALMA observations to image high energy rotational transitions of cyanide-bearing molecules in the inner envelope (< 8") of the carbon star IRC+10216. The observed lines include the J = 38 - 37 and J = 28 - 27 transitions of cyanoacetylene (HC$_3$N), and the J = 18 - 17 (K = 0 - 9) transition of methyl cyanide (CH_3CN). In contrast to previous observations of photochemical products in the same source, the maps of these molecular lines show spatially coincident, compact morphologies comprising various arcs and loops, with significant enhancement in dense clumps at an angular distance of $\sim$3" (350 AU) from the central AGB star. Considering the known gas phase formation mechanisms of these molecules, our results are consistent with photochemistry occurring in warm ($\sim$200 K) knots present in the inner regions of this circumstellar envelope. Using visibility sampled LIME radiative transfer models accompanied by the results of a specialized photochemical model, we explore the possibility that the enhanced HC$_3$N abundances in the inner wind are due to a binary companion supplying UV photons to this region. In this talk, I will discuss the results of this analysis, and demonstrate how they may impact our understanding of circumstellar carbon chemistry at the final stages of stellar evolution.

MN09   4:48–5:03

ALMA REVEALS THE MOLECULAR OUTFLOWS IN THE ENVELOPE OF HYPERGIANT VY CANIS MAJORIS

AMBESH PRATIK SINGH, *Department of Chemistry and Biochemistry, University of Arizona, Tucson, AZ, USA*; ANITA M RICHARDS, *Physics, University of Manchester , Manchester , UK*; ROBERTA M. HUMPHREYS, *Minnesota Institute for Astrophysics, University of Minnesota, Minneapolis, MN, USA*; LUCY M. ZIURYS, *Dept. of Astronomy, Dept. of Chemistry, Arizona Radio Observatory, The University of Arizona, Tucson, AZ, USA.*

Extreme supergiant stars, or hypergiants, are thought to undergo extensive, chaotic mass loss events in their later stages, with complex envelope structures composed of arcs, clumps, and knots. The red hypergiant VY CMa is one of the best examples of these types of stars. Previous studies in the infrared of VY CMa of dust emission have shown the presence of distinct arcs to the southwest (Arc 1, Arc 2), a NW arc, and another clumps and knots, many extending several arcseconds from the central star. Using ALMA, we imaged the envelope of VY CMa in multiple molecular lines at Band 6 (1 mm) with 0.25 arcsecond resolution and with the sensitivity to structures as large as 3-4 arcseconds. While some observations are still in progress, preliminary maps of SO$_2$, H^{13}CN, and PO have been produced. From SO$_2$ emission, a map of the global molecular outflow structure of VY CMa has been obtained for the first time on scales of 6-8 arcseconds. These molecular data show the striking morphology seen in dust emission in VY CMa, including Arc 1, Arc 2, and the NW Arc, among other features. These new images will be presented, as well as other new data, and the implications for the evolution of massive stars will be discussed.

MN10   5:06 – 5:21

REEXAMINING THE CHEMISTRY IN PROTOPLANETARY NEBULAE: M1-92, COTTON CANDY NEBULA, AND IRAS22036

<u>KATHERINE R. GOLD</u>, *Department of Chemistry and Biochemistry, The University of Arizona, Tucson, AZ, USA*; DEBORAH SCHMIDT, *Department of Physics and Astronomy, Franklin and Marshall College, Lancaster, PA, USA*; LUCY M. ZIURYS, *Dept. of Astronomy, Dept. of Chemistry, Arizona Radio Observatory, The University of Arizona, Tucson, AZ, USA.*

Protoplanetary nebulae (PPNe) are an important step in stellar evolution as they bridge the asymptotic giant branch (AGB) and planetary nebulae phases. Observations have demonstrated that planetary nebulae are rich in molecular content which varies considerably from the AGB phase; therefore, significant chemical changes must occur in the PPNe stage. To examine this issue, we have conducted observations of M1-92, the Cotton Candy Nebula, and IRAS22036+5306, all PPN sources in which CO had previously been detected. Measurements were conducted with the 12-meter antenna and the Sub-millimeter Telescope (SMT) of the Arizona Radio Observatory at 3, 2, and 1 mm. Towards M1-92 we have thus far detected CN, HCO$^+$, H^{13}CO$^+$, HCN, and HNC. Towards the Cotton Candy Nebula, we have identified CN, HCN, and HNC. In IRAS22036+5306, H$_2$S and SO have been observed. Abundances in these PPNe appear to vary from those in circumstellar AGB envelopes. The detailed chemistry in these sources will be discussed.

MN11   5:24 – 5:39

AN ABSORPTION SURVEY OF C$_3$H$^+$ AND C$_4$H IN DIFFUSE CLOUDS TOWARD GALACTIC CONTINUUM REGIONS

<u>HARSHAL GUPTA</u>, *Division of Astronomical Sciences, National Science Foundation, Alexandria, VA, USA*; KELVIN LEE, *Accelerated Computing Systems and Graphics, Intel Corporation, Hillsboro, OR, USA*; MARYVONNE GERIN, *LERMA, Observatoire de Paris, Paris, France*; MICHAEL C McCARTHY, *Center for Astrophysics, Harvard & Smithsonian, Cambridge, MA, USA.*

Observations of the diffuse interstellar gas over the past few decades have revealed a surprisingly rich molecular inventory comprising over 25% of all known interstellar molecules. While the molecules observed in diffuse clouds are small relative to ones found in dark clouds, considerable progress has been made in recent years towards detecting larger, more complex molecules.[a,b] There is also clear evidence at optical wavelengths for a very large molecule—the fullerene ion C$_{60}^+$—in the diffuse gas.[c] Using the 100-m Green Bank Telescope, we undertook observations of 8 sightlines toward bright centimeter continuum regions in the Galaxy, and detected the C$_3$H$^+$ ion and the C$_4$H radical in absorption from foreground diffuse clouds along 7 sightlines.[d] Both molecules are thought to be key intermediates in the carbon chemistry of the interstellar medium, and to our knowledge C$_3$H$^+$ is currently the largest carbon chain ion and C$_4$H the largest carbon chain radical detected by radio astronomy in the diffuse gas. I will discuss our results within the context of understanding hydrocarbon chemistry, establishing the limits of molecular complexity, and bridging the gap between small molecules and very large molecules in the diffuse gas. I will also discuss the prospects of enlarging the molecular inventory of diffuse clouds, particularly large polyatomic ions and radicals,[e] by means of absorption surveys exploiting long pathlengths toward bright continuum sources.

---

[a]Liszt, H. S., Gerin, M., Beasley, A., & Pety, J., 2018, Astrophysical Journal, 856, 151; *and references therein.*

[b]Gerin, M., Liszt, H., Neufeld, D., et al. 2019, Astronomy & Astrophysics, 622, A26; *and references therein.*

[c]Maier, J. P. & Campbell, E. K. 2016, Phil. Trans. R. Soc. A, 374, (issue 2076), 1

[d]Our sample includes two sightlines where millimeter-wave absorption from C$_3$H$^+$ has previously been detected.[b]

[e]Molecular ions such as C$_3$H$^+$ are far more challenging to produce in the laboratory than carbon chain radicals, and might first be found in space.

TA. Mini-symposium: Spectroscopy meets Chemical Dynamics

Tuesday, June 21, 2022 – 8:30 AM

Room: 100 Noyes Laboratory

Chair: Nathanael M. Kidwell, The College of William and Mary, Williamsburg, VA, USA

TA01   **INVITED TALK**   8:30 – 9:00

X-RAY MOLECULAR SPECTROSCOPIC DYNAMICS

STEPHEN R. LEONE, *Department of Chemistry, The University of California, Berkeley, CA, USA.*

Ultrafast X-ray spectroscopic investigations and molecular dynamics are now approachable with short pulses of laboratory, laser-produced high-order harmonics. Those X-rays probe transitions from localized inner shells of specific atomic sites in the molecules to valence orbitals, conveying new information about photochemical transformations. The interpretations of these spectra involve a new regime of core-to-valence X-ray probing that depends on energy shifts due to the surrounding electronic densities, spin coupling effects, energy shifts due to bond elongation with vibrational excitation, and even Jahn-Teller distortions. Coherent vibrational superpositions reveal different slopes of inner shell potentials with bond extension and Fermi resonance coupling, for the first time, in the X-ray. Open shell radicals have characteristic features of singly occupied orbitals and energetic shifts upon bond cleavage, which can be viewed from the localized atomic perspective. Corresponding theory work by collaborators provides a powerful assessment of the X-ray spectroscopic dynamics. Progress for revealing the full potential of time-resolved X-ray spectroscopy for the investigation of numerous novel features in molecular photochemistry is discussed.

TA02   9:06 – 9:21

ULTRAFAST XUV MAGNETIC CIRCULAR DICHROISM: OBSERVING SPIN TRANSPORT AT INTERFACES

ROBERT BAKER, *Department of Chemistry and Biochemistry, The Ohio State University, Columbus, OH, USA*; MARTIN SCHULTZE, *Institute of Experimental Physics, Graz University of Technology, Graz, Austria*; HARSHAD GAJAPATHY, *Chemistry and Biochemistry, The Ohio State University, Columbus, OH, USA*; SAVINI SANDUNIKA BANDARANAYAKE, EMILY B HRUSKA, STEPHEN LONDO, *Department of Chemistry and Biochemistry, The Ohio State University, Columbus, OH, USA.*

In time resolved spectroscopy of molecular systems, spectral signatures are directly correlated with processes such as charge migration, intra and intermolecular vibrational relaxation, internal conversion, and intersystem crossing. However, the challenge of probing these analogous processes in material systems with surface sensitivity and ultrafast time resolution motivates the goal to extend a molecular-level understanding to dynamics at surfaces and interfaces.

In this talk, we describe the recent ability to directly observe spin-polarized electron transport at semiconductor surfaces using XUV Magnetic Circular Dichroism (XUV-MCD) in a reflection geometry. The ability to produce spin polarized currents at interfaces underlies many promising applications ranging from spintronics to enantioselective photocatalysis, but designing materials capable of these applications requires an improved understanding of spin-dependent electron dynamics at interfaces. Towards this goal, XUV-MCD reflection-absorption spectroscopy provides direct observation of spin dynamics in magnetic materials with ultrafast time resolution and surface sensitivity.

Yttrium iron garnet ($Y_3Fe_5O_{12}$, YiG) is a ferrimagnetic semiconductor, consisting of two sub-lattices based on octahedrally and tetrahedrally coordinated Fe(III) centers. A combination of linearly and circularly polarized XUV measurements at the Fe $M_{2,3}$-edge of YiG provides a detailed picture of these lattice-dependent electron dynamics, which give rise to spin polarized current at the YiG surface upon band gap excitation. These findings have important applications towards the development of spin selective photocatalysts as well as new platforms for light-induced control of ultrafast spin polarization at material interfaces.

TA03 9:24 – 9:39

ULTRAFAST ELECTRON TRANSFER AND SPIN FLIP IN A HETEROBIMETALLIC COMPLEX

<u>JOHN H BURKE</u>, JOSH VURA-WEIS, *Department of Chemistry, University of Illinois at Urbana-Champaign, Urbana, IL, USA*.

A major channel of energy loss in solar energy conversion is nonradiative charge recombination, whereby photochemical or photovoltaic energy is lost to the surroundings as heat. Understanding the mechanism of charge recombination, particularly the timescale and coupling to nuclear and spin degrees of freedom, is critical for understanding how to promote long-lived charge separation. In this regard, bimetallic molecules with metal-to-metal charge transfer (MMCT) transitions are valuable model systems because the charge recombination reaction can be initiated with light by directly populating the charge transfer state.

We employed femtosecond optical transient absorption (OTA) spectroscopy to monitor charge recombination following MMCT excitation in a heterobimetallic Fe(II)Co(III) complex. The measurements uncovered a long-lived excited state with a 500 ps lifetime. Time-dependent density functional theory (DFT) allowed for assignment of this state as a metal-centered high spin state. The combined experimental and theoretical approach pointed to an ultrafast intersystem crossing and charge recombination to a local, intermediate-spin, metal-centered excited state, followed by a slower intersystem crossing to the long-lived high-spin state. These results uncover the intricate mechanism of charge recombination in this molecule by elucidating the spectral signatures, lifetimes, assignments, energetics, and nuclear geometries of the states involved. The coupling of the electron transfer to vibrations and spin in this complex could account for the ultrafast timescale of the charge recombination and could be a target for promoting long-lived charge transfer states through synthetic tuning.

TA04 9:42 – 9:57

MONITORING VALENCE-ELECTRON DYNAMICS IN MOLECULES WITH ULTRAFAST X-RAY DIFFRACTION

<u>HAIWANG YONG</u>, STEFANO M. CAVALETTO, *Department of Chemistry, UC Irvine, IRVINE, CA, USA*; SHAUL MUKAMEL, *Department of Chemistry, University of California, Irvine, Irvine, CA, USA*.

Ultrafast x-ray diffraction has been used to directly observe excited state electron density distributions in molecule upon photoexcitation (1). Theoretical studies have shown that its signal contains mixed elastic-inelastic coherence term originating from electronic coherence (2,3). In this study, we present a simulation study of valence-electron dynamics of oxazole using time-resolved off-resonant x-ray diffraction (4). A valence-state electronic wavepacket is prepared with an attosecond soft x-ray pulse through a stimulated resonant x-ray Raman process (5), and then probed with off-resonant single-molecule x-ray diffraction. We find that the time dependent diffraction signal originates solely from the electronic coherences and can be detected by existing experimental techniques. The present study thus provides a practical way of imaging electron dynamics in free molecules. In addition, the created electronic coherences and subsequent electron dynamics can be manipulated by resonant x-ray Raman excitations tuned to different core-excited states.

(1) H. Yong, N. Zotev, J. M. Ruddock, B. Stankus, M. Simmermacher, A. Moreno Carrascosa, W. Du, N. Goff, Y. Chang, D. Bellshaw, M. Liang, S. Carbajo, J. E. Koglin, J. S. Robinson, S. Boutet, M. P. Minitti, A. Kirrander, P. M. Weber, Observation of the molecular response to light upon photoexcitation. Nat. Commun. 11, 2157 (2020)

(2) K. Bennett, M. Kowalewski, J. R. Rouxel, S. Mukamel, Monitoring molecular nonadiabatic dynamics with femtosecond x-ray diffraction. Proc. Natl. Acad. Sci. U.S.A. 115, 6538-6547 (2018).

(3) M. Simmermacher, N. E. Henriksen, K. B. Moller, A. Moreno Carrascosa, A. Kirrander, Electronic coherence in ultrafast x-ray scattering from molecular wave packets. Phys. Rev. Lett. 122, 073003 (2019).

(4) H. Yong, S. M. Cavaletto, S. Mukamel, Ultrafast valence-electron dynamics in oxazole monitored by x-ray diffraction following a stimulated x-ray Raman excitation. J. Phys. Chem. Lett. 12, 9800-9806 (2021).

(5) D. Healion, Y. Zhang, J. D. Biggs, N. Govind, S. Mukamel, Entangled valence electron-hole dynamics revealed by stimulated attosecond x-ray Raman scattering. J. Phys. Chem. Lett. 3, 2326-2331 (2012).

TA05   10:00 – 10:15

ULTRAFAST DYNAMICS OF TWO- AND THREE-BODY DISSOCIATION CAPTURED BY CORE-TO-VALENCE TRANSIENT ABSORPTION SPECTROSCOPY

<u>JAN TROSS</u>, NEIL C. COLE-FILIPIAK, PAUL SCHRADER, LAURA M McCASLIN, KRUPA RAMASESHA, *Combustion Research Facility, Sandia National Laboratories, Livermore, CA, USA.*

Molecular photodissociation is central to numerous photochemical processes relevant to atmospheric chemistry and photocatalysis. As platforms to understand the ultrafast excited state dynamics underlying complex molecular photodissociation mechanisms, we studied the ultraviolet photodissociation of two gas-phase molecules: acetyl iodide[a], which is a photolytic precursor for the acetyl radical, and iron pentacarbonyl[b], which is a model photocatalyst system. Using ultrafast extreme ultraviolet transient absorption spectroscopy, we followed the photodissociation dynamics of these molecules via core-to-valence transitions of their respective heavy atom constituents (I and Fe), giving access to atom-specific signatures of excited electronic states.

In acetyl iodide, we observe transient features with sub-100 fs lifetimes associated with the excited state wavepacket evolution prior to dissociation. These features then evolve to yield spectral signatures corresponding to the dissociation of the C-I bond. In iron pentacarbonyl, we observe transient features evolving on 100 fs to few-picosecond timescales due to excited state loss of carbonyl groups. We combine experimental findings with quantum chemical calculations to gain insight into the photodissociation dynamics.

SNL is managed and operated by NTESS under DOE NNSA contract DE-NA0003525.
SAND No. SAND2022-2283 A

---

[a] P. M. Kroger and S. J. Riley J. Chem. Phys. 67, 4483 (1977); https://doi.org/10.1063/1.434589

[b] M. Poliakoff and E. Weitz, Acc.Chem.Res. 1987, 20, 11, 408-414; https://doi.org/10.1021/ar00143a004

TA06   10:18 – 10:33

MAPPING COMPLEX PHOTOCHEMICAL REACTIONS USING FEMTOSECOND UV-PUMP XUV-PROBE PHOTOELECTRON SPECTROSCOPY

<u>DANIEL HORKE</u>, GRITE L. ABMA, *Institute for Molecules and Materials (IMM), Radboud University Nijmegen, Nijmegen, Netherlands.*

Time-resolved photoelectron spectroscopy has emerged as one of the premier tools to study the complex coupled motion of electrons and nuclei that underlies ultrafast photochemical processes. To study the entire reaction pathway from reactants through intermediates to products, however, requires sufficiently energetic photons to ionise all species involved. The advent of high-flux high-harmonic generation sources now puts this within reach, and we present here femtosecond photoelectron spectroscopy studies using UV-pump XUV-probe pulses. We used this approach to probe the dynamics of dissociating CS_2 molecules across the entire reaction pathway upon excitation, Figure 1. Dissociation occurs either in the initially excited singlet manifold or, via intersystem crossing, in the triplet manifold. Both product channels are monitored and we show that, despite being more rapid, the singlet dissociation is the minor product and that triplet state products dominate the final yield. We will also show first results of our recent UV-pump XUV-probe studies of acetaldehyde photodissociation and aim to unravel the complex competing direct and roaming dissociation channels.

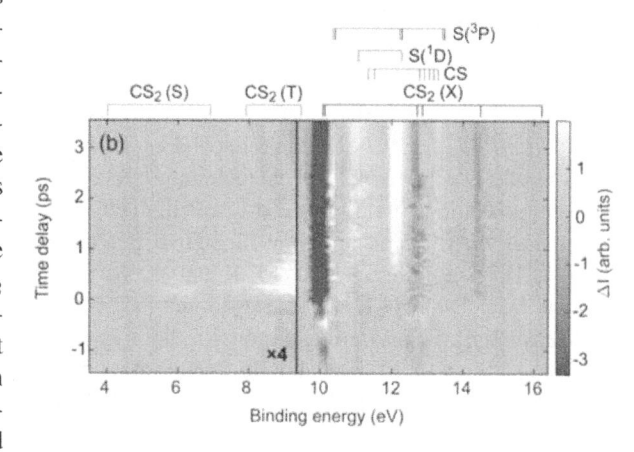

Figure 2: Time-resolved photoelectron spectroscopy of CS_2 dissociation. XUV probe pulses allow us to map all intermediate and final states.

Intermission

TA07   11:15 – 11:30
ELECTRON LOCALIZATION IN MOLECULES INTERACTING WITH INTENSE LASER PULSES

AGNIESZKA JARON, *JILA and Department of Physics, University of Colorado, Boulder, CO, USA*; LAUREN BAUERLE, *JILA and the Department of Chemistry, Universityy of Colorado, Boulder, CO, USA*.

We theoretically study dynamic localization in molecules interacting with intense laser pulses. Mechanism is responsible for the effect of Charge Resonance Enhanced Ionization (CREI) studied for H_2^+ and I_2^+ for over 2 decades within the field of ultrafast intense laser AMO. Here we focus on the multielectron aspects and the attosecond electron dynamics.

Calculations are performed for di- and polyatomic molecules at equilibrium internuclear distances and we discuss multielectron, or more precisely multi-orbital character of the process. CREI has been connected to the dynamic electron localization as well as to the multiple ionization bursts over one laser field cycle. We discuss the similarities and differences between CREI and results for multielectron molecules at equilibrium distances. Results obtained within TDDFT show that as expected if we use laser wavelength tuned to the resonance one could observe resonance enhancement of multiphoton ionization of valence orbitals, analogous to CREI. But calculations also reveal that in contrast to CREI studied for H_2^+ and I_2^+, the resonance one photon transition acts as a trigger for other excitations and leads to enhancement of ionization from multiple inner valence orbitals and the dynamical properties exhibit more complicated behavior than expected from simple '2-level'-H_2^+ picture of CREI.

TA08   11:33 – 11:48
PROBING SPATIAL EVOLUTION OF ULTRAFAST ELECTRONIC WAVEPACKETS WITH TWO-ELECTRON ANGULAR STREAKING

GABRIEL A. STEWART, *Chemistry, Wayne State University, Detroit,, MI, USA*; DUKE A. DEBRAH, *Chemistry, Wayne State University, Detroit, MI, USA*; GIHAN BASNAYAKE, *Chemistry, Wayne State University, Detroit,, MI, USA*; SUK KYOUNG LEE, *Chemistry Department, Wayne State University, Detroit, MI, USA*; WEN LI, *Department of Chemistry, Wayne State University, Detroit, MI, USA*.

Coherence among several electronic states can produce electronic wavepackets. Due to the delocalized nature of electronic orbitals, electronic wavepackets initiated by strong field ionization have significant spatial evolution. However, the spatial evolution was not previously accessible to experimental investigations at the attosecond time scale. Using the two-electron-angular-streaking (2eAS) method, we carried out measurements on xenon and krypton, in which the yields of double ionization were measured with a time range between 0 and 2.4 fs. A clear difference in the time-resolved double ionization yield between xenon and krypton was observed: at around 1.3 fs, xenon shows a higher double ionization yield than that of krypton. At this time, the ionization site by the laser field is roughly about 180 degrees from that of the first ionization. This suggests that the second ionization is modulated by a dynamical process evolving at one femtosecond time scale. We attribute this to a spin-orbit electronic wave packet produced by the first ionization. A simulation using the time dependent configurational interaction with single excitation (TDCIS-IP-CAP) method was carried to model the ionization yield of a coherent superposition between two spin-orbit (SO) states. The calculation shows that due to the energy difference in SO splitting, the wavepackets evolves different temporally and spatially and the measured ionization yields have captured these detailed dynamics.

TA09 11:51 – 12:06

SIMULATING PHOTOEXCITATION WITH A LASER PULSE BEYOND THE PERTURBATIVE LIMIT

DIPTESH DEY[a], GRAHAM WORTH, *Department of Chemistry, University College London, London, UK.*

The advent of ultrashort laser pulses in the femtosecond to attosecond regime allows the study of ultrafast molecular dynamics with unprecedented time resolution [1,2]. These powerful modern light sources can result in the ionization of matter and thereby trigger electronic and nuclear dynamics [3,4]. In my talk, I will give an overview of the ongoing research efforts in the Worth group at UCL addressing the following fundamental questions: (i) Can we control photochemical processes by creating/manipulating a quantum superposition state with a laser pulse? (ii) Can we understand the coupled electron-nuclear motion and the associated ultrafast decoherence? (iii) Can we design laser pulses in a simple way to make use of the quantum interference pathways? (iv) Can we simulate an experimental photoelectron spectrum by developing simple theoretical models?

These elementary aspects of laser-matter interactions are governed by quantum mechanics and therefore we solve the time-dependent Schrödinger equation using state-of-the-art quantum dynamics method, MCTDH [5], in combination with vibronic coupling Hamiltonian [6]. This further allows us to deal with the non-adiabatic coupling between the electrons and the nuclei [6]. The ionized electron is modeled explicitly by incorporating the continuum of free-electron states [7]. The QUANTICS suite of programs are used to run the dynamical simulations [8].

References

[1] M. Nisoli, P. Decleva, F. Calegari, A. Palacios and F. Martín, Chem. Rev. 117, 10760 (2017).
[2] H. H. Fielding and G. A. Worth, Chem. Soc. Rev. 47, 309 (2018).
[3] V. Despré, N. V. Golubev and A. I. Kuleff, Phys. Rev. Lett. 121, 203002 (2018).
[4] A. Henley, J. W. Riley, B. Wang and H. H. Fielding, Faraday Discuss. 221, 202 (2020).
[5] M. H. Beck, A. Jäckle, G. A. Worth and H.-D. Meyer, Phys. Rep. 324, 1 (2000).
[6] G. A. Worth and L. S. Cederbaum, Annu. Rev. Phys. Chem. 55, 127 (2004).
[7] M. Seel and W. Domcke, J. Chem. Phys. 95, 7806 (1991).
[8] QUANTICS, http://www2.chem.ucl.ac.uk/quantics/doc/index.html

[a] d.dey@ucl.ac.uk

TA10 12:09 – 12:24

IMAGING THE REACTIVE RADICAL-CATION COMPLEX IN THE IONIZED LIQUID WATER

MING-FU LIN, *Linac Coherent Light Source, SLAC National Accelerator Laboratory, Menlo Park, CA, USA.*

Liquid water is important in nature and plays a critical role in numerous chemical and biological applications. The elementary reaction pathways for ionized water have been extensively studied, however, the short-lived reactive complex and its structural dynamic response after the proton transfer reaction remain illusive. Using a liquid-phase ultrafast electron diffraction technique to study the intermolecular oxygen-oxygen and oxygen-hydrogen bonds, we captured the short-lived radical-cation complex OH(H3O+) that was formed within 140 fs through a direct and fast oxygen-oxygen bond contraction and proton transfer, followed by the radical-cation pair dissociation and the subsequent structural relaxation of water shells within 250 fs. These studies provide direct evidence of this short-lived metastable radical-cation complex before separation, therefore improving our fundamental understanding of elementary reaction dynamics in ionized liquid water.

TB. Mini-symposium: Benchmarking in Spectroscopy
Tuesday, June 21, 2022 – 8:30 AM
Room: 116 Roger Adams Lab

Chair: L. H. Coudert, Université Paris-Saclay, CNRS, Orsay, France

TB01   *INVITED TALK*   8:30 – 9:00

EXTENDING ACCURATE QUANTUM CHEMISTRY TO HEAVY ELEMENTS

XUECHEN ZHENG, CHAOQUN ZHANG, LAN CHENG, *Department of Chemistry, Johns Hopkins University, Baltimore, MD, USA.*

The presentation will be focused on development and applications of relativistic wave function-based approaches aiming to extend the accuracy and applicability of quantum chemistry to heavy elements. An atomic mean-field spin-orbit approach within exact two-component theory, the X2CAMF scheme, is shown to enhance the computational efficiency while retaining the accuracy of the parent four-component Dirac-Coulomb-Breit approach. An efficient implementation of the X2CAMF scheme together with analytic energy gradients for spin-orbit coupled-cluster methods enables accurate calculations of geometries and properties for molecules containing heavy atoms. The applicability of these relativistic quantum-chemical methods is demonstrated with applications in heavy-element chemistry and spectroscopy.

TB02   9:06 – 9:21

ELECTRONIC STRUCTURE OF RuO

YAO YU, LEI ZHANG, XINWEN MA, JIE YANG, *Atomic Physics Center, Institute of Modern Physics, Chinese Academy of Sciences, Lanzhou, CHINA.*

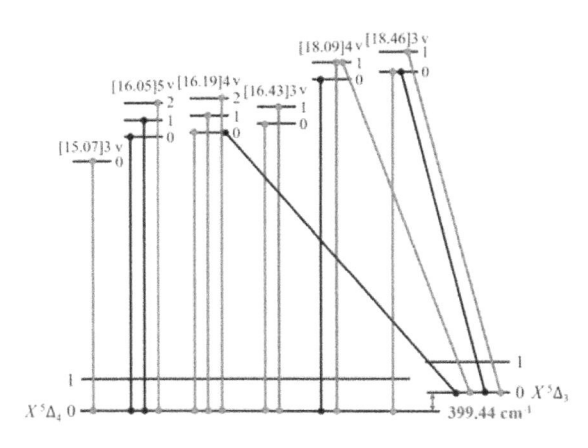

The laser-induced fluorescence (LIF) excitation spectra of jet-cooled ruthenium monoxide (RuO) molecule in the gas phase have been investigated in the range of 13,800 to 19,250 cm^{-1}. As shown in the figure, a total of sixteen vibronic bands were experimentally observed and grouped into the transition systems from the ground $X^5\Delta_4$ and $X^5\Delta_3$ states to six excited electronic states, labeled as $[15.07]3 - X^5\Delta_4$, $[16.05]5 - X^5\Delta_4$, $[16.43]3 - X^5\Delta_4$, $[16.19]4 - X^5\Delta_{4,3}$, $[18.09]4 - X^5\Delta_{4,3}$, $[18.46]3 - X^5\Delta_{4,3}$. The spin-orbit splitting and the rotational constants in the lower and upper states were obtained accurately by the rotationally and isotopically resolved LIF spectra. In addition, the single-vibronic-level (SVL) emission spectra from the excited states were recorded, and the vibrational constants in the ground $X^5\Delta_4$ and $X^5\Delta_3$ states were obtained. Our results are sufficiently reliable and accurate to guide spectroscopists on further studies of RuO molecule.

TB04   9:42 – 9:57

ACCURATE PREDICTION OF EQUILIBRIUM STRUCTURE FOR HEAVY ELEMENT CONTAINING MOLECULES

CHAOQUN ZHANG, LAN CHENG, *Department of Chemistry, Johns Hopkins University, Baltimore, MD, USA.*

Accurate prediction of molecular geometries is a central subject in electronic structure theory. For accurate calculations of vibronic branching ratios in laser coolable molecules, it requires accurate calculations of molecular geometries for both electronic ground states and excited states. Using exact two-component theory with atomic-mean-field (X2CAMF) framework and analytical gradient techniques for spin-orbit coupled-cluster (SO-CC) method, we can obtain molecular equilibrium structures with accurate treatment of electron correlation and relativistic effects. By comparing with the experimental measurements of period-four-element containing diatomic molecules, the calculated bond lengths are accurate to 0.001 Å and the calculated harmonic frequencies are accurate to a few cm^{-1}.

TB05　　　　　　　　　　　　　　　　　　　　　　　　　　　　　　　　　　　　　10:00 – 10:15

LaO LINE LIST FOR THE $B^2\Sigma^+$- $X^2\Sigma^+$ BAND SYSTEM

PETER F. BERNATH, *Department of Chemistry and Biochemistry, Old Dominion University, Norfolk, VA, USA*; RANDIKA DODANGODAGE, *Physics, Old Dominion University, Norfolk, VA, USA*; JACQUES LIÉVIN, *Service de Chimie Quantique et Photophysique, Université Libre de Bruxelles, Brussels, Belgium*.

LaO bands appear in the optical spectra of S-type stars. The formation of the elements can be studied by measuring the stellar abundances of heavy metals such as La. For cooler stars, the visible and near-infrared electronic transitions of LaO are more useful than La atomic lines.

We have analyzed the LaO $B^2\Sigma^+$-$X^2\Sigma^+$ band system up to v=5 in both ground and excited states. The rotational analysis of the $B^2\Sigma^+$-$X^2\Sigma^+$ transition was carried out using the PGOPHER program. Most of the ground state spectroscopic parameters and hyperfine parameters of the excited $B^2\Sigma^+$ state were taken from literature and kept fixed. The equilibrium constants for $X^2\Sigma^+$ and $B^2\Sigma^+$ states were determined. The line strengths were calculated based on the ab initio transition dipole moment and RKR potential curves. We also provide radiative lifetimes of the $B^2\Sigma^+$ state for v=0 to v=4. With this work, we provide a modern line list for the LaO $B^2\Sigma^+$-$X^2\Sigma^+$ transition that can be used to simulate LaO spectra of cool S-type stars to determine La abundances.

A similar analysis is in progress for the LaO $A^2\Pi$-$X^2\Sigma^+$ transition.

Intermission

TB06　　　　　　　　　　　　　　　　　　　　　　　　　　　　　　　　　　　　　10:57 – 11:12

PREDICTION AND INTERPRETATION OF TRANSITION METAL X-RAY SPECTRA USING REAL-TIME TIME-DEPENDENT DENSITY FUNCTIONAL THEORY

JUN YI, ZHOU LIN, *Department of Chemistry, University of Massachusetts, Amherst, MA, USA*; YING ZHU, *Department of Chemistry and Biochemistry, The Ohio State University, Columbus, OH, USA*.

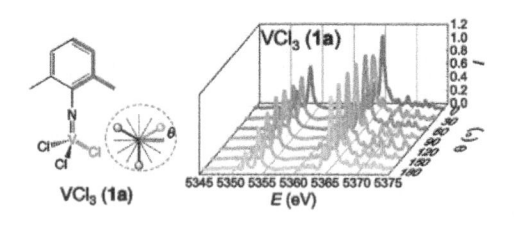

Many transition metal complexes are popular catalysts for homogeneous organic synthesis. Their instantaneous geometric and electronic configurations and roles in the reaction mechanisms can be directly probed by *in-situ* K-edge X-ray absorption near-edge structure (XANES) spectroscopy. First-principles modeling is indispensable to translate the frequencies and lineshapes of K-edge absorptions into orbital and structural configurations. In the present study, we performed real-time time-dependent density functional theory (RT-TDDFT) calculations for (2,6-dimethylphenyl)imino)vanadium(V) trichloride and its methyl-substituted derivatives, and obtained time-dependent electronic densities and transition dipole moments by solving the time-dependent Kohn–Sham equations under an applied electromagnetic field. Compared to traditional linear-response TDDFT (LR-TDDFT), RT-TDDFT allows a significant rearrangement of electronic densities after photoexcitations and provides a broadband spectrum in the frequency domain after the Fourier transform. Based on our RT-TDDFT calculations, we managed to reproduce the pre-edge peaks for these species and assigned them to the dipole-allowed transitions of electrons from $1s$ orbital to the $3d4p$ hybridized orbitals of vanadium. Both characters align with the results from LR-TDDFT. In addition, RT-TDDFT leads to important features from the shoulder peaks, which correspond to the dipole-allowed, density-rearranging transitions of electrons from $1s$ orbital of vanadium to its $4p$ orbitals or the $3p$ orbitals of chlorine. These shoulder peak features have never been provided by LR-TDDFT. From the present study, we provided a proof-of-concept that the next-generation RT-TDDFT approach is a versatile and powerful computational tool for the prediction and interpretation of X-ray spectroscopy of transition metal complexes.

TB07 11:15 – 11:30

SIMPLIFIED LR-TDDFT/ZORA APPROACH FOR GENERATING SPIN-ORBIT COUPLINGS FOR X-RAY ABSORPTION SPECTRA

SARAH PAK, DANIEL R. NASCIMENTO, *Chemistry, University of Memphis, Memphis, TN, USA.*

Transition metals represent a space of continual interest due to their complex electronic structure and the diverse range of possible ligands and oxidation states. Studies of transition metal complexes often rely on X-ray spectroscopies (usually at the L or M edges) and computational methods to explain spectral features and help design new experiments. Most computational approaches either account for relativistic effects at the scalar level, by omitting spin-orbit coupling terms, or completely neglect them sacrificing accuracy in favor of a lower computational cost. On the other hand, explicit ab-initio treatments of spin-orbit couplings are costly and labor intensive, restricting their applications to smaller atomic systems. In the present work, we propose a simplified approach based on linear-response time-dependent density functional theory (LR-TDDFT) and the relativistic two-component zeroth order regular approximation (ZORA) to generate spin-orbit couplings of closed-shell molecular systems. The proposed approach was validated by computing the L-edge absorption spectra of several first and second row transition metal complexes. The method reproduces experimental data with satisfactory accuracy at a fraction of the cost of exact two-component or fully relativistic methods.

TB08 11:33 – 11:48

VIBRONIC ANALYSIS OF MOLECULES WITH QUASI-DEGENERATE ELECTRONIC STATES

KETAN SHARMA, TERRY A. MILLER, *Department of Chemistry and Biochemistry, The Ohio State University, Columbus, OH, USA;* JINJUN LIU, *Department of Chemistry, University of Louisville, Louisville, KY, USA.*

Progress in laser cooling and trapping molecules has lead to a renewed interest in alkaline earth monoalkoxide (MOR) free radicals as promising candidates for direct laser-cooling of polyatomic molecules. Theoretical understanding of these molecules is challenging due to the presence of quasi-degenerate electronic states in these molecules. In addition to that, pseudo-Jahn Teller interactions and spin-orbit coupling also play a very important role. Understanding these couplings and their effects on the molecular spectra will provide critical information for future direct laser cooling of MORs and similar radicals. In this talk we discuss the theoretical intricacies involved in calculating the spin-vibronic spectra of such molecules from first principles. A Hamiltonian has been developed in a spin-vibronic representation for molecules with quasi-degenerate electronic states. We will describe calculating the parameters in this Hamiltonian using ab-initio methods and the software developed for solving such Hamiltonians (SOCJT3). Our discourse includes both frequency calculations and relative transition intensities from first principles for both excitation and emission spectra which can be compared to experimentally observed using LIF and DF spectra of $CaOCH_3$, $CaOC_2H_5$, and iso-$CaOC_3H_7$ to be reported in succeeding talk. Typical Franck-Condon factor calculations done under the Born-Oppenheimer approximation reproduce the dominant features of these spectra, but the inclusion of Jahn-Teller and pseudo-Jahn-Teller couplings and spin-orbit interactions in the calculations not only improves the accuracy of simulation but also leads to additional vibronic transitions that help to explain the finer structure observed in the spectra. A major limitation of these methods is the amount of computational resources required as the molecules become larger. Efforts to minimize the amount of resources required as well as approximations involved in simulating the spin-vibronic spectra for larger molecules like iso-$CaOC_3H_7$ have also been discussed.

TB09 11:51 – 12:06

ELECTRONIC SPECTROSCOPY OF THE $\tilde{A} - \tilde{X}$ TRANSITIONS OF JET-COOLED CALCIUM MONOALKOXIDE RADICALS: SPIN-VIBRONIC STRUCTURE OF NONLINEAR MOLECULES AS CANDIDATES FOR DIRECT LASER COOLING

ANAM C. PAUL, HAMZEH TELFAH, *Department of Chemistry, University of Louisville, Louisville, KY, USA*; KETAN SHARMA, *Department of Chemistry and Biochemistry, The Ohio State University, Columbus, OH, USA*; S M SHAH RIYADH, *Department of Physics and Astronomy, University Of Louisville, Louisville, KY, USA*; TERRY A. MILLER, *Department of Chemistry and Biochemistry, The Ohio State University, Columbus, OH, USA*; JINJUN LIU, *Department of Chemistry, University of Louisville, Louisville, KY, USA*.

We report a combined experimental and computational study of spin-vibronic structure and transition intensities of the lowest electronic states of nonlinear alkaline earth monoalkoxide (MOR) radicals, including calcium methoxide (CaOCH$_3$), calcium ethoxide (CaOC$_2$H$_5$), and calcium isopropoxide [CaOCH(CH$_3$)$_2$]. Experimentally, laser-induced fluorescence/dispersed fluorescence (LIF/DF) and cavity ring-down (CRD) spectra of the $\tilde{A}^2E$–$\tilde{X}^2A_1$ electronic transition of CaOCH$_3$ (C_{3v}), the $\tilde{A}_1{}^2A''/\tilde{A}_2{}^2A'$–$\tilde{X}^2A'$ transition of CaOC$_2$H$_5$ (C_s), and the $\tilde{A}_1{}^2A'/\tilde{A}_2{}^2A''$–$\tilde{X}^2A'$ transition of [CaOCH(CH$_3$)$_2$] were recorded under jet-cooled conditions. An essentially constant $\tilde{A}_2 - \tilde{A}_1$ energy separation for different vibronic levels is observed in the LIF spectrum of each radical, attributed to the spin-orbit (SO) interaction and, in the case of the two C_s molecules, the zero-point-energy-corrected "difference potential". The complete active space self-consistent field (CASSCF) and the coupled-cluster (CC) methods are used to calculate electronic transition energies and vibrational frequencies and to predict parameters governing the spin-vibronic energy level structure and simulate the recorded LIF/DF spectra. The Jahn-Teller (JT), pseudo-Jahn-Teller (pJT), and SO interactions, especially those between the $\tilde{A}_1/\tilde{A}_2$ and the neighboring $\tilde{B}$ states, induce a number of off-diagonal Franck-Condon (FC) matrix elements leading to additional vibronic transitions. The spin-vibronic Hamiltonian presented in the preceding talk has been employed for the spectral simulation. Computational and experimental results on all three free radicals will be compared, and the implications for future laser cooling experiments will be discussed.

TB10 12:09 – 12:24

ALKALI DIATOMICS: ASYMPTOTIC LONG RANGE BEHAVIOR OF ELECTRONIC MATRIX ELEMENTS BASED ON AB INITIO CALCULATIONS

EKATERINA A. BORMOTOVA, ANDREY STOLYAROV, *Department of Chemistry, Lomonosov Moscow State University, Moscow, Russia*.

Ultracold molecules have been widely utilized in various fields of study from the search for new physics in the ultracold regime to ultracold chemistry. Systems at such ($< 1\mu$K) temperatures are usually made with laser cooling techniques, i.e. photoassociation and stimulated Raman adiabatic passage, which utilize closed optical schemes with rovibronic levels of electron-excited states serving as intermediate steps to create ultracold molecules from pre-cooled atoms. This process requires full and detailed data for the ground and excited states in a wide range of internuclear distances, R. Sufficiently accurate data requires going beyond the adiabatic approximation, calculating non-adiabatic interaction matrix elements (IME), i.e. the spin-orbit (SO) and L-coupling (LC) IMEs, with special attention paid to correct long-range behavior.

Here, the asymptotic behavior near the dissociation limit (DL) of IMEs is studied focusing on the transition-dipole moment (TDM), SO and LC IMEs [a]. These were calculated for LiNa, LiK, LiRb, LiCs using spin-averaged wavefunctions corresponding to Hund's case (a) and effective core pseudopotentials. The electronic correlation is accounted for using a 2 valence electron multi-reference configuration interaction calculation. Core-polarization potentials take the core–valence effect into account. Where possible, theoretical curves were compared to ones derived from experiment. The leading asymptotic trends for the TDMs, and SO and LC IMEs, have been determined for three groups of state pairs: (a) dipole allowed transitions between an excited state and one converging to the first DL; (b) forbidden transitions between two states converging to the same DL>1; (b) forbidden transitions between two states converging to different DL>1. Thus, for the TDMs type (a) pairs converge as R^{-3} to the atomic dipole moment, while type (b,c) pairs converge to zero as R^{-4}. The SO IMEs converge: as R^{-7} to zero for (a); as R^{-6} to the atomic SO splitting for (b); as R^{-3} to zero for (c). Finally, the LC functions: approach infinity linearly for (a); converge as R^{-6} to a constant for (b); converge as R^{-3} to zero for (c).

---

[a] Phys. Chem. Chem. Phys. 20, 1889–1896 (2018); Phys. Rev. A 99, 012507 (2019).; Phys. Chem. Chem. Phys. 23(9), 5187–5198 (2021).

TB11 12:27 – 12:42

RELATIVISTIC DELTA-COUPLED-CLUSTER CALCULATIONS OF K-EDGE CORE-IONIZATION ENERGIES FOR THIRD-ROW ELEMENTS

<u>XUECHEN ZHENG</u>, CHAOQUN ZHANG, LAN CHENG, *Department of Chemistry, Johns Hopkins University, Baltimore, MD, USA.*

Core-valance separated delta-coupled-cluster (CVS-ΔCC) with spin-free exact two-component theory in its one-electron variant (SFX2C-1e) has been shown to provide quantitative description of core-ionization energies for second-row elements [1]. Here we extend the applicability of CVS-ΔCC calculations to K-edge core-ionization energies for third-row elements. We develop a revised CVS scheme to make it applicable in larger basis sets. Basis-sets effects have been demonstrated to be important. The use of uncontracted cc-pCVTZ basis sets for target atom and cc-pVTZ sets for the other atoms appears to be an efficient and accurate approach (cc-pCVTZ-unc*). High-level relativistic (HLR) corrections beyond the SFX2C-1e, including two-electron picture change, spin-orbit coupling, Breit interaction and QED effects have been taken into account and shown to play an important role. SFX2C-1e CVS-ΔCCSD(T)/cc-pCVTZ-unc* calculations augmented with high-level relativistic corrections can provide highly accurate K-edge core-ionization energies of third-row elements with deviation of less than 0.5 eV from experimental values.

Reference

[1] Zheng, Cheng, J. Chem. Theory Comput. **15**, 4945–4955 (2019).

TC. Linelists

Tuesday, June 21, 2022 – 8:30 AM

Room: B102 Chemical and Life Sciences

Chair: Holger S. P. Müller, Universität zu Köln, Köln, NRW, Germany

TC01 8:30 – 8:45
HIGH-ACCURACY LINE LISTS OF METHANE AND FORMALDEHYDE BETWEEN 1240 AND 1380 cm^{-1} FROM FOURIER-TRANSFORM OPTICAL FREQUENCY COMB SPECTROSCOPY

MATTHIAS GERMANN, ADRIAN HJÄLTÉN, ISAK SILANDER, ALEKSANDRA FOLTYNOWICZ, *Department of Physics, Umea University, Umea, Sweden*; VINCENT BOUDON, CYRIL RICHARD, *Laboratoire ICB, CNRS/Université de Bourgogne, DIJON, France*; KAROL KRZEMPEK, ARKADIUSZ HUDZIKOWSKI, ALEKSANDER GLUSZEK, GRZEGORZ SOBOŃ, *Faculty of Electronics, Photonics and Microsystems, Wrocław University of Science and Technology, Wrocław, Poland.*

Many small molecules have strong vibrational bands between 1000 to 1500 cm^{-1}. This spectral range overlaps with the atmospheric water window and lies within the sensitivity range of space observatories such as the James Webb Space Telescope. Therefore, it is well suited for detecting such molecules in the Earth's atmosphere or on celestial bodies. However, the current line lists in this range are still largely based on conventional FTIR measurements. Optical frequency comb spectroscopy offers superior frequency accuracy and precision but was hindered by the lack of comb sources in that spectral range. We recently developed a Fourier-transform spectrometer [a] based on an 8-μm difference-frequency-generation comb source[b]. Here, we present low-pressure spectra of methane (CH$_4$), a potent greenhouse gas and constituent of (exo-) planetary atmospheres, and formaldehyde (H$_2$CO), an atmospheric pollutant and constituent of the interstellar medium, measured with this spectrometer using the sub-nominal resolution sampling-interleaving method[c]. From these spectra, we retrieved line positions and intensities of several hundred rovibrational transitions of the ^{12}CH$_4$ and ^{13}CH$_4$ ν_4 fundamental bands and two ^{12}CH$_4$ hot bands, as well as of the H$_2$CO ν_4 and ν_6 bands, achieving uncertainties of line positions and line intensities of a few hundred kilohertz and a few percent, respectively. The line positions and intensities of ^{12}CH$_4$ were used to improve the global fit of the effective Hamiltonian and dipole-operator parameters, leading to a reduction of the line-position fit residuals by over one order of magnitude relative to the previously used data[d].

---
[a] A. Hjältén, M. Germann, K. Krzempek et al., J. Quant. Spectrosc. Radiat. Transfer 271, 107734 (2021).
[b] K. Krzempek, D. Tomaszewska, A. Gluszek et al., Opt. Express 27, 37435 (2019).
[c] L. Rutkowski, P. Maslowski, A. C. Johansson et al., J. Quant. Spectrosc. Radiat. Transfer 204, 63 (2018).
[d] B. Amyay, A. Gardez, R. Georges et al., J. Chem. Phys. 148, 134306 (2018).

TC02

IMPROVED CO_2 IR LINE LIST FOR 1500K - 3000K

XINCHUAN HUANG, *Carl Sagan Center, SETI Institute, Moutain View, CA, USA*; DAVID SCHWENKE, *MS 258-2, NAS Facility, NASA Ames Research Center, Moffett Field, CA, USA*; RICHARD S FREEDMAN, *Carl Sagan Center, SETI Institute, Moutain View, CA, USA*; TIMOTHY J. LEE, *Space Science and Astrobiology Division, NASA Ames Research Center, Moffett Field, CA, USA*.

Previously published high temperature CO_2 IR line lists either do not cover the region >10,000 cm^{-1}, or lack convergence due to cutoffs, or have noticeable noises. We report a new CO_2 IR line list improved for applications in the range from 1500K to 3000K, denoted Ames-3000K.[a] With at least 7 billion lines of CO_2 626, 636, 628 and 627, it covers the whole range from 0 to 20,000 cm^{-1}. We estimate it is converged up to 20,000 cm^{-1} at 1000K, up to 10,000-15,000 cm^{-1} at 2000K, or up to 5000-8000 cm^{-1} at 3000K, but needs further PES and DMS improvements for 4000K and above. Compared to our earlier CO_2 line list work, e.g., Ames-296K/1000K and Ames-4000K, the Ames-3000K combines the advantages of two sets of IR line lists. The 1st set focuses on the low energy region, with intensity computed using the best available Ames-2 PES, and the best available ab initio DMS, Ames-2021. The Ames-2021 DMS based IR intensity represents a major improvement for theoretical CO_2 intensity calculations. Our predictions for the CO_2 2001x and 3001x bands matched high accurate experiments to -0.1±0.1% (NIST) or 0.2±0.4% (DLR). But the Ames-2021 DMS was fit only up to 30,000 cm^{-1}. The 2nd set of line lists provides reliable prediction for IR transitions with E' up to 36,000 cm^{-1}. Related calculations were run on a different PES, X01d. To enhance the success rate of Ames vs. CDSD matches in the range of 15,000 - 22,000 cm^{-1}, the X01d PES was refined specifically using selected CDSD Effective Hamiltonian model levels up to 24,000 cm^{-1}, but at a price of the accuracy reduced for lower energy levels and transitions. The ab initio dipole dataset of Ames-2021 DMS was refitted with 40,000 cm^{-1} cutoff to generate an DMS suitable for the intensity calculation at higher energy, denoted Ames-2021-40K. The two sets of line lists are then combined and updated using the CDSD energy levels to get accurate line positions for E' <15,000 cm^{-1} and J<150 transitions. The accuracy, consistency, and issues of the Ames-3000K IR line list will be evaluated by comparing with high temperature experiments and databases.

[a] Funded by NASA Grants 18-APRA18_0013 and NASA/SETI Co-op Agreements 80NSSC20K1358 & 80NSSC19K1036.

TC03

AMES-1 296K IR LINE LISTS FOR CS_2 ISOTOPOLOGUES

XINCHUAN HUANG, *Carl Sagan Center, SETI Institute, Moutain View, CA, USA*; DAVID SCHWENKE, *MS 258-2, NAS Facility, NASA Ames Research Center, Moffett Field, CA, USA*; TIMOTHY J. LEE, *Space Science and Astrobiology Division, NASA Ames Research Center, Moffett Field, CA, USA*.

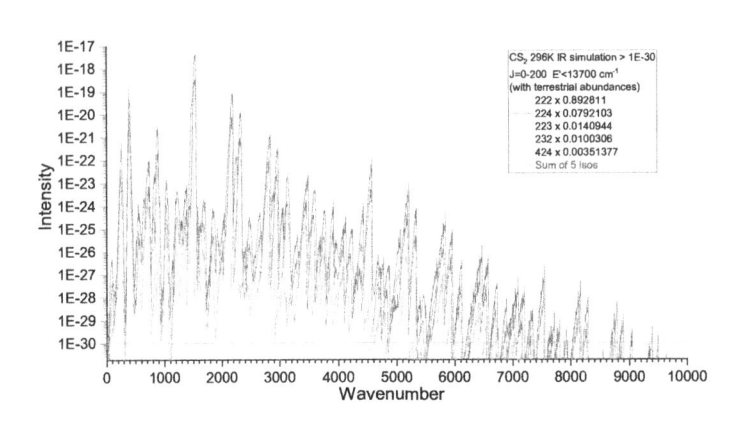

To fill in the CS_2 data gaps in IR databases, Ames-1 296K IR Line lists are reported in the range of 0 - 10,000 cm^{-1}, with line intensity cut off at 1E-30 cm/molecule.[a] Five most abundant isotopologues (222, 224, 223, 232, and 424) are included in a "natural" CS_2 combo list with their terrestrial abundances. The Ames-1 potential energy surface (PES) for CS_2 was refined using experimental levels compiled in Karlovets et al [JQSRT 258:1, 2021], with fitting σ_{rms}=0.02 cm^{-1}. The Ames-1 dipole moment surface (DMS) was fit from extrapolated CCSD(T)/aug-cc-pV(T,Q,5+d)Z dipoles, with fitting σ_{rms} = 5.2E-6 a.u. for 2416 points in 0 - 25,000 cm^{-1}. The "Ames-1 PES + Ames-1 DMS" intensity should be consistently reliable with better than 95% accuracy, but needs more experiment evaluation beyond a few strong peaks below 5000 cm^{-1}. Differences between Ames and HITRAN model extrapolations increase to 0.2-0.7 cm^{-1} at J=150. We plan to update the 222 line list with Tashkun's EH model levels [JQSRT 279:108072, 2022]. Future work may focus on states >10,000 cm^{-1}, the accuracy for J>100, and high density of states for high temperature line lists. See http://huang.seti.org for latest update.

[a] Funded by NASA Grant 18-XRP18_2-0029 and through NASA/SETI Co-operative Agreement 80NSSC19M0121.

TC04

AMES-1 296K IR LINE LISTS FOR OCS ISOTOPOLOGUES

<u>XINCHUAN HUANG</u>, *Carl Sagan Center, SETI Institute, Moutain View, CA, USA*; DAVID SCHWENKE, *MS 258-2, NAS Facility, NASA Ames Research Center, Moffett Field, CA, USA*; TIMOTHY J. LEE, *Space Science and Astrobiology Division, NASA Ames Research Center, Moffett Field, CA, USA*.

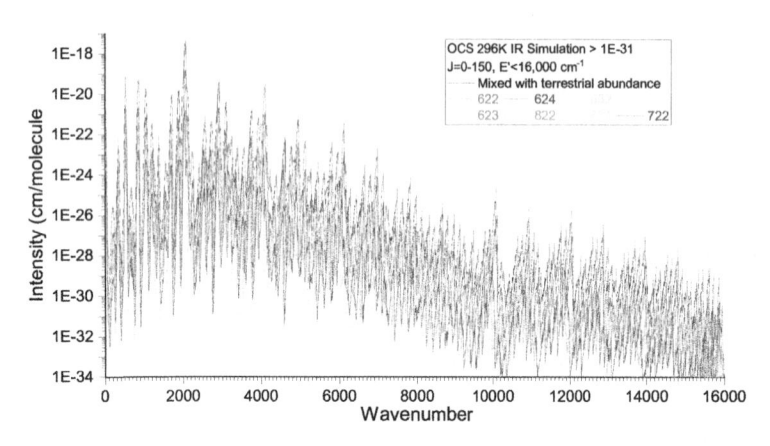

To fill in the OCS data gaps in IR databases, Ames-1 296K IR line lists are reported for OCS isotopologues in the range of 0 - 16,000 cm^{-1}, with line intensity cut off at 1E-30 cm/molecule.[a] Seven isotopologues (622,624,632,623,822,634,and 722) are included in a "natural" OCS line list with their terrestrial abundances. The Ames-1 potential energy surface (PES) for OCS was refined using selected HITRAN data and band origins up to 13,952 cm^{-1}(with reduced weight). It can reproduce most HITRAN levels with σ_{rms} <0.01 cm^{-1}, except a few bands of the main isotopologue: 5002, 4112 and 9110. The Ames-1 dipole moment surface (DMS) was fit from extrapolated CCSD(T)/aug-cc-pV(T,Q,5+d)Z dipoles, with fitting σ_{rms} = 5.8E-7 a.u. for 1862 points in 0 - 20,000 cm^{-1}. In general, the Ames-1 296K intensity finds good agreement with experiment and HITRAN. Agreements for bands >10,000 cm^{-1} are also reasonable. In future, we need to identify the source of discrepancies observed in the Ames-1 vs Expt/HITRAN comparisons, and focus on higher energy and higher temperature line lists. See http://huang.seti.org for latest update.

[a]Funded by NASA Grant 18-XRP18_2-0029 and through NASA/SETI Co-operative Agreement 80NSSC19M0121.

TC05

AMES-1 296K IR LINE LISTS FOR N$_2$O ISOTOPOLOGUES

<u>XINCHUAN HUANG</u>, *Carl Sagan Center, SETI Institute, Moutain View, CA, USA*; DAVID SCHWENKE, *MS 258-2, NAS Facility, NASA Ames Research Center, Moffett Field, CA, USA*; TIMOTHY J. LEE, *Space Science and Astrobiology Division, NASA Ames Research Center, Moffett Field, CA, USA*.

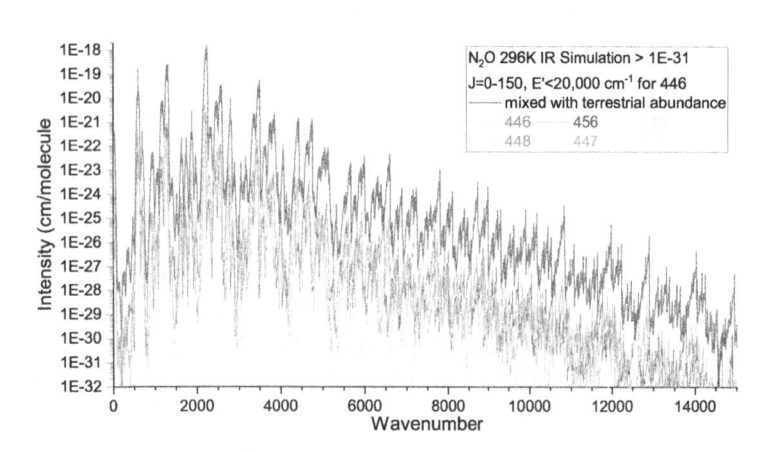

Ames-1 296K IR Line lists are reported for N$_2$O in the range of 0 - 15,000 cm^{-1}, with line intensity cut off at 1E-30 cm/molecule.[a] Six isotopologues (446,456,546,448,447 and 556) are included in a "natural" N$_2$O combo list with their terrestrial abundances. The Ames-1 potential energy surface (PES) for N$_2$O was refined using selected HITRAN data (J<80) up to 8000 cm^{-1}and additional levels (J=0-1) up to 15,000 cm^{-1}with reduced weights. For 6908 J=0-98 levels of ^{14}N$_2^{16}$O in HITRAN2020, the Ames-1 based levels agree with σ_{rms}=0.021 cm^{-1}. The Ames-1 dipole moment surface (DMS) was fit from extrapolated CCSD(T)/aug-cc-pV(T,Q,5)Z dipoles, with fitting σ_{rms} = 2.7E-5 a.u. for 5184 points in 0 - 20,000 cm^{-1}. In general, the "Ames-1 PES + Ames-1 DMS" intensity finds good agreement with HITRAN, and a few bands > 10,000 cm^{-1}. Isotopologue line lists are compared to published Effective Hamiltonian models for potential combination of reliable intensities and accurate line positions. Future improvements are planned for PES, DMS and line lists. See http://huang.seti.org for latest update.

[a]Funded by NASA Grant 18-APRA18-0013 and through NASA/SETI Co-operative Agreement 80NSSC20K1358.

Intermission

TC06   10:39 – 10:54

ROVIBRONIC INFRARED AND VISIBLE LINE LIST FOR O_2

<u>WILFRID SOMOGYI</u>, SERGEI N. YURCHENKO, *Department of Physics and Astronomy, University College London, London, UK*; GAP-SUE KIM, *Dharma College, Dongguk University, Seoul, Korea.*

The increasingly frequent observations of hot, rocky, Earth-like exoplanets make the production of hot high-resolution line lists for geo-chemically relevant species all the more important. Furthermore, molecular oxygen (O_2) is a critical biosignature molecule in atmospheric exoplanet retrievals and plays an important role in many chemical processes.

Ab initio spectroscopy of the O_2 molecule is uniquely challenging due to the fact that dipole transitions are forbidden within the three lowest lying electronic levels of, and thus transitions in infrared and visible regions are due solely to higher order electric quadrupole and magnetic dipole moments. Nonetheless, accurate line lists for these spectral regions are vital for astronomical applications.

We present results of MRCI calculations on the the $X^3\Sigma_g^-$, $a^1\Delta_g$, $b^1\Sigma_g^+$ and $d^1\Pi_g$ states, and related spin-orbit, and electric quadrupole couplings. Using the Duo program we then obtain a variational solution to the rovibronic Schrödinger equation, and perform empirical refinement of the energy levels by fitting a Morse/Long-range potential energy curve, along with spin-orbit and spin-spin coupling functions. We also discuss ongoing and future work for the magnetic dipole moment transitions.

TC07   10:57 – 11:12

EXOMOL ROVIBRONIC LINE LIST AND TEMPERATURE DEPENDENT PHOTODISSOCIATION CROSS SECTION CALCULATIONS FOR OH FROM *AB INITIO* ELECTRONIC STRUCTURE CALCULATIONS

<u>GEORGI B MITEV</u>, JONATHAN TENNYSON, SERGEI N. YURCHENKO, *Department of Physics and Astronomy, University College London, London, UK.*

OH spectroscopy has been heavily studied due to its importance in combustion, atmospheric and interstellar chemistry, and as a key constituent of the Earth's atmosphere. Recently, OH has been detected in the atmosphere of the Ulta-Hot Jupiter WASP-76b and has also been found in the stellar spectra of M-dwarfs[a]. Novel MolPro electronic structure calculations for ground and excited electronic state PECs will be presented along with associated coupling curves and (transition) dipole moments. These *ab initio* calculations are used to produce a ExoMol rovibronic linelist using the programs Duo and ExoCross. Photodissociation is a primary destructor of OH in diffuse interstellar clouds, particularly the direct $X\,^2\Pi \rightarrow 1\,^2\Sigma^-$ photodissociation. A $^2\Sigma^+$ predissociation is also studied. Temperature-dependent photodissociation cross sections using the method established by Pezzella et al.[b] are calculated and presented. Gaussian line profile optimization of photodissociation cross sections has been automated and applied to the cases of direct photodissociation for OH, HCl, and HCN.

---

[a]R. Landman, A. Sánchez-López, P. Mollière, A. Y. Kesseli, A. J. Louca, I. A. G. Snellen, *A&A*, 2021, **656**, A119
[b]M. Pezzella, J. Tennyson, S. N. Yurchenko, *Phys. Chem. Chem. Phys.*, 2021, **23**, 16390

TC08 11:15–11:30

HIGH LEVEL AB INITIO STUDY OF THE ROVIBRONIC SPECTRUM OF SULFUR MONOXIDE (SO): DIABATIC REPRESENTATION

RYAN BRADY, *Department of Physics and Astronomy, University College London, London, UK*; GAP-SUE KIM, *Dharma college of Dongguk, University in Seoul, Seoul, Korea*; WILFRID SOMOGYI, SERGEI N. YURCHENKO, JONATHAN TENNYSON, *Department of Physics and Astronomy, University College London, London, UK*.

We present a high level ab initio study of the rovibronic spectra of Sulfur Monoxide (SO) using internally contracted multireference configuration interaction (IC-MRCI) method using aug-cc-pv5z basis sets and a fully diabatised model for the molecule. The diabatic model covers the lowest 13 singlet and triplet electronic states of SO $X^3\Sigma^-$, $a^1\Delta$, $b^1\Sigma^+$, $c^1\Sigma^-$, $A^{3\prime}\Delta$, $A^{3\prime\prime}\Sigma^+$, $A^3\Pi$, $B^3\Sigma^-$, $C^3\Pi$, $C^{3\prime}\Pi$, $d^1\Pi$, $e^1\Pi$, and $(3)^1\Pi$ ranging up to 66,800 cm^{-1}. The ab initio spectroscopic model includes potential energy curves, dipole and transition dipole moment curves, spin-orbit curves and electronic angular momentum curves. A diabatic representation is built by removing avoiding crossings between the $C^3\Pi$–$C^{3\prime}\Pi$ and $e^1\Pi$–$(3)^1\Pi$ states through a unitary transformation who's rotation angle is determined on the fly by enforcing smoothness properties of the diabatic potential energy curves. A rovibronic line list of SO is computed covering the wavelength range up to 167 nm.

TC09 11:33–11:48

VISIBLE OPACITY OF M DWARFS AND HOT JUPITERS: THE TiO $B^3\Pi$- $X^3\Delta$ BAND SYSTEM

WILLIAM D CAMERON, *Physics, Old Dominion University, Norfolk, VA, USA*; PETER F. BERNATH, *Department of Chemistry and Biochemistry, Old Dominion University, Norfolk, VA, USA*.

The TiO $B^3\Pi$- $X^3\Delta$ electronic transition (γ' system) is an important opacity source in the atmospheres of M dwarfs and hot Jupiter exoplanets. The 0–0, 1–0, and 2–1 bands of the $B^3\Pi$- $X^3\Delta$ band system have been analyzed using a TiO emission spectrum recorded at the McMath-Pierce Solar Telescope, operated by the National Solar Observatory at Kitt Peak, Arizona. Improved spectroscopic and equilibrium constants were determined. Line strengths were calculated from an *ab initio* transition dipole moment function scaled using an experimental lifetime. A new line list for v' = 0-2 and v''= 0-4 of the $B^3\Pi$- $X^3\Delta$ band system is provided.

TC10 11:51 – 12:06

RECENT UPDATES TO THE HITEMP DATABASE

ROBERT J. HARGREAVES, IOULI E GORDON, *Atomic and Molecular Physics, Harvard-Smithsonian Center for Astrophysics, Cambridge, MA, USA*; XINCHUAN HUANG, *Space Science and Astrobiology Division, NASA Ames Research Center, Moffett Field, CA, USA*; EAMON K CONWAY, *Atomic and Molecular Physics, Harvard-Smithsonian Center for Astrophysics, Cambridge, MA, USA*; LAURENCE S. ROTHMAN, *Atomic and Molecular Physics, Harvard-Smithsonian Center for Astrophysics, Cambridge, MA, USA*.

The HITEMP database [1] provides line-by-line spectroscopic parameters for use at high temperatures. HITEMP line lists are used for numerous applications that include spectral modeling of exoplanets, brown dwarfs, and stellar atmospheres, as well as the high-resolution remote sensing of combustion environments. It is therefore necessary that these spectroscopic line lists are sufficiently complete in order to reproduce high-temperature spectra, but it is also essential that the line positions, intensities, and broadening parameters are accurate for high-resolution studies. Over recent years, HITEMP has been undergoing a significant upgrade that has improved the quality and extent of the available spectroscopic data and the number of line lists available: H_2O, CO_2, N_2O, CO, CH_4, NO, NO_2, OH [1-4]. HITEMP line lists are typically built upon a state-of-the-art *ab initio* (or semi-empirical) line list that is cross-evaluated against other works. The line list is then combined with HITRAN (when possible), and broadening parameters are applied for each line. The resultant line list is validated against available high-resolution experimental studies at elevated temperatures, and improvements are incorporated where necessary. This methodology will be presented for the recent additions to HITEMP [3,4], along with an "effective line" technique that was used for CH_4 [4]. The presentation will also discuss the forthcoming planned updates for the H_2O and CO_2 line lists.

[1] Rothman, et al. (2010), *JQSRT* **111**, 2139
[2] Li, et al. (2015), *ApJS* **216**, 15
[3] Hargreaves, et al. (2019), *JQSRT* **232**, 35
[4] Hargreaves, et al. (2020), *ApJS* **247**, 55

TC11 12:09 – 12:24

A DIGITAL TELLURIUM ATLAS FOR SPECTRAL CALIBRATION, 19000 – 24000 cm^{-1}

JOSEPH M. CARDON, TONY SMITH, DENNIS CLOUTHIER, *Laser Research Laboratory, Ideal Vacuum Products, LLC, Albuquerque, NM, USA*; AMANDA J. ROSS, *Inst. Lumière Matière, Univ Lyon 1 & CNRS, Université de Lyon, Villeurbanne, France*.

We propose a digital record of the absorption spectrum of $^{130}Te_2$ vapour as an aid to calibration of laboratory spectra currently referenced to the paper atlas of Cariou and Luc[a]. The strong and crowded $A0_u^+ - X0_g^+$ bands of Te_2 have long provided useful benchmarks for calibration beyond 20000 cm^{-1}, where room-temperature $B - X$ I_2 absorption cuts off. Molecular tellurium offers more lines per wavenumber than atomic uranium, whose atlas is also useful in this region[b].

Absorption spectra were recorded through the emission port of a Fourier transform spectrometer, using an external sample and light source. The sample was a sealed, evacuated 10-cm cell containing a small quantity of $^{130}Te_2$. The cell was heated to temperatures between 600 and 640 °C, generating tellurium vapour pressures 8-11 Torr, to produce strong absorption without saturation. Optical filters were used to select 2000 cm^{-1} spectral sections; interferograms were taken at nominal apodized resolution of 0.02 to 0.033 cm^{-1}. The pieces were spliced together to cover the range 19000 – 24000 cm^{-1}. The wavenumber scale was fine-tuned to match earlier (and sometimes absolute) reference data[acde]. Measured linewidths of isolated peaks vary from 0.04 to 0.09 cm^{-1}, *i.e.* broader than expected from Doppler broadening and instrumental resolution considerations, but we believe the wavenumber scale to be good to ± 0.005 cm^{-1}.

Ascii data files with Te_2 transmittance and absorbance data are freely available for download from J. Mol. Spectrosc.[f] and from the Mendeley database, at https://data.mendeley.com/datasets/kmkbwtjhd3/1.

[a] Atlas du spectre d'absorption de la molécule de téllure, Luc & Cariou, Laboratoire Aimé Cotton, CNRS publications, (1980)
[b] A uranium atlas, from 365 to 505 nm; Ross *et al.* J Mol Spectrosc **369** 111270 (2020)
[c] Absolute wavelength determinations in molecular tellurium: new reference lines for precision laser spectroscopy, Gillaspy and Sansonetti, J. Opt. Soc. Am. B 8, 2414 (1991)
[d] Absolute wavenumber measurements in $^{130}Te_2$: reference lines in the 420.9 to 464.6-nm region, Scholl *et al* J. Opt. Soc. Am. B 22(5), 1128 (2005)
[e] Cavity dispersion tuning spectroscopy of tellurium near 444.4 nm, Coker *et al* J. Opt. Soc. Am. B 28 (12), 2934 (2011)
[f] Te_2 absorption spectrum from 19000 to 24000 cm^{-1}, Ross and Cardon, J. Mol. Spectrosc. **384** (2022) 111589

TC12
LINE LISTS FOR $X^3\Sigma^-$ AND $a^1\Delta$ VIBRATION-ROTATION BANDS OF SO

PETER F. BERNATH, *Department of Chemistry and Biochemistry, Old Dominion University, Norfolk, VA, USA*; RYAN JOHNSON, *Physics Department, Old Dominion University, Norfolk, VA, USA*; JACQUES LIÉVIN, *Service de Chimie Quantique et Photophysique, Université Libre de Bruxelles, Brussels, Belgium.*

Sulfur monoxide (SO) is found in several astronomical sources including the atmospheres of Io and Venus. Continuing our previous work[a] to make a more complete line list for SO, we used our previous fits of rotational constants for v=0-6 for the $X^3\Sigma^-$ state and v=0-5 for the $a^1\Delta$ state along with high-level *ab initio* calculations to produce line strengths and positions for the all of the vibration-rotation transitions. All possible vibrational bands were calculated and line strengths included the Herman-Wallis effect caused by vibration-rotation interaction.

---

[a]P.F. Bernath, R.M. Johnson, J. Liévin. Line Lists for the $b^1\Sigma^+ - X^3\Sigma^-$ and $a^1\Delta - X^3\Sigma^-$ Transitions of SO. JQSRT 272,107772(2021)

TD. Rotational structure/frequencies
Tuesday, June 21, 2022 – 8:30 AM
Room: 217 Noyes Laboratory

Chair: Kyle N. Crabtree, University of California, Davis, CA, USA

TD01   8:30 – 8:45

MICROWAVE SPECTROSCOPY OF ISOTHIAZOLE

HOGA FURUKAWA, <u>KAORI KOBAYASHI</u>, *Department of Physics, University of Toyama, Toyama, Japan*; MARIA ZDANOVSKAIA, BRIAN J. ESSELMAN, R. CLAUDE WOODS, ROBERT J. McMAHON, *Department of Chemistry, University of Wisconsin-Madison, Madison, WI, USA.*

Recently, cyclic molecules such as benzonitrile [a] and 2-cyanocyclopentadiene [b] have been discovered in the interstellar medium. Cyclic molecules with large dipole moments are considered good candidates for future search. Isothiazole (C_3H_3NS) is a five-membered ring molecule with two adjacent hetero atoms, nitrogen and sulfur. Previous studies of millimeter-wave spectroscopy have been conducted below 35 GHz [c, d, e], and data at higher frequencies are desired. Therefore, we performed a new measurement in the region of 40-360 GHz at room temperature.

The ground state, and the vibrational excited states ($\nu_{18} = 1$, $\nu_{17} = 1$, $\nu_{13} = 1$, $\nu_{16} = 1$, $\nu_{12} = 1$, $\nu_{11} = 1$, $\nu_{15} = 1$, $\nu_{10} = 1$, and $\nu_{14} = 1$) were analyzed by using AABS [f], and SPFIT/SPCAT [g] packages. More than 10000 lines were assigned and analyzed using Watson's A-reduced Hamiltonian.

[a] B.A. McGuire, A.M. Burkhardt, S. Kalenskii, C.N. Shingledecker, A.J. Remijan, E. Herbst, M.C. McCarthy, *Science* **359**, 202 (2018).
[b] M.C. McCarthy, K.L.K. Lee, R.A. Loomis, A.M. Burkhardt, C.N. Shingledecker, S.B. Charnley, M.A. Cordiner, E. Herbst, S. Kalenskii, E.R. Willis, C. Xue, A.J. Remijan, B.A. McGuire, *Nat. Astron.* **5**, 176 (2021).
[c] J.H. Griffiths, A. Wardley, V.E. Williams, N.L. Owen, and J. Sheridan, *Nature* **216**, 1301 (1967).
[d] J. Wiese, D.H. Sutter, *Z. Naturforsch. A* **35**, 712 (1980).
[e] Gripp, U. Kretschmer, H. Dreizler *Z. Naturforsch. A* **49**, 1059 (1994).
[f] Z. Kisiel, L. Pszczółkowski, I. R. Medvedev, M. Winnewisser, F. C. De Lucia, E. Herbst, *J.Mol.Spectrosc.* **233**, 231 (2005).
[g] H. M. Pickett, *J.Mol.Spectrosc.* **148**, 371 (1991).

TD02   8:48 – 9:03

EXTENDED LABORATORY INVESTIGATION OF THE PURE ROTATIONAL SPECTRUM OF THE CH_2CN RADICAL IN THE (SUB-)MILLIMETER REGION (79-860 GHz)

<u>OLIVIA CHITARRA</u>, THOMAS SANDOW HEARNE, OLIVIER PIRALI, MARIE-ALINE MARTIN-DRUMEL, *Institut des Sciences Moléculaires d'Orsay, Université Paris Saclay, CNRS, Orsay, France.*

The cyanomethyl radical, CH_2CN, is considered a key reactive intermediate in the interstellar medium (ISM) since its first detection [1]. To date, the radical has been detected in several environments of the ISM using pure rotational data available in the literature, limited to frequencies below 280 GHz [2,3]. The radical is also postulated to participate to the formation of complex organic molecules, such as cyanoacetaldehyde [4]. To enable the detection of the CH_2CN radical in current high frequency astronomical surveys, laboratory re-investigation of its spectrum at submillimeter wavelengths appears essential. We have investigated the pure rotational spectrum of CH_2CN at room temperature in the 75-900 GHz domain. The radical was produced using a H-abstraction method from CH_3CN using F atoms. To record pure rotational transitions, we used two spectrometers: a commercial broadband chirped-pulse (CP) spectrometer covering the 75-110 GHz spectral region and a tunable single-frequency absorption spectrometer exploiting a frequency multiplication chain with a large spectral coverage (here, 140-900 GHz). A combined fit of the literature data and our newly measured transitions (involving N'' and K_a'' up to 42 and 8, respectively) yields to an improvement of the rotational parameters; in particular the A rotational constant and K-dependent parameters. This work allows for confident searches of the radical in cold to warm environments of the ISM, over a wide frequency range. In addition, the broadband capacities of the CP spectrometer has also revealed very efficient in the study of discharge products (synthesized by the reaction between CH_3CN and F atoms in this work). I will present both aspects of this work: the improvement of the spectroscopy of CH_2CN and the analysis of the chemical composition of the discharge by CP spectroscopy.

[1] W. M. Irvine et al., The Astrophysical Journal Letters (1988) 334, L107 [2] S. Saito et al., The Journal of Chemical Physics (1997) 107, 1732 [3] H. Ozeki et al., American Astronomical Society (2004) 617, 680 [4] B. Ballotta et al., ACS Earth and Space Chemistry (2021) 5, 1071

TD03　　　　　　　　　　　　　　　　　　　　　　　　　　　　　　　　　　　9:06 – 9:21

ELECTRICAL DISCHARGE OF NITROGEN CONTAINING MOLECULES: A DETAILED STUDY OF THE DISCHARGE PRODUCTS OF PYRROLE AND PYRIDINE

EVA GOUGOULA, DONATELLA LORU, GAYATRI BATRA, MELANIE SCHNELL, *FS-SMP, Deutsches Elektronen-Synchrotron (DESY), Hamburg, Germany.*

Five- and six-membered aromatic rings have received significant attention in the exploration of interstellar space. Not only have recent detections expanded our understanding of interstellar chemistry but also highlight the timeliness and importance of investigation of the laboratory rotational spectra of such molecules. Following the detections of cyclopentadiene[1] and benzene[2] via rotational and infrared spectroscopies, respectively, their respective nitrogen containing analogues, pyrrole (C_4H_5N) and pyridine (C_5H_5N), call for extensive investigation of their rotational spectra as well as their chemistry under harsh energetic conditions.

Here, we present a detailed study of the products of pyrrole (C_4H_5N) and pyridine (C_5H_5N) generated through electrical discharge of the precursors and supersonic expansion. The spectra of the resulting species are simultaneously recorded with a Chirped Pulse Fourier Transform Microwave (CP-FTMW) Spectrometer operating in the 18-26 GHz frequency region.[3] The observed species, varying from cyclopropene to linear cyanopolyynes, contain both fewer and more, or the same number of carbons as their respective precursors suggesting that both fragmentation and recombination processes take place during electrical discharge. Our results support the detection of related molecules in the interstellar medium which may also provide an insight into potential pathways around their formation.

[1] Cernicharo, J., Agúndez, M., Cabezas, C., Tercero, B., Marcelino, N., Pardo, J. R. & de Vicente P. A&A. 649, L15 (2021)

[2] Cernicharo, J., Heras, A. M., Tielens, A. G. G. M., Padro, J. R., Herpin, F., Guelin, M. & Waters, L. B. M. Astrophys. J. 546, L123 (2001)

[3] Fatima, M., Perez, C., Arenas, B. E., Schnell, M. & Steber, A. Phys. Chem. Chem. Phys. 22, 17042-17051 (2020)

TD04　　　　　　　　　　　　　　　　　　　　　　　　　　　　　　　　　　　9:24 – 9:39

ACCURATE SPECTROSCOPIC CHARACTERIZATION OF UNSATURATED CARBON-CHAINS OF ASTROCHEMICAL IMPORTANCE

ALESSIO MELLI, SILVIA ALESSANDRINI, VINCENZO BARONE, *Scuola Normale Superiore, Scuola Normale Superiore, Pisa, Italy*; MATTIA MELOSSO, NINGJING JIANG, LUCA DORE, *Dept. Chemistry "Giacomo Ciamician", University of Bologna, Bologna, ITALY*; CRISTINA PUZZARINI, *Dep. Chemistry 'Giacomo Ciamician', University of Bologna, Bologna, Italy*; LUCA BIZZOCCHI, *Dipartimento di Chimica G. Ciamician, Università di Bologna, Bologna, Italy*; J.-C. GUILLEMIN, *Ecole Nationale Supèrieure de Chimie de Rennes, Univ. Rennes, Rennes, France.*

The molecular universe of Astrochemistry is expanding at a surprisingly rapid pace. However, to univocally identify the transitions of the studied molecule within an astronomcial survey –which are, typically, densely packed with lines– an extremely accurate knowledge of the rotational frequencies is required. Therefore, an accurate spectroscopic characterization of *E*- and *Z*-cyanovinylacetylene (CVA), allenylacetylene (AA) and propadienone (PD) has been carried out to guide their detection in the interstellar medium. An eventual first detection, as it would be for PD and *Z*-CVA, as well as new findings (on *E*-CVA and AA, which have been recently identified in TMC-1) in different astronomical regions, can be of great help in the refining of the models of the interstellar objects. Indeed, PD is the only isomer of the [H_2C_3O] family which has not been observed in the ISM, while unsaturated carbon chains like CVA and AA can play important roles in reactivity, e.g., the pathways leading to the formation of aromatic molecules.

In this work, we relied on a solid computational study to complete the experimental data available in literature. The accurate equilibrium geometries of the four species have been determined, exploiting composite schemes rooted in the coupled-cluster theory. Harmonic and anharmonic force field calculations gave access to the set of centrifugal distortion parameters; the importance of an accurate estimate of the sextic ones is presented. Exploiting a pyrolysis system to generate the four species in the gas-phase and using a frequency-modulation spectrometer working in the millimeter/sub-millimeter wave range, we were able to record and analyze the rotational spectrum up to 400 GHz, providing accurate rotational frequencies and a thorough characterization of the spectroscopic parameters.

TD05 9:42 – 9:57

SPECTROSCOPIC AND COMPUTATIONAL CHARACTERIZATION OF 2-AZA-1,3-BUTADIENE, A MOLECULE OF ASTROCHEMICAL SIGNIFICANCE

NINGJING JIANG, MATTIA MELOSSO, *Dept. Chemistry "Giacomo Ciamician", University of Bologna, Bologna, ITALY*; LUCA BIZZOCCHI, *Dipartimento di Chimica G. Ciamician, Università di Bologna, Bologna, Italy*; SILVIA ALESSANDRINI, *Scuola Normale Superiore, Scuola Normale Superiore, Pisa, Italy*; J.-C. GUILLEMIN, *Ecole Nationale Supèrieure de Chimie de Rennes, Univ. Rennes, Rennes, France*; LUCA DORE, *Dept. Chemistry "Giacomo Ciamician", University of Bologna, Bologna, ITALY*; CRISTINA PUZZARINI, *Dep. Chemistry 'Giacomo Ciamician', University of Bologna, Bologna, Italy*.

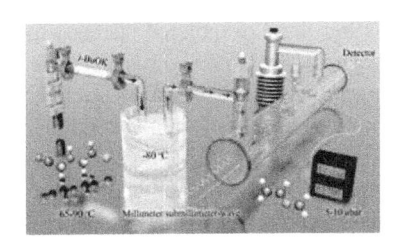

Being N-substituted unsaturated species, azabutadienes are molecules of potential relevance in astrochemistry, ranging from the interstellar medium to Titan's atmosphere. 2-azabutadiene and butadiene share a similar conjugated π system, thus allowing the investigation of the effects of heteroatom substitution. More interestingly, 2-azabutadiene can be used to proxy the abundance of interstellar butadiene. To enable future astronomical searches, the rotational spectrum of 2-azabutadiene has been investigated up to 330 GHz. Experiment has been supported and guided by an accurate computational characterization of the molecular structure, energetics, and spectroscopic properties of the two possible forms, *trans* and *gauche*. The *trans* species, more stable by about 7 kJ/mol than *gauche*-2-azabutadiene, has been experimentally observed and its rotational and centrifugal distortion constants obtained with remarkable accuracy, while theoretical estimates of the spectroscopic parameters are reported for *gauche*-2-azabutadiene.

Intermission

TD06 10:39 – 10:54

THE MILLIMETER/SUBMILLIMETER SPECTRUM OF 3-HYDROXYPROPANAMIDE

COLTON MOORE, HAYLEY BUNN, CHASE P SCHULTZ, *Department of Chemistry, University of Wisconsin-Madison, Madison, WI, USA*; SUSANNA L. WIDICUS WEAVER, *Chemistry and Astronomy, University of Wisconsin-Madison, Madison, WI, USA*.

3-hydroxypropanamide (HOCH$_2$CH$_2$CONH$_2$), has primarily been used in drug synthesis and is an isomer of the amino acid β-alanine. Due to its structural similarity to β-alanine, it is a key target for tracing the formation of important biomolecules in astrochemistry. 3-hydroxypropanamide has a low vapor pressure and readily decomposes when heated to temperatures above $\sim 80°$C. Therefore, no rotational spectroscopic investigation has yet been conducted. We report the rotational spectrum of 3-hydroxypropanamide collected from 140-460 GHz using a long-pathlength direct absorption millimeter/submillimeter spectrometer. To aid in its characterization, the gas sample was held at a static pressure of ~ 40 mTorr at 70°C; these conditions could be held for several hours so that broadband spectra could be acquired. We will report in this talk on the 3-hydroxypropanamide spectra obtained and the progress of spectral analysis.

TD07 10:57 – 11:12

ANALYSIS OF THE HIGH RESOLUTION ROTATIONAL SPECTRUM OF 2-CHLOROETHANOL

<u>HAYLEY BUNN</u>, BRIAN J. ESSELMAN, *Department of Chemistry, University of Wisconsin-Madison, Madison, WI, USA*; ANDI WRIGHT, STEVEN SHIPMAN, *Department of Chemistry, New College of Florida, Sarasota, FL, USA*; SUSANNA L. WIDICUS WEAVER, *Chemistry and Astronomy, University of Wisconsin-Madison, Madison, WI, USA*.

2-Chloroethanol ($HOCH_2CH_2Cl$) is the smallest terrestrially stable chlorohydrin and is predicted to exist in the interstellar medium, forming from HCl with either oxirane or ethylene glycol, each of which are known interstellar constituents. Rotational[a] and ro-vibrational [b, c] spectra of 2-chloroethanol have been previously reported from 9-40 GHz and 100-500 cm^{-1}, respectively. However, attempts at the detection of 2-chloroethanol towards Sgr B2(N) have been unsuccessful. It is uncertain if the lack of detection arises from its lack of presence in this sightline, or whether the extrapolated spectral information for 2-cholorethanol is not of sufficient accuracy to guide astronomical searches. Therefore, we have measured the spectrum of 2-chloroethanol from 140 to 700 GHz to further improve the molecular constants and provide spectral frequencies directly comparable to radio telescope data. Analysis of this spectrum has resulted in the determination of refined rotational constants and centrifugal distortion constants up to the octic level for both naturally occurring Cl isotolopologues. Partially resolved nuclear quadrupole coupling arising from the presence of the chlorine atom is observed throughout the spectral range. New spectra from 8 to 26 GHz have been obtained to refine the quadrupole coupling constants with well resolved microwave transitions. We also have tentative least-squares fits of transitions for all vibrationally excited states below 500 cm^{-1} for each isotopologue, where the majority appear to be perturbed by Coriolis interactions. Analysis of the vibrationally excited states will be facilitated by the previously published high resolution far-IR data and may provide new insights into the vibrational energies and coupling interactions of these states. Here we will report the in-depth spectral analysis of the rotational spectrum of 2-chloroethanol.

---

[a] Azrak, R. G.; Wilson, E. B. The Journal of Chemical Physics, 1970 52 (10), 5299–5316
[b] Soliday, R. M.; Bunn, H.; Sumner, I.; Raston, P. L. The Journal of Physical Chemistry A, 2019 123 (6), 1208–1216
[c] Hull, K.; Soliday, R. M.; Raston, P. L. Journal of Molecular Structure, 2020, 1217:128369

TD08 11:15 – 11:30

FOURIER TRANSFORM MICROWAVE SPECTRA OF *cis*-3-HEXENAL, *trans*-3-HEXENAL, *cis*-2-HEXENAL AND *trans*-2-HEXENAL: STRUCTURAL ISOMERS AND ISOMERIZATION

<u>RYOTO OZAWA</u>, NOBUHIKO KUZE, YOSHIYUKI KAWASHIMA, *Department of Materials and Life Sciences, Sophia University, Tokyo, Japan*.

cis-3-Hexenal (*c*3-HA; $O=CH-CH_2-CH=CH-CH_2-CH_3$) is known as an odor molecule of grass and the *c*3-HA easily isomerizes to *trans*-2-hexenal (*t*2-HA). Rotational spectra of the *c*3-HA and its structural isomers were observed by Fourier transform microwave (FTMW) spectroscopy in the frequency region 4.8-23 GHz. We reported that two conformers of the *c*3-HA, *SG'cS* and *CScS*, were assigned[a]: in *SG'cS*, *S*, *G'*, *c*, and *S* in order denote the *skew*, *gauche'*, *cis* and *skew* around the dihedral angles OC(1)C(2)C(3), C(1)C(2)C(3)=C(4), C(2)C(3)=C(4)C(5) and C(3)=C(4)C(5)C(6), respectively. We found other four conformers which were assigned to the *SStS* and *S'S'tS* conformers of *trans*-3-hexenal (*t*3-HA), and the *TcSG'* and *TcST* conformers of *cis*-2-hexenal (*c*2-HA) by comparing from the results of ab initio calculation. We also observed the rotational spectra of the *t*2-HA which had been reported in 2015[b]. The spectra of the *c*3-HA and *t*3-HA were observed in room temperature. When the nozzle temperature increased, the maximum of spectral intensities of the *c*3-HA and *t*3-HA reach at around 350 K while the intensities of the *t*2-HA and *c*2-HA are stronger. This evidence shows that the *c*3-HA and *t*3-HA isomerized into the *t*2-HA and *c*2-HA.

---

[a] S. Yoshizawa, N. Kuze and Y. Kawashima, ISMS2019, P3866 (2019).
[b] R. Yokoyama, Y. Kawashima, and E Hirota, 9th Annual Meeting on Molecular Science, Tokyo, 4P008 (2015).

TD09 11:33 – 11:48

DECIPHERING THE COMPLETE NUCLEAR QUADRUPOLE COUPLING TENSOR OF IODINE WITH THE ROTATIONAL SPECTRUM OF 2-IODOETHANOL

MICHAEL J. CARRILLO, LINDSEY ANN SPEARE, DINESH MARASINGHE, MICHAEL TUBERGEN, *Department of Chemistry and Biochemistry, Kent State University, Kent, OH, USA.*

High level ab initio calculations at the CCSD(T)//MP2/6-311++ level were used to model the rotational constants and hyperfine constants of 2-iodoethanol. A potential energy surface scan was performed at the B3LYP/6-311G++ level of theory to obtain a better understanding of the conformational landscape and possible conformations. The B3LYP/6-311G++ level of theory was also used to calculate centrifugal distortion constants and zero-point vibrational corrections. We report for the first time the rotational spectroscopic observation on the gauche hydrogen bonding conformer of 2-iodoethanol using a molecular beam, cavity-based Fourier transform microwave spectrometer in the frequency range of 9.4-18.0 GHz. A semi-rigid rotor Hamiltonian perturbed by nuclear quadrupole hyperfine interactions was used to fit the spectrum. 20 rotational transitions split into 104 hyperfine components by the 5/2 nuclear spin of iodine have been measured. A least-squares fit of 3.9 kHz provided the fitted rotational constants which are A = 11369.8531(10), B = 1833.107(5), C = 1654.322 (5) MHz, and the nuclear quadrupole coupling constants which are χ_{aa} = -1476.693(9) MHz, χ_{bb}-χ_{cc} = -189.0537(2) MHz, χ_{ab} = -1180.354(12) MHz, χ_{ac} = 332.17(6) MHz, and χ_{bc} = 243.862(24) MHz. The spectrum of 2-iodoethanol is consistent with the theoretical model structure which predicts a 2.91Å intramolecular hydrogen bond.

TD10 11:51 – 12:06

CENTIMETER-WAVE SPECTROSCOPY OF SEVERAL NEW SILICON-BEARING CARBON CHAINS

MICHAEL C McCARTHY, BRYAN CHANGALA, BRANDON CARROLL, *Atomic and Molecular Physics, Harvard-Smithsonian Center for Astrophysics, Cambridge, MA, USA.*

The rotational spectra of several new silicon-bearing carbon chains were detected by means of Fourier-transform microwave spectroscopy in a supersonic jet source equipped with an electrical discharge. The newly detected species are HSiCCH, H_2C_3Si, and the SiC_5H radical. Precise rotational constants have been determined for all three, and as have fine and hyperfine constants for SiC_5H. Using samples enriched in carbon-13 and D, it has also been possible to detect several rare isotopic species and in turn derive an experimental structure for HSiCCH. Isotopic spectroscopy also provides clues as to the formation pathways that may be operative in our discharge. Finally, because these chains are both polar and closely related in structure and composition to other small Si-bearing chains and rings that have been detected in the circumstellar envelope of the evolved carbon star IRC+10216, they may be of astronomical interest.

TD11 12:09 – 12:24

A HIGH SPEED FITTING PROGRAM FOR ROTATIONAL SPECTROSCOPY

BRANDON CARROLL, MICHAEL C McCARTHY, *Atomic and Molecular Physics, Harvard-Smithsonian Center for Astrophysics, Cambridge, MA, USA.*

The ongoing development of rotational spectroscopy through the growth of broadband capabilities and automated acquisition schemes regularly generates a wealth of data to be analyzed. However, assigning these data is often a bottleneck to obtaining useful chemical information. This is particularly true for unknown carriers for which no initial guess or constraint is available. Development of automated spectral analysis tools is therefore critical to fully utilize rotational spectroscopy data.

We have previously reported the development of a high speed algorithm for the calculation of asymmetric rotor spectra. Previous versions of this software included basic search and assignment features that were capable of producing a list of probable matches that can be readily evaluated by hand. Since its original release, we have added several new features, including more advanced and automated searching, significant performance increases, multithreading support, and new calculation types. We will discuss the program, improvements, and implementation of its new features.

TE. Chirality and stereochemistry

Tuesday, June 21, 2022 – 8:30 AM

Room: 1024 Chemistry Annex

Chair: Ha Vinh Lam Nguyen, Université Paris-Est Créteil, Créteil, France

TE01   8:30–8:45

HIGH RESOLUTION INFRARED SPECTROSCOPY OF AZIRIDINE-2-CARBONITRILE ($C_3H_4N_2$)

<u>KAREN KEPPLER</u>, SIEGHARD ALBERT, CARINE MANCA TANNER, MARTIN QUACK, *Laboratorium für Physikalische Chemie, ETH Zurich, Zurich, Switzerland*; JÜRGEN STOHNER, *ICBT Institut für Chemie und Biotechnologie, ZHAW, Wädenswil, Switzerland.*

Molecular parity violation has been critically discussed in relation to biomolecular homochirality in the early evolution of life [a]. In this context molecules of potential importance for prebiotic chemistry like the small, chiral three-membered heterocyclic molecule aziridine-2-carbonitrile (2-cyanoaziridine) are of interest [b]. Indeed, this molecule has been previously examined [c] and the parity violating energy difference between the enantiomers in their ground state has also been calculated [d]. Molecular parameters for the ground state of this molecule are available from earlier microwave studies [e], and its conformations have been examined by *ab initio* theory [f]. Here we report initial results of a high resolution spectroscopic study of cyanoaziridine, carried out at room temperature with an instrumental resolution of 0.0011 cm^{-1} in the 800-1000 cm^{-1} region using the Bruker IFS125 Zurich Prototype (ZP2001) Fourier transform spectrometer [g]. Transitions in the ν_{15} and ν_{16} bands have been assigned, and molecular parameters have been determined using the Watson Hamiltonian. Simulations performed using these parameters reproduce the observed spectra well. The results are discussed in relation to astrophysical spectroscopy and recent efforts on parity violation in chiral molecules [h].

---

[a] M. Quack, *Angew.Chem.Intl.Ed.(Engl.)* **2002**, 41(24), 4618; *Adv.Chem.Phys.* **2014**, 157, 249, www.ir.ETHz.CH.

[b] A. Eschenmoser and E. Loewenthal, *Chem.Soc.Rev.* **1992**, 21, 1.

[c] S. Drenkard, J. Ferris, and A. Eschenmoser, *Helv.Chim.Acta* **1990**, 73, 1373.

[d] R. Berger, M. Quack and G.S. Tschumper, *Helv.Chim.Acta* **2000**, 83(8), 1919.

[e] R.D. Brown, P.D. Godfrey, and A.L. Ottrey, *J.Mol.Spectrosc.* **1980**, 82, 73.

[f] G.S. Tschumper, *J.Chem.Phys.* **2001**, 114(1), 225.

[g] S. Albert, K. Albert and M. Quack, *Trends in Optics and Photonics* **2003**, 84, 177; S. Albert, K. Keppler Albert, M. Quack, Ch. 26, Handbook of High-Resolution Spectroscopy, Vol. 2, p. 965–1019, M. Quack, F. Merkt, Eds., Wiley, Chichester (2011).

[h] M. Quack and G. Seyfang,"Tunnelling and Parity Violation in Chiral and Achiral Molecules: Theory and High-Resolution Spectroscopy," Chapter 6, Tunnelling in Molecules: Nuclear Quantum Effects from Bio to Physical Chemistry, p.192–244, J. Kästner, S. Kozuch, Eds., RSC, Cambridge (2020), ISBN: 978-1-78801-870-8; M. Quack, G. Seyfang, G. Wichmann, *Adv.Quantum Chem.* **2020**, 81, 51–104.

TE02   8:48 – 9:03

TRANSIENT CHIRALITY AND MICROSOLVATION IN p-ETHYLPHENOL

JUAN CARLOS LOPEZ, *Departamento de Química Física y Química Inorgánica - I.U. CINQUIMA, Universidad de Valladolid, Valladolid, Spain*; FERNANDO GONZALEZ, ALBERTO MACARIO, *Departamento de Química Física y Química Inorgánica, Universidad de Valladolid, Valladolid, Spain*; SUSANA BLANCO, *Departamento de Química Física y Química Inorgánica - I.U. CINQUIMA, Universidad de Valladolid, Valladolid, Spain*.

p-Ethylphenol (PEP) and other volatile phenols appear in wines contaminated with Brettanomyces yeast giving undesirable off-aromas ("Brett" or phenolic character) which spoil wines even at very low concentrations. These phenols are produced by an enzymatic transformation of the hydroxycinnamic acids present in wines. In this work, we have analyzed the rotational spectrum of PEP and its microsolvated complexes using CP-FTMW spectroscopy in the 2-8 GHz region. The equilibrium configuration of PEP has the ethyl group carbon plane perpendicular to the phenyl ring while the OH group lies in the ring plane. The two possible orientations of the OH group originate two non-superposable enantiomeric forms, energetically equivalent, but with opposite signs for the μ_b electric dipole component. The interconversion of both enantiomers by the OH internal rotation leads to a situation of transient chirality. This motion is expected to have a two-fold periodic potential energy function with the torsional states appearing as doublets as happen in phenol. The rotational spectrum reflects this behavior. The μ_a spectrum consists of single lines resulting from the collapse of the individual torsional 0^+ and 0^- spectra. The μ_b transitions, forbidden within each torsional state, are allowed as chiral $0^+ \leftrightarrow 0^-$ transitions. Therefore, the μ_b-type spectrum consists of doublets spaced twice the energy difference between the 0^+ and 0^- torsional states. We have observed the ^{13}C and OD isotopologues and have determined the molecular structure of PEP along with the internal rotation potential energy profile. In addition, we have measured the spectra of the PEP-H$_2$O, PEP-Ne-H$_2$O, and PEP-(H$_2$O)$_2$ complexes. The PEP-H$_2$O and PEP-Ne-H$_2$O spectra show doublets with 1:3 intensities revealing the water rotation dynamics exchanging the H atoms. For these species the spectra of different isotopologues ^{13}C, D, ^{18}O, and ^{22}Ne have been also measured to determine their structures.

TE03   9:06 – 9:21

THE MICROWAVE SPECTRA AND MOLECULAR STRUCTURES OF THE CHIRAL AND ACHIRAL ROTAMERS OF 2,3,3-TRIFLUOROPROPENE AND THEIR GAS PHASE HETERODIMERS WITH THE ARGON ATOM

HELEN O. LEUNG, MARK D. MARSHALL, TAHA AHMAD, DAVID W. BORDEN, CAITLIN HOFFMAN, NAVIE KIM, *Chemistry Department, Amherst College, Amherst, MA, USA*.

The three minima obtained upon rotation of the difluoromethyl group in 2,3,3-trifluoromethylpropene correspond to a higher energy, achiral rotamer that contains a plane of symmetry while the two minima that share a lower energy value characterize a chiral, enantiomeric pair. Four isotopologues of each form are observed in the microwave rotational spectrum obtained using a pulsed-jet, chirped pulse Fourier transform spectrometer and the spectra of all eight have been assigned and analyzed. Additionally, spectra for four isotopologues of the gas phase heterodimer formed between the chiral rotamer and an argon atom have been obtained and analyzed using a narrowband, Balle-Flygare cavity Fourier transform instrument. For the heterodimer of the achiral rotamer with argon, only the spectrum of the most abundant isotopologue has been observed.

TE04   9:24 – 9:39

HIGH PRECISION SPECTROSCOPY AND CONTROLLED DIMER FORMATION IN A CRYOGENIC ENVIRONMENT

DAVID PATTERSON, *Physics, University of California, Santa Barbara, CA, USA*; GRETA KOUMARIANOU, *Chemistry and Biochemistry, UCSB, Santa Barbara, CA, USA*; LINCOLN SATTERTHWAITE, DANIEL SORENSEN, *Physics, University of California, Santa Barbara, CA, USA*.

A cryogenic buffer gas cell at a few degrees Kelvin provides a bright source of internally cold and slow moving molecules. I will be presenting recent results from our buffer gas spectrometers, including direct observation of dimer formation with conformationally selected reagents and high-resolution spectroscopy in slow, bright buffer-gas cooled molecular beams.

TE05 9:42 – 9:57

BROADBAND MICROWAVE 3-WAVE MIXING: ASSIGNMENT-FREE CHIRALITY DETECTION IN UNKNOWN SAMPLES

GRETA KOUMARIANOU, *Chemistry and Biochemistry, UCSB, Santa Barbara, CA, USA*; IRENE WANG, *Physics, University of California, Santa Barbara, CA, USA*; LINCOLN SATTERTHWAITE, *Chemistry and Biochemistry, UCSB, Santa Barbara, CA, USA*; DAVID PATTERSON, *Physics, University of California, Santa Barbara, CA, USA*.

Straightforward identification of chiral molecules in multi-component mixtures of unknown composition is extremely challenging. Current spectrometric and chromatographic methods cannot unambiguously identify components while the state of the art spectroscopic methods are limited by the difficult and time-consuming task of spectral assignment. Here, we introduce a highly sensitive generalized version of microwave three-wave mixing that uses broad-spectrum fields to detect chiral molecules in enantiomeric excess without any prior chemical knowledge of the sample. This method does not require spectral assignment as a necessary step to extract information out of a spectrum. We demonstrate our method by recording three-wave mixing spectra of multi-component samples that provide direct evidence of enantiomeric excess. Our method opens up new capabilities in ultrasensitive phase-coherent spectroscopic detection that can be applied for chiral detection in real-life mixtures, raw products of chemical reactions and difficult to assign novel exotic species.

Intermission

TE06 10:39 – 10:54

THE MICROWAVE SPECTRA AND MOLECULAR STRUCTURES OF THE CHIRAL TAGGING CANDIDATE *CIS*-1,3,3,3-TETRAFLUORO-1,2-EPOXYPROPANE AND ITS GAS PHASE HETERODIMER WITH THE ARGON ATOM

JONAH R. HOROWITZ, HELEN O. LEUNG, MARK D. MARSHALL, *Chemistry Department, Amherst College, Amherst, MA, USA*.

We are exploring how argon binding to substituted oxiranes, which have potential applications as chiral tags, is modulated by varying the identity of the substituents on the epoxy ring. Previously studied systems generally showed close contacts primarily to atoms contained in the ring. However, for complexes with *cis*-1,3,3,3-tetrafluoro-1,2-epoxypropane (cFTFO) multiple minima with similar energies are predicted by quantum chemistry calculations including some with significant interactions between the argon atom and substituents on the oxirane. Analysis of the rotational spectra obtained using chirped pulse Fourier transform microwave spectroscopy for four isotopologues of Ar-cFTFO reveals that the argon atom binds to the back of the ring; very different from Ar-3,3,3-trifluoro-1,2-epoxypropane (Ar-TFO) and Ar-3,3-difluoro-1,2-epoxypropane, but similar to Ar-*trans*-1,3,3,3-tetrafluoro-1,2-epoxypropane. The utility of cFTFO in chiral analysis is explored via quantum chemistry calculations on the TFO-cFTFO heterodimer and progress on the observation and analysis of the two diastereomeric forms of this species will be reported.

TE07 10:57 – 11:12

THE MICROWAVE SPECTRA AND MOLECULAR STRUCTURES OF *CIS*- and *TRANS*-1,1,1-TRIFLUORO-2,3-EPOXYBUTANE

MARK D. MARSHALL, HELEN O. LEUNG, CAITLIN KNIGHT, *Chemistry Department, Amherst College, Amherst, MA, USA*.

Connected to our efforts in characterizing substituted oxiranes for use as potential chiral tags for the conversion of enantiomeric molecules into spectroscopically distinct diastereomeric complexes for chiral analysis, we have obtained and analyzed the spectra of both the *cis* and *trans* isomers of 1,1,1-trifluoro-2,3-epoxybutane. Although the spectrum of the *trans* isomer and all four of its singly-substituted ^{13}C isotopologues, obtained in natural abundance, could be satisfactorily analyzed as a centrifugally-distorting rigid rotor asymmetric top, the spectrum of the *cis* isomer showed the effects of methyl group internal rotation. Progress on assigning and analyzing the spectrum of this isomer will be reported.

TE08 11:15 – 11:30

ENHANCED ENANTIOMER-SELECTIVE POPULATION ENRICHMENT USING MICROWAVE SPECTROSCOPY WITH RAPID ADIABATIC PASSAGE

FREYA E. L. BERGGÖTZ, HIMANSHI SINGH, WENHAO SUN, *FS-SMP, Deutsches Elektronen-Synchrotron (DESY), Hamburg, Germany*; CRISTOBAL PEREZ, *Faculty of Science - Department of Physical Chemistry, University of Valladolid, Valladolid, Spain*; MELANIE SCHNELL, *FS-SMP, Deutsches Elektronen-Synchrotron (DESY), Hamburg, Germany.*

Chirality is ubiquitous in nature since most biologically active molecules are chiral. The two mirror images of a chiral molecule, which are called enantiomers, have almost identical physical properties, however, their chemical and biochemical properties can differ tremendously. Thus, beyond the structural analysis, enantiomer differentiation and separation are essential for a deeper understanding of their functionality.

Over the past decade, microwave three-wave mixing has emerged as a chiral-sensitive technique enabling the differentiation of enantiomers using a sequence of microwave pulses.[1] This technique was further extended to achieve enantiomer-selective population transfer in chiral molecules, that is, the energetic separation of enantiomers in a specific rotational state of interest.[2–4] The efficiency of the enantiomer-selective population transfer is mainly limited by two factors: the spatial degeneracy and the thermal population of the rotational levels. To deal with the latter issue, we applied a chirped microwave pulse within the rapid adiabatic passage (RAP) regime to depopulate the initial thermal population in the relevant rotational state. The effect of the RAP pulse on the enantiomer-selective enrichment will be presented, in combination with a theoretical simulation.

[1] D. Patterson, M. Schnell, J. M. Doyle, *Nature* **2013**, *497*, 475–477.
[2] S. Eibenberger, J. Doyle, D. Patterson, *Phys. Rev. Lett.* **2017**, *118*, 123002.
[3] C. Pérez, A. L. Steber, S. R. Domingos, A. Krin, D. Schmitz, M. Schnell, *Angew. Chem. Int. Ed.* **2017**, *56*, 12512–12517.
[4] J. Lee, J. Bischoff, A. O. Hernandez-Castillo, B. Sartakov, G. Meijer, S. Eibenberger-Arias, *arXiv:2112.09058 [physics.chem-ph]* **2021**.

TE09 11:33 – 11:48

INSIGHT INTO CHIRAL RAMAN SIGNALS UNDER RESONANCE CONDITION.

GUOJIE LI, YUNJIE XU, *Department of Chemistry, University of Alberta, Edmonton, AB, Canada.*

Resonance Raman optical activity (RROA) measures the small intensity difference between right circularly polarized light, I_R, versus left circularly polarized light, I_L, when a randomly polarized light is in resonance with a chiral molecule. Researchers have explored RROA as a mean to significantly enhance the weak ROA response for the past two decades, although the progress has been severely hampered by the lack of agreement between theoretical and experimental RROA spectra so far. After examining a series of light-matter events which can occur simultaneously under a typical RROA experimental condition, we discovered a new form of chiral Raman spectroscopy, eCP-Raman-a combination of electronic circular dichroism (ECD) and circularly polarized Raman (CP Raman).[1] Further analyses of the I_R-I_L spectra of three resonating chiral molecules revealed that all of the I_R-I_L spectra observed can be satisfactorily explained by the novel eCP Raman mechanism without any detectable contributions from natural RROA.[2] The discovery of eCP-Raman allows one to extract true RROA contribution from the I_R-I_L signal obtained under resonance to facilitate the current theoretical RROA development. Furthermore, eCP-Raman offers a new way for sensitive chirality detection of molecular systems in biology and chemistry.

1. G. Li, M. Alshalalfeh, J. Kapitán, P. Bouř, Y. Xu, Chem. Eur. J. 2022, doi.org/10.1002/chem. 202104302. 2. a) G. Li, M. Alshalalfeh, Y. Yang, J. R. Cheeseman, P. Bouř, Y. Xu, Angew. Chem. Int. Ed. 2021, 60, 22004-22009. b) T. Wu, G. Li, J. Kapitán, J. Kessler, Y. Xu, P. Bouř, Angew. Chem. Int. Ed. 2020, 59, 21895-21898.

TE10 11:51 – 12:06

ANISOTROPIC CIRCULAR DICHROISM SPECTROSCOPY OF JET-COOLED CHIRAL MOLECULES

<u>CHANGSEOP JEONG</u>, NAM JOON KIM, *Chemistry/Lab. of ion and laser chemistry, Chungbuk National University, Cheongju, Chungbuk, Republic of Korea.*

Circular dichroism (CD) spectroscopy is one of the most powerful methods to investigate the structures and reactions of chiral molecules. The CD of molecules with fixed spatial distribution is called anisotropic CD (ACD). ACD spectroscopy has been extensively used to probe the orientation of macromolecules in anisotropic medium. Here, we have obtained the resonant two photon ionization CD (R2PICD) spectra of (-)PED using a dual laser beam method. It is found that the CD values of the P-, Q-, and R-branch transitions of the origin bands are different from each other. Furthermore, the CD values of the rotational transitions of conformers A and C do not exhibit mirror images between (+) and (-)PED. These results are explained by ACD phenomena of jet-cooled molecules undergoing the P-, Q-, and R-branch transitions.

TF. Comparing theory and experiment

Tuesday, June 21, 2022 – 8:30 AM

Room: 124 Burrill Hall

Chair: Rebecca A. Peebles, Eastern Illinois University, Charleston, IL, USA

TF01   8:30 – 8:45

THE INTRIGUING $F_{bc}(P_bP_c + P_cP_b)$ TERM IN THE INTERACTION HAMILTONIAN FOR TUNNELING BETWEEN EQUIVALENT GAUCHE CONFORMERS

PETER GRONER, *Department of Chemistry, University of Missouri - Kansas City, Kansas City, MO, USA.*

This study was triggered by the results of the microwave investigation of triflic acid (TA), $CF_3 - SO_2 - OH$, and its deuterated (TA-d) and ^{34}S (TA-S) isotopologues by Huff et al.[a] To fit the observed transitions split by gauche-gauche tunneling due to the CS-OH internal rotation, the interaction Hamiltonians for TA and TA-S required the term $F_{bc}(P_bP_c + P_cP_b)$. In contrast, the Coriolis term g_aP_a had to be used for TA-d.

The F_{bc} term results from two facts: 1) The moment of inertia tensor I and its inverse, the μ-tensor, of both the right- and left-handed forms of the gauche conformers need to be expressed in the same molecule-fixed axis system; 2) The Cartesian coordinates of some or all atoms and the components of I depend on the internal rotation coordinate τ. If we define a Cartesian axis system with two of the axes in the symmetry plane of the transition state between the two conformers, the third axis is perpendicular to it. When τ changes, the moving atoms will eventually cross the symmetry plane and their 3rd Cartesian coordinate will change its sign and with it also the signs of two off-diagonal components of I and the μ-tensors.

The rotational Hamiltonian in a 2-by-2 block format contains the contributions of the right and left gauche conformers (H_R and H_L, respectively) on the diagonal and the Coriolis interactions in the off-diagonal blocks. If the internal rotation wave functions ϕ_R and ϕ_L are symmetrized to $\phi_{A'}$ and $\phi_{A''}$ to conform with C_s symmetry, the diagonal blocks of the Hamiltonian become $H_{A'}$ and $H_{A''}$. The off-diagonal blocks contain now the Coriolis terms and the contributions from the sign-changing μ-tensor components.

Detailed explanations and a demonstration that this particular interaction may be especially important for $K_a = 1$ energy levels will be presented.

---

[a]A.K. Huff, N. Love, C.J. Smith, K.R. Leopold, (2022) submitted for publication.

TF02   8:48 – 9:03

A LOCAL MODE STUDY OF PSEUDOROTATIONAL EFFECTS IN THE INFRARED SPECTRA OF THE SCISSOR AND CH STRETCH VIBRATIONS OF CYCLOPENTANE

EDWIN SIBERT, *Department of Chemistry, University of Wisconsin–Madison, Madison, WI, USA*; PETER F. BERNATH, *Department of Chemistry and Biochemistry, Old Dominion University, Norfolk, VA, USA.*

We report and interpret recently recorded high resolution infrared spectra for the fundamentals of the CH_2 scissors and CH stretches at -50 ^oC of gas phase cyclopentane. We extend previous theoretical studies of this molecule, which is known to undergo barierless pseudorotation, by constructing local mode Hamiltonians of the stretching and scissor vibrations for which the frequencies, couplings, and linear dipoles are calculated as functions of the pseudorotation angle using B3LYP/6-311++(d,p) and MP2/cc-pvtz levels of theory. Symmetrization (D_{5h}) of the vibrational basis sets leads to simple vibration/pseudorotation Hamiltonians whose solutions lead to good agreement with experiment at medium resolution, but which miss interesting line fractionation when compared to the high resolution spectra. In contrast to the scissor motion, pseudorotation leads to significant state mixing of the CH stretches which themselves are Fermi coupled to the scissor overtones.

TF03 9:06 – 9:21

ROTATIONAL AND PHOTOELECTRON SPECTROSCOPIES MEET QUANTUM CHEMISTRY: N,N-DIETHYLHYDROXYLAMINE

GIOVANNA SALVITTI, ASSIMO MARIS, SONIA MELANDRI, LUCA EVANGELISTI, FABRIZIA NEGRI, *Dipartimento di Chimica G. Ciamician, Università di Bologna, Bologna, Italy*; MARCELLO CORENO, *LD2 Unit, c/o Basovizza Area Science Park, ISM-CNR, Trieste, Italy*; ALESSANDRA CIAVARDINI, *Laboratory of Quantum Optics, University of Nova Gorica, Nova Gorica, Slovenia*; HANAN SA'ADEH, *Department of Physics, University of Jordan, Amman, Jordan.*

We report a combination of quantum mechanical calculations and different spectroscopic techniques used to investigate in the gas phase N,N-diethylhydroxylamine (DEHA), an important scavenger compound. The molecule has been first studied by rotational spectroscopy using Pulsed Jet Fourier Transform Microwave (PJ-FTMW) spectrometer in the 6.5-18.5 GHz frequency range and Stark modulated Free Jet Absorption Millimeter-Wave (FJ-AMMW) spectrometer in the 59.6-74.4 GHz range. Three conformers have been overall observed. They are all characterized by the hydroxyl hydrogen atom being in trans isomerism with respect to the bisector of the CNC angle. For the global minimum, also the ^{13}C and ^{15}N isotopologues have been observed in natural abundance, allowing for a partial structure determination. Ultraviolet Photoelectron Spectroscopy (UPS) and X-ray Photoelectron spectroscopy (XPS) measurements have been performed at the Gas Phase Photoemission beamline (GasPhase) of the Elettra Synchroton light laboratory (Trieste, Italy). The core (C(1s), N(1s) and O(1s)) photoemission spectra have been assigned with the support of SAC-CI/cc-pVTZ calculations. Density Functional Theory (DFT) approaches, including Time-Dependent DFT, have been exploited to reproduce the outer valence electron binding energies and peaks profiles, through the calculation of the Huang-Rhys factors. Interestingly, the structure of the first ionized cation is not that of an amine but it is similar to an N-oxoammonium compound.

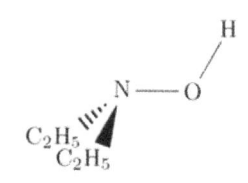

trans-DEHA

TF04 9:24 – 9:39

CONFORMATIONAL EQUILIBRIUM OF THE CHALCOGEN-BRIDGED COMPOUNDS ALLYL ETHYL ETHER AND ALLYL ETHYL SULFIDE REVEALED BY MICROWAVE SPECTROSCOPY AND COMPUTATIONAL CHEMISTRY

TAMANNA POONIA, JENNIFER VAN WIJNGAARDEN, *Department of Chemistry, University of Manitoba, Winnipeg, MB, Canada.*

The conformational landscapes of allyl ethyl ether (AEE) and allyl ethyl sulfide (AES) were investigated using Fourier transform microwave spectroscopy in the frequency range of 5-23 GHz aided by the density functional theory (DFT) B3LYP-D3(BJ)-aug-cc-pVTZ calculations. The quantum chemical calculations identified a rich conformational equilibrium with 14 stable conformers for AEE and 13 for AES within 14 kJ/mol. Experimentally, rotational transitions corresponding to three low energy conformers of AEE and two forms of AES were assigned. Interconversion pathways were modelled to understand the relaxation of the higher energy conformers to the more stable forms in the supersonic jet expansion and to explain the observed tunneling splitting in one conformer of AEE. To better understand the stereoelectronic effects and topology of the interactions governing the conformational preferences of AEE and AES, natural bond orbital (NBO) and non-covalent interaction (NCI) analyses were performed. For the lowest energy conformers of AEE and AES, ground state effective (r_0) and substitution (r_s) structures were derived using the spectral data collected for the ^{13}C and ^{34}S isotopologues in natural abundance. The results confirm the theoretical predictions that the lowest energy geometries are surprisingly different depending on the identity of the bridging chalcogen atom.

TF05 9:42 – 9:57

MILLIMETER-WAVE SPECTRUM OF THE LOWEST ENERGY, VIBRATIONALLY EXCITED COUPLED DYAD OF S-TRANS-Z-1-CYANO-1,3-BUTADIENE

P. MATISHA DORMAN, BRIAN J. ESSELMAN, ROBERT J. McMAHON, R. CLAUDE WOODS, *Department of Chemistry, University of Wisconsin-Madison, Madison, WI, USA.*

Recently, the ground state spectroscopic constants of three cyanobutadiene isomers (C_5H_5N) were reported as plausible targets for detection in the interstellar medium.[1] Many hundreds of transitions were collected in the 130 – 375 GHz range for each isomer, but s-trans-Z-1-cyano-1,3-butadiene is the only isomer with an isolated ground state. s-trans-Z-1-Cyano-1,3-butadiene (μ_a = 3.6 D, μ_b = 2.3 D, MP2/6-311+G(2d,p)) is a prolate (κ = -0.91), asymmetric top with C_s symmetry, and its ground state was fit to a partial octic, distorted rotor Hamiltonian model with over 5500 distinct transitions. The lowest-energy vibrationally excited state (ν_{19}, B_1) is predicted to be 129 cm^{-1} higher in energy than the ground state and is close in energy to the second-lowest energy vibrationally excited state (ν_{27}, B_2, 135 cm^{-1}, MP2/6-311+G(2d,p)). These states form a Coriolis coupled dyad with intense coupling along the *a*- and *b*- principal axes causing the formation of sharp local resonances hundreds of MHz away from their unperturbed predicted frequencies. This presentation will detail the effects of strong Coriolis coupling in a dyad of vibrational states < 6 cm^{-1} apart and the strategies used to assign and least-squares fit these transitions.

1. Zdanovskaia, M. A.; Dorman, P. M.; Orr, V. L.; Owen, A. N.; Kougias, S. M.; Esselman, B. J.; Woods, R. C.; McMahon, R. J. Rotational Spectra of Three Cyanobutadiene Isomers (C_5H_5N) of Relevance to Astrochemistry and Other Harsh Reaction Environments. *J. Am Chem. Soc.* **2021**, *143*, 9551-9564.

TF06 10:00 – 10:15

THE ROTATIONAL SPECTRA OF 2-CYANOPYRIMIDINE ($C_5H_3N_3$) AND 2-CYANOPYRAZINE ($C_5H_3N_3$): VIBRATIONAL GROUND STATES AND DYAD OF LOWEST-ENERGY VIBRATIONALLY EXCITED STATES

HOUSTON H. SMITH, BRIAN J. ESSELMAN, MARIA ZDANOVSKAIA, R. CLAUDE WOODS, ROBERT J. McMAHON, *Department of Chemistry, University of Wisconsin-Madison, Madison, WI, USA.*

2-Cyanopyrimidine and 2-cyanopyrazine are heterocyclic analogs of the known interstellar molecule benzonitrile. They are attractive molecules for interstellar detection *via* radioastronomy because they have substantial dipole moments (μ_a = 6.47 D and μ_a = 4.22 D, respectively) and could serve as tracer molecules for both pyrimidine and pyrazine. In the present work, we analyzed and assigned the rotational spectra of 2-cyanopyrimidine ($C_5H_3N_3$) and 2-cyanopyrazine ($C_5H_3N_3$) for the first time. From 130 – 500 GHz, the vibrational ground state transitions of each molecule have been least-squares fit to partial octic, distorted-rotor Hamiltonian with each fit containing several thousand transitions. The resulting spectroscopic constants are sufficient for radioastronomical searches for these molecules. Further similar to benzonitrile, the two lowest-energy vibrationally excited states form Coriolis coupled dyads for both 2-cyanopyrimidine and 2-cyanopyrazine. Several thousand transitions of each vibrationally excited state have been assigned and analyzed with a partial octic, distorted-rotor Hamiltonian with a- and/or b-axis Coriolis coupling. The complete analysis of these states is expected to yield a highly precise energy separation between these vibrationally excited states and allow for an interesting comparison to the analogous dyads of benzonitrile and the cyanopyridines.

Intermission

TF07 10:57 – 11:12

HYDROXYL GROUPS TORSIONAL MOTION IN CATECHOL MOLECULE.

<u>DARYA KISURYNA</u>, *Physics, University of Maryland, College Park, MD, USA*; ALEX MALEVICH, ARYNA KHRAPUNOVA, *Physics, Belarusian State University, Minsk, Belarus*; ULADZIMIR SAPESHKA, *Department of Physics, University of Illinois at Chicago, Chicago, IL, USA*; GEORGE PITSEVICH, *Physics, Belarusian State University, Minsk, Belarus*.

Catechol molecule $C_6H_4(OH)_2$ is the representative of a separate class of aromatic hydrocarbons. It is an important component of biochemical, industrial and commercial products. In a recently published article [1] rotationally resolved Fourier Transform far-infrared spectrum of the free and bonded $O-H$ groups forming the intramolecular hydrogen bond was recorded. The authors were also able to measure pure rotational spectrum in the 70–220 GHz frequency range using a millimeter–wave spectrometer. Splitting due to tunneling was resolved for free $O-H$ torsional state. Having this solid experimental background, we have performed extensive calculations of the kinetic parameters and 2D potential energy surfaces formed by variation of the $O-H$ torsional coordinates of the catechol molecule at few levels of theory. It was found that almost all used levels of theory very well predict the frequency value of the fundamental torsional vibration of the free hydroxyl group: 224–227 cm^{-1}, while experimental value is 221.9 cm^{-1}. At the same time calculated frequencies of the H–bonded hydroxyl group torsional fundamental vibration is higher (422–425 cm^{-1}) than experimental one (415 cm^{-1}). We associate this difference with overestimating intramolecular H–bond energy in the frame of used levels of theory. It is also worth noting that there was a good agreement between calculated and experimental tunneling splitting of the first excited torsional state of free $O-H$ group (3.6×10^{-6} and 1×10^{-5} respectively). Besides, complete information about the second conformer of the catechol molecule with C_{2V} symmetry has been obtained.

[1] J. Bruckhuisen and etc, Molecules 26 (2021) 3645

TF08 11:15 – 11:30

ORIGINS OF THE INTENSITY OF THE STRETCH-BEND COMBINATION TRANSITION IN WATER CLUSTERS AND IMPLICATIONS FOR CHARACTERIZING HYDROGEN BONDING

<u>RACHEL M. HUCHMALA</u>, ANNE B McCOY, *Department of Chemistry, University of Washington, Seattle, WA, USA*.

Water and hydrogen bonding have been actively studied for many years. The unique features of hydrogen bonding lead to processes such as proton transport which is essential to a variety of chemical, biochemical, and electrochemical processes. Despite the long-standing interest, many questions still remain surrounding the intricacies of hydrogen bonding. One goal of this study is to understand how the strength and other properties of hydrogen bonding can be extracted from the spectral signatures near 5000 cm^{-1}, which corresponds to combination transitions involving the HOH bend and the OH stretch. This region is of interest because, like the bend region, the intensities are relatively insensitive to the hydrogen bonding environment. At the same time, unlike the bend fundamental region, the frequencies of the transitions reflect the hydrogen bond strength as they follow the trends for the ν=1 levels of the OH stretches. This makes interpretation easier and introduces an interesting question, what are the origins of the intensities of the bend and the combination transitions? In order to investigate this question, we use various structures of water clusters, and dissect the intensity of the combination transition into mechanical and electrical contributions. Through this process, we are able to gain insights into the origin of the intensities. Further for the electrical contributions, we explore how the bending vibration is tuning the transition moment for the OH stretch.

TF09 11:33 – 11:48

SPECTROSCOPY AND BRAIN CHEMISTRY Of SEROTONIN AND DOPAMINE CONFORMERS

VIPIN BAHADUR SINGH, *Department of Physics, Udai Pratap Autonomous College, Varanasi, India.*

The neurotransmitters Serotonin and Dopamine are thought to play a distinct role in brain chemistry and human behavior. In the Present work we will discuss the Conformer specific spectroscopic signatures of protonated Serotonin and Dopamine in the gas phase and aqueous media. A comparison of the computed frequencies of protonated Dopamine with the observed Raman spectrum indicates that gauche and trans conformers coexist in the liquid dopamine and exhibit population redistribution upon a change in pH during stress. Since the trans-conformers have more affinity for the receptor site than the gauche conformers, the higher population distribution of trans conformers is hypothesized to be associated with efficient neurotransmission and normal human behavior. The strong cation-pi interaction in the isolated gauche conformers of serotonin in the gas phase is predicted to be a possible cause of human aggression. 1. Vipin Bahadur Singh, ACS Chem Neuroscience, 12,613-625 (2021)

TF10 11:51 – 12:06

TORSIONAL POTENTIALS, BARRIER TO INTERNAL ROTATION, MOLECULAR STRUCTURE, VIBRATIONAL PROPERTIES, NLO BEHAVIOUR AND NBO CHARACTERISTICS OF 2-(PHENYLSULFONYL)VINYLBENZENE AND 2-(TOSYL)VINYLBENZENE EMPLOYING FT-IR, FT RAMAN SPECTRAL TECHNIQUES AND DFT APPROACH

K SRISHAILAM, *PHYSICS, SR UNIVERSITY, HANAMKONDA, TELANGANA, INDIA*; BALAKRISHNA AEGURLA, *Department of Chemistry, Indian Institute of Technology , Roorkee, Uttarakhand, India*; BYRU VENKATRAM REDDY, G. RAMANA RAO, *Department of Physics, KAKATIYA UNIVERSITY, WARANGAL, India.*

2-(Phenylsulfonyl)vinylbenzene (2PVB) and 2-(Tosyl)vinylbenzene(2TVB) molecules were characterized, by recording their FT-IR(4000-400 cm^{-1}) and FT Raman(4000-50 cm^{-1}) spectra. Torsional potentials, barrier to internal rotation around phenyl-sulfonyl C-S bond, sulfonyl-vinyl S-C bond, vinyl-benzene C-C bond, and phenyl-methyl C-C bond (this bond is relevant for 2TVB only). Optimized structure parameters, general valence force field, harmonic vibrational fundamentals, potential energy distribution, infrared and Raman intensities, frontier molecular orbital parameters, NLO behaviour and NBO characteristics were determined using density functional theory, employing B3LYP exchange-correlation in conjunction with functional 6-311++G(d,p) basis set. Time dependent DFT was made use of to compute absorption maxima (λmax) and oscillator strengths, for both molecules, in their electronic transitions, in DMSO-d6 solution. Good agreement was found, between measured and computed parameters involving structure parameters, IR and Raman spectra and UV-Vis transitions. The rms error between experimental and theoretical vibrational frequencies was 6.4 and 4.35 cm^{-1}), for 2PVB and 2TVB, respectively. With the help of PED and eigenvectors, all vibrational fundamentals of both the molecules were assigned for the first time. The computations demonstrated that both the molecules were good for NLO applications, that was substantiated by NBO analysis for both 2PVB and 2TVB.

TF11   **12:09 – 12:24**

THEORETICAL AND EXPERIMENTAL ROTATIONAL SPECTROSCOPIC STUDIES OF SUBSTITUTED BENZOIC ACID HETERODIMERS

<u>MOHAMAD H. AL-JABIRI</u>, *Department of Chemistry, University of Alberta, Edmonton, AB, Canada*; MIHAEL ERAKOVIĆ, *Department of Physical Chemistry, Ruder Boskovic, Zagreb, Croatia*; ARAN INSAUSTI, *Departamento de Química Física, Universidad del País Vasco (UPV-EHU), Bilbao, Spain*; MARKO CVITAŠ, *Department of Physical Chemistry, Ruder Boskovic, Zagreb, Croatia*; WOLFGANG JÄGER, *Department of Chemistry, University of Alberta, Edmonton, AB, Canada.*

The complex tunnelling dynamics of double proton transfer in carboxylic acid dimers has been the focus of many theoretical and experimental studies.[1,2] Here we combine spectroscopic and computational approaches to model and understand how functional groups in substituted benzoic acid heterodimers can influence these dynamics. Dimers of benzoic acid with its 4-chloro-, 4-nitro-, and 4-amino-analogues were studied using a 2 to 6 GHz chirped-pulse Fourier transform microwave spectrometer, which is based on the design by Pates et al.,[3] to obtain experimental tunneling line splittings. Jacobi field instanton theory (JFI)[4,5] was used to compute tunneling splittings in the ground vibrational state. The use of the JFI method, which necessitates a smaller number of potential energy and gradient calculations compared to other methods, enabled us to use ab initio on-the-fly potentials and compute the splitting in full dimensionality, in spite of the large system sizes. Furthermore, final expressions for the tunneling splittings provided a way to examine the influence of substituents on both the potential energy barrier height and shape, and on the vibrational modes, which can either promote or inhibit tunnelling.

(1) Evangelisti, L.; Écija, P.; Cocinero, E. J.; Castaño, F.; Lesarri, A.; Caminati, W.; Meyer, R. J. Phys. Chem. Lett. 2012, 3 (24), 3770–3775. (2) Tautermann, C. S.; Voegele, A. F.; Liedl, K. R. J. Chem. Phys. 2004, 120 (2), 631–637. (3) Pérez, C.; Lobsiger, S.; Seifert, N. A.; Zaleski, D. P.; Temelso, B.; Shields, G. C.; Kisiel, Z.; Pate, B. H. Chem. Phys. Lett. 2013, 571, 1–15. (4) Eraković, M.; Vaillant, C. L.; Cvitaš, M. T. J. Chem. Phys. 2020, 152 (8), 084111. (5) Mil'nikov, G. V.; Nakamura, H. J. Chem. Phys. 2001, 115 (15), 6881–6897.

TG. Vibrational structure/frequencies
Tuesday, June 21, 2022 – 8:30 AM
Room: 274 Medical Sciences Building

Chair: Stephen J. Daunt, University of Tennessee, Knoxville, TN, USA

TG01   8:30 – 8:45

IS IT POSSIBLE TO IMPROVE THEORETICAL PREDICTION OF THE FREQUENCIES OF THE TORSIONAL VIBRATIONS BY ACCOUNTING ZPVE? TESTING MOST SIMPLE MOLECULES

GEORGE PITSEVICH, ALEX MALEVICH, ARYNA KHRAPUNOVA, *Physics, Belarusian State University, Minsk, Belarus*; ULADZIMIR SAPESHKA, *Department of Physics, University of Illinois at Chicago, Chicago, IL, USA*; DARYA KISURYNA, *Physics, University of Maryland, College Park, MD, USA.*

Torsional vibrations and internal rotation are the one kind of large amplitude motion in polyatomic molecules and clusters. It is well known that the standard approach within the frame of harmonic approximation to calculating the frequencies of torsional vibrations is unworkable. In this case, one must calculate full potential energy surface (PES) while varying torsional coordinates throughout all intervals of their determination. Recently, when calculating PES, some authors took into account zero-point vibrational energy (ZPVE). Sometimes it leads to an improvement in the agreement between calculated and experimental data, and sometimes it rather worsens the agreement between them [1,2]. To obtain more complete information on the efficiency of taking into account ZPVE, we have made a calculation of energy of stationary torsional states for hydrogen peroxide and methyl alcohol molecules with and without taking into account ZPVE. It is well known that there is much more experimental data about the energy of excited torsional states for these molecules than for any others. The calculations were performed on several levels of theory.

[1] S. Dalbouha, M.L. Senent, N. Komiha J.Chem.Phys., 142(7) 2015 074304.
[2] G.A. Pitsevich, A.E. Malevich, U.V. Lazicki, U.U. Sapeshka Journal of the Belarusian State University. Physics. 2 2021 15.

TG02   8:48 – 9:03

FIRST HIGH-RESOLUTION STUDY OF VIBRATIONALLY EXCITED STATES ν_{17} AND ν_{12} OF PROPYLENE OXIDE

KAREL VÁVRA, EILEEN DÖRING, JAN JAKOB, GUIDO W. FUCHS, PASCAL STAHL, ARNE VEREIJKEN, MARCEL SCHLESAG, THOMAS GIESEN, *Institute of Physics, University of Kassel, Kassel, Germany.*

Propylene oxide, $CH_3C_2H_3O$, is a stable chiral molecule that gained new attention through its recent radio astronomical discovery in the interstellar medium toward the galactic center[a]. Subsequently, extensive laboratory data on rotational transitions in the ground state and in the lowest vibrationally excited ν_{24} torsion state were published[b,c]. Previously, only the 3 μm spectral range of the four C-H stretching vibration modes was measured with high spectral resolution at mid-infrared wavelength[d].

In the present study we used two quantum cascade laser spectrometers at 8 and 10 μm to record ro-vibrational spectra of the ν_{17} fundamental mode (CH_2 rock) at 1023 cm^{-1} and the ν_{12} ring breathing mode at 1266 cm^{-1}. The spectra were measured in a static cell at room temperature and in a supersonic jet expansion at low temperatures. The room temperature measurement allowed a quick assignment via graphical techniques (Loomis-Wood diagram) and determination of the molecular parameters using the SPFIT/SPCAT program package[e]. In the supersonic jet spectrum line splittings could be observed for certain transitions. The combination of measurements at low temperature (30K) and at room temperature conditions led to an assignment of hundreds of transitions of the very dense infrared spectrum and covers quantum numbers from lowest J and K up to $J = 55$ and $K_a = 36$.

---

[a] B.A. McGuire, P.B. Carroll, R.A. Loomis, I.A. Finneran, P.R. Jewell, A.J. Remijan, G., A. Blake, Science **352**, 1449–1452 (2016)
[b] A.J. Mesko, L. Zou, P.B. Carroll, S.L. Widicus Weaver, J. Mol. Spectrosc. **335**, 49–53 (2017)
[c] P. Stahl, B. E. Arenas, O. Zingsheim, M. Schnell, L. Margulès, R. A. Motiyenko, G. W. Fuchs, T. F. Giesen, J. Mol. Spectrosc. **378**, 111445 (2021)
[d] F.X. Sunahori, Z. Su, C. Kang, Y. Xu. Chem. Phys. Lett. **494**, 14-20 (2010)
[e] H.M. Pickett, J. Mol. Spectrosc. **148**, 371–377 (1991)

TG03

CHARACTERIZATION OF 4-PYRONE PYROLYSIS PRODUCTS VIA MATRIX-ISOLATION FT-IR

KHALED ALEY EL-SHAZLY, HEATHER LEGG, KATHRYN NARKIN, ELIZABETH RENEE SPARKS, LAURA R. McCUNN, *Department of Chemistry, Marshall University, Huntington, WV, USA.*

The characterization of the byproducts of biomass pyrolysis is an integral part in the development of viable biofuels and renewable energy sources. 4-Pyrone, (IUPAC name: 4-pyran-1-one) is one of the byproducts observed in the pyrolysis of many forms of biomass, such as wood chips, straw, and cotton husks. Using the technique of argon matrix-isolation FT-IR spectroscopy, the pyrolysis products of 4-pyrone were characterized by passing a diluted sample of 4-pyrone through a heated silicon carbide tube onto a cold window that captures the products and allows for their analysis via FT-IR spectroscopy. Computational analysis using Gaussian 09 was also utilized to model the unimolecular decomposition pathways, and these results were compared to the experimental spectra for product identification. Current data collected at pyrolysis temperatures ranging between 900 K and 1400 K indicate the formation of acetylene, vinylacetylene, propyne, and carbon monoxide. The formation of formylketene is also likely, as some peaks have been observed that match computational predictions.

TG04

WEAKLY-BOUND COMPLEX FORMATION BETWEEN HCN AND CH$_3$Cl: A MATRIX-ISOLATION AND COMPUTATIONAL STUDY

EMILY K HOCKEY, *Department of Chemistry and Biochemistry, University of Maryland, College Park, College Park, MD, USA*; KORINA VLAHOS, *Chemistry and Biochemistry, University of Maryland, College Park, College Park, MD, USA*; THOMAS HOWARD, JESSICA PALKO, LEAH G DODSON, *Department of Chemistry and Biochemistry, University of Maryland, College Park, MD, USA.*

Matrix-isolation spectroscopy is used to characterize the weakly-bound complex(es) of hydrogen cyanide with methyl chloride, two astrophysically relevant molecules. HCN and its polymers captivate interstellar discussions of prebiotic monomers and other life-bearing polymers, while CH$_3$Cl leads as the first organohalogen detected in space. This highlights the importance of studying their reactivity. In this talk, we will describe our new matrix-isolation instrument, constructed at the University of Maryland, and how we identify the structure of the weakly-bound complexes [(HCN)$_n$CH$_3$Cl] that form upon co-condensation of HCN and CH$_3$Cl in an argon matrix. Infrared spectroscopy is used in tandem with quantum chemistry calculations to characterize the vibrational spectrum of the resulting complexes. Our work reveals preferential formation of matrix-isolated HCN trimer species in the presence of CH$_3$Cl, qualitatively characterized by non-covalent interactions though natural bond orbital calculations. Finally, we will discuss the astrochemical implications of the resulting complexes and HCN trimer formation.

TG05

GAS-PHASE CH-OVERTONE BAND SPECTRA OF METHYL ACETATE AND ETHYL ACETATE VIA INCOHERENT BROAD-BAND CAVITY-ENHANCED ABSORPTION SPECTROSCOPY

TAKERU SATO, MITSUNORI ARAKI, TAKAHIRO OYAMA, SHOMA HOSHINO, KOICHI TSUKIYAMA, *Faculty of Science Division I, Tokyo University of Science, Shinjuku-ku, Tokyo, Japan.*

Gas-phase CH-stretching overtone bands of the two volatile organic compounds methyl acetate and ethyl acetate were detected for up to v = 6–0 by incoherent broad-band cavity-enhanced absorption spectroscopy. To obtain high sensitivity, short-pass and long-pass filters were used to cut background light out of a high reflection range of the dielectric multilayer mirrors consisting of the cavity. Hence, the signal-to-noise ratios of v = 4–0 were achieved to be 40–50 by the 100s integration time, suggesting an application possibility of this spectroscopic technique for environmental monitoring. Profiles of the observed overtone bands were analyzed in detail with the aid of theoretical calculations and their prominent peaks were assigned to the progressions starting from the bundles of the symmetric CH-stretching bands starting at 2964 cm^{-1}. Based on the local-mode analysis, the harmonic frequencies and the anharmonicities were determined and the dissociation energies were derived.

TG06 10:00 – 10:15

SUPERSONIC JET CAVITY RING DOWN SPECTROSCOPY OF MOLECULES IN THE MID INFRARED

FABIAN PETERß, GUIDO W. FUCHS, *Institute of Physics, University of Kassel, Kassel, Germany.*

Many molecular compounds of spectroscopic interest are difficult to produce or can only be produced *in situ* with low production rates, e.g., transient species. One way to produce such species is to use a discharge nozzle in combination with a supersonic jet expansion. The hereby rotationally cooled spectra increase the line intensity at low rotational quantum numbers and ease the detection of absorption features. Nevertheless, the detection of rare species remains difficult and requires an extremely sensitive detection scheme. The Cavity Ringdown (CRD) technique with its high sensitivity is ideally suited to address this kind of problem. In addition, CRD spectroscopy can also be used to detect very weak molecular rovibrational transitions of otherwise well-known stable molecules.

While CRD spectroscopy of supersonic jets is no new idea, the application to wavelengths in the mid-IR (2.5μm - 4.5μm), where -O-H, -N-H and $\equiv$ C-H stretching vibrations can be investigated, only got possible in recent times with the availability of suitable laser sources and highly reflective dielectric mirrors for this wavelength region.

Here, we report about our progress in building up a CRD spectrometer operating in the mid infrared range utilizing a tunable cw-OPO laser system with high-quality cavity mirrors (R>99.99%) between 3μm - 3.4μm. First spectroscopic results will be presented.

Intermission

TG07 10:57 – 11:12

UNRAVELING HYDROGEN-BONDING INTERACTION, FERMI RESONANCES AND SOFT-MODE COUPLING IN PHENOL-BENZIMIDAZOLE PROTON-COUPLED ELECTRON TRANSFER MODEL COMPLEXES WITH CRYOGENIC ION VIBRATIONAL SPECTROSCOPY

LIANGYI CHEN, JOSEPH FOURNIER, *Department of Chemistry, Washington University, St. Louis, MO, USA.*

Proton-coupled electron transfer (PCET) has been of great interest in chemical and biochemical catalysis. The electron transfer process in numerous biomimetic systems has been investigated in solution, but direct interrogation of the proton transfer coordinate remains largely unexplored. We have measured cryogenic ion vibrational spectra of a series of phenol-benzimidazole PCET model compounds to explore the nature of the strong OH—N H-bond in the ground electronic state. Highly redshifted and broadened H-bonded OH stretch transitions were observed throughout the model series. Isotopic substitution and anharmonic vibrational calculations suggest that the breadth arises from an interplay between strong OH stretch-bend Fermi resonance interactions and coupling of the OH stretch to low frequency H-bond soft-mode motions accessible at the zero-point level. The effects of steric hindrance, resonance stabilization and charge distribution are also investigated through systematic structural variation of the model compounds.

TG08 11:15 – 11:30

STRUCTURAL DEFORMATION OF 4-BENZOYLBENZOATE UPON COMPLEXATION WITH METAL IONS AND SOLVENT UTILIZING MASS-SELECTED CRYOGENIC IR

ANNA GABRIELLA DEL ROSARIO RULLÁN BUXÓ, EVAN H PEREZ, JOSEPH P. MESSINGER, SEAN COLEMAN EDINGTON, FABIAN MENGES, MARK JOHNSON, *Department of Chemistry, Yale University, New Haven, CT, USA.*

4-benzoylbenzoate (4BBA$^-$, $C_{14}H_9O_3$) serves as a model system for the marine organic material in sea-spray aerosols (SSAs), which are highly heterogeneous and complex. SSAs are primarily composed of salt water, which affects the behavior of the marine organic material contained within it. Here, we investigate how addition of metal ions and solvent (H$_2$O, CH$_3$CN) modify the structure of 4BBA$^-$ by use of cryogenic ion vibrational predissociation spectroscopy. Upon addition of Ca^{2+} to 4BBA$^-$, we observe the collapse of the asymmetric and symmetric CO$_2$ stretching modes due to the bidentate complexation of Ca^{2+} to the carboxylate head group. Upon addition of high dielectric solvent (H$_2$O or CH$_3$CN) the vibrational modes are seen to slowly relax towards the vibrational modes of 4BBA$^-$. This behavior is explained by electronic structure calculations, showing that the skeletal structure of 4BBA$^-$ relaxes towards its original structure with increasing solvation.

TG09   11:33–11:48

CRYOGENIC IR SPECTROSCOPY OF CARBANION INTERMEDIATES: CIRCUMAMBULATORY REARRANGEMENT FOLLOWING DECARBOXYLATION OF BENZOIC ACID DERIVATIVES

<u>OLIVIA MOSS</u>, JOSEPH P. MESSINGER, EVAN H PEREZ, ANNA GABRIELLA DEL ROSARIO RULLÁN BUXÓ, TIM SCHLEIF, *Department of Chemistry, Yale University, New Haven, CT, USA*; KIM GREIS, *Department of Molecular Physics, Fritz-Haber-Institut der Max-Planck-Gesellschaft, Berlin, Germany*; MARK JOHNSON, *Department of Chemistry, Yale University, New Haven, CT, USA*.

Collision induced dissociation (CID) of benzoates, the conjugate bases of benzoic acids, tend to form highly reactive carbanion intermediates. This study specifically investigates a series of formylbenzoic acid (FBA) isomers and their respective decarboxylated phenides. Cryogenic ion vibrational predissociation spectroscopy (1000 cm^{-1}- 4200 cm^{-1}) reveals the spectroscopic signatures of the 2, 3, and 4-FBA anions as well as those of the decarboxylates resulting from heterolytic C-C bond cleavage. Comparison of quantum chemical calculations with the isomer selective two color IR-IR photobleaching experiments confirms that the phenides isomerize after ddecarboxylation such that the anionic charge center migrates around the ring from its initial location corresponding to the carboxylate position. The propensity for site-to-site interconversions are observed to strongly depend on the starting location of the anionic charge center. These trends are considered in the context of the calculated barriers for charge migration by H-atom transfers and the initial energy content of the nascent species created by CID.

TG10   11:51–12:06

PROTON, HYDRIDE, OR NEITHER? THE IDENTITY OF H IN THE Au$_9$(PPh$_3$)$_8$H^{2+} CLUSTER

<u>HANNA MORALES HERNANDEZ</u>, JONATHAN WOOD FAGAN, CHRISTOPHER J. JOHNSON, *Chemistry, Stony Brook University, Stony Brook, NY, USA*.

The diverse tunability of gold nanoclusters via size, geometry, and ligand chemistry allows them to be optimized for greater catalytic activity, selectivity, and optoelectronic properties. The binding of a hydride to Au$_9$(PPh$_3$)$_8^{3+}$ to form Au$_9$(PPh$_3$)$_8$H^{2+} has raised the question of whether the hydride behaves as a metal dopant which donates its two electrons to the Au core or whether it behaves as an electron-withdrawing ligand such as Cl$^-$ and Br$^-$. We previously showed significant similarities between its electronic absorption spectrum to that of Au$_9$(PPh$_3$)$_8$Cl^{2+} and Au$_9$(PPh$_3$)$_8$Br^{2+}, but follow-up theoretical work suggested that this was a coincidence. Here we analyze the infrared absorption spectra of Au$_9$(PPh$_3$)$_8$H^{2+} with a single N$_2$ or H$_2$O molecule physiosorbed onto the cluster to further elucidate the role of the hydride in Au$_9$(PPh$_3$)$_8$H^{2+}.

TG11   12:09–12:24

INFRARED SPECTROSCOPY OF CARBOCATIONS UPON ELECTRON IONIZATION OF ETHYLENE IN HELIUM NANODROPLETS

SWETHA ERUKALA, ALEXANDRA J FEINBERG, <u>AMANDEEP SINGH</u>, ANDREY VILESOV[a], *Department of Chemistry, University of Southern California, Los Angeles, CA, USA*.

The electron impact ionization of helium droplets doped with ethylene molecules and clusters yields diverse C$_X$H$_Y^+$ cations embedded in the droplets. The ionization primarily produces C$_2$H$_2^+$, C$_2$H$_3^+$, C$_2$H$_4^+$, and CH$_2^+$, whereas larger carbocations are produced upon the reactions of the primary ions with ethylene molecules. The vibrational excitation of the cations leads to the release of bare cations and cations with a few helium atoms attached. The laser excitation spectra of the embedded cations show well resolved vibrational bands with a few wavenumber widths—an order of magnitude less than those previously obtained in solid matrices or molecular beams by tagging techniques. Comparison with the previous studies of free and tagged CH$_2^+$, CH$_3^+$, C$_2$H$_2^+$, C$_2$H$_3^+$, and C$_2$H$_4^+$ cations shows that the helium matrix typically introduces a shift in the vibrational frequencies of less than about 20 cm-1, enabling direct comparisons with the results of quantum chemical calculations for structure determination. This work demonstrates a facile technique for the production and spectroscopic study of diverse carbocations, which act as important intermediates in gas and condensed phases.

---

[a]Corresponding author

TH. Mini-symposium: Spectroscopy meets Chemical Dynamics
Tuesday, June 21, 2022 – 1:30 PM
Room: 100 Noyes Laboratory

Chair: Bryan Changala, Ctr for Astrophysics/Harvard & Smithsonian, Cambridge, MA, USA

TH01 *INVITED TALK* 1:30 – 2:00

ULTRAFAST SPECTROSCOPY WITH FREQUENCY COMBS: ENABLING NEW MEASUREMENTS OF DILUTE SPECIES IN MOLECULAR BEAMS

NICHOLAS D. COOPER, WALKER M. JONES, TODD ELIASON, MELANIE A.R. REBER, *Department of Chemistry, University of Georgia, Athens, GA, USA.*

Initially developed as a tool for metrology, frequency combs are most often used for precision, frequency-resolved spectroscopy. The utility of frequency combs in ultrafast spectroscopy is just beginning to be explored. By exploiting the properties of frequency combs, we are improving the sensitivity, spectral resolution, and detection of ultrafast spectroscopies. The first technique discussed will be cavity-enhanced transient absorption spectroscopy, which uses fiber-laser frequency combs coupled to external enhancement cavities to increase the sensitivity of ultrafast transient absorption spectroscopy. A home-built Ytterbium fiber-laser frequency comb and amplifier system provide a stable source of ultrafast pulses. External enhancement cavities increase both the laser power and effective absorption path length, thus improving the signal by several orders of magnitude over traditional transient absorption spectroscopy. Altogether the sensitivity is more than four orders-of-magnitude better than the previous best transient absorption techniques, which allows for the study dilute samples in molecular beams on the femtosecond timescale with transient absorption spectroscopy. The second technique discussed will be the application of cavity-enhancement and frequency-comb techniques, including dual-comb spectroscopy, to two-dimensional spectroscopy. Initial results and current progress towards ultrafast two-dimensional spectroscopy of dilute species in molecular beams will be presented.

TH02 2:06 – 2:21

REAL-TIME TRACKING OF COHERENT VIBRATIONAL MOTION IN GROUND AND EXCITED ELECTRONIC STATES

SHAINA DHAMIJA, GARIMA BHUTANI, *Department of Chemical Sciences, Indian Institute of Science Education & Research, Mohali, Punjab, India*; AJAY JAYACHANDRAN, *Institut für Physikalische und Theoretische Chemie, Ludwig-Maximilians Universität Würzburg, Würzburg, Germany*; ARIJIT K DE, *Department of Chemical Sciences, Indian Institute of Science Education & Research, Mohali, Punjab, India.*

Molecular vibrations, involving both ground and excited electronic states, are at the heart of chemical transformations which necessitates understanding the origin of these vibrations. Femtosecond infrared spectroscopy and frequency- domain coherent Raman spectroscopy successfully captured full vibrational spectra but bear a few limitations like interfering lineshapes, background signals, etc. Time-domain measurement, i.e. impulsive stimulated Raman scattering employs a short Raman pump pulse, creating a nuclear wavepacket which evolves as a function of time and is interrogated using a probe pulse and Fourier transform of the temporal interferogram yields the Raman spectrum whereas the scattering background can be easily removed as a zero frequency component. However, separation of vibrational coherences in ground and excited electronic states even for small chromophores in condensed phase still remains challenging. Recently, we showed how 'spectrally dispersed' impulsive stimulated Raman spectroscopy can be employed to track time evolution of vibrational coherences in ground as well as excited states, distinctly, under non-resonant/resonant impulsive excitation [1-4]. More specifically, separation of excited-state, ground-state and solvent coherences for diatomic as well as polyatomic molecules in solution is demonstrated, which I will discuss in this presentation. The origin of spectral patterns corresponding to certain vibrational modes of the solute as well as the solvent will be presented. In addition to this, density functional theory is employed to identify the Raman active modes, which nicely correlates with the experimental observations. Details of this method as an emerging technique will be discussed.

References: [1] S. Dhamija, G. Bhutani, and A. K. De, Asian Journal of Physics, 255-260, 29 (3 and 4), 2020. [2] S. Dhamija, G. Bhutani, and A. K. De, Frontiers in Optics + Laser Science 2021, paper JW7A.70, 2021. [3] S. Dhamija, G. Bhutani, A. Jayachandran, and A. K. De, The Journal of Physical Chemistry A, 1019-1032, 126(7), 2022. [4] S. Dhamija, G. Bhutani, and A. K. De, Chemical Physics Letters, Under review (Manuscript ID: CPLETT-22-308).

TH03   2:24 – 2:39

PHOTOPHYSICS OF Ni^{II} PYRIDINOPHANE PHOTOCATALYSTS USED FOR C-O CROSS-COUPLING REACTIONS PROBED VIA FEMTOSECOND OPTICAL ABSORPTION SPECTROSOCPY

<u>RACHEL WALLICK</u>, JOSH VURA-WEIS, *Department of Chemistry, University of Illinois at Urbana-Champaign, Urbana, IL, USA*; RENSKE VAN DER VEEN, *Photovoltaics, Helmholtz Zentrum Berlin, Berlin, Germany*.

Ni catalysis has garnered much attention over the past decades as a low-cost, abundant alternative to Pd catalysis. Ni$^{I/III}$ cycles are thought to be critically important to the cross-coupling step in the catalytic cycle, but typical Ni catalysts contain bipyridine ligands which are generally unable to stabilize high-valent Ni^{III}. Tridentate pyridinophane ligands, on the other hand, are able to stabilize both high- and low-valent Ni, making them optimal ligands to use in Ni catalysis. Tridentate pyridinophane Ni^{II} dichloride complexes form a highly reactive Ni^{I} catalyst upon photoexcitation of the metal-to-ligand charge transfer (MLCT) band. This process is thought to occur from the ^{3}d-d charge transfer state, though there is no experimental evidence for this and little is known about the photophysics following photoexcitation of the MLCT transition. Optical transient absorption gives insight into the photophysics of the catalyst formation. We report highly-efficient back electron transfer (BET) following MLCT excitation. We will vary the excitation energy to investigate if the BET is suppressed or enhanced. We will perform transient XUV spectroscopy to probe the dynamics at the Ni M-edge and determine the states that are involved in the Ni^{I} catalyst formation.

TH04   2:42 – 2:57

ULTRAFAST VIBRATIONAL DYNAMICS OF THE INTRAMOLECULAR H-BOND IN ACETYLACETONE INVESTIGATED WITH 2D IR SPECTROSCOPY

<u>JESSIKA L.S. DEAN</u>, *Chemistry, Washington University in St. Louis, St. Louis, MO, USA*; JOSEPH FOURNIER, *Department of Chemistry, Washington University, St. Louis, MO, USA*.

We report ultrafast transient absorption and 2D IR spectra of the light and deuterated isotopologues of acetylacetone to study the vibrational coupling and dynamics of the strong intramolecular hydrogen bond. Strong 2D IR cross-peaks in the fingerprint region reveal a high level of OH bend character throughout this region. This mode mixing gives rise to a large manifold of OH bend overtone and combination bands in the OH stretch region as evidenced by a highly elongated OH bend excited state absorption transition. As a consequence, strong OH stretch/bend Fermi resonance interactions contribute to a broad OH stretch absorption band that exhibits ultrafast population dynamics on a time scale less than 100 fs. The deuterated species displays similarly strong anharmonic coupling and relaxation dynamics, in addition to coherent oscillations corresponding to the O-O hydrogen bond stretch motion which are absent in the light isotopologue. Polarization anisotropy measurements shows a fast 200 fs reorientation relaxation of the OH stretch while the OD stretch displays a slow 1 ps component. The large isotopic dependence of the anisotropy dynamics is attributed to a combination of differences in anharmonic couplings and proton/deuteron transfer dynamics in the vibrationally hot molecules.

TH05   3:00 – 3:15

RAPID FREQUENCY-COMB INFRARED SPECTROSCOPY WITH CROSS-DISPERSED SPECTROMETERS

D. MICHELLE BAILEY, JOSEPH T. HODGES, <u>ADAM J. FLEISHER</u>, *Material Measurement Laboratory, National Institute of Standards and Technology, Gaithersburg, MD, USA*.

Time-resolved spectroscopy with optical frequency combs combines rapid acquisition with high sensitivity, broad bandwidth, and high resolution.[a] This presents an opportunity to study chemistry on a microsecond timescale with molecular specificity and multiplexing. Here we introduce two cross-dispersed frequency comb spectrometers operating in two wavelength regions of the infrared: one from 1.5 μm to 1.7 μm and another from 4.4 μm to 4.7 μm. In the latter mid-infrared region, we resolve the ro-vibrational lines of several isotopocules of nitrous oxide (N$_2$O), demonstrating a spectrometer-limited resolution of 725 MHz.[b] Improvements in spectrometer design, beginning in the former near-infrared region, allow for individual frequency-comb teeth to be resolved. Applied in combination with fast-frame-rate camera technology and emerging solid-state or frequency-agile comb sources, the result is a high-throughput spectroscopic technique that is well-suited for investigating the dynamic chemistry of individual events.

---

[a] A. J. Fleisher, B. J. Bjork, T. Q. Bui, K. C. Cossel, M. Okumura, J. Ye, *J. Phys. Chem. Lett.* **5**, 2241–2246 (2014)
[b] D. M. Bailey, G. Zhao, A. J. Fleisher, *Anal. Chem.* **92**, 13759–13766 (2020)

Intermission

TH06 3:39 – 3:54

SIMULATING FRANCK-CONDON SPECTRA WITH IMAGINARY-FREQUENCY VIBRATIONS

BRYAN CHANGALA, *Atomic and Molecular Physics, Harvard-Smithsonian Center for Astrophysics, Cambridge, MA, USA*; NADAV GENOSSAR, JOSHUA H BARABAN, *Chemistry, Ben-Gurion University of the Negev, Beer-Sheva, Israel.*

Vibronic spectra simulated under the harmonic Franck-Condon approximation are an ubiquitous tool for interpreting the structure of optical, photoelectron, and photoionization spectra. For transitions to bound final states located in a well on their potential energy surface, it is straightforward to calculate overlap integrals between discrete vibrational eigenstates, but this approach breaks down when the surface has locally negative curvature, such as near transition states. Time-dependent methods based on the vibrational autocorrelation function alleviate many of these difficulties, but suffer from certain analytical and technical deficiencies, including branch-cut discontinuities (associated with bound, periodic vibrations) and unstable finite-precision arithmetic (associated with unbound, imaginary-frequency modes). In this talk, we present a new derivation of the multidimensional, harmonic autocorrelation function that resolves these issues. An application is illustrated with the cyclopropyl radical, c-C_3H_5, which undergoes prompt ring-opening to allyl upon photoionization. We will also discuss progress towards perturbative anharmonic corrections within the time-dependent approach.

TH07 3:57 – 4:12

PROTON TRANSFER AND INTERSYSTEM CROSSING IN 2-NITROPHENOL PROBED BY GAS-PHASE TRANSIENT ABSORPTION SPECTROSCOPY

MYLES C SILFIES, ARSHAD MEHMOOD, GRZEGORZ KOWZAN[a], BENJAMIN G LEVINE, THOMAS K ALLISON, *Departments of Physics and Chemistry, Stony Brook University, Stony Brook, NY, USA.*

Recent work in both experiment and ab-initio theory indicates that intersystem crossing (ISC) can occur on ultrafast timescales in certain organic compounds, offering a relaxation channel competing with internal conversion. In particular, many nitroaromatic compounds are being investigated for this behavior. 2-nitrophenol (2NP) is one such system; after UV excitation the S1 state has both strong spin-orbit coupling to neighboring triplet states allowing for fast ISC and a low barrier to excited-state intramolecular proton transfer. Recent trajectory surface hopping calculations indicate that both of these relaxation channels occur on similar sub-picosecond timescales[b]. Both transient absorption spectroscopy (TAS) in solution and time-resolved photoelectron spectroscopy (TRPES) were used to probe the dynamics but the measured time constants were not consistent between methods which makes interpretation more difficult[c].

To further elucidate the dynamics in 2NP, we perform gas-phase TAS measurements using a newly-developed broadband cavity-enhanced ultrafast transient absorption spectrometer[d]. The spectrometer has a pump wavelength of 350 nm and a tunable probe from 450 to 700 nm with a demonstrated detection limit of $\Delta OD < 1 \times 10^{-9}/\sqrt{Hz}$. This technique serves as a complement to both solution-phase TAS and TRPES and provides additional information for comparison with theory. Using molecular beam techniques we are able to vary the sample vibrational/rotational temperature or change the solvent environment with clustering to observe the effects on 2NP relaxation dynamics. In this talk, we will discuss results from 2NP under various conditions and compare to previous experiments and theory.

---

[a]Second affiliation: Institute of Physics, Faculty of Physics, Astronomy and Informatics, Nicolaus Copernicus University, Torun, Poland
[b]C. Xu et al., Sci Rep 6, 26768 (2016).
[c]H. A. Ernst et al., J. Phys. Chem. A 119, 9225 (2015).
[d]M. C. Silfies et al., PCCP 23, 9743 (2021).

TH08
SOLVENT DRIVEN COHERENT POPULATION TRANSFER IN TRYPTOPHAN

4:15 – 4:30

VISHAL K. JAISWAL, MARZIOGIUSEPPE GENTILE, IRENE CONTI, ARTUR NENOV, MARCO GARAVELLI, *Dipartimento di Chimica Industriale "Toso Montanari", Università di Bologna, Bologna, Italy*; PIOTR KABACIŃSKI, ROCIO BORREGO-VARILLAS, GIULIO CERULLO, *Dipartimento di Fisica, Politecnico di Milano, Milano, Italy.*

The environment has a profound effect on the ultrafast photophysics of tryptophan due to radically different electronic nature of the lowest two singlets(La/Lb) which make up the first absorption band. In aqueous environment the polar La state becomes fluorescent. Therefore previous works have attributed the ultrafast dynamics to a sub-50fs Lb→La internal conversion followed by picosecond relaxation of solvent around the La-state.

We have investigated the primary photoinduced processes in solvated tryptophan by combining UV transient absorption spectroscopy with sub-30 fs temporal resolution and CASPT2/MM calculations and unveil a richer mechanism comprising of two population transfer events involving the La and Lb electronic state.

Our results reveal two consecutive coherent population transfer events involving the lowest two singlet states: a sub-50-fs nonadiabatic La →Lb through a conical intersection and a subsequent 220 fs reverse Lb→La due to solvent assisted adiabatic stabilization of La state. Vibrational fingerprints present in the transient spectra show compelling evidence of the vibronic coherence established between the two states from the earliest times after excitation and lasting till the back-transfer to La is complete.

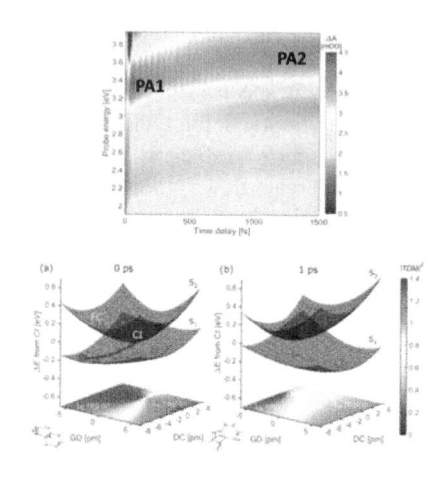

I will present how the delayed response of solvent causes a dynamic inversion of the energetic order of the vibronically coupled states, which determines the direction of the population transfer.

TH09
TWO-DIMENSIONAL TRANSIENT UV INVESTIGATION OF REDUCED FLAVINS

4:33 – 4:48

ERIC YOKIE, *Department of Chemistry and Biochemistry, Kent State University, Kent, OH, USA*; ARKAPRABHA KONAR, *Chemistry and Biochemistry, Kent State University, Kent, OH, USA.*

UV radiation in sunlight is responsible for DNA damage. It leads to the formation of photoproducts. Photolyases, a class of flavoproteins and photoenzymes repair the DNA lesions upon absorption of blue light. Photolyase contain two non-covalently bound chromophore, one is fully reduced Flavin Adenine Dinucleotide (FAD) and the other is an antenna pigment complex. The isoalloxazine ring in FAD plays a very important role in the repair mechanism. Understanding the role and nature of excited states is required to properly interpret kinetics due to electron transfer, solvation etc. Controversy surrounding the nature of excited states was put to rest recently by Stanley et. al. who used Stark spectroscopy to determine the presence of two nearly parallel electronic states around 360 nm and 425 nm. Here we use wavelength scanning pump-probe spectroscopy in the UV region to determine the effect of excitation wavelength on the observed excited state dynamics. We chose Flavin mononucleotide as a model system for preliminary studies. The complete two-dimensional dataset is used to extract 2D decay associated difference spectra to gain important insights into the presence of distinct electronic states in reduced Flavins.

TI. Mini-symposium: Benchmarking in Spectroscopy
Tuesday, June 21, 2022 – 1:30 PM
Room: 116 Roger Adams Lab

Chair: Eva Gougoula, Deutsches Elektronen-Synchrotron DESY, Hamburg, Germany

TI01   1:30 – 1:45

THE "LEGO BRICK" APPROACH AT WORK: A COST-EFFECTIVE STRATEGY FOR PREDICTING ACCURATE ROTATIONAL CONSTANTS

HEXU YE, *Dept. Chemistry "Giacomo Ciamician", University of Bologna, Bologna, ITALY*; SILVIA ALESSANDRINI, *Scuola Normale Superiore, Scuola Normale Superiore, Pisa, Italy*; MATTIA MELOSSO, *Dept. Chemistry "Giacomo Ciamician", University of Bologna, Bologna, ITALY*; CRISTINA PUZZARINI, *Dep. Chemistry 'Giacomo Ciamician', University of Bologna, Bologna, Italy*.

The "Lego brick" model [a] is based on the idea that a molecular system can be seen as formed by different fragments ("Lego bricks"). If accurate semi-experimental equilibrium geometries are available for these fragments, then the template molecule approach [b] can be used to account for the modifications occurring when going from the isolated fragment to the molecular system under investigation. The linear regression model [c] can be employed to correct the linkage between the different fragments. The application of the "Lego brick" approach to substituted (mainly CN and CCH) benzenes and small PAHs will be presented. Rotational constants will be used to test the accuracy of these structures.

[a] A. Melli, F. Tonolo, V. Barone, C. Puzzarini, J. Phys. Chem. A **125**, 9904 (2021)
[b] M. Piccardo, E. Penocchio, C. Puzzarini, M. Biczysko, V. Barone, J. Phys. Chem. A **119**, 2058 (2015)
[c] G. Ceselin, V. Barone, N. Tasinato, J. Chem. Theory Comput. **17**, 7290 (2021)

TI02   1:48 – 2:03

CONCENTRATION DETERMINATIONS FOR REACTIVE CHEMICAL INTERMEDIATES USING EMPIRICALLY DETERMINED AND THEORETICALLY CALCULATED TRANSITION PROBABILITIES

IAN JONES, JONATHAN SWIFT BERSSON, JINJUN LIU, *Department of Chemistry, University of Louisville, Louisville, KY, USA*; KETAN SHARMA, TERRY A. MILLER, *Department of Chemistry and Biochemistry, The Ohio State University, Columbus, OH, USA*; JOHN F. STANTON, *Quantum Theory Project, University of Florida, Gainesville, FL, USA*.

It has long been recognized that the Beer-Lambert law allows the determination of molecular concentrations from experimentally measured transition intensities of absorption spectra provided the absorption cross section and path length are known, with the latter typically easily measured experimentally. For non-reactive molecules, a suitable standard of known concentration/pressure can provide the cross section if it is not already available from published molecular line lists. However, for many chemical intermediates, their reactivity precludes preparing such a standard and accounts for their frequent absence in molecular line lists. Nonetheless, such molecules play important roles in chemical reactions of significance both economically and environmentally; hence spectroscopic measurements of their concentrations can be very valuable. Historically such cross sections have been determined empirically by "on-the-fly" concentration measurements, mostly depending on the sometimes questionable assumption that the chemistry of these intermediates is thoroughly understood. For example, if the self-reaction rate constant of an isolated intermediate is accurately known, measurement of its temporal decay yields its concentration, thereby providing the line's cross section from its intensity measurement. Alternatively, if a reaction mechanism is assumed that determines the stoichiometry of a reactive intermediate and a non-reactive byproduct with a known cross section, the measurement of their relative transition intensities provides the cross section of the intermediate. While such empirical cross sections have proven quite useful, it is worthwhile to note that it is also possible to calculate cross sections for individual rovibronic transitions using a combination of quantum chemistry methods and spectral simulation software. The peroxy radicals, RO_2 (R=H or alkyl group), are important intermediates in combustion and tropospheric chemistry with considerable work reported on their chemistry and spectroscopy. For the peroxy radicals, we compare results obtained from empirical cross sections measured by cavity ringdown spectroscopy with theoretically calculated values using the CFOUR quantum chemistry suite and the PGOPHER spectral simulation software.

TI03
AMINO ACIDS AND PEPTIDES (AAP) STRUCTURES, ENERGETICS AND SPECTROSCOPY (SES) DATABASE

2:06 – 2:21

MALGORZATA BICZYSKO, *International Centre for Quantum and Molecular Structures, Shanghai University, Shanghai, China.*

Derivation of structural, energetic, and spectroscopic properties for amino acids and polypeptide conformers from highly accurate theoretical approaches or mixed experimental-theoretical ones allows to set-up a database consistent with experiments *https : //github.com/VibESLab/AAP_SES_DataBase.*

In this work, we present works towards the set-up of database, which will extend over purely computational databases available so far. Both semi-experimental and accurate theoretical data make a reliable reference and their combination allows an extensive benchmark exploration of DFT methodologies. In fact, the application of DFT for specific properties usually requires careful benchmarking, but the databases available in literature usually tend to focus on the DFT performance for the computation of atomic and molecular energies rather than on structural and spectroscopic parameters. In this work we focus on the structural and spectroscopic properties as well as conformational energies suggesting that desired accuracy can be obtained by means of dispersion-corrected double hybrid functionals (DHF).

1. P. Wang, C. Shu, H. Ye, M. Biczysko, J. Phys. Chem. A 125, 45, 9826-9837, 2021
2. M. Sheng, F. Silvestrini, M. Biczysko, C. Puzzarini, J. Phys. Chem. A 125, 41, 9099–9114, 2021
3. C. Shu, Z. Jiang, M. Biczysko, Journal of Molecular Modeling, 26(6), 129, 2020
4. Z. Jiang, M. Biczysko, N. W. Moriarty, Proteins: Structure, Function, and Bioinformatics, 86, 273-278, 2018
5. C. Puzzarini, M. Biczysko, V. Barone, L. Largo, I. Pena, C. Cabezas, J.L. Alonso, J. Phys. Chem. Lett. 5, 534-540, 2014
6. V. Barone, M. Biczysko, J. Bloino, C. Puzzarini, Phys. Chem. Chem. Phys 15, 10094-10111, 2013

TI04
COMPUTATIONAL STUDIES OF MGC$_4$H ISOMERS

2:24 – 2:39

ALAND SINJARI, *Chemistry and Biochemistry, San Diego State University, San Diego, CA, USA*; TARUN ROY, SUBHAS GHOSAL, *Chemistry, National Institute of Technology Durgapur, Durgapur, West Bengal, INDIA*; VENKATESAN S. THIMMAKONDU, *Chemistry and Biochemistry, San Diego State University, San Diego, CA, USA.*

Constitutional isomers of MgC$_4$H elemental composition are theoretically investigated in this work using density functional theory at various levels. The linear doublet ($^2\Sigma^+$) isomer, 1-magnesapent-2,4-diyn-1-yl (**1**), was identified not only in the laboratory but also in the evolved carbon star, IRC+10216. While zero-point vibrational energy corrected relative energies obtained at the ROB3LYP/6-311++G(2d,2p) and ROωB97XD/6-311++G(2d,2p) levels correctly predict that isomer **1** is the global minimum geometry, the same obtained with UHF wavefunctions predict that a cyclic isomer, 1-ethynyl-1-λ^3-magnesacycloprop-2-yne (**2**), is the global minimum structure. Further electronic structure calculations carried out with GGA-functional, such as PBE0-D3 with def-TZVP basis set predict that isomer **1** is the global minimum irrespective of whether the solutions are based on ROHF or UHF wavefunctions. It is outlined here that the issue of spin-contamination (though under 5 %) becomes a serious one affecting the relative energies dramatically while using hybrid functionals such as B3LYP and ωB97XD in this case.

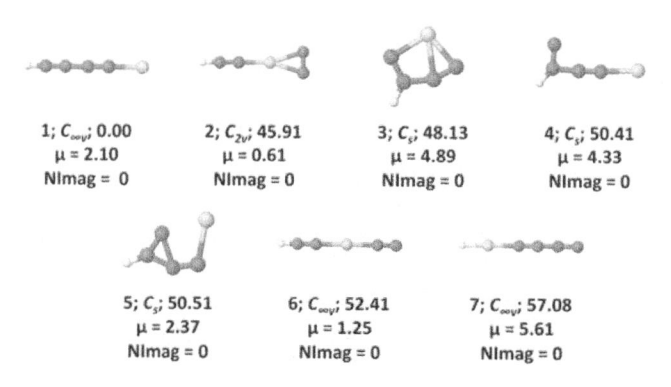

Figure 1: Isomers of MgC$_4$H. Relative energies (in kcal mol^{-1}) and dipole moments (in Debye) are computed at the UPBE0-D3/Def2-TZVP level. All isomers are minima.

TI05   2:42 – 2:57

ULTRAHIGH FINESSE CAVITY-ENHANCED SPECTROSCOPY OF DEUTERIUM MOLECULE FOR QED TESTS

MIKOŁAJ ZABOROWSKI, MICHAŁ SŁOWIŃSKI, <u>KAMIL STANKIEWICZ</u>, *Institute of Physics, Faculty of Physics, Astronomy and Informatics, Nicolaus Copernicus University, Torun, Poland*; FRANCK THIBAULT, *Institute of Physics of Rennes, Univ. Rennes, CNRS, Rennes, France*; AGATA CYGAN, HUBERT JÓŹWIAK, GRZEGORZ KOWZAN, PIOTR MASLOWSKI, AKIKO NISHIYAMA, NIKODEM STOLARCZYK, SZYMON WOJTEWICZ, ROMAN CIURYLO, DANIEL LISAK, PIOTR WCISLO, *Institute of Physics, Faculty of Physics, Astronomy and Informatics, Nicolaus Copernicus University, Torun, Poland.*

Molecular hydrogen, in the view of its simplicity, is well suited for testing quantum electrodynamics (QED) for molecules as well as for searching for new physics beyond the standard model such as new forces or extra dimensions. Furthermore, molecular hydrogen possesses a wide structure of ultranarrow rovibrational transitions with different sensitivities to the proton charge radius and proton-to-electron mass ratio. Therefore, the recent large progress in both theoretical and experimental determinations of the rovibrational splitting in different isotopologues of molecular hydrogen makes it a promising system for determination of some physical constants.

We present the most accurate measurement of the position of the weak quadrupole S(2) 2–0 line in molecular deuterium. We have collected the spectra with a frequency-stabilized cavity ring-down spectrometer (FS-CRDS) with an ultrahigh finesse optical cavity (F = 637 000), optical frequency comb and operating in the frequency-agile, rapid scanning spectroscopy (FARS) mode. To reduce the systematic errors in line position determination, we analyzed our spectra with one of the most physically justified line-shape model describing the collisional effects, the speed-dependent billiard-ball profile (SDBBP), parameters of which are derived from *ab initio* quantum-scattering calculations.

Despite working in the Doppler-limited regime, we reached 40 kHz of statistical uncertainty and 161 kHz of absolute accuracy. The accuracy of our measurement corresponds to the fifth significant digit of the leading term in QED correction. We were also able to test two other higher-order QED terms. We observed 2.3σ discrepancy with the recent theoretical value.

Intermission

TI06   3:21 – 3:36

RESONANT INELASTIC X-RAY SCATTERING CALCULATIONS OF Ru COMPLEXES WITHIN A SIMPLIFIED TIME-DEPENDENT DENSITY FUNCTIONAL THEORY FRAMEWORK

<u>DANIEL R. NASCIMENTO</u>, *Department of Chemistry, The University of Memphis, Memphis, TN, USA.*

Resonant inelastic x-ray scattering (RIXS) provides valuable information on the electronic structure of molecules and materials that is not easily accessible by one-photon spectroscopies due to selection rule restrictions. With the continuing development in light source technologies, RIXS is rapidly becoming an important technique for the study of gas- and solution-phase molecular systems, and the need for reliable and inexpensive electronic structure methods to aid in the prediction and interpretation of complicated spectral features is becoming apparent. In this work, we present a simplified approach based on the linear-response time-dependent density functional theory (LR-TDDFT) formalism to simulate RIXS in 4d transition metal complexes without the need to solve the costly TDDFT quadratic-response equations. As an illustrative example, we simulate the 2p4d RIXS maps of three representative ruthenium complexes. The method is able to capture all experimental features in all three complexes with relative energies correct to within 0.6 eV, and at the cost of roughly two independent LR-TDDFT calculations.

TI07 3:39 – 3:54

DECONVOLUTING VIBRATIONAL PROBE RESPONSES USING CRYOGENIC ION INFRARED SPECTROSCOPY

AHMED MOHAMED, SEAN COLEMAN EDINGTON, MARK JOHNSON, *Department of Chemistry, Yale University, New Haven, CT, USA.*

Noncovalent interactions between metal ions and complex molecules play a central role in condensed matter systems from enzyme catalysis to membrane permeability. Vibrational probes are used to gain information on the local electrostatic environment during such condensed phase phenomena. While this approach has proven successful, there are shortcomings that have not been addressed. In the condensed phase, the intrinsic molecular level response (polarization, isomerization, etc.) is obscured by the effects of hydrogen bonding, solvent exchange, and other external factors such as heterogeneity in the medium.

Cryogenic ion vibrational predissociation spectroscopy (CIVP) is a useful way to obtain the detailed information needed to unambiguously measure the intrinsic response of vibrational electric field probes. In particular, this paper describes how CIVP can be used to quantify the separate roles of proximal molecular ions and interactions with solvent. We apply this approach to monitor the responses of palmitic acid and benzo-15-crown-5-nitrile to various metals in the +1 and +2 charge states. Both of these species contain popular vibrational probes (carboxylate in the former and nitrile in the latter), and are relevant, molecular-level models of scaffolds present in biological systems. Vibrational spectra of the cold (20K), H2 or He tagged ions are collected and assignments are made with the assistance of electronic structure calculations. This technique provides a new window into the intrinsic response of vibrational probes that are widely used in biophysical applications.

TI08 3:57 – 4:12

QUARANTINED CC-STRETCHED FORMIC ACID: MOLECULAR WORK-OUT IN (SELF) ISOLATION

KATHARINA A. E. MEYER, *Department of Chemistry, University of Wisconsin-Madison, Madison, WI, USA*; ARMAN NEJAD, *Institute of Physical Chemistry, Georg-August-Universität Göttingen, Göttingen, Germany.*

Vibrational spectra of small molecules effectively probe the underlying potential energy hypersurface, which can be tested when combined with accurate anharmonic calculations.[a] Particularly suited for a performance test of quantum chemical gas phase calculations are spectra recorded in a supersonic expansion, as significant rotational cooling is achieved while the molecules or molecular clusters remain isolated in the gas phase. One of the smallest reference systems for such a benchmarking study is the formic acid monomer with its cis-$trans$-torsional isomerism.[b] Recently, new vibrational reference data on the stretching vibrations of all four H/D isotopologues of the higher-energy cis-conformer were provided *via* the combination of Raman jet spectroscopy with thermal excitation.[c] Another very interesting carboxylic acid for such a study is the smallest acetylenic acid, HCC-COOH, whose cis- and $trans$-rotamers will be discussed in this contribution. Of particular interest are two almost isoenergetic $trans$-fundamentals of different symmetry which are shown to be a particularly useful benchmarking target, but also the dimers of the CC-stretched formic acid prove to be an insightful reference system for benchmarking.[d]

---

[a] P. R. Franke, J. F. Stanton, G. E. Douberly, *J. Phys. Chem. A* **2021**, *125*, 1301–1324; J. M. Bowman, T. Carrington, H.-D. Meyer, *Mol. Phys.* **2008**, *106*, 2145–2182.

[b] D. P. Tew, W. Mizukami, *J. Phys. Chem. A* **2016**, *120*, 9815–9828; F. Richter, P. Carbonnière, *J. Chem. Phys.* **2018**, *148*, 064303; A. Nejad, E. L. Sibert III, *J. Chem. Phys.* **2021**, *154*, 064301.

[c] A. Nejad, M. A. Suhm, K. A. E. Meyer, *Phys. Chem. Chem. Phys.* **2020**, *22*, 25492–25501.

[d] K. A. E. Meyer, A. Nejad, *Phys. Chem. Chem. Phys.* **2021**, *23*, 17208–17223.

TI09   **4:15 – 4:30**

THE FORMIC ACID MONOMER: EXTENSION OF THE VIBRATIONAL DATABASE AND RIGOROUS ELECTRONIC AND NUCLEAR VIBRATIONAL STRUCTURE BENCHMARKS

<u>ARMAN NEJAD</u>, *Institute of Physical Chemistry, Georg-August-Universität Göttingen, Göttingen, Germany*; EDWIN SIBERT, *Department of Chemistry, University of Wisconsin–Madison, Madison, WI, USA*; MARTIN A. SUHM, *Institute of Physical Chemistry, Georg-August-Universität Göttingen, Göttingen, Germany*.

The vibrational spectroscopy of formic acid, F, has seen new and important experimental and theoretical impulses in the past six years.[a] In a combined experimental and theoretical approach, the vibrational database of F below 4000 cm^{-1} is reviewed and extended to 189 band centres [∼300% increase], including a plethora of highly-excited vibrational states, both torsional conformers, and several isotopologues [^{1}H, ^{2}H, ^{12}C, ^{13}C, and ^{16}O].[b] Essentially, the vibrational characterisation of its skeletal modes below 3500 cm^{-1} can be regarded as complete which is also an important stepping stone in understanding the complex vibrational dynamics of its cyclic dimer.[c] A new key insight is that the impact of the OH bend-torsion resonance [ν_5 and $2\nu_9$] on the entire vibrational dynamics of *trans*-HCOOH is more far-reaching than previously believed. Beyond 3500 cm^{-1}, which is also near the expected *trans*→*cis* isomerisation threshold, this resonance polyad is indicated to play an important role in the perturbations of the OH stretching fundamental [ν_1]. In this contribution, new spectroscopic developments are summarised and promising future research directions for F are discussed. In particular, its importance and suitability for the purpose of benchmarking electronic and nuclear vibrational methodologies are highlighted.

---

[a](exp) K. Hull, T. Wells, B. E. Billinghurst, H. Bunn, P. L. Raston, *AIP Adv.* **2019**, *9*, 015021; K. A. E. Meyer, M. A. Suhm, *Chem. Sci.* **2019**, *10*, 6285; A. Nejad, M. A. Suhm, K. A. E. Meyer, *Phys. Chem. Chem. Phys.* **2020**, *22*, 25492. (theo) D. P. Tew, W. Mizukami, *J. Phys. Chem. A* **2016**, *120*, 9815; F. Richter, P. Carbonnière, *J. Chem. Phys.* **2018**, *148*, 064303; A. Aerts, P. Carbonnière, F. Richter, A. Brown, *J. Chem. Phys.* **2020**, *152*, 024305; A. Nejad, E. L. Sibert III, *J. Chem. Phys.* **2021**, *154*, 064301.

[b] A. Nejad, PhD thesis, submitted (2022).

[c] A. Nejad, K. A. E. Meyer, F. Kollipost, Z. Xue, M. A. Suhm, *J. Chem. Phys.* **2021**, *155*, 224301

TJ. Photodissociation and photochemistry
Tuesday, June 21, 2022 – 1:30 PM
Room: B102 Chemical and Life Sciences

Chair: Fleming Crim, The University of Wisconsin, Madison, WI, USA

TJ01 1:30–1:45

RESONANCE ENHANCED PHOTODISSOCIATION SPECTROSCOPY OF AuAg+ REVEALS ISOTOPIC DEPENDANCE ON PHOTODISSOCIATION

<u>SAMUEL JACK PALMER MARLTON</u>, CHANG LIU, PATRICK WATKINS, JACK T BUNTINE, EVAN BIESKE, *School of Chemistry, The University of Melbourne, Melbourne, Victoria, Australia.*

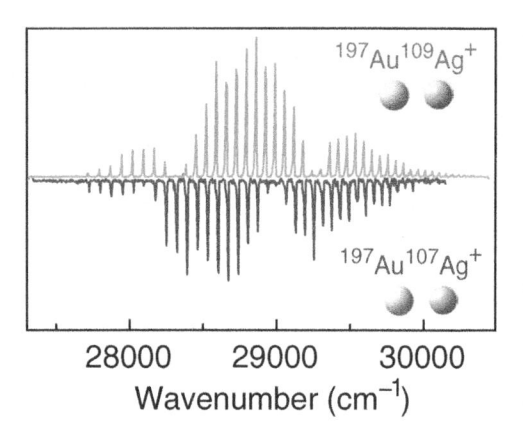

Bimetallic materials comprised of gold and silver have useful optical and electronic properties, which are complicated by quantum mechanical, relativistic, and isotopic effects. To provide a bottom-up perspective on these larger systems, the smallest monocation comprised of gold and silver—diatomic AuAg+—is spectroscopically probed using resonance enhanced photodissociation (REPD). The ^{197}Au^{107}Ag$^+$ and ^{197}Au^{109}Ag$^+$ isotopologues are confined in a cryogenically cooled (ca. 5 K) quadrupole ion trap and are exposed to tunable light while detecting Au+ photofragment ions using a time-of-flight mass spectrometer. Electronic spectra in the UV exhibit a transition from the $X^2\Sigma^+_{1/2}$ ground state to an excited state that is yet to be assigned. Vibronic progressions for this transition extend over more than 30 quanta for both isotopologues, but with striking differences in band intensities (see Figure). This difference in photodissociation yield between the two isotopologues arises because the vibronic energies and associated wavefunctions depend on the reduced mass, leading to a difference in the coupling of the excited state levels and the repulsive electronic state that leads to dissociation. The observed photodissociation intensities for ^{197}Au^{107}Ag$^+$ and ^{197}Au^{109}Ag$^+$ are successfully modelled by calculating respective vibronic energies and wavefunctions of their bound and dissociative electronic states.

TJ02 1:48–2:03

PHOTODISSOCIATION SPECTRUM OF Au$_2^+$N$_2$

<u>NIMA-NOAH NAHVI</u>, MARKO FÖRSTEL, KAI POLLOW, TAARNA STUDEMUND, OTTO DOPFER, *Institut für Optik und Atomare Physik, Technische Universität Berlin, Berlin, Germany.*

The binding motif of nitrogen on transition metals is an interesting issue. Here we present the electronic spectrum of the $\tilde{A}^2\Sigma^+ \to \tilde{X}^2\Sigma^+$ transition of Au$_2^+$N$_2$, which was measured via photodissociation spectroscopy. The spectrum contains a long progression, caused by symmectric and asymmetric strech vibrations. We extract harmonic frequencies, anharmonicities and cross-anharmonicities of the excited state via a Dunham expansion and harmonic frequencies of the ground state via Franck-Condon simulations. In comparison to density functional theory calculations, the observed frequencies agree well with the theory. We also discuss the binding motif of Au$_2^+$N$_2$ in the ground and excited state.

[1] M. Förstel, K. Pollow, T. Studemund, O. Dopfer, Chem. Eur. J. 2021, 27, 15075-15080.

[2] M. Förstel, K. M. Pollow, K. Saroukh, E. A. Najib, R. Mitric, O. Dopfer, Angew. Chem. Int. Ed. 2020, 123, 21587-21592.

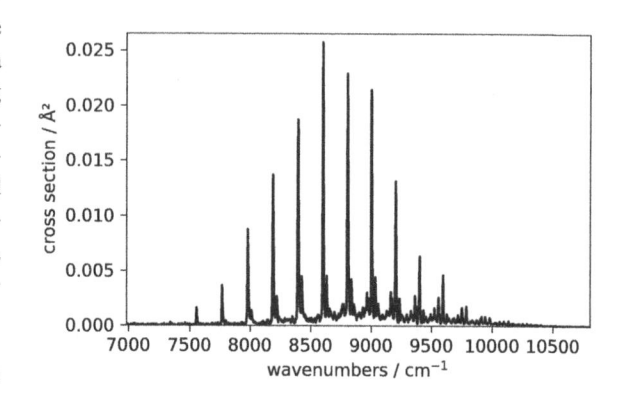

Figure 3: Electronic spectrum of Au$_2^+$N$_2$.

TJ03 2:06 – 2:21

GAS-PHASE ELECTRONIC SPECTROSCOPY OF C_6^+

JASON E. COLLEY, DYLAN S. ORR, MICHAEL A DUNCAN, *Department of Chemistry, University of Georgia, Athens, GA, USA.*

Electronic spectrum measurements are reported for mass selected C_6^+ in the gas phase using photodissociation spectroscopy. Carbon cluster cations are produced by laser vaporization and mass selected using a time-of-flight mass spectrometer. Photodissociation of C_6^+ measured a strong absorption at 417.1 nm. Experimental results are accompanied with calculations at the B3LYP/Def2TZVP level that explores predicted isomeric structures, their energetics, and vibrational and electronic spectra. Electronic excitations and vibrational hot bands in the spectrum agree more with frequencies predicted for the linear structure than those of the cyclic structure.

TJ04 2:24 – 2:39

$Si_2O_2^+$ - PHOTODISSOCIATION AND OPTICAL ABSORPTION PROPERTIES

TAARNA STUDEMUND, MARKO FÖRSTEL, KAI POLLOW, EMIL MICKEIN, OTTO DOPFER, *Institut für Optik und Atomare Physik, Technische Universität Berlin, Berlin, Germany.*

Interstellar dust consists mainly of μm-sized silicate particles. Their origin and evolutionary development processes are still poorly understood. So far, only molecular SiO as a possible precursor has been observed and identified in a circumstellar disk [1]. We present experimental data and quantum chemical calculations of absorption and dissociation properties of $Si_2O_2^+$ clusters. These cations represent possible intermediates between the circumstellar diatomic SiO molecule and the silicate grains observed in the interstellar medium. These optical spectra provide the first spectroscopic information for any $Si_nO_m^+$ cation larger than SiO^+. These spectra are the first optical absorption spectra of $Si_2O_2^+$ cations. We were able to obtain those by photodissociation spectroscopy of mass-selected ionsin a tandem mass spectrometer coupled to a laser vaporization source [2]. Here, the experimental results will be compared with TD-DFT calculations and discussed in an astrophysical context.

Literature:

[1] R. Wilson et al., Astrophys. J., 1971, 167, L97.
[2] M. Förstel et al., Rev. Sci. Instrum., 2017, 88, 123110.

Intermission

TJ05 3:03 – 3:18

SPECTROSCOPIC STUDIES OF π-BACKDONATING EARLY TRANSITION METAL AND MONOVALENT LANTHANIDE DIBORIDES

DAKOTA M. MERRILES, *Chemistry, University of Utah, Salt Lake City, UT, USA*; KIMBERLY H. TOMCHAK, *Department of Chemistry, University of Utah, Salt Lake City, UT, USA*; CHRISTOPHER NIELSON, *Chemistry, University of Utah, Salt Lake City, UT, USA*; MICHAEL D. MORSE, *Department of Chemistry, University of Utah, Salt Lake City, UT, USA.*

The second period p-block elements reign as mainstays in a plethora of scientific disciplines due to their varied chemical bonding and significant natural abundance. Indeed, the range of chemistries of these p-block elements is profoundly expanded when these atoms, particularly electron deficient boron, bond with transition metals and lanthanides. Exotic metallaboron compounds have been demonstrated to participate in a wide array of bonding schemes, mechanisms, and geometries. Here, resonant two-photon ionization spectroscopy and ab initio quantum chemical calculations are used to elucidate the chemical bonding and electronic structure of triatomic metal diboride complexes. These previously unstudied species are demonstrated to require an extension of the Dewar-Chatt-Duncanson bonding model of organometallic chemistry. Instead of weakening the bond in the diboron ligand via backdonation into the pi* antibonding orbital, the metal-boron and boron-boron bonds are strengthened by backdonation into the pi bonding orbital of diboron. Moreover, it is shown that the lanthanide atoms in these species exhibit a rare +1 oxidation state, further defining this family of molecules as a special class of monovalent lanthanide compounds.

TJ06　　3:21–3:36
BOND DISSOCIATION ENERGIES AND IONIZATION ENERGIES OF RHENIUM CONTAINING SMALL MOLECULES

KIMBERLY H. TOMCHAK, ERICK TIEU, THOMAS T. KAWAGOE, JORDAN DERBIDGE, KEITH T. CLARK, MICHAEL D. MORSE, *Department of Chemistry, University of Utah, Salt Lake City, UT, USA.*

Resonant two-photon ionization spectroscopy has been used to determine the bond dissociation energies (BDEs) and ionization energies (IEs) of rhenium containing small molecules. The ultraviolet spectra of these molecules display a highly congested collection of indeterminate vibronic states. Couplings among these states allow the molecule to find a path to dissociation as soon as the ground separated atom limit is exceeded in energy, allowing a precise measurement of the bond energy from the observation of a sharp predissociation threshold. Measurements provide BDE values of 5.731(3) eV (ReC), 5.359(3) eV (ReC$_2$), 5.635(3) eV (ReN), 5.510(3) eV (ReO), and 3.947(3) eV (ReS). The ionization energy of ReC, 8.425(15) eV, was determined from the observed onset of one-color two-photon ionization. By combining our ReC results with the ionization energy of Re (7.83352(11) eV) in a thermochemical cycle, the BDE of cationic ReC+ was determined as 5.140(15) eV.[a] This is in excellent agreement with that measured using guided ion beam mass spectrometry, 5.13(12) eV.[b]

---

[a] Kramida, A.; Ralchenko, Y.; Reader, J.; NIST ASD Team, NIST Atomic Spectra Database (version 5.9). National Institute of Standards and Technology, Gaithersburg, MD: 2019.

[b] Kim, J.; Cox, R. M.; Armentrout, P. B., Guided ion beam and theoretical studies of the reactions of Re+, Os+, and Ir+ with CO. J. Chem. Phys. 2016, 145 (19), 194305/1-194305/13.

TJ07　　3:39–3:54
ULTRAFAST CARRIER DYNAMICS IN QUANTUM DOT SENSITIZED ZnO

CONNER DYKSTRA, *Chemistry, University of Illinois Champaign - Urbana, Champaign, Il, USA*; THOMAS ROSSI, RENSKE VAN DER VEEN, *Photovoltaics, Helmholtz Zentrum Berlin, Berlin, Germany*; JOSH VURA-WEIS, *Department of Chemistry, University of Illinois at Urbana-Champaign, Urbana, IL, USA.*

Quantum dot sensitized solar cells have been a rising star in in the field of photovoltaics and materials science. Here, UV probe transient spectroscopy is employed to directly investigate the metal oxide dynamics in CdSe sensitized ZnO. The excitonic transition in ZnO lays at 365 nm, and charge injection results in a bleaching of this transition due to phase space filling. Combining UV and visible probe transient spectroscopy allows direct comparison between the spectrally separated CdSe and ZnO signals.

The two regions show a difference in kinetics, with the ZnO showing a delayed signal from charge injection contrary to the abrupt decay of the quantum dot signal, which has been attributed to the formation of an interfacial exciton at the boundary of the ZnO and CdSe. High fluence measurements with band edge excitation gives evidence that charge injection follows a second mechanism that does not show delayed charge separation, indicating the interfacial exciton state is not forming. Understanding this effect could pave the way for more effective photovoltaics.

TJ08　　3:57–4:12
PHOTOCHEMISTRY OF CYANOMETHYLENE CYCLOPROPANE (C$_5$H$_5$N) IN A LOW TEMPERATURE RARE GAS MATRIX

SAMUEL A. WOOD, SAMUEL M. KOUGIAS, BRIAN J. ESSELMAN, *Department of Chemistry, University of Wisconsin-Madison, Madison, WI, USA*; R. CLAUDE WOODS, *Department of Chemistry, University of Wisconsin, Madison, WI, USA*; ROBERT J. McMAHON, *Department of Chemistry, University of Wisconsin-Madison, Madison, WI, USA.*

We are interested in the photochemistry and spectroscopy of interstellar molecules, and recently focused on isomers of pyridine. We examined the photochemistry of cyanomethylene cyclopropane in low temperature conditions relevant to the interstellar medium. Cyanomethylene cyclopropane was mixed with argon prior to deposition onto a CsI window at temperatures below 30 K. We collected IR spectra in the range of 400-4,000 cm^{-1}. We irradiated the molecule at $\lambda >$200 nm using a Xe/Hg arc lamp, and observed IR bands indicative of a new organic nitrile develop over time; no change to the IR spectrum of cyanomethylene cyclopropane was observed when a $\lambda >$295 nm UV cut-off filter was used. The new IR bands produced from this process were compared to other experimental and predicted IR spectra of C$_5$H$_5$N isomers to interrogate the C$_5$H$_5$N potential energy surface.

TJ09 4:15 – 4:30

UV PHOTOLYSIS STUDY OF *PARA*-AMINOBENZOIC ACID USING PARAHYDROGEN MATRIX ISOLATED SPECTROSCOPY

ALEXANDRA McKINNON, BRENDAN MOORE, PAVLE DJURICANIN, TAKAMASA MOMOSE, *Department of Chemistry, University of British Columbia, Vancouver, BC, Canada.*

Para-aminobenzoic acid (PABA) is one of the original sunscreen chemical agents. As these agents often undergo photodissociation during the process of UV absorption, understanding the photochemical behaviour of sunscreen agents is highly important. In this study, the photolysis of PABA was studied at three different UV ranges (UVA: 355 nm, UVB: >280 nm, and UVC: 266 nm and 213 nm) using parahydrogen (pH_2) matrix isolation Fourier-Transform infrared (FTIR) spectroscopy. Parahydrogen has weak cage effects that allow radicals to escape the lattice site and therefore prevent further radical recombination reactions. PABA was found to be stable under UVA irradiation. However, PABA dissociated into 4-aminylbenzoic acid (the PABA radical) through amino hydrogen atom loss under UVB and UVC irradiation.[1] The production of the PABA radical supports a previously proposed mechanism of the formation of the carcinogenic PABA-thymine adduct. The infrared spectrum of the PABA radical was analyzed with quantum chemical calculations. Two conformers of this radical were observed in the pH_2 matrix. Both conformers of the PABA radical were stable in solid pH_2 for hours after irradiation. This work displays that pH_2 matrix isolation spectroscopy is effective for sunscreen agent photochemical studies.

1. McKinnon, A.; Moore, B.; Djuricanin, P.; Momose, T. UV Photolysis Study of *Para*-Aminobenzoic Acid Using Parahydrogen Matrix Isolated Spectroscopy. *Photochem.* **2022**, *2*, 88 – 101.

TJ10 4:33 – 4:48

UV PHOTOLYSIS OF AMINO ACIDS IN A SOLID PARAHYDROGEN MATRIX

BRENDAN MOORE, SHIN YI TOH, *Department of Chemistry, University of British Columbia, Vancouver, BC, Canada*; TERMEH BASHIRI, *Chemistry, Caltech, Pasadena, CA, USA*; KYLE MAHONEY, ALEXANDRA McKINNON, MEI FEI ZENG, YING-TUNG ANGEL WONG, PAVLE DJURICANIN, TAKAMASA MOMOSE, *Department of Chemistry, University of British Columbia, Vancouver, BC, Canada.*

Matrix isolation has recently proven successful for the spectroscopic characterization of amino acids in their neutral form. Here, we utilize solid parahydrogen, a cage-free matrix host, to study the photochemistry of a number of amino acids. The photochemistry of alanine, glycine, leucine, proline, and serine will be presented. Irradiation by 213 nm light resulted in α-carbonyl C-C bond cleavage and hydrocarboxyl (HOCO) radical production from all five amino acids. The temporal behavior of the Fourier-transform infrared spectra revealed that HOCO radicals rapidly reach a steady state, which occurs predominantly due to photodissociation of HOCO into CO + OH or CO_2 + H. In alanine, glycine, and leucine, the amine radicals generated by the α-carbonyl C-C bond cleavage rapidly undergo hydrogen elimination to yield ethanimine, methanimine and 3-methylbutane-1-imine, respectively. As an analogue to gas phase photochemistry, the photodissociation pathways identified here provide new insights into the behavior of amino acids in interstellar space.

TK. Mini-symposium: Machine Learning

Tuesday, June 21, 2022 – 1:30 PM

Room: 217 Noyes Laboratory

Chair: Andrew White, University of Rochester, Rochester, NY, USA

TK01   *INVITED TALK*   1:30 – 2:00

AN OVERVIEW OF MACHINE LEARNING IN ROTATIONAL SPECTROSCOPY

<u>STEVEN SHIPMAN</u>, *Department of Chemistry, New College of Florida, Sarasota, FL, USA.*

Over the last several years, particularly with the advent of well-documented open source libraries, it has become increasingly easier to apply machine learning techniques to a wide range of problems. Spectroscopy has not been immune to this, and literature searches for "machine learning" and "spectroscopy" return thousands of hits. However, these techniques have not yet found widespread use in the area of high-resolution rotational spectroscopy. In this talk, I will give an overview of the current work in the field and highlight some of the challenges that make this a difficult problem. Along the way, I hope to also provide a kind of "baseline", showing what can be done without the use of machine learning techniques and where they may be particularly applicable.

TK02   2:06 – 2:21

DEVELOPMENT OF HIGH-SPEED AB INITIO CCSD(T) LEVEL NEURAL NETWORK POTENTIAL ENERGY SURFACES FOR DIFFUSION MONTE CARLO

<u>FENRIS LU</u>, ANNE B McCOY, *Department of Chemistry, University of Washington, Seattle, WA, USA.*

Diffusion Monte Carlo (DMC) is a general statistical method that is capable of providing an accurate ground-state solution to the molecular Schrodinger equation of the system of interest. The approach is particularly well suited for systems like water clusters and CH_5^+ that undergo large amplitude vibrational motions, providing a way to gain insights into their vibrational and rotational spectra that are difficult to achieve by other methods. The ability to perform DMC simulations is predicated by the availability of a fast and reliable Potential Energy Surface(PES), as billions of structures with energies up to ten times the zero point energy will be evaluated in a typical DMC simulation. Such strenuous demands for speed, accuracy and extrapolability to high-energy regions of the potential pose major challenges to most current PES developed by conventional methods.

To address these issues, we have developed a Neural Network(NN) architecture and training protocol to generate CCSD(T) level NN-PES specifically to meet all the demands of DMC. We validated this approach with CH_5^+ and $(H_2O)_2$, and applied it to protonated ethylene $(C_2H_5^+)$. This proposed NN-PES is trained solely with *ab initio* data, and is versatile, so it can be applied to any small-to-medium-sized systems. Powered by the robust parallel computing ability of Graphics Processing Units (GPUs), this approach can be used to evaluate the energy of a single geometry with a microsecond. Its architecture also ensures remarkable extrapolability and no unphysical energy predictions (e.g. 'holes' in the potential) even in high energy regions of the potential where training data are extremely scarce. In this talk we will focus on the procedures taken to develop such NN-PES, and in the accompanying talk, we will share the results of DMC studies of $C_2H_5^+$ that use a NN-PES, which has been developed using this approach.

TK03   2:24 – 2:39

DIFFUSION MONTE CARLO STUDY OF $C_2H_5^+$ USING AN AB INITIO POTENTIAL ENERGY SURFACE

PATTARAPON MOONKAEN, FENRIS LU, ANNE B McCOY, *Department of Chemistry, University of Washington, Seattle, WA, USA.*

Carbocations are a class of important organic intermediates, which exist in hydrocarbon plasmas and are believed to play a role in the chemistry in the interstellar medium. Protonated ethylene ($C_2H_5^+$) is one such carbocation, which is formed from the smallest alkene family. It is also important in mass spectrometry as it appears in the mass spectra of many organic molecules and it is used as the protonating agent in chemical-ionization mass spectrometry. High-level electronic structure calculations predict that the minimum energy structure is the non-classical one in which the excess proton is equidistant from the two carbon atoms. This was confirmed by the IR spectrum of $C_2H_5^+$ obtained by the Dopfer and Duncan groups.

In this work, the ground state wavefunction and structure of $C_2H_5^+$ is obtained from Diffusion Monte Carlo (DMC) based on a potential with CCSD(T)-level accuracy, evaluated using several machine learning approaches. The effect of the shared proton motion on the IR spectrum as well as the coupling between the vibration of the shared proton and other higher frequency motion will be discussed. The impact of deuteration on these couplings also will be described. Lastly, the excited state for the shared proton motion can be obtained by fixed-node DMC, allowing us to explore the excited state wave functions, and particularly the possibility of accessing the classical carbocation structure through vibrational excitation.

Intermission

TK04   *INVITED TALK*   3:03 – 3:33

PUTTING DENSITY FUNCTIONAL THEORY TO THE TEST WITH MACHINE LEARNING

HEATHER J KULIK, *Chemical Engineering, MIT, Cambridge, MA, USA.*

Accelerated simulation with machine learning (ML) has begun to provide the advances in efficiency to make property prediction tractable at an unprecedented scale. Nevertheless, ML-accelerated workflows both inherit the biases of training data derived from density functional theory (DFT) and leads to many attempted calculations that are doomed to fail. Many compelling molecular systems involve strained chemical bonds, open shell radicals and diradicals, or metal–organic bonds to open-shell transition-metal centers. Although promising targets, these materials present unique challenges for electronic structure methods and combinatorial challenges for their discovery. I will describe some of my group's recent advances in using artificial intelligence to address challenges in accuracy and efficiency beyond conventional DFT-based ML workflows. I will describe how we have developed ML models trained to predict the results of multiple methods or the differences between them, enabling quantitative sensitivity analysis. I will then describe ML models we have developed on a series of chemical and electronic structure descriptors that predict the likelihood of calculation success and detect the presence of strong correlation. Combining novel descriptors and developing consensus from multiple levels of theory empowers decision engines that represent the first steps toward autonomous workflows that avoid the need for expert determination of the robustness of DFT-based computational modeling.

TK05
PARTITION FUNCTION ESTIMATION FROM INCOMPLETE SPECTROSCOPIC GRAPHS

<u>KELVIN LEE</u>, *Accelerated Computing Systems and Graphics, Intel Corporation, Hillsboro, OR, USA*; KYLE N. CRABTREE, *Department of Chemistry, University of California, Davis, Davis, CA, USA*.

Statistical mechanical treatment of molecules is a crucial part of the analysis workflow for many fields, ranging from reaction dynamics, spectral intensity simulation, to abundance characterization in the interstellar medium, to materials research and simulation. At the heart of this is computation of the partition function—the statistical equivalent to the quantum mechanical wavefunction—which involves summation over thermally relevant energy levels. Despite being conceptually straightforward, calculation of the partition function can be a challenging task: at high temperatures, the number of contributing states grows exponentially, and often the list of states is truncated for computational and portability reasons.

Here, we propose the use of physics informed graph neural networks to parameterize the partition function calculation based off incomplete spectroscopic graphs, and as a proof-of-concept, demonstrate its applicability and weaknesses through the study of pure rotational energy levels. In contrast to approximate analytical expressions based on the principal rotational constants, graph structures natively capture effects such as centrifugal distortion of varying degrees, which otherwise significantly undermine the accuracy of calculated partition functions at elevated temperatures. As part of our study, we discuss implications on computational performance, data requirements, and applicability in typical workflows.

TK06
ACCURATE PHOTOPHYSICS OF ORGANIC RADICALS FROM MACHINE LEARNED RANGE-SEPARATED FUNCTIONALS

<u>CHENGWEI JU</u>, *Pritzker School of Molecular Engineering, The University of Chicago, Chicago, IL, USA*; YILI SHEN, *College of Software Engineering, Tongji University, Shanghai, China*; AARON TIAN, *N/A, Massachusetts Academy of Math and Science, Worcester, MA, USA*; ETHAN FRENCH, HONGSHAN BI, ZHOU LIN, *Department of Chemistry, University of Massachusetts, Amherst, MA, USA*.

Luminescent doublet-spin organic semiconducting radicals are emergent and unique candidates for organic light-emitting diodes because their internal quantum efficiency is not limited by intersystem crossing into any non-emissive high-spin state. The multi-configurational nature of their electronic structures challenges the usage of single-reference density functional theory (DFT), but the problem can be mitigated by designing more powerful exchange–correlation (XC) functionals. In an earlier study, we developed a molecule-dependent range-separated functional, referred to as ML-ωPBE, using a stacked ensemble machine learning framework.[a] In the present study, we assessed the performance ML-ωPBE for 64 organic semiconducting radicals from four categories, when similar radicals are absent from the training set. Compared to the first-principles OT-ωPBE functional, ML-ωPBE reproduced the molecule-dependent range-separation parameter, ω, with a small mean absolute error (MAE) of **0.0214** a_0^{-1}. Using single-reference time-dependent DFT (TDDFT), ML-ωPBE exhibited outstanding behaviors in absorption and fluorescence energies for most radicals in question, with small MAEs of 0.22 and 0.12 eV compared to experimental sources, and approached the accuracy of OT-ωPBE (0.22 and 0.11 eV). Our results demonstrated excellent generalizability and transferability of our ML-ωPBE functional from closed-shell organic semiconducting molecules to open-shell doublet-spin organic semiconducting radicals.

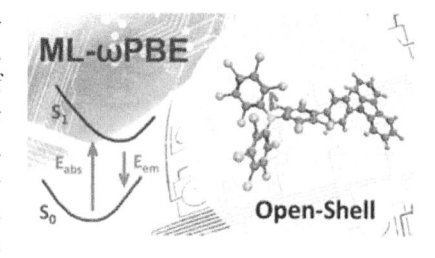

---

[a] Ju et al. *J. Phys. Chem. Lett.*, **2021** 12, 9516.

TL. Theory and Computation
Tuesday, June 21, 2022 – 1:30 PM
Room: 1024 Chemistry Annex

Chair: János Sarka, Texas Tech University, Lubbock, TX, USA

TL01 1:30 – 1:45

CALCULATIONS OF ACTINIDE- AND LANTHANIDE-CONTAINING SMALL MOLECULES USING SPINOR-BASED RELATIVISTIC COUPLED-CLUSTER METHODS

TIANXIANG CHEN, CHAOQUN ZHANG, LAN CHENG, *Department of Chemistry, Johns Hopkins University, Baltimore, MD, USA.*

Neodymium and uranium mono-oxide (NdO and UO) and the corresponding anions and cations are of interest to both experimental and theoretical studies. These systems exhibit a high density of low-lying electronic states and strong correlation among valence f-type electrons. They thus emerge as challenging examples for electronic-structure calculations. In this presentation, we demonstrate the usefulness of coupled-cluster techniques in understanding many properties of low-lying electronic states including ionization energies, electron affinities, and geometrical constants. We show that the inclusion of spin-orbit coupling in orbitals plays an important role in the capability to treat dense electronic states using single reference methods. Possible extension to treat transuranium-containing small molecules is discussed.

TL02 1:48 – 2:03

THEORETICAL INVESTIGATION OF THE X-RAY STARK EFFECT IN SMALL MOLECULES

CATHERINE WRIGHT, AVDHOOT DATAR, DEVIN A. MATTHEWS, *Department of Chemistry, Southern Methodist University, Dallas, TX, USA.*

We perform a computational study of the Stark effect for X-ray absorption spectra, and analyze the electric field response through the orbital and geometry variation with the electric field strength and orientation. We utilize a combination of Q-Chem and CFOUR, using the powerful CVS-EOM-CCSD/aug-cc-pCVTZ method for treating the vertical x-ray absorption energies and transition properties. External electric fields are applied collinear to the molecular dipole moment and the molecular geometry and orientation (when allowed by symmetry) are optimized in the presence of the field. We discuss how the symmetry of the molecule affects the X-ray spectra and identify characteristic features for the finite-field spectra. A rich structure is observed in the variation of X-ray spectra with varying electric field strength.

TL03 2:06 – 2:21

AB INITIO INVESTIGATION OF INTRAMOLECULAR CHARGE TRANSFER IN DMABN BY CALCULATION OF TRANSIENT X-RAY ABSORPTION FEATURES

AVDHOOT DATAR, SAISRINIVAS GUDIVADA, DEVIN A. MATTHEWS, *Department of Chemistry, Southern Methodist University, Dallas, TX, USA.*

Dual fluorescence in dimethylaminobenzonitrile (DMABN) and its derivatives in polar solvents, has been studied extensively for the past several years. Intramolecular charge transfer (ICT), in addition to the localized low-energy (LE) valence minimum, has been proposed as a mechanism for this dual fluorescence, with large geometric relaxation and molecular orbital reorganization a key feature of the ICT pathway. Herein, we have used both equation-of-motion coupled-cluster singles and doubles (EOM-CCSD) and time-dependent density functional (TD-DFT) methods to investigate the landscape of excited state potential energy surfaces across the several geometric conformations proposed as ICT structures, including Franck-Condon (FC), twisted (TICT), partially twisted (PTICT), wagged (WICT), and rehybridized (RICT) structures. Initial geometries for each type of structure were selected for excited state PES optimizations, as well as a systematic exploration of the low-lying PESs starting from the FC geometry. We find a number of minimum-energy (near)-crossing points among the lowest three excited states leading to the eventual ICT minima. Finally, we have calculated the carbon and nitrogen K-edge transient absorption spectra for all important "signpost" structures in order to investigate the differential pump-probe features along the LE and ICT pathways.

TL04   2:24 – 2:39

ENHANCING THERMALLY ACTIVATED DELAYED FLUORESCENCE THROUGH STRUCTURAL AND ENERGETIC FLEXIBILITY: THEORETICAL STUDIES

<u>DIEAA H ALHMOUD</u>, ZHOU LIN, *Department of Chemistry, University of Massachusetts, Amherst, MA, USA.*

Thermally activated delayed fluorescence (TADF) is one of the most promising routes to enhance the luminescent efficiency of an organic light-emitting diode (OLED) device by converting a non-emissive triplet exciton (T_1) back to an emissive singlet configuration (S_1) through reverse intersystem crossing (RISC) before it fluoresces back to the ground state (S_0). However, the TADF rate is generally restricted if only the highest occupied molecular orbital (HOMO) and the lowest unoccupied molecular orbital (LUMO) are involved. This is due to the conflict between a fast RISC rate between S_1 and T_1 (which requires a small HOMO–LUMO overlap), and a large transition dipole moment (μ_T) between S_1 and S_0 (which requires a large HOMO–LUMO overlap).[a] In the present study, we proposed two solutions to enhance the overall fluorescent rate: an inclusion of higher-lying singlet and triplet states ($S_{n \geq 2}$ and $T_{n \geq 2}$) in ISC–RISC routes to avoid the trade-off, and a fluxional molecular conformation to sample a broad range of HOMO–LUMO overlap. We provided a proof-of-concept for our solutions based on computational modeling of sample di-tert-butyl carbazole derivatives with the pyrazine or dipyrazine substituents (DTCz-Pz or DTCz-Pz), using a combination of density functional theory (DFT) and molecular dynamics (MD). Our study will provide a computational and quantitative strategy for the design of new TADF emitters with maximum luminescent efficiency.

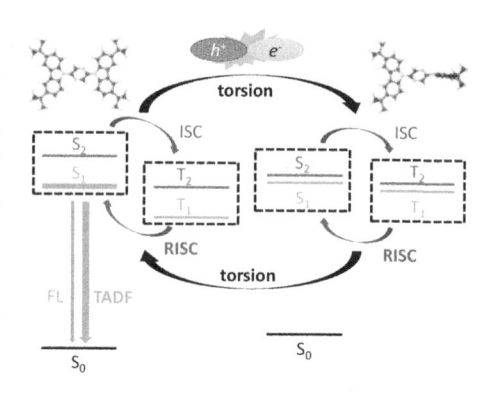

---

[a] A. Endo et al., *Appl. Phys. Lett.* **2011**, 98, 083302.

TL05   2:42 – 2:57

AB INITIO MODELING OF ULTRAFAST NONLINEAR OPTICAL SIGNALS IN MOLECULAR SYSTEMS INVOLVING ELECTRONIC TRANSITIONS

<u>RICHARD THURSTON</u>, THORSTEN WEBER, *Chemical Science Division, Lawrence Berkeley National Laboratory, Berkeley, CA, USA*; LIANG Z. TAN, *Molecular Foundry Division, Lawrence Berkeley National Laboratories, Berkeley, CA, USA*; DANIEL S. SLAUGHTER, *Chemical Science Division, Lawrence Berkeley National Laboratory, Berkeley, CA, USA.*

The observation of ultrafast time-resolved molecular dynamics after electronic excitation often relies on the measurement and interpretation of nonlinear optical signals. These signals can be very challenging to interpret without the aid of a theoretical model. A common approach to understand these signals is by using parameterized semi-empirical models that describe the specific process under study. These methods can be very useful and are very flexible but finding appropriate parameter values can be challenging, and the physical interpretation of these parameters can be ambiguous. Ab initio calculations can reduce the number of free parameters. However, available quantum chemistry packages like Dalton, QChem, and others, typically report frequency domain information, and tracking the evolution of the target usually requires the mapping of time onto a nuclear reaction coordinate which may not be observable. Here we present an ab initio approach to modeling time domain ultrafast nonlinear optical signals that addresses these issues by using the Dalton quantum chemistry package to parameterize a general N-level model which is then evaluated using a Liouville space representation. We compare these results to recent Ultrafast Transient Polarization Spectroscopy measurements of nitrobenzene.

This work was supported by the U.S. Department of Energy, Office of Science, Office of Basic Energy Sciences, Chemical Sciences, Geosciences, and Biosciences Division. Work at the Molecular Foundry was supported by the Office of Science, Office of Basic Energy Sciences of the U.S. Department of Energy under Contract no. DE-AC02-05CH11231.

Intermission

TL06 3:21 – 3:36

VIBRATIONALLY UNUSUAL BEHAVIORS PREDICTED FOR (XeHXe)$^+$: COMPUTATIONAL MOLECULAR SPECTROSCOPY STUDY

TSUNEO HIRANO, *Department of Chemistry, Ochanomizu University, Tokyo, Japan*; UMPEI NAGASHIMA, *Graduate school of Nanobioscience, Yokohama City University, Yokohama, Japan*; MASAAKI BABA, *Graduate School of Science, Kyoto University, Kyoto, Japan.*

We have reported on the vibrationally averaged structure and frequencies of (XeHXe)$^+$ at ISMS2021[a]: (a) (XeHXe)$^+$ is a linear molecule having a bent vibrationally averaged structure, (b) the ultra-heavy Xe atoms keep almost standstill during vibration, (c) severe matrix-effect for the ν_1 symmetric stretching mode, (d) $\nu_3 > \omega_{e,3}$ for the antisymmetric stretching mode, and (e) the zero-point structure has non-equivalent two r(Xe–H) bond distances irrespective of the potential being symmetrical for the bond-distance of these two bonds. We proposed in the previous report[a] that the unusual features (d) and (e) are characteristic for the [ultra-heavy]-[light]-[ultra-heavy] system. In this report, we disclose, from the viewpoint of computational molecular spectroscopy, why features (d) and (e) become characteristic for this system.

Based on the 3D vibrational potential energy surface (PES) calculated at the valence-CCSD(T)_DK3/[ANO-RCC 5ZP(Xe), cc-pV5Z-DK(H)] level, ro-vibrational wavefunctions (DVR3D wavefunction) were derived by the Discrete Variable Representation (DVR) method. In the antisymmetric stretching mode of a [ultra-heavy]-[light]-[ultra-heavy] system, the central light atom moves back and forth between the almost standstill ultra-heavy atoms just like a ball in catch-ball play. We will show this is the key for understanding unusual features (d) and (e), using the results of the PES and vibrational wavefunction analyses. We will also show why the symmetric stretching mode ν_1 is severely affected[b] by the molecular mass of the matrix medium.

---

[a]T. Hirano, U. Nagashima, M. Baba. ISMS2021, WA07.
[b]M. Tsuge, J. Kalinowski, R.B. Gerber, Y-P. Lee, J. Phys. Chem. A **119**, 2651 (2015).

TL07 3:39 – 3:54

FINE AND HYPERFINE RESOLVED EMPIRICAL ENERGY LEVELS OF VANADIUM OXIDE (VO)

CHARLES A BOWESMAN, *Department of Physics and Astronomy, University College London, London, UK*; SCOTT HOPKINS, *Department of Chemistry, University of Waterloo, Waterloo, ON, Canada*; SERGEI N. YURCHENKO, JONATHAN TENNYSON, *Department of Physics and Astronomy, University College London, London, UK.*

Vanadium oxide (VO) is believed to play an important role in driving temperature inversion in the atmospheres of hot-Jupiters. It also characterises the spectra of late M and early L dwarfs and subdwarfs, where it is understood to be a significant opacity source. A MARVEL (measured active rotational-vibrational energy levels) analysis of the spectra of VO is performed, involving thirteen electronic states (6 quartets and 7 doublets). ^{51}V^{16}O data from 14 sources are used to form three networks: hyperfine-resolved quartets, hyperfine-unresolved quartets and hyperfine-unresolved doublets. A single quartet network is formed by deperturbing the hyperfine lines and 191 lines are assigned to an intercombination 2 $^2\Pi$–X $^4\Sigma^-$ band system in the visible region previously recorded by Hopkins et al. (2009), allowing the doublet and quartet networks to be merged. As a result 6535/4393 and 8610/4641 validated transitions/final energies were obtained from analysis of the hyperfine-resolved/unresolved networks. T_0 energy values are determined for the 2 $^2\Pi_{1/2}$, $\nu = 0, 1$ and 2 $^2\Pi_{3/2}$, $\nu = 0$ states.

TL08 3:57 – 4:12

USING ASIMUT-ALVL TO MODEL THE VIS-NIR SPECTRUM OF JUPITER'S ATMOSPHERE

MIRIAM E. CISNEROS-GONZÁLEZ, *Institute of Condensed Matter and Nanosciences (IMCN), Université catholique de Louvain, Louvain-la-Neuve, Belgium*; MANUEL LÓPEZ-PUERTAS, *Terrestrial Planetary Atmospheres, Astrophysics Institute of Andalusia (IAA), Granada, Spain*; JUSTIN ERWIN, ANN CARINE VANDAELE, *Planetary Aeronomy, Royal Belgian Institute for Space Aeronomy (BIRA-IASB), Brussels, Belgium*; CLÉMENT LAUZIN, *Institute of Condensed Matter and Nanosciences (IMCN), Université catholique de Louvain, Louvain-la-Neuve, Belgium*; SÉVERINE ROBERT[a], *Planetary Aeronomy, Royal Belgian Institute for Space Aeronomy (BIRA-IASB), Brussels, Belgium*.

MAJIS (Moons And Jupiter Imaging Spectrometer) is one of the key scientific instruments on board the Jupiter ICy Moons Explorer (JUICE), the next mission to the Jovian system. A reliable determination of H_2O and CH_4 densities in the vertical structure and distribution of Jupiter's atmosphere is one of our main goals. In order to achieve this, we implemented the current knowledge of physical and chemical properties of Jupiter in ASIMUT-ALVL to perform simulations with different viewing geometries of the MAJIS instrument from $0.5\mu m$ to $2.5\mu m$. ASIMUT-ALVL is a Radiative Transfer (RT) code developed at BIRA-IASB that has been extensively used to characterize Mars and Venus atmospheres.[b,c] Our simulations are benchmarked to those from KOPRA, another RT software previously used for the study of Titan, Mars and Jupiter.[d] The next step is to validate our model against Jupiter observational data to finally assess the performances of the MAJIS VIS-NIR channel[e] to characterize the vertical structure of the Jovian atmosphere.[f]

---

[a] Also part of the Institute of Condensed Matter and Nanosciences (IMCN), Université catholique de Louvain, Louvain-la-Neuve, Belgium.
[b] Vandaele, A.C., et al., Optics Express. 2013, 21(18), 21148
[c] Vandaele, A.C., et al., Icarus. 2017, 295, 1-15.
[d] López-Puertas, M., et al., The Astronomical Journal. 2018, 156.4, 169.
[e] Cisneros-González, M.E., et al., SPIE Astronomical Telescopes and Instrumentation. 2020, 114431L.
[f] This project acknowledges the funding provided by the Belgian National Scientific Research Fund (FNRS by its acronym in french) through the Aspirant-Renewal Grant "34828872 MAJIS detectors and Impact on Science".

TL09 4:15 – 4:30

THE GPU ACCELERATED ABSORPTION SIMULATION (GAAS) PLATFORM

CHARLIE SCOTT CALLAHAN, *Mechanical Engineering, University of Colorado Boulder, Boulder, CO, USA*; SEAN COBURN, GREGORY B RIEKER, *Department of Mechanical Engineering, University of Colorado Boulder, Boulder, CO, USA*.

We present the GPU Accelerated Absorption Simulation (GAAS). GAAS is an open-source software package for simulating broadband absorption spectra rapidly using Nvidia graphics processing units (GPUs). GAAS is intended to provide a fast alternative to HAPI [1], capable of simulating absorbance spectra given a pressure, temperature, and concentration. GAAS is written in C++ and C and comes with a python interface so that it can be easily integrated into existing codebases. GAAS supports Voigt lineshape profiles and primarily contains a python function to replace HAPI's absorptionCoefficientVoigt. GAAS uses spectroscopic data in HITRAN's "par" format in order to be compatible with existing codebases that use HAPI. The software realizes up to a 100x reduction in computation time by simulating each Voigt lineshape in the spectrum on its own GPU thread, achieving enough parallelization for full utilization of GPU resources for spectra containing a few thousand absorption lines.

[1] R.V. Kochanov, I.E. Gordon, L.S. Rothman, P. Wcisło, C. Hill, J.S. Wilzewski, HITRAN Application Programming Interface (HAPI): A comprehensive approach to working with spectroscopic data, Journal of Quantitative Spectroscopy and Radiative Transfer, Volume 177, 2016, Pages 15-30, ISSN 0022-4073

TL10 QUANTUM SCRAMBLING IN MOLECULES

<u>CHENGHAO ZHANG</u>, *Department of Physics, University of Illinois at Urbana-Champaign, Urbana, IL, USA*; MARTIN GRUEBELE, *Department of Chemistry, University of Illinois at Urbana-Champaign, Urbana, IL, USA*; PETER GUY WOLYNES, *Department of Chemistry, Rice University, Houston, TX, USA.*

In quantum systems, out of time order correlators (OTOCs) can be used to probe the sensitivity of the dynamics to perturbing the Hamiltonian or changing the initial conditions ordinarily associated with classical chaos or its quantum analog. The vibrations of polyatomic molecules are known to undergo a transition from regular dynamics at low energy to facile energy flow at sufficiently high energy. Molecules therefore represent ideal quantum systems to study the transition to chaos in many-body systems of moderate size (here 6 to 36 degrees of freedom). By computing quantum OTOCs and their classical counterparts we quantify how information becomes 'scrambled' quantum mechanically in molecular systems.

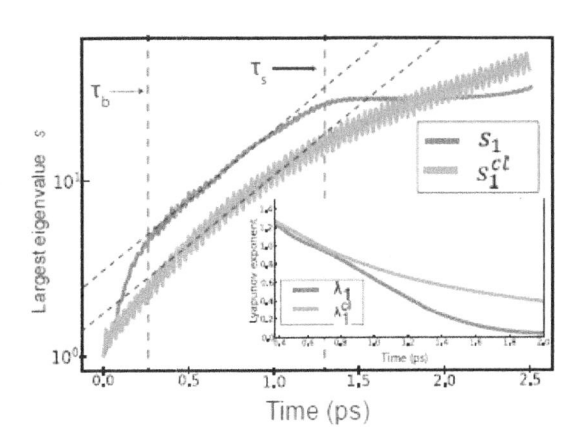

TM. Clusters/Complexes

Tuesday, June 21, 2022 – 1:30 PM

Room: 124 Burrill Hall

Chair: G. S. Grubbs II, Missouri University of Science and Technology, Rolla, MO, USA

TM01 1:30 – 1:45

PURE ROTATIONAL SPECTROSCOPY OF RARE GAS DIMERS BASED ON ROTATIONAL WAVE PACKET IMAGING

KENTA MIZUSE, *Department of Chemistry, School of Science, Kitasato University, Sagamihara, Japan*; YUYA TOBATA, *Department of Chemistry, Tokyo Institute of Technology, Tokyo, Japan*; URARA SATO, *Department of Chemistry, Kitasato University, Sagamihara, Japan*; YASUHIRO OHSHIMA, *Department of Chemistry, Tokyo Institute of Technology, Tokyo, Japan*.

We report time-domain rotational spectroscopy of argon dimer and krypton dimer by implementing time-resolved Coulomb explosion imaging of rotational wave packets. The rotational wave packets are created in the dimers with a ultrashort laser pulse, and their spatiotemporal evolution is fully characterized by measuring angular distribution of the fragment ions. The pump-probe measurements have been carried out up to a delay time of 16 ns. The alignment parameters, derived from the observed images, exhibit periodic oscillation lasting for more than 15 ns. Pure rotational spectrum of Ar_2 is obtained by Fourier transformation of the time traces of the alignment parameters. The frequency resolution in the spectrum is about 90 MHz, the highest ever achieved for Ar_2. The rotational constant and the centrifugal distortion constant are determined with much improved presision than the previous experimental results: $B_0 = 1.72713(9)$ GHz and $D_0 = 0.0310(5)$ MHz. The present B_0 value does not match within the quoted experimental uncertainty with that from the VUV spectroscopy, so far accepted as an experimental reference to assess theories. Spectrum of the krypton dimer will be also reported.

TM02 1:48 – 2:03

PARTIAL PROTON TRANSFER IN THE TRIFLUOROACETIC ACID - TRIMETHYLAMINE COMPLEX

AARON J REYNOLDS, NATHAN LOVE, KENNETH R. LEOPOLD, *Chemistry Department, University of Minnesota, Minneapolis, MN, USA*.

Chirped-pulse and cavity microwave spectra are presented for the complex formed from trifluoroacetic acid (TFA) and trimethylamine (TMA). Both the parent complex and that formed from deuterated TFA have been observed. Based on measured ^{14}N nuclear quadrupole coupling constants and supplemental computations at the MP2/6-311++G(df,pd) level of theory, the complex is shown to involve partial transfer of the TFA proton to the amine. Structural indicators of the degree of proton transfer are used to support this conclusion and comparisons with other related hydrogen bonded systems are presented. The relatively strong acidity of TFA as compared with other carboxylic acids, together with the relatively strong Brønsted basicity of TMA, likely underlie the ability of this system to undergo partial proton transfer in the gas phase without the aid of microsolvation.

TM03
ALTERNATING 1-PHENYL-2,2,2-TRIFLUOROETHANOL CONFORMATIONAL LANDSCAPE WITH THE ADDITION OF ONE WATER: TUNNELLING AND LARGE AMPLITUDE MOTIONS

COLTON CARLSON, DANIEL MASON, QIAN YANG, *Department of Chemistry, University of Alberta, Edmonton, AB, Canada*; NATHAN A. SEIFERT, *Department of Chemistry, University of New Haven, West Haven, CT, USA*; YUNJIE XU, *Department of Chemistry, University of Alberta, Edmonton, AB, Canada.*

The 1:1 adduct of 1-phenyl-2,2,2-trifluoroethanol (PhTFE) with water was investigated using chirped pulse Fourier transform microwave spectroscopy and computational methods. PhTFE itself was previously reported to have two stable conformations, I (gauche) and II (trans), however, only the most stable conformer, PhTFE I, was experimentally observed.[1] Rotational spectra of the two most stable PhTFE-H_2O conformers along with several deuterium and oxygen-18 isotopologues were assigned and their structures analyzed. The most stable complex exhibits PhTFE in the gauche configuration with water inserted into the existing intramolecular OH-F hydrogen bond. This conformer is stabilized by two intermolecular hydrogen bonds in addition to the intramolecular interactions present in the PhTFE monomer. Those being a strong interaction between the alcohol hydrogen on PhTFE and the oxygen on water OH-OH_2 and a weaker interaction between a fluorine on PhTFE and a water hydrogen F-HOH. Water tunnelling splitting was identified in the rotational spectrum showing the characteristic ortho versus para intensity ratio, which was attributed to the interchange of bonded and nonbonded hydrogen atoms of the water subunit. The second observed complex exhibits PhTFE in the trans configuration, indicating that complexation with water sufficiently stabilized PhTFE II such that it can survive the supersonic expansion. Stabilization is achieved by water interacting with both the alcohol hydrogen and the phenyl ring of PhTFE. The nonbonded hydrogen of the water subunit was shown to exhibit a large amplitude motion in both conformers.

1. Carlson, C. D.; Seifert, N. A.; Heger, M.; Xie, F.; Thomas, J; Xu, Y. J. Mol. Spectrosc., 2018, 351, 62–67.

TM04
CONFORMATIONAL BEHAVIOUR OF m-ANISALDEHYDE AND ITS MICROSOLVATES

ANDRES VERDE, JUAN CARLOS LOPEZ, SUSANA BLANCO, *Departamento de Química Física y Química Inorgánica - I.U. CINQUIMA, Universidad de Valladolid, Valladolid, Spain.*

The rotational spectra of m-anisaldehyde and its microsolvated complexes generated in a supersonic jet have been studied by chirped-pulse Fourier transform microwave spectroscopy (CP-FTMW) in the 2-8 GHz region. Four conformers have been detected for the monomer. The three most intense rotamers have line intensities high enough to allow the observation of the monosubstituted ^{13}C isotopologues in natural abundance allowing the determination of their r_e, r_s and r_m structures. When allowing water vapor to expand in the supersonic jet, the spectra of ten new species assigned to microsolvated complexes appear. Seven monohydrated species have been identified reflecting the two possible interactions of water and the aldehyde group. The two dihydrated species observed are related to the most stable m-anisaldehyde conformer. The most abundant dihydrated complex presents a structure with water dimer closing a cycle with the aldehyde and methoxy groups which confers high stability. In the less abundant dihydrate, water dimer closes a cycle with the aldehyde group, a structure of great interest to better understand the solvation of aldehydes. Additionally, one complex of m-anisaldehyde with four molecules of water has been detected. In this species, the most stable conformer of m-anisaldehyde captures the tetramer of water adopting a stacked configuration. Work is in progress.

Intermission

TM06 3:21 – 3:36

POINT MUTATION CHANGES VIBRATIONAL COUPLING IN LEPIDIUM VIRGINICUM WATER SOLUBLE CHLOROPHYLL BINDING PROTEIN

GALINA GRECHISHNIKOVA, AMIT SRIVASTAVA, SAFA AHAD, MIKE EARL REPPERT, LIBAI HUANG, *Department of Chemistry, Purdue University, West Lafayette, IN, USA.*

Low temperature photoluminescence spectroscopy (PL) revealed a change in vibrational coupling of mutated Water soluble chlorophyll binding protein complexes (WSCPs) with Chlorophyll a. Pigment-protein systems can adjust the range of absorbed wavelengths according to living conditions. However, the mechanism of spectral tuning is unclear. A study of point mutations in the Q57 site of the Lepidium virginicum (Lv) WSCP is expected to shed light on how hydrogen bonds and electrostatic interactions influence the emission spectrum of Chlorophyll a (Chl a) bound to WSCP. Steady state PL revealed the change of the electron-phonon coupling strength within the mutants at 7 K. Time-resolved (TR) PL detected the difference in the lifetimes of the WSCP mutants at 7 K. Both PL and TRPL results cannot be ascribed to the charge difference in the Q57 site of Lv WSCP alone. The influence of hydrogen bonding together with electrostatic interactions and geometry changes should be considered to correctly describe the mechanism of tuning of vibrational coupling in WSCP bound with Chl a complex.

TM07 3:39 – 3:54

STABILITY OF NEUTRAL MANGANESE OXIDE CLUSTERS

CHASE H ROTTEGER, SHAUN SUTTON, SCOTT G SAYRES, *School of Molecular Sciences and Biodesign Center for Applied Structural Discovery, Arizona State University, Tempe, AZ, USA.*

Manganese oxides are among the most widely explored transition metal oxides for diverse biomedical applications and are also employed in a wide number of industrial processes. Its wide range of oxidation states provide manganese with extreme flexibility in electron occupancy that has also attracted increasing attention for use in photocatalytic processes. Neutral clusters are excellent mimics of the active sites of bulk materials, and can be employed to understand the local geometric and electronic structure properties, and oxidation states that provide the best charge carrier lifetimes and by extension optimal photochemical efficiency. Here, I will present our ongoing work on the ultrafast relaxation dynamics of neutral manganese oxide clusters, which are prepared through the laser ablation of a pure metal rod with a 532 nm Nd:YAG laser. A synchronized pulse of He seeded with 5% oxygen enables cluster formation through supersonic expansion. The neutral clusters are then studied through by combining two-color femtosecond spectroscopy with time-of-flight mass spectrometry. Our cluster distribution shows that manganese has a large range of oxidation states. The clusters are excited by the second harmonic of a Ti:Sapphire femtosecond (fs) laser system (400 nm = 3.1eV) and subsequently ionized through strong field ionization with the fundamental laser beam (800 nm = 1.55 eV). The subtle changes in the ultrafast dynamics upon the addition/subtraction of each atom are being evaluated to provide new understanding to the flow of energy through a material.

TM08   3:57 – 4:12

EXCITED STATE PHOTODYNAMICS OF SUB-NANOMETER METAL OXIDE CLUSTERS

SCOTT G SAYRES, *School of Molecular Sciences and Biodesign Center for Applied Structural Discovery, Arizona State University, Tempe, AZ, USA.*

I will present our recent work[1–3] on the ultrafast dynamics of sub-nanometer neutral metal oxide clusters investigated with femtosecond pump-probe spectroscopy and supported by theoretical calculations. Absorption of a UV (400 nm) photon initiates several relaxation processes, with excited state lifetimes that are strongly dependent on the nature of the electronic transition. The atomic precision and tunability of gas phase clusters highlights how the simple picture of sequential oxidation of the metal atoms reveals a linear tunability to the contributions of each relaxation component to the total transient signal. In chromium oxides, a 30 fs transient signal fraction grows linearly with oxidation, matching the amount of O to Cr charge transfer character of the photoexcitation and highlighting a gradual transition between semiconducting and metallic behavior at the molecular level. The lifetimes of nickel oxide clusters exhibit a unique reliance on the nature of the atomic orbital contributions, providing new insights to the analogous band edge excitation dynamics of strongly correlated bulk material. Short lived dynamics in stoichiometric (NiO)n clusters are attributed to excitation between Ni-3d and Ni-4s orbitals, where their strong exchange coupling produces metallic-like electron-electron scattering. Oxygen vacancies introduce 3d to 4p transitions, which increases the lifetimes of the sub-picosecond component by 20-60 percent and enables the formation of long-lived (lifetimes greater than 2.5 ps) states.

(1) Garcia, J. M.; Heald, L. F.; Shaffer, R. E.; Sayres, S. G. Oscillation in Excited State Lifetimes with Size of Sub-Nanometer Neutral $(TiO_2)_n$ Clusters Observed with Ultrafast Pump–Probe Spectroscopy. J. Phys. Chem. Lett. 2021, 12, 4098–4103.

(2) Garcia, J. M.; Sayres, S. G. Increased Excited State Metallicity in Neutral Cr_2O_n Clusters (n < 5) upon Sequential Oxidation. J. Am. Chem. Soc. 2021, 143 (38), 15572–15575.

(3) Garcia, J. M.; Sayres, S. G. Orbital-Dependent Photodynamics of Strongly Correlated Clusters. Phys.Chem.Chem.Phys. 2022, 24, 5590-5597.

TM09   4:15 – 4:30

THE MILLIMETER-WAVE SPECTRUM OF THE WEAKLY BOUND ARGON-METHANOL CLUSTER

CONNOR J. WRIGHT, *Department of Chemistry, University of Wisconsin-Madison, Madison, WI, USA*; KEVIN ROENITZ, *Department of Chemistry, Emory University, Atlanta, GA, USA*; JONATHAN REBELSKY, *Department of Chemistry, University of Wisconsin-Madison, Madison, WI, USA*; ANNA KAY GEROSOLINA, MORGAN GIESE, *Chemistry and Astronomy, University of Wisconsin-Madison, Madison, WI, USA*; STEVEN SHIPMAN, *Department of Chemistry, New College of Florida, Sarasota, FL, USA*; SUSANNA L. WIDICUS WEAVER, *Chemistry and Astronomy, University of Wisconsin-Madison, Madison, WI, USA.*

The study of the structure and internal motion of weakly bound gas-phase clusters is of considerable interest in understanding the nature of intermolecular bonding. Van der Waals clusters with rare gas atoms such as argon are particularly interesting due to their ability to freely internally rotate about the host molecule. Additionally, many experiments that utilize argon as the buffer gas for supersonic expansions suffer from subsequent clustering of the argon to the sample of interest. In high-resolution spectroscopy, this can cause difficulties with line identification and assignment. Therefore, it is useful to have a complete and accurate characterization of the rotational transitions for such complexes. In our research, nearly all of our supersonic expansions involve the use of argon gas, and methanol is often a molecular starting material for the chemistry that we wish to study making the target of this study the $Ar-CH_3OH$ cluster. The spectrum from 140-335 GHz was collected via direct absorption spectroscopy using a supersonic expansion of argon seeded with vapor from a pure methanol sample. Numerous spectral lines were detected across this frequency range. Spectral analysis was conducted using the Effective Rotational Hamiltonian program (ERHAM) due to the presence of a low barrier methyl rotor, which ERHAM is well-suited to address. The spectral results and associated analysis for $Ar-CH_3OH$ will be presented here.

TN. Radicals
Tuesday, June 21, 2022 – 1:30 PM
Room: 274 Medical Sciences Building

Chair: Ugo Jacovella, CNRS, Université Paris-Saclay, Orsay, France

TN01　　　　1:30–1:45
HIGH-RESOLUTION INFRARED SPECTROSCOPY OF GAS-PHASE CYCLOBUTYL RADICAL IN THE α-CH STRETCH REGION: STRUCTURAL AND DYNAMICAL INSIGHTS

YA-CHU CHAN, *JILA and the Department of Chemistry, University of Colorado Boulder, Boulder, CO, USA*; DAVID NESBITT, *JILA, Department of Chemistry, and Department of Physics, University of Colorado Boulder, Boulder, CO, USA.*

Gas-phase cyclobutyl radical ($\cdot C_4H_7$) is generated at a rotational temperature of 15 K in a slit-jet discharge mixture of 70% Ne/30% He and 0.5-0.6% cyclobutyl bromide (C_4H_7Br). The fully rovibrationally resolved absorption spectra of the α-CH stretch fundamental band are observed and analyzed, yielding the first precision structural information for this radical species. The band origin is determined to be 3068.7801(25) cm^{-1}, which from previous infrared spectroscopic studies of cyclobutyl radicals in droplets[a] implies a 0.8 cm^{-1} blue shift due to the presence of liquid helium. This value is also in good agreement with high-level *ab initio* calculations at CCSD(T) level of theory with a PVnZ (n = 2,3) and ANOn (n = 0,1) basis set, which predicts an anharmonic frequency of 3076.4 cm^{-1} from second-order vibrational perturbation theory (VPT2).[b] A complete rovibrational analysis is underway, progress toward which will be reported. Of particular dynamical interest in such results will be the large amplitude nature of the ring puckering motion, specifically whether this radical possesses a planar (C_{2v}) or puckered (C_s) geometry. While CCSD(T) theoretical calculations predict a C_s electronic minimum and a C_{2v} first-order saddle point, the ratio of out-of-plane puckering frequency to interconversion barrier constitutes the dominant influence on the vibrationally averaged molecular geometry and dynamics of large amplitude motion for cyclobutyl radical.

[a] A. R. Brown, P. R. Franke and G. E. Douberly, "Helium nanodroplet isolation of the cyclobutyl, 1-methylallyl, and allylcarbinyl radicals: Infrared spectroscopy and *ab initio* computations," J. Phys. Chem. A 121, 7576-7587 (2017).
[b] D. A. Matthews, L. Cheng, M. E. Harding, F. Lipparini, S. Stopkowicz, T.-C. Jagau, P. G. Szalay, J. Gauss and J. F. Stanton, "Coupled-cluster techniques for computational chemistry: The CFOUR program package," J. Chem. Phys. 152, 214108 (2020).

TN02　　　　1:48–2:03
EXTENDING PURE ROTATIONAL MEASUREMENTS OF THE CH_3O RADICAL TOWARD THE TERAHERTZ DOMAIN

MARIE-ALINE MARTIN-DRUMEL, OLIVIA CHITARRA, JEAN-THIBAUT SPANIOL, THOMAS SANDOW HEARNE, OLIVIER PIRALI, *Institut des Sciences Moléculaires d'Orsay, Université Paris Saclay, CNRS, Orsay, France*; J.-C. LOISON, *Institut des Sciences Moléculaires, Université de Bordeaux, Talence, France.*

Current astronomical observations, for instance with ALMA and NOEMA, extend well into the submillimeter-wave frequency domain. For many molecules, including some that have already been detected in the interstellar medium, laboratory data remain limited to the microwave and millimeter-wave regions. This is particularly striking for numerous reactive species difficult to produce in the laboratory. Considering that frequency extrapolation in absence of laboratory data is particularly unreliable, this lack of measurements surely prevents a thorough analysis of the observational data at high frequencies. The CH_3O radical is one such species: it is a known interstellar molecule [1] for which laboratory measurements do not extend beyond 370 GHz [2].

In this work, we have investigated the pure rotational spectrum of CH_3O toward the terahertz domain. The radical was produced by H-abstraction from methanol using atomic fluorine, itself produced using a microwave discharge in F_2 diluted in He, a method that we successfully used recently to investigate the rotation-tunneling spectrum of the CH_2OH radical [3]. Compared to that previous work, several enhancements have been made to our (sub)millimeter-wave spectrometer that now allows for double-pass into the absorption cell and magnetic-field modulation. The strength of the double-modulation (source frequency and magnetic field) scheme is that only transitions of open-shell species are visible over a completely flat baseline, a feature that has proven invaluable in the case of CH_3O to disentangle an otherwise dense spectrum with numerous strong transitions arising from the precursor or other reaction products (such as H_2CO). Overall, about 500 lines of CH_3O have been recorded up to 900 GHz, with accuracies ranging from 10 to 200 kHz. These transitions have been fit, together with available pure rotation literature data, to a rigid-rotor Hamiltonian using the SPFIT/SPCAT software.

[1] J. Cernicharo *et al.*, *Astrophys. J.* **759** L43 (2012)　　[2] Y. Endo *et al.*, *J. Chem. Phys.* **81**, 122 (1984); T. Momose *et al.*, *J. Chem. Phys.* **88** 5338 (1988) & **90** 8 (1990); J. C. Laas, S. L. Widicus Weaver, *Astrophys. J.* **835** 46 (2017)　　[3] O. Chitarra *et al.*, *Astron. Astrophys.* **644** A123 (2020)

TN03

THE MICROWAVE SPECTRUM OF THE DIFLUOROCYANOMETHYL RADICAL, ĊF$_2$CN

LU KANG, *Department of Chemistry and Biochemistry, Kennesaw State University, Kennesaw, GA, USA*; HA VINH LAM NGUYEN, *Université Paris-Est Créteil et Université de Paris, Laboratoire Interuniversitaire des systèmes atmosphériques (LISA), CNRS UMR7583, Creteil, France*; CHRISTOPHER FALLS, ALEXANDER SEYS, WALLACE C. PRINGLE, *Department of Chemistry, Wesleyan University, Middletown, CT, USA*; THOMAS A. BLAKE, *Chemical Physics and Analysis, Pacific Northwest National Laboratory, Richland, WA, USA*; STEWART E. NOVICK, *Department of Chemistry, Wesleyan University, Middletown, CT, USA*; S. A. COOKE, *Natural and Social Science, Purchase College SUNY, Purchase, NY, USA.*

The pure rotational spectrum of the open shell difluorocyanomethyl radical, ĊF$_2$CN, has been measured using two Balle-Flygare-type cavity Fourier-Transform-Microwave (FTMW) spectrometers both equipped with pulsed discharged nozzles. A total of 156 transitions (from $N = 1 - 0$ to $6 - 5$, and $K_a = 0, 1, 2, 3$) in the electronic ground state were observed between 6.5 GHz and 38.4 GHz with a typical linewidth of approximately 5 kHz full-width-half-maximum. A Hamiltonian that included semi-rigid rotor, spin-rotation, and nuclear hyperfine parameters was fit to the observed data set and these parameters have been interpreted and compared to similar radicals. Excellent agreement between experimental and uB3LYP/aug-cc-pVQZ calculated rotational constants, the experimental inertial defect, -0.6858(2) uÅ^2, and the failure of a coupling scheme in which the fluorine nuclei are treated as identical and related by a C$_{2v}$ symmetry axis combine to indicate a nonplanar structure for the ĊF$_2$CN radical.

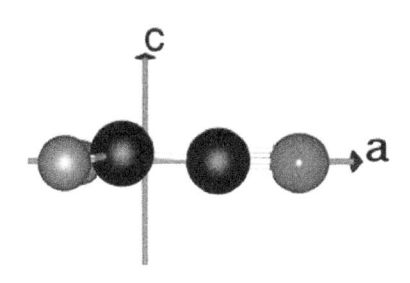

TN04

IMPROVEMENTS TO NEW PROGRAM FOR SPIN-TORSION-ROTATION & THE METHYL-PHENOXYL RADICALS

J. H. WESTERFIELD, *Department of Chemistry, University of California, Davis, Davis, CA, USA*; BLAIR WELSH, TIMOTHY S. ZWIER, *Combustion Research Facility, Sandia National Laboratories, Livermore, CA, USA*; KYLE N. CRABTREE, *Department of Chemistry, University of California, Davis, Davis, CA, USA.*

A new program, written in Julia, has been written to simulate and fit spectra of radicals with 3-fold internal rotors. The program now uses a single diagonalization stage implementation of the Rho Axis Method to provide more direct usage of the wavefunction symmetries for the A states. The three different methyl positions provided test cases of potential spin-torsion coupling with varying internal barrier heights of about $V_3 \approx 206$ cm^{-1} in ortho, $V_3 \approx 64$ cm^{-1} in meta, and $V_6 \approx 7$ cm^{-1} in para. Spectroscopic parameters determined from CCSD(T)/ANO0 calculations provided test cases for assigning states and simulating the spectra. The rotational spectra of ortho-, meta-, and para-methyl-phenoxyl radicals was collected through Chirped-Pulse Fourier Transform Microwave Spectroscopy. The radicals were produced from the appropriate methyl anisole precursors through pyrolysis in a SiC pyrolysis source attached to a pulsed valve. The temperature of the reactor was monitored with an infrared camera and the production of the radicals was monitored with 118 nm photoionization -Time of Flight Mass Spectrometry. Once the optimal temperature of the pyrolysis source was determined, the rotational spectrum was recorded from 7.5 – 17.5 GHz. Each radical was fit as a closed-shell species using RAM36 and as an open-shell species using the new program which also included spin-torsion coupling terms.

TN05　　2:42 – 2:57
PRODUCT-SPECIFIC REACTION KINETICS OF CN WITH PROPENE PROBED BY CHIRPED-PULSE FOURIER TRANSFORM MILLIMETER WAVE SPECTROSCOPY

DIVITA GUPTA[a], BRIAN M HAYS, MYRIAM DRISSI, THEO GUILLAUME, OMAR ABDELKADER KHEDAOUI, ILSA ROSE COOKE, IAN R. SIMS, *CNRS, IPR (Institut de Physique de Rennes) - UMR 6251, Univ Rennes, F-35000 Rennes, France.*

Studying the different possible reactions and their dynamics under the low-temperature conditions of the interstellar medium and various planetary atmospheres is essential to understand the chemical evolution of various species detected in these environments. I will discuss the CPUF (Chirped Pulse in Uniform supersonic Flow) technique, which is a combination of the CRESU (Cinétique de Réaction en Ecoulement Supersonique Uniforme or Reaction Kinetics in Supersonic Uniform Flow) method to provide a low temperature environment and chirped-pulse Fourier transform millimeter spectroscopic detection. This technique has been further modified with an additional expansion chamber to enhance the detection of a wider variety of species and to overcome pressure effects in a CRESU flow. I will show our measurements for the reaction of CN radical with propene down at 35 K. I will discuss the impact of these experimental measurements, their application to astrochemical studies, and the future outlook for this technique at Rennes.

---

[a]Current Affiliation: I. Physikalisches Institut, Universität zu Köln, Köln, Germany

TN06　　3:00 – 3:15
EXAMINING METHYLAMINE DISSOCIATION PRODUCTS USING THEORY AND ROTATIONAL SPECTROSCOPY: THE CH_2NH_2 RADICAL

CONNOR J. WRIGHT, JONATHAN REBELSKY, *Department of Chemistry, University of Wisconsin-Madison, Madison, WI, USA*; ANNA KAY GEROSOLINA, *Chemistry and Astronomy, University of Wisconsin-Madison, Madison, WI, USA*; JOHN F. STANTON, *Physical Chemistry, University of Florida, Gainesville, FL, USA*; SUSANNA L. WIDICUS WEAVER, *Chemistry and Astronomy, University of Wisconsin-Madison, Madison, WI, USA*.

Studying the chemical inventory of the interstellar medium (ISM) is critical to developing new theories of molecular formation and evolution. Furthermore, the search for biologically-relevant species and their precursors has been at the forefront of astrobiology and astrochemistry in recent years. As such, this work focuses on the dissociation products of methylamine (CH_3NH_2), a known precursor to the simplest amino acid, glycine ($C_2H_5NO_2$). It is likely that the radical products of cosmic-ray induced photodissociation of methylamine are important in prebiotic interstellar pathways as well as atmospheric models of planetary bodies such as Titan. Therefore, we are studying the radical species produced in a methylamine discharge as a guide for future studies of methylamine photodissociation. Our initial molecular target is the CH_2NH_2 radical, for which no rotational spectroscopic information is available. We examined the structure of this radical using high-level computational methods and then predicted the rotational spectrum based off of this information. We then compared these predictions to the rotational spectra of species obtained using a high voltage discharge of methylamine in argon at the throat of a supersonic expansion. Here we will present the spectroscopic predictions and the initial experimental results for CH_2NH_2, and discuss the implications of this work for astrochemistry and astrobiology.

Intermission

TN07 3:39 – 3:54

PRODUCTION OF •CH$_2$NH$_2$ AND CH$_2$NH IN THE REACTIONS OF METHYLAMINE (CH$_3$NH$_2$) WITH •H OR •OH IN SOLID p-H$_2$ AND ITS IMPLICATION IN ASTROCHEMISTRY

PRASAD RAMESH JOSHI, *Department of Applied Chemistry, National Yang Ming Chiao Tung University, Hsinchu, Taiwan*; YUAN-PERN LEE, *Department of Applied Chemistry, Institute of Molecular Science, and Centre for Emergent Functional Matter Science, National Yang Ming Chiao Tung University, Hsinchu, Taiwan.*

Methylamine (CH$_3$NH$_2$) is considered to be a potential precursor for the formation of interstellar glycine through the reaction between aminomethyl radical (•CH$_2$NH$_2$) and HOCO, but direct evidence of the formation and spectral identification of •CH$_2$NH$_2$ remains unreported. Taking advantage of unique properties associated with the *para*-hydrogen (p-H$_2$) matrix, we performed the reaction H + CH$_3$NH$_2$ in solid p-H$_2$ at 3.2 K. To generate H atoms, photolysis at 365 nm of a co-deposited mixture of CH$_3$NH$_2$/p-H$_2$ and Cl$_2$ to produce Cl atoms and subsequent IR irradiation for promoting the Cl + H$_2$ ($\nu = 1$) → H + HCl reaction were carried out. IR spectra of •CH$_2$NH$_2$ and CH$_2$NH were observed upon UV/IR irradiation and when the matrix was maintained in darkness. The new IR spectrum of •CH$_2$NH$_2$ clearly indicates that •CH$_2$NH$_2$ can be formed from the reaction H + CH$_3$NH$_2$ in dark interstellar clouds. Experiments on CD$_3$NH$_2$ produced CHD$_2$NH$_2$, in addition to •CD$_2$NH$_2$ and CD$_2$NH, confirming the occurrence of H addition to •CD$_2$NH$_2$. The potential-energy scheme of H + CH$_3$NH$_2$ reactions reveals the feasibility of sequential H-abstraction and H-addition reactions for the formation of products observed in this study. The observed dual-cycle mechanism containing two consecutive H-abstraction and two H-addition steps chemically connects CH$_3$NH$_2$ and CH$_2$NH and might imply their quasi-equilibrium. In another experimental method, photolysis at 250 nm of a H$_2$O$_2$-doped CH$_3$NH$_2$/p-H$_2$ matrix was performed to generate •OH to facilitate the •OH + CH$_3$NH$_2$ reaction; further reaction of •OH + H$_2$ → H$_2$O + H might also trigger the H + CH$_3$NH$_2$ reaction. Significantly more •CH$_2$NH$_2$ was produced than in CH$_3$NH$_2$/Cl$_2$/p-H$_2$ experiments, consistent with a barrier predicted for •OH + CH$_3$NH$_2$ much smaller than that for H + CH$_3$NH$_2$. All species observed herein are plausible starting materials for interstellar glycine in molecular clouds.

TN08 3:57 – 4:12

ORIENTATION DYNAMICS OF CH$_3$, CH$_4$, AND CD$_4$ QUANTUM ROTORS IN SOLID METHANES AT CRYOGENIC TEMPERATURES

YURIJ DMITRIEV, *Division of Plasma Physics, Atomic Physics and Astrophysics, Ioffe Institute, St. Petersburg, Russia.*

High-resolution EPR spectra of CH$_3$ radicals in the solid CH$_4$ and CD$_4$ matrices were obtained and analyzed. The change in the symmetry of a small impurity molecule freely embedded in the matrix crystal lattice in comparison with the symmetry of this molecule in the gas phase, which we found on the example of the CH$_3$ radical in the CH$_4$ and CD$_4$ solids, is expected to be a fairly general and important effect for spectroscopy. The data we obtained on the orientation mobility of methyl radical in the methane matrices in comparison with the results for other matrices indicate a sufficiently rapid sub-barrier reorientation of the methyl radical and the correlated tunneling reorientation of the methane molecules, which occurs even at helium temperatures in an orientationally ordered solid.

TN09   4:15–4:30

FORMATION REACTION MECHANISM AND INFRARED SPECTRA OF CRIEGEE INTERMEDIATE ANTI-TRANS-METHACROLEIN OXIDE [CH$_2$C(CH$_3$)CHOO] AND ITS ASSOCIATED PRECURSOR AND ADDUCT RADICALS

<u>YUAN-PERN LEE</u>, JIA-RONG CAI, JUNG-HSUAN SU, CHEN-AN CHUNG, *Department of Applied Chemistry, National Yang Ming Chiao Tung University, Hsinchu, Taiwan.*

Methacrolein oxide (MACRO, CH$_2$C(CH$_3$)CHOO) is an important Criegee intermediate produced in ozonolysis of isoprene, the most abundantly-emitted non-methane hydrocarbon in the atmosphere. We employed a step-scan Fourier-transform infrared spectrometer to investigate the source reaction of MACRO in laboratories. Upon UV irradiation of precursor 1,3-diiodo-2-methyl-prop-1-ene CH$_2$IC(CH$_3$)CHI (**1**), the 3-iodo-2-methyl-prop-1-en-3-yl CH$_2$C(CH$_3$)CHI radical (**2**) was detected, confirming the fission of the allylic C-I bond rather than the vinylic C-I bond. Upon UV irradiation of (**1**) and O$_2$ near 21 Torr, *anti-trans*-MACRO (**3a**) was observed to have an intense OO-stretching band near 917 cm^{-1}, much greater than those of *syn*-CH$_3$CHOO and (CH$_3$)$_2$COO, supporting a stronger O-O bond in MACRO because of resonance stabilization. At increased pressure (86-346 Torr), both reaction adducts CH$_2$C(CH$_3$)CHIOO (**4**) and (CHI)C(CH$_3$)CH$_2$OO (**5**) radicals were observed, indicating that O$_2$ can add to either carbon of the delocalized propenyl radical moiety of (**2**). We also employed a quantum-cascade laser and an UV laser to investigate the yield and kinetics of MACRO. The yield of MACRO is only 5 % from the source reaction, significantly smaller than other carbonyl oxides. The rate coefficients of the formation reaction and the self-reaction of MACRO will also be discussed.

TN10   4:33–4:48

STUDY OF THE KINETICS AND PRODUCT YIELDS FOR THE REACTION OF CRIEGEE INTERMEDIATE CH$_2$OO WITH HNO$_3$ USING MID-INFRARED TIME-RESOLVED DUAL-COMB SPECTROSCOPY

<u>PEI-LING LUO</u>, *Institute of Atomic and Molecular Sciences, Academia Sinica, Taipei, Taiwan.*

The reaction of Criegee intermediates with HNO$_3$ have been thought to be important in the oxidation of atmospheric HNO$_3$ because of the fast reaction rates, over 3 orders of magnitude larger than that of the OH + HNO$_3$ reaction.[a] In particular, a new catalytic conversion of the simplest Criegee intermediate CH$_2$OO to OH and HCO radicals by HNO$_3$ was proposed in recent theoretical study.[b] Herein, the mid-infrared dual-comb spectrometers[c] with the capability of widely wavelength tunability and switchable dual-comb and continuous-wave operation modes were employed to investigate the reaction kinetics and determine the branching ratios of the primary product channels in the reaction CH$_2$OO + HNO$_3$. Based on quantitative determinations of CH$_2$OO, CH$_2$O, OH and HO$_2$ radicals under various experimental conditions, the pressure-dependent yields of the OH and HO$_2$ product channels of the reaction CH$_2$OO + HNO$_3$ were evaluated in this work.

---

[a] Khan, M. A. H.; Percival, C. J.; Caravan, R. L.; Taatjes, C. A.; Shallcross, D. E. Environ. Sci.: Processes Impacts 2018, 20, 437–453.
[b] Raghunath, P.; Lee, Y.-P.; Lin, M. C. J. Phys. Chem. A 2017, 121, 3871–3878.
[c] Luo, P.-L.; Horng, E.-C. Commun Chem 2020, 3, 95; Luo, P.-L. Opt. Lett. 2020, 45, 6791–6794.

TO. Plenary Special Session
Tuesday, June 21, 2022 – 5:15 PM
Room: 2025A/B/C Ikenberry Commons

Chair: Helen O. Leung, Amherst College, Amherst, MA, USA

TO01   5:20 – 5:55

SPECTROSCOPY TODAY: THE URGENT NEED FOR SCIENCE AND INNOVATION TO SAVE THIS WARMING PLANET

GERALDINE RICHMOND, *Under Secretary of Science and Innovation, U.S. Department of Energy, Washtington, DC, USA.*

In this year that we celebrate the 75th anniversary of the International Symposium on Molecular Spectroscopy we find ourselves on a very different planet. Carbon dioxide, a favorite of many molecular spectroscopy studies over these years, is a major contributor to the rising global temperature and climate change as its concentration in the atmosphere continues to rise. We all, and especially scientists like ourselves, can play a role in slowing and hopefully reversing these rising temperature trends. In this session I will talk about what we are doing at the Department of Energy to support all who want to contribute to helping in this critical task at hand, and how my career in molecular spectroscopy helps me every day in this new role.

TO02   6:00 – 6:35

ISMS AND NSF: SOME HISTORY AND A LOOK FORWARD

FLEMING CRIM, *Department of Chemistry, The University of Wisconsin, Madison, WI, USA.*

The International Symposium on Molecular Spectroscopy is celebrating its 75th anniversary, and the National Science Foundation recently celebrated its 70th. The two organizations have many confluences, and support from the NSF has enabled the research of many ISMS contributors. Both the Foundation and the Symposium have evolved over the years while adhering to a their organizing principles. From the perspective of a former leader of the Mathematical and Physical Sciences Directorate of NSF (2013-2017) and a former Chief Operating Officer of NSF (2018-2021), I will discuss some of that history, the current state, and speculate on the future.

WA. Mini-symposium: Spectroscopy meets Chemical Dynamics
Wednesday, June 22, 2022 – 8:30 AM
Room: 100 Noyes Laboratory

Chair: Melanie A.R. Reber, University of Georgia, Athens, GA, USA

WA01   *INVITED TALK*   8:30 – 9:00

MICROBUBBLE RESONATORS FOR FUN AND PROFIT

RANDALL GOLDSMITH, *Department of Chemistry, University of Wisconsin-Madison, Madison, WI, USA.*

In recent years, optical microresonators with exquisite sensitivity have grown into powerful platforms for label-free sensing and imaging, including reaching the single-molecule detection limit. Combining optical microresonators with spectroscopic measurements on nanoscale objects adds chemical identification to label-free detection schemes, offering deeper insights into their fundamental chemical, biological, material, and photonic properties. Particularly, single-molecule measurements allow distinct observations of unsynchronized chemical dynamics, properties otherwise obscured in bulk measurements. Simultaneously, optical microresonators are also flexible playgrounds for exploring nanophotonic phenomena and quantum optics. I will tell two stories focusing on microbubble resonators. In the first, I will describe how microbubble resonators can be used to watch chemical dynamics of single nanoparticles. In the second, I will describe how microbubble resonators allow solvent control of photonic-plasmonic hybridization.

WA02   9:06 – 9:21

PHOTOELECTRON SPECTROSCOPIC STUDY ON DIPOLE-BOUND STATES: INTRAMOLECULAR ELECTRIC FIELD INDUCED ELECTRONIC CORRELATION

DAOFU YUAN, *Department of Chemistry, Brown University, Providence, RI, USA*; YUE-ROU ZHANG, *Chemistry department, Brown university, Providence, RI, USA*; LAI-SHENG WANG, *Department of Chemistry, Brown University, Providence, RI, USA.*

Polar molecules with sufficiently large dipole moments can form highly diffuse dipole-bound anions. Dipole-bound anions possess noncovalent dipole-bound states (DBSs) just below the detachment threshold by the long-range electron-dipole interaction. The diffuse electron in a DBS is spatially well separated from the valence electrons and is known to have negligible effects on the DBS's molecular structure. Electron correlation effects between the distant dipole-bound electron and the valence electrons of the neutral cores are known to be important for the accurate calculation of the binding energies of the dipole-bound electron. However, how the oriented intramolecular electric field of the dipole-bound electron influences the valence electrons has not been examined. We present the observation of a DBS in deprotonated 4-(2-phenylethynyl)-phenoxide anions. The photodetachment of the dipole-bound electron is observed to accompany a simultaneous shakeup process in valence orbitals in this aromatic molecular anion. This shakeup process is due to configuration mixing as a result of valence orbital polarization by the intramolecular electric field of the dipole-bound electron.

WA03   9:24 – 9:39

SINGLE-CONFORMATION SPECTROSCOPY AND DYNAMICS ON MULTIPLE POTENTIAL ENERGY SURFACES: FLEXIBLE NITROGEN-HETEROCYCLE CHROMOPHORES AND COMPLEXES IN AEROSOLS

NATHANAEL M. KIDWELL, *Department of Chemistry, William & Mary, Williamsburg, VA, USA.*

The interplay between chemical functionality and structure is a key factor in the photophysics and photochemistry of complex, flexible molecules, often giving rise to multiple potential energy surfaces. Adequate description of this relationship to understand the outcomes and properties of polyatomic molecules is made even more difficult as the number of isomers and conformations increase substantially with the size of the system. The inclusion of water-mediated interactions is often needed due to dramatic effects on the conformational preferences and photophysics. Therefore, the synergy between spectroscopy and chemical dynamics methods is required to obtain a molecular-level view of such complex chemical systems. To address these opportunities, we will illustrate our efforts to investigate the intermolecular interactions of molecular complexes using single-conformation spectroscopy and dynamics techniques to probe the photo-initiated outcomes on multiple potential energy surfaces. Thus, the photophysical, photochemical and structural details of the target conformational isomers and complexes enable multifaceted comparisons to several theoretical predictions.

WA04   9:42 – 9:57

DEVELOPMENT OF STRUCTURAL COMPLEXITY IN BARE AND HYDROGENATED CARBON CLUSTERS

SAMUEL JACK PALMER MARLTON, JACK T BUNTINE, CHANG LIU, PATRICK WATKINS, EVAN BIESKE, *School of Chemistry, The University of Melbourne, Melbourne, Victoria, Australia.*

The importance of bare and hydrogenated carbon clusters in combustion and in the chemistry of interstellar space has motivated numerous spectroscopic studies, most of which have focused on smaller neutral and charged clusters with fewer than 10 carbon atoms and on the C_{60} and C_{70} fullerenes. Recently, we have obtained electronic spectra of bare and hydrogenated carbon cation clusters containing between up to 36 carbon atoms. Spectroscopically interrogating carbonaceous molecules containing more than 10 carbon atoms is complicated by the coexistence of different isomers possessing unique spectroscopic properties. To address this issue, we have developed an apparatus that allows formation and selection by ion mobility of a particular $C_xH_y^+$ isomer population, which is incarcerated in a cryogenically cooled ion trap and subjected to tunable radiation. Resonant excitation of an electronic transition leads to cluster fragmentation, which when monitored as a function of wavelength, yields an action spectrum. We have used this approach to obtain electronic spectra for monocyclic C_n^+ clusters with $12 \leq n \leq 36$, which exhibit sharp transitions that progressively shift to longer wavelength with increasing cluster size. We have also probed C_nH^+ clusters, which are shown to exist as linear and cyclic isomers with distinct electronic spectra. Linear isomers ($7 \leq n \leq 17$), feature sharp, intense absorptions across the UV and visible range, whereas cyclic isomers ($n \geq 15$) have much weaker, and broader absorptions. Addition of more hydrogen atoms precipitates formation of bi-cyclic structures that may be precursors of polycyclic aromatic hydrocarbons.

WA05   10:00 – 10:15

POLYCYCLIC AROMATIC HYDROCARBON GROWTH IN A PLASMA REVEALED BY IR-UV ACTION SPECTROSCOPY

ALEXANDER KAREL LEMMENS, *FELIX Laboratory, Institute for Molecules and Materials (IMM), Radboud University, Nijmegen, Netherlands*; DANIEL RAP, SANDRA BRÜNKEN, *FELIX Laboratory, Radboud University, Nijmegen, The Netherlands*; WYBREN JAN BUMA, *Van' t Hoff Institute for Molecular Sciences, University of Amsterdam, Amsterdam, Netherlands*; ANOUK RIJS, *Division of BioAnalytical Chemistry, AIMMS Amsterdam Institute of Molecular and Life Sciences, Vrije Universiteit Amsterdam, Amsterdam, Netherlands.*

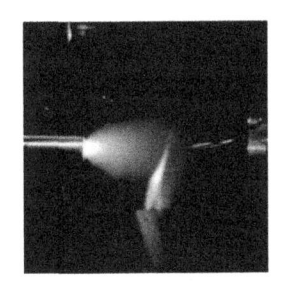

The bottom-up formation of polycyclic aromatic hydrocarbons (PAHs) in combustion and interstellar gas-phase environments is still subject of extensive debate. As a result, accounting for PAH abundance in soot and the interstellar medium is far from trivial. Over the past years, a number of new reaction mechanisms have been proposed, spectroscopically identified and added as possible growth routes for larger PAHs.[a] These include reactions with radical phenyl rings and several small hydrocarbon radicals. We show here that a combination of these barrierless reactions is necessary to fully describe the chemistry leading to PAH growth.

To this purpose we follow and characterize in our experiments the formation of PAHs in an electrical discharge. The fragments, products and reactive intermediates that are produced in this discharge are entrained in a molecular beam and structurally identified by mass selective IR-UV spectroscopy using an IR Free Electron Laser. Comparison of the mass-selected IR absorption spectra with IR spectra calculated for potential species associated with each of these spectra enables us to identify products including larger PAHs, radicals, and intermediates. The assigned structures serve as promising candidates for radio astronomical searches and highlight the necessity of describing PAH growth by an interconnected network of pathways.[b]

---
[a] Kaiser, R. I., Hansen, N. (2021), JPC A, 125(18), 3826-3840
[b] Lemmens, A. K., Rap, D. B., Thunnissen, J. M., Willemsen, B., Rijs, A. M. (2020), Nat. Comm., 11(1), 1-7

Intermission

WA06 10:57 – 11:12
CONFORMATION-SPECIFIC INSIGHTS INTO THE CHEMICAL DYNAMICS OF NO:CH$_4$ MOLECULAR COMPLEXES

<u>JOHN PATRICK DAVIS</u>, NATHANAEL M. KIDWELL, *Department of Chemistry, William & Mary, Williamsburg, VA, USA.*

The photochemistry of flexible molecular complexes, such as a nitric oxide:methane (NO:CH$_4$), are defined by potential energy surfaces that depend on the chemical functionality and the relative orientation of conformational isomers. Experimental results are required to test and improve modern theoretical methods for accurate prediction of photoinitiated processes and chemical mechanisms. A thorough understanding of the intermolecular interactions and reaction mechanism outcomes can be obtained by elucidating the conformations adopted by NO:CH$_4$ molecular complexes. Moreover, by investigating the specific vibrational modes inherent to NO:CH$_4$ conformational isomers, we can assess their impact on energy transfer following fragmentation of the molecular complex isomers. We will leverage a synergy of laser-induced spectroscopy and chemical dynamics techniques, in particular conformation-specific infrared spectroscopy and velocity map imaging, to understand these fundamental mechanisms and dynamics at play within NO:CH$_4$ and NO:alkane complexes more broadly. Ultimately, we will gain insights into the mode-specific energy transfer pathways following fragmentation of NO:CH$_4$ molecular complex isomers. Furthermore, our experimental results will be compared to several theoretical approaches in order to reveal the multifaceted signatures of dynamical events using spectroscopy probes.

WA07 11:15 – 11:30
DFT INVESTIGATION ABOUT ELECTRONIC AND VIBRATIONAL PROPERTIES OF CHROMONE SCHIFF BASE LIGANDS WITH METAL COMPLEXES, SQM ANALYSIS

<u>BERNA CATIKKAS</u>, *Department of Physics, Mustafa Kemal University, Hatay, Turkey.*

This research attempts to electronic and vibrational properties of metal complexes of chromone Schiff base ligands were calculated using the gauge independent atomic orbital (GIAO) method. Using time-dependent density functional theory, the theoretical electronic absorption spectra were determined. To obtain information about the ability of the molecule to react with chemicals, Frontier Molecular Orbital properties, energies, descriptors, and total/partial state density diagram were obtained. The charge distribution and chemical reactivity sites were visualized monitored by mapping electron density isosurface with electrostatic potential surfaces (ESP). To learn nonlinear optical properties (NLO), the polarizability and hyper polarizability tensors of the complexes were computed using density functional (DFT) theory at mPW1PW91 6-311+G(d,p) and LanL2DZ level. The study's second section focused on vibrational spectroscopic analysis. To fit the calculated harmonic wavenumbers with the observed Fourier Transform Infrared (FT-IR) and Raman spectra in the solid phase of the complexes, the calculated harmonic force constants were refined using the Scaled Quantum Mechanical Force Field (SQM-FF) procedure. When combined with the results of the SQM approach, it is possible to create a comprehensive assignment of the observed spectra.

WA09

IR INDUCED ISOMERIZATION AND ITS BACKWARD REACTION OF COLD PHENOL-METHANOL CLUSTER CATIONS

MASAYOSHI OZEKI, MASATAKA ORITO, HIKARU SATO, KENTA MIZUSE, HARUKI ISHIKAWA, *Department of Chemistry, School of Science, Kitasato University, Sagamihara, Japan.*

Since gas-phase hydrogen-bonded clusters are treated as a microscopic model of hydrogen bond networks, a huge number of spectroscopic studies have been performed, so far. Structural fluctuations are one of features of hydrogen bond network. Such fluctuations correspond to isomerizations among isomers having distinct hydrogen bond structures in the cases of clusters. To elucidate dynamical aspects of microscopic hydrogen-bond networks, we have been investigating an IR-induced isomerization of phenol-methanol cluster cations, $[PhOH(MeOH_3)]^+$, trapped in a cold ion trap, and its backward reaction. In our experiment, we recorded UV-photodissociation (PD) spectra of $[PhOH(MeOH_3)]^+$ with and without IR excitation. An isomerization from the ring- to chain-type isomers can be observed as a decrease in the band intensity of the ring-type isomer and also an increase in that of the chain-type isomer in the UV-PD spectra. In the last symposium, we reported a clear evidence of the isomerization process and also its backward reaction.[a] In the present experiment, we carefully examined time propagations of the spectra. As a result, we observed a rapid generation of the chain-type isomers and a change in the UV-PD spectral profiles of the chain-type isomer in the order of 10 μs. This is due to the re-cooling and the backward reaction of the chain-type isomers within a cold trap. We estimated the temperatures of the chain-type isomers during the re-cooling process by referring to the UV-PD spectra of $[PhOH(MeOH_3)]^+$ measured at various temperatures.[b] Details of the observations are presented in the paper.

---

[a] M. Ozeki, *et al.* RM14, *International Symposium on Molecular Spectroscopy*, (2021).
[b] M. Orito, *et al.* RM13, *International Symposium on Molecular Spectroscopy*, (2021).

WB. Mini-symposium: Benchmarking in Spectroscopy

Wednesday, June 22, 2022 – 8:30 AM

Room: 116 Roger Adams Lab

Chair: Juan Carlos Lopez, Universidad de Valladolid, Valladolid, Spain

---

WB01 *INVITED TALK* 8:30 – 9:00

A NEW STANDARD OF AGREEMENT OF SEMI-EXPERIMENTAL EQUILIBRIUM (r_e^{SE}) AND COMPUTED EQUILIBRIUM (r_e) STRUCTURES

<u>BRIAN J. ESSELMAN</u>, *Department of Chemistry, University of Wisconsin-Madison, Madison, WI, USA.*

Recently, the CCSD(T) equilibrium (r_e) structures and the Semi-Experimental Equilibrium (r_e^{SE}) structures of several small molecules (hydrazoic acid, benzene, pyridazine, pyrimidine, thiophene, thiazole, etc.) demonstrated a new standard of agreement between theory and experiment (typically 0.001 Å for bond distances and 0.04° for bond angles). In each of these examples, all or nearly all of the computed parameters fell within the 2σ statistical uncertainties of their corresponding experimental values. This agreement is typically possible by obtaining an r_e^{SE} structure based upon many isotopologues beyond single-isotopic substitution from many hundreds or thousands of transitions for each isotopologue. The resulting rotational constants are corrected using CCSD(T) calculations for the impact of the vibration-rotation interaction and for the electron-mass distribution. Additionally, we have found that such close agreement requires an r_e structure calculated at the CCSD(T)/cc-pCV5Z level further corrected to account for an incomplete basis set, untreated correlation, and relativistic effects. This talk will feature examples to demonstrate the agreement possible, current best practices, and the tools used to analyze these structures. Outstanding questions and future investigations will be discussed.

WB02 9:06 – 9:21

THE PREFERRED CONFORMATION AND NON-COVALENT INTERACTIONS OF THE METHYL ALLYL DISULFIDE-FORMALDEHYDE COMPLEX REVEALED BY ROTATIONAL SPECTROSCOPY

<u>ZHEN WANG</u>, YUAGO XU, GANG FENG, *School of Chemistry and Chemical Engineering, Chongqing University, Chongqing, China.*

The methyl allyl disulfide-formaldehyde adduct were probed using Fourier transform microwave spectroscopy and quantum chemical computations. The low energy isomers of the adduct were sampled using the conformer-rotamer ensemble sampling tool (CREST) and geometrically optimized at the B3LYP-D3BJ/def2-TZVP level of theory. Although many isomers of the adduct were theoretically predicted to have close stability, only one isomer of the methyl allyl disulfide-formaldehyde adduct have been detected in the helium supersonic jet. Each observed transition exhibited multiple splitting arising from internal rotation of formaldehyde and methyl internal rotations. In the observed isomer, the non-covalent bonding distance between the carbon atom of formaldehyde and the nearest sulfur atom of methyl allyl disulfide has been found to be well within the corresponding sum of van der Waals radii, indicating the existence of a n $\rightarrow \pi^*$ interaction. Also, formaldehyde acts as a lone pair donor forming a weak CH...O hydrogen bond with methyl allyl disulfide. Detailed spectral analysis, spectroscopic and computational results will be presented.

WB03　　9:24 – 9:39

MILLIMETER/SUBMILLIMETER SPECTRUM AND PRECISE EQUILIBRIUM STRUCTURE OF 1H-1,2,4-TRIAZOLE

HAYLEY BUNN, BRIAN J. ESSELMAN, SAMUEL M. KOUGIAS, *Department of Chemistry, University of Wisconsin-Madison, Madison, WI, USA*; JOHN F. STANTON, *Physical Chemistry, University of Florida, Gainesville, FL, USA*; R. CLAUDE WOODS, ROBERT J. McMAHON, *Department of Chemistry, University of Wisconsin-Madison, Madison, WI, USA*; SUSANNA L. WIDICUS WEAVER, *Chemistry and Astronomy, University of Wisconsin-Madison, Madison, WI, USA*.

1H-1,2,4-Triazole is a five membered aromatic heterocycle with 3 inequivalent nitrogen atoms. This molecule exists as an equilibrium of two tautomers; 1H-1,2,4-Triazole (C_s) and 4H-1,2,4-triazole (C_{2v}), with the 1H tautomer being dominant. 1,2,4-Triazole is predicted to exist in the atmosphere of Titan, forming in aerosols containing known constituents HNC and NH_3, where identification relies on accurate spectral information. The rotational spectrum of 1H-1,2,4-triazole was reported by Bolton et al.[a], but only the ground state rotational constants were determined. Here we present the 70-700 GHz spectrum of 1H-1,2,4-triazole with spectral frequencies comparable to telescopes such as ALMA. Analysis of this spectrum resulted in improved rotational constants and an accurate determination of the sextic and quartic centrifugal constants. We also obtained tentative least-squares fits of transitions for all vibrationally excited states below 1200 cm^{-1}, where the majority appear to be perturbed by Coriolis interactions. A partial structure determination of 1H-1,2,4-triazole, derived from three isotopologues, has been reported previously. Recent work on other heteroatomatic compounds has achieved impressive accuracy and precision in the determination of semi-experimental (r_e^{SE}) equilibrium structures. Using deuterium-enriched triazole samples, we have determined rotational constants for 27 isotopologues of 1H-1,2,4-triazole including multiple isotopic substitutions of all atoms. As a result, we have obtained a complete r_e^{SE} structure that is in full agreement with an r_e structure determined with high-level quantum chemistry. Here we will report on the spectroscopic and structural analysis of 1H-1,2,4-triazole.

---

[a]Bolton, K.; Brown, R. D.; Burden, F. R.; Mishra, A. The microwave spectrum and structure of 1,2,4 triazole. J. Mol. Struc. 1975, 27 (2), 261–266

WB04　　9:42 – 9:57

ON THE NATURE OF THE INTERACTION OF CO WITH PERFLURINATED AROMATICS: NEW INSIGHTS FROM THE EXPERIMENTA DATA AND THEORETICAL STUDY

LUCA EVANGELISTI, ASSIMO MARIS, *Dipartimento di Chimica G. Ciamician, Università di Bologna, Bologna, Italy*; CAMILLA CALABRESE, IMANOL USABIAGA, *Departamento de Química Física, Universidad del País Vasco (UPV-EHU), Bilbao, Spain*; WEIXING LI, *Fudan University, Department of Chemistry, Shanghai, China*; GIOVANNI BISTONI, *Department of chemistry, biology and biotechnology, Università degli Studi di Perugia, Perugia, Italy*; SONIA MELANDRI, *Dipartimento di Chimica G. Ciamician, Università di Bologna, Bologna, Italy*.

The rotational spectra of pentafluoropyridine-CO and hexafluorobenzene-CO have shown unambiguously that substitution by fluorine atoms on the ring strongly influences the binding abilities of the aromatic ligand. Differently from their non-substituted counterparts, both molecules interact with CO forming a perpendicular lp···π interaction between the carbon and the ring. We report earlier the rotational spectroscopy studies performed with a Molecular Beam Fourier Transform Microwave spectrometer in which we have tested the binding abilities of the fluorine substituted aromatics molecules with CO. Now local energy decomposition analysis of the relative conformational energies shows the interplay between the non-covalent interactions which led to the final configuration preference of CO with respect to the aromatic rings in the supersonic expansion. Although the relative complexity of the non-covalent interactions made these molecular systems challenging to study, the progress in theoretical modelling have shown to physical explain the origin of the molecular binding.

WB05 10:00 – 10:15

ROTATIONAL SPECTROSCOPIC STUDY OF MICROSOLVATED CLUSTERS OF 1- AND 2-NITRONAPHTHALENE

SHEFALI SAXENA, M. EUGENIA SANZ, *Department of Chemistry, King's College London, London, United Kingdom.*

Polycyclic aromatic hydrocarbons containing the nitro group (nitro-PAHs) are pollutants found in the atmosphere as the result of direct release from exhaust or of radical reactions on naphthalene involving hydroxyl radical (daytime), nitrate radical (night time) and nitrogen dioxide. Among them, the nitro-PAHs 1-nitronaphthalene (1NN) and 2-nitronaphthalene (2NN) are relevant as they are highly toxic and major environmental contaminants in urban areas. We have investigated 1NN and 2NN and their complexes with water by broadband rotational spectroscopy and determined their structures. Water primarily interacts with the –NO2 group forming an O-H···O hydrogen bond. Experimental observations are compared with predictions by theoretical methods to evaluate the performance of the latter. Our results contribute to understanding the microsolvation processes of atmospheric pollutants in the gas phase.

Intermission

WB06 10:57 – 11:12

SUB-PERMILLE MEASUREMENTS AND CALCULATIONS OF 3-0 BAND CO LINE INTENSITIES

ZACHARY REED, *Chemical Sciences Division, National Institute of Standards and Technology, Gaithersburg, MD, USA*; KATARZYNA BIELSKA, *Institute of Physics, Faculty of Physics, Astronomy and Informatics, Nicolaus Copernicus University, Torun, Poland*; ALEKSANDRA A. KYUBERIS, *Van Swinderen Institute, Universiteit Groningen, Groningen, Netherlands*; GANG LI, *PTB, Physikalisch-Technische Bundesanstalt, Braunschweig, Germany*; AGATA CYGAN, ROMAN CIURYLO, DANIEL LISAK, *Institute of Physics, Faculty of Physics, Astronomy and Informatics, Nicolaus Copernicus University, Torun, Poland*; ERIN M. ADKINS, JOSEPH T. HODGES, *Chemical Sciences Division, National Institute of Standards and Technology, Gaithersburg, MD, USA*; LORENZO LODI, *Department of Physics and Astronomy, University College London, London, UK*; NIKOLAY F. ZOBOV, *Microwave Spectroscopy, Institute of Applied Physics, Nizhny Novgorod, Russia*; VOLKER EBERT, *PTB, Physikalisch-Technische Bundesanstalt, Braunschweig, Germany*; JONATHAN TENNYSON, OLEG L. POLYANSKY, *Department of Physics and Astronomy, University College London, London, UK.*

Here we present new measurements and calculations of line intensities in the 3 - 0 band of $^{12}C^{16}O$. These experimental results and calculations exhibit unprecedented consistency and low uncertainty. Calibration-free agreement at the 1 permille level relative standard deviation level has been demonstrated between theoretical ab initio calculations and three sets of independent experiments, corresponding to a nearly twenty-fold reduction in uncertainty by comparison to literature values. The experimental techniques cover a broad range of rotational quantum numbers from J = 5 to 30, including three separate laser-based measurements of high-J lines performed at two institutions, along with independent Fourier transform spectroscopy measurements for J = 5 to 18. The most accurately determined intensity is that of the R23 transition determined to within 0.4 permille. The intensity of this transition is a possible intrinsic reference for evaluating and reducing biases in future spectroscopic determinations of molecular line intensities.

WB07

QUANTUM CHEMICAL INVESTIGATION OF INTRAMOLECULAR HYDROGEN BONDS IN OXYGENATED AROMATIC MOLECULES: INFLUENCE OF RING SIZE, DONOR/ACCEPTOR GROUPS AND SUBSTITUTANTS

JONAS BRUCKHUISEN, CECILIA GOMEZ-PECH, GUILLAUME DHONT, ARNAUD CUISSET, *Laboratoire de Physico-Chimie de l'Atmosphère, Université du Littoral Côte d'Opale, Dunkerque, France*; MALGORZATA OLEJNICZAK, *Centre of New Technologies, University of Warsaw, Warsaw, Poland*; MANUEL GOUBET, VALÉRIE VALLET, *Laboratoire PhLAM, UMR 8523 CNRS - Université Lille 1, Villeneuve d'Ascq, France.*

Hydrogen bonds (HBs) are important for a broad range of applications and play a fundamental role in structural chemistry and biology. HB interactions, dynamics and their directionality are discussed for almost one century and there is still a need for further experiments and theoretical investigations to fully encompass this complex interaction. Especially the experimental investigation of weak intramolecular HBs of isolated molecules in the gas phase remains challenging. Quantum chemical tools are needed to support high resolution THz and IR spectroscopies which can reveal the influence of intramolecular HBs on the rovibrational dynamics[1].

In this work we focus on intramolecular HBs of oxygenated aromatic molecules. They are investigated through a combination of quantum theory of atoms in molecules QTAIM[2], non-covalent interactions NCI[3], natural bond orbitals NBO[4], and topological data analysis TDA[5]. We studied the influence of the substitutants, of the donor or acceptor groups and of the number of atoms included in the ring formed by the HB. We relate our findings with recent rovibrational measurements in catechol (1,2-dihydroxybenzene) and guaiacol. We provide an overview of the problems arising while studying weak intramolecular HBs stabilizing oxygenated aromatic compounds and we discuss the performance of the different quantum chemical tools.

[1] J. Bruckhuisen, *Molecules*, **2021**, 26, 3645; [2] R. Bader, *International series of monographs on chemistry*, **1994**, 22; [3] C. Narth, *Challenges and advances in computational chemistry and physics*, **2016**, 491-527; [4] E. Glendening, *NBO 6.0*, **2013**; [5] N. Otter, *EPJ Data Sci.*, **2017**, 6, 17.

WB08

INFRARED PREDISSOCIATION SPECTROSCOPY OF PROTONATED METHYL CYANIDE

ARAVINDH NIVAS MARIMUTHU, FRANK HUIS IN'T VELD, *FELIX Laboratory, Radboud University, Nijmegen, The Netherlands*; SVEN THORWIRTH, *I. Physikalisches Institut, Universität zu Köln, Köln, Germany*; BRITTA REDLICH, SANDRA BRÜNKEN, *FELIX Laboratory, Radboud University, Nijmegen, The Netherlands.*

Methyl cyanide (CH_3CN) was among the first polyatomic molecules detected by radio-astronomical observations of the interstellar medium (ISM)[1]. As methyl cyanide has a proton affinity much larger than that of H_2, its protonated version (CH_3CNH^+) is postulated to form efficiently via exothermic proton transfer from H_3^+ to CH_3CN in the interstellar medium. In this talk, we present a comprehensive experimental and quantum-chemical study of the gas phase vibrational spectrum of CH_3CNH^+ [2]. We employed the widely tuneable free electron lasers for infrared experiments (FELIX) coupled to a cryogenic ion trap instrument [3] for our measurements. The spectrum was recorded in the 300-1700 and 2000-3300 cm^{-1} spectral regions using infrared predissociation (IRPD) action spectroscopy with neon as a weakly bound messenger atom. The assignment of the vibrational modes is based on anharmonic frequency calculations performed at the CCSD(T)/ANO2 level of theory. We demonstrate that the comparatively low-cost ANO0 basis-set provides accurate estimates on the influence of the weakly-bound neon atom as a tag in the IRPD experiments. The data presented here will support astronomical searches for the CH_3CNH^+ ion in space.

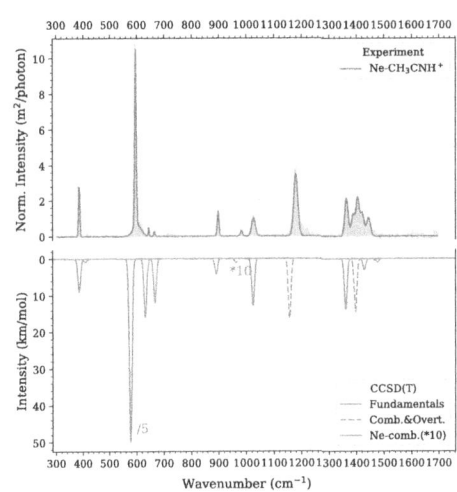

[1] P.M. Solomon, K.B. Jefferts, A.A. Penzias and R.W. Wilson, Astrophys. J. 168 (1971) L107
[2] A. N. Marimuthu, F. Huis in't Veld, S. Thorwirth, B. Redlich and S. Brünken, J. Mol. Spec. 379 (2021) 111477
[3] P. Jusko, S. Brünken, O. Asvany, S. Thorwirth, A. Stoffels, L. van der Meer, G. Berden, B. Redlich, J. Oomens and S. Schlemmer, Faraday Discuss. 217, (2019), 172

WB09   11:51 – 12:06

AUTOMATED SEARCH ALGORITHMS FOR STRUCTURAL ISOMERISM: THE PROS AND CONS

<u>VENKATESAN S. THIMMAKONDU</u>, *Chemistry and Biochemistry, San Diego State University, San Diego, CA, USA.*

Although automated search algorithms are highly powerful tools to find out various structural isomers for a given elemental composition, human chemical intuition still delivers more geometries than automated searches once we know the initial geometries. This indirectly emphasizes the fact that creating an unbiased algorithm for structural isomerism is simply difficult. Moreover, it also outlines that an integrated approach is necessary between search algorithms and chemical intuition to further our knowledge of chemical space for any given elemental composition.

WC. Electronic structure, potential energy surfaces
Wednesday, June 22, 2022 – 8:30 AM
Room: B102 Chemical and Life Sciences

Chair: Lan Cheng, The Johns Hopkins University, Lutherville Timonium, MD, USA

WC01 8:30 – 8:45

ROTATIONAL ANALYSIS OF HIGH RESOLUTION LASER EXCITATION AND DISPERSED FLUORESCENCE SPECTRA FROM THE $B^1\Sigma^+ - A^1\Pi$, $B^1\Sigma^+ - X^1\Sigma^+$, AND $B^1\Sigma^+ - a^3\Pi_1$ SYSTEMS OF MgS.

NICHOLAS CARON, *Department of Physics, University of New Brunswick, Fredericton, NB, Canada*; BRADLEY GUISLAIN, *Department of Physics, University of New Brunswick, Saint John, NB, Canada*; DENNIS W. TOKARYK, *Department of Physics, University of New Brunswick, Fredericton, NB, Canada*; ALLAN G. ADAM, *Department of Chemistry, University of New Brunswick, Fredericton, NB, Canada*.

Magnesium Sulfide (MgS) is an astrophysically interesting molecule. Its solid form is the main component of the mineral niningerite (found in enstatite chondrite meteorites) and the MgS component of solid dust grains has generally been agreed upon as the carrier of the 30 μm feature seen in the emission spectra of some carbon-rich stars[a]; however, investigations of the visible spectrum of gas phase MgS remain relatively sparse in the literature.

The first analysis of a rotationally-resolved spectrum of MgS in the gas phase was undertaken by Marcano and Barrow in 1970[b], who investigated the $B^1\Sigma^+ - X^1\Sigma^+$ system in absorption. Our group at UNB previously reported the first experimental observation and rotational analysis of the low-lying $A^2\Pi$ state of MgS at 4531.94 cm^{-1} from a series of laser-induced dispersed fluorescence spectra taken using a grating spectrometer. Since then we have extended this work by recording a series of dispersed fluorescence spectra of the $B^1\Sigma^+ - A^1\Pi$ and $B^1\Sigma^+ - X^1\Sigma^+$ systems at higher resolution using a BOMEM DA3 Fourier transform interferometer. The weak $B^1\Sigma^+ - a^3\Pi_1$ transition was also observed. We present here our extended analyses of the $B^1\Sigma^+ - A^1\Pi$ and $B^1\Sigma^+ - X^1\Sigma^+$ systems, as well as the first analysis of the $B^1\Sigma^+ - a^3\Pi_1$ system in MgS.

[a]Volk, Kevin; Sloan, G. C.; Kraemer, Kathleen E. (2020). The 21 μm and 30 μm emission features in carbon-rich objects. Astrophysics and Space Science, Volume 365 (Issue 5), article id.88. DOI: 10.1007/s10509-020-03798-2.

[b]Marcano, M; Barrow, R. F. (1970). Rotational Analysis of Bands of the $B^1\Sigma^+ - X^1\Sigma^+$ system of gaseous MgS. Transactions of the Faraday Society, Volume 66, pages 2936-2938. DOI: 10.1039/TF9706602936.

WC02 8:48 – 9:03

EXTENSION OF AN ATOMIC-IONS-IN-MOLECULE ELECTRONIC STRUCTURE MODEL FROM CALCIUM MONOXIDE TO SCANDIUM MONOXIDE

ROBERT W FIELD[a], *Department of Chemistry, MIT, Cambridge, MA, USA*; SANJAY G. NAKHATE[b], *Atomic and Molecular Physics Division, Bhabha Atomic Research Centre, Mumbai,400085, Maharastra, India*.

The electronic spectrum of CaO is so complicated that it had been dismissed as uninterpretable random fragments from a polyatomic molecule. An atomic-ions-in-molecule model, which employs foundational concepts from Inorganic Chemistry, provides the "why" as well as the "what." There are two oxidation states, Ca^{2+}O^{2-} and Ca$^+$O$^-$, the latter manifest in O$^-$ 2pπ-hole (π^{-1}) and 2pσ-hole (σ^{-1}) "hard/soft" forms. These three families of electronic structure states are co-present in the low-energy region, and their large differences in molecular structure (R_e and ω_e) result in a dense web of perturbations. But all is now understood. Going from CaO to ScO, the addition of a single valence electron awakens the sleeping giant of complexity, bellowing "you ain't seen nothin' yet." The number of low-lying electronic states in each of the three families increases significantly. Can an atomic-ions-in-molecule model guide the interpretation of the ScO spectrum?

New Laser Induced Fluorescence (LIF), Dispersed LIF, and lifetime-gated LIF spectra offer insights into the electronic structure of ScO. These spectra sample the ScO A$^2\Pi$, C$^2\Pi$ and D$^2\Sigma^+$ states over a wide range of vibrational levels. Of special importance is the A(v=6) C(v=16) perturbation and two previously unobserved, closely-spaced, long-lived, Ω=1/2 states that lie near, and are probably made visible by their interaction with the C$^2\Pi_{1/2}$(v=6) and A$^2\Pi_{3/2}$(v=16) states.

[a]rwfield@mit.edu

[b]Infrared Laser Spectroscopy Section, Physics Group, Bhabha Atomic Research Centre, Mumbai 400 085, India and Homi Bhabha National Institute, Bhabha Atomic Research Centre, Mumbai 400 085, India Email: nakhate@barc.gov.in

WC03　9:06 – 9:21

ELECTRONIC STRUCTURE OF THE GROUND AND EXCITED STATES OF EUROPIUM OXIDE (EuO)

BRADLEY WELCH, *Chemistry, Michigan State University, East Lansing, MI, United States*; NUNO M. S. ALMEIDA, ANGELA K. WILSON, *Department of Chemistry, Michigan State University, East Lansing, MI, USA*.

Despite being subject to numerous single reference computations, Europium Oxide (EuO) to date has not had its electronic structure studied with multireference methods. High-level ab initio approaches were performed detailing its numerous excited states, and spin multiplicities. Complete active space self-consistent field (CASSCF) and multireference configuration interaction (MRCI) was utilized to compute the ground and excited state properties of EuO. The potential energy curves for the ground, excited states, and different dissociation channels are explored. Spin-orbit corrections were performed with the Breit-Pauli hamiltonian. When available comparisons to experiment are made.

WC04　9:24 – 9:39

MULTIREFERENCE CALCULATIONS ON THE GROUND AND EXCITED STATES AND DISSOCIATION ENERGIES OF LrF AND LrO

NUNO M. S. ALMEIDA, SASHA C. NORTH, TIMOTHÉ R. L. MELIN, ANGELA K. WILSON, *Department of Chemistry, Michigan State University, East Lansing, MI, USA*.

High-level ab initio approaches were performed on LrF and LrO detailing their numerous excited states, and spin multiplicities. Herein, multi reference methodologies such as the complete active space self-consistent field (CASSCF) and multireference configuration interaction (MRCI) were utilized to calculate ground and excited state properties of LrF and LrO. The potential energy curves for the ground, several excited states, and different dissociation channels are explored at CASSCF and MRCI+Q. Spin-orbit corrections were performed by diagonalizing the MRCI wavefunction on the basis of the Breit-Pauli Hamiltonian. For the second part of this work the bond dissocation energies (BDEs) of LrO and LrF were performed at different levels of theory using a range of basis sets. Core-valence, relativistic effects and spin-orbit contributions to the ground state are discussed. In addition, density functional theory (DFT) is also compared against wavefunction methods. Detailed spectra for intricate diatomic complexes such as actinide oxides and fluorides are essential for future experimental studies on heavy metal containing species.

WC05　9:42 – 9:57

SPECTROSCOPIC CHARACTERIZATION OF THE [H, P, S, O] MOLECULAR SYSTEM AND CHEMICAL INSIGHTS INTO THE NON-DETECTION OF PHOSPHORUS- AND SULFUR-BEARING DIATOMIC MOLECULES PS AND PH

VINCENT J. ESPOSITO, *Department of Chemistry, University of Pennsylvania, Philadelphia, PA, USA*; JACQUELINE M. FRISKEY, *Chemistry, University of Pennsylvania, Philadelphia, PA, USA*; TAREK TRABELSI, JOSEPH S FRANCISCO, *Department of Earth and Environmental Science and Department of Chemistry, University of Pennsylvaina, Philadelphia, PA, USA*.

Phosphorus and sulfur are integral to life on Earth, and their role in the chemistry of the interstellar medium is highly debated and unknown. Only a handful of phosphorus-bearing species have been detected thus far, with the most recent confirmed detection taking place in 2014. The simultaneous detection of molecules such as PO, SH, and OH indicate the possibility of reactive intermediate species existing in the interstellar medium and circumstellar envelopes of evolved stars. To explore this possibility, we have characterized the [H, P, S, O] tetratomic isomer family using high level ab initio methods. We provide rotational, vibrational, and electronic spectroscopic data to help drive experimental and observational detection of new phosphorus and sulfur-bearing molecules and explore chemical and photochemical pathways to explain possible reservoirs and sources for the as of yet undetected PH and PS diatomic molecules.

Intermission

WC06   10:39 – 10:54
COMPUTATIONAL AND SPECTROSCOPIC STUDIES OF NITROGEN-CONTAINING DIPOLE BOUND ANIONS

NICHOLAS A. KRUSE, NATHAN I HAMMER, *Chemistry and Biochemistry, University of Mississippi, Oxford, MS, USA.*

Nitrogen is an essential ingredient in molecules that support life. Its presence also typically leads to the delocalization of electrons, causing large dipole and quadrupole moments. Such molecules are sometimes able to form negative ions through the electrostatic binding of an excess electron via a process known as Rydberg Charge Exchange. These so-called multipole-bound (dipole-bound, quadrupole-bound, etc.) anions have been shown to be important in radiation damage in biology as well as electron transport processes. Here, we present our recent computational and experimental results studying the creation of new multipole-bound anions.

WC07   10:57 – 11:12
LOW AND HIGH-RESOLUTION LASER-INDUCED FLUORESCENCE (LIF) of JET-COOLED NdO

JOEL R SCHMITZ, ARIANNA RODRIGUEZ, *Department of Chemistry, Emory University, Atlanta, GA, USA*; TIMOTHY STEIMLE, *School of Molecular Sciences, Arizona State University, Tempe, AZ, USA*; MICHAEL HEAVEN, *Department of Chemistry, Emory University, Atlanta, GA, USA.*

The chemi-ionization reactions of atomic lanthanides M + O $\rightarrow$ MO + e$^-$ are currently being investigated as a method to artificially increase the ion density in the ionosphere for uniform radio wave propagation. Recent experiments involving the release of atomic neodymium (Nd) into the upper atmosphere have resulted in the production of a cloud with green emission[1]. Based on the cloud emission, it is believed that NdO was the primary product, but spectroscopic characterization of NdO is needed to properly identify the emitting species. While NdO is well characterized above 590 nm, little spectroscopic data exits at emission wavelengths below 590 nm[2,3]. In this work, jet-cooled NdO was produced and low- and high-resolution laser-induced fluorescence (LIF) and dispersed laser-induced fluorescence (DLIF) techniques were used to characterize the electronic structure of NdO from 15,500-21,000 cm^{-1}. Congested DLIF spectra allowed vibrational characterization of the ground X4 state as well as five low-lying states for the first time. By employing high-resolution LIF, the hyperfine structure of the ground X4 state was obtained. Data and analysis of the ground and low-lying states of NdO will be presented.

[1] Ard, S.G. et al. J. Chem. Phys.2015, 143, 204303.
[2] Kaledin, L.A. et al. Acta Physica Hungarica 1983, 54, 189-212.
[3] Linton, C. et al. J. Mol. Spec. 2004, 225, 132-144.
[4] VanGundy, R.A. et al. J. Chem. Phys. 2019, 114302.

WC08   11:15 – 11:30
PHOTOPHYSICS OF A RIGID MACROCYCLE Fe^{II} COMPLEX WITH A NANOSECOND LIFETIME MLCT EXCITED STATE

JUSTIN THOMAS MALME, *Department of Chemistry, University of Illinois at Urbana-Champaign, Urbana, IL, USA*; RYAN T ASH, *Physics, University of Wisconsin-Madison, Madison, WI, USA*; REESE CLENDENING, *Department of Chemistry, Purdue University, West Lafayette, IN, USA*; JOSH VURA-WEIS, *Department of Chemistry, University of Illinois at Urbana-Champaign, Urbana, IL, USA*; TONG REN, *Department of Chemistry, Purdue University, West Lafayette, IN, USA.*

Replication of the long lifetimes of 4d transition metal complexes in their 3d counterparts is desirable for both cost reduction and environmental concerns. Fe^{II}(rac-HMTI)(CN)$_2$ is an Fe^{II} complex with a remarkable nanosecond lifetime metal-to-ligand charge transfer (MLCT) state in low polarity solvents. Architecturally, the Fe^{II} center is ligated to axially-oriented strong field cyano ligands, and equatorially to a rigid [14]-tetracene-N4 macrocycle. This rigidity enforces poor vibrational overlap of excited states, significantly raising the barrier of vibrational relaxation and extending their lifetimes. Fe(HMTI)(CN)$_2$ is studied by optical transient absorption, and spectroelectrochemical studies reproduce the features of the OTA at potentials consistent with metal oxidation and ligand reduction, confirming the attribution of MLCT character to the transition. DFT, TDDFT and CASSCF computational methods are also used to create a theoretical potential energy manifold, to better describe the deactivation mechanism of the excited state. Further understanding of this molecule's photophysics will allow for more targeted development of longer-lived Fe^{II} complexes.

WC09 11:33 – 11:48

MECHANISM AND KINETICS OF THE REACTION OF CRIEGEE INTERMEDIATE CH$_2$OO WITH ACETIC ACID STUDIED WITH A STEP-SCAN FOURIER-TRANSFORM IR SPECTROMETER

BEDABYAS BEHERA, *Department of Applied Chemistry, National Yang Ming Chiao Tung University, Hsinchu, Taiwan*; KAITO TAKAHASHI, *Institute of Atomic and Molecular Sciences, Academia Sinica, Taipei, Taiwan*; YUAN-PERN LEE, *Department of Applied Chemistry, Institute of Molecular Science, and Centre for Emergent Functional Matter Science, National Yang Ming Chiao Tung University, Hsinchu, Taiwan.*

Acetic acid CH$_3$C(O)OH plays an important role in the acidity in the troposphere. The reaction of Criegee intermediate with CH$_3$C(O)OH was proposed to be a potential source of secondary organic aerosol in the atmosphere. We investigated the detailed mechanism and kinetics of the reaction of Criegee intermediate CH$_2$OO with CH$_3$C(O)OH. The time-resolved infrared absorption spectra of transient species produced upon irradiation at 308 nm of a flowing mixture of CH$_2$I$_2$/O$_2$/CH$_3$C(O)OH at 298 K were recorded with a step-scan Fourier-transform infrared spectrometer. Bands of CH$_2$OO were observed initially upon irradiation; their decrease in intensity was accompanied with the appearance of bands near 886, 971, 1021, 1078, 1160, 1225, 1377, 1402, 1434, and 1777 cm^{-1}, assigned to the absorption of hydroperoxymethyl acetate [CH$_3$C(O)OCH$_2$OOH, HPMA], the hydrogen-transferred adduct of CH$_2$OO and CH$_3$C(O)OH. Two conformers of HPMA, an open form and an intramolecularly hydrogen-bonded form, were identified. At a later reaction period, bands of the open-form HPMA became diminished and new bands appeared at 930, 1045, 1200, 1378, 1792, and 1810 cm^{-1}, assigned to the formic acetic anhydride [CH$_3$C(O)OC(O)H, FAA], a dehydrolysis product of HPMA. The intramolecularly hydrogen-bonded HPMA is stable. From the temporal profiles of HPMA and FAA, we derived a rate coefficient k = (1.3 ± 0.3) × 10^{-10} cm^3 molecule^{-1} s^{-1} for the reaction CH$_2$OO + CH$_3$C(O)OH to form HPMA and a rate coefficient k = 980 ± 40 s^{-1} for the dehydration of the open-form HPMA to form FAA. Theoretical calculations were performed to elucidate the CH$_2$OO + CH$_3$C(O)OH reaction pathway and to understand the different reactivity of the two forms of HPMA.

WC10 11:51 – 12:06

A MICROWAVE AND COMPUTATIONAL STUDY OF PIVALIC SULFURIC ANHYDRIDE AND THE PIVALIC ACID MONOMER: MECHANISTIC INSIGHTS INTO THE RCOOH + SO$_3$ REACTION

NATHAN LOVE, KENNETH R. LEOPOLD, *Chemistry Department, University of Minnesota, Minneapolis, MN, USA.*

Recent microwave studies in our laboratory have explored a series of carboxylic sulfuric anhydrides (RCOOSO$_2$OH, CSAs) that are formed from a cyclic reaction between carboxylic acids and SO$_3$. These studies have shown that the reaction occurs readily with a wide range of carboxylic acids. Moreover, the zero-point corrected activation energies are typically small and, in some cases even negative, but there remains uncertainty as to the factors which control the size and sign of the barrier. In this talk we present chirped-pulse and cavity microwave spectra of pivalic sulfuric anhydride, (CH$_3$)$_3$CCOOSO$_2$OH (PivSA), and explore the reaction pathway for its formation using computational chemistry. The reaction is found to be best described as a pericyclic heteroene reaction coupled with a 60 degree rotation of the t-butyl group. The process can occur through either a sequential (two-step) or a concerted (one-step) pathway. Based on zero-point corrected single-point CCSD(T) calculations, the sequential pathway has the lowest energy transition state, with a value of -0.52 kcal/mol relative to that of a pivalic acid - SO$_3$ precursor complex. This value represents the lowest barrier for SO$_3$ + carboxylic acid reactions studied to date. When compared with CF$_3$COOSO$_2$OH, which has the highest barrier among the systems previously studied, the results provide insight into the relative influence of the electronic and mass effects on the reaction energetics. Additional computational studies further explore the effects of the R group of the RCOOH reactants. Finally, as a precursor to the experimental work on PivSA, the microwave spectrum of the pivalic acid monomer was also recorded and is reported here as well.

WC11   12:09 – 12:24

INVESTIGATING STRUCTURE AND REACTIVITY RELATIONSHIPS OF NITROGEN-CONTAINING RADICALS WITH COMPUTATIONAL CHEMISTRY AND PHOTOIONIZATION MASS SPECTROMETRY

<u>SOMMER L. JOHANSEN</u>, JUDIT ZADOR, LEONID SHEPS, *Combustion Research Facility, Sandia National Laboratories, Livermore, CA, USA.*

Nitrogen-containing organic molecules play significant roles within atmospheric and combustion chemistry due to their presence as volatiles emitted during wildfires, significant components of crude biofuels, and their use in carbon capture technology. The historical focus of gas-phase nitrogen chemistry was on small molecules formed during high-temperature combustion, where the molecular structure of fuel-N has a limited effect on the chemistry due to significant fragmentation. At lower temperatures relevant to Earth's atmosphere and modern combustion technology, oxidation out-competes thermal decomposition and fuel-N structure can have a substantial effect on reactivity. However, the degree to which chemical pathways differ between N-containing compounds is unclear due to the lack of detailed kinetic studies and potential energy surfaces, resulting in poor representation of these pathways within chemical kinetics models. Here, we present the first set of results in a research program designed to build a comprehensive understanding of the structure and reactivity relationships for model nitrogen-containing compounds, with a focus on differences between radical isomers. Five-membered rings pyrrole (c – C_4H_5N) and pyrrolidine (c – C_4H_9N) serve as model compounds due to their broad chemical importance and ability to form three different radicals. Using KinBot, a computational tool that automatically locates kinetically important stationary points, we have developed potential energy surfaces for reactions of the pyrrolyl and pyrrolidinyl radicals with O_2 at the B3LYP/6-31G level of theory for reaction searches, conformational analyses, and IRC calculations, followed by reoptimization of the most relevant stationary points at ωB97X-D/6-311++G(d,p) with energies refined at CCSD(T)-F12/cc-pVDZ-F12. These results indicate stark differences in reactivity between radical isomers and support our ongoing experimental kinetics studies using a high-pressure laser photolysis reactor coupled to a photoionization mass spectrometer. Characterization of pyrrole and pyrrolidine oxidation will not only provide a detailed knowledge base for future studies of N-containing compounds, but also will allow for comparison to well-studied oxidation pathways of isoelectronic species, such as furan and tetrahydrofuran. Such comparisons will give us a better understanding of the key differences in reactivity between nitrogenated, oxygenated, and pure hydrocarbon volatiles.

WD. Clusters/Complexes

Wednesday, June 22, 2022 – 8:30 AM

Room: 217 Noyes Laboratory

Chair: Josh Vura-Weis, University of Illinois at Urbana-Champaign, Urbana, IL, USA

WD01   8:30 – 8:45

MAPPING ELECTRONIC RELAXATION DYNAMICS IN METAL NANOCLUSTERS USING POLARIZATION-SELECTIVE TWO-DIMENSIONAL ELECTRONIC SPECTROSCOPY

WILLIAM R. JEFFRIES, *Chemistry, The Pennsylvania State University, University Park, PA, USA*; KENNETH L. KNAPPENBERGER, JR., *Department of Chemistry, Pennsylvania State University, University Park, PA, USA*.

Gold monolayer protected clusters (MPCs) are a class of quantum-confined metal nanostructures that span the transition from molecular to metallic electron dynamics. MPCs are well-described by three structural motifs that include (i) an all-metal atom core, (ii) an inorganic semiring of alternating Au-S staple units, and (iii) passivating organic ligands. The structure and composition of these domains influence the nanocluster optical and electronic properties, providing a well-defined platform to elucidate structure-dependent energy relaxation mechanisms in quantum confined metals. In this presentation, ultrafast electronic and charge carrier relaxation will be discussed. Coherent two-dimensional electronic spectroscopy (2DES) provides an excitation-detection frequency-frequency correlation by spreading the transient signal over two axes that spectrally and temporally resolves state-to-state electron dynamics on the femtosecond timescale. Here, 2DES was used to distinguish several electronic fine-structure peaks that comprise a charge transfer resonance in molecular-like $Au_{38}(SC_6H_{13})_{24}$ nanoclusters. By manipulating the polarization vector of the femtosecond pulses, additional insights on the coupling of transition dipole moments were obtained from cross-peak specific spectra. These results revealed a low-amplitude excited state absorption signal that uniquely relaxed through a charge transfer resonance within 150 femtoseconds. Evidence of population changes of excited vibrational states within the electronic manifold, which undergo intramolecular vibrational relaxation (IVR), were quantified by fitting time-dependent amplitudes of 2DES-detected cross-peaks spanning a frequency range of 1000 cm^{-1}. Anisotropy and orientation parameters obtained from polarization-selective 2DES were applied to better understand state-specific relaxation through coupled electronic states. Solvent dependences on charge carrier relaxation will be discussed. These results demonstrate the ability of polarization-selective 2DES to map state-resolved electron dynamics in molecular-like metal nanoclusters.

WD02   8:48 – 9:03

PHOTOELECTRON SPECTROSCOPY OF THE BERYLLIUM PENTAMER ANION

NOAH B JAFFE, DAVID ARCHIE STEWART, *Department of Chemistry, Emory University, Atlanta, GA, USA*; JOHN F. STANTON, *Quantum Theory Project, University of Florida, Gainesville, FL, USA*; MICHAEL HEAVEN, *Department of Chemistry, Emory University, Atlanta, GA, USA*.

Beryllium is known to be a challenging test for even high level ab initio methods due to high electron correlation contributions. There is fundamental interest in understanding how well computational methods can predict physical properties of beryllium containing molecules, but very little available experimental data on these molecules. We have continued in our exploration of pure beryllium clusters, and have acquired preliminary spectra for the beryllium pentamer Be_5. In this talk we will present our work to date on Be_5, with comparisons to theory and the Beryllium tetramer

WD03
9:06 – 9:21

A SPECTROSCOPIC INVESTIGATION OF THE EFFECTS OF SPIN STRAIN ON LN_3O^- CLUSTERS

CALEB D HUIZENGA, CAROLINE CHICK JARROLD, *Department of Chemistry, Indiana University, Bloomington, IN, USA*; SHIVANGI VAISH, *Chemistry, Indiana University, Bloomington, IN, USA*.

In the world of single molecule magnets (SMMs), lanthanide-based single molecule magnets have proven to be potential source of strong anisotropic magnetic moments and recent research has sought to harness these properties in the creation of SMMs with long spin relaxation lifetimes and high blocking temperatures. The properties of these lanthanide SMMs are dictated by both the lanthanide identity as well as the structure of the magnetic core, and SMMs with odd-numbers of metal centers have been seen to exhibit exciting magnetic properties such as spin frustration and toroidal spin moments. Expanding on previous studies of bimetallic lanthanide oxide clusters we employ anion photoelectron spectroscopy and computational modelling of gas-phase Ln_3O^- (Ln = Ce, Sm, Gd) clusters to better understand the effects of spin strain on the electronic and magnetic properties of ligand-free SMM cores. Spectra exhibit the typical binding energies of lanthanide oxide clusters (between 0.7eV and 1.2 eV) and photoelectron angular distribution anomalies we attribute to interactions between departing photoelectrons and remnant neutral clusters are observed.

WD04
9:24 – 9:39

ZINC OXIDE ELECTRONIC STRUCTURE STUDY USING PES

SHIVANGI VAISH, *Chemistry, Indiana University, Bloomington, IN, USA*; CAROLINE CHICK JARROLD, *Department of Chemistry, Indiana University, Bloomington, IN, USA*.

As the global energy landscape currently dominated by the fossil fuels is causing environmental and energy issues, there is an urgent need to shift to renewable energy sources. Production of Hydrogen gas a source of energy from water is by far the cleanest renewable energy source. Transition metal oxides are effective catalysts for the hydrogen evolution reaction. Small metal oxide clusters are used as a model to understand the catalytically active sites in bulk. In this study we use anion photoelectron spectroscopy as a means of understanding the electronic structure of the anionic and neutral species of the Zinc oxide clusters.

WD05
9:42 – 9:57

SPECTROSCOPIC STUDY OF THE N_2-H_2O COMPLEX IN THE 2 OH STRETCHING REGIONS

ROBIN GLORIEUX, *Institute of Condensed Matter and Nanosciences (IMCN), Université catholique de Louvain, Louvain-la-Neuve, Belgium*; ALEXANDR BOGOMOLOV, *Institute of Chemical Kinetics and Combustion, Novosibirsk State University , Novosibirsk, Russia*; BRIAN M HAYS, *Institute of Condensed Matter and Nanosciences (IMCN), Université catholique de Louvain, Louvain-la-Neuve, Belgium*; THOMAS VANFLETEREN, *Service de Chimie Quantique et Photophysique, Université Libre de Bruxelles, Brussels, Belgium*; MICHEL HERMAN, *SQUARES, Université Libre de Bruxelles, Brussels, Belgium*; NASSER MOAZZEN-AHMADI, *Physics and Astronomy/Institute for Quantum Science and Technology, University of Calgary, Calgary, AB, Canada*; CLÉMENT LAUZIN, *Institute of Condensed Matter and Nanosciences (IMCN), Université catholique de Louvain, Louvain-la-Neuve, Belgium*.

Rovibrational spectra of N_2-H_2O van der Waals complexes were measured in the overtone range, around the 2 OH stretching regions. The rotationally resolved $(\nu_1', \nu_2', \nu_3') \leftarrow (\nu_1'', \nu_2'', \nu_3'') = (2,0,0) \leftarrow (0,0,0)$ and $(1,0,1) \leftarrow (0,0,0)$ vibrational bands were observed; where ν_1, ν_2, ν_3 are the vibrational quantum numbers of the isolated water molecule. As well, a combination band involving the (1,0,1) state and the intermolecular in-plane N_2 bending vibration will be presented. The spectra were measured using continuous wave cavity ringdown spectroscopy in a supersonic expansion, as implemented in the FANTASIO+ setup [1,2]. These spectra were analyzed by considering the feasible tunneling motions of this complex, fitted as separate asymmetric rotors for the four observed tunneling states. The tunneling splittings are discussed as a function of the vibrational state and compared with other isotopologues. The assignment of a rovibrational perturbation will also be discussed.

[1] M. Herman, K. Didriche, D. Hurtmans, B. Kizil, P. Macko, A. Rizopoulos, P.V. Poucke, Molecular Physics, 2007, 105 (5-7), 815-823.

[2] A.S. Bogomolov, A. Roucou, R. Bejjani, M. Herman, N. Moazzen-Ahmadi, C. Lauzin, Chemical Physics Letters, 2021, 774, 138606.

WD06   10:00–10:15

WEAKLY BOUND CLUSTERS OF ATMOSPHERIC MOLECULES: INFRARED SPECTRA AND STRUCTURAL CALCULATIONS OF $(CO_2)_n$-$(CO)_m$-$(N_2)_p$, (n,m,p) = (2,1,0), (2,0,1), (1,2,0), (1,0,2), (1,1,1), (1,3,0), (1,0,3), (1,2,1), (1,1,2)

A. J. BARCLAY, *Physics and Astronomy/Institute for Quantum Science and Technology, University of Calgary, Calgary, AB, Canada*; A.R.W. McKELLAR, *Steacie Laboratory, National Research Council of Canada, Ottawa, ON, Canada*; ANDREA PIETROPOLLI CHARMET, *Dipartimento di Scienze Molecolari e Nanosistemi, Università Ca' Foscari, Venezia, Italy*; NASSER MOAZZEN-AHMADI, *Physics and Astronomy/Institute for Quantum Science and Technology, University of Calgary, Calgary, AB, Canada*.

Structural calculations and high-resolution infrared spectra are reported for trimers and tetramers containing CO_2 together with CO and/or N_2. Among the 9 clusters studied here, only $(CO_2)_2$-CO was previously observed by high-resolution spectroscopy. The spectra, which occur in the region of the ν_3 fundamental of CO_2 (~2350 cm^{-1}), were recorded using a tunable optical parametric oscillator source to probe a pulsed supersonic slit jet expansion. The trimers $(CO_2)_2$-CO and $(CO_2)_2$-N_2 have structures in which the CO or N_2 is aligned along the symmetry axis of a staggered side-by-side CO_2 dimer unit. The observation of two fundamental bands for $(CO_2)_2$-CO and $(CO_2)_2$-N_2 shows that this CO_2 dimer unit is non-planar, unlike $(CO_2)_2$ itself. For the trimers CO_2-$(CO)_2$ and CO_2-$(N_2)_2$, the CO or N_2 monomers occupy equivalent positions in the 'equatorial plane' of the CO_2, pointing toward its C atom. To form the tetramers CO_2-$(CO)_3$ and CO_2-$(N_2)_3$, a third CO or N_2 monomer is then added off to the 'side' of the first two. In the mixed tetramers CO_2-$(CO)_2$-N_2 and CO_2-CO-$(N_2)_2$, this 'side' position is taken by N_2 and not CO. In addition to the fundamental bands, combination bands are also observed for $(CO_2)_2$-CO, CO_2-$(CO)_2$, and CO_2-$(N_2)_2$, yielding some information about their low-frequency intermolecular vibrations.

Intermission

WD07   10:57–11:12

MATRIX ISOLATION FTIR ANALYSIS OF WEAKLY-BOUND COMPLEXES OF WATER WITH γ-LACTONES

ANNABELLE N CARNEY, KENNETH C MOGAURO, EMILY M WEAVER, JOSH NEWBY, *Chemistry, Nazareth College, Rochester, NY, USA*.

The interaction preferences of water with small molecules has been an area of interest for many years as we endeavor to better understand solvation at the molecular scale. Here, a study of weakly-bound complexes of γ-lactones with water is presented. In this study, matrix isolation FTIR and computational methods were used to examine stable 1:1 complexes of γ-butyrolactone, γ-valerolactone, and Angelica lactone complexes with water. These five-membered heterocycles contain multiple regions that could serve as binding sites for a single water molecule including two chemically distinct oxygen atoms and a π-cloud. Matrix isolation FTIR experiments identified several peaks that were not associated with isolated water or lactone, implying the bands are due to weakly-bound complexes of the two. In addition to normal water, D_2O and HDO complexes with the lactones were also observed. The spectra can be interpreted with the aid of computational chemistry. In this work, multiple density functional theories along with MP2 calculations were used to find minimum energy configurations and vibrational structure of the complexes that can be directly compared to our spectra. Possible interpretations of the experimental and computational results are presented.

WD08
11:15 – 11:30

VIBRATIONAL SPECTROSCOPY OF BENZONITRILE–(WATER)$_{1-2}$ CLUSTERS IN HELIUM DROPLETS

<u>JAI KHATRI</u>, TARUN KUMAR ROY, KUNTAL CHATTERJEE, GERHARD SCHWAAB, MARTINA HAVENITH, *Physikalische Chemie II, Ruhr University Bochum, Bochum, Germany.*

Polycyclic aromatic hydrocarbons are considered as primary carriers of the unidentified interstellar bands. The recent discovery of the first interstellar aromatic molecule, benzonitrile (C_6H_5CN), suggests a repository of aromatic hydrocarbons in the outer earth environment. Herein, we report an infrared (IR) study of benzonitrile–(D_2O)$_n$ clusters using mass-selective detection in helium nanodroplets. In this work, we use isotopically substituted water, D_2O, instead of (H_2O) because of our restricted IR frequency range (2565–3100 cm^{-1}). A comparison of the experimental and predicted spectra computed at the MP2/6-311++G(d,p) level of benzonitrile–(water)$_{1-2}$ clusters reveals the formation of a unique local minimum structure, which was not detected in previous gas-phase molecular beam experiments. Here, the solvent water forms a nearly linear hydrogen bond (H-bond) with the nitrile nitrogen of benzonitrile, while the previously reported most stable cyclic H-bonded isomer is not observed. This can be rationalized by the stepwise aggregation process of precooled monomers. The addition of a second water molecule results in the formation of two different isomers. In one of the observed isomers, a H-bonded water chain binds linearly to the nitrile nitrogen similar to the monohydrated benzonitrile–water complex. In the other observed isomer, the water dimer forms a ring-type structure, where a H-bonded water dimer simultaneously interacts with the nitrile nitrogen and the adjacent ortho CH group. Finally, we compare the water-binding motif in the neutral benzonitrile–water complex with the corresponding positively and negatively charged benzonitrile–water monohydrates to comprehend the charge-induced alteration of the solvent binding motif.

WD09
11:33 – 11:48

MICROSOLVATION AND PHOTODYNAMICS IN FORMIC ACID-WATER CLUSTERS

<u>SHAUN SUTTON</u>, CHASE H ROTTEGER, *School of Molecular Sciences and Biodesign Center for Applied Structural Discovery, Arizona State University, Tempe, AZ, USA*; TARAKESHWAR PILARISETTY, DANE MILLER, *School of Molecular Sciences, Arizona State University, Tempe, AZ, USA*; SCOTT G SAYRES, *School of Molecular Sciences and Biodesign Center for Applied Structural Discovery, Arizona State University, Tempe, AZ, USA.*

Formic acid is the simplest carboxylic acid and plays a pivotal role in atmospheric chemistry. It is an intermediate in the Water-Gas-Shift reaction, decomposing into either CO_2 and H_2 or into H_2O and CO under ionizing radiation. Furthermore, it is important in acid rain and seeding the nucleation of water molecules in cloud formation. Here, I will present our recent work, where femtosecond lasers are applied to study the microsolvation and photodynamics of molecular gas-phase formic acid-water clusters using time-of-flight mass spectrometry. Our cluster distribution confirms the enhanced stability of $(FA)_5(H_2O)_1H^+$, where the formic acid cluster forms a cage-like structure surrounding the water molecule. Upon exposure to high laser intensities (400 nm, 200 fs, laser intensities of 1.9×10^{15} W/cm^2), the clusters undergo an enhanced ionization which produces multiply charged ions of C, O, and CO. Coulomb explosion of these ions leads to a large kinetic energy release that is shown to increase with the size of clusters. The measured values are in agreement with a Molecular Dynamics simulation of the Coulomb explosion for the mean size of the clusters within the cluster distribution, suggesting that no movement occurs during ionization. Of particular relevance, we record a large amount of signal for the carbon monoxide trication. KER values were recorded as high as 44 eV for CO^{3+} for $(FA)_2$, but increases to 75.3 eV when the cluster distribution is shifted toward $(FA)_5$ as the largest signal. Potential energy curves for CO^{3+} are calculated using the multireference configuration interaction (MRCI+Q) method to confirm the existence of metastable states with a large potential barrier with respect to dissociation. This combined experimental and theoretical effort confirms the existence of metastable CO^{3+}.

WD10   11:51 – 12:06

THE 2OH OVERTONE SPECTRUM OF H_2O-CO_2 VAN DER WAALS COMPLEX: SEARCH FOR INTERMOLECULAR MODES EXCITATION AND LARGER COMPLEXES

<u>BRIAN M HAYS</u>, ROBIN GLORIEUX, *Institute of Condensed Matter and Nanosciences (IMCN), Université catholique de Louvain, Louvain-la-Neuve, Belgium*; MICHEL HERMAN, *Laboratoire de Chimie Quantique et Photophysique, Universite Libre de Bruxelles, Brussels, Belgium*; CLÉMENT LAUZIN, *Institute of Condensed Matter and Nanosciences (IMCN), Université catholique de Louvain, Louvain-la-Neuve, Belgium.*

The H_2O-CO_2 van der Waals complex is a rich chemical system composed of two major constituents of the atmosphere. To further expand the knowledge surrounding the structure of this system, the rovibrational spectrum of the H_2O-CO_2 complex was explored around the 2OH stretching region using the FANTASIO+ set-up [1]. The complex was formed in a pulsed slit supersonic expansion and was probed using continuous-wave cavity ringdown spectroscopy in the near infrared range. Combination bands that include intermolecular modes will be reported and compared to recent high-level ab initio calculations [2]. The frequency of such modes is very sensitive to the potential energy surface morphology. Improvements of the FANTASIO+ experimental set-up allowing such observation and the search for larger clusters will be presented.

[1] Bogomolov, A. S.; Roucou, A.; Bejjani, R.; Herman, M.; Moazzen-Ahmadi, N.; Lauzin, C. Chem. Phys. Lett 2021, 774, 138606

[2] Felker, P. M.; Bačić, Z. J. Chem. Phys. 2022, 156, 064301

WE. Coblentz Special Session
Wednesday, June 22, 2022 – 8:30 AM
Room: 1024 Chemistry Annex

Chair: Zachary Schultz, The Ohio State University, Columbus, OH, USA

WE01   8:30 – 8:45

UNDERSTANDING THE SURFACE ENHANCED RAMAN SPECTROSCOPY (SERS) SIGNALS OF AMINO ACIDS, PEPTIDES, AND PROTEINS FOR BIOSENSING APPLICATIONS

TAYLOR PAYNE, ZACHARY SCHULTZ, *Department of Chemistry and Biochemistry, The Ohio State University, Columbus, OH, USA.*

One promising diagnostic tool for viral infection is surface enhanced Raman spectroscopy (SERS), which is a quick, sensitive light scattering technique that uses the energy of the bonds as a fingerprint to identify molecules. SERS yields enhanced Raman signals by positioning analytes near the surface of metal nanostructures and creating localized, electric fields around the metal with a resonant laser. Fundamentally, the vibrational signatures of peptides and proteins rely on their amino acid composition, secondary structure, and local environment. The SERS signals of these species are further complicated by interactions with the metal nanostructures. For instance, the SERS signals of a peptide can differ if the peptide is adsorbed to a gold nanostructured substrate versus a gold nanoparticle. As another example, tryptophan is an important aromatic residue within the binding domain of many proteins, but its SERS signal shows distinct differences from its Raman signal. These changes in tryptophan's signal can impact the overall signal from the peptides or proteins it comprises. Using SERS for biosensing requires determining the vibrational signature of the target molecule, which then allows for identification. In SERS sensing of viruses, a common concern is signal variability based on the orientation of these large species on the nanostructure surface. Fortunately, capture molecules can improve signal reproducibility by forcing the analyte into a consistent surface orientation, as well as by selectively targeting the analyte to avoid interference. Peptides can be used to bind the surface proteins of viruses and capture them on SERS surfaces to identify their SERS signatures. In this work, we investigate the SERS signals of a SARS-CoV-2 spike-binding peptide both before and after spike protein binding, along with those of tryptophan and tryptophan-containing peptides, on gold SERS surfaces. Understanding the origins of these signals will provide a basis for the design of a peptide-surface protein-based SERS assay for SARS-CoV-2, along with other potential viruses in the future.

WE02   8:48 – 9:03

APTAMER BASED MICROPARTICLES IMMUNOASSAY METHOD FOR CA125 DETECTION USING RAMAN SPECTROSCOPY

ROBINSON KARUNANITHY, TORREY E. HOLLAND, P SIVAKUMAR, *Physics, Southern Illinois University Carbondale, Carbondale, IL, USA.*

Epithelial ovarian cancer (EOC) is considered to have higher mortality, with no or few symptoms at an early stage and a poor prognosis. The treatments and survival solely depend on the stage of cancer at diagnosis. Developing a non-invasive technique that can detect biomarkers (antigens) with sufficient sensitivity, selectivity, and reproducibility is a promising approach to overcome the challenges in the early diagnosis of EOC. The bioconjugation technique is a promising approach to detecting cancer antigens such as CA125 and HE4 at low concentrations. Typically, antibodies are used to recognize the specific type of cancer antigens. However, aptamers have been recently shown to work similarly to antibodies for recognizing antigens, with some advantages over antibodies, including relatively smaller size compared to antibodies that make them recognize the target molecules relatively accurately and chemically synthesized and modified easily according to the target. In this work, we evaluate the affinity and specificity of aptamer towards CA 125 using an aptamer-based affinity purification with gold nanoparticles (AuNps) Raman-label. For this purpose, Ni-NTA (Nickel-nitrilotriacetic acid) microparticles, used for the magnetic separation process, were conjugated to CA 125-Histidine (CA 125 His Tag). It was then allowed to bind biotinylated aptamer. Later, this conjugate was incubated with gold nanoparticles pre-modified with streptavidin and a Raman label. The final conjugate was investigated with surface enhanced Raman spectroscopy following the magnetic separation process. The Raman signatures from the label verified the sandwich-type conjugation of the CA 125-aptamer complex in between Ni-NTA and AuNPs.

WE03   9:06 – 9:21

CELL PHASE IDENTIFICATION IN A THREE-DIMENSIONAL TUMOR CELL CULTURE MODEL BY FOURIER TRANSFORM INFRARED (FT-IR) SPECTROSCOPIC IMAGING

PEI-HSUAN HSIEH, *Bioengineering, University of Illinois at Urbana-Champaign, Urbana, IL, USA*; ROHIT BHARGAVA, *Department of Chemical and Biomolecular Engineering, University of Illinois at Urbana-Champaign, Urbana, IL, USA.*

Cell cycle progression plays a vital role in regulating proliferation, metabolism and apoptosis. Specifically, assessing cell phase is of significant importance since the development of cancer is tightly linked with the dysregulation of cell cycle. However, investigating the cellular status in three-dimensional in vitro models and tissue is often limited to the complexity of sample preparation and the loss of structural integrity. The most common technique nowadays is flow cytometry, which requires a full disintegration of cellular organization and additional fluorescence staining. To overcome these challenges, Fourier transform infrared (FT-IR) spectroscopic imaging is introduced in this study. It is a powerful approach for analyzing biological samples by detecting the vibrational modes of indigenous molecules, thereby eliminating the need for stains and greatly expanding information beyond phase or intensity contrast of optical imaging. Drawing upon these advantages, we apply FT-IR imaging integrated with unsupervised learning technique to distinguish subtle biochemical compositions between cell phases while retaining a spatial distribution of the innate constituents. The spectral variation in DNA quantity from 2D cell culture is served as an indicator to understand the relative cell cycle stages in a 3D MCF10A acini model. We further evaluate the temporal dependence of these spectral changes throughout the acini formation and validate that cells present to be more proliferative in the early stages of acini formation compared to fully developed acini. Taken altogether, our study presents a computational approach to provide a comprehensive cell phase in tissue-like structure without any requisite for specific biomarker staining, which has the potential to accelerate pharmaceutical agents design with more defined targeted effects. Moreover, the integration of FT-IR spectroscopy and computational methodologies could also expand to the field of pathology and lead to an improvement for clinical diagnostics.

WE04   9:24 – 9:39

LABEL-FREE AUTOFLUORESCENCE-DETECTED MID-IR PHOTOTHERMAL MICROSCOPY

ALEKSANDR RAZUMTCEV, GARTH SIMPSON, *Department of Chemistry, Purdue University, West Lafayette, IN, USA.*

The instrumentation and methods to perform autofluorescence-detected photothermal mid-IR (AF-PTIR) microscopy are demonstrated experimentally and applied for chemically-selective label-free imaging of an active pharmaceutical ingredient (API) within a mixture with common pharmaceutical excipients. In AF-PTIR, the heat released from mid-IR absorption induces changes in two-photon excited UV-fluorescence (TPE-UVF) intensity. The spectral dependence of the fluorescence modulation locally informs on chemical composition with a spatial resolution dictated by the diffraction limit of visible light. AF-PTIR is shown to provide an additional level of selectivity in nonlinear optical imaging by mid-IR spectroscopy enabling mapping of the API distribution in the presence of TPE-UVF and second harmonic generation active excipients (**Fig. 1**). AF-PTIR provides high selectivity and sensitivity in image contrast for aromatic APIs, complementing broadly applicable commercial methods such as optical photothermal mid-IR (O-PTIR) microscopy.

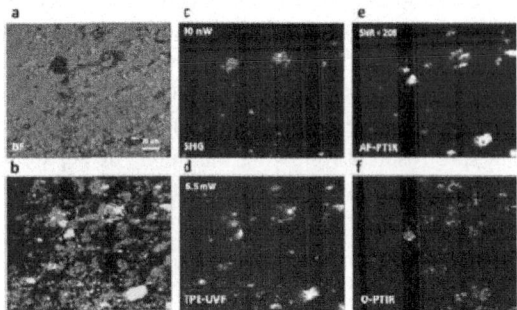

Figure 1. (a), (c – f) – Bright field, second harmonic generation (SHG), TPE-UVF, AF-PTIR and O-PTIR images of the field of view respectively. (b) – Segmentation results showing the spatial distribution of individual components (lactose particles are shown in blue, indomethacin in green, TiO_2 in yellow and Mg stearate is shown in red).

WE05 9:42 – 9:57

A WIDE-FIELD IMAGING APPROACH FOR SIMULTANEOUS SUPER-RESOLUTION SURFACE-ENHANCED RAMAN SCATTERING IMAGING AND SPECTROSCOPY

<u>DEBEN SHOUP</u>, ZACHARY SCHULTZ, *Department of Chemistry and Biochemistry, The Ohio State University, Columbus, OH, USA.*

The ability to simultaneously obtain high spatial resolution images and chemical specific information is of interest in a variety of biological and physical processes. Surface-enhanced Raman scattering (SERS) is particularly suited for this purpose due to its ability to enhance signal from Raman vibrational modes by probing molecules near the surface of plasmonic metal nanostructures. The spatial resolution in SERS imaging is limited by the diffraction limit of light, limiting the resolution to hundreds of nanometers. However, Raman reporter molecules adsorbed to single nanoparticles experience temporal intensity fluctuations that enable the SERS signal to be fit with localization algorithms, such as stochastic optical reconstruction microscopy (STORM). STORM fittings can be applied to generate images with sub-diffraction limited localization of the emitting centers from the nanoparticles. In this work, we demonstrate a wide-field spectrally resolved SERS imaging approach where a transmission diffraction grating placed before the imaging array detector captures the image and first-order diffraction on the same detector. The first-order diffraction corresponds to the SERS spectrum and can be directly correlated to the location and features of a nanoparticle. STORM fitting both the spatial and spectral response results in improved localization in the spatial response and improved peak identification compared to the measured spectra in the spectral response. We show that spatially correlated Raman spectra from multiple nanoparticles in a wide-field of view are readily obtained on a 10-100 ms time scale, which enables spatially resolved monitoring of chemical processes.

WE06 10:00 – 10:15

ISOLATING THE INTRINSIC SPECTRAL RESPONSES OF VIBRATIONAL PROBES: BENCHMARKS FOR REPORTERS OF CONDENSED PHASE AND BIOLOGICAL PROCESSES

<u>SEAN COLEMAN EDINGTON</u>, AHMED MOHAMED, MARK JOHNSON, *Department of Chemistry, Yale University, New Haven, CT, USA.*

We use cryogenic infrared vibrational predissociation spectroscopy of isolated, nitrile-containing vibrational probe molecules to provide benchmarks for the probe molecule spectral response. Popular probes, such as paracyanophenylalanine, and other nitrile-containing molecules are manipulated in solution to modify conformation and charge state prior to extraction and isolation using electrospray ionization and He buffer gas cooling to 10 K. The vibrational spectra of the cold, He- or H2-tagged molecules are collected in a linear predissociation regime and interpreted with the aid of electronic structure calculations. The results provide insight into the intrinsic spectral response of isolated nitrile vibrational reporters decoupled from solvent effects.

Vibrational probe molecules are popularly employed to provide spectroscopic readouts of local electrostatic environments in phenomena including bulk solvation dynamics, interfacial proton transfer, and enzyme catalysis. A range of these molecules has been developed, allowing investigators to exploit absorption-free "windows" in the infrared spectrum to ease measurement. However, in the condensed phase it is often a challenge to separate the components of the reporter's response arising from external factors, such as local electric fields or hydrogen bonding, from those due to intrinsic factors such as molecular electrostatic potential or reporter isomerization.

Intermission

WE07 10:57–11:12
HIGH-THROUGHPUT MICROPLASTIC MONITORING IN MICROFLUIDICS BY RAPID COHERENT RAMAN SCATTERING SPECTROSCOPY

MINJIAN LU, YUJIA ZHANG, YAN LI, HAOYUN WEI, *Department of Precision Instrument, Tsinghua University, Beijing, China.*

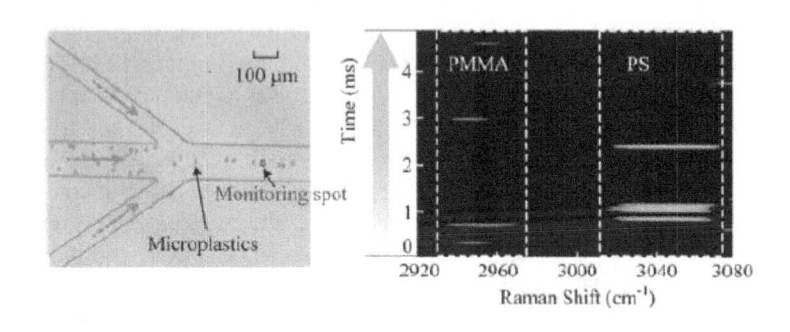

Although small microplastics pose a huge threat to aquatic environment and biological health, current microplastic monitoring procedures are rather time-consuming and laborious. With the help of the rapid coherent anti-Stokes Raman scattering microspectroscopy as a label-free molecular identification approach, we achieved microplastic monitoring in microfluidics with a high throughput of ~2150 events/s. The spectral refresh rate, i.e. the theoretical highest throughput, is 35 000 events/s by the apparatus, which is the highest speed for flow device monitoring up to the present. Also, we classified PS and PMMA microbeads based on their unique spectral peaks, and the classification was further verified by principal component analysis (PCA). Other sets of results under different flow velocities are further classified and verified by the PCA model trained by the first set of data, with a consistency more than 99%, which demonstrates the repeatability and consistency of our system in rapid monitoring.

WE08 11:15–11:30
UNDERSTANDING POLARIZATION EFFECTS ON ABSORPTION SPECTRA MEASURED USING A QUANTUM CASCADE LASER-BASED SPECTROMETER

RUO-JING HO, *Bioengineering, University of Illinois at Urbana-Champaign, Urbana, IL, USA*; YAMUNA DILIP PHAL, *Electrical and Computer Engineering, University of Illinois Urbana-Champaign, Urbana, IL, USA*; ROHIT BHARGAVA, *Department of Chemical and Biomolecular Engineering, University of Illinois at Urbana-Champaign, Urbana, IL, USA.*

Infrared (IR) spectroscopy using Quantum Cascade Lasers (QCLs) is an emerging technology that has opened new possibilities due to its numerous advantages such as shorter acquisition times and high signal-to-noise-ratio measurements. Furthermore, the intrinsic polarized source allows direct probing of other parameters, for instance, the dichroic properties of the samples. In particular, polarimetric detection can enhance structural and chemical contrasts and has been applied for imaging, chemical sensing, and biological tissue classification. While specific optical configurations are known to introduce polarization deviation and thus, less sensitivity in anisotropy detection, the influence on absorbance measurements has been downplayed as a systematic error. In this work, we characterize the polarization effects introduced by optical components. Using full-Stokes' measurements, we investigate the polarization scrambling and other effects introduced by various factors such as focusing optics, optical coatings, and incident source polarization. With this thorough analysis, we account for most of the polarization deviation factors introduced in typical experimental systems. Lastly, we optimize spectrometer design based on the characterization and demonstrate infrared absorbance spectra of polymer films with higher precision and anisotropy sensitivity.

WE09 11:33 – 11:48
DETECTION OF MEDICAL INHALER USE VIA TERAHERTZ SPECTROSCOPY

DANIEL J TYREE, IVAN MEDVEDEV, *Department of Physics, Wright State University, Dayton, OH, USA*; STEVE S KIM, *711th Human Performance Wing, Air Force Research Laboratory, WPAFB, USA*; MICHAEL C BROTHERS, *Integrative Health and Performance Sciences, UES Inc., Dayton, OH, USA.*

HFA134a (aka 1,1,1,2 tetrafluoroethane) is the most common propellant in pressure metered dose medical inhalers (PMDIs). Rapid and easy detection of this compound can benefit various human health and performance sectors to identify an unintended medication and confirm adherence. Current medical screening is commonly performed by urinalysis which can be significantly influenced by the rate at which the target compound is processed into urine. As an alternative to urine, breath represents a readily available, easily obtained, and relevant biofluid for airway medication screening while detection of PMDI propellant serves as a more general marker of use. In this study, we demonstrate the novel use of THz spectroscopy, performed with a recently developed table-top THz chemical sensor, to detect and quantify HFA134a in breath as a marker of recent inhaler use at physiologically relevant concentrations. THz chemical analysis facilitates a near instantaneous (few minutes up to 30 minutes) post inhalation detection of propellant. These time scales are shorter than most urinalysis. The compact, and semiautomated nature of the sensor is amenable to rapid analysis on-site with minimal supporting material and components. In this study, we analyzed breath from 10 human subjects. Samples were obtained prior to and after a single dose of an albuterol inhaler. Analysis of the breath samples was performed by the table-top THz sensor and gas chromatography coupled to mass spectrometry (GC-MS) for validation. THz sensing demonstrated reliable detection of HFA134a in nearly all samples. The breath concentrations determined by the THz sensor and GC-MS exhibited exponential decay of breath-HFA134a with time constants varying between 2.5 to 6 minutes. The current sensitivity of the THz sensor allows to monitor HFA143a levels up to 30 minutes post inhalation.

WE10 11:51 – 12:06
A PHOTONIC GAS SENSOR FOR THE MID-INFRARED

TRAVIS A GARTNER, *Department of Physics and Astronomy, University of Calgary, Calgary, AB, Canada*; NASSER MOAZZEN-AHMADI, *Physics and Astronomy/Institute for Quantum Science and Technology, University of Calgary, Calgary, AB, Canada*; A. J. BARCLAY, *Department of Physics and Astronomy, University of Calgary, Calgary, AB, Canada.*

The mid-infrared (MIR) contains the strong absorption signatures of many molecules that are of extreme interest in real-world sensing applications. The miniaturization of spectroscopic sensing equipment made possible by silicon photonics has the potential to revolutionize emission sensing in the MIR.

Nanophotonic devices have greatly benefited from telecommunication technology in the near infrared (NIR) region. The industry has reached a level of maturity where high volume production of integrated circuitry can be done at low cost. Silicon based photonic devices can now support optical signals in the MIR past 8 microns with losses approaching those of the telecommunications band [1] making the region attractive for sensing applications.

Absorption sensing with photonic devices has been demonstrated in silicon on sapphire, silicon nitride [2], and other silicon-on-insulator platforms. These methodologies have demonstrated the ability to sense analyte concentrations as low as 5000 ppmv (parts per million by volume), which is the workplace limit in many constituencies [3].

We present our current state of research on the development of a high-quality factor MIR silicon-on-sapphire (SOS) photonic gas sensor for use in lab-on-a-chip sensing applications. An optical parametric oscillator (OPO) will be used as a MIR source to pump a grating coupled SOS ring cavity immersed in a controlled CO_2 environment. The cavity will be geometrically engineered to allow for high sensitivity spectroscopy of trace CO_2 near 2350cm-1. Design was conducted in COMSOL Multiphysics and Lumerical software suites. The sensor was patterned at Applied Nanotools in Edmonton, AB and is currently undergoing characterization in the laboratory at the University of Calgary.

[1] R. Shankar et al., Applied Physics Letters, 102, 051108, 2013
[2] C. Ranacher et al., IEEE Photonics Journal, 10 (5), 2018
[3] C. Ranacher et al., Sensors and Actuators A: Physical, 277, pp. 117-123, 2018

WE11

THE IMPACT OF PLASMONICALLY GENERATED HOT-CARRIERS ON SERS ANALYSIS

<u>CHELSEA M. ZOLTOWSKI</u>, ZACHARY SCHULTZ, *Department of Chemistry and Biochemistry, The Ohio State University, Columbus, OH, USA.*

Plasmonic nanostructures have paved the way for the development of surface enhanced Raman spectroscopy (SERS); a technique that takes advantage of the Raman signal specific to the molecular vibrational modes. SERS enhances the Raman signal up to 109-fold allowing for lower limits of detection. Through the illumination of the nanostructure with a laser, a localized surface plasmon resonance (LSPR) is excited and further the enhances the electric field at the surface of the nanostructure. While the excitation of the LSPR enhances the Raman signal, it can also generate hot carries that cause the formation of photoproducts that can change the Raman signal. Photoproducts have been reported for various nanostructures in different SERS experiments and can include cross-linking/dimerization, fragmentation, and radical formation. Understanding the parameters and occurrences of these photoproducts will allow for the ability to prevent them when not desired and generate them for further applications. Previously, our group has reported on radical formation with the amino acid tryptophan as well as 4-mercaptobenzoic acid, a common Raman reporter molecule. This work will use changes in the SERS signal to elaborate on the conditions and dynamics of these radical formation reactions associated with the plasmonic activity of nanostructures.

WF. Large amplitude motions, internal rotation
Wednesday, June 22, 2022 – 8:30 AM
Room: 124 Burrill Hall

Chair: Mark D. Marshall, Amherst College, Amherst, MA, USA

WF01   8:30 – 8:45

A GLOBAL RAM METHOD FOR FITTING ASYMMETRIC TOPS WITH ONE METHYL INTERNAL ROTOR AND TWO ^{14}N NUCLEI: APPLICATION OF THE BELGI-2N CODE TO THE MICROWAVE SPECTRA OF THE METHYLIMIDAZOLE ISOMERS.

HA VINH LAM NGUYEN, ISABELLE KLEINER, MARTIN SCHWELL, *Université Paris-Est Créteil et Université de Paris, Laboratoire Interuniversitaire des systèmes atmosphériques (LISA), CNRS UMR7583, Creteil, France*; EVA GOUGOULA, *Photon Science - Spectroscopy of Molecular Processes, Deutsches Elektronen-Synchrotron DESY, Hamburg, Germany*; NICK WALKER, *School of Natural and Environmental Sciences, Newcastle University, Newcastle-upon-Tyne, UK*.

A number of internal rotation codes can deal with the combination of one or two internal rotor(s) with one ^{14}N quadrupole nucleus, but not many treats the internal rotations with two ^{14}N nuclei. Here we present the extended version of our internal rotor program (BELGI-C$_s$), called BELGI-2N using the Rho-Axis Method (RAM)[a] global approach to deal with the compounds containing one methyl top and two weakly coupling ^{14}N nuclei. For molecules containing a ^{14}N nucleus with a nuclear spin I equal to 1, all rotational transitions of the rigid rotor split into several hyperfine components. The quadrupole moment is relatively small and can be treated using a first order perturbation approximation. To test our new code, we applied it to the microwave data previously recorded for N-, 2-, 4- and 5-methylimidazole, using a chirped-pulse Fourier transform microwave spectroscopy in the 7.0–18.5 GHz frequency range[b]. Compared to this study, we were able to perform global fits with root-mean-square deviations within the experimental accuracy and to increase the number of assigned lines with the high predictive power of the fits.

[a] J. T. Hougen, I. Kleiner, and M. Godefroid, J. Mol. Spectrosc. 163, 559 (1994)
[b] E. Gougoula, C. Medcraft, J. Heitkämper, and N. R. Walker, J. Chem. Phys. 151, 144301 (2019)

WF02   8:48 – 9:03

A GLOBAL RAM METHOD FOR FITTING INFRARED AND FAR-INFRARED DATA FOR SMALL VOLATILE ORGANIC COUMPOUNDS: APPLICATION TO TOLUENE

V. ILYUSHIN, *Radiospectrometry Department, Institute of Radio Astronomy of NASU, Kharkov, Ukraine*; ISABELLE KLEINER, SELLITTO PASQUALE, F. KWABIA TCHANA, *Université Paris-Est Créteil et Université de Paris, Laboratoire Interuniversitaire des systèmes atmosphériques (LISA), CNRS UMR7583, Creteil, France*; PIERRE ASSELIN, PASCALE SOULARD, *CNRS, De la Molécule aux Nano-Objets: Réactivité, Interactions, Spectroscopies, MONARIS, Sorbonne Université, PARIS, France*; OLIVIER PIRALI, *Institut des Sciences Moléculaires d'Orsay, Université Paris Saclay, CNRS, Orsay, France*; MANUEL GOUBET, *Laboratoire PhLAM, UMR 8523 CNRS - Université Lille 1, Villeneuve d'Ascq, France*; ROBERT GEORGES, *IPR UMR6251, CNRS - Université Rennes 1, Rennes, France*.

Producing spectroscopic data in the infrared range for a number of VOCs (volatile organic compounds) to be used for detecting and measuring their abundance with remote sensing is highly needed to control air pollution and air quality. Toluene is one of the important VOCs and abundant hydrocarbon in the Earth's atmosphere and it is a major anthropogenic pollutant emitted by various sources. The ultimate goal of our study is twofold: (i) develop an offspring of the RAM36 code[a] capable of simultaneous fitting torsion-rotation spectra in several vibrational states of a molecule with C$_{3v}$ internal rotor and C$_{2v}$ frame, and (ii) build an infrared database for toluene in the spectral range 600-800 cm^{-1} for remote sensing purposes. For the second goal new data were recorded using the JET-AILES experiment at the SOLEIL synchrotron around the band ν_{36} at 729 cm^{-1}. In order to account for possible hot bands in the infrared spectrum we also performed a search for the transitions belonging to the lowest vibration state of toluene ν_{38} at 204 cm^{-1}. The details of the new code and the first assignments of the torsion-rotation spectrum for the lowest vibrational state of toluene in the microwave range will be presented.[b]

[a] V. V. Ilyushin, Z. Kisiel, L. Pszczółkowski, H. Mäder, J. T. Hougen, J. Mol. Spectrosc. 259, 26 (2010)
[b] We acknowledge support by the Dim Qi2 program.

WF03 9:06 – 9:21

AN OH IN FLUORINE'S CLOTHING - THE CURIOUS ROTATIONAL SPECTROSCOPY OF PERFLUOROPHENOL

<u>BLAIR WELSH</u>, AMANDA DEWYER, ANGIE ZHANG, KENDREW AU, NILS HANSEN, TIMOTHY S. ZWIER, *Combustion Research Facility, Sandia National Laboratories, Livermore, CA, USA.*

Perfluorophenol (C_6F_5OH) is analogous to hexafluorobenzene (C_6F_6), with one fluorine atom replaced by a hydroxyl group. This substitution has a threefold effect: it provides a permanent dipole moment, the molecule remains very close to the oblate symmetric top limit, and intramolecular hydrogen bonds between the H and adjacent fluorine atoms are formed. Hydrogen can tunnel through the barrier to internal rotation of the OH group, lifting the degeneracy of the torsional states. These factors result in the unusual case of a polar, tunneling, near-symmetric top.

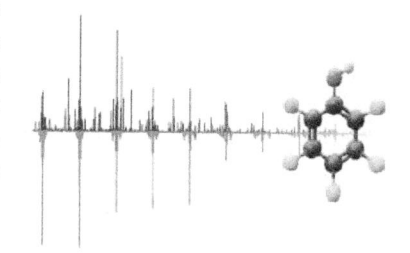

To probe these effects, the 1 K rotational spectrum of perfluorophenol between 7.5 and 17.5 GHz has been measured using chirped-pulse Fourier transform microwave (CP-FTMW) spectroscopy. The asymmetry parameter (κ) was experimentally determined to be 0.944, in agreement with the near-oblate geometries predicted by MP2/6-311++G(d,p) calculations. Tunneling splitting was observed for both a-type and b-type transitions due to the C-O bond axis lying between the a and b inertial axes; a consequence of the near-symmetry of perfluorophenol. The energy difference between the split 0^+ and 0^- tunnelling levels was established to be 24.850 MHz. Preliminary wB97XD/6-311++G** calculations estimate a barrier to internal rotation (V_2) of approximately 1211 cm^{-1}. The observed energy splitting is much lower than might be expected of this barrier height when compared to other phenolic derivatives, the exact reason for which is still to be understood.

WF04 9:24 – 9:39

MICROWAVE SPECTRA OF DINITROTOLUENE ISOMERS: A NEW STEP TOWARDS THE DETECTION OF EXPLOSIVE VAPORS

<u>MHAMAD CHRAYTEH</u>, *Laboratoire de Physico-Chimie de l'Atmosphère, Université du Littoral Côte d'Opale, Dunkerque, France*; PASCAL DRÉAN, MANUEL GOUBET, *UMR 8523 - PhLAM - Physique des Lasers Atomes et Molécules, University of Lille, CNRS, F-59000 Lille, France*; ANTHONY ROUCOU, ARNAUD CUISSET, *Laboratoire de Physico-Chimie de l'Atmosphère, Université du Littoral Côte d'Opale, Dunkerque, France.*

The spectroscopic characterization of explosives taggants, like nitrotoluenes (NT) used for the TNT detection, is a research subject of growing interest. Recently, the spectroscopic studies of the three NT isomers in the microwave and millimeter-wave ranges were reported[1,2]. We present the gas-phase rotational spectroscopic study of weakly volatile dinitrotoluenes (DNT) isomers. The pure rotational spectrum of, 2,4-DNT and 2,6-DNT was recorded in microwave range (2-20 GHz) using a Fabry-Perot Fourier-transform microwave (FP-FTMW) technique coupled to a pulsed supersonic jet. The spectral analysis was supported by quantum chemical calculations carried out at the B98/cc-pvtz and MP2/cc-pvtz levels of theory. The spectra of DNT were complicated by the presence of two ^{14}N nucleus giving rise to congested hyperfine structures. The methyl group internal rotation barriers were calculated at the B98/cc-pvtz level of theory to be V_3=563 cm^{-1} and V_3= 696 cm^{-1} for 2,4- and 2,6-DNT, respectively. Although no splitting due to internal rotation was observed for 2,6-DNT, several splittings were observed for 2,4-DNT and their analysis in under progress. The semi-rigid and the nuclear quadrupole couplings descriptions obtained from the spectral analysis are presented. An anisotropic internal rotation of the coupled -CH_3 and -NO_2 torsional motions, as already mentioned for 2-NT[1], will be discussed for 2,4-DNT.

[1] Roucou et al., CHEMPHYSCHEM, 21, 2523-2538, (2020). [2] Roucou et al., CHEMPHYSCHEM, 19, 1056-1067, (2018). Acknowledgment: This work received financial support from the French Agence Nationale de la Recherche via funding of the project Millimeter-wave Explosive Taggant vapors Investigations using Spectral taxonomy (METIS) under contract number ANR-20-ASTR-0016-03.

WF05 9:42 – 9:57
CONFORMATIONAL ANALYSIS OF VALINE METHYL ESTER BY MICROWAVE SPECTROSCOPY

DINESH MARASINGHE, MICHAEL TUBERGEN, *Department of Chemistry and Biochemistry, Kent State University, Kent, OH, USA*.

The rotational spectra of two conformers of valine methyl ester (ValOMe) have been measured and assigned using a cavity based Fourier-transform microwave spectrometer in the range of 9-18 GHz as a part of a project investigating the structures of a series of amino acid methyl esters. We modeled 15 possible conformers of ValOMe using the ωB97XD/6-311++G(d,p)) level of theory. 59 rotational transitions assigned to conformer I were fit to Watson's A-reduced Hamiltonian: A = 2552.01(1) MHz, B = 1041.821(2) MHz, and C = 938.549(2) MHz. ^{14}N nuclear quadrupole hyperfine splittings were resolved, and the 137 hyperfine components were fit to χ_{aa} = -4.20(2) MHz and $\chi_{bb} - \chi_{cc}$ = 1.26(1) MHz. The spectrum of conformer I also reveals tunneling splittings from the ester methyl rotor. The *XIAM*[a] program was used to fit the barrier to the internal rotation of the methyl rotor. The best fit V_3 barrier was found to be 387.8(8) cm^{-1}. 20 rotational transitions were assigned for conformer II and the fitted rotational constants are A = 2544.405(9) MHz, B = 1092.337(2) MHz, and C = 896.301(1) MHZ. The transitions were split by nuclear quadrupole coupling and tunneling, and complete assignment of these components is ongoing.

---
[a]H. Hartwig and H. Dreizler, Z. Naturforsch. **51a**, (1996) 923.

Intermission

WF06 10:39 – 10:54
ROTATIONAL SPECTRUM OF ACETOIN (CH$_3$COCH(OH)CH$_3$)

JONATHAN REBELSKY, *Department of Chemistry, University of Wisconsin Madison, Madison, WI, USA*; CHASE P SCHULTZ, *Department of Chemistry, University of Wisconsin-Madison, Madison, WI, USA*; STEVEN SHIPMAN, *Department of Chemistry, New College of Florida, Sarasota, FL, USA*; SUSANNA L. WIDICUS WEAVER, *Chemistry and Astronomy, University of Wisconsin-Madison, Madison, WI, USA*.

Acetoin (CH$_3$COCH(OH)CH$_3$) is a common additive to e-cigarette fluids. Though not toxic itself, it decomposes into diacetyl (CH$_3$COCOCH$_3$), which is known to cause lung damage. Diacetyl may be important in interstellar chemistry because it has been observed as a VUV desorption product from an interstellar ice analog experiment studying acetaldehyde-based ices. We reported on an attempt to study this molecule at this conference in 2021. Given its extremely small dipole moment and multiple methyl rotors, the study of diacetyl is challenging. Acetoin, conversely, has a strong dipole moment of 2.55 D, which allows its spectrum to be easily observed. The microwave spectrum of acetoin has been collected by Gou and coworkers as reported in the Microwave Newsletter. We extended measurements of rotational lines from 70 to 115 GHz and from 140 to 800 GHz. These data were collected using a long-path length direct absorption flow cell spectrometer. The spectral analysis is underway. The results of this spectrum will enable astronomical observations for both acetoin and, by proxy, diacetyl. Here we will report on the millimeter/submillimeter spectrum of acetoin and our progress towards its analysis and comparison to observations.

WF07

ON THE CHOICE OF HAMILTONIAN REDUCTION AND REPRESENTATION FOR THE ROTATIONAL SPECTRUM OF 1,1-DIFLUOROACETONE RECORDED UP TO 640 GHz

S. A. COOKE, *Natural and Social Science, Purchase College SUNY, Purchase, NY, USA*; PETER R. FRANKE, *Department of Chemistry, University of Florida, Gainesville, FL, USA*; PETER GRONER, *Department of Chemistry, University of Missouri - Kansas City, Kansas City, MO, USA*; L. MARGULÈS, R. A. MOTIYENKO, *UMR 8523 - PhLAM - Physique des Lasers Atomes et Molécules, University of Lille, CNRS, F-59000 Lille, France.*

While recording the cm-wave spectrum of the title compound[a] we discovered that the Watson A reduction in the I^r representation resulted in a poorly fitting Hamiltonian to the observed ground state transitions. However, the Watson S reduction in the I^r representation gave satisfactory results as did both reductions in the III^r representation. The prior work used only measurements between 6 GHz and 16 GHz and only quartic centrifugal distortion (CD) constants were needed in the fits. In order to further explore the reduction/representation-dependence of the spectroscopic fits quartic and sextic CD constants have been obtained from quantum chemical calculations. Furthermore higher frequency measurements have been recorded which i) provide greater certainty in the experimental CD constants, and ii) now require up to decadic CD constants in the Hamiltonian. Further insights into the failure of the A-I^r approach will be presented. In the course of performing this work the methyl group barrier to internal rotation has been improved and will also be discussed.

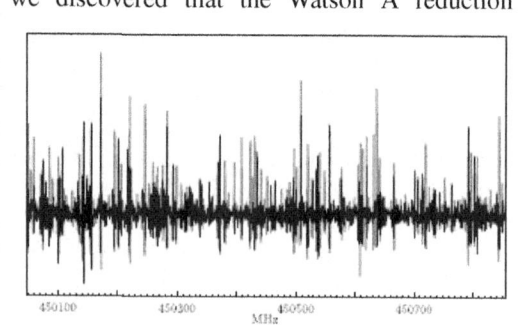

[a]G.S. Grubbs, P. Groner, Stewart E. Novick, S.A. Cooke, "Methyl group internal rotation and the choice of Hamiltonian for the rotational spectrum of 1,1-difluoroacetone", Journal of Molecular Spectroscopy, Volume 280, 2012, Pages 21-26

WF08

THE FAR-INFRARED SPECTRA OF CYCLOPROPYLAMINE

YUE LIANG, *College of Chemistry and Chemical Engineering, Lanzhou University, Lanzhou, Gansu, China*; BRANT E. BILLINGHURST, *EFD, Canadian Light Source Inc., Saskatoon, Saskatchewan, Canada*; BOWEN LIU, ZIQIU CHEN, *College of Chemistry and Chemical Engineering, Lanzhou University, Lanzhou, Gansu, China.*

The infrared spectra of cyclopropylamine (c-$C_3H_5NH_2$) in the region of 35-600 cm^{-1} have been measured at 298K with a resolution of 0.00096 cm^{-1} using the far-infrared beamline at the Canadian Light Source synchrotron. We report here the results of the rovibrational analysis of the ν_{27} (253.87 cm^{-1}) –NH_2 torsional fundamental, as well as the pure rotational analysis of transitions associated with the ground state and the first excited state of the –NH_2 torsional mode between 35 and 60 cm^{-1}. The ongoing assignment and analysis of hot bands and overtones involving higher torsional states will also be discussed.

WF09 11:33–11:48

LINE POSITION AND LINE INTENSITY ANALYSES OF $H_2^{18}O$ UP TO THE FIRST TRIAD AND $J = 20$[a]

L. H. COUDERT, *Institut des Sciences Moléculaires d'Orsay, Université Paris-Saclay, CNRS, Orsay, France*; GEORG CH. MELLAU, *Physikalisch Chemisches Institut, Justus Liebig Universitat Giessen, Giessen, Germany*; SEMEN MIKHAILENKO, *Atmospheric Spectroscopy Div., Institute of Atmospheric Optics, Tomsk, Russia*; ALAIN CAMPARGUE, *UMR5588 LIPhy, Université Grenoble Alpes/CNRS, Saint Martin d'Hères, France*.

We present a line position analysis of a large body of data pertaining to $H_2^{18}O$ and involving all 5 vibrational states up to the First Triad, namely, the lowest lying states (000), (010), (020), (100), and (001). The data set contains infrared lines retrieved in this work, from FTS and from high-temperature emission spectra, and already published high-resolution measurements including microwave and THz transitions, and kHz accuracy transitions.[b] The analysis, carried out with the Bending-Rotation fitting Hamiltonian,[c] allows us to reproduce more than 11700 data with a unitless standard deviation of 1.6 up to $J = 20$ and $K_a = 16$. The highly accurate THz transitions[b] are reproduced with an RMS of 0.2 MHz and the kHz accuracy transitions[b] with an RMS better than 0.3 MHz.

A line intensity analysis of absorption transitions involving the same vibrational states will also be presented. FIR line intensities measured in this work using FTS were fitted in addition to previously measured line intensities. 3890 line intensities are accounted for with a unitless standard deviation of 1.4.

The absorption line list calculated using these results will be compared to that recently obtained from theoretical calculations.[d] With the present set of spectroscopic parameters, discrepancies up to 0.09 cm^{-1} are noted for the line positions.

---
[a]Financial support from the French Programme National de Physique et Chimie du Milieu Interstellaire is acknowledged
[b]Kyrö, *J. Mol. Spec.* **88** (1981) 167; Matsushima *et al.*, *J. Mol. Spec.* **193** (1999) 217; and Diouf *et al.*, *J. Phys. Chem. Ref. Data* **50** (2021) 023106
[c]Coudert and Chélin, *J. Mol. Spec.* **326** (2015) 130
[d]Conway *et al.*, *J. Quant. Spec. Rad. Trans.* **241** (2020) 106711

WF10 11:51–12:06

HIGH-RESOLUTION LASER SPECTROSCOPY OF THE $S_1 \leftarrow S_0$ TRANSITION OF ACETALDEHYDE

KOSUKE NAKAJIMA, *Graduate School of Science, Kobe University, Kobe, Japan*; SHUNJI KASAHARA, *Molecular Photoscience Research Center, Kobe University, Kobe, Japan*; AKIRA SHIMIZU, RIN TANIGUCHI, *Graduate School of Science, Kobe University, Kobe, Japan*; MASAAKI BABA, *Graduate School of Science, Kyoto University, Kyoto, Japan*.

Acetaldehyde is one of a prototype molecule to study large amplitude motion. In the ground state, the energy level structure were well understood by considering the methyl torsional motion (ν_{15} mode). [a] On the other hand, in the S_1 state, it is necessary to consider the aldehyde-hydrogen inversion mortion (ν_{14} mode) [b][c] in addition to the methyl torsion. Rotationally-resolved spectrum of the $S_1 \leftarrow S_0$ transition were observed by using a pulsed amplified CW laser, and obtained effective rotational constants. [d][e] In this work, rotationally-resolved high-resolution fluorescence excitation spectra of the $S_1 \leftarrow S_0$ transition of acetaldehyde have been observed. Sub-Doppler excitation spectra were measured by crossing a single-mode UV laser beam perpendicular to a collimated molecular beam. The typical linewidth of observed spectra was about 40 MHz. The absolute wavenumber was calibrated with accuracy 0.0002 cm^{-1} by measurement of the Doppler-free saturation spectrum of iodine molecule and fringe pattern of the stabilized etalon. The observed spectra around 30118 cm^{-1} and 30375 cm^{-1} correspond to $14_0^0 - 15_0^2$ and $14_0^{0+} 15_0^4$ band, respectively. We are trying to analyze the rotational structure including the interaction with the large amplitude motions and then determine the parameters of the S_1 state.

---
[a]I. Kleiner, J. T. Hougen, J. -U. Grabow, M. Mckhtiev, and J. Cosleou, *J. Mol. Spectrosc.*, **179**, 41 (1996).
[b]M. Baba, I. Hanazaki, U. Nagashima, *J. Chem. Phys.*, **82**, 3938 (1985).
[c]M. Noble and K. C. Lee, *J. Chem. Phys.*, **81**, 1632 (1984).
[d]Y.-C. Chou, C.-L. Huang, I-C. Chen, C.-K. Ni, A. H. Kung, *J. Chem Phys.*, **115**, 5089 (2001).
[e]H. Liu, E. C. Lim, A. Nino, C. Munoz-Caro, R. H. Judge, D. C. Moule, *J. Mol. Spectrosc.*, **190**, 78 (1998).

WF11 12:09 – 12:24

ROTATIONAL SPECTROSCOPY OF *n*-PROPANOL: *Aa* AND *Ag* CONFORMERS

<u>OLIVER ZINGSHEIM</u>, HOLGER S. P. MÜLLER, BETTINA HEYNE, MARIYAM FATIMA, LUIS BONAH, *I. Physikalisches Institut, Universität zu Köln, Köln, Germany*; ARNAUD BELLOCHE, *Millimeter- und Submillimeter-Astronomie, Max-Planck-Institut für Radioastronomie, Bonn, NRW, Germany*; FRANK LEWEN, STEPHAN SCHLEMMER, *I. Physikalisches Institut, Universität zu Köln, Köln, Germany*.

Propanol occurs in two isomers, as a primary alcohol *normal*-propanol ($CH_3CH_2CH_2OH$) and as a secondary alcohol *iso*-propanol ($CH_3CH(OH)CH_3$). Moreover, *normal*-Propanol occurs in five different conformers: *Ga*, *Gg*, *Gg'*, *Aa*, and *Ag*. Rotational spectra of all three conformers of the *G* family are well described [1], hence, an astronomical search of their rotational fingerprints is possible, in contrast to *Aa* and *Ag*.

Rotational spectra of *normal*-propanol were recorded in the frequency region of 18 to 500 GHz. Double-modulation double-resonance (DM-DR) measurements were performed additionally, in particular to unambiguously assign weak transitions of the *Aa* and to verify assignments of the *Ag* conformer. An extended quantum mechanical model for *Aa* was derived, based on Ref. [2]. Furthermore, the existence of two tunneling states, Ag^+ and Ag^-, has been proven by unambiguously assigned transitions, but a quantum mechanical model description for *Ag* could not be given yet. The astronomical detection of all five conformers is now possible, but the quantum mechanical description of the *A* family should still be improved in the future.

[1] Kisiel, Z., Dorosh, O., Maeda, A., et al., *Phys. Chem. Chem. Phys.* **12** (2010) 8329.
[2] Dreizier, H. & Scappini, F. Z., *Naturforsch. A* **36** (1981), 1187.

WG. Ions

Wednesday, June 22, 2022 – 8:30 AM

Room: 274 Medical Sciences Building

Chair: Harshal Gupta, National Science Foundation, Alexandria, VA, USA

WG01   8:30 – 8:45

OPTICAL SPECTRUM OF Si_2^+

<u>EMIL MICKEIN</u>, TAARNA STUDEMUND, KAI POLLOW, SOPHIE VERHOEVEN, MARKO FÖRSTEL, OTTO DOPFER, *Institut für Optik und Atomare Physik, Technische Universität Berlin, Berlin, Germany.*

Silicon is very important in the modern electrical industry, for example for the production of solar cells. To improve their efficiency the newest generation of solar cells consists of nanostructures like quantum dots. Therefore studies about optical properties of silicon nanoclusters are of particular interest [1]. These characteristics for the smallest cluster Si_2, which is necessary for the formation of larger clusters, are not well established yet [1].
In this talk, experimental data and quantum chemical calculations on the absorption and dissociation properties of Si_2^+ are presented. The spectrum of Si_2^+ was obtained by photodissociation of mass-selected Si_2^+ cations in a tandem mass spectrometer, which are created in a laser vaporization source [2]. The experimental results are compared and discussed with theoretical results of TD-DFT calculations. Significantly, our optical spectrum provides the first spectroscopic information for this simple diatomic cation.

Literature:

[1] L.-Z. Zhao et al. J. Phys. Chem. A 2017, 121, 34, 6388–6397
[2] M. Förstel et al., Rev. Sci. Instrum., 2017, 88, 123110.

WG02   8:48 – 9:03

INTERESTING BEHAVIOR OF THE $Si_3O_2^+$ SILICON OXIDE CLUSTER CATION

<u>KAI POLLOW</u>, TAARNA STUDEMUND, EMIL MICKEIN, MARKO FÖRSTEL, OTTO DOPFER, *Institut für Optik und Atomare Physik, Technische Universität Berlin, Berlin, Germany.*

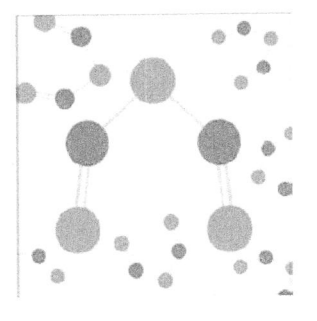

Silicon oxide cluster cations $Si_nO_m^+$ are especially interesting in the context of interstellar dust particles and might be carriers of the diffuse interstellar bands (DIBs). To date, SiO and different Si_nC_m clusters were found in circumstellar envelopes.

In this talk we present our results on the fairly small but nevertheless complicated $Si_3O_2^+$ system. We discuss the optical spectrum obtained by photodissociation in the gas phase and compare that to quantum chemical calculations.

Spoiler, the observed spectrum of $Si_3O_2^+$ does not match any known DIB.

WG03

ON THE SPECTROSCOPY OF ACYLIUM IONS: INFRARED ACTION SPECTROSCOPIC DETECTION OF NCCO$^+$

OSKAR ASVANY, MARCEL BAST, STEPHAN SCHLEMMER, SVEN THORWIRTH, *I. Physikalisches Institut, Universität zu Köln, Köln, Germany.*

The linear N≡C–C≡O$^+$ ion has been studied spectroscopically for the first time using the Free Electron Laser for Infrared eXperiments, FELIX, at Radboud University (Nijmegen, The Netherlands) in combination with the 4K 22-pole ion trap facility FELion.[a] The vibrational spectrum of NCCO$^+$ was observed in the range from 500 to 1500 and 2000 to 2500 cm^{-1} using resonant photodissociation of the correponding Ne-complex while monitoring the depletion of the ion-Ne cluster signal as a function of wavenumber. Spectroscopic assignment of vibrational bands relies on comparison against results from high-level quantum-chemical calculations performed at the CCSD(T) level of theory and very good agreement is found.

[a] Jusko et al. 2019, Faraday Discuss. 217, 172

WG04

HIGH-RESOLUTION SPECTROSCOPY OF MgKr$^+$ IN ITS GROUND AND LOW-LYING ELECTRONICALLY EXCITED STATES

CARLA KREIS, *Laboratory of Physical Chemistry, ETH Zurich, Zürich, Switzerland*; MATTHIEU GÉNÉVRIEZ, *Institute of Condensed Matter and Nanosciences (IMCN), Université catholique de Louvain, Louvain-la-Neuve, Belgium*; FRÉDÉRIC MERKT, *Laboratorium für Physikalische Chemie, ETH Zurich, Zurich, Switzerland.*

Diatomic molecules RgM consisting of a rare-gas atom Rg and an alkaline-earth-metal atom M and their singly and doubly-charged cations RgM$^+$ and RgM^{2+} have unusual chemical properties that are related to the low first and second ionization energies of M and the high ionization energy of Rg. In MgAr the second ionization energy of Mg is lower than the first ionization energy of Ar. Consequently, MgAr^{2+} is thermodynamically stable and Rydberg series of MgAr$^+$ can be observed that converge on the X^{2+} $^1\Sigma^+$ ground state of MgAr^{2+}.[a] In this contribution, we present the results of spectroscopic investigations of MgKr$^+$ in its ground and low-lying electronically excited states that complement earlier studies of this cation.[b,c] Pulsed-field-ionization zero-kinetic-energy (PFI-ZEKE) photoelectron spectra of the X$^+$ $^2\Sigma^+$ ground state of MgKr$^+$ were recorded following single-photon excitation from the a $^3\Pi_0$ metastable state of MgKr. Vibrational channel interactions enabled the observation of the lowest vibrational levels of MgKr$^+$ and the determination of an accurate value of the adiabatic ionization energy of metastable MgKr (38183 ± 2 cm^{-1}). Using isolated-core multiphoton Rydberg dissociation (ICMRD) spectroscopy,[d] spectra of several low-lying electronically excited states of MgKr$^+$ were observed that are associated with the Kr + Mg$^+(nl)$ dissociation limits with $n = 3, 4$ and $l = s, p$ and d. These states may be regarded as the lowest members of Rydberg series converging on the ground state of MgKr^{2+}. These studies represent first steps towards studying the doubly charged cation MgKr^{2+}.

[a] D. Wehrli, M. Génévriez and F. Merkt, Phys. Chem. Chem. Phys., 23, 10978, (2021) and references therein
[b] J. G. Kaup and W. H. Breckenridge, J.Chem. Phys. 107, 2180, 1997
[c] J. S. Pilgrim, C. S. Yeh, K. R. Berry, M. A. Duncan, J. Chem. Phys., 100, 7945, (1994)
[d] M. Génévriez, D. Wehrli and F. Merkt, Mol. Phys. 118, e1703051 (2019)

WG05   9:42 – 9:57
RO-VIBRATIONAL SPECTROSCOPY OF LINEAR C_3H^+

<u>PHILIPP C SCHMID</u>, THOMAS SALOMON, SVEN THORWIRTH, OSKAR ASVANY, STEPHAN SCHLEMMER, *I. Physikalisches Institut, Universität zu Köln, Köln, Germany.*

The C_3H^+ ion has been identified as an important reaction intermediate in the carbon chemistry network in the interstellar medium and was recently detected via its rotational lines[a]. Laboratory measurements on the rotational spectrum of linear C_3H^+ provided accurate spectroscopic parameters for the vibrational ground state[b]. In addition, vibrational pre-dissociation spectroscopy of the linear C_3H^+-Ne complex offered first insights on the vibrational band positions of this molecule[c]. Here, we report on the first infrared study of C_3H^+ at high spectral resolution that was targeted at the C−H stretching mode ν_1 located around 3170 cm^{-1}. The experiment was performed in our cryogenic multipole 22-pole ion trap instrument LIRtrap. In addition to the vibrational fundamental, the associated $\nu_1 + \nu_5 \leftarrow \nu_5$ hot band originating from the energetically lowest bending mode could be detected. Both spectra are in good agreement with estimates based on previous quantum-chemical calcultions and low-resolution measurements.

[a] J. Pety et al., A&A 548(2012)A68., B. McGuire et al., Ap. J. 774(2013)56.
[b] S. Brünken et al., Ap. J. Lett. 783(2014)L4.
[c] S. Brünken et al., J. Phys. Chem. A 123(2019)8053.

WG06   10:00 – 10:15
GAS-PHASE CHARGE TRANSFER ELECTRONIC SPECTROSCOPY OF AG+-BENZENE COMPLEX

<u>DYLAN S. ORR</u>, JASON E. COLLEY, MICHAEL A DUNCAN, *Department of Chemistry, University of Georgia, Athens, GA, USA.*

Charge transfer electronic spectroscopic results were reported for the Ag+-benzene complex in the gas phase using photodissociation. The Ag+-benzene complex was generated by laser vaporization of a silver rod in combination with pulsing an inert gas seeded with benzene then mass selected and probed using a time-of-flight mass spectrometer. The mass-selected ions were then fragmented and scanned using a solid state OPO capable of scanning through the UV-Visible range. A high-resolution electronic spectrum of Ag+-benzene was reported in the UV-Visible range to determine the upper threshold for the dissociation energy of the Ag+-benzene complex which were compared with previous velocity map imaging results. An unexpected feature was observed in the lower UV region which was attributed to the HOMO-LUMO absorption on an excited benzene ligand.

Intermission

WG07   10:57 – 11:12

HIGH-RESOLUTION INFRARED SPECTRA OF THE OH-STRETCHING BANDS OF PROTONATED WATER DIMER, $H_5O_2^+$

THOMAS SALOMON, OSKAR ASVANY, *I. Physikalisches Institut, University of Cologne, Cologne, Germany*; CHARLES R. MARKUS, *Division of Chemistry and Chemical Engineering, California Institute of Technology, Pasadena, CA, USA*; STEPHAN SCHLEMMER, *I. Physikalisches Institut, University of Cologne, Cologne, Germany.*

We present high-resolution infrared action spectra of cold $H_5O_2^+$. For this purpose the mass selected parent ions are stored in a cryogenically cooled 22-pole ion-trap (COLtrap). There we employ a two-color-photodissociation scheme where first the symmetric or the anti-symmetric O-H-stretching band is excited by a narrow linewidth cw-OPO. Then, Light from a CO_2 laser is used to efficiently dissociate the parent molecule. The infrared-absorption of the parent ion is recorded by the appearance of H_3O^+ photoproducts. This procedure follows the seminal approach first invented in the group of Y.T. Lee [a,b]. The rotationally resolved and basically background-free spectrum exhibits a complex structure, making the assignment of individual ro-vibrational tunneling features challenging. Nonetheless, recurring spectral spacings are used to start to unfold the rotational/tunneling structure. Moreover, spectral indicators are found that support the assumption of hydrazine-like tunnelling dynamics being present in this peculiar molecule of fundamental interest.

[a] L. I. Yeh, M. Okumura, J. D. Myers, J. M. Price, and Y. T. Lee, *Vibrational spectroscopy of the hydrated hydronium cluster ions $H_3O^+(H_2O)_n$ (n=1,2,3)*, J. Chem. Phys. 91, 7319-7330 (1989)

[b] L. I. Yeh, Y. T. Lee, and J. T. Hougen. *Vibration-rotation spectroscopy of the hydrated hydronium ions $H_5O_2^+$ and $H_9O_4^+$.* Journal of Molecular Spectroscopy 164.2 (1994): 473-488.

WG08   11:15 – 11:30

PROBING THE DEGREE OF NITROGEN ACTIVATION BY TRIDENTATE COPPER(I) COMPLEXES USING CIVP SPECTROSCOPY

ALEXANDRA TSYBIZOVA, VLADIMIR GORBACHEV, PETER CHEN, *Department of Chemistry and Applied Biosciences, ETH Zurich, Zurich, Switzerland.*

The activation and utilization of N_2 have become attractive areas of research, with the ultimate goals of dinitrogen fixation and reduction. A deep understanding of the interaction and electronic influences between transition metal atoms and the inert N2 molecule would allow facilitating the transformation of inert molecular nitrogen to useful nitrogen-containing chemicals. In this work, we used cryogenic ion vibrational predissociation (CIVP) spectroscopy to experimentally probe the activation of the molecular nitrogen by copper complexes bearing terpyridine and pyridine-2,6-bis(oxazoline) ligands. We used the N_2 stretching vibration as a reporter chromophore to estimate how electronic and steric effects affect the activation of the molecular nitrogen by these copper complexes. In contrast to the previous studies on nitrogen activation that probe "late activation" of the nitrogen molecule, our cryogenic studies give access to the "early activation" states that otherwise difficult to access. Our data show that the electronic character, as well as position and number of substituents, can affect the N-N vibrational frequency, leading either to a bigger or to a lesser degree of N_2 activation.

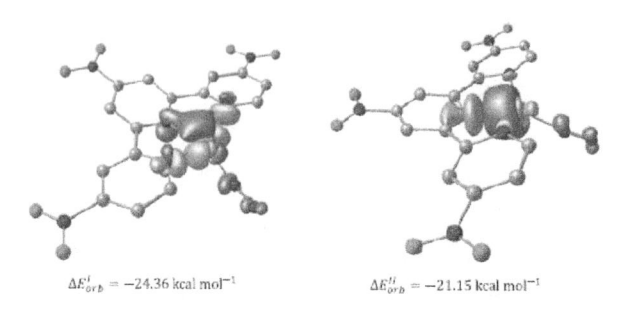

WG09   11:33–11:48

ANIONIC REARRANGEMENTS FOLLOWING DECARBOXYLATION OF BENZOPHENONE DERIVATIVES WITH CRYOGENIC IR SPECTROSCOPY

JOSEPH P. MESSINGER, EVAN H PEREZ, ANNA GABRIELLA DEL ROSARIO RULLÁN BUXÓ, TIM SCHLEIF, OLIVIA MOSS, *Department of Chemistry, Yale University, New Haven, CT, USA*; KIM GREIS, *Department of Molecular Physics, Fritz-Haber-Institut der Max-Planck-Gesellschaft, Berlin, Germany*; MARK JOHNSON, *Department of Chemistry, Yale University, New Haven, CT, USA*.

Carbanions are highly reactive intermediates that are commonly used in organic synthesis. Here, we investigate the fundamental gas phase spectroscopy and isomerization of substituted aromatic phenides (deprotonated benzene derivatives) using isomer-selective cryogenic ion vibrational predissociation spectroscopy (1000 cm^{-1}– 4200 cm^{-1}). The phenide is formed by the decarboxylation of the 4-benzoyl benzoate anion (4BBA$^-$, $C_{14}H_9O_3^-$), a substituted benzophenone, in a commercial Orbitrap mass spectrometer before being transferred to the triple focusing time-of-flight photofragmentation mass spectrometer. The resulting spectra are congested, suggesting the presence of multiple isomers. They are revealed by quantum chemical calculations in conjunction with two color IR-IR photobleaching spectroscopy to be the expected phenide, and a new molecule formed by multiple steps of isomerization that end in ring-closed product. The identities of these compounds and the proposed mechanism are confirmed by additional experiments using 4BBA$^-$-d_9 and 2BBA$^-$.

WG10   11:51–12:06

CARBOXYLATE STRETCHING MODES ARE STRUCTURAL PROBES FOR ION-DEPENDENT BINDING PROPERTIES IN ALKALI EARTH METAL-EDTA COMPLEXES

MADISON M. FOREMAN, J. MATHIAS WEBER, *JILA and Department of Chemistry, University of Colorado, Boulder, CO, USA*.

Ethylenediaminetetraacetic acid (EDTA) can be used as a chelating agent for binding metal ions in solution. In addition, its binding pocket is a model for the interactions between carboxylate groups and the divalent ions they often bind in some biological systems.[a,b,c] With its four carboxyl groups and two nitrogen atoms, EDTA can chelate nearly any metal cation to form water-soluble complexes, making it a robust model system for studying biologically relevant divalent ion-carboxylate interactions.

Here, we present cryogenic gas-phase infrared spectra of a series of alkaline earth metal-EDTA complexes of the form [M(II)·EDTA]$^{2-}$ and assign spectral features using density functional theory calculations. The vibrational spectra encode structural and electrostatic information, reflecting the geometry of each metal ion within the EDTA binding pocket and its relation to ionic radius.

[a] S. Mitra, K. Werling, E. Berquist. D. S. Lambrecht, S. Garrett-Roe, J. Phys. Chem. A 125 (2021) 4867-4881
[b] S. C. Edington, C. R. Baiz, J. Phys. Chem. A 122 (2018) 6585-6592
[c] Q. Yuan, X. T. Kong, G. L. Hou, L. Jiang, X. B. Wang, Faraday Discuss. 217 (2019) 383

WG11 — *Post-Deadline Abstract* — 12:09 – 12:24

FIRST LABORATORY DETECTION OF N^{13}CO$^-$ AND SEMIEXPERIMENTAL EQUILIBRIUM STRUCTURE OF THE NCO$^-$ ANION

LUCA DORE, *Dept. Chemistry "Giacomo Ciamician", University of Bologna, Bologna, ITALY*; LUCA BIZZOCCHI, *Dipartimento di Chimica G. Ciamician, Università di Bologna, Bologna, Italy*; VALERIO LATTANZI, *The Center for Astrochemical Studies, Max-Planck-Institut für extraterrestrische Physik, Garching, Germany*; MATTIA MELOSSO, *Dept. Chemistry "Giacomo Ciamician", University of Bologna, Bologna, ITALY*; FILIPPO TAMASSIA, *Dipartimento di Chimica Industriale "Toso Montanari", Università di Bologna, Bologna, Italy*; MICHAEL C McCARTHY, *Center for Astrophysics, Harvard & Smithsonian, Cambridge, MA, USA*.

The cyanate anion NCO$^-$ is a species of considerable astrophysical relevance. It is widely believed to be embedded in interstellar ices present in young stellar objects but has not yet been detected in the dense gas of the interstellar medium. Here, very accurate laboratory measurements of the rotational spectrum of the N^{13}CO$^-$ isotopologue at submillimeter wavelengths and three additional lines of the parent isotopologue up to 437.4 GHz are reported. With this new data, the rotational spectrum of both isotopologues can be predicted to better 0.25 km s^{-1} in equivalent radial velocity up to 1 THz. Moreover, a semiexperimental equilibrium structure of the anion is derived by combining the experimental ground-state rotational constants of the two isotopologues with theoretical vibrational corrections, obtained by using the coupled-cluster method with inclusion of single and double excitations and perturbative inclusion of triple excitations (CCSD(T)). The estimated accuracy of the two bond distances is on the order of 5×10^{-4} Å.

WLUN. Plenary Panel Discussion

Wednesday, June 22, 2022 – 12:35 PM

Room: Ballroom Illini Union

Chair: Anthony Remijan, NRAO, Charlottesville, VA, USA

WLUN01   12:35 – 1:30
A PERSONAL VIEW OF THE ISMS

TERRY A. MILLER, *Department of Chemistry and Biochemistry, The Ohio State University, Columbus, OH, USA.*

The 75th international symposium on molecular spectroscopy (ISMS) is an appropriate time for remembrance and celebration. This talk provides my personal view of ISMS, both from the perspective of a conferee who has attended over 50 meetings and from the perspective of one who has served as Symposium Chair for 22 of them. I will describe the growth and evolution of the Symposium since the first meeting in 1946 at The Ohio State University in Columbus, Ohio, USA. This description will include some statistical data and organizational information but will focus on the people and events that created the culture of the Symposium, which indeed reflects the culture of the molecular spectroscopy community. Photos from previous Symposia will be shown to provide context and hopefully capture some of the flavor of these meetings. The photos will also serve as a backdrop to the personal stories that the panelists can relate from firsthand experience of nearly the past 60 years of the Symposium. Most of all, I want to convey the excitement and joy of the pursuit of scientific accomplishment that ISMS has exemplified to me and to emphasize the strong professional and personal bonds that I have formed with conferees from around the world because of these meetings.

WLUN02   12:35 – 1:30
THANK YOU ISMS!

TAKESHI OKA, *Department of Astronomy and Astrophysics and Department of Chemistry, The Enrico Fermi Institute, University of Chicago, Chicago, IL, USA.*

Molecular spectroscopists are blessed because they can attend the annual international symposium throughout their lives. I am grateful to David Dennison, Harald Nielsen, Gerhard Herzberg, Bright Wilson and Charlie Townes who initiated the ISMS in 1947, and chairmen Harald Nielsen, Narahari Rao, Terry Miller, Ben McCall, and Josh Vura-Weis who maintained the high standard. Although the basic organization and the spirit of the symposium remained the same there were a few major changes. The biggest change was of course the change of venue from the Ohio State University to the University of Illinois Urbana Champaign in 2014. Thus Columbus meeting changed to the UIUC meeting. We are grateful to Ben McCall for undertaking this big task. Other big change I remember was change of dinner and after dinner speech to picnic.

My first ISMS was the 17th in 1964 when I was a postdoc in Ottawa. When I started my search for the laboratory spectrum of H_3^+, I stopped attending conferences so I missed ISMS for 6 years from 1976 to 1981 but otherwise attended all meetings till this year. John Johns and Jon Hougen also from Ottawa started attending the ISMS several years before me. Hougen never missed the meeting till he passed away in 2019. Hougen was the champion attendee of the ISMS.

I have given 6 plenary talks: in 1969 (collision selection rules), 1975 (forbidden rotational transitions), 1984 (H_3^+ in the laboratory plasmas), 1986 (IR spectra of molecular ions), 1999 (H_3^+ in interstellar plasmas), and 2008 (H_3^+ in the Galactic center). I also gave an after dinner speech with the title Astronomy and Spectroscopy. One scientific change of ISMS has been introduction of astronomy. This gradually happened but was accelerated around 2014. This was convenient for me because my reseach moves from spectroscopy to astronomy. Recently my papers have been exclusively presented in astronomy session. I shall be 90 years old at the symposium this year. Perhaps I am the oldest participant of this symposium.

WLUN03   12:35 – 1:30
MY ISMS

<u>YASUKI ENDO</u>, *Department of Applied Chemistry, National Yang Ming Chiao Tung University, Hsinchu, Taiwan.*

My first ISMS was 35th meeting in 1980. At that time I was working at Institute for Molecular Science as a research associate of prof. Hirota's group, mainly doing mm-wave spectroscopy of short lived species. In that meeting Terry A. Miller gave a plenary talk, where the word Jahn-Teller interaction attracted me.

A few years later I was able to observe a Jahn-Teller molecule, CH_3O. Results were presented at my second attendence in 1984. In the meeting, spectroscopy of molecular ions are hot topics, and impressive plenary talks were given by T. Oka and R. J. Saykally.

My next attendance was 1990, six years later. In the meantime, I moved to the University of Tokyo and started a new laboratory, where I constructed an FTMW spectrometer. At the 1990 meeting, there was a presentation by T. A. Miller and V. E. Bondybey's group showing a pulsed discharge nozzle (PDN) to produce short lived species in the supersonic jet. Since I was looking for an effective method to produce short lived species for my FTMW spectrometer, the PDN seemed to be quite attractive. When I came back to Japan, we started to combine the PDN with our FTMW spectrometer. Soon we were able to observe a number of short lived species. The PDN-FTMW system gave me a chance to give my first plenary talk at 1993 ISMS meeting. Since the 1990 meeting, I or my colleagues, students attended the meeting almost every year.

Another important meeting for me was the 2012 ISMS, where M. I. Lester gave a plenary talk mentioning the importance of so called Criegee intermediates. Inspired by her talk, we started FTMW study of the Criegee intermediates.Until now we were able to write more than 20 papers for the Criegee intermediates. Futhermore, the results led me to give my third plenary talk in 2014. After my retirement from the University of Tokyo in 2015, I moved to National Yang Ming Chiao Tung University with my FTMW spectrometer, and I am still working in the microwave region.

WH. Mini-symposium: Spectroscopy meets Chemical Dynamics

Wednesday, June 22, 2022 – 1:45 PM

Room: 100 Noyes Laboratory

Chair: Krupa Ramasesha, Sandia National Laboratories, Livermore, CA, USA

WH01   1:45 – 2:00
PHOTODISSOCIATION AND VELOCITY-MAP IMAGING OF CARBON CLUSTER CATIONS

NATHAN JOHN DYNAK, BRANDON M. RITTGERS, JASON E. COLLEY, DOUGLAS J. KELLAR, MICHAEL A DUNCAN, *Department of Chemistry, University of Georgia, Athens, GA, USA*.

Carbon cluster cations are generated in the gas phase by laser vaporization of a carbon rod in a pulsed supersonic expansion. C_n^+ clusters (n = 6,7,10,11,12,15,20) are mass selected using a reflectron time-of-flight mass spectrometer and photodissociated at 355 nm. The main channel for this multiphoton dissociation process is the loss of neutral C_3, resulting in C_{n-3}^+ cation fragments. The cationic fragments are reaccelerated into an imaging flight tube with velocity-map imaging grids and detected with an imaging detector. Significant kinetic energy release (KER) is observed for all of these cations, but with much greater KER values detected for the larger species. Specifically, the n = 10,11,12,15 and 20 species known to have monocyclic ring structures produce much greater KER than the n = 6 and 7 species known to have linear structures. Consideration of photon energies for two- or three-photon processes, together with the KER values and estimates for ring strain energies allows investigation of the energetics of the bonding and dissociation in these systems.

WH02   2:03 – 2:18
PHOTODISSOCIATION DYNAMICS OF CH_2OO ON MULTIPLE POTENTIAL ENERGY SURFACES: EXPERIMENT AND THEORY

VINCENT J. ESPOSITO, TIANLIN LIU, GUANGHAN WANG, ADRIANA CARACCIOLO, *Department of Chemistry, University of Pennsylvania, Philadelphia, PA, USA*; MICHAEL F. VANSCO, *Chemical Dynamics Group, Argonne National Laboratory, Lemont, IL, USA*; ERNEST ANTWI, *Department of Chemistry, University of Louisiana at Lafayette, Lafayette, LA, USA*; OLIVIA WERBA, *Department of Chemistry, University of Pennsylvania, Philadelphia, PA, USA*; SARAH A. BUSH, RACHEL E. BUSH, BARBARA MARCHETTI, TOLGA N. V. KARSILI, *Department of Chemistry, University of Louisiana at Lafayette, Lafayette, LA, USA*; MARSHA LESTER, *Department of Chemistry, University of Pennsylvania, Philadelphia, PA, USA*.

Criegee intermediates are zwitterionic carbonyl oxide species that result from alkene ozonolysis in the Earth's troposphere. UV excitation of the simplest Criegee intermediate, CH_2OO, across most of the broad span of the (B $^1A'$) - (X $^1A'$) spectrum results in prompt dissociation to two energetically accessible asymptotes: O (^1D) + H_2CO (X $^1A_1$) and O (^3P) + H_2CO (a $^3A''$). Dissociation proceeds on multiple singlet potential energy surfaces that are coupled by two regions of conical intersection (CoIn). Velocity map imaging studies reveal a bimodal total kinetic energy (TKER) distribution for the O (^1D) + H_2CO (X $^1A_1$) products. The unexpected low TKER component corresponds to highly internally excited H_2CO (X $^1A_1$) products. Full dimensional trajectory calculations suggest that the bimodal TKER distribution of the O (^1D) + H_2CO (X $^1A_1$) products originates from two different dynamical pathways: a primary pathway evolving through one CoIn region to products and a smaller component sampling both CoIn regions during the dissociation process. Those that access both CoIn regions likely give rise to the more highly internally excited H_2CO (X $^1A_1$) products. The remaining trajectories dissociate to O (^3P) + H_2CO (a $^3A''$) products after traversing through both CoIn regions. No trajectories follow the more thermodynamically favorable spin-forbidden pathway to O (^3P) + H_2CO (X $^1A_1$) products. This complementary experimental and theoretical investigation provides insight into the photodissociation of CH_2OO via multiple dissociation pathways through two regions of CoIn that control the branching and energy distributions of products

WH03　　2:21 – 2:36

OZONE PHOTODISSOCIATION IN THE SINGLET CHANNEL AT 226 NM

MEGAN AARDEMA, *Department of Chemistry, Texas A & M University, College Station, TX, USA*; GEORGE McBANE, *Department of Chemistry, Grand Valley State University, Allendale, MI, USA*; SIMON NORTH, *Department of Chemistry, Texas A & M University, College Station, TX, USA*.

Ozone photodissociation plays an important role in atmospheric chemistry and has been the focus of many experimental and theoretical studies. In the Hartley band (200-300 nm) there are two spin-allowed dissociation channels, one forming excited state, singlet products (O2(a 1Δg) + O($1D$)), and one forming ground state, triplet products (O2(X 3Σg-) + O($3P$)). The singlet channel is the primary dissociation channel in the Hartley band, and numerous studies have characterized the dissociation at longer wavelengths within the Hartley band. There has been considerable interest in the triplet channel dissociation at 226 nm following the observation of low velocity O($3P$) fragments, but the singlet channel dissociation dynamics at 226 nm has not been previously reported. We report the rotational state distribution and vector correlations of the O2(a 1Δg, v=0) fragments arising from the 226 nm photodissociation of jet-cooled O3. Consistent with previously reported trends, the rotational distribution is shifted to higher rotational states with decreasing wavelength. We observe highly suppressed odd rotational state populations due to a strong Λ-doublet propensity. The measured rotational distribution is in agreement with classical trajectory calculations for the v=0 products, although the distribution is narrower than predicted. The spatial anisotropy follows the previously observed trend of decreasing β with increasing photon energy with $\beta = 0.72 \pm 0.14$ for v=0, j=38. As expected for a triatomic molecule, the v-j correlation is consistent with v perpendicular to j, but the measured correlation is non-limiting due to rotational and translational depolarization. The j-dependent linewidth of the O2(a 1Δg) REMPI spectrum is also discussed in connection with the lifetime of the resonant O2(d 1Πg) state and predissociation via the II 1Πg valence state.

WH04　　2:39 – 2:54

RAPID ALLYLIC 1,6 H-ATOM TRANSFER IN A CRIEGEE INTERMEDIATE WITH UNSATURATED SUBSTITUENTS

ANNE S HANSEN, *Chemistry, University of Pennsylvania, Philadelphia, PA, USA*; YUJIE QIAN, *Department of Chemistry, University of Pennsylvania, Philadelphia, PA, USA*; STEPHEN J. KLIPPENSTEIN, *Chemical Science and Engineering Division, Argonne National Laboratory, Lemont, IL, USA*; MARSHA LESTER, *Chemistry, University of Pennsylvania, Philadelphia, PA, USA*.

A new allylic 1,6 H-atom transfer mechanism is established through infrared (IR) excitation of the 2-butenal-oxide Criegee intermediate [$CH_3CH=CHCHOO$]. Rapid 1,6 H-atom transfer is facilitated for certain conformers of 2-butenal oxide by extended conjugation across the vinyl and carbonyl oxide groups. A low-energy conformer (*tZZ*) of 2-butenal oxide is identified by IR action spectroscopy in the fundamental CH region with ultraviolet (UV) detection of OH products by laser-induced fluorescence (LIF). The strongest observed IR transition at 2996 cm^{-1} is consistent with the anharmonic frequency computed for the *tZZ* conformer. A low energy reaction pathway involving isomerization of 2-butenal oxide from a lower energy conformer (*tZZ*) to a higher energy conformer (*cZZ*), followed by 1,6 H-atom transfer via a 7-membered ring transition state with relatively low ring strain, is theoretically predicted and shown experimentally to yield the OH products. The rapid appearance of OH products (ca. $2.3 \pm 1.0 \times 10^8$ s^{-1}) agrees with a statistical RRKM calculation for an effective reaction rate (k_{eff}(E) on the order of 10^8 s^{-1} at ca. 3000 cm^{-1}) including tunneling. Unimolecular decay involves a combination of conformational isomerization and unimolecular dissociation via 1,6 H-atom transfer. The excellent agreement between experiment and theory confirms the allylic 1,6 H-atom transfer mechanism in 2-butenal-oxide Criegee intermediate and provides a novel pathway for non-photolytic OH generation upon alkene ozonolysis in the troposphere.

WH05   2:57 – 3:12

THE VIBRATIONAL PREDISSOCIATION OF THE Ã STATE OF THE C_3Ar VAN DER WAALS COMPLEX WITH VIBRATIONAL ENERGIES OF 1558-1660 cm^{-1}

SHENG-CHANG HSIAO, *Department of Physics, National Central University, Taoyaun, Taiwan*; YEN-CHU HSU, *Department of Physics, National Central University, Jhongli, Taiwan*.

The laser-induced fluorescence (LIF) and wavelength-resolved emission spectroscopic techniques have been used to study the rotational levels, the vibrational predissociation (VP) products and the product-state branching ratios of the Ã state of the C_3Ar van der Waals complex. The excited states were prepared by exciting the complex bands associated with 0 8$^-$ 0-000, 0 4$^+$ 0-000 and 0 0 2-000 bands of the Ã $^1\Pi_u$ - X̃ $^1\Sigma_g$ system of C_3. The superscripts "-" and "+" denote the lower and upper Renner components, respectively. The type A and C bands of the complex bands are in pairs and they are separated by $2\nu_b$ (b, van der Waals bending vibration).[a] Of 11 bands, only two, associated with the 002-000 band of C_3, are rotationally resolved with a laser of 0.04 cm^{-1} resolution. The lifetimes of these complex bands are in the order of a few to a few tens of picoseconds estimated from the rotational linewidths of the LIF spectra. The VP processes are quite complex; more than one vibrational state of the C_3 fragments was identified from each upper complex level. The fragment states were the pure bending levels (0 v$_2$ 0) and the combination levels (1 v$_2$ 0) of the Ã state.

---

[a] A.J. Merer, Y.-C. Hsu, Y.-R. Chen, and Y.-J. Wang, J. Chem. Phys. 143, 194304(2015).

WH06   3:15 – 3:30

THE VIBRATIONAL PREDISSOCIATION AND INTRAMOLECULAR VIBRATIONAL REDISTRIBUTION OF THE Ã STATE OF THE C_3Ar VAN DER WAALS COMPLEX

SHENG-CHANG HSIAO, *Department of Physics, National Central University, Taoyaun, Taiwan*; YEN-CHU HSU, *Department of Physics, National Central University, Jhongli, Taiwan*.

The vibrational predissociation (VP) products of eighteen rovibrational levels of the Ã state of the C_3Ar complex have been studied.[a,b] These complex levels are associated with the 0 2$^-$ 0, 0 2$^+$ 0, 0 4$^-$ 0, 0 8$^-$ 0, 0 4$^+$ 0, and 0 0 2 vibrational levels of C_3(Ã). The distributions of the fragment branching ratios versus the square root of the excess energies (the sum of the translational and rotational energy of the VP product) obtained from these complex levels do not necessarily follow the momentum gap law [c] or energy gap law. [d] Effects such as spectroscopic perturbation,[e] energy gap,[c,d] angular momentum,[a] threshold predissociation,[a] and intramolecular vibrational redistribution[f] on the VP processes have been previously reported. In this work, these effects will be examined and the VP mechanism of the Ã state of the C_3Ar complex will be proposed.

---

[a] Y.-J. Wang and Y.-C. Hsu, J. Chem. Phys. 153, 124303(2020).
[b] S.-C. Hsiao and Y.-C. Hsu, to be published.
[c] G.E. Ewing, J. Chem. Phys. 71, 3143(1979).
[d] J.A. Beswick and J. Jortner, J. Chem. Phys. 69, 512(1979).
[e] E.J. Bohac, M.D. Marshall, and R.E. Miller, J. Chem. Phys. 98,6642(1993) and references therein.
[f] A. Buchachenko, N. Halberstadt, B. Lepetit, and O. Roncero, Int. Rev. Phys. Chem. 22, 153(2003).

Intermission

WH07 4:12 – 4:27
DETECTION OF NASCENT PRODUCTS FROM THE PHOTOLYSIS OF ACRYLONITRILE VIA TIME-RESOLVED MILLIMETER WAVE SPECTROSCOPY

<u>NATHAN A. SEIFERT</u>, *Department of Chemistry, University of New Haven, West Haven, CT, USA*; KIRILL PROZUMENT, *Chemical Sciences and Engineering Division, Argonne National Laboratory, Lemont, IL, USA.*

In 2017, we presented at ISMS a new Time-Resolved Kinetic Chirped-Pulse (TReK-CP) spectrometer.[a] By coupling a UV photolysis source to a chirped pulse millimeter-wave (mm-wave) spectrometer, we demonstrated the ability to measure kinetic and thermodynamic properties of the photolysis of acrylonitrile (CH_2CHCN), including product branching ratios and rotational and vibrational thermalization rates at reasonable time resolution (ca. 10 μs). However, sensitivity to vibrationally excited states and pre-collisional dynamics was limited, so the observation of truly nascent molecules was still out of reach.

Here, we present improvements to the TReK-CP design that enables detection of nascent product molecules from the photolysis of acrylonitrile, with particular focus on the formation of cyanoacetylene (HC_3N). Moving to the 260-295 GHz mm-wave band significantly improves sensitivity to small polyatomics, enabling detection of HC_3N within 1 μs after photolysis in a variety of vibrational states. We have also devised a new detection scheme that enables a time resolution of 1 μs, amongst other improvements.

Revisiting the photolysis of acrylonitrile with these improvements has led to surprising observations. We will present evidence that HC_3N has different dynamics than the primary photoproduct, HCN, which clearly forms rotationally hot and is undetectable until the first collisional event takes place. Meanwhile, cyanoacetylene forms slower, exhibiting low temperature state distributions, a large kinetic isotopic effect, and strong kinetic dependence on the initial temperature of the precursor. This is consistent with the theoretical prediction that the final step, $CH_2CCN \rightarrow HC_3N + H$, occurs with little excess energy.[b] We will also show that we are, in fact, detecting truly nascent cyanoacetylene, in that the kinetics show a distinct change from first to second order on the collisional timescale of the reactor.

---
[a]Zaleski, D. P.; Prozument, K.; *ISMS* **2017**, *WH02*.
[b]Zaleski, D. P.; Harding, L. B.; Klippenstein, S. J.; Ruscic, B.; Prozument, K. *J. Phys. Chem. Lett.* **2017**, *8*, 6180.

WH08 4:30 – 4:45
EXOMOLHD: RECENT PROGRESSES ON PHOTODISSOCIATION OF SMALL MOLECULES

<u>MARCO PEZZELLA</u>, JONATHAN TENNYSON, *Department of Physics and Astronomy, University College London, London, UK*; SERGEI N. YURCHENKO, *Physics and Astronomy, University College London, London, United Kingdom.*

The destruction of hot molecules by photodissociation influences the composition and dynamics of exoplanets, particularly in the presence of a UV-rich stellar environments. We compute temperature-dependent photodissociation cross sections and rates for molecules found in these atmospheres, for building a more realistic model of the planetary chemistry. The cross sections are calculated by solving the nuclear-motion Schrödinger equation as part of the ExoMol project using codes Duo, DVR3D and Exocross[a], using the methodology previously described[b]. Photodissociation rates are computed integrating the cross section with different stellar field models representing different star types.
New tools and results for HF, HCl and HCN. Cross sections and rates for the diatomics are compared with previously available data[c], finding a good agreement for the interstellar medium for low temperatures. Both cross sections and rates have a dramatic temperature dependence for temperatures above 1000 K. Our results for HCN are compared with the results obtained by previous works employing the time dependent Schrödinger equation[d].

---
[a]Yurchenko *et al* Comput Phys Commun 2016 **202** 262–275; Tennyson *et al* Comput Phys Commun 2004 **163** 85-116; Yurchenko *et al* A&A 2018 **614** A131
[b]Pezzella *et al* Phys. Chem. Chem. Phys. 2021 **23** 16390–16400
[c]Heays *et al* A&A 2017 **602** A105
[d]Chenel *et al* J. Chem. Phys. 2016 **144** 144306; Aguado *et al* Astrophys. J. 2017 **838** 33

WH09   4:48 – 5:03

CO FORMATION FROM ACETONE PHOTOLYSIS: THE ROAMING PATHWAY

<u>LORRIE S. D. JACOB</u>, *Yusuf Hamied Department of Chemistry, University of Cambridge, Cambridge, Cambridgeshire, United Kingdom*; KELVIN LEE, *Accelerated Computing Systems and Graphics, Intel Corporation, Hillsboro, OR, USA*; TIMOTHY SCHMIDT, KLAAS NAUTA, SCOTT KABLE, *School of Chemistry, UNSW, Sydney, NSW, Australia.*

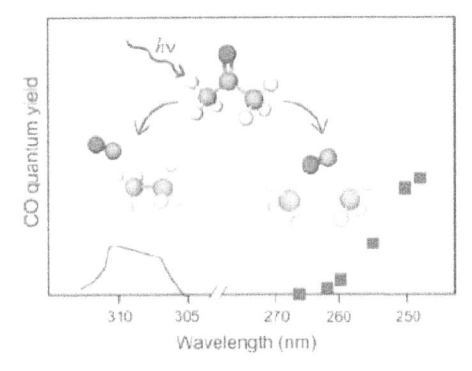

Acetone is one of the most abundant ketones in the atmosphere, with 73 million tonnes emitted or formed in the atmosphere annually. Additionally, as the simplest ketone, understanding the photodynamics of acetone can improve our understanding of the photolysis pathways of other ketones.

CO formation from acetone photolysis was studied over the whole $S_1 \leftarrow S_0$ absorption spectrum,[a] however, this talk focuses on the longer wavelengths (305-320 nm). Resonance enhanced photoionisation (REMPI) and photofragment excitation (PHOFEX) of the CO photofragment at photolysis wavelengths longer than 300 nm, combined with laser-induced fluorescence (LIF) of acetone, found CO was forming from a unimolecular pathway, attributed to roaming. Although roaming is often associated with 'cold' rotational distributions, this does not seem to be the case for CO formed from roaming in acetone. The CO products had significant rotational excitation up to $J \sim 80$.

Fourier transform infrared spectroscopy was used to obtain quantum yields of the photolysis products of acetone from 285 – 325 nm at various pressures of synthetic air and nitrogen bath gas (3-760 Torr total pressure). Carbon monoxide was found to have a quantum yield of up to 10% in non-oxidative conditions at 3 Torr and 760 Torr. In an atmosphere of synthetic air at actinic wavelengths, this pathway was reduced to a maximum of 3%.

---

[a] Jacob, L.S.D.; Lee, K.L.K.; Schmidt, T.W.; Nauta, K.; Kable, S.H. *J. Chem. Phys.* **2022**, *156*, 094303

WH10   5:06 – 5:21

SPECTROSCOPY AND PREDISSOCIATION DYNAMICS OF SH RADICALS VIA THE $A^2\Sigma^+$ STATE

<u>YUAN QIN</u>, XIANFENG ZHENG, YU SONG, GE SUN, *Department of Chemistry, University of California, Riverside, CA, USA*; JINGSONG ZHANG, *Department of Chemistry and Air Pollution Research Center, University of California, Riverside, CA, USA.*

The spectroscopy and predissociation dynamics of several vibronic levels ($v' = 0$-6) of the SH $A^2\Sigma^+$ state have been studied using the high-n Rydberg atom time-of-flight (HRTOF) technique. By measuring the product translational energy distributions as a function of excitation wavelength, the H + S(^3P_J) photofragment yield (PFY) spectra are obtained across the various $A^2\Sigma^+ \leftarrow X^2\Pi$ bands. The PFY spectra of the $A^2\Sigma^+$ $v' = 3$-6 states exhibit broad linewidths (> 4 cm^{-1}), indicating that these levels undergo rapid predissociation with lifetimes on the order of picosecond. The measured spin-orbit branching fractions of the H + S($^3P_{J=2,1,0}$) product channels provide insights to the predissociation dynamics of the $A^2\Sigma^+$ state, which change dramatically as the vibrational level v' increases. The $A^2\Sigma^+$ $v' = 0$ state of SH predissociates mainly through adiabatic coupling to the $^4\Sigma^-$ repulsive state, while all three repulsive states ($^4\Sigma^-$, $^2\Sigma^-$, and $^4\Pi$) are involved in the dissociation pathways for higher vibrational levels.

WH11
VELOCITY MAP IMAGING OF GOLD ION - LIGAND COMPLEXES

BRANDON M. RITTGERS, MICHAEL A DUNCAN, *Department of Chemistry, University of Georgia, Athens, GA, USA.*

$Au^+(L)$ (L = H_2O, NH_3, O_2, formaldehyde, or acetone) complexes are generated in the gas phase by laser vaporization off of a gold rod during a supersonic expansion of rare gases seeded with the ligand of interest and detected using time-of-flight mass spectrometry. Metal ionization potentials are typically lower than that of many molecules, leading to the charge being localized on the metal in a cation-molecule complex. Gold has a relatively high ionization potential that is closer to that of molecules, and laser excitation of a gold ion – molecule complex can lead to a charge transfer dissociation channel that produces the molecular ion fragment. If the excitation wavelength is sufficiently high, excess kinetic energy release above the dissociation threshold can be detected using velocity map imaging. This energy release is then be used to determine an upper bound on the gold ion – molecule binding energy.

WI. Mini-symposium: Benchmarking in Spectroscopy

Wednesday, June 22, 2022 – 1:45 PM

Room: 116 Roger Adams Lab

Chair: Cristina Puzzarini, University of Bologna, Bologna, Italy

---

WI01   1:45 – 2:00

NON-ADIABATIC COUPLING IN NO@C$_{60}$: PREDICTION OF A RENNER-TELLER LIKE EFFECT FOR SPHERICALLY ENCAPSULATED DIATOMIC MOLECULES

ANDREAS W. HAUSER, JOHANN V. POTOTSCHNIG, *Institute of Experimental Physics, Graz University of Technology, Graz, Austria.*

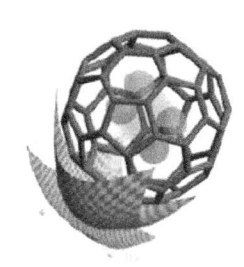

The Renner-Teller effect describes the coupling of a symmetry-reducing molecular vibration with a two-fold degenerate electronic state. Its discovery goes back to work of Herzberg and Teller, who realized in 1933 that the potential energy surface of a triatomic, linear molecule splits into two as soon as the molecule is bent. In this work, we show that a very similar, yet unknown type of non-adiabatic coupling can even occur for diatomic (!) molecules.

This seems absurd at first sight, but becomes possible as soon as the diatomic molecule ist embedded in a spherically symmetric confinement. In this case, its translational degrees of freedom become quantized and can couple to electronically degenerate states in a very similar fashion as predicted by Renner-Teller effect theory. To our knowledge, it is the first time that this novel type of non-adiabatic coupling has been investigated either in theory or experiment.[1]

We demonstrate this effect for the experimentally accessible case of NO embedding in a C$_{60}$. Endofullerenes, in particular those carrying a radical molecule, are highly topical objects of ongoing research in molecular spectroscopy, reaction chemistry and carbon-based nanomaterial design. Also, suitable confinements in molecular traps for quantum information and quantum computing will produce a similar effect of nonadiabatic coupling as predicted by our study.

[1] A.W. Hauser and J.V. Pototschnig, J.Phys. Chem. A, 2022, DOI:10.1021/acs.jpca.1c10970

WI02   2:03 – 2:18

USING HIGH-RESOLUTION PHOTOELECTRON IMAGING TO PROBE THE SPECTROSCOPY OF CRYOGENICALLY COOLED AZOLIDE MOLECULES

YUE-ROU ZHANG, *Chemistry department, Brown university, Providence, RI, USA*; DAOFU YUAN, LAI-SHENG WANG, *Department of Chemistry, Brown University, Providence, RI, USA.*

Photoelectron spectroscopy is a powerful technique to investigate the electronic structure and chemical bonding of anions and the corresponding neutrals upon electron detachment. Here, we use our electrospray ionization photoelectron spectroscopy apparatus, which couples a cryogenically-cooled 3D Paul trap and a high resolution imaging system to get the vibrational and electronic information about three azolide: pyrazolide, pyrrolide and imidazolide. Besides the expected conventional dipole bound state, a core-excited dipole bound state is observed in pyrazolide with the neutral core in its first excited electronic state. And a completely different threshold behavior is observed for pyrrolide and imidazolide with a similar pi type HOMO: a d-wave-dominated spectrum is found for pyrrolide and an s-wave-dominated spectrum is found for imidazolide.

WI03
CAN LONDON DISPERSION OVERRIDE CATION-π INTERACTIONS?

<u>VLADIMIR GORBACHEV</u>, ALEXANDRA TSYBIZOVA, LARISA MILOGLYADOVA, PETER CHEN, *Department of Chemistry and Applied Biosciences, ETH Zurich, Zurich, Switzerland.*

We report an evaluation of the importance of London dispersion in moderately large (up to 32 heavy atoms) organic molecules by means of a molecular torsion balance[a] whose conformations "weigh" London forces against cation-π(aryl) in the absence of solvent. The experimental gas-phase study is performed using cryogenic ion vibrational predissociation (CIVP) spectroscopy covering both the N-H and the effectively "deperturbed" N-D[b] stretching modes, taking into account possible perturbation due to the tag molecule.[c] The gas-phase data is supported by solid-state FT-IR spectroscopy, single-crystal x-ray crystallography, and is accompanied by DFT calculations, including an extensive search and analysis of the accessible conformations. We begin with the unsubstituted molecular torsion balance, and then step up the complexity systematically by adding alkyl groups incrementally as dispersion energy donors (DEDs) to achieve a degree of chemical complexity comparable to what is typically found in transition states for many regio- and stereoselective reaction in organic and organometallic chemistry. We find clear evidence for the small attractive contribution by DEDs, as had been reported in other studies, but we also find that small individual contributions by London dispersion, when they operate in opposition to other weak non-covalent interactions, produce composite effects on the structure that are difficult to predict intuitively, or by modern quantum chemical calculations. The experimentally observed structures, together with a reasonable value for a reference cation-π interaction, indicate that the pairwise interaction between two *tert*-butyl groups, in the best case, is modest. Moreover, the visualization of the conformational space, and comparison to spectroscopic indicators of structure, as one steps up the complexity of the manifold of non-covalent interactions, makes clear that *in silico* predictive ability for the structure of moderately large, flexible, organic molecules falters sooner than one might have expected.[d]

---

[a]Tsybizova‡, A.; Fritshe‡, L.; Gorbachev‡, V.; Miloglyadova, L.; Chen, P. *J. Chem. Phys.* **2019**, *151*, 234304
[b]Gorbachev, V.; Miloglyadova, L.; Tsybizova, A.; Chen, P. *Rev. Sci. Instrum.* **2021**, *92*, 083002
[c]Tsybizova, A.; Paenurk, E.; Gorbachev, V.; Chen, P. *J. Phys. Chem. A* **2020**, *124*, 41, 8519, 234304
[d]Gorbachev, V.; Tsybizova, A.; Miloglyadova, L.; Chen, P. *J. Am. Chem. Soc.* **2022**, *submitted*

WI04
ELECTRONIC SPECTROSCOPY OF THE PREVIOUSLY UNKNOWN PALLADIUM MONOSULFIDE (PdS) RADICAL

<u>LEI ZHANG</u>, YAO YU, XINWEN MA, JIE YANG, *Atomic Physics Center, Institute of Modern Physics, Chinese Academy of Sciences, Lanzhou, CHINA.*

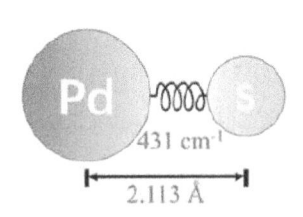

The optical spectra of the diatomic PdS radical in the gas phase have been investigated for the first time through a combination of laser-induced fluorescence (LIF) and single vibronic level emission spectroscopy. The $[22.3]\,^3\Sigma^- - X\,^3\Sigma^-$ transition system containing sixteen vibrational bands was identified in the LIF spectra in the energy range of 22,030 − 23,400 cm^{-1}. Rotationally resolved spectra and analysis enabled a determination of the molecular structures in the upper and lower states, involving the rotational constants, the vibrational constants, the spin-orbit splittings, and the vibrational isotope shifts. The emission transitions from the [22.3] state down to the ground state and to the low-lying $A\,^3\Pi$ state were recorded, by which the spin-orbit splittings of $A\,^3\Pi_{2,1,0^-,^+}$ were determined. A comparison of the bond lengths (and the vibrational frequencies) of the VIII group monosulfide radicals (NiS/PdS/PtS) reveals the relativistic effects in the Pd and Pt atoms.

WI05   2:57 – 3:12

NEW METHODS FOR CORE-HOLE SPECTROSCOPY BASED ON COUPLED CLUSTER

<u>MEGAN SIMONS</u>, DEVIN A. MATTHEWS, *Department of Chemistry, Southern Methodist University, Dallas, TX, USA.*

Equation-of-Motion Coupled cluster (EOM-CC) is a preferred method for high-precision electronic spectroscopy due to its size-extensivity and implicit inclusion of higher-order excitation effects in the electronic wavefunction. The accuracy of the EOM-CC wave function can be controlled by truncating the cluster operator, T, and/or excitation operator, R, at increasing levels of excitation. Within core-hole calculations (XPS, XAS/NEXAFS, XES, and RIXS), the inclusion of triple excitations, in concert with the core-valence separation (CVS), is critical in order to accurately treat orbital relaxation effects; however, including triple excitations unavoidably leads to high computational cost. Instead, we propose two alternative approaches: first, in Transition-Potential Coupled Cluster (TP-CCSD), orbital relaxation is explicitly included in the reference orbitals through the use of a fractional-occupation SCF calculation followed by CVS-EOM-CCSD. Second, the CVS-STEOMEE-CCSD+cT method extends the similarity-transformed EOM-CC approach of Nooijen with triple excitations, but only for the inexpensive core ionization potentials. We benchmark both methods for first-row K-edge vertical ionization and excitation energies of 14 small molecules, compared to the accurate but extremely expensive CVS-EOMEE-CCSDT method, as well as select comparisons to experimental gas-phase XAS. We find that both methods are effective in treating the orbital relaxation of core-hole states, with absolute energy errors below 0.5 eV and relative errors for peak positions typically below 0.3 eV. Both methods are also computationally efficient: TP-CCSD has the same computational cost as the less-accurate CVS-EOM-CCSD method, while CVS-STEOMEE-CCSD+cT is only marginally more expensive for a small number of excitations. For large numbers of excited states, the STEOM-based approach may be significantly faster.

WI06   3:15 – 3:30

GENERALIZED OSCILLATOR STRENGTH OF THE INNER SHELL EXCITATION OF NITROGEN STUDIED BY NONRESONANT INELASTIC X-RAY SCATTERING

<u>LIHAN WANG</u>, *Hefei National Laboratory for Physical Science at Microscale, University of Science and Technology of China, Hefei, China.*

The inner shell excitation process is a good probe to investigate internuclear potential, the core-hole decay mechanisms, and the electronic configuration of highly excited molecules. Experimentally, the electron scattering method is usually used to study the dynamic parameters of excitation process. Through the scattering of high-energy electrons with the target gas, we can measure its generalized oscillator strength. For a long time, the results obtained by this method were used as the benchmark data. However, recent studies have shown that the differential scattering cross sections obtained by the electron scattering method include the contribution of intermolecular scattering, and the GOS derived from it is not suitable as a benchmark for experiments and theory.

In this study, we measured the generalized oscillator strength of the $\sigma_u 1s \rightarrow \pi_g 2p$ and $\sigma_g 1s \rightarrow \pi_g 2p$ transitions of N_2 based on the nonresonant inelastic X-ray scattering method. The range of momentum transfer of the generalized oscillator strength measured by this method is wide, and the results strictly follow the first-order Born approximation. The results can be used as benchmark data for inner shell excitation of N_2, and can rigorously test the theoretical wave functions of the inner shell.

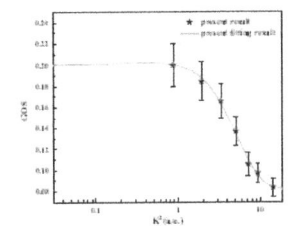

Intermission

WI07
FESCHBACH RESONANCE IN TETRACENE RADICAL ANION: THE SECRET TO A LONG LIFETIME OF NEGATIVITY

<u>COLE R SAGAN</u>, ETIENNE GARAND, *Department of Chemistry, University of Wisconsin–Madison, Madison, WI, USA.*

Polycyclic aromatic hydrocarbons (PAH) have been surmised as carriers of the diffuse interstellar bands (DIB), hundreds of unidentified spectral lines in the infrared through ultraviolet regions. These PAH are often thought to be in their cationic or neutral forms in the interstellar medium, although there have been models that feature these molecules as the primary carriers of negative charge in dense interstellar clouds, rather than just free electrons. We monitored the photodetachment cross section as a function of wavelength for tetracene radical anion ($C_{18}H_{12}^-$) to explore the resonances of the tetracene radical anion above the detachment threshold. The observed electronic states closely align with a previously reported absorption spectrum of the molecule, with one major exception. Sharp features (less than 10 cm^{-1}) corresponding to a long-lived Feschbach resonance of the molecule were found in the near-IR. This corresponds to a lifetime of no faster than 600 fs, a much longer lifetime than typically observed for above detachment resonances. These features can potentially be used to detect the presence of anionic polyaromatic species in the interstellar medium. However, we were not able to make any assignments based on our spectra for tetracene and available DIB data. Still, by acquiring photoelectron spectra at these anion excited electronic states, we identify specific photodetachment channels by which these resonances relax to the ground neutral electronic state. These features will be compared to the anthracene radical anion ($C_{14}H_{10}^-$) and the tetracenyl anion to explore the effect of PAH size and dehydrogenation on these resonances. In addition, we will report on possible fragmentation in the UV spectral region mediated by these resonances. Finally, photoelectron spectra are collected using slow electron velocity-map imaging (SEVI), yielding high precision electron affinity values and T_1 term energies for tetracene, as well as identifying active vibrations in these transitions. Interestingly, the T_1 state in the tetracene radical anion photoelectron spectrum features highly non-Franck Condon activity, most likely due to vibronic coupling. The anion resonances shown here along with the photoelectron spectra acquired have interesting implications for the possibility of tetracene as a negative charge carrier in the interstellar medium.

WI08
FLUORESCENCE-DETECTED MID-INFRARED PHOTOTHERMAL MICROSCOPY

<u>MINGHE LI</u>, ALEKSANDR RAZUMTCEV, GARTH SIMPSON, *Department of Chemistry, Purdue University, West Lafayette, IN, USA.*

Fluorescence-detected photothermal mid-infrared (F-PTIR) spectroscopy is demonstrated and used to characterize chemical composition within phase-separated domains of pharmaceutical materials. Infrared and Raman spectroscopic imaging are powerful techniques for generating detailed chemical images based on a sample's spectrum. Previous study on optically detected photothermal infrared (O-PTIR) improved the spatial resolution by probing the temperature-induced refractive index change but are potentially prone to the high background in scattering media. Fluorescence-detected photothermal mid-infrared (F-PTIR) spectroscopy (Fig. 1) is proposed, providing dual-level chemical discrimination based on both fluorescence and infrared absorption. F-PTIR relies on the intrinsic sensitivity of the fluorescence quantum efficiency to temperature. Therefore, fluorescence can serve as a sensitive probe (SNR over 100) for reporting on highly localized and selective infrared absorption. The theoretical spatial resolution of F-PTIR is ultimately limited by fluorescence microscopy and the thermal diffusivity of the sample instead of the infrared wavelength. Following proof-of-concept measurements with model systems of silica gel and polyethylene glycol particles, F-PTIR measurements were used to probe chemical composition within phase-separated domains of ritonavir within copovidone polymer matrices of relevance in the production of pharmaceutical final dosage forms.

WI09 4:48 – 5:03

THE COUPLED-CHANNEL DEPERTURBATION ANALYSIS OF THE A∼B∼X STATES MANIFOLD OF CN WITH ALMOST SPECTROSCOPIC ACCURACY

VERA TERASHKEVICH, ELENA ALEXANDROVNA PAZYUK, ANDREY STOLYAROV, *Department of Chemistry, Lomonosov Moscow State University, Moscow, Russia.*

A direct deperturbation analysis for the experimental rovibronic term values belonging to the first three electronic states of the CN radical has been performed using an iterative solution of the inverse spectroscopic problem based on a rigorous coupled-channel approximation. Besides potential energy curves (PECs), the non-adiabatic energy matrix explicitly included the spin-orbit and Coriolis coupling functions between the $X^2\Sigma^+$, $A^2\Pi$ and $B^2\Sigma^+$ states. The regular perturbation caused by the remote doublet states was taken into account by the introduction of so-called Λ-doubling parameters as an implicit function of the interatomic distance. The initial set of the deperturbed PECs was defined in analytical extended Morse oscillator (EMO) form while the non-adiabatic coupling functions were given as the properly morphed *ab initio* electronic matrix elements [a]. The resulting PECs and non-adiabatic parameters reproduce the overall set of experimental energy levels with an accuracy of about 0.01-0.02 cm^{-1}, which is almost comparable with their uncertainty of measurement.[b] .

[a] V. A. Terashkevich, E.A. Pazyuk, and A.V. Stolyarov. *Journal of Quantitative Spectroscopy and Radiative Transfer*, **276**, 107916, 2021
[b] The work was supported by the Russian Science Foundation (RSF) (grant No.22-23-00272)

WI10 5:06 – 5:21

CAVITY RING-DOWN SPECTROSCOPY OF WATER VAPOR IN THE NEAR-UV REGION

Q.-Y. YANG, Y. TAN, SHUI-MING HU, *Department of Chemical Physics, University of Science and Technology of China, Hefei, China*; EAMON K CONWAY, *Atomic and Molecular Physics, Harvard-Smithsonian Center for Astrophysics, Cambridge, MA, USA*; IOULI E GORDON, *Atomic and Molecular Physics, Harvard-Smithsonian Center for Astrophysics, Cambridge, MA, USA.*

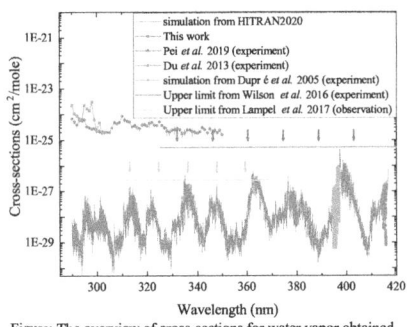

Figure: The overview of cross-sections for water vapor obtained in this work and those reported in previous works, as well as the simulation from HITRAN2020.

Water vapor absorption in the near-ultraviolet region is essential to describing the energy budget of Earth, but little spectroscopic information is currently available since it is a challenging spectral region for both experimental and theoretical studies. A continuous-wave cavity ring-down spectroscopic experiment was built to record the weak absorption of water vapor in the *near*-UV region around 415 nm. This is a region that is still missing in laboratory measurements. A minimum absorption coefficient detection of around 4×10^{-10} cm^{-1} was reached and over 40 ro-vibrational transitions of $H_2^{16}O$ determined in this work. A comparison of line positions and intensities determined in this work to the most recent HITRAN2020 database will be presented. We calculate water vapor absorption cross-sections from our measurements and compare them with recent observations (Pei et al., 2019[a]; Du et al., 2013[b]; Dupré et al., 2005[c]; Wilson et al., 2016[d]; Lampel et al., 2017[e]) and simulations (Gordon et al., 2022[f]).

[a] Pei, et al., Journal of Geophysical Research: Atmospheres; 124(24):14310-14324.
[b] Du et al., Geophysical Research Letters; 40(17):4788-4792.
[c] Dupré et al., The Journal of Chemical Physics; 123(15): 154307
[d] Wilson et al., Journal of Quantitative Spectroscopy and Radiative Transfer; 295(170): 194-199.
[e] Lampel et al., Atmospheric Chemistry and Physics; 17(2): 1271–1295.
[f] Gordon et al., Journal of Quantitative Spectroscopy and Radiative Transfer; 277.

WI11 5:24 – 5:39

IN SITU SPECTROSCOPIC DIAGNOSTIC OF SHOCK INDUCED DECOMPOSITION OF C_{60}

SHUBHADIP CHAKRABORTY, *Université de Rennes 1, Institut de Physique de Rennes,UMR CNRS 6251, Rennes, France*; SERGEI N. YURCHENKO, *Department of Physics and Astronomy, University College London, London, UK*; ROBERT GEORGES, *IPR UMR6251, CNRS - Université Rennes 1, Rennes, France*; VIJAYANAND CHANDRASEKARAN, *Department of Chemistry, School of Advanced Sciences, Vellore Institute of Technology, Vellore, India*; V JAYARAM, *Shock Induced Materials Chemistry Lab, Solid State and Structural Chemistry Unit, Indian Institute of Science, Karnataka, India*; ELANGANNAN ARUNAN, *Department of Inorganic and Physical Chemistry, Indian Institute of Science, Bangalore, India*; LUDOVIC BIENNIER, *IPR UMR6251, CNRS - Université Rennes 1, Rennes, France*.

The applications of the shock wave research are multi modal. The potential of the shock wave is a large amount of energy is transferred to the material within a very short timescale, leading to the formation of new chemical species and the kinetics of product formation can be studied.

Far from the laboratory, shock waves play an important role in controlling the physical and chemical evolution of the interstellar medium (ISM). In the ISM, shock waves are generated due to supernovae explosions, bipolar outflows and stellar winds. However, the application of shock waves to study the chemistry of the ISM is a relatively new area of research. One of the objectives of our research is to identify new possible shock tracers in the low velocity shocked regions of the ISM.

Shock induced decomposition of C_{60} (one of the interstellar building blocks of dusts) was explored in situ with the help of a UV-Vis spectrometer and a monochromator. The integrated emission spectrum reveals the presence of C_2 features with a broad continuum and was affected by self-absorption. The broad continuum is likely due to the combined effect of the black-body emission from small carbon particles and the recurrent fluorescence of various carbon clusters produced via the dissociation of C_{60}. The emission spectrum of C_2 was computed using Exocross module and the column density of the C_2 units were determined.

WJ. Instrument/Technique Demonstration

Wednesday, June 22, 2022 – 1:45 PM

Room: B102 Chemical and Life Sciences

Chair: Deacon J Nemchick, Jet Propulsion Laboratory, Pasadena, CA, USA

WJ01   1:45 – 2:00

INFRARED HIGH RESOLUTION COHERENT 2D SPECTROSCOPY

DeAUNNA A DANIELS, *Chemistry, Spelman College, Atlanta, GA, USA*; THRESA WELLS, PETER CHEN, *Department of Chemistry, Spelman College, Atlanta, GA, USA.*

High resolution coherent multidimensional spectroscopy is a powerful tool that can be used to overcome difficulties encountered when using 1D spectroscopy. The 2D spectra have reduced congestion and show easily recognizable patterns, even for molecules that yield patternless 1D spectra. Furthermore, the peaks are automatically sorted by quantum number and species. A new infrared version of this technique has been developed. This talk provides background behind how the technique works and how to interpret the results.

WJ02   2:03 – 2:18

A NEW FEMTOSECOND XUV SOURCE AT THE UNIVERSITY OF WISCONSIN

RYAN T ASH, ZAIN ABHARI, UWE BERGMANN, *Physics, University of Wisconsin-Madison, Madison, WI, USA.*

In this presentation, we discuss a femtosecond tabletop extreme ultraviolet (XUV) source using high-harmonic generation in a gas target and its application towards studying the ultrafast dynamics of condensed matter systems. We will overview the building and design of the instrument, characterization of the source, preliminary data of systems containing first-row transition metals, and plans for future experiments.

WJ03   2:21 – 2:36

DEVELOPMENT OF A CRYOGENIC, MASS SELECTIVE, MULTI-REACTION TRAP ION SPECTROMETER

GINA ROESCH, ETIENNE GARAND, *Department of Chemistry, University of Wisconsin–Madison, Madison, WI, USA.*

Development of cryogenic ion traps have greatly enhanced the ability to control ion-neutral chemistry and spectroscopically probe the resulting reaction products. Currently, our lab uses a dual cryogenic ion trap instrument for controlled ion manipulation and subsequent tagging in preparation for infrared action spectroscopy studies. This allows, for example, the study of microsolvated ionic species and catalytic reaction intermediates. The first ion trap is a liquid nitrogen cooled "reaction trap". It is the sole location for ion manipulation and thus limits us to a single chemical reaction or the addition of a single type of solvent molecule. To overcome this limitation, we have developed a cryogenic, mass selective, sequential multi-reaction trap setup with a modular housing design. Mass selectivity is achieved via frequency and duty cycle manipulations of the RF square wave trapping potential. In addition, the modular design reduces the cost and allows for easier adaptability and expansion.

We show that such digital linear quadrupole can efficiently form clusters at low temperature and subsequently mass-select a single species within a series of different cluster sizes before ion transfer. Additionally, we show that manipulation of the square wave duty cycle during the clustering process can be used to enhance the formation of a specific cluster size. This single species enhancement and selection is expected to decrease the amount of time required for spectroscopic characterization. Careful ion transfer into a second reaction trap can be done to cluster a different species and simulate more complex ion environments. Future plans for the multi-reaction trap instrument include characterizing water networks around small peptides by inserting a D_2O as a position sensitive spectroscopic molecular probe.

WJ04　　　　　　　　　　　　　　　　　　　　　　　　　　　　　　　　　　　　2:39 – 2:54
DEMONSTRATION OF CRESU-REMPI FOR REACTION KINETIC MEASUREMENTS IN THE GAS-PHASE

RANIL GURUSINGHE, NURESHAN DIAS, JINXIN LANG, *Department of Chemistry, University of Missouri, Columbia, MO, USA*; MATTHEW L EDLIN, *Chemistry, University of Missouri, Columbia, MO, USA*; ARTHUR SUITS, *Department of Chemistry, University of Missouri, Columbia, MO, USA*.

The CRESU technique (French acronym for "reaction kinetics in uniform supersonic flows") provides a wall-less gas-phase reactor to measure low-temperature reaction kinetics. In the past, probing methods such as laser-induced fluorescence (LIF), mass spectrometry, and chirped-pulse uniform flow (CPUF) microwave spectroscopy have been successfully used to measures reaction kinetics in CRESU flows, but the latter two call for sampling of the flow prior to detection. Here we show a selective, low-cost, and highly sensitive probing tool to measure the kinetics of reactions that involve both molecular and atomic species. This new detection method uses resonance-enhance multi-photon ionization (REMPI) and an electron capture probe, adapted from approaches successfully used in flames, to selectively identify atomic and molecular species. A negative-biased high voltage applied to two electrodes, that are placed on either side of a grounded probe, enables rapid capture of electrons produced by the selective ionization from the REMPI spectroscopy. The performance of this setup was verified by recording the (1+1) REMPI spectra of nitric oxide in 20 K and 50 K uniform supersonic flows. The REMPI probe response is proportional to the number of electrons produced by ionization, and therefore to the concentration of ionized species. Thus, the time-dependent REMPI signal can be used to measure the rate of decay or growth of a reactant or product in fast chemical reactions in CRESU flows.

WJ05　　　　　　　　　　　　　　　　　　　　　　　　　　　　　　　　　　　　2:57 – 3:12
TOWARDS THE RESOLUTION LIMIT OF PFI-ZEKE PHOTOELECTRON SPECTROSCOPY

HOLGER HERBURGER, VINCENT WIRTH, URS HOLLENSTEIN, FRÉDÉRIC MERKT, *Laboratorium für Physikalische Chemie, ETH Zurich, Zurich, Switzerland*.

The spectral resolution in Pulsed-Field Ionization Zero-Kinetic Energy (PFI-ZEKE) photoelectron spectroscopy is related to the state selectivity in the ionization process of the Rydberg states. The selectivity is determined by the applied electric field pulse sequence. Hollenstein et al.[a] used discrete electric field pulses with increasing field strength in combination with a preceding field pulse of opposite polarity. By using such field pulse sequences with the smallest possible field step size (i.e., approximately 9 mV/cm), a spectral resolution of 0.06 cm^{-1} could be achieved. To improve the resolution further Harper et al.[b] recently suggested replacing the sequence of field steps by a linearly increasing field, as used earlier by Reiser et al.[c], in combination with a prepulse of opposite polarity and obtained promising results on the PFI-ZEKE photoelectron spectrum of NO and CO$_2$. Using a home-built narrow-bandwidth long-pulse laser system (pulse lengths up to 50 ns) in combination with a field pulse ramp[b,c], we explore the resolution limit of this approach. To avoid overlap of spectral lines, we chose an atomic system, Ar, as test system and recorded PFI-ZEKE photoelectron spectra of transitions from the metastable states $(3p)^5(4s)[3/2]_2$ ($^3P_2$) and $(3p)^5(4s)'[1/2]_0$ ($^3P_0$) to the $(3p)^5$ $^2P_{3/2,1/2}$ states of Ar$^+$. This system also offers the advantage of a precisely known ionization energy[d] with which the ionization energy determined with the new method can be compared.

---

[a]U. Hollenstein, R. Seiler, H. Schmutz, M. Andrist, and F. Merkt, *J. Chem. Phys.* **115**, 5461–5469 (2001).
[b]Oliver J. Harper, Ning L. Chen, Séverine Boyé-Péronne, and Bérenger Gans, *Phys. Chem. Chem. Phys.* **24**, 2777–2784 (2022).
[c]G. Reiser, W. Habenicht, K. Müller-Dethlefs, and E. W. Schlag, *Chem. Phys. Lett.* **152**, 119–123 (1988).
[d]V. L. Sukhorukov, I. D. Petrov, M. Schäfer, F. Merkt, M.-W. Ruf, and H. Hotop, *J. Phys. B: At. Mol. Opt. Phys.* **45**, 092001 (2012) and references therein.

Intermission

WJ06   3:54 – 4:09
MID-INFRARED CW OPTICAL PARAMETRIC OSCILLATOR PUMPED BY AN ELECTRO-OPTIC FREQUENCY COMB

MATTHEW J. CICH, ADAM HEINIGER, DAVID B. FOOTE, WALTER HURLBUT, CHRIS HAIMBERGER, *TOPTICA Photonics, Inc, Farmington, NY, USA*; DAVID A. LONG, *Material Measurement Laboratory, National Institute of Standards and Technology, Gaithersburg, MD, USA.*

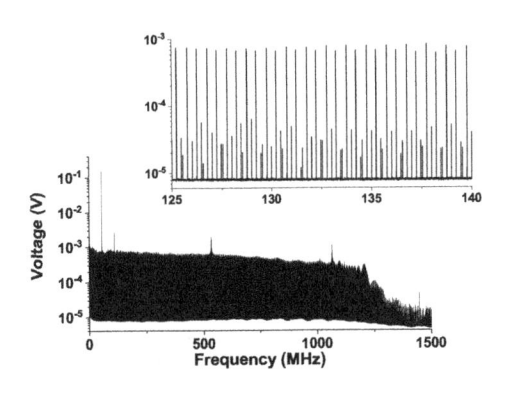

Optical frequency comb (OFC) spectroscopy in the mid-infrared (MIR) promises faster, more precise, and more sensitive molecular spectroscopy. To date, demonstrations of MIR OFCs have suffered from low power, poor wavelength coverage, or low sensitivity. Systems that do excel in these areas have high cost and complexity. The technique and measurements reported here demonstrate that singly resonant, single frequency optical parametric oscillators (OPO's) are a powerful platform for generating MIR OFC's with properties not shown by other MIR light sources.

An EOM frequency comb is first generated via phase modulation of CW light near 1064 nm. An inexpensive direct digital synthesizer (DDS)-based scheme is used to generate chirped modulation resulting in a 2 GHz-wide frequency comb with ultraflat comb teeth and frequency agile repetition rates between 1 MHz and 10 MHz. This comb pumps the OPO, resulting in an idler output that is a MIR OFC tunable between 2200 - 4000 nm with >1 W output power (figure). This technique is utilized to perform frequency comb spectroscopy on select rovibrational features near 3 μm in methane and acetylene.

WJ07   4:12 – 4:27
CAVITY RING-DOWN SPECTROSCOPY WITH INTERBAND CASCADE OPTICAL FREQUENCY COMBS

TZULING CHEN, CHARLES R. MARKUS, DOUGLAS OBER, *Division of Chemistry and Chemical Engineering, California Institute of Technology, Pasadena, CA, USA*; LUKASZ A. STERCZEWSKI, *Instruments Division, Jet Propulsion Laboratory/Caltech, Pasadena, CA, USA*; CHADWICK L CANEDY, IGOR VURGAFTMAN, *Optical Sciences, U.S. Naval Research Laboratory, Washington, DC, USA*; CLIFFORD FREZ, *Instruments Division, Jet Propulsion Laboratory/Caltech, Pasadena, CA, USA*; JERRY R MEYER, *Optical Sciences, U.S. Naval Research Laboratory, Washington, DC, USA*; MAHMOOD BAGHERI, *Instruments Division, Jet Propulsion Laboratory/Caltech, Pasadena, CA, USA*; MITCHIO OKUMURA, *Division of Chemistry and Chemical Engineering, California Institute of Technology, Pasadena, CA, USA.*

The spectrum of an optical frequency comb is composed of many equidistant lines, which is a natural match for enhancement cavities. Cavity ring-down spectroscopy is known to be a robust and highly sensitive technique, although it is challenging to implement with optical frequency combs. Here we demonstrate a new approach to performing direct frequency comb cavity ring-down spectroscopy in the CH stretching region using an interband cascade optical frequency comb. These chip-scale devices generate combs with large repetition rates (10 GHz), which enables mode-resolved detection using Vernier spectroscopy. The decay of each comb mode can be obtained as the comb is being scanned, providing sensitive and broadband detection. Here we demonstrate the effectiveness of this technique for trace gas detection and discuss the overall performance.

WJ08　4:30 – 4:45
MID-INFRARED SPECTROSCOPY OF TRANSIENT SPECIES USING A CHIP-SCALE MID-INFRARED OPTICAL FREQUENCY COMB

CHARLES R. MARKUS, TZULING CHEN, DOUGLAS OBER, *Division of Chemistry and Chemical Engineering, California Institute of Technology, Pasadena, CA, USA*; LUKASZ A. STERCZEWSKI, *Instruments Division, Jet Propulsion Laboratory/Caltech, Pasadena, CA, USA*; CHADWICK L CANEDY, IGOR VURGAFTMAN, *Optical Sciences, U.S. Naval Research Laboratory, Washington, DC, USA*; CLIFFORD FREZ, *Instruments Division, Jet Propulsion Laboratory/Caltech, Pasadena, CA, USA*; JERRY R MEYER, *Optical Sciences, U.S. Naval Research Laboratory, Washington, DC, USA*; MAHMOOD BAGHERI, *Instruments Division, Jet Propulsion Laboratory/Caltech, Pasadena, CA, USA*; MITCHIO OKUMURA, *Division of Chemistry and Chemical Engineering, California Institute of Technology, Pasadena, CA, USA*.

Optical frequency combs have become a promising tool for sensitive and broadband spectroscopy. They are especially attractive for investigations of the structure and reactivity of transient species, where multiplexed detection provides information regarding reactive intermediates and product branching ratios. However, the cost and complexity of conventional frequency combs has inhibited their widespread use in chemistry laboratories. Frequency combs generated using semiconductor lasers, such as quantum or interband cascade lasers, offer an alternative that is compact and less technically demanding. We have employed interband cascade lasers, which provide coverage in the CH stretching region, to monitor reactions initiated by pulsed-laser photolysis using Vernier spectroscopy. The reaction between 1-hydroxyethyl radical and oxygen forms acetaldehyde, and is an ideal test-case for the newly constructed instrument. We will discuss the performance characteristics and applications of this new and promising technique.

WJ09　4:48 – 5:03
HIGH-SPEED, HIGH-RESOLUTION, BROADBAND DUAL-COMB SPECTROMETER FROM 3-5 μm

SCOTT C EGBERT, *Mechanical Engineering, University of Colorado Boulder, Boulder, CO, USA*; PETER CHANG, *Physics, University of Colorado at Boulder, Boulder, CO, USA*; SCOTT DIDDAMS, *Time and Frequency Division, National Institute of Standards and Technology, Boulder, CO, USA*; GREGORY B RIEKER, *Mechanical Engineering, University of Colorado Boulder, Boulder, CO, USA*; NAZANIN HOGHOOGHI, *Department of Mechanical Engineering, University of Colorado Boulder, Boulder, CO, USA*.

Dual Comb Spectroscopy (DCS) is an emerging technique for measuring infrared molecular absorption at higher speeds and spectral resolution than historically possible using Michelson interferometer-based Fourier Transform Spectroscopy. While Quantum Cascade Laser (QCL) DCS is capable of fast acquisition speeds and the ability to probe between 4-10 μm, these benefits also come at the cost of a low instantaneous bandwidth, spectral resolution, and coherence time over which measurements can be averaged.

Here we present the development of a GHz repetition rate intra-pulse DFG mid-IR DCS system. This system is based on mode-locked lasers simultaneously spanning 3-5 μm with 0.03 cm^{-1} comb tooth spacing, μs acquisition speeds, and single-cycle residual noise below 10^{-1}. Spectra and noise characteristics from a static spectroscopy cell containing various hydrocarbons are reported and discussed. The system shows promise for sensing in rapid transient systems given the high single shot signal to noise ratio and rapid interferogram acquisition time afforded by the GHz pulse repetition rates.

WJ10 5:06 – 5:21

RAPID DUAL-COMB COHERENT RAMAN SPECTROSCOPY IN THE HIGH-WAVENUMBER REGION

<u>YUJIA ZHANG</u>, MINJIAN LU, YAN LI, HAOYUN WEI, *Department of Precision Instrument, Tsinghua University, Beijing, China.*

Delay-spectral focusing dual-comb coherent anti-Stokes Raman spectroscopy is proposed and performed, realizing a 40000 spectra/s acquisition rate, which is the fastest Raman spectral detection in the high-wavenumber region up to the present. The spectral resolution (~10 cm^{-1}) and the signal-to-noise ratio (~260) keep stable along the detection process.

This novel spectroscopic technique avoids the invalid scanning time wasted in waiting for the superposition in time of the dual-comb pulses by actively modulating the repetition frequency difference and thus the relative delay. An intracavity electro-optic modulator (EOM), with high modulation amplitude and response frequency, is applied for fast repetition frequency modulation. Delay-spectral focusing method also helps to obtain the high-wavenumber region spectrum, which is difficult to realize for previously-used Fourier transform CARS (FT-CARS) due to the intrinsic coherence of ultrabroadband pulses. This technique shows huge potentials in which both high speed and high-wavenumber region detection are required, such as fast microspectroscopic imaging and flow cytometry.

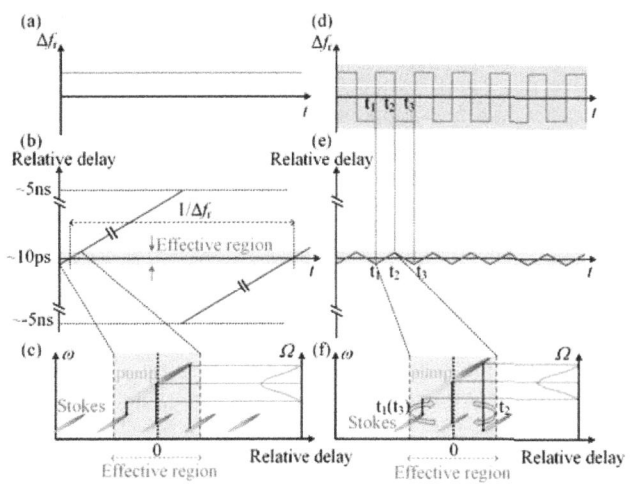

WJ11 5:24 – 5:39

ABSOLUTE FREQUENCY SCALE FOR HIGH-RESOLUTION QUANTUM CASCADE LASER DUAL-COMB SPECTROMETER

<u>MICHELE GIANELLA</u>, *Laboratory for Air Pollution / Environmental Technology, Empa, Dubendorf, Switzerland*; KENICHI KOMAGATA, *Laboratoire Temps-Fréquence, Université de Neuchâtel, Neuchâtel, Switzerland*; SIMON VOGEL, *Laboratory for Air Pollution / Environmental Technology, Empa, Dubendorf, Switzerland*; JÉRÔME FAIST, *Institute for Quantum Electronics, ETH Zurich, Zurich, Switzerland*; THOMAS SÜDMEYER, *Laboratoire Temps-Fréquence, Université de Neuchâtel, Neuchâtel, Switzerland*; LUKAS EMMENEGGER, *Laboratory for Air Pollution / Environmental Technology, Empa, Dubendorf, Switzerland.*

Dual-comb spectroscopy with quantum cascade lasers is an inherently high-speed spectroscopic technique for the mid-infrared spectral region, as the sample is probed simultaneously at all the frequencies of the comb teeth. With typical beat note spacing of few MHz, the temporal resolution is of the order of microseconds and the spectral point spacing is typically 10 GHz. By interleaving several thousand spectra, the spectral point spacing is reduced to less than 10 MHz, suitable for spectroscopy of Doppler-broadened gases, within a measurement time of a few milliseconds. The above-mentioned interleaving is easily achieved by ramping the current of the lasers.

We seek the frequencies of every comb tooth at every instant of the ramp in order to produce a frequency axis for the interleaved spectra. We continuously measure the spectral point spacing of the interrogating comb (i.e., its repetition frequency) by pointing a directional microwave antenna at the laser and picking up the intermode beat, which oscillates at the repetition frequency. We further measure the optical frequency of one comb tooth by beating the comb with a frequency-locked distributed feedback laser, acting as the optical reference frequency. We test the accuracy of the computed frequency axis by measuring the well-known positions of the P and R lines of the ν_1 fundamental band of N_2O near 1300 cm^{-1}. The spectral coverage is 1265-1305 cm^{-1}, and the measurement (scan) duration is varied from 27 to 215 ms. We find that the frequency scale is accurate within 1 MHz.

WK. Mini-symposium: Machine Learning
Wednesday, June 22, 2022 – 1:45 PM
Room: 217 Noyes Laboratory

Chair: Daniel R. Nascimento, The University of Memphis, Memphis, TN, USA

WK01   *INVITED TALK*   1:45 – 2:15

INTERPRETABLE DEEP LEARNING FOR MOLECULES AND MATERIALS

ANDREW WHITE, *Chemical Engineering, University of Rochester, Rochester, NY, USA.*

Deep learning has begun a renaissance in chemistry and materials. We can devise and fit models to predict molecular properties in a few hours and deploy them in a web browser. We can create novel generative models that were previously PhD theses in an afternoon. In my group, we're exploring deep learning in soft materials and molecules. We are focused on two major problems: interpretability and data scarcity. Now that we can make deep learning models to predict any molecular property ad naseum, what can we learn? I will discuss our recent efforts on interpreting deep learning models through symbolic regression and counterfactuals. Data scarcity is a common problem in chemistry: how can we learn new properties without significant expense of experiments? One method is in judicious choose of experiments, which can be done with active learning. Another approach is self-supervised learning and constraining symmetries, which both try to exploit structure in data. I will cover recent progress in these areas. Finally, one consequence of the state of deep learning is that you can just make cool things in chemistry with minimal effort. I'll review a few fun projects, including making molecules by banging on the keyboard, doing math with emojis, and doing molecular dynamics with ImageNet derived potentials.

WK02   2:18 – 2:33

SUPERVISED LEARNING FOR SELECTIVE MULTI-SPECIES QUANTIFICATION FROM NOISY INFRARED SPECTROSCOPY DATA

EMAD AL IBRAHIM, AAMIR FAROOQ, *Clean Combustion Research Center, King Abdullah University of Science and Technology (KAUST), Thuwal, Saudi Arabia.*

A supervised learning approach is implemented to extract information from noisy vibrational spectroscopy data. Our method tackles two of the main problems in any commercial sensing application: sensitivity and selectivity. First, an encoder takes in noisy spectra of complex mixtures and learns reduced representations referred to as embeddings. The learned embeddings are then used in the decoder to filter out noise and unwanted species. Embeddings are also simultaneously used as input to a regression network for the prediction of concentrations and baseline shift. The model was applied for gas sensing using Fourier-Transform Infrared spectroscopy (FTIR) data. We focus on identifying common volatile organic compounds (VOCs) in a realistic scenario. The multitask nature of the model gives better results compared to single task denoising followed by regression and classical techniques like non-negative linear regression. The denoising capability was also compared to other denoising methods like Savitzky-Golay filters (SVG) and wavelet transformations (WT).

WK03   2:36 – 2:51

COMPUTATIONAL OPTIMAL TRANSPORT FOR MOLECULAR SPECTRA

NATHAN A. SEIFERT, *Department of Chemistry, University of New Haven, West Haven, CT, USA*; KIRILL PROZUMENT, MICHAEL J. DAVIS, *Chemical Sciences and Engineering Division, Argonne National Laboratory, Lemont, IL, USA.*

The use of computational optimal transport for the comparison of molecular spectra is presented. Computational optimal transport provides a comparator, the transport distance, which can be used in machine learning applications and for the comparison of theoretical and experimental spectra. Unlike many other comparators, the transport distance encodes line positions and intensities. It can be used to compare two discrete spectra, a discrete spectrum and a continuous spectrum, as well as two continuous spectra. Because the transport distance reflects the movement of density from one spectrum to another, the two spectra being compared do not have to have the same number of lines or features and need not closely match up in frequency space.

Several well-chosen examples will be shown to demonstrate how computational optimal transport is used and its overall utility. In addition, it is used to make quantitative comparisons between theoretical and experimental spectra including a rotational spectrum of 1-hexanal and an electronic absorption spectrum of SO_2.[a]

---

[a]This work was supported by the U. S. Department of Energy, Office of Basic Energy Sciences, Division of Chemical Sciences, Geosciences, and Biosciences operating under Contract Number DE-AC02-06CH11357.

Intermission

WK04   3:33 – 3:48

INVERSE INFRARED SPECTROSCOPY WITH BAYESIAN METHODS

<u>JEZRIELLE R. ANNIS</u>, DANIEL P. TABOR, *Department of Chemistry, Texas A & M University, College Station, TX, USA*.

While calculating theoretical harmonic IR spectra is straightforward for most molecules, nearly all methods for incorporating anharmonic effects add a substantial computational footprint. For large systems such as molecular clusters, the brute force assignment of experimental spectra by computationally iterating over all candidate structures is infeasible at the anharmonic level. However, the developments of machine learning methods have provided an alternative route to evaluating the anharmonicities of new molecules and larger clusters, which is the subject of this talk. In this talk, we demonstrate that Bayesian optimization enables real time spectral evaluation of a range of anharmonic values applied to a calculated Hamiltonian. The Bayesian Optimization algorithm can be applied to explore anharmonic value ranges to minimize the integrated difference between the calculated and theoretical spectra. Further, this same computational framework can be adapted to assign spectra that originate from multiple isomers or cluster sizes.

WK05   3:51 – 4:06

SEQUENCE-TO-SEQUENCE LEARNING FOR MOLECULAR STRUCTURE DERIVATION FROM INFRARED SPECTRA

<u>ETHAN FRENCH</u>, ZHOU LIN, *Department of Chemistry, University of Massachusetts, Amherst, MA, USA*.

Fully identifying unknown molecules via infrared spectroscopy can be a challenging task for even the most experienced researchers. Current data-driven computational methods usually identify unknown spectra by matching them against databases of known spectra. However, this method can be problematic for novel complex molecules given the relative lack of information. Deep learning provides a potential solution to this problem. Sequence-to-sequence learning has had great success in a wide range of areas such as language translation and speech recognition.[a] In this work, an unsupervised sequence-to-sequence model was extended to chemical systems and used to derive complete molecular structures from infrared spectra. The model was trained on the infrared spectra of small organic molecules containing C, H, O, N, and F atoms. These molecules were represented using SELFIES, an improved version of the SMILES string molecular fingerprint descriptor.[b] Our model is able to achieve state-of-the-art results in successfully identifying a wide variety of molecules from their infrared spectra.

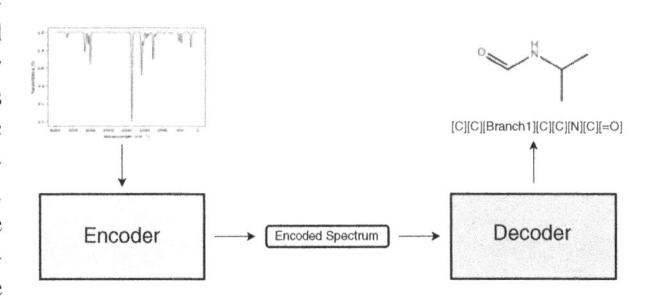

---

[a] Ilya Sutskever, Oriol Vinyals, Quoc V. Le, "Sequence to Sequence Learning with Neural Networks", *NeurIPS*, 2014, **27**.
[b] Mario Krenn, Florian Häse, AkshatKumar Nigam, Pascal Friederich, and Alan Aspuru-Guzik, "Self-referencing embedded strings (SELFIES): A 100% robust molecular string representation", *Mach. Learn.: Sci. Technol.* 2020, **1**, 045024

WK06 4:09 – 4:24
GAS-PHASE INFRARED SPECTRA ANALYSIS VIA DEEP NEURAL NETWORKS

ABIGAIL A ENDERS, NICOLE NORTH, HEATHER C. ALLEN, *Department of Chemistry and Biochemistry, The Ohio State University, Columbus, OH, USA.*

Infrared spectroscopy provides unique molecular vibrational information that is molecule and environment specific. Spectral responses, as images rather than array-based data, were used to train a deep neural network to develop analytical methods capable of large-scale information processing. We label spectra based on the present and absent functional groups, but the model must determine the frequencies, peak shape, and variability of each molecular response to identify functional groups. The resultant machine learning models significantly reduce the time required for traditional infrared spectral analysis and the functional group assignments is found to be more accurate than expert chemists. Application of machine learning methods to spectroscopic data is made approachable by a straightforward model system that is generalizable, broad, and well-performing on thousands of gas-phase infrared spectra from the NIST spectral database. Future improvement will involve more specific and applied models, such as the investigation of field samples for environmental contaminants or component identification, with increased solvent complexity to continue developing a broad range of models. To the best of our knowledge, this is the first presentation of a generalizable machine learning model for infrared analysis because it is capable of analyzing a diverse spectral database.

WK07 4:27 – 4:42
COMPARISON OF EXPERIMENTAL AND SIMULATED RAMAN SPECTRA THROUGH REVERSE SELF MODELING CURVE RESOLUTION FOR REGRESSION-BASED MACHINE LEARNING

NICOLE NORTH, ABIGAIL A ENDERS, HEATHER C. ALLEN, *Department of Chemistry and Biochemistry, The Ohio State University, Columbus, OH, USA.*

Raman spectroscopy utilizes inelastic scattering to provide information about the vibrational environment of bonds within molecules. The intensity of vibrations can be cautiously used to determine relative concentrations of compounds. Machine learning methods are used to find patterns within datasets and commonly work better with large datasets, such as those from Raman spectral acquisitions; however, the generation of these large datasets is time consuming and the data manipulation is cumbersome. This work seeks to circumvent these issues by determining if experimental data can be fortified or substituted with simulated data. To initiate this process, Raman spectra were collected on a variety of different molecules in solutions made of 2-3 chemical species. These spectra were then used to simulate data with the same concentrations using Reverse Self Modeling Curve Resolution (RSMCR). The experimental and the RSMCR simulated data were used to train regression-type machine learning models. Models were then validated using previously withheld experimental Raman spectral data to determine how well each dataset worked as a generalizable basis for the regression model. We found that the RSMCR simulated data closely represents the experimental Raman spectral data with an approximate 2% error in the relative intensity.

WL. Conformers and isomers

Wednesday, June 22, 2022 – 1:45 PM

Room: 1024 Chemistry Annex

Chair: Isabelle Kleiner, CNRS, UPEC et Université de Paris, Créteil, France

---

WL01   1:45 – 2:00

FOURIER TRANSFORM MICROWAVE SPECTRA OF 1-PENTANETHIOL-d

<u>NOBUHIKO KUZE</u>, YOSHIYUKI KAWASHIMA, *Department of Materials and Life Sciences, Sophia University, Tokyo, Japan.*

We have been observing the rotational spectra of the 1-pentanethiol (1-C$_5$SH; C(5)H$_3$C(4)H$_2$-C(3)H$_2$C(2)H$_2$C(1)H$_2$SH) by Fourier transform microwave (FTMW) spectroscopy. So far, eight conformers of the normal species for 1-C$_5$SH have been identified by FTMW spectroscopy and the quantum chemical calculations[a]. They are *TTTg*, *TTTt*, *TTGg*, *TTGg'*, *TGTg*, *TGTg'*, *GTTg*, and *GTTg'*. The nomenclature of the conformer such as *TTGg'* is based on the conformation of the molecular skeleton around the C(4)-C(3), C(3)-C(2), C(2)-C(1), and C(1)-S axis, respectively. This means that *TTGg'* represents trans (*T*), trans (*T*), clockwise gauche (*G*) and anti-clockwise gauche (*g'*) conformers.

In this work, we observed the isotopologues the 1-pentanethiol such as the deuterated species in the thiol group, 1-C$_5$SD. The rotational spectral lines of the seven conformers in 1-C$_5$SD, except for *TTTt*, were assigned as in 1-C$_5$SH. In the *TTTg* conformer of 1-C$_5$SH, characteristic splittings were observed in the rotational spectral lines of the *c*-type transitions. They are due to the tunneling splitting by the torsional motion of the SH group. Therefore, we focused on the line spllitings in the *c*-type transition of the *TTTg* conformer of 1-C$_5$SD and compared our results with data from 1-C$_5$SH and related compounds, 1-butanethiol[b], 1-propanethiol and 1-ethanethiol.

---

[a] K. Suzuki, N. Kuze and Y. Kawashima, ISMS, WI05 (2019).

[b] Y. Kawashima, Y. Tanaka, T. Uzuyama, and E. Hirota. *J. Phys. Chem. A*, 125, 1166-1183 (2021).

WL02   2:03 – 2:18

MICROWAVE SPECTRUM OF ACETIC DIFLUOROACETIC ANHYDRIDE

<u>KAITLYN BELMONT</u>, NATHAN LOVE, KENNETH R. LEOPOLD, *Chemistry Department, University of Minnesota, Minneapolis, MN, USA.*

The rotational spectrum of acetic difluoroacetic anhydride, (CH$_3$COOCOCHF$_2$) was recorded by microwave spectroscopy and the A and E internal rotor states of the methyl group were analyzed. The A state was easily assigned using the assignment/fitting program DAPPERS, and a combined fit for the A and E state transitions was performed using XIAM. The fitted internal rotation barrier of the methyl group was determined to be 252.646(19) cm^{-1}. Using the M06-2X/6-311++G(d,p) level of theory, one non-planar cis conformer and two non-planar trans conformers of the anhydride were predicted. Agreement between theoretical and experimental rotational constants indicate that the non-planar trans conformer with the difluoromethyl alpha hydrogen participating in a hydrogen bond with a C=O oxygen is the form observed. The differences in the hydrogen bonding ability of the alpha hydrogens in the CH$_3$ and CHF$_2$ groups are a result of the differences in electron density.

WL03   2:21 – 2:36

FLUORINATION AND DEOXYGENATION AS CHEMICAL TOOLS TO STUDY THE CONFORMATIONAL PREFERENCES OF HEXOPYRANOSES: A JOURNEY FROM GAS PHASE TO SOLUTION

ELENA R. ALONSO, ARAN INSAUSTI, CAMILLA CALABRESE, FRANCISCO J. BASTERRETXEA, *Departamento de Química Física, Universidad del País Vasco (UPV-EHU), Bilbao, Spain*; FRANCISCO CORZANA, *CISQ, Chemistry Department, University of La Rioja, Logroño, Spain*; OMAR BOUTUREIRA, *Department of Analytical and Organic Chemistry, Universidad Rovira i Virgili, Tarragona, Spain*; EMILIO J. COCINERO, *Departamento de Química Física, Universidad del País Vasco (UPV-EHU), Bilbao, Spain.*

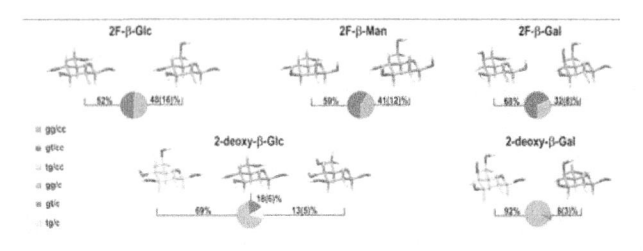

The 3D-arrangement of carbohydrates and, particularly, the orientation of their hydroxymethyl groups are structural features crucial for their biological activities. In this work, we investigate the influence of water on the conformational preferences of model hexopyranoses by performing a comprehensive analysis in the gas phase via microwave spectroscopy[a,b] of different fluorinated and deoxygenated carbohydrate analogues and comparing the results with those obtained in solution using a combination of NMR data and molecular dynamics simulations. The gg conformation is stabilized in the gas phase by intra molecular HBs that lock this conformation when oriented clockwise. However, and contrary to previously reported data, the conformation of the hydroxymethyl group in D-gluco and D-mannopyranose series follows a similar tendency in the gas phase and in solution, indicating the importance of stereo electronic and minimizing the importance of competing water molecules against stabilizing intra molecular HBs.

[a] C. Calabrese, I. Uriarte, A. Insausti, M. Vallejo-Lopez, F. J. Basterretxea, S. A. Cochrane, B. G. Davis, F. Corzana and E. J. Cocinero *ACS Cent. Sci.*, **6**, 293-303, 2020.
[b] E. J. Cocinero, A. Lesarri, P. Ecija, F. J. Basterretxea, J.-U. Grabow, J. A. Fernandez, F. Castaño *Angew. Chem. Int. Ed.*, **51**, 3119, 2012.

WL04   2:39 – 2:54

UNVEILING THE EIGHT FORMS OF CAFFEIC ACID

GABRIELA JUÁREZ[a], MIGUEL SANZ-NOVO[b], ELENA R. ALONSO, IKER LEÓN, SANTIAGO MATA, JOSÉ L. ALONSO, *Grupo de Espectroscopia Molecular, Lab. de Espectroscopia y Bioespectroscopia, Unidad Asociada CSIC, Universidad de Valladolid, Valladolid, Spain.*

Herein we report a complete conformational analysis of caffeic acid, a relevant polyphenol[1], and the main hydroxycinnamic acid found in humans' diet using laser ablation chirped-pulse Fourier transform microwave (LA-CP-FTMW) spectroscopy. The entire conformational space consisting of eight distinct rotameric species has been fully deciphered based on a thorough inquiry of the trend of the rotational constants supported by high-level theoretical computations.

[1] A. M. Boudet, 2007, Phytochemistry, 68, 22-24, 2722-2735

[a] G.J.L. acknowledges funding from the Spanish "Ministerio de Ciencia, Innovación y Universidades" under predoctoral FPI Grant (BES-2017-082173). M.S.N.
[b] M.S.N. acknowledges funding from the Spanish "Ministerio de Ciencia, Innovacion y Universidades" under predoctoral FPU Grant (FPU17/02987).

WL05   2:57 – 3:12

THE MICROWAVE SPECTRUM OF PIPERONAL: DESIGNING AND TESTING A NEW HEATED NOZZLE ASSEMBLY

BRAYDEN CARTY, *Department of Natural Sciences, University of Virginia's College at Wise, Wise, VA, USA*; GALEN SEDO, *Department of Natural Sciences, University of Virginia's College at Wise, Wise, VA, USA*; AMANDA DUERDEN, JOSHUA E. ISERT, NICOLE MOON, G. S. GRUBBS II, *Department of Chemistry, Missouri University of Science and Technology, Rolla, MO, USA.*

A modular heated nozzle assembly with an open source external temperature control unit was designed for use in a new broadband microwave spectrometer under construction at Missouri University of Science and Technology. The first version of the heated source was tested using MS&T's existing cp-FTMW. As an initial proof of concept, the microwave spectrum of molecular piperonal was collected in the 5.5 to 18.75 GHz region. The parent isotopologues of two conformers, s-cis- and s-trans-piperonal, were observed and an analysis of the ^{13}C substituted species are ongoing.

WL06   3:15 – 3:30

THE JET-COOLED ROTATIONAL SPECTRUM OF N,N'-BIS(HYDROXYMETHYL)UREA AND ITS PHOTO-FRAGMENTED SPECIES

<u>LUCIE KOLESNIKOVÁ</u>, *Department of Analytical Chemistry, University of Chemistry and Technology, Prague, Prague, Czech Republic*; SANTIAGO MATA, IKER LEÓN, ELENA R. ALONSO, JOSÉ L. ALONSO, *Grupo de Espectroscopia Molecular, Lab. de Espectroscopia y Bioespectroscopia, Unidad Asociada CSIC, Universidad de Valladolid, Valladolid, Spain.*

A novel approach based on laser ablation of solid organic precursors has been recently proposed for the laboratory *in situ* generations of new chemical species.[a] The chemical compounds generated in the laser ablation process are cooled in a supersonic expansion and probed by eyes of high-resolution microwave spectroscopy. This "micro-laboratory" enhances the scope of *in situ* experiments using precursors not typically accessible to traditional techniques such as electric discharge and pyrolysis. In this contribution, N,N'-Bis(hydroxymethyl)urea is chosen as a precursor. It contains a C=O functional group and two pairs of –NH and –OH groups, very appealing from the astrochemical point of view. Guided by the theoretical predictions, we assigned the precursor's rotational spectrum (four conformers), and then we focused on tuning up our experiment to achieve the experimental conditions that maximize the photo-fragmentation. A detailed analysis of the spectrum revealed the generation of hydroxymethylurea and the simultaneous formation of other species in the jet, showing that the laser ablation of solid organic precursors constitutes an innovative tool in generating new chemical species.

Acknowledgments: The authors thank the financial fundings from the Czech Science Foundation (GACR, grant 19-25116Y), Ministerio de Ciencia e Innovación (grant PID2019-111396GB-I00), Junta de Castilla y León (grants VA244P20), and European Research Council under the European Union's Seventh Framework Programme ERC-2013-SyG, Grant Agreement n. 610256 NANOCOSMOS.

---

[a]L. Kolesniková, I. León, E. R. Alonso, S. Mata, and J. L. Alonso, *Angew. Chem. Int. Ed.* 2021, 60, 24461.

Intermission

WL07   4:12 – 4:27

ROTAMERS OF METHANEDIOL: COMPOSITE AB INITIO PREDICTIONS OF FUNDAMENTAL FREQUENCIES AND ROVIBRATIONAL CONSTANTS

<u>PETER R. FRANKE</u>, *Department of Chemistry, University of Florida, Gainesville, FL, USA*; JOHN F. STANTON, *Quantum Theory Project, University of Florida, Gainesville, FL, USA.*

The class of geminal diols comprises molecules known to be intermediates in atmospheric ozonolysis and the aerosol cycle. Owing to their thermodynamic propensity to decompose into water and an aldehyde/ketone, geminal diols have proved difficult to isolate and characterize. Recently, experimental evidence was published for the existence of methanediol, the simplest member of this class, in ices of methanol and oxygen following electron bombardment.[a] To aid in future spectroscopic investigations of methanediol in the gas phase, we report fundamental frequencies and rovibrational constants for the two rotamers of methanediol using *ab initio* composite methods along with vibrational perturbation theory. Sensitivity of the predictions to the level of theory and the treatment of anharmonic resonances are carefully assessed. The OH stretching harmonic frequencies of both rotamers are particularly sensitive to the level of theory. The CH stretches of the C_s rotamer are sensitive to the treatment of anharmonic resonances with VPT2-based effective Hamiltonian models. Equilibrium bond distances and harmonic frequencies are converged to within 0.0001 Å and 1 cm^{-1}, respectively. The effect of tunneling on the rotational constants is investigated with a 2D variational calculation, based on a relaxed hydroxyl torsional potential energy surface. Tunneling is found to be negligible in the lower energy C_2 rotamer but should modify the rotational constants of the C_s rotamer on the order of MHz, giving rise to rotational line splittings of the same order. The rovibrational constants of the C_s rotamer are dominated by torsional effects, and here we see evidence for the breakdown of vibrational perturbation theory.

---

[a]Zhu, C.; Kleimeier, N. F.; Turner, A. M.; Singh, S. K.; Fortenberry, R. C.; Kaiser, R. I. *Proc. Natl. Acad. Sci. U. S. A.* 2022, 119, e2111938119.

WL08   4:30–4:45

CONFORMATIONAL DIVERSITY OF NON-AROMATIC HETEROCYCLIC MOLECULAR COMPOUNDS AS STUDIED BY MEANS OF MATRIX ISOLATION INFRARED SPECTROSCOPY

JOANNA STOCKA, *Institute of Chemical Physics at Faculty of Physics, Vilnius University, Vilnius, Vilnius, Lithuania*; RASA PLATAKYTE, JUSTINAS CEPONKUS, *Physics, Vilnius University, Vilnius, Lithuania*; JOGILE MACYTE, *Institute of Chemical Physics at Faculty of Physics, Vilnius University, Vilnius, Vilnius, Lithuania*; DANIEL VINCENT HICKMAN, THEODORE JACOB CARRIGAN-BRODA, *Department of Chemistry and Biochemistry, College of Charleston, Charleston, SC, USA*; PAWEL RODZIEWICZ, *Faculty of Natural Sciences, Jan Kochanowski university of Kielce, Kielce, Poland*; GAMIL A GUIRGIS, *Department of Chemistry and Biochemistry, College of Charleston, Charleston, SC, USA*; VALDAS SABLINSKAS, *Institute of Chemical Physics at Faculty of Physics, Vilnius University, Vilnius, Vilnius, Lithuania*.

Non-aromatic heterocyclic molecular compounds due to their π electron orbitals have potential to be used in the surface science as coatings with good surface adhesion properties. Such properties are even more pronounced when silicon atom is present in the ring. It is due to formation of stable covalent bonding between the coating and an inorganic substrate. The objective of this study is to elucidate conformational diversity of newly synthesized five and six membered non-aromatic cyclic compounds, namely 1-chloromethyl-1-fluorosilacyclohexane, 1-chloro-1-chloromethylsilacyclohexane, 1-chloromethyl-1-fluorosilacyclopentane and 1-chlorosilacyclopentane. In order to obtain structural parameters and to perform conformational analysis of such yet unknown molecules detailed computational and experimental studies were performed. The samples were investigated by means conventional IR and Raman spectroscopy as well as matrix isolation FTIR spectroscopy, solid nitrogen acting as matrix medium. Calculations were performed using ORCA 4.1.1 software package. Geometry of different conformers, their stability, normal vibrations and the potential barriers for the conformational interconversions were calculated using density functional theory (DFT) and utilizing augmented B3LYP hybrid functional and Dunning's augmented double zeta correlation consistent basis sets. Additionally, the Carr-Parinello Molecular Dynamics was used to mimic theoretically the matrix isolation conditions and to describe the molecular behavior in the systems with finite temperature. It was found that conformational equilibrium in the non-aromatic heterocyclic molecular compounds under study strongly depends on type of radical attached to the ring.

WL09   4:48–5:03

STRUCTURAL ELUCIDATION OF IONS USING CHEMICAL REACTIONS

UGO JACOVELLA, *Institut des Sciences Moléculaires d'Orsay, Université Paris Saclay, CNRS, Orsay, France*; CORENTIN ROSSI, CLAIRE ROMANZIN, CHRISTIAN ALCARAZ, ROLAND THISSEN, *Institut de Chimie Physique, Université Paris Saclay, CNRS, Orsay, France*.

A general method is proposed to disentangle isomeric structures by combining mass spectrometry, tunable synchrotron light source, and quantum-chemistry calculations. Reactive chemical monitoring technique is used and consists in tracking reactivity changes as a function of photoionization energy *i.e.*, internal energy related to isomerization barriers. The capability of this technique will be illustrated with charge transfer reactions of $C_6H_4^+$ isomers with allene and propyne.[a] The methodology can be generalized using neutral reaction partners with ionization energies forming a chemical ruler to elucidate the ionic structure. It can also serve as a structural probe as a function of photoionization energy, unveiling isomerization routes.

[a] Jacovella *et al.* Structural elucidation of $C_6H_4^+$· using chemical reaction monitoring: Charge transfer versus bond forming reactions, ChemPhysChem (2021), doi: 10.1002/cphc.202100871
Article picked to be the cover feature

WL10 5:06 – 5:21

VISUALIZING ELECTRON DYNAMICS FOR A PHOTOISOMERIZATION REACTION

LAUREN BAUERLE, *JILA and the Department of Chemistry, Universityy of Colorado, Boulder, CO, USA*; AGNIESZKA JARON, *JILA and Department of Physics, University of Colorado, Boulder, CO, USA*.

Using time-dependent density functional theory, we probe the electron dynamics involved in the photo-chemical isomerization of 1,3-cyclohexadiene to 1,3,5-hexatriene by analyzing changes to the harmonic spectra. The reaction is often used as an analog for the photo-induced reaction of provitamin D_3 to vitamin D_3 in the skin, as that reaction proceeds through a similar scheme.

Calculations are performed for 1,3-cyclohexadiene and 1,3,5-hexatriene as well as two intermediate conformers. There are distinct changes in the harmonic spectra that could be used to mark reaction progress. As expected, the breaking of the molecular symmetry leads to peaks outside of the expected odd harmonics.

In addition to the harmonic spectra, we discuss the dynamical changes to the electron density and electron localization function (ELF). From these measures of electron probability, we can see ionization and recombination occur throughout the pulse, from each of the isomers.

WL11 5:24 – 5:39

STRUCTURE AND SPECTRA OF A COMPLEX BIOCHROMOPHORE - DEPROTONATED BILIVERDIN IX

WYATT ZAGOREC-MARKS, *JILA and Department of Chemistry, University of Colorado, Boulder, CO, USA*; LEAH G DODSON, *JILA and NIST, University of Colorado, Boulder, CO, USA*; ERIK K. SCHNEIDER, PATRICK WEIS, MANFRED M KAPPES, *Institute of Physical Chemistry, Karlsruhe Institute of Technology, Karlsruhe, Germany*; J. MATHIAS WEBER, *JILA and Department of Chemistry, University of Colorado, Boulder, CO, USA*.

Biliverdin (BV) is an attractive candidate for use in fluorescence microscopy applications, because it can be genetically encoded (and engineered) as a red fluorescent biomarker by binding to cysteine and including it in fluorescent proteins. An important step towards rational design of a biomarker with specific desired properties is to study the intrinsic properties of the molecule, i.e., in the absence of any chemical environment. In the present work, we focus on the singly and doubly deprotonated forms of the position isomer biliverdin IX (see Figure). The structural flexibility of this molecule makes structural identification of its conformation in vacuo rather challenging. Ion mobility and cryogenic infrared spectroscopy allow us to obtain structural information. The electronic spectrum depends strongly on the deprotonation state of the molecule. We interpret the data with density functional theory calculations.

WM. Non-covalent interactions

Wednesday, June 22, 2022 – 1:45 PM

Room: 124 Burrill Hall

Chair: Steven Shipman, New College of Florida, Sarasota, FL, USA

WM01   1:45 – 2:00

HELIUM NANODROPLET ISOLATION SPECTROSCOPY OF METHANOL AND METHANOL-WATER CLUSTERS IN THE SYMMETRIC METHYL STRETCHING BAND

MAAMEYAA ASIAMAH, PAUL RASTON, *Chemistry and Biochemistry, James Madison University, Harrisonburg, VA, USA.*

The mid-infrared spectra of helium solvated methanol and methanol-water clusters have been investigated in the symmetric CD_3 stretching band of CD_3OH and CD_3OD. We find that the position of this band provides a useful signature of the general type of hydrogen-bonded cluster it is associated with. Our results are consistent with those previously reported in the OH stretching region [1], in that methanol clusters from the trimer to the pentamer are cyclic, and that mixed clusters with one water molecule (and at least two methanol molecules) are also cyclic. We additionally provide evidence that the methanol trimer adopts a chair-like structure (as opposed to bowl-like), that mixed clusters with a larger number of water molecules are also cyclic, and that branched methanol clusters contribute to the depletion signal in larger methanol clusters. We performed DFT calculations which support these interpretations.

[1] Sulaiman, M. I., Yang, S., Ellis, A. M., J. Phys. Chem. A, 2017, 121, 771-776.

WM02   2:03 – 2:18

CHARACTERISATION OF THE STRUCTURE OF THE HYDROGEN-BONDED COMPLEX, THIAZOLE...$(H_2O)_2$, BY FOURIER-TRANSFORM MICROWAVE SPECTROSCOPY

CHARLOTTE NICOLE CUMMINGS, *School of Chemistry, Newcastle University, Newcastle-upon-Tyne, United Kingdom*; EVA GOUGOULA, *Photon Science - Spectroscopy of Molecular Processes, Deutsches Elektronen-Synchrotron DESY, Hamburg, Germany*; YUAGO XU, GANG FENG, *School of Chemistry and Chemical Engineering, Chongqing University, Chongqing, China*; NICK WALKER, *School of Natural and Environmental Sciences, Newcastle University, Newcastle-upon-Tyne, UK.*

The microsolvation of aromatic and heteroaromatic rings has been the subject of many microwave spectroscopy studies in recent years. In 2020, Li et al. reported the geometry of the monohydrate complex of thiazole.[a] Since thiazole contains multiple sites at which intermolecular bonds can form, a complex of thiazole with two water molecules was subsequently searched for. The rotational spectrum of thiazole...$(H_2O)_2$ was recorded over the frequency range 6.5-18.5 GHz while analysing a gaseous sample containing thiazole, water and argon by Chirped-Pulse, Fourier-Transform Microwave (CP-FTMW) spectroscopy at Newcastle University and by COBRA (coaxially oriented beam-resonator arrangement)-FTMW spectroscopy at Chongqing University. Aided by density functional theory (DFT) calculations, the spectrum of thiazole...$(H_2O)_2$ was assigned and rotational constants (A_0, B_0 and C_0), centrifugal distortion constants (D_J, D_{JK}, d_1 and d_2) and nuclear quadrupole coupling constants (χ_{aa} and χ_{bb-cc}) of nitrogen atoms were determined. The microwave spectra of four isotopologues of thiazole...$(H_2O)_2$ have been assigned allowing the determination of structural parameters which include intermolecular bond lengths and angles.

---

[a] W. Li, J. Chen, Y. Xu, T. Lu, Q. Gou and G. Feng, *Spectrochimica Acta - Part A: Molecular and Biomolecular Spectroscopy*, 2020, **242**, 118720

WM03 2:21 – 2:36

MULTIPLE WATER CONFIGURATIONS IN FENCHONE⋯(H$_2$O)$_{1-6}$ HYDRATES REVEALED BY ROTATIONAL SPECTROSCOPY

ECATERINA BUREVSCHI, *Department of Chemistry, King's College London, London, United Kingdom*; MHAMAD CHRAYTEH, *UMR 8523 - PhLAM - Physique des Lasers Atomes et Molécules, University of Lille, CNRS, F-59000 Lille, France*; DONATELLA LORU, *Department of Chemistry, King's College London, London, United Kingdom*; PASCAL DRÉAN, *UMR 8523 - PhLAM - Physique des Lasers Atomes et Molécules, University of Lille, CNRS, F-59000 Lille, France*; M. EUGENIA SANZ, *Department of Chemistry, King's College London, London, United Kingdom*.

Fenchone is a bicyclic monoterpenoid that is released to the atmosphere by natural and anthropogenic sources, where it interacts with other atmospheric molecules such as water. Here we present the investigation of the hydrates of fenchone C$_{10}$H$_{16}$O⋯(H$_2$O)$_n$ (n = 1-6) by microwave spectroscopy, in the frequency range 2 to 20 GHz, and computational calculations[1]. Several isomers of each hydrated complex have been observed and their rotational and centrifugal distortion constants determined. For fenchone⋯(H$_2$O)$_{1-4}$ complexes, observation of the ^{18}O isotopologues allowed us to determine the location of the oxygen atoms of water and the configuration of water molecules around fenchone. Water binds to fenchone through O–H⋯O and C–H⋯O hydrogen bonds. In the mono-, di- and trihydrates water molecules arrange in open chains around fenchone, while for the higher order hydrates water molecules adopt distorted tetramer, pentamer and hexamer configurations. The various configurations as well as the relevant intermolecular interactions, and their modelling by computational methods, will be discussed.

[1] M. Chrayteh, E. Burevschi, D. Loru, T. R. Huet, P. Dréan, M. E. Sanz, *PCCP*, 23, 20686 (2021).

WM04 2:39 – 2:54

TOWARDS UNDERSTANDING THE SOLVENT-ROLE IN THE CATALYSIS OF THE BIOMASS-MOLECULE 6-AMYL-α-PYRONE USING MICROWAVE SPECTROSCOPY

HIMANSHI SINGH, *FS-SMP, Deutsches Elektronen-Synchrotron (DESY), Hamburg, Germany*; MARIYAM FATIMA, *I. Physikalisches Institut, Universität zu Köln, Köln, Germany*; MD. ALI HAIDER, *Department of Chemical Engineering, Indian Institute of Technology Delhi, Delhi, Delhi, India*; MELANIE SCHNELL, *FS-SMP, Deutsches Elektronen-Synchrotron (DESY), Hamburg, Germany*.

6-amyl-α-pyrone (6PP) is a biomass molecule that is widely used in the synthesis of industrial and pharmaceutical products. 6PP offers a green and sustainable route in the preparation of industrial chemicals such as linear ketones and hydrocarbon fuels. It is catalytically hydrogenated to produce δ-decalactone (DDL). This reaction, carried out in different solvents under similar conditions, is reported to produce significant variation in DDL yield varying from 6% to 79%.[1] Such dramatic variations in yield during the reaction can be attributed to numerous reasons, such as the dielectric constant of solvents, or different kinds of solute-solvent interactions during the reaction.
In this work, we study the structure of 6PP and its solute-solvent interactions using chirped-pulse Fourier transform microwave (CP-FTMW) spectroscopy. This technique coupled with supersonic expansion reveals accurate structures of molecules and weakly bound complexes isolated in the gas phase. 6PP is highly flexible due to the presence of the pentyl chain. We first investigate the conformational flexibility in 6PP and then its complexes to understand the effect of the solvent molecule on the structure of 6PP. We choose two solvents, ethanol and cyclohexane one giving the best yield and the other one giving moderate results to study how the inter-molecular interactions affect the reaction yield. The observed structural changes in 6PP upon complexation, as well as the preferred intra- and intermolecular interactions, will be discussed.

[1] M. I. Alam, T. S. Khan, M. A. Haider, *ACS Sustainable Chemistry and Engineering* **2019**, *7*, *3*, 2894-2898.

WM05 2:57 – 3:12
A NOVEL STRUCTURE FOR THE GAS PHASE HETERODIMER FORMED BETWEEN (Z)-1-CHLORO-3,3,3-TRIFLUOROPROPENE AND ACETYLENE

SEOHYUN (CECE) HONG, MARK D. MARSHALL, HELEN O. LEUNG, *Chemistry Department, Amherst College, Amherst, MA, USA.*

Our characterization of the structures of gas phase heterodimers formed between haloethylenes and the three protic acids, hydrogen fluoride, hydrogen chloride, and acetylene, provided a wealth of information regarding intermolecular forces and the relative effects of electrostatic, dispersion and steric forces. By and large all of these species shared the common structural feature of a hydrogen bond formed between the protic acid donor and a halogen acceptor on the ethylene. The extension of the carbon chain by one atom via the addition of a trifluoromethyl group provides a wider variety of possible interactions and binding sites. For the heterodimer formed between (Z)-1-chloro-3,3,3-trifluoropropene and acetylene, a novel structure with no hydrogen bond but rather an interaction between the acetylenic triple bond and the two hydrogen atoms of the propene is obtained from the analysis of the microwave rotational spectra of the ^{35}Cl and ^{37}Cl isotopologues of the complex.

WM06 3:15 – 3:30
AN INTERNAL AFFAIR: THE INFLUENCE OF INTRAMOLECULAR HYDROGEN BONDING ON THE STRUCTURE OF METAL-ION-PEPTIDE COMPLEXES

KATHARINA A. E. MEYER, *Department of Chemistry, University of Wisconsin-Madison, Madison, WI, USA;* KATHLEEN ANN NICKSON, ETIENNE GARAND, *Department of Chemistry, University of Wisconsin–Madison, Madison, WI, USA.*

Understanding the interplay of the various non-covalent interactions present in biomolecular systems is important as these are the driving forces of the structure of these systems. In the condensed phase, however, it is difficult to disentangle the individual contributions of these interactions due to the plethora of structures present, which ultimately limits any systematic studies. One popular way of bypassing this is to study relevant model complexes in the gas phase where these can be mass-isolated and spectroscopically interrogated. In this way, one can obtain an in-depth understanding of the competing non-covalent interactions on a molecular level and correlate structural changes systematically, for example by increasing the system size or changing interaction partners. Due to their structural flexibility, popular model systems for such studies are small amino acids or peptides and their complexes with water or metal ions. In this contribution, we will study the complexes of three alkali metal ions (Li$^+$, Na$^+$, K$^+$) with di- and tripeptides with cryogenic ion vibrational spectroscopy illustrating how the interaction strength changes with the size of the cation and peptide chain length by analyzing their OH, NH, and C=O stretching as well as NH bending vibrations. Of particular interest is the interplay of metal ion peptide interaction with internal NH$\cdots$NH$_2$ hydrogen bonding of the neutral peptide itself, whose strength is modulated by the metal cation interaction.

Intermission

WM07 4:12 – 4:27
MOLECULAR RECOGNITION IN OLFACTION: INTERACTIONS OF THE ODORANT CARVONE WITH ETHANOL

S. INDIRA MURUGACHANDRAN, DONATELLA LORU, ISABEL PEÑA, M. EUGENIA SANZ, *Department of Chemistry, King's College London, London, United Kingdom.*

Non-covalent interactions are vitally important for molecular recognition in many biological and chemical processes. Understanding the interplay between intra- and intermolecular forces is crucial for advancing our knowledge on these events and how they are influenced by slight changes. Here we report the interactions of the common odorant carvone with ethanol, a mimic to the amino acid side chain serine. It has been studied through combination of chirped-pulse Fourier transform microwave spectroscopy and computational calculations, including density functional theory and ab initio methods. Seven carvone-ethanol complexes have been observed showing an O$\cdots$H-O primary bond between the carbonyl group of carvone, acting as a hydrogen bond acceptor, and the hydroxyl group of ethanol as the hydrogen bond donor. Secondary C-H$\cdots$O dispersion interactions anchoring ethanol to carvone are also established. Changes in the conformational preferences of the monomers upon complexation will be discussed.

WM08   4:30 – 4:45

EXAMINING INTERMOLECULAR INTERACTIONS BETWEEN HYDROCARBONS AND WATER: A BROADBAND ROTATIONAL SPECTROSCOPIC STUDY OF THE α-PINENE – WATER COMPLEX

ARSH SINGH HAZRAH, MOHAMAD H. AL-JABIRI, WOLFGANG JÄGER, *Department of Chemistry, University of Alberta, Edmonton, AB, Canada.*

Released into the atmosphere by vegetation, biogenic volatile organic compounds (VOCs) contribute substantially to yearly carbon emission, amounting to approximately 1150 Tg of carbon per year.[1] α-pinene, a bicyclic monoterpene, is not only one of the most abundant biogenic VOCs released, but also plays a critical role in the generation of secondary organic aerosol. Once released, α-pinene can be photo-oxidized by atmospheric species such as ozone or various radical species.[2] Water is relatively abundant in the atmosphere and has therefore a high probability of a close contact with α-pinene. Complexation with water may affect the reactivity with species such as ozone, thus altering product yield, and ultimately the rate of aerosol formation. It is difficult to predict a preferred structure for the α-pinene-water cluster using chemical intuition alone, and a study of its structure and energetics can provide insights into intermolecular interactions between weakly-polar hydrocarbons and hydrogen bonding capable species, as well as data relevant to atmospheric processes. To experimentally identify α-pinene-water clusters we used a chirped pulse Fourier transform microwave spectrometer in the 2-6 GHz range[3] and the experiments were supplemented with electronic structure calculations. Two potential conformers were theoretically identified, both of which involve the formation of an O-H — π bond between water and α-pinene. However, only the higher energy conformer could be assigned experimentally. From various one-dimensional energy scans along internal rotation coordinates, the absence of the lower energy conformer is most likely due to a large amplitude O-H wagging motion, which leads to a partial dipole moment cancellation. The O-H — π interaction in both complexes was then visualized and quantified using non-covalent interactions[4] and natural bond orbital analyses[5], respectively.

1. A. Guenther, C. N. Hewitt, D. Erickson, R. Fall, C. Geron, T. Graedel, P. Harley, L. Klinger, M. Lerdau and W. A. McKay, J. Geophys. Res. Atmos., 1995, 100, 8873–8892.; 2. J. H. Seinfeld and J. F. Pankow, Annu. Rev. Phys. Chem., 2003, 54, 121–140.; 3. N. A. Seifert, J. Thomas, W. Jäger and Y. Xu, Phys. Chem. Chem. Phys., 2018, 20, 27630–27637.; 4. J. Contreras-García, E. R. Johnson, S. Keinan, R. Chaudret, J.-P. Piquemal, D. N. Beratan and W. Yang, J. Chem. Theory Comput., 2011, 7, 625–632.; 5. E. D. Glendening, C. R. Landis and F. Weinhold, J. Comput. Chem., 2013, 34, 1429–1437.

WM09   4:48 – 5:03

THE 3-METHYLCATECHOL-$(H_2O)_{N=1-4}$ COMPLEXES: STUDYING MICROSOLVATION USING BROADBAND ROTATIONAL SPECTROSCOPY

ARSH SINGH HAZRAH, *Department of Chemistry, University of Alberta, Edmonton, AB, Canada*; ARAN INSAUSTI, *Departamento de Química Física, Universidad del País Vasco (UPV-EHU), Bilbao, Spain*; MOHAMAD H. AL-JABIRI, JIARUI MA, YUNJIE XU, WOLFGANG JÄGER, *Department of Chemistry, University of Alberta, Edmonton, AB, Canada.*

Biomass burning greatly influences the Earth-cloud-climate system by releasing complex mixtures of organic and inorganic species into the atmosphere.[1] During biomass burning, lignin, an organic polymer and a major component of wood,[2] undergoes pyrolysis resulting in the direct release of substituted catechols.[3] 3-methylcatechol (3MC), a common substituted catechol, may be photo-oxidized or aggregates with other atmospherically relevant molecules, such as water, forming small molecular clusters or hydrates. These hydrates play an important role in the early phases of aerosol particle formation, and can provide valuable thermodynamic data for modelling. To elucidate the conformationally complex hydrate structures we analyzed rotational spectra measured with a chirped-pulse Fourier transform microwave spectrometer in the 2-6 GHz range.[4] To aid in spectral assignment, we used the Conformer–Rotamer Ensemble Sampling Tool (CREST)[5] to generate an ensemble of conformers. Two monomer conformations with their respective ^{13}C isotopologues were assigned, followed by the determination of substitution structures and semi-experimental effective structures. With the aid of the CREST results, transitions of several hydrates, 3MC-$(H_2O)_{N=1-4}$, were also assigned in the experimental spectrum. For the monohydrate and dihydrate, splittings of rotational transitions into quartets were observed. These splittings are a consequence of methyl internal rotation (MIR) and the proton exchange motion of water. Only MIR splittings are present for the trihydrate, while no MIR or proton exchange splitting is present for the tetrahydrate. Non-covalent interactions[6] and natural bond orbital analyses[7] were used to visualize and quantify the intermolecular interactions within each cluster. 1. M. Fromm et al., J. Geophys. Res. Atmospheres, 2019, 124, 13254–13272.; 2. A. V. Bridgewater, Therm. Sci., 2004, 8, 21–50.; 3. M. Asmadi et al., J. Anal. Appl. Pyrolysis, 2011, 92, 88–98.; 4. N. A. Seifert et al., Phys. Chem. Chem. Phys., 2018, 20, 27630–27637.; 5. P. Pracht et al., Phys. Chem. Chem. Phys., 2020, 22, 7169–7192.; 6. J. Contreras-García et al., J. Chem. Theory Comput., 2011, 7, 625–632.; 7. E. D. Glendening et al., J. Comput. Chem., 2013, 34, 1429–1437.

WM10   5:06–5:21

INTERMOLECULAR FREQUENCIES OF N$_2$O–KR AND SYMMETRY BREAKING OF THE N$_2$O BENDING MODE IN THE PRESENCE OF A RARE GAS

CHRIS GERGESS, M. DEHGHANY, *Department of Chemistry and Physics, Mount Royal University, Calgary, AB, Canada*; K. H. MICHAELIAN, *CanmetENERGY, Natural Resources Canada, Edmonton, Alberta, Canada*; A.R.W. McKELLAR, *Steacie Laboratory, National Research Council of Canada, Ottawa, ON, Canada*; NASSER MOAZZEN-AHMADI, *Department of Physics and Astronomy, University of Calgary, Calgary, AB, Canada.*

Rotationally-resolved infrared spectra of N$_2$O–Ar and N$_2$O-Kr van der Waals clusters are studied in the region of the N$_2$O ν_1 vibration ($\approx$ 2224 cm^{-1}) using a tunable Quantum Cascade laser source to probe a pulsed supersonic jet. The N$_2$O-Kr ν_1 fundamental band is re-analyzed, together with previous ν_3 band data, using a unified scheme to fit the (small) observed Kr isotope splittings. This scheme is then transferred to analyze the bending combination band of N$_2$O-Kr near 2257 cm^{-1} where isotope effects are much larger due to stretch-bend Coriolis interactions. As a result, N$_2$O–Kr intermolecular bend (33.29 cm^{-1}) and stretch (34.48 cm^{-1}) frequencies are directly determined for the first time.

We also report observation of weak spectra for both N$_2$O-Ar and -Kr corresponding to the $(\nu_1, \nu_2^{l_2}, \nu_3) = (1,1^1,0) \leftarrow (0,1^1,0)$ hot band of N$_2$O, located around 2209.8cm^{-1}. In the presence of Argon/Krypton atom, the doubly-degenerate ν_2 bending mode of the N$_2$O monomer splits into an in-plane and an out-of-plane mode. These two infrared bands are heavily linked by Coriolis interactions and their analysis yields the magnitude of the splitting of the bending modes which are significantly smaller than those observed in the analogous CO$_2$-containing dimers [a]. The experimental results obtained here are valuable for testing the accuracy of theoretical calculation toward a better understanding of intermolecular interactions.

---

[a] T.A. Gartner, A.J. Barclay, A.R.W. McKellar, and N. Moazzen-Ahmadi, Phys. Chem. Chem. Phys. 22, 21488-21493 (2020).

WM11   5:24–5:39

AB INITIO INVESTIGATIONS ON THE TRIMERS CONTAINING HC$_3$N IN COMBINATION WITH H$_2$C$_2$ AND/OR HCN

ANDREA PIETROPOLLI CHARMET, *Dipartimento di Scienze Molecolari e Nanosistemi, Università Ca' Foscari, Venezia, Italy.*

The present contribution focuses on the main results coming from ab initio investigations carried out on the mixed trimers containing (at least one molecule of) cyanoacetylene in combination with acetylene and/or hydrogen cyanide units. The several optimized structures corresponding to true minima on the PES of these complexes have been characterised at different levels of theory, and a set of their spectroscopic parameters relevant to rotational and vibrational spectroscopies have been determined. Besides, by employing different approaches, also the kinds and the topologies of the interactions present in each of these minima have been investigated.

WN. Astronomy
Wednesday, June 22, 2022 – 1:45 PM
Room: 274 Medical Sciences Building

Chair: Brett A. McGuire, Massachusetts Institute of Technology, Cambridge, MA, USA

WN01 1:45 – 2:00

SUBMILLIMETER WAVE STUDY OF NITROSOMETHANE (CH$_3$NO)

L. MARGULÈS, LUYAO ZOU, R. A. MOTIYENKO, *UMR 8523 - PhLAM - Physique des Lasers Atomes et Molécules, University of Lille, CNRS, F-59000 Lille, France*; J.-C. GUILLEMIN, *UMR 6226 CNRS - ENSCR, Institut des Sciences Chimiques de Rennes, Rennes, France.*

The knowledge of synthetic routes of complex organic molecules is still far to be fully understood. The creation of reliable models is particularly challenging. Hollis et al.[a] pointed out that the observations of molecular isomers provides an excellent tool to evaluate the hypothesis of the synthetic pathways. Formamide (HC(O)NH$_2$) is an abundant molecule in ISM detected in 1971 in SgrB2[b]. We decided to investigate two isomers of formamide some years ago: formaldoxime and nitrosomethane, like they are interesting ISM targets. Formaldoxime is a classic asymmetrical spinning top, its spectrum does not present any identification difficulties, it has been published recently[c]. Concerning nitrosomethane, the methyl top internal rotation should be taken into account, therefore the analysis is not obvious. We have been working on the project for several years. Analysis is performed using the version of RAM36 coded which includes the treatment of the nuclear quadrupole hyperfine structure[d]. Up to now the spectroscopic studies are only available up to 40 GHz [e]. We recently recorded the spectra in Lille from 225 to 660 GHz using the bolometric detection in order to improve the signal to noise ratio. The new spectroscopic results will be presented. Its presence in ISM will also be discussed. *This work was supported by the CNES and the Action sur Projets de l'INSU, PCMI.*

[a] Hollis, J. M.; et al., 2006, *ApJ* **642**, 933
[b] Rubin, R. H. ; et al., 1971, *ApJ* **169**, L39
[c] Zou L. ; et al., 2021, *A&A* **649**, A60
[d] Ilyushin, V.V. et al, 2010, *J. Mol. Spectrosc.* **259**, 26
[e] Turner P. H. et al., 1978, *J. Chem. Soc., Faraday Trans. 2* **74**, 533

WN02 2:03 – 2:18

MILLIMETER AND SUB-MILLIMETER SPECTROSCOPY OF DOUBLY DEUTERATED ACETALDEHYDE (CD$_2$HCHO)

JUDIT FERRER ASENSIO, SILVIA SPEZZANO, CHRISTIAN ENDRES, VALERIO LATTANZI, *The Center for Astrochemical Studies, Max-Planck-Institut für extraterrestrische Physik, Garching, Germany*; L. H. COUDERT, *Institut des Sciences Moléculaires d'Orsay, Université Paris-Saclay, CNRS, Orsay, France*; PAOLA CASELLI, *The Center for Astrochemical Studies, Max-Planck-Institut für extraterrestrische Physik, Garching, Germany.*

In the last years the number of multi-deuterated molecules detected in the Interstellar Medium (ISM) increased substantially. These molecules are found to be more abundant than expected when taking into account the ISM deuterium abundance (D/H = $2.0 \pm 0.1 \times 10^{-5}$, Drozdovskaya et al.[a] and references therein). In order to better understand the nature of deuterium fractionation, and the interplay of the chemistry in the gas phase and on the surface of dust grains, chemical models need to be constrained by observations of singly- and multi-deuterated molecules. Doubly deuterated acetaldehyde (CD$_2$HCHO) has not been detected in the ISM yet as it has been studied in the laboratory only up to 40 GHz (Turner & Cox[b], Turner et al.[c]) and hence lacks an extensive spectroscopic study, in contrast with the singly-deuterated forms CH$_2$DCHO and CH$_3$CDO that were detected towards the protostellar core IRAS16293-2422B (Coudert et al.[d]). In order to allow the first detection of CD$_2$HCHO in the ISM, and to understand its deuterium fractionation, we are studying the rotational spectrum of CD$_2$HCHO in the millimetre and sub-millimeter frequency range. This work should allow us to obtain an accurate spectral catalogue for CD$_2$HCHO, which we will use to search for this molecule in star-forming regions.

[a] Drozdovskaya, M. N., Coudert, L. H., Margulès, L., Coutens, A., Jorgensen, J. K., Manigand, S., 2022, *A&A*, in press
[b] Turner, P. H., Cox, A. P., 1976, *Chem. Phys. Lett.*, 42, 1
[c] Turner, P. H., Cox, A. P., Hardy, J. A., 1981, *J. Chem. Soc.*, 77, 1217-1231
[d] Coudert, L. H., Margulès, L., Vastel, C., Motiyenko, R., Caux, E., Guillemin, J.-C., 2019, *A&A*, 624, A70

WN03

THE ROTATION-TUNNELING SPECTRUM OF DIMETHYLAMINE, $(CH_3)_2NH$

<u>HOLGER S. P. MÜLLER</u>, FRANK LEWEN, STEPHAN SCHLEMMER, *I. Physikalisches Institut, Universität zu Köln, Köln, Germany.*

Methylamine (CH_3NH_2) was among the molecules detected early by means of radio astronomy. Detected initially only toward the giant star-forming region Sagittarius B2 close to the Galactic center. Recently, vinylamine ($C_2H_3NH_2$) and ethylamine ($C_2H_5NH_2$) were detected securely and tentative, respectively, toward the cold Galactic center source G+0.693−0.03,[a] making $(CH_3)_2NH$ a prime target for searches in space.

The microwave spectrum of dimethylamine was studied more than 50 years ago up to 45 GHz and $J = 8$.[b] The spectrum displays an inversion splitting of the amino H atom of 2646 MHz, and the ^{14}N hyperfine splitting was well resolved for transitions with $J \leq 1$. The internal rotation splitting of the two equivalent methyl rotors was not resolved. Very recently, a Fourier transform microwave spectroscopic (FTMW) study (2 − 40 GHz) of secondary amines[c] revealed a small internal rotation splitting of order of ∼200 kHz in dimethylamine.

We have studied the rotation-inversion spectrum of dimethylamine between 76 and 1091 GHz covering quantum numbers up to $J = 60$ and $K_a = 21$. Hyperfine splitting was resolved at least partly for many transitions and was treated in the analysis. The small internal rotation splitting was resolved in particular for transitions at lower frequencies or with lower quantum numbers, but was not considered thus far. The analysis was carried out with Pickett's spfit program. As the program is capable of treating internal rotation, we want to combine our data with the FTMW data.

---

[a] S. Zeng et al., *Astrophys. J. Lett.* **920** (2021) L27.
[b] J. E. Wollrab and V. W. Laurie, *J. Chem. Phys.* **48** (1968) 5058.
[c] K. J. Koziol, W. Stahl, H. V. L. Nguyen, Contribution WH19, 74th ISMS, June 21−25, 2021, Urbana-Champaign, IL, USA

WN04

RE-INVESTIGATION OF THE CYANOACETALDEHYDE ($NCCH_2CHO$) ROTATIONAL SPECTRUM

<u>L. MARGULÈS</u>, LUYAO ZOU, R. A. MOTIYENKO, *UMR 8523 - PhLAM - Physique des Lasers Atomes et Molécules, University of Lille, CNRS, F-59000 Lille, France*; J.-C. GUILLEMIN, *UMR 6226 CNRS - ENSCR, Institut des Sciences Chimiques de Rennes, Rennes, France.*

Cyanoacetaldehyde could be present in interstellar space or in planetary atmospheres, because of the facile hydrolysis of cyanoacetylene, which is prevalent in the interstellar medium, and found in comets and in Titan's atmosphere. We already studied its rotation spectrum ten years ago[a]. The two lowest energy rotamers were studied, Rotamer I was found to be 2.9(8) kJ/mol more stable than II by relative intensity measurements. There was no major difficulties with assignment of the conformer II for the ground and the two lowest energy vibrational states. On the other hand, the analysis of the most stable conformer is not satisfactory. This is due to the existence of tunnelling effect between two equivalent configurations, which makes the analysis of the spectra tricky. The assignment is actually limited to data up to 80 GHz and with Ka<3. It should be noted that the synthesis of cyanoacetaldehyde is not straightforward, and non negligeable amount of the precursor, isoxazole, is present in the final mixture. We re-examined the millimeter wave spectra (150-330 GHz) as our DDS spectrometer is now faster and particularly suitable for unstable species. We also have more experience with analyzing Coriolis interaction from tunnelling motion.[b]. The new spectroscopic results will be presented. Its presence in ISM will also be discussed. *This work was supported by the CNES and the Action sur Projets de l'INSU, PCMI.*

---

[a] Møllendal, H.; *et al.*, 2012, *J. Phys. Chem. A* **116**, 4047
[b] Margulès, L.; *et al.*, 2017, *A&A* **601**, A50

WN05   2:57 – 3:12

ROTATIONAL SPECTRUM OF CD$_3$OD: NEW MEASUREMENTS AND ASSIGNMENTS IN THE $v_t = 0$, 1 and 2 TORSIONAL STATES

V. ILYUSHIN, R. POROHOVOI, E. A. ALEKSEEV, OLGA DOROVSKAYA, *Radiospectrometry Department, Institute of Radio Astronomy of NASU, Kharkov, Ukraine*; HOLGER S. P. MÜLLER, FRANK LEWEN, STEPHAN SCHLEMMER, *I. Physikalisches Institut, Universität zu Köln, Köln, Germany*; CHRISTOF MAUL, *Institut für Physikalische und Theoretische Chemie, Technische Universität Braunschweig, Braunschweig, Germany*; RONALD M. LEES, *Department of Physics, University of New Brunswick, Saint John, NB, Canada*.

We present[a] the results of our new study of the torsion-rotation spectrum of the fully deuterated isotopolog of methanol (CD$_3$OD). The new measurements were carried out from the millimeter wave range (starting at 34.5 GHz) to the terahertz range (up to 1.1 THz) using spectrometers in Kharkiv and Köln. We extend the rotational quantum number coverage up to $J_{max} = 50$ in this work. The analysis is done using the rho axis method and the RAM36 program code, as in our earlier studies on CD$_3$OH[b] and CH$_3$OD. Our preliminary fits show that the $v_t = 2$ torsional state is affected by intervibrational interactions with non-torsional vibrational modes which propagate down through intertorsional interactions, similar to the cases of CD$_3$OH and CH$_3$OD. Taking into account the astrophysical significance of methanol and its isotopologs, we decided at this stage of the analysis to concentrate our fitting attempts on the ground and first excited torsional states of CD$_3$OD. We will present the status of our investigations.

[a] We are grateful for the support of the Deutsche Forschungsgemeinschaft and the Volkswagen foundation. The assistance of the Science and Technology Center in Ukraine is acknowledged (STCU partner project P756).
[b] V. V. Ilyushin et al., *Astron. Astrophys.* **658** (2022) A127

WN06   3:15 – 3:30

LABORATORY MEASUREMENT OF MILLIMETER-WAVE TRANSITIONS OF ^{13}CH$_2$DOH FOR ASTRONOMICAL USE

TAKAHIRO OYAMA, *Cluster for Pioneering Research, RIKEN, Saitama, Japan*; YUKI OHNO, *Faculty of Science Division I, Tokyo University of Science, Shinjuku-ku, Tokyo, Japan*; AKEMI TAMANAI, SHAOSHAN ZENG, *Cluster for Pioneering Research, RIKEN, Saitama, Japan*; YOSHIMASA WATANABE, *Materials Science and Engineering, College of Engineering, Shibaura Institute of Technology, Koto-ku, Tokyo, JAPAN*; RIOUHEI NAKATANI, *Cluster for Pioneering Research, RIKEN, Saitama, Japan*; TAKESHI SAKAI, *Graduate School of Informatics and Engineering, The University of Electro-Communications, Chofu, Japan*; NAMI SAKAI, *Cluster for Pioneering Research, RIKEN, Saitama, Japan*.

Methanol (CH$_3$OH) is known to be an important precursor of various interstellar complex organic molecules. As a monodeuterated methanol, CH$_2$DOH is one of the most abundant isotopologues of CH$_3$OH which is often used to study the deuterium fractionation of CH$_3$OH in interstellar medium.[a] One of the problems regarding CH$_2$DOH is that its emission lines are sometimes optically thick, and thus the derivation of its abundance is very difficult and frequently unreliable. Observations of its presumably optically thin ^{13}C substituted species, ^{13}CH$_2$DOH, would give us an opportunity to overcome this issue. In this study, the rotational transitions of ^{13}CH$_2$DOH have been measured in the millimeter wave region between 216 GHz and 264 GHz with an emission type millimeter and submillimeter-wave spectrometer, SUMIRE,[b] by using a deuterium and ^{13}C enriched samples.[c] The absolute intensities for the a-type transitions are within 10% from their theoretical values except for perturbed lines, whereas large differences are seen in the b-type transitions. Our experimental results will contribute to identify ^{13}CH$_2$DOH in observational spectra from respective astronomical environments, and thereby allow us to study the deuterium fractionation of CH$_3$OH in various sources with accurate determination of the CH$_2$DOH abundance.

[a] e.g., Jørgensen *et al.* 2018, A&A, **620**, A170.
[b] Watanabe *et al.* 2021, PASJ, **72**, 372.
[c] Ohno, Oyama *et al.*, submitted to ApJ.

Intermission

WN07   4:12 – 4:27

MILLIMETER-WAVE SPECTRUM OF 2-PROPANIMINE AND ITS SEARCH IN THE INTERSTELLAR MEDIUM

LUYAO ZOU, L. MARGULÈS, R. A. MOTIYENKO, *UMR 8523 - PhLAM - Physique des Lasers Atomes et Molécules, University of Lille, CNRS, F-59000 Lille, France*; J.-C. GUILLEMIN, *Institut des Sciences Chimiques de Rennes, UMR 6226 CNRS - ENSCR, Rennes, France*; ARNAUD BELLOCHE, *Millimeter- und Submillimeter-Astronomie, Max-Planck-Institut für Radioastronomie, Bonn, NRW, Germany*; JES JORGENSEN, *Niels Bohr Institute, University of Copenhagen, Copenhagen, Denmark*.

Imines are believed to be important prebiotic molecules that lead to the synthesis of amino acids in the interstellar medium (ISM). However, only four aldimine molecules, methanimine (CH_2=NH), ethanimine (CH_3CH=NH), cyanomethanimine (NCCH=NH), and propargylimine (HCCCH=NH), have been detected so far in the ISM, resulting in a poor understanding of their interstellar chemistry. The lack of high resolution spectroscopy data, which are partially caused by the chemical instability of imines under terrestrial conditions, hinders the search for other imines. Calculations suggested that 2-propanimine ((CH_3)$_2$C=NH) is the most stable isomer in the group of 3-carbon imine with a molecular formula of C_3H_7N. Following the lowest energy principle, it is a good target for astronomical search. If found, it would also be the first ketenimine detected in space. The rotational spectrum of 2-propanimine is not available currently, because of its chemical instability under room temperature. In addition, the two methyl internal rotors in 2-propanimine also complicate its rotational spectrum due to internal rotation, and make the spectral assignment and analysis non-trivial. In this work, we successfully measured and assigned the millimeter-wave spectrum of 2-propanimine between 50 and 500 GHz using a cryogenic preserved fresh sample from dedicated chemical synthesis. The spectroscopic results and the search for 2-propanimine in imaging spectral line surveys of SgrB2(N) and IRAS16293-2422 performed with ALMA will be presented.

This work was supported by the CNES and the Action sur Projets de l'INSU, PCMI. L. Zou thanks the financial support from the European Union's Horizon 2020 research and innovation programme under the Marie Skłodowska-Curie grant agreement (H2020-MSCA-IF-2019, Project no. 894508).

WN08   4:30 – 4:45

MILLIMETER AND SUBMILLIMETER SPECTROSCOPY OF ISOBUTENE

MARIYAM FATIMA, OLIVER ZINGSHEIM, HOLGER S. P. MÜLLER, DIRK HOPPEN, STEPHAN SCHLEMMER, *I. Physikalisches Institut, Universität zu Köln, Köln, Germany*.

Propene is among the largest saturated or nearly saturated hydrocarbons that have been detected not only toward TMC-1[a], but also in the warmer environment of the solar-type protostellar system IRAS 16293-2422[b]. Isobutene, also known as 2-methylpropene, $(CH_3)_2C=CH_2$, is thus a promising candidate to be searched for in space.
Its rotational spectrum was studied in the microwave region to some extent[c]. In this work, we have extended the measurement up to 370 GHz employing the Cologne (Sub-)Millimeter spectrometer. The molecule has two equivalent methyl rotors. The barrier height of the tops is high enough that the internal rotation splittings could either not be resolved or occur as symmetrical triplets. A few quartets are also assigned, where splittings are up to ∼10 MHz. The analysis has been carried out with the ERHAM program[d] using the previous data as well. We have accessed transitions up to $J = 60$ and $K_c = 41$, greatly improving the spectroscopic parameters for this molecule and thus paving the way to search for it in space.

---
[a] N. Marcelino et al., *ApJ* **665** (2007) L127.
[b] S. Manigand et al., *A&A* **645** (2021) A53.
[c] H. S. Gutowsky et al., *J. Mol. Spec.* **147** (1991) 91-99 and references therein.
[d] P. Groner, *J. Chem. Phys.* **107** (1997) 4483-4498.

WN09

EXTENSION OF THE MILLIMETER AND SUBMILLIMETER SPECTRUM OF GLYCOLIC ACID: ROTATIONAL SPECTROSCOPIC STUDY OF A POTENTIAL PREBIOTIC INTERSTELLAR MOLECULE

<u>CHASE P SCHULTZ</u>, HAYLEY BUNN, *Department of Chemistry, University of Wisconsin-Madison, Madison, WI, USA*; SUSANNA L. WIDICUS WEAVER, *Chemistry and Astronomy, University of Wisconsin-Madison, Madison, WI, USA.*

Glycolic acid (HOCH$_2$CO$_2$H) is a promising candidate for interstellar detection because it is the next step in molecular complexity from known interstellar species such as formic acid and methyl formate. Glycolic acid has also been confirmed as a product of the UV photolysis of simple (H$_2$O:CO:NH$_3$) interstellar ice analogues. Glycolic acid has two conformers: The SSC, or syn-syn-cis, conformer is the most stable species, followed by the trans conformer ATT, anti-trans-trans. Previous rotational spectral study of glycolic acid reported lines in the range of 113 – 318 GHz. We have extended the spectra of both the SSC and ATT conformers from 318 GHz to 1 THz using long-pathlength direct absorption flow cell spectroscopy. Here we will report on the spectroscopic results and the associated analysis for glycolic acid.

WN10

THE MILLIMETER WAVE SPECTRA OF VINYL ISOCYANATE AND VINYL KETENE, CANDIDATES FOR ASTRONOMICAL OBSERVATIONS

<u>LUCIE KOLESNIKOVÁ</u>, JAN KOUCKÝ, KAREL VÁVRA, KATEŘINA LUKOVÁ, TEREZA UHLÍKOVÁ, PATRIK KANIA, *Department of Analytical Chemistry, University of Chemistry and Technology, Prague, Prague, Czech Republic*; J.-C. GUILLEMIN, *ISCR - UMR6226, Univ. Rennes. Ecole Nationale Supérieure de Chimie de Rennes, Rennes, France*; STEPAN URBAN, *Department of Analytical Chemistry, University of Chemistry and Technology, Prague, Prague, Czech Republic.*

Interstellar detections of isocyanic acid[a], methyl isocyanate[b], and very recently also ethyl isocyanate[c] open the question of the possible detection of the related molecule vinyl isocyanate in the interstellar medium. Similarly, astronomical observations of ketene[d] places vinyl ketene among the species of potential interstellar relevance. In the present work, both vinyl species were generated by thermolysis of suitable precursors at 500°C and their room-temperature rotational spectra were recorded between 218 and 330 GHz using the Prague millimeter wave spectrometer[e]. The spectroscopic measurements and analyses presented here will allow to search for both molecules in the millimeter wave surveys of interstellar sources such as those recorded by Atacama Large Millimeter/submillimeter Array.

Acknowledgments: L.K., J.K., K.V., K.L., and P.K. acknowledge the financial fundings from the Czech Science Foundation (GACR, grant No. 19-25116Y) and the Ministry of Education, Youth and Sports of the Czech Republic (MSMT, grant No. 8J21FR006). J.C.G. thanks the Barrande project No. 46662VH and the Centre National d'Etudes Spatiales (CNES) for a grant BC U32-4500065585.

---

[a] Snyder, L. E. & Buhl, D. 1972, ApJ, 177, 619.
[b] Halfen, D. T., Ilyushin, V. V., & Ziurys, L. M. 2015, ApJ, 812, L5. Cernicharo, J., Kisiel, Z., Tercero, B., et al. 2016, A&A, 587, L4.
[c] Rodríguez-Almeida, L. F., Rivilla, V. M., Jiménez-Serra, I., et al. 2021, A&A, 654, L1.
[d] Turner, B. E. 1977, ApJ, 213, L75.
[e] Kania, P., Stříteská, L., Šimečková, M., & Š. Urban. 2006, J. Mol. Struct., 795, 209.

WN11

ROTATIONAL SPECTROSCOPY AND INTERSTELLAR SEARCH FOR N- AND I-BUTYRALDEHYDE

<u>MIGUEL SANZ-NOVO</u>[a], JOSÉ L. ALONSO, *Grupo de Espectroscopia Molecular, Lab. de Espectroscopia y Bioespectroscopia, Unidad Asociada CSIC, Universidad de Valladolid, Valladolid, Spain*; ARNAUD BELLOCHE, KARL M. MENTEN, *Millimeter- und Submillimeter-Astronomie, Max-Planck-Institut für Radioastronomie, Bonn, NRW, Germany*; VICTOR MANUEL RIVILLA, LUCAS RODRÍGUEZ-ALMEIDA, IZASKUN JIMÉNEZ-SERRA, JESÚS MARTÍN-PINTADO, *Departamento de Astrofísica, Centro de Astrobiología CAB, CSIC-INTA, Madrid, Spain*; ROBIN T. GARROD, *Departments of Chemistry and Astronomy, The University of Virginia, Charlottesville, VA, USA*; PILAR REDONDO, CARMEN BARRIENTOS, JUAN CARLOS VALLE, *Departamento de Química Física y Química Inorgánica, Universidad de Valladolid, Valladolid, Spain*; LUCIE KOLESNIKOVÁ, *Department of Analytical Chemistry, University of Chemistry and Technology, Prague, Prague, Czech Republic*; HOLGER S. P. MÜLLER, *I. Physikalisches Institut, Universität zu Köln, Köln, Germany*.

Large organic molecules of extraordinary complexity have recently been found in diverse regions of the interstellar medium (ISM). In this context, we aim to provide accurate frequencies of the ground vibrational state of two key aliphatic aldehydes, n-butyraldehyde, and its branched-chain isomer i-butyraldehyde. We employed a frequency modulated millimeter-wave absorption spectrometer to measure the rotational features of n- and i-butyraldehyde; several thousands of transitions belonging to the lower-energy conformers have been assigned up to 325 GHz. A precise set of the relevant rotational spectroscopic constants have been determined for each structure as a first step to identifying both molecules in the ISM. We then used the spectral line survey named Re-Exploring Molecular Complexity with ALMA (REMoCA), performed toward the star-forming region Sgr B2(N) with ALMA to search for n- and i-butyraldehyde. We also searched for both aldehydes toward the molecular cloud G+0.693-0.027 with IRAM 30m and Yebes 40m observations. We report the nondetection of these isomers toward both astronomical sources. Our astronomical results indicate a leap around one order of magnitude in the aldehyde's abundance while increasing the level of complexity.

---

[a] M.S.N. acknowledges funding from the Spanish "Ministerio de Ciencia, Innovacion y Universidades" under predoctoral FPU Grant (FPU17/02987).

RA. Plenary
Thursday, June 23, 2022 – 8:30 AM
Room: Foellinger Auditorium

Chair: Anne B McCoy, University of Washington, Seattle, WA, USA

RA01 8:30 – 9:10

SPECTROSCOPY OF METAL AND PHOSPHORUS BEARING MOLECULES: A WINDOW ON THE UNIVERSE

LUCY M. ZIURYS, *Dept. of Astronomy, Dept. of Chemistry, Arizona Radio Observatory, The University of Arizona, Tucson, AZ, USA.*

Small molecules containing refractory elements such as metals and phosphorus hold important clues to understanding astrochemistry and the connection between gas-phase matter and solid-state constituents of the interstellar medium. They also are extremely relevant for the origin of life and the delivery of the biogenic elements to planet surfaces. Studies of these types of molecules in interstellar space have clearly been driven by laboratory spectroscopy. For over three decades, the Ziurys laboratory has been conducting measurements of rotational spectra of highly reactive metal and phosphorus-bearing species, and subsequently searching for these molecules in the interstellar medium with radio telescopes. These studies have led to the interstellar detection of exotic metal-bearing radicals such as FeCN and VO, and new phosphorus compounds, for example, CCP. Critical to this endeavor has been the development of unusual synthetic methods to create these unstable molecules, and the challenge of unraveling spectra of states with high spin and orbital angular momenta. Molecules of recent interest include metal dicarbide species, including TiCC. An overview of this laboratory spectroscopy effort will be presented, and the implications of this work in unraveling the chemistry between the stars.

RA02 9:15 – 9:55

THEORETICAL DESCRIPTIONS OF THE FUNDAMENTALS OF CH, NH AND OH STRETCH VIBRATIONS WITH SIMPLE MODELS THAT INCLUDE ANHARMONIC EFFECTS

EDWIN SIBERT, *Department of Chemistry, University of Wisconsin–Madison, Madison, WI, USA.*

In this talk I review our work on theoretically modeling of spectra in the frequency range of the fundamentals of high-frequency XH vibrations (where X = C, N, or O) of medium size molecules. These vibrations are often coupled to nearly degenerate overtone and combination bands, and this coupling complicates the interpretation of many spectral features. When a molecule contains multiple XH groups, assigning the spectrum is more difficult, especially when multiple conformers are present. I will present experimental/theoretical collaborative approaches appropriate for addressing these challenges. Our work focuses on molecules for which the densities of states is sufficiently high at the energies of the fundamentals that calculating eigenstate-resolved spectra is not useful due to long time state-mixing effects. Nonetheless, using ideas based on perturbation theory, local modes, effective Hamiltonians, the transferability of anharmonic couplings, and empirical scalings of vibrational frequencies we have developed approaches for modeling complex spectra with Hamiltonians that approach the simplicity of Hückel Hamiltonians. Several molecular systems will be presented to illustrate these ideas as well as one for which is fails entirely.

Intermission

JON T. HOUGEN MEMORIAL AWARDS 10:30
Introduction of Award by Isabelle Kleiner, CNRS, UPEC et Universite de Paris, Creteil, France

2022 Jon T. Hougen Memorial Award Winners
Kenneth Koziol, RWTH Aachen University
Lorrie Jacob, University of Cambridge

SNYDER AWARD 10:35
Presentation of Award by Anthony Remijan, NRAO

2021 Snyder Award Winner
Divita Gupta, Institut de Physique de Rennes

RAO AWARDS 10:40
Presentation of Awards by Timothy Zwier, Sandia National Laboratories

2021 Rao Award Winners
Parker Crandall, Technische Universität Berlin
Nicholas Hölsch, ETH Zuerich
Wey-Wey Su, Stanford University
James Thorpe, University of Florida

MILLER PRIZE 10:50
Introduction by Michael Heaven, Emory University

RA03 *Miller Prize Lecture* 10:55 – 11:10

DIABATIC VALENCE-HOLE STATES IN THE C_2 MOLECULE: "PUTTING HUMPTY DUMPTY TOGETHER AGAIN"

JUN JIANG, *Center for Accelerator Mass Spectrometry, Lawrence Livermore National Laboratory, Livermore, CA, USA*; HONG-ZHOU YE, *Department of Chemistry, Massachusetts Institute of Technology, Cambridge, MA, USA*; KLAAS NAUTA, *School of Chemistry, UNSW, Sydney, NSW, Australia*; TROY VAN VOORHIS, *Department of Chemistry, Massachusetts Institute of Technology, Cambridge, MA, USA*; TIMOTHY SCHMIDT, *School of Chemistry, UNSW, Sydney, NSW, Australia*; ROBERT W FIELD, *Department of Chemistry, MIT, Cambridge, MA, USA*.

Each of the six C,N,O diatomic molecules has a unique role in shaping our intuitive understanding of electronic structure theory. In this work, the pathologically pervasive configuration interactions that occur in four electronic symmetry manifolds ($^1\Pi_g$, $^3\Pi_g$, $^1\Sigma_u^+$, and $^3\Sigma_u^+$) of the C_2 molecule are disentangled by a global multi-state diabatization scheme. The key concept of our model is the existence of two "valence-hole" configurations, $2\sigma_g^2 2\sigma_u^1 2\pi_u^3 3\sigma_g^2$ ($^{1,3}\Pi_g$) and $2\sigma_g^2 2\sigma_u^1 2\pi_u^4 3\sigma_g^1$ ($^{1,3}\Sigma_u^+$) that derive from a $3\sigma_g \leftarrow 2\sigma_u$ electron promotion. The lowest energy state from each of the four C_2 symmetry species is dominated by this type of valence-hole configuration at its equilibrium internuclear separation. These valence-hole configurations have a nominal bond order of 3 and correlate with the $2s^2 2p^2 + 2s 2p^3$ separated-atom configurations. Facilitated by chemical intuition, the diabatic picture uncovers the disruptive impact of the valence-hole configurations on the global electronic structure and unimolecular dynamics of C_2. In each of the four symmetry manifolds studied in this work, the strongly-bound diabatic valence-hole state, the energy of which starts low and ends high, crosses multiple weakly-bound and repulsive states that are composed of electron configurations with a $2\sigma_g^2 2\sigma_u^2$ valence-core. These diabatic crossings result in an extensive, interconnected network of avoided-crossings among the low-lying electronic states of C_2. The C_2 molecule behaves "badly", yet its secrets are revealed by diabatic modeling of their lumpy adiabatic potentials and broken spectroscopic patterns. Based on our demonstration of the importance of valence-hole configurations in C_2, we propose a diabatic model re-analysis of similar interactions in the other second-row diatomic molecules, for which the valence-hole states are expected to have a similar impact on their global electronic structure.

COBLENTZ AWARD **11:15**
Presentation of Award by Zac Schultz, Coblentz Society

RA04 *Coblentz Society Award Lecture* **11:20 – 12:00**

ADVANCING DYNAMIC METHODS FOR COMPUTATIONAL SPECTROSCOPY IN THE GAS AND CONDENSED PHASE

SANDRA LUBER, *Department of Chemistry, University of Zurich, Zurich, Switzerland.*

I will give an overview about our work on development of novel computational methods for spectroscopy with emphasis on dynamic methods and approaches for the condensed phase.

I will describe the efficient calculation of Infrared spectra for periodic systems using subsystem density functional theory (DFT) as well as Raman and sum frequency generation spectra by means of DFT-based molecular dynamics. This has allowed a realistic description of (large) compounds including finite temperature and environmental effects. Moreover, pioneering Raman optical activity spectra for the investigation of chiral compounds using DFT-based molecular dynamics have been presented and a novel approach for vibrational circular dichroism. In addition, I will show our developments for excited state dynamics and using real time propagation for the study of absorption and vibrational spectra for (chiral) compounds in the gas and condensed phase.

RH. Mini-symposium: Spectroscopy meets Chemical Dynamics

Thursday, June 23, 2022 – 1:45 PM

Room: 100 Noyes Laboratory

Chair: Timothy S. Zwier, Sandia National Laboratories, Livermore, CA, USA

RH01   1:45 – 2:00

A DFT STUDY: SPECTROSCOPIC ANALYSIS OF SCHIFF BASE LIGAND WITH FE(II) COMPLEX

BERNA CATIKKAS, *Department of Physics, Mustafa Kemal University, Hatay, Turkey.*

In this study, the molecular geometry, electronic, magnetic, and vibrational spectra of Schiff base ligand with Fe(II) Complexes were simulated by using density functional theory hybrid methods. NMR, UV-Vis, Raman, Infrared Spectroscopic investigations were carried out. The calculated values have been compared with the corresponding experimental results. Molecular orbital properties, descriptors, the mapping molecular electrostatic potential surface (MEP), and nonlinear optical (NLO) properties have been reported for better understanding at the molecular level. Normal modes analysis and their vibrational assignments were searched by using the Scaled Quantum Mechanical Force Field (SQM-FF) method based on total energy distribution (TED).

RH02   2:03 – 2:18

HIGH-RESOLUTION LASER SPECTROSCOPIC STUDIES OF UROCANIC ACID AND DERIVATIVES: TOWARDS NOVEL NATURE-INSPIRED SUNSCREENS

JIAYUN FAN, *Van' t Hoff Institute for Molecular Sciences, University of Amsterdam, Amsterdam, Netherlands*; LAURA FINAZZI, *FELIX Laboratory, Radboud University, Nijmegen, The Netherlands*; ALEXANDER KAREL LEMMENS, *FELIX Laboratory, Institute for Molecules and Materials (IMM), Radboud University, Nijmegen, Netherlands*; WYBREN JAN BUMA, *Van' t Hoff Institute for Molecular Sciences, University of Amsterdam, Amsterdam, Netherlands.*

Trans-urocanic acid (UA) is found in the outer layer of human skin, where -due to its favorable UV absorption properties- it is thought to act as a natural sunscreen protecting DNA from photodamage. In recent decades it has become clear, however, that the cis-isomer produced upon irradiation has immunosuppressive properties, which is the main reason that UA is no longer employed in commercial sunscreen formulations. As a basic chromophore UA is nevertheless an excellent starting point for the development of potentially harmless nature-inspired sunscreens. Key to such efforts is a fundamental understanding of the photochemistry and photophysics of UA on which there are still quite a number of unresolved questions, and how substitutions affect these properties. Here we report on molecular beam studies of (substituted) UA compounds using Resonance Enhanced MultiPhoton Ionization (REMPI) spectroscopic techniques that demonstrate that previous conclusions need to be revised. Together with FT-IR and UV/Vis absorption studies of these compounds in various solvents they provide a comprehensive view on the photoactive properties of these compounds, as well as the influence of the presence of different conformers and tautomers.

RH03   2:21 – 2:36

HIGH-RESOLUTION LASER SPECTROSCOPIC STUDIES OF CINNAMATE-BASED MOLECULAR HEATERS

<u>I. ROMANOV</u>, Y. BOEIJE, *Van't Hoff Institute for Molecular Sciences, University of Amsterdam, Amsterdam, Amsterdam, Netherlands*; WYBREN JAN BUMA, *Van' t Hoff Institute for Molecular Sciences, University of Amsterdam, Amsterdam, Netherlands*; JOSENE MARIA TOLDO, MARIANA TELLES DO CASAL, MARIO BARBATTI, *Institut de Chimie Radicalaire (ICR), Aix-Marseille University, Marseille, France.*

Food security is one of the major challenges society is currently facing. One of the approaches to meet this challenge is to use molecular light-to-heat converters to extend the growth season and to allow utilization of geographical locations that are currently not suitable. Cinnamates -chromophores used already in nature as sunscreens against damage by UV radiation - from in this respect an attractive starting point for the development of such 'molecular heaters'. Here we report molecular beam studies on judiciously substituted cinnamates in which we study their spectroscopy and excited-state dynamics using Resonance Enhanced MultiPhoton Ionization (REMPI) spectroscopic methods focussing in particular on how substitutions affect their photophysics and photochemistry. One particularly interesting aspect of these studies is the use of Velocity Map Imaging (VMI) electron detection which allows us to study in much more detail than before the properties of the initially excited state as well as energy dissipation pathways involving 'dark' electronically excited states. In combination with advanced quantum chemical calculations, a comprehensive view is obtained of how photon energy is converted into heat, and how these pathways might be optimized.

RH04   2:39 – 2:54

HYPERFINE EXCITATION OF HC^{17}O$^+$ WITH p-H$_2$ COLLISIONS

<u>FRANCESCA TONOLO</u>, *Scuola Normale Superiore, Scuola Normale Superiore, Pisa, Italy*; LUCA BIZZOCCHI, *Dipartimento di Chimica G. Ciamician, Università di Bologna, Bologna, Italy*; FRANÇOIS LIQUE, *CNRS, IPR (Institut de Physique de Rennes) - UMR 6251, Univ Rennes, F-35000 Rennes, France*; MATTIA MELOSSO, *Dept. Chemistry "Giacomo Ciamician", University of Bologna, Bologna, ITALY*; VINCENZO BARONE, *Scuola Normale Superiore, Scuola Normale Superiore, Pisa, Italy*; CRISTINA PUZZARINI, *Chemistry G. Ciamician, University of Bologna, Bologna, Italy.*

The formyl ion (HCO$^+$) is one of the most abundant ions in molecular clouds and represents an excellent candidate to trace dense molecular gas through the evolutionary stages of the interstellar medium (ISM). For this reason, the accurate rotational rate coefficients of HCO$^+$ and its isotopes with the most abundant perturbing species in the ISM are crucial in non-local thermal equilibrium (LTE) models and deserve special attention. To this end, many efforts have been made in order to retrieve accurate collisional parameters of HCO$^+$ interacting with the He and H$_2$ colliders as well as for some of its isotopologues[a,b]. However, in spite of laboratory and observational studies on HC^{17}O^{+}[c,d], to the best of our knowledge, an accurate characterization of its collisional parameters has not been carried out yet. Although rarer, the HC^{17}O$^+$ isotope assumes a prominent role to avoid problems due to the optical thickness of the parent species emissions. With the aim of filling this lack, this work reports the first calculations of hyperfine resolved rate coefficients for the excitation of HC^{17}O$^+$ by p-H$_2$ ($J = 0$).

We characterized the potential energy surface of the HCO$^+$ and H$_2$ collisional system by means of the CCSD(T)-F12a/aug-cc-pVQZ level of theory. The interaction energy has been averaged over five H$_2$ orientations and then fitted as an expansion of angular functions. Finally, state-to-state rate coefficients between the lower hyperfine levels have been computed using recoupling techniques for temperature ranging from 5 to 100 K.

---

[a]Tonolo F., Bizzocchi L., Melosso M., Lique F., Dore L., Barone V., Puzzarini C., 2021, *The Journal of Chemical Physics*, **155**, 234306.
[b]Denis-Alpizar O., Stoecklin T., Dutrey A., Guilloteau S., 2020, *Monthly Notices of the Royal Astronomical Society*, **497**, 4276.
[c]Plummer G., Herbst E., De Lucia F., 1983, *The Astrophysical Journal*, **270**, L99.
[d]Dore L., Cazzoli G., Caselli P., 2001, *Astronomy & Astrophysics*, **368**, 712.

RH05   2:57 – 3:12
EXTENDED PREDICTION OF CAF ELECTRONIC STATES: ENERGIES, MULTIPOLE MOMENTS, AND A SHAPE RESONANCE STATE

STEPHEN L COY, TIMOTHY J BARNUM, ROBERT W FIELD, *Department of Chemistry, MIT, Cambridge, MA, USA*; JOHN F. STANTON, *Physical Chemistry, University of Florida, Gainesville, FL, USA*.

The alkaline earth monohalides have a number of applications. They are a continuing focus of ultracold experiments; they provide insight into the calcium ionic bonding of biological relevance; and they are molecular prototypes for Rydberg spectroscopy. In Rydberg spectroscopy, a MQDT model is extremely effective, but not all states are of purely Rydberg type since a lifetime matrix calculated in Serhan Altunata's work describes a shape resonance that couples Σ states to dissociation. To explore this, a wide range of CaF properties have been obtained in a series of UHF-CCSD(T) calculations extending to nearly 40,000 cm-1 above the ground state. Excited states were converged from QRHF initial guesses and extended to include CCSD(T) first-order properties, computed analytically. Remarkably accurate results are obtained for dipole moments known from molecular beam experiments, as well as very good results found for known values of bond length, vibrational frequency and anharmonicity. Several new states are predicted. In general, it is not possible for two states of the same symmetry to be quite close in energy and yet cross unless electronic configurations are very different. The calculation finds that to be the case for two higher $^2\Sigma^+$ states that differ dramatically in electron density and bond length, one with a short bond length and electron density along the axis far away from the center of mass, and a second with a long bond length with density in a ring close to the center of mass. The states have large quadrupole moments of opposite signs. The long bond length state may be related to the predicted shape resonance.

Intermission

RH06   3:54 – 4:09
STATE-RESOLVED MODELING FOR THE ENERGY TRANSFER PROCESSES IN LASER-INDUCED FLUORESCENCE OF DIATOMIC MOLECULES

SHENGKAI WANG[a], *State Key Laboratory for Turbulence and Complex Systems, College of Engineering,, Peking University, Beijing, China*.

This work presents a generic framework for modeling the energy transfer processes between rovibronic quantum states in diatomic molecules upon laser excitation. A comprehensive set of rate equations (denoted here as the master equation) was developed to describe the interactions between radiation processes (i.e. absorption, stimulated emission and fluorescence), collision processes (including rotational energy transfer, vibrational energy transfer, and electronic quenching), and losses such as inter-system crossing an chemical reactions (including predissociation and ionization). The rate coefficients were fully parameterized using physical quantities such as the transnational temperature of the exited molecule, the energy gap and the start/end quanta across the transfer process, and the numerical expressions of parameterization were guided by a critical review of the existing literature. A stiff ODE solver with adjustable step-size was implemented to accommodate the wide range of physical timescales involved in the master equation. To demonstration the utility of the current modeling approach, simulations were performed for OH and NO molecules excited by selected transitions in the A-X (0,0) and (1,0) bands, and the spectro-temporal features of the predicted fluorescence signals were analyzed and validated against previous experimental results. Additional simulations were also conducted at extreme conditions of ultra-short laser pulses and very high laser energies, which revealed non-monotonic trends resulting from complications of strong non-linearity and spectral-temporal correlation at these conditions, indicating the existence of an optimal pulse length or laser energy (not necessarily the shorter or higher the better) for typical LIF applications. This modeling framework will be released online soon and should prove useful in aiding the design and analysis of modern quantitative LIF measurements.

---
[a]Corresponding Email: sk.wang@pku.edu.cn

RH07 4:12 – 4:27

PRESSURE AND TEMPERATURE DEPENDENCE OF ABSORPTION CROSS-SECTION OF HCN IN THE LONG-WAVE MID-INFRARED REGION

ALI ELKHAZRAJI, MOHAMMAD ADIL, MHANNA MHANNA, NAWAF ABUALSAUD, AHMED AYIDH ALSULAMI, MOHAMMAD KHALED SHAKFA, *Clean Combustion Research Center, King Abdullah University of Science and Technology (KAUST), Thuwal, Saudi Arabia*; MARCO MARANGONI, *Dipartimento di Fisica, Politecnico di Milano, Milano, Italy*; BINOD GIRI, AAMIR FAROOQ, *Clean Combustion Research Center, King Abdullah University of Science and Technology (KAUST), Thuwal, Saudi Arabia.*

Hydrogen cyanide (HCN) is extensively studied in combustion and exoplanetary research for its important role in both fields. Laser-based detection of HCN in both fields, among other applications, necessitates quantifying the pressure and temperature dependence of its absorption cross-section. Here, we introduce a method to access HCN's strongest IR band, ν_2, near 712 cm^{-1} *via* a high-resolution custom-designed laser source. Difference-frequency generation (DFG) between a cw EC-QCL and a pulsed CO$_2$ gas laser in an orientation-patterned GaAs crystal is employed to generate laser light in the long-wavelength mid-IR region. The DFG laser can be wavelength-tuned over 667 - 865 cm^{-1}. We employed our DFG laser to quantify the pressure dependence of absorption cross-section of the Q-branch of the ν_2 band of HCN over the range 100 - 800 Torr. Furthermore, we exploited the developed laser source in conjunction with a shock tube to measure the temperature dependence of absorption cross-section of the peak of the Q-branch behind reflected shock waves over the temperature range 850 - 3000 K. We compared our results with HITRAN simulations. Ultimately, we utilized these results in measuring HCN formation time-histories in a reactive environment behind reflected shock waves.

RH08 4:30 – 4:45

HITTING THE TRIFECTA: HOW TO SIMULTANEOUSLY PUSH THE LIMITS OF SCHRÖDINGER SOLUTION WITH RESPECT TO SYSTEM SIZE, CONVERGENCE ACCURACY, AND NUMBER OF COMPUTED STATES

JÁNOS SARKA, BILL POIRIER, *Department of Chemistry and Biochemistry, Texas Tech University, Lubbock, Texas, USA.*

Methods for solving the Schrödinger equation have seen an explosive growth in recent years, as the importance of incorporating quantum effects in numerical simulations in order to obtain experimentally accurate data becomes increasingly recognized. In practical terms, there are just three primary factors that currently limit what can be achieved. These are: (a) SYSTEM SIZE, i.e., the number of degrees of freedom that can be treated explicitly quantum mechanically; (b) NUMERICAL ACCURACY, measured in terms of convergence with respect to ALL POSSIBLE computational parameters such as basis sizes; (c) ENERGY EXCITATION or the total number of accurately computed states. Broadly speaking, current methods can deliver on any two of these goals, but achieving all three at once remains an enormous challenge.

In this presentation, we shall describe just such a method, and demonstrate how it can be used to "hit the trifecta" in the context of molecular vibrational spectroscopy calculations.[a] In particular, we compute thousands of vibrational states for the 12D acetonitrile molecule (CH$_3$CN), to a target numerical convergence of a few 10^{-2} cm^{-1} or better. In other words, we compute ALL vibrational states for this six-atom system in full quantum dimensionality, and throughout the entire dynamically relevant spectral range, to near spectroscopic accuracy. To our knowledge, no such vibrational spectroscopy calculation has ever previously been performed–although given the generality of the method, we anticipate there will be many more such calculations to follow.

---

[a] J. Sarka and B. Poirier, J. Chem. Theory Comput. 17, 7732-7744 (2021).

RH09 — 4:48–5:03
ANALOG QUANTUM SIMULATION OF MOLECULAR DYNAMICS AND SPECTROSCOPIC OBSERVABLES

RYAN J MacDONELL, IVAN KASSAL, *School of Chemistry, University of Sydney, Sydney, NSW, Australia.*

Modern computational techniques used to simulate quantum chemistry are on the boundary of tractability due to the exponential growth of the molecular wavefunction, requiring a careful balance between molecule size and simulation accuracy. In recent years, quantum computing has risen in popularity as a potential alternative to conventional (classical) techniques; however, most methods rely on access to "digital" quantum computers composed of qubits and quantum gates, which at present are severely limited by noise. We have developed a real-time, analog approach to simulate vibronic chemical dynamics with existing quantum technology. Our approach uses an intuitive mapping of molecular electronic and vibrational degrees of freedom onto quantum resonators and qudit (d-level system) states, with controllable couplings between degrees of freedom. The measurement output can be mapped onto different time-dependent observables, including the time-domain simulation of vibronic spectra. Our approach can also incorporate controlled sources of noise to simulate system-bath interactions and dissipative dynamics at a minimal cost. We present experimental results using a trapped-ion device, thus showing the potential for near-term simulation of chemical dynamics in complex environments beyond the abilities of classical computers.

RH10 — 5:06–5:21
MEASUREMENTS OF HIGH-TEMPERATURE ABSORPTION SPECTRA OF DIMETHYL ETHER AND DIETHYL ETHER BETWEEN 950 AND 1190 cm^{-1} AND THEIR DIRECT PYROLYSIS STUDY IN A SHOCK TUBE

MOHAMMAD ADIL, BINOD GIRI, AAMIR FAROOQ, *Clean Combustion Research Center, King Abdullah University of Science and Technology (KAUST), Thuwal, Saudi Arabia.*

Laser absorption spectroscopy has been proved to be a powerful diagnostic tool for high enthalpic systems like exoplanets, combustion applications and hypersonic flows. But there is a scarcity of high-temperature absorption data, especially for large molecules due to technical challenges like limited availability of optical materials necessary to withstand high temperatures. Furthermore, generating a chemically stable, homogeneous and steady gas state for a sufficient duration to carry out such high-temperature measurements is rather complicated and most experimental approaches satisfy only a few of these requirements. In this work, we present measurements of temperature-dependent absorption cross-section between 950-1190 cm^{-1} of dimethyl ether (DME) and diethyl ether (DEE) and their direct pyrolysis study. The methodology employed here consists of rapid tuning, wide range/fixed wavelength MIRcat-QT laser in conjugation with shock tube. The spectral measurements are performed between 600-900 K, at around 1.2 bar. The measured IR absorption spectra are the first experimental measurements of high-temperature spectra of these species and show strong temperature dependence. For the first time absorption cross-section correlation has been provided for a wide range of spectra over a wide range of temperatures. These measured spectra have provided a significant idea about the trend in spectra at elevated temperatures and helped in the selection of promising wavelengths for sensitive detection. DME and DEE pyrolysis studies are performed at 1121.7 cm^{-1} and 1115 cm^{-1} respectively by providing the marginal temperature dependence absorption cross-section correlations.

RH11 5:24–5:39

MECHANISTIC STUDY OF PHOTOCHEMICAL [2+2] CYCLOADDITION BETWEEN 1,5-CYCLOOCTADIENE AND MALEIC ANHYDRIDE

<u>JUN YI</u>, ZHOU LIN, *Department of Chemistry, University of Massachusetts, Amherst, MA, USA*; JUNPENG WANG, *School of Polymer Science and Polymer Engineering, The University of Akron, Akron, OH, USA.*

One famous family of chemically recyclable polymers are produced from fused-ring cyclooctene monomers, and their chemical properties are highly tunable by modifying the functional groups from the monomers. The photochemical [2+2] cycloaddition is crucial to synthesizing such a fused-ring cyclooctene monomer, but its mechanistic details remain mysterious. Recently we observed a significant isomerization probability in the photochemical [2+2] cycloaddition between 1,5-cyclooctadiene and maleic anhydride, which produces more *trans*-fused-ring cyclooctene than the *cis* counterpart. In the present work, we investigated the photochemical mechanism (figure) of this reaction using density functional theory (DFT), with the aim of decoding when this isomerization happens and how it is correlated to the yields of products. We found that the isomerization occurs only at the first excited state after a charge transfer photoexcitation from 1,5-cyclooctadiene to maleic anhydride, and its activation barrier depends on the structure and orientation of the reactant complex. After the isomerization, the reactant complex barrierlessly reaches a conical intersection (CI) between the ground and the first excited states and quickly passes to the ground state of the product after climbing over an affordable activation barrier. Compared to a *cis* counterpart, the *trans* product exhibits a slightly lower total energy and a significantly lower activation barrier, indicating its *trans* configuration is favorable both thermodynamically and kinetically. Our model has been effectively extended to various functional groups and can be used to guide the rational design of photochemically synthesized fused-ring monomers.

RI. Mini-symposium: Benchmarking in Spectroscopy
Thursday, June 23, 2022 – 1:45 PM
Room: 116 Roger Adams Lab

Chair: Daniel A. Obenchain, Georg-August-Universität Göttingen, Göttingen, Germany

---

RI01   *INVITED TALK*   1:45 – 2:15

THE HyDRA BLIND CHALLENGE: INVITING THEORY TO PREDICT UNKNOWN VIBRATIONAL SPECTROSCOPY DATA

TAIJA L. FISCHER, MARAGRETHE BÖDECKER, SOPHIE M. SCHWEER, *Institute of Physical Chemistry, Georg-August-Universität Göttingen, Göttingen, Germany*; ANNE ZEHNACKER-RENTIEN, *Institut des Sciences Moléculaires d'Orsay, Université Paris Saclay, CNRS, Orsay, France*; RICARDO A MATA, MARTIN A. SUHM, *Institute of Physical Chemistry, Georg-August-Universität Göttingen, Göttingen, Germany*.

There is a myriad of quantum-chemical methods which can be used to predict the OH stretching spectrum of cold, vacuum-isolated hydrate clusters, with a perspective to deepen our understanding of aqueous solution dynamics. They range from uniformly scaled harmonic DFT predictions to fully anharmonic high level wave function theory treatments.

Fortuitous error compensation is a major issue in such a situation, in particular if the experimental result is known beforehand. The HyDRA (Hydrate Donor Redshift Anticipation) blind challenge is an effort to circumvent previous knowledge, by inviting theory groups to make predictions for 10 not yet vibrationally characterized organic monohydrates and performing the corresponding experiments in parallel.

This contribution will present the procedure[a] and discuss results of the recently finished blind challenge HyDRA by comparing the theoretical predictions to our experimental results.

---

[a] Taija L. Fischer, Margarethe Bödecker, Anne Zehnacker-Rentien, Ricardo A. Mata, Martin A. Suhm, ChemRxiv, 2021, DOI: 10.26434chemrxiv-2021-w8v42.

RI02   2:21 – 2:36

NEW JET-COOLED VIBRATIONAL SPECTROSCOPIC BENCHMARK DATA OF THE CYCLIC DIMER AND TRIMER OF FORMIC ACID

ARMAN NEJAD, *Institute of Physical Chemistry, Georg-August-Universität Göttingen, Göttingen, Germany*; KATHARINA A. E. MEYER, *Department of Chemistry, University of Wisconsin-Madison, Madison, WI, USA*; MARTIN A. SUHM, *Institute of Physical Chemistry, Georg-August-Universität Göttingen, Göttingen, Germany*.

Using well-established FTIR and Raman jet spectroscopic set-ups, the gas phase vibrational database of the cyclic formic acid dimer, (FF), has been reviewed and updated for the slow fingerprint vibrations [below $1500\,\text{cm}^{-1}$] of the main and its three symmetrically deuterated isotopologues.[a] Experimental benchmarks validate the popular second-order vibrational perturbation theory approach in combination with high-level [hybrid] force fields which is shown to provide accurate predictions for moderate excitations of the intermolecular van der Waals[b] and intramolecular fingerprint vibrations[a] of (FF). The new and extended benchmark-quality database of (FF) is particularly useful to guide recent efforts[c] to accurately model the 24-dimensional vibrational dynamics of this prototypical model system in a 'bottom-up' approach. As a byproduct, the number of assigned vibrational fundamentals [and selected overtone bands] of the vacuum-isolated formic acid trimer, F(FF), has been drastically increased.[a] Since the polar dimer, FF, is a fragment of the trimer, the experimentally validated theoretical description of F(FF) promises to provide reliable spectral predictions for future gas phase spectroscopic searches of FF.

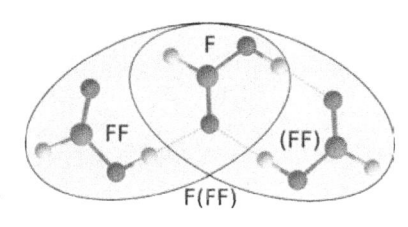

---

[a] A. Nejad, K. A. E. Meyer, F. Kollipost, Z. Xue, M. A. Suhm, *J. Chem. Phys.* **2021**, *155*, 224301 and A. Nejad, PhD thesis, submitted (2022).
[b] A. Nejad, M. A. Suhm, *J. Indian Inst. Sci.* **2020**, *100*, 5.
[c] C. Qu, J. M. Bowman, *Phys. Chem. Chem. Phys.* **2019**, *21*, 3397 and A. M. Santa Daría, G. Avila, E. Mátyus, *Phys. Chem. Chem. Phys.* **2021**, *23*, 6526.

RI03　　2:39 – 2:54

A VIBRATIONAL ACTION SPECTROSCOPIC STUDY OF THE RENNER-TELLER AND SPIN-ORBIT AFFECTED CYANOACETYLENE RADICAL CATION HC_3N^+ ($^2\Pi$)

<u>KIM STEENBAKKERS</u>, ARAVINDH NIVAS MARIMUTHU, *FELIX Laboratory, Institute for Molecules and Materials (IMM), Radboud University, Nijmegen, Netherlands*; GERRIT GROENENBOOM, *Institute for Molecules and Materials (IMM), Radboud University Nijmegen, Nijmegen, Netherlands*; BRITTA REDLICH, SANDRA BRÜNKEN, *FELIX Laboratory, Institute for Molecules and Materials (IMM), Radboud University, Nijmegen, Netherlands.*

The linear radical cation of cyanoacetylene, HC_3N^+ ($^2\Pi$), is of fundamental spectroscopic interest due to its strong spin-orbit and Renner-Teller interactions, which have been investigated previously in several high-resolution photoelectron spectroscopic (PES) studies[a,b,c]. Here, we present the first broadband vibrational action spectroscopic investigation of this ion through the infrared pre-dissociation (IRPD) method using a Ne tag. Experiments have been performed using the FELion cryogenic ion trap instrument in combination with the Free Electron Lasers for Infrared eXperiments (FELIX) Laboratory at the Radboud University (Nijmegen, The Netherlands)[d]. The vibronic splitting patterns of the 3 interacting bending modes (ν_5,ν_6,ν_7), ranging from 180-1600 cm^{-1}, could be fully resolved revealing several bands that were previously unobserved. The associated Renner-Teller and cross-coupling constants were determined by fitting an effective Hamiltonian to the experimental data, and the obtained spectroscopic constants were in reasonable agreement with previous studies of the HC_3N^+ ion. The influence of the attached Ne atom on the infrared spectrum was investigated by *ab initio* calculations at the CCSD(T) level of theory, showing that the discrepancies between the IRPD and PES data can be explained by the effect of the Ne binding.

[a] Dai, Z. Sun, W. Wang, J. Mo, Y., J. Chem. Phys. **2015**, 143, (5), 054301.
[b] Desrier, A. Romanzin, C. Lamarre, N. Alcaraz, C. Gans, B. Gauyacq, D. Liévin, J. Boyé-Péronne, S., J. Chem. Phys. **2016**, 145, (23), 234310.
[c] Gans, B. Lamarre, N. Broquier, M. Liévin, J. Boyé-Péronne, S., J. Chem. Phys. **2016**, 145, (23), 234309.
[d] Jusko, P. Brünken, S. Asvany, O. Thorwirth, S. Stoffels, A. van der Meer, L. Berden, G. Redlich, B. Oomens, J. Schlemmer, S., Faraday Discuss. **2019**, 217, 172-202.

RI04　　2:57 – 3:12

MODEL CHEMISTRY RECOMMENDATIONS FOR HARMONIC FREQUENCY CALCULATIONS: A BENCHMARK STUDY

<u>JUAN C. ZAPATA TRUJILLO</u>, LAURA K McKEMMISH, *School of Chemistry, University of New South Wales, Sydney, NSW, Australia.*

While harmonic frequency calculations are widespread across chemistry[1], sparse benchmarking is available to guide users on appropriate model chemistry recommendations (i.e., a method and basis set pair). Instead, studies exploring the dependence of harmonic frequencies on model chemistry have focused on producing multiplicative scaling factors to match the calculated harmonic frequencies to experimental fundamental frequencies[2].

Along with the scaling factor, it is often common to calculate the root-mean-squared error (RMSE) between the scaled harmonic and experimental fundamental frequencies, and use this value as metric of model chemistry performance. We recently compiled a set of over 1,400 scaling factors[3] spanning hundreds of methods and basis sets, thus allowing approximate comparisons between different model chemistries[2]. However, initial recommendations from this analysis can only be preliminary, as the differences in the benchmark databases used means that the RMSE metrics cannot be fairly compared across different publications.

Here, we introduce a new benchmark database for vibrational frequency calculations (VIBFREQ1292) containing 1,292 experimental fundamental frequencies and CCSD(T)-F12c/cc-pVDZ-F12 harmonic frequencies for 141 molecules. Assuming that our ab initio calculations reduce model chemistry error to a minimum, and noting the importance of using frequency-range-specific scaling factors, our analysis shows that the intrinsic error between the scaled harmonic and experimental frequencies usually lies below 15 cm^{-1}.

Thus, using VIBFREQ1292 as our reference set, we have rigorously assessed the performance of over 300 general-purpose model chemistry choices for harmonic frequency calculations. Model chemistry recommendations, as well as expected computational errors will be presented in this talk.

1. Scott, A.; Radon, L., J. Phys. Chem. 1996, 41, 16502-16513.
2. Zapata Trujillo, J. C.; McKemmish, L. K., Wiley Interdiscip. Rev.: Comput. Mol. Sci. 2021, e1584.
3. Zapata Trujillo, J. C.; McKemmish, L. K., Harvard Dataverse, V1, 2021, https://doi.org/10.7910/DVN/SQK6YU.

RI05　　3:15 – 3:30
NON-LTE INFRARED SPECTRUM OF JET-COOLED NAPHTHALENE

SHUBHADIP CHAKRABORTY, *Université de Rennes 1, Institut de Physique de Rennes,UMR CNRS 6251, Rennes, France*; GIACOMO MULAS, *Osservatorio Astronomico di Cagliari, Istituto Nazionale di Astrofisica (INAF), Selargius, Italy*; OLIVIER PIRALI, *Institut des Sciences Moléculaires d'Orsay, Université Paris Saclay, CNRS, Orsay, France*; PASCALE SOULARD, PIERRE ASSELIN, *CNRS, De la Molécule aux Nano-Objets: Réactivité, Interactions, Spectroscopies, MONARIS, Sorbonne Université, PARIS, France*; MANUEL GOUBET, *UMR 8523 - PhLAM - Physique des Lasers Atomes et Molécules, University of Lille, CNRS, F-59000 Lille, France*; LUDOVIC BIENNIER, ROBERT GEORGES, *IPR UMR6251, CNRS - Université Rennes 1, Rennes, France.*

Polycyclic aromatic hydrocarbons (PAHs) are responsible for the aromatic infrared bands (AIBs) observed in various astronomical objects. Studying their sharp Q-branches associated with the out-of-plane bending vibrational modes under low rotational excitation might be a key for their identification in the interstellar medium (ISM).

IR spectrum of naphthalene was recorded around 12.7 μm using the jet-AILES setup, coupled to the Fourier transform spectrometer (Bruker IFS 125 HR) equipping the AILES beamline of the synchrotron SOLEIL. In the jet, an efficient rotational relaxation of naphthalene occurs resulting in a rotational temperature of about 25 K, while the vibrational cooling is limited due to an insufficient number of two-body collisions in the supersonic expansion. This leads to an interesting non-LTE situation, favorable for the detection of hot bands: the low rotational temperature drastically simplifies the rotational structure and magnifies the Q-branches, while the higher vibrational excitation allows the presence of many transitions from moderately excited vibrational states. To assign the observed hot bands we have used the AnharmoniCaOs code, which explicitly considers Fermi and Darling Dennison resonances for a better accuracy of the band positions, and the second order dipole derivatives to simulate intensities of overtone, combination, and difference bands. Our program is unique in the sense that it can produce spectrum at a non-zero kelvin temperature unlike standard commercially available quantum chemistry packages. It also enables us to assign arbitrary (non-thermal) populations to individual vibrational states from which transitions originate, allowing us to simulate non-LTE spectra.

Intermission

RI06　　4:12 – 4:27
PROBING HALOGEN BONDING INTERACTIONS BETWEEN HEPTAFLUORO-2-IODOPROPANE AND THREE AZABENZENES WITH RAMAN SPECTROSCOPY AND DENSTIY FUNCTIONAL THEORY

ETHAN CHASE LAMBERT, ASHLEY E. WILLIAMS, RYAN C. FORTENBERRY, NATHAN I HAMMER, *Chemistry and Biochemistry, University of Mississippi, Oxford, MS, USA.*

The potential formation of halogen bonded complexes between a donor, heptafluoro-2-iodopropane (HFP), and the three acceptor heterocyclic azines (azabenzenes: pyridine, pyrimidine, and pyridazine) is investigated herein through normal mode analysis via Raman spectroscopy, density functional theory, and natural electron configuration analysis. Theoretical Raman spectra of the halogen bonded complexes are in good agreement with experimental data providing insight into the structure of these complexes. The exhibited shifts in vibrational frequency of as high as 8 cm-1 for each complex demonstrate, in conjunction with NEC analysis, significant evidence of charge transfer from the halogen bond acceptor to donor. Here, an interesting charge flow mechanism is proposed involving a conduit-like flow of electron density from each azabenzenes' interacting nitrogen atom through the halogen bond and iodine atom to the highly electron-withdrawing fluorine atoms. This mechanism provides further insight into the formation and fundamental nature of halogen bonding and its effects on neighboring atoms. The present findings provide novel and deeper characterization of halogen bonding with applications in supramolecular and organometallic chemistry.

RI07   4:30 – 4:45

VIBRATIONAL CHARACTERIZATION OF HEMI-BONDED HALIDE-THIOCYANATE DIMER RADICAL ANIONS (XSCN)$^{\cdot-}$ IN WATER

IRENEUSZ JANIK, SUSMITA BHATTACHARYA, *Radiation Laboratory, University of Notre Dame, Notre Dame, IN, USA.*

Time resolved Raman studies of halide-thiocyanate dimer radical anions, (X-SCN)$^{\cdot-}$ (for X=Cl, Br, I), were performed in resonance with their peak of light absorption wavelength at 415 nm. In two of the experiments (for X$^-$=Br$^-$ or I$^-$) the apparent Raman spectrum contains signatures of three hemibonded intermediates present simultaneously in mutual equilibria with their precursor and successor hemibonded radical counterparts: $X_2^{\cdot-} + SCN^- = (XSCN)^{\cdot-} + X^- = (SCN)_2^{\cdot-} + X^-$. In order to extract (X-SCN)$^{\cdot-}$ (for X=Br, I) from the composite spectrum additional experiments were performed to generate pre-resonance spectra of $X_2^{\cdot-}$ and $(SCN)_2^{\cdot-}$ at 415 nm in order to collect and then subtract their contributions from the composite spectrum. Ten Stokes Raman bands of the halide-thiocyanate radical anions (X-SCN)$^{\cdot-}$ (for X=Br, I) were observed in the 60-2400cm^{-1} region. They were assigned in terms of the strongly enhanced 198 and 174cm^{-1}, weakly enhanced 719.5 and 729cm^{-1}, and moderately enhanced 2069 and 2078cm^{-1} fundamentals, their overtones, and combinations in BrSCN$^{\cdot-}$ and ISCN$^{\cdot-}$, respectively. On attempt to record chloride intermediate only characteristic bands coming from the mixed contributions of $Cl_2^{\cdot-}$ and $(SCN)_2^{\cdot-}$ have been apparent. Quantum chemical calculations using a range-separated hybrid density functional (ωB97x) with flexible augmented correlation-consistent basis sets support the spectroscopic assignments of the strongest fundamental vibrations to a predominantly S-X (X = Br, I) stretching mode and the features around 720cm^{-1} and 2070cm^{-1} to CS and CN symmetric stretching modes, respectively. Interestingly, CS and CN bond stretching vibrational frequencies in asymmetrical (X-SCN)$^{\cdot-}$ anion radicals are shifted a few wavenumbers down or up in comparison to the symmetrical $(SCN)_2^{\cdot-}$ molecule in BrSCN$^{\cdot-}$ or ISCN$^{\cdot-}$, respectively. Considering that ClSCN$^{\cdot-}$ seems to have vibrational frequencies almost identical to $(SCN)_2^{\cdot-}$ does not grant any systematic correlation between hemi-bond polarization in this array of molecules and vibrational frequencies of CS and CN bonds. A possible explanation of such an observation can relate to a counteracting induction and migration effects in σ and π bonds, respectively, upon charge migration across the molecule.

RI08   4:48 – 5:03

THE HIGHER TORSIONAL STATES OF METHYLAMINE - PRELIMINARY ANALYSIS

IWONA GULACZYK, MAREK KREGLEWSKI, *Faculty of Chemistry, Adam Mickiewicz University, Poznan, Poland.*

Methylamine is a molecule performing two strongly coupled large amplitude motions: CH_3 internal rotation and NH_2 inversion. The rovibrational spectrum of the methylamine molecule has been extensively studied both experimentally and theoretically. The analyses of infrared bands such as NH_2 inversion or CN stretching show significant perturbations from highly excited torsional states. In order to untangle the interactions in the 700-1200 cm^{-1} region of the methylamine spectrum, it is crucial to assign the perturbing excited torsional states ($3\nu_{15}$ and $4\nu_{15}$). Both states are located well above the top of the torsional barrier. Thus, the splittings between the lower and upper sublevels are very large (80 to 180 cm^{-1}) and only low lying sublevels of $3\nu_{15}$ or $4\nu_{15}$ will be experimentally identified. The spectra were recorded with a resolution of 0.00125 cm^{-1} using Bruker IFS-120HR spectrometer at the University of Oulu. The accurate energy levels of the first excited torsional state, ν_{15},[a][b] were used as reference values for lower state combination differences in the assignments of the third and fourth torsional hot bands, $3\nu_{15}$-ν_{15} and $4\nu_{15}$-ν_{15}. After the complete analysis in the second torsional overtone region (360-720 cm^{-1}) was performed [c], many of the remaining unassigned lines in this region could be assigned to v=3-1 and v=4-1 bands. Earlier, about 200 transitions of B, E_{1+1} and E_{1-1} symmetry for the $3\nu_{15}$ and 28 transitions of B symmetry for $4\nu_{15}$ were found [d]. On the basis of the calculated energy levels for the third and fourth excited torsional states, many transitions of the hot band v=3-1, not assigned previously, have been identified (over 1500 transitions for all symmetry species). As for v=4-1, so far, the previously assigned series were only extended to higher J values (over 100 transitions assigned of B symmetry), but the analysis is in progress. All the assignments were confirmed by the LSCD. Each set of the experimental data was fit to a single state model based on the group theoretical formalism [e].

---

[a] I. Gulaczyk, M. Kreglewski, V-M. Horneman, J. Mol. Spectrosc. 342 (2017) 25-30
[b] I. Gulaczyk, M. Kreglewski, JQSRT 252 (2020) 107097
[c] I. Gulaczyk, M. Kreglewski, V-M. Horneman, JQSRT 217 (2018) 321–328
[d] N. Ohashi, H. Shimada, W. B. Olson, K. Kawaguchi, J. Mol. Spectrosc. 152 (1992) 298
[e] N. Ohashi and J.T. Hougen, J. Mol. Spectrosc. 121 (1987) 474

RI09 5:06 – 5:21

COMPLETION OF THE FIRST SOLVATION SHELL OF CARBON DIOXIDE IN ARGON: ROTATIONALLY RESOLVED INFRARED SPECTRA OF CO_2-AR_{15} AND CO_2-AR_{17}

A. J. BARCLAY, *Physics and Astronomy/Institute for Quantum Science and Technology, University of Calgary, Calgary, AB, Canada*; A.R.W. McKELLAR, *Steacie Laboratory, National Research Council of Canada, Ottawa, ON, Canada*; NASSER MOAZZEN-AHMADI, *Physics and Astronomy/Institute for Quantum Science and Technology, University of Calgary, Calgary, AB, Canada.*

There have been a number of theoretical papers on the structures and energetics of CO_2-Ar_n clusters. But in terms of experiment, the only previous spectroscopic results are for n = 1 (extensive work on the CO_2-Ar dimer) and n = 2 (microwave and infrared spectra of CO_2-Ar_2). We have now obtained and analyzed infrared spectra in the CO_2 ν_3 region for a number of clusters in the range n = 3 to 17. Notable among these are CO_2-Ar_{15} and CO_2-Ar_{17}, which mark completion of the first solvation shell for CO_2 in argon. These clusters have highly symmetric structures with D_{3h} and D_{5h} symmetry, respectively, in good agreement with theory. For n = 15, CO_2 is surrounded by five argon rings, each containing three Ar atoms. For n = 17, there are three rings of five atoms each, plus two additional Ar atoms located on the symmetry axis at each end. The observed spectra are symmetric top parallel bands, and both exhibit distinct intensity alternation which helps to confirm their assignment. Observed B-values are 69.93 MHz for CO_2-Ar_{15} and 54.52 MHz for CO_2-Ar_{17}. As usual for symmetric rotors, the spectra are not sensitive to the A constant, but we do obtain precise values for the band origins, and hence the vibrational shifts (relative to free CO_2) as induced by the argon cages.

RI10 5:24 – 5:39

HIGH RESOLUTION INFRARED SPECTROSCOPY OF DIBORANE DISPERSED IN SOLID PARAHYDROGEN

AARON I. STROM, IBRAHIM MUDDASSER, DAVID T. ANDERSON, *Department of Chemistry, University of Wyoming, Laramie, WY, USA.*

Few polyatomic molecules have been the subject of more *ab initio* studies than B_2H_6, diborane. The earliest studies were focused on elucidating the structure of its prototypical three-center, two-electron "banana" bonds. Information about the force field and motion of atoms in B_2H_6 can be most directly derived from its vibrational frequencies. However, with eight atoms, high symmetry, and significant vibrational anharmonicities, an exclusively spectroscopic determination of its anharmonic force field is nearly an intractable problem. However, with advances in *ab initio* methods and the development of methods to treat vibrational frequencies and intensities beyond the harmonic approximation, this challenging system is now amenable to deeper understanding. We decided to use parahydrogen (pH_2) matrix isolation infrared spectroscopy to measure the vibrational wavenumbers and intensities of as many infrared absorptions of B_2H_6 as possible in the 800 to 5000 cm^{-1} region to compare with more recent *ab initio* studies by Ziegler and Rauhut that go beyond the double harmonic approximation.[a] Our studies show nearly quantitative agreement between theory and experiment for the allowed infrared vibrational modes in the surveyed region. We devised a scheme to assign peaks in our spectra that then can be compared directly with computational predictions. Indeed, earlier spectroscopic assignments were hampered by not knowing the anharmonic contributions to the measured vibrational frequencies. We are currently investigating the analogous spectra of the B_2D_6 isotopolog and will present out latest findings and comparisons with available theory at the meeting.

---

[a] B. Ziegler, G. Rauhut, *J. Phys. Chem. A* **123**, 3367 (2019).

RI11
TRIHYBRID LINE LIST CONSTRUCTION FOR NH AND ZrO

ARMANDO N. PERRI, LAURA K McKEMMISH, *School of Chemistry, University of New South Wales, Sydney, NSW, Australia.*

Accurate and comprehensive diatomic molecular spectroscopic data is essential to the measuring and monitoring of gaseous environments, the computational benchmarking of theoretical approaches and, increasingly, in ultracold physics. The recent search for unusual transition metal diatomics, such as TiO and VO, in hot Jupiter exoplanets has demanded spectra of sub 0.1 cm^{-1} accuracy. This experimental need has motivated significant developments in line list construction.

A line list contains the assigned rovibronic energy levels of a molecule, as well as the transition frequencies and intensities between these energy levels. Here, I will discuss the new trihybrid construction of line lists, specifically for NH and ZrO. This trihybrid methodology is advantageous as precedence is given to experimental energy levels that independently form a self-consistent network. This list of energy levels is subsequently interpolated with perturbative calculations using model Hamiltonians and extrapolated with variational calculations using fitted potential energy and coupling curves.

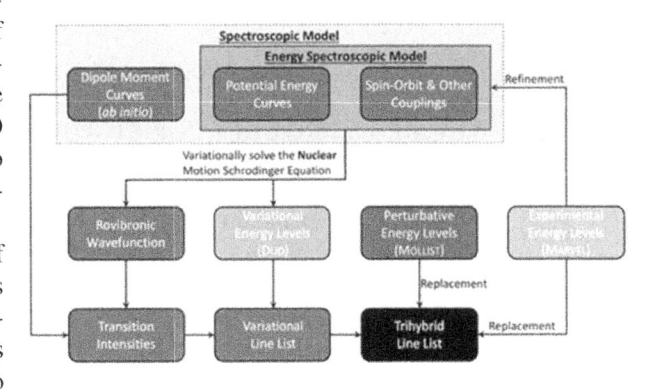

The exemplar cases of NH and ZrO highlight the diversity of electronic structures encountered in line list construction. For NH, only the uncoupled ground and first excited triplet electronic states are considered, as direct transitions to other states are either forbidden or negligible in intensity. Alternatively, for ZrO, eleven highly coupled electronic states are considered as many transitions are allowed and intense, especially in the hot stellar environment of S-type stars that ZrO characterises.

RJ. Instrument/Technique Demonstration

Thursday, June 23, 2022 – 1:45 PM
Room: B102 Chemical and Life Sciences

Chair: Jacob Stewart, Connecticut College, New London, CT, USA

RJ01   1:45 – 2:00

PROGRESS ON SHOCKGAS-IR: MEASUREMENTS OF METHYL FORMATE AT ELEVATED TEMPERATURES

<u>WEY-WEY SU</u>, YIMING DING, CHRISTOPHER L STRAND, RONALD K HANSON, *Mechanical Engineering, Stanford University, Stanford, CA, USA.*

Methyl formate plays an important role in multiple combustion mechanisms, such as the oxidation of dimethoxymethane, warranting further study of its absorbance spectra at elevated temperatures. However, pyrolysis reactions make broadband measurements at elevated temperatures difficult, and currently available spectra are mostly limited to lower temperatures around 296 K. In this study, we have shock heated methyl formate, dilute in argon, at temperatures up to 1000 K and measured the cross sections from 1655 to 1875 cm^{-1}. Measurements within the short ms-scale test times were achieved through a rapid-tuning, broad-scan external-cavity quantum-cascade laser. We have also supplemented these elevated temperature measurements with elevated pressure cross sections at room temperature in a static cell, at pressures up to 35 atm. Our measurements were validated through excellent 296 K agreement with that in the literature. The elevated temperature cross sections reveal an additional absorbance structure near 1800 cm^{-1}, possibly the emergence of a combination band. Interestingly, the cross sections at elevated pressure conditions display a dependence on pressure, contrary to its common use and implementation in previous literature. These cross sections expand our ShockGas-IR database (https://searchworks.stanford.edu/view/wt021dc3029), containing elevated temperature cross sections of many other molecules important for combustion mechanisms.

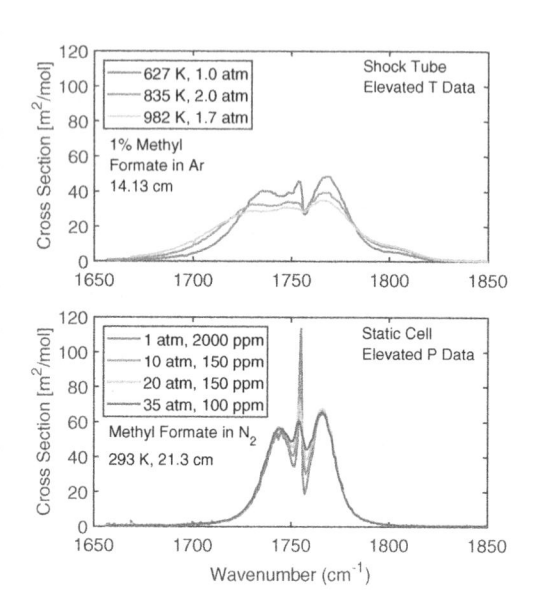

RJ02   2:03 – 2:18

CO2 COLLISIONAL BROADENING OF THE 557 GHz WATER ABSORPTION FEATURE PROFILED WITH A DIFFERENTIAL ABSORPTION RADAR PLATFORM

KEN COOPER, <u>DEACON J NEMCHICK</u>, OMKAR PRADHAN, ROBERT DENGLER, RAQUEL RODRIQUEZ MONJE, BRIAN DROUIN, JOSE SILES, LESLIE TAMPPARI, *Jet Propulsion Laboratory, California Institute of Technology, Pasadena, CA, USA.*

Millimeter and sub-millimeter differential absorption radar (DAR) systems, which measure the attenuation of a transmitted beam as function of both frequency and range, are currently in development for a variety of Earth and planetary science applications. This talk will summarize efforts to realize a portable DAR system optimized to profile the 557 GHz 1_{10}-1_{01} pure rotational transition of water that is suited for humidity measurements between scatter targets in low-pressure Martian-like environments. This emerging class of active remote sensing instrumentation, if deployed on future Mars lander/rover missions, could provide local near-surface humidity profiles that are unresolvable to the current generation of passive orbiting sensors. This presentation will include an overview of DAR operational principles, system architecture, and deployment scenarios. Room temperature laboratory measurements recorded with the DAR prototype system of the 557 GHz pure rotational water transition broadened by carbon dioxide in a sample mixture that is reasonably analogous to that found on Mars (∼200 ppm H_2O in 5 Torr CO_2) will be presented. Observed results will be discussed in the context of previously measured lineshape parameters with extrapolation made to the lower surface temperatures (200 - 250 K) found on Mars.

RJ03 2:21 – 2:36

ROOM-TEMPERATURE QUANTIFICATION OF $^{14}CO_2$ BELOW THE NATURAL ABUNDANCE WITH TWO-COLOR, CAVITY RINGDOWN SPECTROSCOPY

JUN JIANG, A. DANIEL McCARTT, *Center for Accelerator Mass Spectrometry, Lawrence Livermore National Laboratory, Livermore, CA, USA.*

In this talk, we report the first room-temperature optical detection of radiocarbon dioxide ($^{14}CO_2$) samples at concentrations below the natural abundance level (1.2 parts per trillion, $^{14}C/C$), using the recently-developed two-color, mid-IR, pump-probe, cavity ringdown (CRD) technique. With 3 minutes of averaging, our two-color CRD method successfully differentiates, with an accuracy of 8% of the ^{14}C natural abundance, five combusted ^{14}C standards with $^{14}CO_2$ concentrations ranging from petrogenic (zero $^{14}C/C$) to approximately double the contemporary abundance. Room-temperature quantification of $^{14}CO_2$ is not possible with any existing one-photon cavity-enhanced techniques at our demonstrated ^{14}C concentration levels, due to severe spectral overlap between the very weak target $^{14}CO_2$ ν_3-band transitions ($\sim$5/s ringdown rate at natural abundance) and the strong hot-band transitions of CO_2 isotopologues (>10000/s). All previous CRD-based, one-photon $^{14}CO_2$ measurements at the sub-natural-abundance level required cooling of the test gas (-20 to -100°C) to mitigate the strong background absorption.

Our unprecedented high-sensitivity, high-selectivity detection of $^{14}CO_2$ at room temperature is made possible by the dual-background compensation capabilities of the two-color CRD technique. The two-color measurement utilizes two cavity-enhanced pump and probe lasers to excite, respectively, the $\nu_3 = 1\leftarrow 0$, P(14) and $\nu_3 = 2\leftarrow 1$, R(13) rovibrational transitions of $^{14}CO_2$. With the pump radiation switched off during every other probe ringdown events (>2 kHz rate), the CRD rate fluctuations and strong one-photon absorption interference are effectively cancelled out during the two-color measurements. Highly-selective, room-temperature detection of weak $^{14}CO_2$ absorption signals reduces the technical and operational burdens for cavity-enhanced measurements of radiocarbon. This is a crucial achievement that will enable laser-based radiocarbon quantification outside a laser laboratory setting, and benefit a wide range of scientific applications, such as ^{14}C-labeling analysis of biomedical samples and field monitoring of fossil fuel emission.

RJ04 2:39 – 2:54

SELECTIVE PRODUCTION OF HCN MONOMER AND EVIDENCE FOR GAS-PHASE DIMERIZATION

THOMAS HOWARD, *Department of Chemistry and Biochemistry, University of Maryland, College Park, MD, USA*; EMILY K HOCKEY, *Department of Chemistry and Biochemistry, University of Maryland, College Park, College Park, MD, USA*; DARYA KISURYNA, *Physics, University of Maryland, College Park, MD, USA*; JESSICA PALKO, LEAH G DODSON, *Department of Chemistry and Biochemistry, University of Maryland, College Park, MD, USA.*

Hydrogen cyanide (HCN) is a molecule of importance in astrochemistry. To prepare for experiments to study its reactivity, we selectively produced a molecular beam of monomeric HCN using a cryogenic buffer-gas source. The HCN beam was first interrogated by condensing it on a 10K substrate using argon as a bath gas to create an inert matrix. Based on a comparison of the resulting infrared spectrum with experiments that use conventional effusive sources, HCN polymers can be nearly eliminated from the matrix using a cryogenic buffer-gas beam source. Our experiments suggest that HCN undergoes polymerization in the gas phase and may exist, to some extent, as a dimer under ambient conditions. We will discuss further investigations using continuous-wave cavity ringdown spectroscopy to examine the first vibrational overtone of the alkynyl C-H stretch of HCN monomer and dimer in the near infrared.

RJ05
INSTRUMENT DESIGN AND PREPARATION OF *PARA*-HYDROGEN FOR MATRIX EXPERIMENTS

<u>KORINA VLAHOS</u>, *Chemistry and Biochemistry, University of Maryland, College Park, College Park, MD, USA*; EMILY K HOCKEY, *Department of Chemistry and Biochemistry, University of Maryland, College Park, College Park, MD, USA*; LEAH G DODSON, *Department of Chemistry and Biochemistry, University of Maryland, College Park, MD, USA*.

Para-hydrogen (p-H_2) is used as a host matrix in matrix-isolation experiments because of its unique properties to act as a quantum solid. However, p-H_2 is not commercially available and needs to be produced in house with a custom-built p-H_2 converter. Throughout this presentation, we will describe the design and building phases of the custom-built p-H_2 converter at the University of Maryland. Instrument drawings, schematics, and preliminary results will be presented. This talk will also explore the spectroscopic techniques that are used to both prove the enrichment of p-H_2 and determine the purity of p-H_2. The p-H_2 will be used in future experiments to study novel astrochemistry interactions and reactions in the interstellar medium (ISM). The production of p-H_2 is critical for future astrochemistry relevant experiments as its properties as a quantum solid allow us to further understand molecular properties and interactions that would be otherwise unattainable with rare-gas host matrices.

RJ06
W BAND CHIRPED-PULSE: THE BEAUTY OF COHERENT SPECTROSCOPY

<u>BETTINA HEYNE</u>, MARIUS HERMANNS, *I. Physikalisches Institut, University of Cologne, Cologne, Germany*; NADINE WEHRES, *I. Physikalisches Institut, Universität zu Köln, Köln, Germany*; STEPHAN SCHLEMMER, *I. Physikalisches Institut, University of Cologne, Cologne, Germany*.

We built a chirped-pulse Fourier transform millimeter-wave spectrometer (CPFTS) [1], which is operational between 75 and 110 GHz. The design and operation of the instrument (excitation, optical path and detection scheme) will be discussed. The detector is based on a heterodyne receiver of an emission spectrometer [2] which we built and used before to sensitively record rotational spectra of complex molecules. The performance of the CPFTS instrument is analysed by recording spectra of methyl cyanide as well as products from a DC discharge of this molecule. Based on the quantitative calibration of the detector we compare the operation of the instrument as CPFTS with that of the emission spectrometer. We find molecular signals much higher in intensity and much lower in noise for the CPFTS operation. We demonstrate how the detection of the coherent molecular signal (FID) reduces the noise more efficiently compared to the detection of the emitted power when operating the system as an emission spectrometer.

References

[1] M. Hermanns, N. Wehres, B. Heyne, C. E. Honingh, U. U. Graf and S. Schlemmer, in preparation

[2] N. Wehres, B. Heyne, F. Lewen, M. Hermanns, B. Schmidt, C. Endres, U. U. Graf, D. R. Higgins and S. Schlemmer, IAU Symposium, 2018, pp. 332-345

Intermission

RJ07

LLWP – UPDATES ON A NEW LOOMIS-WOOD SOFTWARE AT THE EXAMPLE OF ACETONE-$^{13}C_1$

<u>LUIS BONAH</u>, OLIVER ZINGSHEIM, HOLGER S. P. MÜLLER, SVEN THORWIRTH, *I. Physikalisches Institut, Universität zu Köln, Köln, Germany*; J.-C. GUILLEMIN, *ENSC, Univ. Rennes, Rennes, France*; FRANK LEWEN, STEPHAN SCHLEMMER, *I. Physikalisches Institut, Universität zu Köln, Köln, Germany*.

Acetone-$^{13}C_1$ is a complex organic molecule with two internal methyl (-CH_3) rotors having relatively low barriers to internal rotation of 251 cm^{-1} [1]. This leads to two low-lying torsional modes and five internal rotation components resulting in a dense and complex spectrum. Similar conditions can be found in many complex molecules, with isotopologues, hyperfine structure, and interactions being additional factors for the presence of even more crowded spectra than that of acetone.

Measurements of acetone-$^{13}C_1$ were performed with an isotopically enriched sample in the frequency range from 37-1102 GHz. Loomis-Wood plots (LWPs) are one approach to improve and fasten the analysis of such crowded spectra. Here, an updated version of the LLWP software was used which relies on LWPs for fast and confident assignments. Additionally, LLWP focuses on being user-friendly, intuitive, and applicable to a broad range of assignment tasks. The software will be presented here and is available together with its full documentation at llwp.astro.uni-koeln.de. Predictions of acetone-$^{13}C_1$ created with ERHAM [2] allow for future radio astronomical searches.

[1] P. Groner, *J. Mol. Struct.* **550-551** (2000) 473-479.
[2] P. Groner, *J. Chem. Phys.* **107** (1997) 4483-4498.
[3] P. Groner, *J. Mol. Spectrosc.* **278** (2012) 52-67.

RJ08

DUAL BAND MINIATURIZED SEMI-CONFOCAL FABRY-PEROT SPECTROMETERS FOR H2O AND HDO MILLIMETER-WAVE SENSING

DEACON J NEMCHICK, ADRIAN TANG, <u>BRIAN DROUIN</u>, *Jet Propulsion Laboratory, California Institute of Technology, Pasadena, CA, USA*; ANANDA Q. NOLE, *College of Engineering and Architecture, Howard University, Washington, DC, USA*; NEDA KHIABANI, CHUNG-TSE MICHAEL WU, *Electrical and Computer Engineering, Rutgers University, Piscataway, NJ, USA*; MARIA ALONSO, *Department of Microelectronics, Delft University of Technology, Delft, The Netherlands*; M.-C. FRANK CHANG, *Electrical Engineering, University of California - Los Angeles, Los Angeles, CA, USA*.

The exploration of icy body composition in the solar system has primarily involved spectroscopic measurements of volatiles through remote sensing, in which materials naturally expelled from the surface enter the exosphere and potentially escape into space. Landed missions on comets have brought focus onto the development of small, sensitive instrumentation capable of similar composition measurements of the nascent surface and near-surface materials. We present an evolution of our compact millimeter-wave cavity spectrometer that is tuned for sensitivity at 80.6 and 183 GHz where HDO and H_2O exhibit resonance features.

In this presentation we will discuss both a low SWaP (size-weight and power) architecture that uses custom micro-chip transceiver elements that is suitable for maturation to deployable systems and a modular configuration using traditional GaAs based millimeter wave hardware suitable for laboratory studies. New design features for these systems including the quartz based coupler, thermal management, and separate clocking board will be discussed in addition to sensitivity studies and preliminary work detecting sublimated ice samples.

RJ09 4:48–5:03

DEVELOPMENT OF A MM-WAVE ULTRA-SENSITIVE SPECTROMETER FOR THE DETECTION OF SEMI-VOLATILE ORGANIC VAPORS

MHAMAD CHRAYTEH, FABIEN SIMON, CORALIE ELMALEH, FRANCIS HINDLE, GAËL MOURET, ARNAUD CUISSET, *Laboratoire de Physico-Chimie de l'Atmosphère, Université du Littoral Côte d'Opale, Dunkerque, France.*

Cavity-Enhanced Absorption Spectroscopy (CEAS) and Cavity Ring-Down Spectroscopy (CRDS) are well established for sensitive infrared measurements of gas phase compounds at trace level using their rovibrational signatures. The recent successful development of a THz Fabry-Perot spectrometer shows that the adaptation of such techniques to the THz and submillimeter is possible[1] by probing rotational transitions of light polar compounds. Here we report on the development of a new millimeter resonator based on a low-loss corrugated waveguide with highly reflective photonic mirrors obtaining a finesse above 3500 around 150 GHz. With an effective path length of one kilometer, a significant sensitivity has been evaluated by the measurement of line intensities as low as 10^{-26} cm^{-1}/(molecule/cm^2). This spectrometer will be used to detect semi-volatile organic vapors at trace level which could not be envisaged with a conventional detection technique.[2,3]

[1] Francis Hindle et al. Optica, vol.6, 1449-1454, (2019).
[2] Gaël Mouret et al. IEEE Sensors, vol.11(1), 133-138, (2013).
[3] Roucou et al., CHEMPHYSCHEM, 19, 1056-1067, (2018).

Acknowledgment: This work received financial support from the French Agence Nationale de la Recherche via funding of the project Millimeter-wave Explosive Taggant vapors Investigations using Spectral taxonomy (METIS) under contract number ANR-20-ASTR-0016-03.

RJ10 5:06–5:21

INTERFERENCE BETWEEN THE $5d_{5/2} - 5p_{3/2}$ AND $5p_{3/2} - 5s_{1/2}$ COHERENCES (386.4 AND 384.1 THz) IN Rb OBSERVED BY ULTRAFAST FOUR-WAVE MIXING SPECTROSCOPY

THOMAS REBOLI, *Department of Electrical and Computer Engineering, University of Illinois at Urbana-Champaign, Urbana, Il, USA*; J. GARY EDEN, *Department of Electrical and Computer Engineering, University of Illinois at Urbana-Champaign, Urbana, IL, USA.*

Coherences at 386.2 THz and 384.1 THz, corresponding to the $5d_{5/2} - 5p_{3/2}$ and $5p_{3/2} - 5s_{1/2}$ difference frequencies, respectively, have been established in the Rb atom during pump-probe experiments involving pairs of identical 150 fs pulses produced by a Ti:Al$_2$O$_3$ laser and a Michelson interferometer. The interference between the two coherences within the atom is observed through a parametric four-wave mixing process in Rb and detection of the signal wave intensity at 420 nm. Scanning the time delay between the pump and probe pulses over a 600 ps interval produces a sampling rate over 300 THz and allows for a spectral domain resolution of 0.05 cm^{-1} to be achieved. The figure at right shows several spectra recorded near 2.1 THz, the $(5d_{5/2} - 5p_{3/2}) - (5p_{3/2} - 5s_{1/2})$ difference frequency, with varying angle between the pump and probe pulses (i.e., the phase matching angle) and varying Rb background density. A Fano interference window is clearly observed, and analysis of these and similar spectra demonstrates that the amplitude and phase of the coherently-coupled, three Rb state system can be controlled precisely.

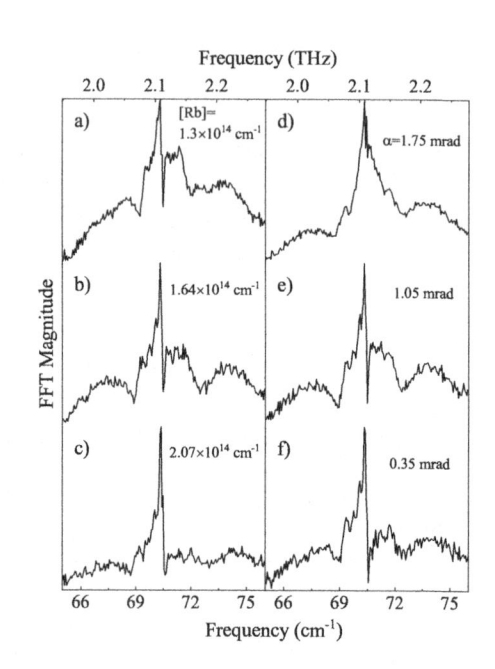

RK. Metal containing

Thursday, June 23, 2022 – 1:45 PM

Room: 217 Noyes Laboratory

Chair: Michael Heaven, Emory University, Atlanta, GA, USA

RK01   1:45 – 2:00

SPECTROSCOPIC CHARACTERIZATION OF REACTIVE INTERMEDIATES IN VARIOUS METAL CATALYSTS

KATHLEEN ANN NICKSON, ETIENNE GARAND, *Department of Chemistry, University of Wisconsin–Madison, Madison, WI, USA.*

In order to improve transition metal catalyst performance, we must first understand the mechanistic features and intermediates in these reactions. Despite great progress in the field, some intermediates can be particularly hard to isolate and investigate. These difficulties can be overcome by forming these intermediates in the gas-phase. Specifically, collision induced dissociation of a precursor creates a vacant ligand position in the precursor which allows for a facile ion-molecule reaction in an ion trap to produce the desired intermediate. These intermediates can then be captured by evaporative quenching of collision complexes and their structures can be probed via cryogenic ion vibrational spectroscopy. In this work, we utilize these gas-phase techniques to focus on two transition metal catalyst systems: a $[Ru^{II}(bpy)(tpy)(H_2O)]^{2+}$ water oxidation catalyst as well as two (N-N)PtCl$_2$ catalysts (N-N= ethylene diamine (en), diamine (NH$_3$)$_2$) for C-H activation and functionalization. For the ruthenium water oxidation catalyst, we have formed the elusive oxo intermediate by reacting $[Ru(bpy)(tpy)]^{2+}$ with O$_3$ to readily produce $[Ru(bpy)(tpy)O]^{2+}$. Interestingly, since the oxo readily forms with ozone but does not with N$_2$O, this indicates that the spin state of the Ru=O is a triplet. This structure is confirmed by the observation of the Ru=O vibration. For the (N-N)PtCl$_2$ catalysts, we prepare the sigma-CH intermediates by reacting $[(N-N)PtCl]^{1+}$ with various alkanes and alkenes such as methane and benzene.

RK02   2:03 – 2:18

THE PURE ROTATIONAL SPECTRUM OF MgCl IN THE $(2)^2\Pi_i$ EXCITED STATE

TYLER J HERMAN, *Department of Chemistry and Biochemistry, University of Arizona, Tucson, AZ, USA*; PARKER CROWTHER, *Chemistry and Biochemistry, University of Arizona, Tucson, AZ, USA*; LUCY M. ZIURYS, *Dept. of Astronomy, Dept. of Chemistry, Arizona Radio Observatory, The University of Arizona, Tucson, AZ, USA.*

The millimeter/submillimeter spectrum of magnesium chloride (MgCl) has been measured in an electronic excited state, using direct absorption spectroscopy in the range of 240-310 GHz. The molecule was synthesized by reacting chlorine gas (Cl$_2$) with magnesium vapor, produced using a Broida-type oven in the presence of argon carrier gas. Seven rotational transitions in each of six isotopologues (^{24}Mg^{35}Cl, ^{24}Mg^{37}Cl, ^{25}Mg^{35}Cl, ^{25}Mg^{37}Cl, ^{26}Mg^{35}Cl, ^{26}Mg^{37}Cl) were measured in the ground vibrational state, with a number of vibrationally excited satellite lines (v=1-4) also being observed for each species. From the data, rotational, fine structure, and ^{25}Mg hyperfine (^{25}MgCl only) parameters were determined for the six isotopologues in this state, as well as equilibrium constants and the equilibrium bond length, r_e = 2.54 Å. Based on theoretical calculations, this excited state has been identified as $(2)^2\Pi_i$, which has never before been observed experimentally. The excited state manifold of MgCl has been the subject of a number of computational studies, and is of interest for laser cooling experiments.

RK03　　　　　　　　　　　　　　　　　　　　　　　　　　　　　　　　　2:21 – 2:36
METAL IDENTITY AND PRODUCT BINDING TUNE STRUCTURE AND CHARGE DISTRIBUTION: INFRARED SPECTRA OF CATALYTICALLY RELEVANT METAL BIPYRIDINE COMPLEXES

<u>MADISON M. FOREMAN</u>, WYATT ZAGOREC-MARKS, J. MATHIAS WEBER, *JILA and Department of Chemistry, University of Colorado, Boulder, CO, USA.*

Electrocatalytic reduction of CO_2 into feedstock for chemical fuels is a promising approach to achieving a carbon neutral fuel cycle.[a] While this has been an active field of study for decades, relatively little is known about the key reaction intermediates and molecular-level processes of proposed catalytic mechanisms, necessitating a deeper understanding to inform the design of future catalysts.

We present cryogenic gas-phase infrared spectra of catalytically relevant model systems consisting of a transition metal center (Co, Ni, or Cu) coordinated to two bipyridine-based ligands, either bare or with a formate adduct.[b] Bipyridine derivatives are frequently ligands for molecular catalysts where a transition metal ion is coordinated to four N atoms. This family of metal-4N catalysts has been studied extensively due to their exceptional performance and ease of synthesis. Formate is one of many possible CO_2 reduction products.[c,d] Density functional theory was used to assign spectral features and calculate charge distributions.

The vibrational spectra inform us of the structure of and intermolecular forces in each complex, revealing the binding motif of the formate adduct to the metal center and the dependence of this arrangement on the identity of the metal. The calculated charge distributions demonstrate the role of the organic ligands to act as charge reservoirs, where they show remarkable electronic flexibility in response to the addition of a formate adduct and the nature of the coordinated metal center. This work showcases the influence of transition metal identity on the formate-metal binding motif and the significant role of the organic ligand framework in adjusting the redox properties of these complexes.

[a] M. M. Foreman, R. J. Hirsch, J. M. Weber, J. Phys. Chem. A 125 (2021) 7297-7302
[b] E. E. Benson, C. P. Kubiak, A. J. Sathrum, J. M. Smieja, Chem. Soc. Rev. 38 (2009) 89–99
[c] J. M. Savéant Chem. Rev. 108 (2008) 2348–2378
[d] T. Shimoda, T. Morishima, K. Kodama, T. Hirose, D. E. Polyansky, G. F. Manbeck, J. T. Mucherman, E. Fujita, Inorg. Chem. 57 (2018) 5486-5498

RK04　　　　　　　　　　　　　　　　　　　　　　　　　　　　　　　　　2:39 – 2:54
HIGH RESOLUTION LASER SPECTROSCOPY OF THE [16.0]5 - $X^5\Delta_4$ ELECTRONIC SYSTEM OF RUTHENIUM MONOXIDE

<u>ALLAN G. ADAM</u>, GEOFFREY M. CHENARD, *Department of Chemistry, University of New Brunswick, Fredericton, NB, Canada*; COLAN LINTON, DENNIS W. TOKARYK, *Department of Physics, University of New Brunswick, Fredericton, NB, Canada.*

At the 2021 ISMS conference, we presented a talk on the high resolution spectroscopy of the RuO molecule.[a] This talk was primarily about the observation of the seven isotopologues of ^{n}RuO (n= 104, 102, 101, 100, 99, 98, and 96) plus hyperfine structure resolved in the ^{101}RuO and ^{99}RuO isotopologues of the 2-0, 1-0, and 0-0 bands of the green [18.1]4 – $X^5\Delta_4$ and [18.1]3 – $X^5\Delta_3$ electronic transitions. Comparison was made to the earlier work of Wang et al.[b] We mentioned that future work would centre on the high resolution spectroscopy of the red [16.0]5 - $X^5\Delta_4$ electronic system. We will now report on the 2-0, 1-0, and 0-0 bands of this system plus our assignments of other spin-orbit transitions associated with this red system. The work has yielded the isotopologues listed above as well as resolved hyperfine structure for the ^{101}RuO and ^{99}RuO isotopologues. The observation of the extra spin-orbit transitions gives us the spin-orbit intervals for the ground and excited states. Results of our hyperfine analysis will be used to discuss the electronic configurations associated with both the red and the green electronic transitions.

[a] A.G. Adam, G.M. Chenard, C. Linton, and D.W. Tokaryk, http://hdl.handle.net/2142/111251.
[b] N. Wang, Y.W. Ng, and A.S.-C. Cheung, J. Phys. Chem. A, <u>117</u>, 13279-13283, (2013).

RK05 2:57 – 3:12

OBSERVATIONS OF THE ZEEMAN/PASCHEN-BACK EFFECT IN THE A-X SYSTEM OF CrH

PATRICK CROZET, JÉRÔME MORVILLE, AMANDA J. ROSS, *Inst. Lumière Matière, Univ Lyon 1 & CNRS, Université de Lyon, Villeurbanne, France*; JULIEN MORIN, *Laboratoire Univers et Particules, Universite de Montpellier, Montpellier, France.*

We present our investigations of the magnetic response of $A^6\Sigma^+ - X^6\Sigma^+$ transitions in CrH, in fields up to 0.5 Tesla, focusing on the strong dissymmetry between σ^+ and σ^- transitions, observed as predicted[a] at modest magnetic field strengths. This dissymmetry is recorded as Stokes V signals in telescope spectropolarimetry, where it gives a sensitive probe of stellar magnetism. CrH (and FeH) bands feature prominently in spectra of cool dwarf stars taken for example on the SPIRou spectropolarimeter (searching for exoplanets at the Canada-France-Hawaii telescope). Ultimately, our work should help to discriminate effects of stellar magnetism from exoplanet presence in radial velocity data derived from telescope spectropolarimetric measurements.

Field-free line positions are well-documented[b] for the 760 and 870 nm bands of the *A–X* system. IR laser magnetic resonance studies[c] provide some ground state Landé factors, but the Zeeman effect has been investigated for only the lowest rotational levels of the *A* state, under molecular beam conditions[d]. To extend these observations, we have recorded cavity-enhanced absorption data (providing relative intensities in zero field conditions) and laser-induced fluorescence spectra using circularly polarised light, with a discharge source producing CrH at around 500 K.

---
[a] Kuzmychov and Berdyugina, Astron. Astrophys. **558**, A120 (2013)
[b] Bauschlicher *et al.*, J. Chem. Phys. **115**, 1312 (2001); Ram *et al.*, J. Mol. Spectrosc. **161** 445 (1993); Chowdhury *et al.*, Phys. Chem. Chem. Phys. **8**, 822 (2006); Kleman and Uhler, Can. J. Phys **37** 537 (1959)
[c] Lipus *et al.*, Mol. Phys. 73 (5), 1041 (1991)
[d] Chen *et al.*, Phys. Chem. Chem. Phys. **8**, 822 (2006).

Intermission

RK06 3:54 – 4:09

TERAHERTZ SPECTROSCOPY OF CaH

SHOTA SUZUKI, TATSUKI SUMI, FUSAKAZU MATSUSHIMA, KAORI KOBAYASHI, YOSHIKI MORIWAKI, *Department of Physics, University of Toyama, Toyama, Japan*; HIROYUKI OZEKI, *Department of Environmental Science, Toho University, Funabashi, Japan.*

Calcium monohydride CaH is an astronomical molecule identified in the Sun and other stars by using the visible transitions. We have found many new vibrational levels of the $A^2\Pi$, $B/B'^2\Sigma^+$, and $1^2\Delta$ state using laser induced fluorescence (LIF) from visible to ultraviolet region. [a,b,c,d] The pure rotational spectra of the ground state have been measured and analyzed, including the hyperfine structure. [e,f] However, the N range was limited to $N = 2 - 1$ and the highest frequency was about 500 GHz. In this study, we will report our new measurement in the terahertz region.

The terahertz spectra were taken by using tunable far-infrared spectrometer at University of Toyama. Calcium monohydride was produced in a quartz cell where Ca vapor was introduced by heating Ca at 750°C and DC discharge was applied under H_2 and He (or Ar) gas environment. The highest frequencies of the ground state and vibrationally excited state are approximately 3.7 THz and 1.9 THz, respectively.

---
[a] K. Watanabe, N. Yoneyama, K. Uchida, K. Kobayashi, F. Matsushima, Y. Moriwaki, S. C. Ross, *Chem. Phys. Lett.* **657**, 1 (2016).
[b] K. Watanabe, I. Tani, K. Kobayashi, Y. Moriwaki, S. C. Ross, *Chem. Phys. Lett.* **710**, 11 (2018).
[c] J. Furuta, K. Watanabe, I. Tani, K. Kobayashi, Y. Moriwaki, S. C. Ross, *International Symposium on Molecular Spectroscopy, 74th meeting*, **T106**, (2019).
[d] S. Yaguramaki, J. Furuta, I. Tani, K. Kobayashi, Y. Moriwaki, S. C. Ross, *The 2021 International Symposium on Molecular Spectroscopy*, **WM11**, (2021).
[e] C. I. Frum, J. J. Oh, E. A. Cohen, H. M. Pickett, *Astrophys. J. Lett.* **408**, L61 (1993).
[f] W. L. Barclay Jr., M. A. Anderson, L. M. Ziurys, *Astrophys. J. Lett.* **408**, L65 (1993).

RK07

ANALYSIS OF THE $A\ ^4\Pi_r - X\ ^4\Sigma^-$ ELECTRONIC TRANSITION OF MOLYBDENUM NITRIDE (MoN)

LEAH C O'BRIEN, *Department of Chemistry, Southern Illinois University, Edwardsville, IL, USA*; GABRIEL A HOTZ, KRISTIN N BALES, JACK C HARMS, JAMES J O'BRIEN, *Chemistry and Biochemistry, University of Missouri, St. Louis, MO, USA*; NYLA S WOODS, *Department of Chemistry, Southern Illinois University, Edwardsville, IL, USA*; WENLI ZOU, *Institute of Modern Physics, Northwest University, Xi'an, China*.

Transition metal nitrides are of growing interest due to their catalytic, energy storage, sensing, superconducting, and mechanical properties. The (0,0) band of the $A\ ^4\Pi_r - X\ ^4\Sigma^-$ transition of MoN was recorded at Doppler-limited resolution using intracavity laser spectroscopy (ILS) integrated with a Fourier-transform spectrometer used for detection (ILS-FTS). The target MoN molecules were produced in the plasma discharge of a molybdenum-lined copper hollow cathode, using a gas mixture of Ar with about 1% N_2 in a reaction chamber with about 1 Torr total pressure. Isotopologue structure in the spectrum is clearly visible and analysis is underway for the five abundant isotopologues with no nuclear spin ($I_{Mo}=0$): ^{92}MoN (14.6%), ^{94}MoN (9.2%), ^{96}MoN (16.7%), ^{98}MoN (24.3%), and ^{100}MoN (9.7%). The progress, preliminary results of this analysis, and comparison to a recent high-level computational study will be provided.

RK08

MASS-INDEPENDENT ROTATIONAL AND DEPERTURBATION ANALYSIS OF THE [15.30]1 AND [14.26]0^+ ELECTRONIC STATES OF TUNGSTEN SULFIDE (WS)

KRISTIN N BALES, JACK C HARMS, JAMES J O'BRIEN, *Chemistry and Biochemistry, University of Missouri, St. Louis, MO, USA*; LEAH C O'BRIEN, *Department of Chemistry, Southern Illinois University, Edwardsville, IL, USA*.

The complex electronic structure of transition metal diatomic molecules, such as tungsten monosulfide (WS), makes them intriguing targets for high level spectroscopic analysis. A plethora of electrons and accessible valence orbitals make WS a difficult molecule to model computationally due to the large number of possible electronic interactions. The (0,0) and (1,0) vibrational bands of the [15.30]1 - X $^3\Sigma^-(0^+)$ transition of WS were recorded in absorption at Doppler-limited resolution using intracavity laser spectroscopy integrated with a Fourier-transform spectrometer used for detection (ILS-FTS). The target WS molecules were produced in the plasma discharge of a tungsten-lined copper hollow cathode, using a gas mixture of approximately 70% Ar and 30% H_2, with a trace amount of CS_2, giving a reaction chamber pressure of about 1 torr total. Within each spectrum, evidence of heterogeneous mass- and J-dependent perturbations were observed across all four abundant isotopologues: ^{182}W^{32}S, ^{183}W^{32}S, ^{184}W^{32}S, and ^{186}W^{32}S. The perturbations observed in the (0,0) and (1,0) bands were attributed to interactions with lines in the v=2 and v=3 vibrational levels of the [14.26]0^+ state of WS. Rotational and deperturbation analyses incorporated a mass-independent Dunham model built into PGOPHER to fit lines from the two [15.30]1 transition bands, as well as line positions from several bands of the [14.26]0^+ - X $^3\Sigma^-(0^+)$ transition previously analyzed by our group (J.C. Harms et al., J. Mol. Spec. 2020 (374), 111378). The results of this analysis and comparison with previous computational work (J. Zhang et al., J. Quant. Spectrosc. Radiat. Transfer. 2020 (256), 107314) will be presented.

RK10 5:06 – 5:21

LOW- AND HIGH-RESOLUTION LASER-INDUCED FLUORESCENCE (LIF) OF JET-COOLED SmO

JOEL R SCHMITZ, ARIANNA RODRIGUEZ, *Department of Chemistry, Emory University, Atlanta, GA, USA*; TIMOTHY STEIMLE, *School of Molecular Sciences, Arizona State University, Tempe, AZ, USA*; MICHAEL HEAVEN, *Department of Chemistry, Emory University, Atlanta, GA, USA*.

The chemi-ionization reactions of atomic lanthanides $M+O \rightarrow MO^+ + e^-$ are currently being investigated as a method to artificially increase the localized electron density in the ionosphere for uniform radio wave propagation. Recent experiments involving the release of atomic samarium (Sm) into the upper atmosphere have resulted in the production of a cloud with blue and red emissions[1]. Spectroscopic characterization of SmO is required to accurately determine the fraction of SmO present in the release cloud. While the low-lying states of SmO have been previously spectroscopically characterized, the analysis was hindered due to the production of SmO under high temperature conditions[2,3]. In this work, jet-cooled SmO was produced and low- and high-resolution laser-induced fluorescence (LIF) as well as dispersed laser-induced fluorescence (DLIF) techniques were employed for electronic structure characterization. For the first time, vibrational constants for several low-lying states have been determined. Using high-resolution LIF, the hyperfine structure of the (1)1 $v = 0$ and [15.35]1 $v = 0, 1$ states was recorded. Data and analysis of ground and low-lying excited states of SmO will be presented.

[1] Ard, S.G. et al. J. Chem. Phys. 2015, 143, 204303.
[2] Hannigan, M. C. J. Mol. Spec. 1983, 99, 235-238.
[3] Linton, C. et al. J. Mol. Spec. 1987, 126, 370-392.

RL. Structure determination
Thursday, June 23, 2022 – 1:45 PM
Room: 1024 Chemistry Annex

Chair: Nathan A. Seifert, University of New Haven, New Haven, CT, USA

RL01   1:45 – 2:00

THE ROTATIONAL SPECTRUM OF SULFANILAMIDE AND ITS HYDRATED CLUSTER [a]

<u>SERGIO MATO</u>, RAÚL AGUADO, JOSÉ L. ALONSO, IKER LEÓN, *Grupo de Espectroscopia Molecular, Lab. de Espectroscopia y Bioespectroscopia, Unidad Asociada CSIC, Universidad de Valladolid, Valladolid, Spain.*

Sulfanilamide (SA, 4-aminobenzenesulfonamide) is an antibacterial drug that interferes with the conversion of para-aminobenzoic acid (PABA) to folate, preventing the synthesis of folic acid (vitamin B9), essential in multiple carbon transfer reactions. Due to its importance, in this work, we characterize sulfanilamide in the isolation conditions of a supersonic expansion using Fourier transform microwave techniques assisted by laser ablation. A single conformer of the bare molecule, stabilized by an N-H•••O=S intramolecular interaction of the sulfonyl group, has been detected. Because the docking process is controlled by the difference in Gibbs free energy between the ligands solvated by the extracellular medium and the ligand interacting with the receptor's active site, we have also studied the sulfanilamide's microsolvation process. Interestingly, a single water molecule is enough to trigger a conformational switch.

---
[a] Acknowledgments: THIS RESEARCH WAS FUNDED BY MINISTERIO DE CIENCIA E INNOVACIÓN, GRANT NUMBER PID2019-111396GB-I00, AND JUNTA DE CASTILLA Y LEÓN, GRANT NUMBER VA244P20. S.M. THANKS CONSEJO SOCIAL FROM UNIVERSIDAD DE VALLADOLID FOR AN UNDERGRADUATE FELLOWSHIP

RL02   2:03 – 2:18

THE ROTATIONAL SPECTRUM OF NONAFLUORO-TERT-BUTYL ALCOHOL

<u>JOSHUA E. ISERT</u>, *Department of Chemistry, Missouri University of Science and Technology, Rolla, MO, USA*; ZAYRA LETICIA GONZALEZ, KARLA V. SALAZAR, DIEGO RODRIGUEZ, *Department of Chemistry, University of Texas Rio Grande Valley, Brownsville, TX, USA*; NICOLE MOON, *Department of Chemistry, Missouri University of Science and Technology, Rolla, MO, USA*; WEI LIN, *Department of Chemistry, University of Texas Rio Grande Valley, Brownsville, TX, USA*; G. S. GRUBBS II, *Department of Chemistry, Missouri University of Science and Technology, Rolla, MO, USA.*

In a collaborative effort with the University of Texas-Rio Grande Valley, a chirped pulse microwave (CP-FTMW) spectroscopy experiment was carried out on nonafluoro-tert-butyl alcohol (NFTBA) monomer from 5.5 to 18.75 GHz. Calculations were run in order to identify the lowest energy conformation and these will be compared to the experimentally determined structure. In addition to the structure, the spectrum of NFTBA exhibits large amplitude motion and these complexities will be examined and discussed. NFTBA exhibits high acidity comparable to carboxylic acids, and this presentation will draw comparisons between these two classes of molecules.

RL03   2:21 – 2:36

INTERNAL ROTATION ANALYSIS AND STRUCTURAL DETERMINATION OF R-CARVONE

<u>NICOLE MOON</u>, G. S. GRUBBS II, *Department of Chemistry, Missouri University of Science and Technology, Rolla, MO, USA.*

When the spectrum of R-carvone was collected at Missouri S&T in preparation for a three-wave mixing experiment, splittings within the rotational transitions were observed that were unreported in the original study of S-carvone by Moreno et al.[a] It was discovered that these splittings were due to internal rotations caused by two non-equivalent methyl rotors. This promoted a re-investigation into the pure rotational spectrum of R-carvone using chirped-pulse, Fourier transform microwave (CP-FTMW) spectroscopy within the 5-18 GHz region of the electromagnetic spectrum. Spectral analyses were performed using a combination of the SPFIT[b] and XIAM[c] software packages. Current work on the parent and singly substituted isotopologue species for the EQ1 and EQ2 conformers will be reported. In addition, the potential energy barrier heights to internal rotation for both rotors have been analyzed and will be discussed.

---
[a] Moreno, J. R. A.; Huet, T. R.; González, J. J. L. Struct Chem. 2013, 24, 1163.
[b] Pickett, H. M. J. Mol. Spectrosc. 1991, 148, 371-377.
[c] H. Hartwig and H. Dreizler, Z. Naturforsch 51a, 923-932 (1996).

RL04   2:39 – 2:54
ROTATIONAL SPECTRUM AND CONFORMATIONAL ANALYSIS OF PERILLARTINE: INSIGHTS INTO THE STRUCTURE-SWEETNESS RELATIONSHIP[a]

<u>GABRIELA JUÁREZ</u>[b], MIGUEL SANZ-NOVO[c], JOSÉ L. ALONSO, ELENA R. ALONSO, IKER LEÓN, *Grupo de Espectroscopia Molecular, Lab. de Espectroscopia y Bioespectroscopia, Unidad Asociada CSIC, Universidad de Valladolid, Valladolid, Spain.*

Perillartine, a solid synthetic sweetener, has been brought into the gas phase using laser ablation techniques, and its conformational panorama has been studied using chirped-pulse Fourier transform microwave spectroscopy (LA-CP-FTMW). Four conformers are detected and characterized under the isolation conditions of the supersonic expansion. The four conformers present an E configuration of the C=N group with respect to the double bond of the ring. The observed structures are verified against the Shallenberger-Acree-Kier's sweetness theory to shed light on the structure-sweetness relationship. The results show that for this particular oxime there is a deluge of possibilities to bind to the receptor.

---

[a] ACKNOWLEDGMENTS: THIS RESEARCH WAS FUNDED BY MINISTERIO DE CIENCIA E INNOVACIÓN, GRANT NUMBER PID2019-111396GB-I00, AND BY JUNTA DE CASTILLA Y LEÓN, GRANT NUMBER VA244P20.

[b] G.J.L. ACKNOWLEDGES FUNDING FROM THE SPANISH "MINISTERIO DE CIENCIA, INNOVACIÓN Y UNIVERSIDADES" UNDER PREDOCTORAL FPI GRANT (BES-2017-082173).

[c] M.S.N. ACKNOWLEDGES FUNDING FROM THE SPANISH "MINISTERIO DE CIENCIA, INNOVACIÓN Y UNIVERSIDADES" UNDER PREDOCTORAL FPU GRANT (FPU17/02987).

RL05   2:57 – 3:12
HIGH-RESOLUTION LASER SPECTROSCOPY OF $S_1 \leftarrow S_0$ TRANSITION OF TRANS-STILBENE : NONPLANAR STRUCTURE IN THE GROUND STATE

<u>AKIRA SHIMIZU</u>, KOSUKE NAKAJIMA, *Graduate School of Science, Kobe University, Kobe, Japan*; SHUNJI KASAHARA, *Molecular Photoscience Research Center, Kobe University, Kobe, Japan*; MASATOSHI MISONO, *Applied Physics, Fukuoka University, Fukuoka, Japan*; MASAAKI BABA, *Graduate School of Science, Kyoto University, Kyoto, Japan.*

We have great interest in the excited-state dynamics of *trans*-stilbene such as *cis-trans* isomerization in the electronic excited state. Zewail et al. reported the results of time-resolved spectroscopy and suggested its nonplanar structure in the ground S_0 state [a]. In contrast, Pratt et al. concluded that the molecule is essentially planar both in the S_0 and S_1 states by analyzing the rotationally resolved high-resolution speoctrum of the $S_1 \leftarrow S_0$ 0_0^0 band [b]. We observed the spectrum with much higher accuracy and quality, and re-determined the rotational constants by high-resolution spectrum of 0_0^0 bannd. Although it is impossible to accurate determine the absoulute value of rotational constant A for the a-type transition, We could conclude that *trans*-stilbene is non-planar in the S_0 state. In addition to estimate the molecular structure from observed rotational constants, we developed program. By this program, we estimated that phenyl rings are rotated approximately ±10 degrees in S_0 state. Theoretical calculation using WB97XD functional provided the phenyl rings are rotated 14 degrees in S_0 state and 2.4 degrees in S_1 state. WB97XD functional evaluate steric repulsion between H atoms of *ortho*-position in a phenyl ring and in an ethylene part by dispersion force potential semi-eprically. This result support non-planar structure revealed from the observed rotational constants.

---

[a] J. A. Syage, P. M. Felker, and A. H. Zewail, J. Chem. Phys. **81**, 4685 (1984).

[b] D. W. Pratt, W. L. Meerts et al., J. Phys. Chem. **94**, 6 (1990).

RL06　　　　　　　　　　　　　　　　　　　　　　　　　　　　　　　　　　　3:15 – 3:30
PROPANE ISOTOPOLOGUES: HIGH RESOLUTION FAR-IR SYNCHROTRON SPECTRA OF PROPANE-D7 (CD3-CDH-CD3) AND PROPANE-D5 (CH3-CD2-CD3)

STEPHEN J. DAUNT, *Department of Physics & Astronomy, The University of Tennessee-Knoxville, Knoxville, TN, USA*; COLIN WESTERN[a], *School of Chemistry, University of Bristol, Bristol, United Kingdom*; BRANT E. BILLINGHURST, JIANBAO ZHAO, *EFD, Canadian Light Source Inc., Saskatoon, Saskatchewan, Canada*; ROBERT GRZYWACZ, *Department of Physics & Astronomy, The University of Tennessee-Knoxville, Knoxville, TN, USA*.

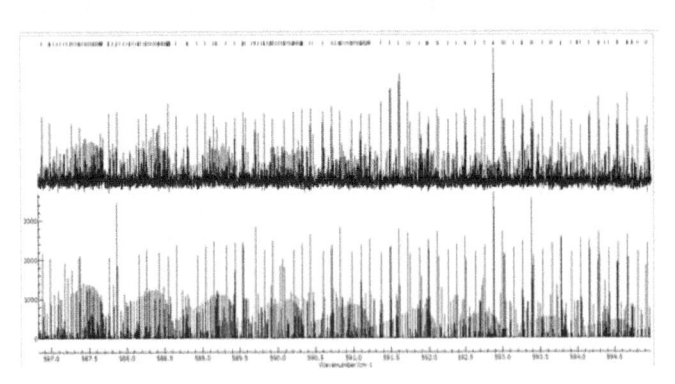

We continue our project of recording spectra and ro-ibrational analyses of propane isotopologues to determine ro-vibrational constants for this family of molecules. No MW, mm or sub-mm studies exist as of yet. IR/R spectra of propane-D_5 do not appear to have ever been reported on in the literature. There are only low/medium resolution data on the -D_7 species.[b] We acquired survey and high resolution (0.002-0.00096 cm^{-1}) synchrotron IR data at the CLS facility in Saskatoon for the -D_5 bands. We also now have preliminary values of its rotational constants from the B-type CCC bending mode near 332.7 cm^{-1}. For the -D_7 species we have preliminary analyses of the B-type ν_{14}(A') CCC bend near 305.24 cm^{-1} and the ν_{13} (A') C-type band near 579.34 cm^{-1}. The figure at the left is a part of the R-side of the ν_{13} band for Propane-D_7. Observed spectrum taken at 0.00096cm^{-1} resolution plotted above the PGOPHER[c] simulation.

[a] Deceased 21- September-2021
[b] Gough, Murphy and Raghavachari, J.Chem. Phys. 87, 3332 (1987) and refs. therein
[c] C. M. Western, B. E. Billinghurst PCCP 21, 13986 (2019) and refs. therein.

RL07　　　　　　　　　　　　　　　　　　　　　　　　　　　　　　　　　　　3:33 – 3:48
SEMI-EXPERIMENTAL EQUILIBRIUM STRUCTURE OF METHACRYLONITRILE (C_4H_5N)

HOUSTON H. SMITH, SAMUEL M. KOUGIAS, DANNY J LEE, BRIAN J. ESSELMAN, *Department of Chemistry, University of Wisconsin-Madison, Madison, WI, USA*; BRYAN CHANGALA, MICHAEL C McCARTHY, *Atomic and Molecular Physics, Harvard-Smithsonian Center for Astrophysics, Cambridge, MA, USA*; R. CLAUDE WOODS, ROBERT J. McMAHON, *Department of Chemistry, University of Wisconsin-Madison, Madison, WI, USA*.

The detection of acrylonitrile (C_3H_3N) in Titan's atmosphere and the interstellar medium suggests methacrylonitrile may also have astronomical relevance. To aid in the astronomical observation, we synthesized methacrylonitrile *via* the hydrocyanation and subsequent dehydration of acetone and obtained its rotational spectrum from 6 – 40 GHz and 130 – 500 GHz. The ground vibrational state of the main isotopologue has been least-squares fit to a sextic Hamiltonian accounting for internal rotation splitting, and the resulting spectroscopic constants compare well with previous literature. The increase in the measured frequency range improved the determination of centrifugal distortion constants, and thus enhances the possibility of detection *via* radioastronomy. Additionally, a semi-experimental equilibrium structure (r_e^{SE}) for methacrylonitrile is sought after due to its small molecular size and accessibility to a wide range of isotopologues. We analyzed the spectra from 6 – 40 GHz and 130 – 360 GHz of all singly-substituted heavy-atom isotopologues (^{13}C and ^{15}N), which were detectable at natural abundance, and least-squares fit them to sextic Hamiltonians accounting for internal rotation. The synthesis of methacrylonitrile was modified by using partially deuterated or fully deuterated acetone to yield samples of varying deuterium incorporation. We will present our analysis of 23 isotopologues, including the main isotopologue, and the resulting (r_e^{SE}) structure.

Intermission

RL08 4:30 – 4:45

SPECTROSCOPIC CONSTANTS AND POTENTIAL FUNCTIONS FOR THE $A^3\Pi_1$ AND $X^1\Sigma^+$ STATES OF IBr BY USING MERGED DATA OF STARK SPECTROSCOPY

NOBUO NISHIMIYA, TOKIO YUKIYA, KATSUKI NOMURA, MASAO SUZUKI, *Faculty of Engineering, Tokyo Polytechnic University, Atsugi, Japan.*

The $A \leftarrow X$ electronic transition spectra of halogen diatomic molecules have been measured to determine the molecular constants and the parameters of potential energy by various researchers.[a,b,c] In 2002, the Dunham coefficients of the X state and rotation-vibration parameters of the A state of IBr were determined by using the assigned line position of spectroscopic data in the range from $v' = 3 - 20$ to $v'' = 1 - 6$ and nuclear quadrupole coupling constants were also reported.[d] An anomalous fluctuations in the v – dependence of the first differences of the inertial rotational constant, $\Delta B'_v = B_{v'+1} - B'_v$ in the $A^3\Pi_1$ was found more than $v = 19$ region. In 2015, we reported a new nonlinear direct potential fitting (DPF) analysis that uses "robust" nonlinear least-squares fits to average properly over the effect of such fluctuations in order to provide an optimum delineation of the underlying potential energy curve(s).[e]

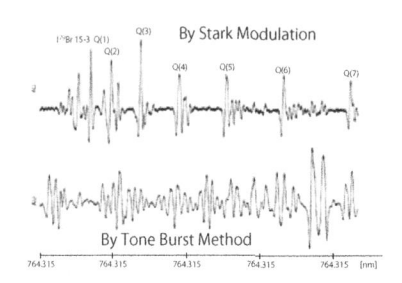

In the near dissociation limit, it would be difficult to assign the spectra, because in that area, too dense spectra would be observed. By adopting Stark spectroscopy, the relatively low J spectra are emphasized and the high J spectra become smaller as shown in the figure. This makes it easier to assign the low J spectra even in dense regions. This work reports the spectroscopic constants refined and the parameters of potential energy curve recalculated.

---

[a] Selin et al, Ark. Fys. **21** (1962) 479.
[b] Coxon et al, JMS **79** (1983) 363, 380.
[c] Heddrich et al, JMS **79** (1992) 384.
[d] Yukiya et al, JMS **214** (2002) 132.
[e] Le Roy, J.Quant.Spectorsc.Rad.Trans. **186**(2017) 179.

RL09 4:48 – 5:03

THE CONFORMATIONAL PANORAMA OF D-PENICILLAMINE: A LASER ABLATION ROTATIONAL STUDY.[a]

DIEGO HERRERAS, ELENA R. ALONSO, IKER LEÓN, JOSÉ L. ALONSO, *Grupo de Espectroscopia Molecular, Lab. de Espectroscopia y Bioespectroscopia, Unidad Asociada CSIC, Universidad de Valladolid, Valladolid, Spain.*

D-Penicillamine, a drug widely used to treat Wilson's disease, removes copper excess from the human body by acting as a chelating agent. In the present work, we address unveiling this molecule's three-dimensional structure as a first approach to shed light on its mechanism of action. Using a laser ablation source, we have transferred solid D-Penicillamine to the gas phase by laser ablation LA and probed it employing CP-FTWM spectroscopy in the isolated conditions of a supersonic jet. Two dominant conformers of the D-Penicillamine have been identified so far.

---

[a] Acknowledgments: THIS RESEARCH WAS FUNDED BY MINISTERIO DE CIENCIA E INNOVACIÓN, GRANT NUMBER PID2019-111396GB-I00, AND BY JUNTA DE CASTILLA Y LEÓN, GRANT NUMBER VA244P20.

RL10   5:06 – 5:21

STRUCTURE AND DYNAMICS OF HHe$_3^+$: THE EMERGENCE OF LARGE-SCALE NUCLEAR DELOCALIZATION

<u>IRÉN SIMKÓ</u>, CSABA FÁBRI, ATTILA CSÁSZÁR, *MTA-ELTE Complex Chemical Systems Research Group, Laboratory of Molecular Structure and Dynamics, ELTE Eötvös Loránd University, Budapest, Hungary*; FABIEN BRIEUC, CHRISTOPH SCHRAN[a], DOMINIK MARX, *Lehrstuhl fuer Theoretische Chemie, Ruhr-Universitaet Bochum, Buchum, Germany*; OSKAR ASVANY, STEPHAN SCHLEMMER, *I. Physikalisches Institut, University of Cologne, Cologne, Germany*.

The HHe$_3^+$ cation is a model system for solvated triatomic molecules, which consists of a (quasi)linear HHe$_2^+$ core (chromophore) and a weakly-bound solvating He.[b] The equilibrium structure is T-shaped, but the "quantum" structure is very different, showing large-scale nuclear delocalization. In order to study the structure and dynamics of HHe$_3^+$ we performed path-integral molecular dynamics and variational nuclear-motion computations,[c] based on a new, highly accurate, neural-network potential-energy surface.[d] We tested the new potential on the HHe$_2^+$ cation. The computed rovibrational transitions have excellent agreement with experimental data, showing the high quality of the potential. As to the HHe$_3^+$, we determined the vibrational states below and above the dissociation limit, corresponding to the solvating He and the chromophore, respectively. The computed chromophore vibrational frequencies have good agreement with the experimental results. Note that, the frequencies of the chromophore vibrations are significantly shifted compared to that of the HHe$_2^+$, because the intermolecular bond is relatively strong. In order to investigate the "quantum" structure, we computed and plotted the nuclear density, which shows the spatial distribution of solvating He with respect to the chromophore. The nuclear density was obtained from path integral molecular dynamics computations and the vibrational wave functions from the nuclear-motion computation. The plots reveal that the true shape of the complex is completely different from the equilibrium structure: the solvating He is fully delocalized, forming a torus around the central proton even in the vibrational ground state. Delocalization is observed for each state, and its exact pattern reflects the type of vibrational excitation.

[a]Current address: Yusuf Hamied Department of Chemistry, University of Cambridge, Lensfield Road, Cambridge, CB2 1EW, UK
[b]*Mol. Phys.* 2019, 117, 9-12, 1559-1583; *J. Phys. Chem. Lett.* 2019, 10, 5325-5330; *Phys. Chem. Chem. Phys.* 2020, 22, 22885-22888
[c]*J. Chem. Phys.* 2009, 130, 134112.; *J Chem Phys.* 2011, 134, 074105.; *J. Chem. Phys.* 2017, 147, 134101.
[d]*Angew. Chem. Int. Ed.* 2017, 56, 12828; *J. Chem. Theo. Comp.* 2020, 16, 88.; https://www.theochem.rub.de/go/rubnnet4md.html

RL11   *Post-Deadline Abstract*   5:24 – 5:39

MID-INFRARED DOPPLER-FREE SATURATION ABSORPTION SPECTROSCOPY OF METHANE FOR FUTURE CAVITY-ENHANCED DOUBLE-RESONANCE SPECTROSCOPY INVESTIGATING ITS HIGH POLYADS.

<u>S M SHAH RIYADH</u>, *Department of Physics and Astronomy, University Of Louisville, Louisville, KY, USA*; HAMZEH TELFAH, MD TOUHIDUL ISLAM, JINJUN LIU, *Department of Chemistry, University of Louisville, Louisville, KY, USA*.

Understanding the rotational structure of molecular spectra requires high resolution and high-frequency accuracy. Furthermore, a capability of high-speed, wide-range spectral scan is strongly desired. We have developed a mid-infrared Doppler-free saturation absorption spectroscopy apparatus using a continuous-wave optical parametric oscillator (CW-OPO).[a] Here we report a comprehensive spectral scan of the $\nu_3 = 1$ band of methane (CH$_4$). The absolute frequency calibration was achieved using previously reported transition frequencies determined using optical frequency combs,[b] while a home-build Fabry-Pérot etalon was used for relative frequency calibration. A linewidth of less than 5 MHz has been reached, and the frequency accuracy is estimated to be better than 1 MHz, both of which can be further improved. We have successfully locked the frequency of the OPO to a Doppler-free line of CH$_4$ using a top-of-fringe locking method. A cavity-enhanced double-resonance spectroscopy apparatus is under construction. It combines the Doppler-free saturation absorption setup and an existing continuous-wave cavity ring-down (CW-CRDS) spectroscopy apparatus. The first mid-infrared photon from the frequency-locked OPO pumps the CH$_4$ molecule to the $\nu_3 = 1$ vibrational levels, followed by a further excitation to high polyads using a Ti:Saphire ring laser.

[a]D. B. Foote, M. J. Cich, W. C. Hurlbut, U. Eismann, A. T. Heiniger, and C. Haimberger, "High-resolution, broadly-tunable mid-IR spectroscopy using a continuous-wave optical parametric oscillator" *Opt. Express* 29, 5295-5303 (2021)
[b]M. Abe, K. Iwakuni, S. Okubo, and H. Sasada, "Accurate transition frequency list of the ν_3 band of methane from sub-Doppler resolution comb-referenced spectroscopy," *J. Opt. Soc. Am. B* 30, 1027-1035 (2013)

RL12 5:42 – 5:57

HIGH-RESOLUTION LASER SPECTROSCOPY AND THE ZEEMAN EFFECT: DIBENZOTHIOPHENE

NAOFUMI NAKAYAMA, *Computational Chemistry, Conflex Cooporation, Tokyo, Japan*; MASAAKI BABA, *Molecular Photoscience Research Center, Kobe University, Kobe, Japan*.

For planar aromatic hydrocarbons, intersystem crossing to the triplet state is expected to be very slow according to El Sayed's rule[a,b]. The fluorescence lifetime in the S_1 state of dibenzothiophene is remarkably shorter compared with the analogous molecules such as dibenzofuran. Pratt et al. suggested that the main fast process was intersystem crossing on the basis of the result of high-resolution laser spectroscopy[c]. We observed the high-resolution spectrum in the external magnetic field in order to confirm the contribution of the triplet state. However, no change has been found in the spectrum up to 1.0 Tesla, indicating that the intersystem crossing is slow and is not the main process for the fluorescence decay in the S_1 state of dibenzothiophene. It should be noted that the spectral feature of the $S_1 \leftarrow S_0$ 0_0^0 band of dibenzothiophene is b-type, whereas that of dibenzofuran is a-type. The relatively faster decay is considered to be the result of different character in the S_1 elecronic state. Several electronic excited states are expected to be located in the lower energy region[d]. Ab initio theoretical calculation of B3LYP/6-311G+(2d,p) accurately reproduced the experimental values of rotational constants and excitation energy. The S_1 state has been assigned to $^1A_1$, which is consistent with the fact that the $S_1 \leftarrow S_0$ transition is b-type.

---

[a] M. Baba, N. Nakayama, et al., J. Chem. Phys. **130**, 134315 (2009).
[b] M. Baba, J. Phys. Chem. A **115**, 9514 (2011).
[c] L. Alvarez-Valtierra, John T. Yi, and David W. Pratt, J. Phys. Chem. A **113**, 2261(1990).
[d] M. Baba, T. Katori, M. Kawabata, S. Kunishige, and T. Yamanaka, J. Phys. Chem. A **117**, 13524 (2013).

RM. Fundamental physics

Thursday, June 23, 2022 – 1:45 PM

Room: 124 Burrill Hall

Chair: Terry A. Miller, The Ohio State University, Columbus, OH, USA

RM01   1:45 – 2:00

ROTATIONAL CLOSURE IN LASER-COOLING NONLINEAR MOLECULES

JINJUN LIU, *Department of Chemistry, University of Louisville, Louisville, KY, USA.*

Laser-cooling molecules relies on rapid and continuous photon scattering events that provide the "momentum kicks" that slow down molecules. Experimental implementation of laser cooling with enough photons scattered per molecule (about 10^4 or 10^5) requires not only a highly diagonal Franck-Condon matrix but also rotational closure. Achieving rotationally closed photon cycling in laser cooling asymmetric-top molecules is nontrivial[a] due to the lowered symmetry and complex intramolecular interactions, including the spin-orbit interaction and vibronic interactions. In this talk, we will discuss transition intensities between rotational energy levels of electronic states involved in laser-cooling asymmetric-top molecules, rotational branching ratios, and selection rules. Using alkaline-earth monoalkoxide radicals as examples, we will predict the rotational branching ratios using a "coupled-state model"[b] and discuss possible pumping and re-pumping schemes.

---

[a] B. L. Augenbraun, J. M. Doyle, T. Zelevinsky, and I. Kozyryev, Phys. Rev. X 10, 031022 (2020).
[b] J. Liu, J. Chem. Phys. 148, 124112 (2018).

RM02   2:03 – 2:18

A NEW UNDERSTANDING OF LAMBDA DOUBLING

ROBERT J GORDON, *Department of Chemistry, University of Illinois at Chicago, Chicago, IL, USA*; ROBERT W FIELD, *Department of Chemistry, MIT, Cambridge, MA, USA.*

Lambda-doubling is the splitting of rotational levels that have the same quantum numbers and differ only in their parity. This phenomenon has been understood for nearly a century to be caused by an asymmetric perturbation by an energetically remote electronic state acting on otherwise degenerate rovibronic states. The terms in the Hamiltonian responsible for this perturbation are $\hat{\mathcal{H}}^c = -B(\hat{J}^+\hat{L}^- + \hat{J}^-\hat{L}^+) + (B + \frac{1}{2}A)(\hat{L}^+\hat{S}^- + \hat{L}^-\hat{S}^+)$, where $\hat{J}^\pm, \hat{L}^\pm$ and $\hat{S}^\pm$ are ladder operators for total, orbital, and spin angular momenta, and B and A are the rotational and spin-orbit coupling constants. The time-honored method for calculating the level-splitting is to calculate off-diagonal matrix elements of this operator that connect macroscopic terms of the form $|^{2S+1}\Lambda_\Omega\rangle_{e,f}$, using second-order perturbation theory (the Van Vleck transformation) to determine the energy difference between states of e- and f-symmetry. We have discovered that neglect of the microscopic electronic structure of the molecule may lead to incorrect values of the level-splitting and erroneous assignment of the parity of some of the levels. The breakdown of the macroscopic method lies in its failure to recognize that the rotational component of $\hat{\mathcal{H}}^c$ contains two-electron operators, whereas the spin-orbit component is a one-electron operator. In addition, the macroscopic formulation fails to account for exchange symmetry of electrons in partially-filled spin-orbitals. We have shown that the macroscopic formulation gives correct results for inhomogeneous (Ω-changing) perturbations and fails for homogeneous (Ω-preserving) perturbations produced by the rotational part of the Hamiltonian. The breakdown is especially marked for the splitting of $^2\Pi_{\frac{1}{2}}$ by $^2\Sigma^\pm_{\frac{1}{2}}$ states, for which both homogeneous and inhomogeneous perturbations are involved.

RM03 2:21 – 2:36

TOWARDS A GLOBAL EIGHT-STATE FIT OF THE ROTATIONAL AND VIBRATIONAL SPECTRA OF HN_3

R. CLAUDE WOODS, *Department of Chemistry, University of Wisconsin-Madison, Madison, WI, USA*; BRENT K. AMBERGER, *Department of Chemistry, University of Wisconsin, Madison, WI, USA*; BRANT E. BILLINGHURST, *EFD, Canadian Light Source Inc., Saskatoon, Saskatchewan, Canada*; BRIAN J. ESSELMAN, *Department of Chemistry, University of Wisconsin-Madison, Madison, WI, USA*; PATRIK KANIA, *Department of Analytical Chemistry, Institute of Chemical Technology, Prague, Czech Republic*; ZBIGNIEW KISIEL, *ON2, Institute of Physics, Polish Academy of Sciences, Warszawa, Poland*; ROBERT J. McMAHON, VANESSA L. ORR, ANDREW N. OWEN, HOUSTON H. SMITH, *Department of Chemistry, University of Wisconsin-Madison, Madison, WI, USA*; STEPAN URBAN, *Department of Analytical Chemistry, Institute of Chemical Technology, Prague, Czech Republic*; KAREL VÁVRA, *Institute of Physics, University of Kassel, Kassel, Germany*; SAMUEL A. WOOD, *Department of Chemistry, University of Wisconsin-Madison, Madison, WI, USA*.

Our longstanding goal has been achieving a global fit of the ground state and seven lowest excited states of HN_3 (ν_5, ν_6, ν_4, ν_3, $2\nu_5$, $2\nu_6$, and $\nu_5+\nu_6$), all of which are strongly connected by Coriolis, anharmonic, and Darling-Dennison resonance perturbations. From the combined effort of the Wisconsin and Prague groups, we observed and assigned most of the millimeter-wave spectrum from low-frequency microwave lines up to 720 GHz. Recently, we have acquired an extensive set of infrared (IR) spectral data at the Canadian Light Source (CLS), 30-5000 cm^{-1} at 0.0009 cm^{-1} resolution and pressures between 1 and 100 mTorr. This data supersedes all previous IR data, in that it provides higher sensitivity (providing transitions with higher J's and K's) and higher frequency accuracy for all the ground and fundamental states. More importantly, it has permitted assignment of thousands of lines in about 30 subbands involving the combination and overtone states. Using linear least-squares treatments of individual subbands (Fortrat or Q-branch plots), we have so far determined absolute energies of K_a = 0-7 of $2\nu_5$, K_a = 2-6 of $\nu_5+\nu_6$, and K_a = 0-6 of $2\nu_6$, using redundant measurements from multiple subbands confirmed by combination differences with known a-type lines in the mm-wave spectrum. Several additional mm-wave series were assigned using improved predictions from the IR spectra, and several others have been reassigned. We present our current spectral analysis and progress on the implementation of an eight-state global fit.

RM05 2:57 – 3:12

A SCALE QUANTIFYING THE STRENGTH OF INTRAMOLECULAR HYDROGEN BONDS FROM IR SPECTROSCOPY

GARRETT D SANTIS, *Department of Chemistry, University of Washington, Seattle, WA, USA*; SOTIRIS XANTHEAS, *Physical Sciences Division, Pacific Northwest National Laboratory, Richland, WA, USA*.

Intramolecular hydrogen bonds are of fundamental importance in chemistry, existing in a range of systems from small medicinal molecules to the macromolecules of DNA, proteins, and plastics. The strengths of these hydrogen bonds have important consequences on the structure, and consequently the function of such chemical systems. However, the strength of intramolecular hydrogen bonds cannot be either directly measured experimentally or computed theoretically through dissociation, like those in regular intermolecular hydrogen bonds. Computational approaches, such as the rotational bond method, can approximate these energies but rely on a series of assumptions that limit their application. This work proposes a scale based on the spectral-energy relationship first studied by Badger and Bauer to estimate the strength of intramolecular hydrogen bonds from the measured experimental infrared (IR) bands of the respective vibrations. A single regression between energy and shifts in vibrational frequency was derived for hydrogen bonds incorporating O, N, and F atoms. The linear regression between energy and underlying frequency was established at the MP2/aug-cc-pVDZ and MP2/aug-cc-pVTZ levels of theory and validated at both higher levels of electron correlation (CCSD(T)) and by using experimental IR spectra and zero-point energies. Our results reproduce the intramolecular hydrogen bond energies of enolones and amino alcohols obtained by the rotational bond method within 1 kcal/mol. We subsequently used our approach to estimate the hydrogen bond strengths of a variety of systems for which the experimental frequencies for the respective intra-molecular hydrogen bonds have been reported. Our results quantify the strengthening of the hydrogen bond in amino-ethanols under fluorination by over 2 kcal/mol and yield hydrogen bond strengths of about 4 kcal/mol in helical poly-peptides, making it possible, for the first time, to quantify the strengths of these elusive interactions in systems of biological importance.

RM06　　　　3:15 – 3:30

PUSHING MULTIPHOTON RESONANT IONIZATION OF ARGON TO LOW-INTENSITY REGIEM

<u>XUAN YU</u>, *Atomic Physics Center, Institute of Modern Physics, Chinese Academy of Sciences, Lanzhou, CHINA*; NA WANG, *College of Physics and Electronic Engineering, Northwest Normal University, Lanzhou, China*; JIANTING LEI, *School of Nuclear Science and Technology, Lanzhou University, Lanzhou, CHINA*; BENNACEUR NAJJARI, SHAOFENG ZHANG, *Atomic and molecular physics, Institute of Modern Physics, Lanzhou, CHINA*; XINWEN MA, *Atomic Physics Center, Institute of Modern Physics, Chinese Academy of Sciences, Lanzhou, CHINA.*

Resonance-enhanced multiphoton ionization process of argon atom by 800 nm, 30 fs linearly polarized laser filed is investigated at an intensity range from 1.1 to 4.55×10^{13} W/cm^2. At 4.55×10^{13} W/cm^2 intensity the experimental photoelectron energy spectrum is in a good agreement with the time-dependent Schrödinger equation (TDSE) calculation where the double structure originating from dressed 4p-4d coupled transition are clearly identified. From the spectrum, it is shown that the pulse duration can obviously influence the resonant ionization yield. At lower intensity of 1.1×10^{13} W/cm^2, the resonant ionization process via 4f state is observed, however, by comparing our results with those given in other papers, the significant differences in the PADs suggest that in the corresponding regime the orbital angular momentum of the intermediate state cannot simply be assigned to the number of jets in the PAD.

Intermission

RM07　　　　4:12 – 4:27

PRECISION MEASUREMENT WITH CAVITY-ENHANCED BUFFER-GAS COOLED MICROWAVE SPECTROSCOPY

<u>LINCOLN SATTERTHWAITE</u>, GRETA KOUMARIANOU, *Chemistry and Biochemistry, UCSB, Santa Barbara, CA, USA*; DANIEL SORENSEN, DAVID PATTERSON, *Physics, University of California, Santa Barbara, CA, USA.*

We report for the first time highly precise differential microwave spectroscopy, carried out in a cavity-enhanced buffer gas cell. We report a statistically limited differential measurement of 0.08 ± 0.72 Hz between (R)- and (S)-1,2-propanediol at frequencies around 15 GHz [a]. This highly repeatable measurement opens new avenues in studying molecular structure at the 10^{-10} level. We also report the coupling of a neon buffer gas beam to this cavity, reaching linewidths of 3 kHz in methyltrioxorhenium, and future modifications to reach 1.5 kHz linewidth.

---

[a] Symmetry 2022, 14(1), 28; https://doi.org/10.3390/sym14010028

RM08　　　　　　　　　　　　　　　　　　　　　　　　　　　　　　　　　　4:30 – 4:45
PRECISION SPECTROSCOPY STUDIES OF RADIOACTIVE MOLECULES FOR FUNDAMENTAL PHYSICS

SILVIU-MARIAN UDRESCU, SHANE WILKINS, RONALD FERNANDO GARCIA RUIZ, ALEX BRINSON, ADAM VERNON, *Physics, MIT, Cambridge, USA*; ALEXANDER A. BREIER, THOMAS GIESEN, *Physics, University Kassel, Kassel, Germany*; ROBERT BERGER, KONSTANTIN GAUL, CARSTEN ZULCH, *Chemistry, Philipps-Universitaet Marburg, Marburg, Germany*; BRAN VAN DEN BORNE, THOMAS COCOLIOS, RUBEN DEGROOTE, ANAIS DORNE, SARINA GELDHOF, LOUIS LALANNE, GERDA NEYENS, *Physics, KU Leuven, Leuven, Belgium*; KIERAN FLANAGAN, HOLLY PERRETT, JORDAN REILLY, JULIUS WESSOLEK, *Physics, University of Manchester, Manchester, UK*; MICHAIL ATHANASAKIS-KAKLAMANAKIS, MIA AU, KATHERINA CHRYSALIDIS, AGOTA KOSZORUS, SEBASTIAN ROTHE, *Physics, CERN, Geneva, Switzerland*; TIMUR A. ISAEV, *Physics, NRC "Kurchatov Institute" PNPI, Gatchina, Russia*; IVANA BELOSEVIC, *Physics, TRIUMF, Vancouver, Canada*; SERGE FRANCHOO, *Physics, Irène Joliot-Curie Lab, Paris, France*; SONJA KUJANPAA, *Physics, University of Jyväskylä, Jyväskylä, Finland* ; MIRANDA NICHOLS, *Physics, University of Gothenburg, Gothenburg, Sweden*; XIAOFEI YANG, *Physics, Peking University, Beijing, China.*

Precision molecular experiments provide a unique tool in the search for physics beyond the Standard Model (SM) and exploration of the fundamental forces of nature. Compared to atoms, certain molecules can offer more than eleven orders of magnitude enhanced sensitivity to violations of fundamental symmetries, enabling precision tests of the SM and the possibility to probe energy scales beyond hundreds of TeV. Containing octupole-deformed nuclei, radium monofluoride (RaF) is expected to be particularly sensitive to symmetry violating nuclear properties [Phys. Rev. A 82, 052521 (2010); J. Chem. Phys. 152, 044101 (2020)]. In this talk, I will present the latest results obtained from a series of laser spectroscopy experiments performed on short-lived RaF molecules at the ISOLDE facility at CERN. Using a collinear resonant ionization setup, the rotational and hyperfine structure of ^{226}RaF and ^{225}RaF were measured with high precision. This allowed us to establish a laser cooling scheme for these molecules, and to explore nuclear structure effects at the molecular level. Our new results represent an increase in precision of at least 3 orders of magnitude compared to our previous studies [Nature 581, 396 (2020); Phys. Rev. Lett. 127, 033001 (2021)] being the first of their kind performed on radioactive, short-lived molecules and opening the way for future precision studies and new physics searches in these systems.

RM09　　　　　　　　　　　　　　　　　　　　　　　　　　　　　　　　　　4:48 – 5:03
CAVITY ENHANCED MICROWAVE SPECTROSCOPY IN A BUFFER GAS CELL

DANIEL SORENSEN, *Physics, University of California, Santa Barbara, CA, USA*; LINCOLN SATTERTHWAITE, GRETA KOUMARIANOU, *Chemistry and Biochemistry, UCSB, Santa Barbara, CA, USA*; DAVID PATTERSON, *Physics, University of California, Santa Barbara, CA, USA.*

Molecular ringdown times place a fundamental upper limit on the precision of measurements in microwave spectroscopy. A Fabry-Perot cavity has been designed and implemented in an existing buffer-gas cell to enhance molecular ringdown signals, allowing for measurements of greatly enhanced precision. This includes a differential measurement of enantiomers of 1,2 - Propanediol with sub-Hz precision. Design elements include: a coupler designed to transmit light out of the cavity proportional to the intensity of Gaussian-Hermite modes; optimization of Q-Factor related to diffractive, reflected, and coupling losses; and a tuning mechanism that allows for full and precise adjustment of resonant frequency in its cryogenic environment. Additionally, work will be presented in ongoing research that implements a columnated molecular beam in a newly-designed cavity with greatly increased mode waist sizes for measurements of groundbreaking precision in a low collision environment.

RM10
A COMBINED mm-WAVE AND FAR-INFRARED STUDY OF PYRAZOLE

5:06 – 5:21

DENNIS W. TOKARYK, *Department of Physics, University of New Brunswick, Fredericton, NB, Canada*; BRIAN J. ESSELMAN, R. CLAUDE WOODS, ROBERT J. McMAHON, *Department of Chemistry, University of Wisconsin-Madison, Madison, WI, USA*; JEFF CROUSE, *Department of Chemistry, University of Waterloo, Waterloo, ON, Canada*; DOYEON KIM, *Department of Physics, University of New Brunswick, Fredericton, NB, Canada.*

Pyrazole ($C_3H_3N_2$, C_s) is an aromatic heterocycle consisting of a 5-membered ring molecule doubly substituted with adjacent nitrogen atoms. Searches for similar heteroaromatic compounds (imidazole, furan, etc.) have been recently conducted in the interstellar medium. This study provides the necessary transition frequencies for a search for pyrazole across the frequency range of available radiotelescopes. We have collected the mm-wave spectrum of pyrazole from 130-750 MHz, which extends the previously published microwave studies from 13 to 35 MHz. The new data greatly expand the range of rotational quantum numbers observed in the ground vibrational state rotational transitions and provide transitions for over a dozen excited vibrational states. These rotational data are simultaneously analyzed with high-resolution rotation-vibration spectra of pyrazole between 500-1300 cm^{-1} that we have obtained at the Canadian Light Source synchrotron's far-infrared beam line. The considerable benefits of simultaneously analyzing mm-wave and high-res IR transitions that cover the same approximate ranges of J and K will be discussed. The results provide a thorough characterization of all eight vibrationally excited states below 950 cm^{-1}, of which the highest energy states (ν_{16}, ν_{15}, and ν_{14}) form a Coriolis-coupled triad.

RM11
COMBINED MILLIMETER WAVE AND FTIR SPECTRA OF DN_3

5:24 – 5:39

R. CLAUDE WOODS, *Department of Chemistry, University of Wisconsin-Madison, Madison, WI, USA*; BRENT K. AMBERGER, *Department of Chemistry, University of Wisconsin, Madison, WI, USA*; BRANT E. BILLINGHURST, *EFD, Canadian Light Source Inc., Saskatoon, Saskatchewan, Canada*; BRIAN J. ESSELMAN, *Department of Chemistry, University of Wisconsin-Madison, Madison, WI, USA*; PATRIK KANIA, *Department of Analytical Chemistry, Institute of Chemical Technology, Prague, Czech Republic*; ZBIGNIEW KISIEL, *ON2, Institute of Physics, Polish Academy of Sciences, Warszawa, Poland*; ROBERT J. McMAHON, VANESSA L. ORR, ANDREW N. OWEN, HOUSTON H. SMITH, *Department of Chemistry, University of Wisconsin-Madison, Madison, WI, USA*; STEPAN URBAN, *Department of Analytical Chemistry, University of Chemistry and Technology, Prague, Prague, Czech Republic*; KAREL VÁVRA, *Institute of Physics, University of Kassel, Kassel, Germany*; SAMUEL A. WOOD, *Department of Chemistry, University of Wisconsin-Madison, Madison, WI, USA.*

We have recently observed the infrared spectrum of DN_3 at a resolution of 0.0009 cm^{-1} using the synchrotron at the Canadian Light Source between 30 and 5000 cm^{-1} at several pressures between 1 and 100 mTorr. A special heavy walled stainless steel apparatus was constructed to perform the synthesis of the highly toxic and explosive substance on site in way that met the stringent safety standards of the facility. We have also measured the millimeter wave spectrum of DN_3 at Wisconsin and at Prague covering altogether the range from 130-730 GHz. We are working toward combining all this spectral data to achieve a global eight state fit with SPFIT. While the many perturbing interactions between these lowest eight vibrational states cause somewhat less dramatic shifts than the same ones do in HN_3, it remains a very challenging problem in spectroscopy. A substantial additional complication in this isotopologue though is the fact that it has proved to be impractical to obtain an isotopically pure sample of DN_3 because of facile H/D exchange on the walls of the absorption cells employed. This makes it desirable at least to assign the HN_3 spectrum first, so that the corresponding features can be eliminated from consideration in the DN_3 work.

RN. Astronomy

Thursday, June 23, 2022 – 1:45 PM

Room: 274 Medical Sciences Building

Chair: Gustavo A. Cruz-Diaz, University of Wisconsin-Madison, Madison, WI, USA

RN01   1:45 – 2:00

LILLE SPECTROSCOPIC DATABASE FOR ASTROPHYSICALLY AND ATMOSPHERICALLY RELEVANT MOLECULES

R. A. MOTIYENKO, L. MARGULÈS, *Laboratoire PhLAM, UMR 8523 CNRS - Université Lille 1, Villeneuve d'Ascq, France.*

The project of Lille Spectroscopic Database (https://lsd.univ-lille.fr) emerged from a large number of molecules of astrophysical and atmospheric interest exhibiting large amplitude motions studied in PhLAM laboratory in the last decade. To fit their spectra and to calculate spectral predictions we used many different codes including SPFIT/SPCAT program suite. While the latter is the main fitting/predicting tool for widely known CDMS and JPL databases, spectral predictions obtained with other codes are somehow scattered in the supplementary data of publications and are eventually available in the another well known Splatalogue database. For this reason, we decided to develop and maintain the Lille Spectroscopic Database which will contain the spectral predictions of the molecules studied by our group in Lille. The new database will provide a typical functionality of other databases: predictions will be available in different formats including different intensity units, and at different temperatures; a search within the full database will be possible to limit the predictions for a particular range of frequencies, intensities or quantum numbers. We will also provide and present an application programming interface (API) that allows the integration of our database into other software.

We thank the Mésocentre de Calcul Scientifique Intensif de l'Université de Lille for hosting the database.

RN02   2:03 – 2:18

A NEW APPROACH FOR AUTOMATED ANALYSIS OF HIGH-RESOLUTION MOLECULAR LINE SURVEYS

SAMER EL-ABD, *Department of Astronomy, The University of Virginia, Charlottesville, VA, USA*; CRYSTAL L. BROGAN, TODD R. HUNTER, *NAASC, National Radio Astronomy Observatory, Charlottesville, VA, USA*; KELVIN LEE, BRETT A. McGUIRE, *Department of Chemistry, Massachusetts Institute of Technology, Cambridge, MA, USA.*

At a distance of 1.3 kpc, NGC 6334I is one of the nearest massive star-forming regions. Previous studies of the source have revealed a number of prodigious hot cores, each of which exhibit a rich molecular inventory. Our previous work on NGC 6334I examined spectra from a limited number of positions scattered throughout the source in order to sample the various physical conditions that can be found. In an effort to better characterize the underlying complex physical and chemical structure of this massive star-forming cluster we have conducted an automated LTE fit of the emission spectra corresponding to each of over 8000 pixels surrounding the hot cores using two ALMA Band 7 tunings with a resolution of 0.26" (340 AU). For each pixel we derive an excitation temperature as well as the column density for each of the 25 most prominent molecular species. Spatial maps of the derived properties for the molecules will be presented with a particular focus on the three $C_2H_4O_2$ isomers and how the clustered star formation appears to impact their abundances. These molecular properties will be discussed within the context of the physical structure of the protocluster.

RN03
REFERENCE DATA FOR AMMONIA SPECTRA IN THE 3900-6300 CM^{-1} RANGE

PETER ČERMÁK, *Department of Experimental Physics, Comenius University, Bratislava, Slovakia*; PATRICE CACCIANI, JEAN COSLEOU, *UMR CNRS 8523 - Université de Lille 1, Laboratoire PHLAM, F-59655 VILLENEUVE D'ASCQ CEDEX, France*; ALAIN CAMPARGUE, SERGE BÉGUIER, *UMR5588 LIPhy, Université Grenoble Alpes/CNRS, Saint Martin d'Hères, France*; JEAN VANDER AUWERA, *SQUARES, Université Libre de Bruxelles, Brussels, Belgium*; ONDŘEJ VOTAVA, JOZEF RAKOVSKÝ, *Heyrovský Institute of Physical Chemistry, Czech Academy of Sciences, Prague, Czech Republic.*

Accurate reference laboratory data represents a key element for understanding any remote observations in particular astrophysical surveys. The subject has grown in importance with the recent discovery of the capability to observe spectra of exoplanets or the ability to closely probe space objects like in the case of the Rosetta mission. This need is even timelier with the James Webb telescope being deployed for operation and the new space missions dedicated to the exoplanetary spectroscopic studies like Twinkle, and the Atmospheric Remote-sensing Infrared Exoplanet Large-survey (ARIEL) destined to be launched in 2024 and 2029, respectively.

The current contribution is an overview of our work concerning the acquisition of such accurate reference data in the case of ammonia molecule based on the combination of room temperature Fourier transform spectra (both old and new), tunable laser spectroscopy in cooled Herriott cell, and in a supersonic expansion. In addition, multiple new techniques to improve the whole process of spectra analysis were used, mainly: the enhanced multi-temperature treatment for determination of empirical lower state energies, intensity-based combination differences process for determination of quantum assignments, or the accurate referenced frequency calibration to verify the absolute line positions with a sub 0.001 cm^{-1} accuracy.

RN04
FORBIDDEN ROTATIONAL TRANSITIONS AND ASTROPHYSICS

TAKESHI OKA, *Department of Astronomy and Astrophysics and Department of Chemistry, The Enrico Fermi Institute, University of Chicago, Chicago, IL, USA.*

When I read Townes and Schawlow's textbook as a beginning student, I was puzzled by the symmetric top selection rule $\Delta K = 0$, because this rule corresponds to cylindrical symmetry C_∞; applying it to NH$_3$ with C_3 symmetry cannot be right. At that time, however, I did not pursue how this wrong rule affect the actual spectrum. 10 years later interstellar NH$_3$ was discovered by Townes' group. When I read the discoverers' claim that lifetimes of $(J, K) = (2,2)$ and $(3,3)$ metastable levels are "longer than the lifetime of the Universe", it was obvious that this wrong statement resulted from the wrong $\Delta K = 0$ selection rule. Accurate theory[a] gave the life times of the (2,2) and (3,3) metastable levels to be 230 years and 44 years, respectively, 10^8 times shorter than the lifetime of the Universe. The theory also predicted $\Delta k = \pm 3$ pure rotational transitions which were observed for PH$_3$, PD$_3$ and AsH$_3$[b]

In this paper[c] I calculate spontaneous emission via forbidden transitions for astrophysically important symmetric tops; oblate tops NH$_3$, H$_3$O$^+$, H$_3^+$, and prolate tops CH$_3$CN. These calculations are preparations for future analyses of ther thermalization.

---
[a] T. Oka, F.O. Shimiza, T. Shimizu, J.K.G. Watson, ApJ 165, L15 (1971)
[b] F.Y. Chu, T. Oka, J. Chem. Phys. 60, 4612 (1974)
[c] T. Oka, J. Mol. Spectrosc. 379, 111482 (2021)

RN05 2:57 – 3:12

EXPERIMENTAL INSIGHTS INTO THE FORMATION OF INTERSTELLAR FULLERENES AND CARBON NANOTUBES

JACOB BERNAL[a], *Department of Chemistry and Biochemistry, University of Arizona, Tucson, AZ, USA*; THOMAS J. ZEGA, *Department of Planetary Science, Lunar and Planetary Laboratory, University of Arizona, Tucson, AZ, USA*; LUCY M. ZIURYS, *Dept. of Astronomy, Dept. of Chemistry, Arizona Radio Observatory, The University of Arizona, Tucson, AZ, USA.*

The detection of the fullerenes C_{60} and C_{70} in the interstellar medium (ISM) has transformed our understanding of chemical complexity in space, and have also raised the possibility for the presence of even larger molecules in astrophysical environments. Here we report in situ heating of analog silicon carbide (SiC) presolar grains using transmission electron microscopy (TEM). These heating experiments are designed to simulate shocks occurring in post-AGB stellar envelopes. Our experimental findings reveal that heating the analog SiC grains yields hemispherical C_{60}-sized nanostructures, which later transform into multi-walled carbon nanotubes (MWCNTs). These MWCNTs are larger than any of the currently- observed interstellar fullerene species, both in overall size and number of C atoms. These experimental results suggest that such MWCNTs are likely to form in post-AGB shocks, where the structures, along with the smaller fullerenes, are subsequently injected into the ISM.

---
[a]Current Affiliation: University of Arizona Department of Planetary Science, Lunar and Planetary Laboratory

Intermission

RN06 3:54 – 4:09

PREBIOTIC MOLECULES IN INTERSTELLAR SPACE: THE ROLE OF ROTATIONAL SPECTROSCOPY AND QUANTUM-CHEMICAL CALCULATIONS

CRISTINA PUZZARINI, *Dep. Chemistry 'Giacomo Ciamician', University of Bologna, Bologna, Italy*; MATTIA MELOSSO, *Dept. Chemistry "Giacomo Ciamician", University of Bologna, Bologna, ITALY*; LUCA BIZZOCCHI, *Dipartimento di Chimica G. Ciamician, Università di Bologna, Bologna, Italy*; SILVIA ALESSANDRINI, *Scuola Normale Superiore, Scuola Normale Superiore, Pisa, Italy.*

While it is now well established that the interstellar medium (ISM) is characterized by a rich and complex chemistry, we are far from a complete census of the interstellar molecules and the understanding about how they form and evolve is at a primitive stage. Concerning the former issue, a significant number of features in radioastronomical spectra are still unassigned. To fill this gap, a huge laboratory effort is required, which is increasingly based on integrated experimental and computational strategies. This contribution aims to present examples of an integrated rotational spectroscopy - quantum chemistry approach for supporting radioastronomical observations. In this respect, a significant example is provided by the recent characterization of (Z)-1,2 ethenediol, a key prebiotic intermediate in the formose reaction [a].

---
[a]Melosso et al. Chem. Commun. **58**, 2750 (2022)

RN07   4:12–4:27
MULTI-WAVELENGTH INVESTIGATION ON NEW MOLECULAR MASERS TOWARD THE GALACTIC CENTER

<u>CI XUE</u>, *Department of Chemistry, MIT, Cambridge, MA, USA*; ALEXANDRE FAURE, *Institut de Planétologie et d'Astrophysique de Grenoble (IPAG), UJF-Grenoble / CNRS-INSU, Grenoble, France*; EMMANUEL MOMJIAN, *NRAO, NRAO, Socorro, NM, USA*; ANTHONY REMIJAN, TODD R. HUNTER, *NAASC, National Radio Astronomy Observatory, Charlottesville, VA, USA*; BRETT A. McGUIRE, *Department of Chemistry, Massachusetts Institute of Technology, Cambridge, MA, USA*.

At the centimeter wavelength, the single-dish observation has suggested that the Sgr B2 molecular cloud at the Galatic center hosts weak maser emission from complex molecules, including CH_2NH, $HNCNH$, and $HCOOCH_3$ (McGuire et al., 2012; Faure et al., 2014, 2018). Because molecular masers often trace specific conditions within the massive star-forming regions, finding new maser transitions and species provides critical insights into the physical structures hidden behind the thick dust. However, the lack of distribution information of these new maser species had prevented us from not only quantitatively assessing the observed spectral profiles but also constraining their pumping mechanisms. In this talk, we present a rigorous mapping study toward the galactic center to resolve the region where the complex maser emission originates. By comparing the distribution of several maser emissions, it is revealed that the new maser species have a close spatial relationship with the CH_3OH Class I masers. This relationship serves as observational evidence to suggest a similar collisional pumping mechanism for these maser transitions.

RN08   4:30–4:45
ASSESSING 27 MOLECULES FOR SENSITIVITY TO PROTON-TO-ELECTRON MASS VARIATION: STRENGTHS AND LIMITATIONS OF A HIGH-THROUGHPUT APPROACH

ANNA-MAREE SYME, <u>LAURA K McKEMMISH</u>, *School of Chemistry, University of New South Wales, Sydney, NSW, Australia*.

Astrophysical molecular spectroscopy is an important method of searching for new physics through probing the variation of the proton-to-electron mass ratio, μ, with existing constraints limiting variation to a fractional change of less than 10^{-17}/year. To improve on this constraint and therefore provide better guidance to theories of new physics, new molecular probes will be useful. These molecular probes must have spectral transitions that are observable astrophysically and have different sensitivities to variation in the proton-to-electron mass ratio.

This talk will focus on the development of a high-throughput methodology to calculate the sensitivities of transitions in diatomic and polyatomic molecules with established spectroscopic models. The calculations required are straightforward; reproducing the line list with a slight increase in nuclear masses and comparing the original and mass-shifted energies and transition frequencies. The major challenge was in matching the quantum states in the original and mass-shifted data as the quantum number descriptions were not always preserved when the state was heavily mixed - unfortunately precisely those states likely to have high sensitivities to μ variation. These challenges were far more severe in polyatomics than diatomics.

Our results found that even a conservative intensity cut-off of 10^{-30} cm/molecule at 100 K (astrophysically relevant interstellar conditions) removed almost all transitions with high sensitivity to μ variation. There were no new clear transitions of interest were identified in the 22 diatomic and 5 polyatomic molecules investigated, with the low-frequency diatomic parity changing and polyatomic inversion transitions having the strongest sensitivities.

In the diatomics we investigated, high sensitivity was observed in low-frequency rovibronic transitions arising from accidental near-degeneracy between electronic states were observed, but these have very low intensity (as the states involved were high in energy) and thus not likely to be observable astrophysically. This insight allows screening of diatomics without spectroscopic models for sensitivity to μ variation; we conclude that no diatomic known extragalactically is likely to have transitions with high sensitivity to μ variation.

RN09 4:48 – 5:03

THE OPTICAL SPECTRUM OF THE DIAMANTANE RADICAL CATION

PARKER B. CRANDALL, ROBERT G. RADLOFF, MARKO FÖRSTEL, OTTO DOPFER, *Institut für Optik und Atomare Physik, Technische Universität Berlin, Berlin, Germany.*

Diamondoids are a class of stable, aliphatic molecules arranged in cage-like structures and serve as a link between small, cyclic hydrocarbons and bulk nanodiamonds. Similarities have been observed between the infrared spectra of diamondoids and unidentified infrared emission bands seen in the spectra of young stars with circumstellar disks.[1] It is also suggested that the radical cations of these molecules could contribute to features in the well-known but largely unassigned diffuse interstellar bands due to their low ionization energy and absorption in the visible range.[2] However, only the optical spectrum of the adamantane cation has been measured so far.[3] Herein, we report the first optical spectrum of the diamantane radical cation ($C_{14}H_{20}^+$) between 400 and 1000 nm in the gas phase. Measurements were taken in a tandem mass spectrometer by photodissociation of mass-selected ions cooled in a cryogenic 22-pole ion trap held at 5 K. The optical spectrum reveals two broad and unresolved bands centered near 760 and 450 nm that are assigned to the $D_2(^2E_u) \leftarrow D_0(^2A_{1g})$ and $D_5(^2A_{2u}) \leftarrow D_0(^2A_{1g})$ transitions using time-dependent density function theory calculations. These calculations also assist to explain the lack of vibrational structure as the result of lifetime broadening and Franck-Condon congestion arising from large geometry changes.

Literature:
[1] O. Pirali, M. Vervloet, J. E. Dahl, R. M. K. Carlson, A. G. G. M. Tielens, J. Oomens, Astrophys. J., 661, 919–925 (2007).
[2] M. Steglich, F. Huisken, J. E. Dahl, R. M. K. Carlson, T. Henning, Astrophys. J., 729, 91–100 (2011).
[3] P. B. Crandall, D. Müller, J. Leroux, M. Förstel and O. Dopfer, 2020, Astrophys. J. Letters, 900, L20

RN10 5:06 – 5:21

CS ABSORPTION AT 140 NM IN SPECTRA ACQUIRED WITH THE HUBBLE SPACE TELESCOPE

STEVEN FEDERMAN, *Physics and Astronomy, University of Toledo, Toledo, OH, USA*; ADAM RITCHEY, , *Eureka Scientific, Seattle, WA, USA*; KYLE N. CRABTREE, ZHONGXING XU, WILLIAM M. JACKSON, *Department of Chemistry, University of California, Davis, Davis, CA, USA.*

We reexamine the abundance of CS in diffuse molecular clouds from lines in the $C-X$ (0, 0) band by including additional sight lines not available in previous work and by extracting information on molecular structure. The analysis incorporates results from our recent large-scale calculations on CS photodissociation and adopts the approach taken in our study of the $F-X$ (0, 0) and (1, 0) bands in C_2. Syntheses of the high-resolution spectra with the best signal to noise yielded wavelengths for the R(0), R(1), and P(1) lines and their widths. Significant line broadening is seen, yielding a predissociation width of 23.7 ± 0.7 mÅ; this value is within a factor of 2 of the predictions from the calculations. The computations also revealed similar rotational constants for the X and C states. The differences in transition frequencies among the three lines then suggest that the P(1) line is shifted by 2.27 cm^{-1}. We also found evidence that the strengths for the R(1) and P(1) lines were affected by the perturbation. The fits to the data for the other directions in the sample adopted these refined line parameters to determine column densities. A comparison of the CS column densities with results for CH, CN, CO, and H_2 helped inform us of the chemical pathways leading to CS in diffuse molecular gas.

RN11   5:24 – 5:39

CAVITY RING DOWN SPECTROSCOPY OF INTERSTELLAR PAHS AND PAH-RELATED ANALOGS - ASTRONOMICAL APPLICATIONS

SALMA BEJAOUI, FARID SALAMA, *Space Science and Astrobiology Division, NASA Ames Research Center, Moffett Field, CA, USA.*

Polycyclic Aromatic Hydrocarbons (PAHs) are ubiquitous in space and most astronomical spectra, from the interstellar medium (ISM) to distant galaxies, including regions of massive star formation, the general ISM, and star forming spiral galaxies out to red-shifts of $z¿4$, are dominated by their ubiquitous infrared emission features. Whether the PAH bands are intimately associated with the object, or foreground/background confounding features, they will have to be understood, separated from other features in the spectra, and analyzed for the information they contain on the physical and chemical properties of their surrounding environments. High-resolution laboratory spectra of PAHs measured in an astrophysically-relevant environment are critical to answer these questions. The most challenging task is to reproduce, as closely as technically possible, the physical and chemical conditions that are present in space (i.e., cold gas phase molecules and ions, isolated in a collision-free environment). Comparable conditions can be achieved using the cosmic simulation chamber (COSmIC) developed at NASA Ames. COSmIC allows to measure gas phase spectra of neutral and ionized interstellar PAH analogs by associating a free supersonic jet with a soft ionizing discharge that generates a cold plasma expansion (100 K). Using the Cavity Ring Down Spectroscopy (CRDS) technique, rovibronic absorption spectra of PAHs and PAH derivatives seeded in Ar supersonic jet expansions are measured in the NUV-Vis-NIR region. The resulting spectra provide a critical tool to identify and characterize specific molecules and ions in astrophysical environments. We intend to expand the capabilities of our current CRDS system to the NIR and MIR up to 3.5 um in order to provide accurate high-resolution laboratory spectra that will help validate the extensive NASA Ames' PAH database and will greatly benefit the interpretation of future James Webb Space Telescope NIRSpec observational data.

FA. Mini-symposium: Spectroscopy meets Chemical Dynamics
Friday, June 24, 2022 – 8:30 AM
Room: 100 Noyes Laboratory

Chair: Ryan T Ash, University of Wisconsin Madison, Madison, WI, USA

FA01 8:30 – 8:45

MULTICHANNEL RADICAL-RADICAL REACTION DYNAMICS OF NO + PROPARGYL PROBED BY ROTATIONAL SPECTROSCOPY

NURESHAN DIAS, RANIL GURUSINGHE, ARTHUR SUITS, *Department of Chemistry, University of Missouri, Columbia, MO, USA.*

Chirped-pulse rotational spectroscopy in a quasi-uniform flow has been used to investigate the reaction dynamics of a multichannel radical-radical reaction of relevance to planetary atmospheres and combustion. In this work, the NO + propargyl (C_3H_3) reaction was found to yield six product channels containing eight detected species. These species, as well as their branching fractions (%), are as follows: HCN (50), HCNO (18), CH_2CN (12), CH_3CN (7.4), HC_3N (6.2), HNC (2.3), CH_2CO (1.3), HCO (1.8). The observed results are discussed in relation to previous unimolecular photodissociation studies of isoxazole and prior potential energy surface calculations of the NO + C_3H_3 system. Furthermore, we show that the observed products and their branching fractions are strongly influenced by the excess energy of the reactant radicals. The implications of the tittle reaction to the planetary atmosphere, particularly to Titan, are discussed.

FA02 8:48 – 9:03

DYNAMICS AND KINETICS STUDIED BY CHIRPED PULSE MICROWAVE SPECTROSCOPY IN COLD UNIFORM SUPERSONIC FLOWS

ALBERTO MACARIO, *CNRS, IPR (Institut de Physique de Rennes) - UMR 6251, Univ Rennes, F-35000 Rennes, France*; MYRIAM DRISSI, *CNRS, IPR (Institut de Physique de Rennes) - UMR 6251, Univ Rennes, Rennes, France*; OMAR ABDELKADER KHEDAOUI, THEO GUILLAUME, *CNRS, IPR (Institut de Physique de Rennes) - UMR 6251, Univ Rennes, F-35000 Rennes, France*; BRIAN M HAYS, DIVITA GUPTA, *IPR UMR6251, CNRS - Université Rennes 1, Rennes, France*; ILSA ROSE COOKE, IAN R. SIMS, *CNRS, IPR (Institut de Physique de Rennes) - UMR 6251, Univ Rennes, F-35000 Rennes, France.*

The vast majority of gas-phase techniques typically employed for studying reaction kinetics follow only the time dependence of one of the reactants or the products and do not allow to distinguish between different isomers, conformers or vibrationally excited states presented in the reaction. However, this has changed in the recent years with the development of the chirped-pulse microwave spectroscopy in uniform supersonic flow (CPUF) technique to study gas phase reaction kinetics. This technique as implemented in Rennes employs the CRESU (a French acronym standing for reaction kinetics in uniform supersonic flow) method coupled with chirped-pulse Fourier transform microwave spectroscopy, combining the power to generate continuous cold uniform supersonic flows with the high selectivity and general applicability of rotational spectroscopy. As a result, it is possible to simultaneously study the time dependence of various species involved in the reaction and to distinguish between different conformers, isomers and vibrationally excited states. The uniform CRESU conditions permit frequent enough collisions to preserve local thermodynamic equilibrium in the flow with regard to translational and rotational degrees of freedom, but vibrational relaxation of some molecules may not be complete. This is a double-edged sword: a challenge for the analysis of product branching ratios, especially for strongly exothermic reactions; but also an opportunity to study vibrational relaxation of polyatomic molecules at low temperatures, a subject of significant theoretical and astrophysical interest. Here we present the time dependent collisional relaxation of some vibrationally excited states of both small molecules produced either by photolysis or chemical reaction in the cold uniform flow, as well as low frequency modes of larger molecules.

FA03　　9:06–9:21

BRANCHING RATIO MEASUREMENTS FOR THE O(^{3}P) + PROPENE REACTION USING CHIRPED PULSE MICROWAVE SPECTROSCOPY AT LOW TEMPERATURE

MYRIAM DRISSI, *CNRS, IPR (Institut de Physique de Rennes) - UMR 6251, Univ Rennes, Rennes, France*; ALBERTO MACARIO, OMAR ABDELKADER KHEDAOUI, BRIAN M HAYS, DIVITA GUPTA, THEO GUILLAUME, ILSA ROSE COOKE, IAN R. SIMS, *CNRS, IPR (Institut de Physique de Rennes) - UMR 6251, Univ Rennes, F-35000 Rennes, France.*

Atomic oxygen can be found in many places in space from interstellar molecular clouds, to planetary systems such as ours. This atom represents an important building block as it is part of many chemical groups and therefore acts as a vector of a rich chemistry in the interstellar medium. Propene (C_3H_6) has been detected in molecular clouds and in Titan's atmosphere. The rate constant of the chemical reaction between these two species has been shown to have a negative temperature dependence at low temperatures, but questions remain on the product branching ratios at low temperature. In this work, we coupled the CRESU (French acronym for Cinétique de Réaction en Ecoulement Supersonique Uniforme) technique to reach low temperatures (below 50 K), with molecular beam sampling into an E-band chirped pulse microwave spectrometer to detect reaction products, in an adaptation of the CPUF (Chirped Pulse in Uniform supersonic Flow) technique. The nature of the reaction products detected at low temperatures will be presented along with their branching ratio. The limitation and impact of vibrational relaxation will be discussed in relation to these values along with future directions of this project.

FA04　　9:24–9:39

CONFORMER SELECTED DIMER FORMATION IN A CRYOGENIC BUFFER GAS CELL

LINCOLN SATTERTHWAITE, GRETA KOUMARIANOU, *Chemistry and Biochemistry, UCSB, Santa Barbara, CA, USA*; DAVID PATTERSON, *Physics, University of California, Santa Barbara, CA, USA.*

Non-covalently bound clusters have long been a target of study in microwave spectroscopy, however, the typical method of forming these small clusters precludes observation of that formation. Here, I present observation of the conformer-selected formation of ethanol-methanol dimers in a cryogenic buffer gas cell via microwave spectroscopy. Use of a buffer gas cell allows for observation of a complete time-domain picture of the reaction of two monomers to form a dimer, as the dimers are formed in the interaction region of the experiment as opposed to just after a pulsed valve. Relaxation cross sections and collisional cross sections are also presented for ethanol.

FA05　　9:42–9:57

ROTATIONAL SPECTROSCOPY OF CHEMICAL REACTIONS IN A CRYOGENIC BUFFER GAS CELL

BRANDON CARROLL, BRYAN CHANGALA, MICHAEL C McCARTHY, *Atomic and Molecular Physics, Harvard-Smithsonian Center for Astrophysics, Cambridge, MA, USA.*

Low temperature reactions play a critical role in the chemistry of the interstellar medium (ISM). Measuring the kinetics of these reactions is key to constraining models of ISM chemistry, and to understanding ISM chemistry at large. However, measuring chemical kinetics at temperatures relevant to the ISM presents numerous experimental challenges, including creating homogeneous and cooled reactants. Buffer gas cooling offers a near universal method of achieving uniform electronic, vibrational, rotational, and translational cooling, while consuming minimal sample. When combined with microwave spectroscopy, buffer gas cooling cells offer a unique method for probing reactions occurring at very low temperatures. We will report our progress in building and characterizing a buffer gas cell configuration capable of measuring bimolecular reactions of thermalized species occurring within the cell, and discuss its applications for studying ISM chemistry.

FA06 10:00 – 10:15

UV PHOTOFRAGMENT SPECTROSCOPY AND ELECTRONIC ENERGY TRANSFER ON A PEPTIDE SCAFFOLD: THE CASE OF NEAR-DEGENERATE UV CHROMOPHORES

<u>CASEY DANIEL FOLEY</u>, *Combustion Research Facility, Sandia National Laboratories, Livermore, CA, USA*; ETIENNE CHOLLET, MATTHEW A. KUBASIK, *Department of Chemistry and Biochemistry, Fairfield University, Fairfield, CT, USA*; TIMOTHY S. ZWIER, *Combustion Research Facility, Sandia National Laboratories, Livermore, CA, USA.*

Some of the most important molecular architectures in nature, such as light harvesting antennae, feature the presence of several nearly identical electronic chromophores in close proximity, in which directed electronic energy transfer plays a key part in the initial events following absorption of a visible photon. This is an area in which spectroscopy and dynamics are inextricably linked, and for which gas phase spectroscopy can play a role in testing model systems in a way not possible in their natural environments. We have studied the UV photofragment spectroscopy of a series of cryo-cooled ions in the gas phase that are close analogs of protonated Leu-enkephalin, the pentapeptide Tyr-Gly-Gly-Phe-Leu-OMe (in short-hand notation, YGGFL-OMe). This protonated ion has been studied previously, and folds into a single peptide backbone conformation that incorporates a beta-turn. We replace the Tyr and Phe UV chromophores with other chromophores chosen to bring their electronic absorptions into near degeneracy. UV photofragmentation reports on the location of the electronic energy via a unique fragmentation pathway involving loss of the resonance-stabilized aromatic, CH2-Phe-X. We identify the chromophore responsible for the UV absorption and map out the efficiency of electronic energy transfer as a function of vibronic state via the fragmentation behavior, a fragmentation based version of fluorescence resonance energy transfer (FRET).

Intermission

FA07 10:57 – 11:12

STRUCTURE AND DYNAMICS OF THE WEAKLY BOUND TRIMER $(H_2S)_2(H_2O)$ OBSERVED USING ROTATIONAL SPECTROSCOPY

<u>ARIJIT DAS</u>, *Department of Inorganic and Physical Chemistry, Indian Institute of Science, Bangalore, India*; EVA GOUGOULA, *Photon Science - Spectroscopy of Molecular Processes, Deutsches Elektronen-Synchrotron DESY, Hamburg, Germany*; NICK WALKER, *School of Natural and Environmental Sciences, Newcastle University, Newcastle-upon-Tyne, UK*; ELANGANNAN ARUNAN, *Department of Inorganic and Physical Chemistry, Indian Institute of Science, Bangalore, India.*

The weakly bound complex between two hydrogen sulfide molecules and one water molecule, $(H_2S)_2(H_2O)$, was identified from its rotational spectrum observed at conditions of supersonic expansion. The spectra of parent species were obtained using a chirped-pulse Fourier transform microwave spectrometer (Newcastle, UK). The isotopologues were identified with Balle-Flygare Fourier transform microwave spectrometer (Bangalore, India). Distinct physical properties of H_2O and H_2S under ambient settings have long been recognized as a result of their significantly different hydrogen-bonding capabilities. It has conclusively shown $(H_2S)_2$ is hydrogen-bonded similar to $(H_2O)_2$ at very low temperature[a]. The break with axial molecular symmetry and the simplified internal dynamics allowed us to investigate $(H_2S)_2(H_2O)$ at a level of structural detail that has not yet been possible for $(H_2O)_3$ and $(H_2S)_3$ with rotational spectroscopy due to their zero-dipole moment. The rotational spectrum of $(H_2S)_2(H_2O)$ shows a doubling of the lines, close to 1:3 relative intensity for the parent species, caused by the internal rotation of the H_2O moiety about its C_2 axis. Analysis of experimental results reveals that the three monomers are bound in a triangular arrangement through the S-H$\cdots$S, O-H$\cdots$S and S-H$\cdots$O hydrogen bonds. The r_s and r_0 structural parameters have been evaluated, and the three heavy atom distances r_s(S-H$\cdots$S)=4.067(2)Å, r_s(O-H$\cdots$S)=3.412(11)Å and r_s(S-H$\cdots$O)=3.454(11)Å are appreciably shorter than the respective distances in $(H_2S)_2$, HOH$\cdots$SH$_2$ and HSH$\cdots$OH$_2$[b]. The geometry contains numerous characteristics that indicate the cooperative nature of the intermolecular interaction. The experimental results for all observables determinable from the rotational spectrum are found to be in excellent agreement with *ab initio* predictions.

---

[a] A. Das, P. K. Mandal, F. J. Lovas, C. Medcraft, N. R. Walker, and E. Arunan. *Angewandte Chemie International Edition*, 2018, 57, 15199-15203.
[b] P. K. Mandal, Ph.D. Dissertation, Indian Institute of Science, 2005.

FA08   11:15 – 11:30
EVIDENCE OF NITROGEN AS ACCEPTOR IN NITROMETHANE-FORMALDEHYDE HETERODIMERS CHARACTERIZED USING MATRIX ISOLATION INFRARED SPECTROSCOPY AND COMPUTATIONAL METHODS

<u>NANDALAL MAHAPATRA</u>, S CHANDRA, NAGARAJAN RAMANATHAN, K SUNDARARAJAN, *Materials Chemistry and Metal Fuel Cycle Group, Indira Gandhi Centre for Atomic Research, Homi Bhabha National Institute, Kalpakkam, Tamilnadu, India.*

Formaldehyde (FA) is a fascinating molecule for astrochemists due to the complex mechanistic pathways leading to its formation. Being a very important prebiotic precursor, understanding its participation in various weak interactions is crucial. FA is well established to form hydrogen bonds. In the present work, the interaction of FA with Nitromethane (NM) was studied at low temperature and supported by ab initio theoretical calculations. The heterodimers of NM and FA, NM-FA, were generated within Ar and N_2 matrices and characterized using infrared spectroscopy. Perturbation in the ν_3 mode of NM and ν_2 mode of FA due to the formation of heterodimers has been investigated, as these infrared spectral signatures were shifted from the monomer absorption of NM and FA. The variation of the intensity of these features, in response to the variation in concentration of FA and NM, additionally supported with computations, affirms the formation NM-FA. The red shifts observed, agree well with the predictions by harmonic frequency calculations on the pnicogen-hydrogen-tetrel bound geometry. Computations indicated three minima on the potential energy surface at MP2/CBS and B2PLYP-GD3/CBS levels of theory. The most stable heterodimer, observed experimentally, was stabilized by cooperative pnicogen (O...N), hydrogen (O...H) and tetrel (O...C) bonds as confirmed by QTAIM and NBO analyses. Dominance of electrostatics over other effects in forming the bonds has been established by energy decomposition analysis (EDA). The ability of FA, as a potential electron donor to pnicogen bonding while being a weak tetrel donor too, in addition to its expected participation in hydrogen bonding, stands established experimentally and computationally.

FA09   11:33 – 11:48
OXYGEN ATOM DIFFUSION BY QUANTUM TUNNELING IN SOLID PARAHYDROGEN: A NEW TOOL TO STUDY LOW TEMPERATURE SOLID STATE REACTIONS

<u>IBRAHIM MUDDASSER</u>, DAVID T. ANDERSON, *Department of Chemistry, University of Wyoming, Laramie, WY, USA.*

In quantum crystals such as solid parahydrogen (pH_2), there is considerable overlap between the wavefunctions of molecules in neighboring lattice sites, such that added chemical impurities can exchange positions with nearest-neighbor pH_2 molecules and thereby quantum diffuse through the solid. Our group and others have taken advantage of the quantum diffusion of hydrogen atoms in solid pH_2 to study various low temperature hydrogenation reactions.[a] In this talk, we report the first experimental evidence of atomic oxygen diffusion in solid pH_2. O_2 doped pH_2 samples are irradiated at 193 nm to produce $O(^3P)$ atoms, and repeated FTIR spectra are collected to map out the temporal behavior during and after photolysis. The experimental proof of mobile O-atoms is provided by the formation of ozone (O_3), which forms via the barrierless $O + O_2 + M \rightarrow O_3 + M$ reaction. After photolysis, while the system is kept in the dark, continued growth in the O_3 concentration with time is detected, indicating that O-atoms are mobile and reacting with O_2 present in the solid. The O_3 growth after photolysis is fit to first-order kinetics equations to extract the rate constant. Kinetics measurements show that the O-atom reaction rate more than doubles in annealed crystals compared to as-deposited crystals. This finding is consistent with the expectation that quantum diffusion is more facile in homogeneous samples with minimum defects. In fact, some proportion of the photo-produced O-atoms get trapped in as-deposited samples and can only be made mobile by annealing the sample. Currently, we are studying the effects of the photolysis conditions, temperature, and doped O_2 concentration on the reaction rate constant. This study shows that O-atoms can be isolated in solid pH_2 and that they are delocalized. Through double doping experiments, we hope to develop this method to study O-atom reactions with other species under controlled low temperature conditions.

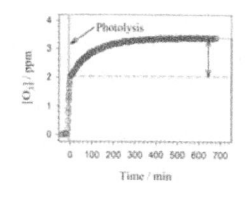

---
[a]F. M. Mutunga et al., *J. Chem. Phys.* **154** (2021) 014302.

FA10 11:51–12:06

USING THE METROPOLIS MONTE CARLO METHOD TO EXTRACT REACTION KINETICS FROM EQUILIBRIUM DISTRIBUTIONS OF STATES

SERGEI F. CHEKMAREV, *Laboratory of Modeling, Institute of Thermophysics, SB RAS, Novosibirsk, Russia.*

Both in experiment and simulations, the kinetics of the mutual interconversion of states in a complex many-body system are usually much more difficult to determine than the equilibrium distribution of states (EDSs). Therefore, it is tempting to find out whether the knowledge of the EDS of a system allows us to obtain information about its kinetics, and if so, to what extent. For this, it is proposed to use the Metropolis Monte Carlo (MMC) method. The EDS plays a roles of the potential of mean force that determines the acceptance probabilities of new states in the MMC simulations.

The approach is illustrated by the protein folding/unfolding reaction. Specifically, two proteins are considered - a model β-hairpin and helical $\alpha_3 D$ protein. For β-hairpin, the free-energy surfaces and free-energy profiles for a set of temperatures are used as the EDSs. It has been found that the rate constants and first-passage time (FPT) distributions obtained in the MMC simulations change with temperature in good agreement with those obtained from molecular dynamics simulations. For $\alpha_3 D$, whose equilibrium folding/unfolding was studied by single-molecule FRET (Chung et al., J. Phys. Chem. A, 115, 2011, 3642), the experimental FRET-efficiency histograms at different denaturant concentrations were used as the EDSs. The rate constants for folding and unfolding obtained in the MMC simulations have been found to change with denaturant concentration in reasonable agreement with the rate constants extracted from the photon trajectories on the basis of theoretical models.

The promising feature of the present approach is that it does not require introducing any additional parameters to perform simulations, which suggests its applicability to other complex systems.

FB. Mini-symposium: Benchmarking in Spectroscopy
Friday, June 24, 2022 – 8:30 AM
Room: 116 Roger Adams Lab

Chair: Brian J. Esselman, The University of Wisconsin, Madison, Madison, WI, USA

FB01   *INVITED TALK*   8:30 – 9:00

ROTATIONAL SPECTROSCOPIC BENCHMARK FOR π INTERATION

HAO WANG, YANG ZHENG, JUAN WANG, *School of Chemistry and Chemical Engineering, Chongqing University, Chongqing, China*; WALTHER CAMINATI, *Dipartimento di Chimica G. Ciamician, Università di Bologna, Bologna, Italy*; JENS-UWE GRABOW, *Institut für Physikalische Chemie und Elektrochemie, Gottfried-Wilhelm-Leibniz-Universität, Hannover, Germany*; JULIEN BLOINO, *Istituto di Chimica dei Composti OrganoMetallici (ICCOM-CNR), UOS di Pisa, Consiglio Nazionale delle Ricerche, Pisa, Italy*; CRISTINA PUZZARINI, *Dep. Chemistry 'Giacomo Ciamician', University of Bologna, Bologna, Italy*; VINCENZO BARONE, *Scuola Normale Superiore, Scuola Normale Superiore, Pisa, Italy*; JUNHA CHEN, QIAN GOU, *School of Chemistry and Chemical Engineering, Chongqing University, Chongqing, China.*

A great deal of attention has been given to noncovalent interactions involving π systems because of their widespread presence in biology as well as materials, where they are pivotal in determining the three-dimensional structures of, e.g., proteins and polymers or the selectivity of molecular affinity. Despite dramatic advances in our understanding over past decades, many aspects of π interactions have only recently been discovered, with many questions remaining. Rotational spectroscopy is arguably the most accurate high resolution molecular spectroscopic technique due to its high sensitivity to mass distributions of molecules and molecular complexes. Since the interaction sites and the relative arrangement of moieties can be determined without environmental bias, rotational spectroscopy allows describing the intermolecular forces at play and enables testing of quantum chemical methods. In this talk, with the recent rotational spectroscopic results we have obtained on π interactions, the comparisons between experimental and computaional data will be discussed.

FB02   9:06 – 9:21

FIRST OBSERVATIONS OF THE HONO · H_2O COMPLEX WITH MICROWAVE SPECTROSCOPY

KENNETH J. KOZIOL, *Institute for Physical Chemistry, RWTH Aachen University, Aachen, Germany*; HA VINH LAM NGUYEN, SAFA KHEMISSI, MARTIN SCHWELL, ISABELLE KLEINER, *Université Paris-Est Créteil et Université de Paris, Laboratoire Interuniversitaire des systèmes atmosphériques (LISA), CNRS UMR7583, Creteil, France*; TAREK TRABELSI, JOSEPH S FRANCISCO, *Department of Earth and Environmental Science and Department of Chemistry, University of Pennsylvaina, Philadelphia, PA, USA.*

The impact of gaseous nitrous acid (HONO) in atmospheric chemistry is well described, being a major source of OH radicals acting as a strong oxidant[a]. In standard conditions, HONO is in equilibrium with various nitrous oxides under rapid decomposition at daytime. However, results by Lammel and Cape describe a steady production of OH radicals by HONO in the atmosphere whose source might be the complex of HONO with water[b]. Recent experiments have revealed that HONO remains stable in an aqeous environment as the HONO · H_2O complex, supporting studies of its greater stability in environments with higher humidity[c]. In the present work, gaseous HONO · H_2O was generated in a laboratory scale and investigated with two molecular jet Fourier transform microwave spectrometers operating from 2 to 40 GHz. To guide the experimental observation, geometry optimizations were performed to obtain rotational constants using the standard coupled-cluster theory with single and double excitations. The HONO · H_2O spectrum has been assigned with the ^{14}N quadrupole coupling taken into account. Further splittings by the ortho-hydrogens, resulting from spin-spin coupling interactions, could be fully resolved. Comparing the results to those of the dimethylamine-water complex[d] confirmed an absence of the water tunnelling motion.

---

[a] N. A. Saliba et. al. *Geophys. Res. Lett.* **27**, 3229-3232, (2000).
[b] G. Lammel, J. N. Cape, *Chem. Soc. Rev.* **25**, 361-369, (1996).
[c] D. Perner, U. Platt, *Geophys. Res. Lett.* **6**, 917-920, (1979).
[d] M. J. Tubergen, R. L. Kuczkowski, *J. Mol. Struct.* **352/353**, 335-344, (1994).

FB03   9:24 – 9:39

INSTRUMENT DEVELOPMENT FOR CHIRPED PULSE FOURIER-TRANSFORM MICROWAVE SPECTROSCOPY OF ALCOHOL:WATER CLUSTERS

S E DUTTON, GEOFFREY BLAKE, *Division of Chemistry and Chemical Engineering, California Institute of Technology, Pasadena, CA, USA.*

This talk will discuss the design and performance of a novel high-throughput instrument for Chirped Pulse Fourier-transform Microwave (CP-FTMW) spectroscopy, and demonstrate its efficacy through the identification of the lowest energy conformers of the ethanol trimer and mixed water:ethanol trimers. Computational characterization of the target clusters will be described, as will experimental details and resulting conclusions as to the structure of the observed clusters. In addition, the increased speed of data collection and resulting sensitivity of the instrument will be addressed, with the new target species made available by these improvements.

FB04   9:42 – 9:57

MULTIDIMENSIONAL TUNNELING IN 2-NITROTOLUENE[a]

ANTHONY ROUCOU, ARNAUD CUISSET, *Laboratoire de Physico-Chimie de l'Atmosphère, Université du Littoral Côte d'Opale, Dunkerque, France*; MANUEL GOUBET, *Laboratoire PhLAM, UMR 8523 CNRS - Université Lille 1, Villeneuve d'Ascq, France*; L. H. COUDERT, *Institut des Sciences Moléculaires d'Orsay, Université Paris-Saclay, CNRS, Orsay, France.*

Although many non-rigid molecules displaying a single LAM have been spectroscopically characterized, less results are available about non-rigid molecules displaying several LAMs, as they are theoretically more challenging. This is confirmed by a recent spectroscopic investigation of nitrotoluene[b] which revealed that its 2-nitrotoluene isomeric species displays two LAMs corresponding to internal rotations of the CH_3 and NO_2 groups. In this investigation,[b] because no approach accounting for two LAMs was available, the microwave spectrum of 2-nitrotoluene was analyzed using a simplified approach accounting only for the torsional motion of the CH_3 group.

In this talk, the IAM water dimer formalism[c] will be applied to 2-nitrotoluene. As this theoretical approach is designed for multidimensional tunneling in the high-barrier limit, it is well suited for this species. Once the equilibrium configurations and the tunneling paths are chosen, the IAM approach[c] allows us to derive a fitting Hamiltonian accounting for the rotational dependence of the tunneling splittings, but not for their magnitude, which should be obtained fitting the spectroscopic data. In 2-nitrotoluene, there are six C_1 symmetry equilibrium configurations and two tunneling paths. The first and most feasible one corresponds to a $2\pi/3$ rotation of the methyl group. The second one is the complicated geared internal rotation of both the CH_3 and NO_2 groups identified using quantum chemistry calculations.[b]

The results of the line position analysis of the available microwave data[b] with the new IAM approach will be presented. It is hoped that the analysis results will be more satisfactory than with the simplified approach[b] and this will provide us with a better understanding of the 2-nitrotoluene multidimensional potential energy surface.

---

[a]This work received financial support from the French ANR. Project METIS under contract number ANR-20-ASTR-0016-03
[b]Roucou, Goubet, Kleiner, Bteich and Cuisset, *ChemPhysChem* **21** (2020) 1
[c]Hougen, *J. Mol. Spec.* **114** (1985) 395; and Coudert and Hougen, *J. Mol. Spec.* **130** (1988) 86

FB05 10:00 – 10:15

DOUBLE-PROTON TRANSFER OVER A PHENYL RING REVEALED BY CP-FTMW SPECTROSCOPY

<u>WEIXING LI</u>, *Department of Chemistry, Fudan University, Shanghai, China*; DENIS TIKHONOV, MELANIE SCHNELL, *FS-SMP, Deutsches Elektronen-Synchrotron (DESY), Hamburg, Germany*; WALTHER CAMINATI, *Dipartimento di Chimica G. Ciamician, Università di Bologna, Bologna, Italy*; DINGDING LV, *Department of Chemistry, Fudan University, Shanghai, China*; GUANJUN WANG, MINGFEI ZHOU, *Fudan University, Department of Chemistry, Shanghai, China.*

Our previous work demonstrated that the measurement of pure rotational spectroscopy of "non-polar" dimer of formic acid can be achieved by means of asymmetric H–D substitution.[1] The concerted double proton transfer of the two hydroxyl hydrogens takes place between two equivalent minima and generates a tunneling splitting of 331.6(5) MHz. In this talk, I will discuss the double proton transfer over a phenyl ring in the complexes of formic acid dimer (FAD) with phenyl compounds. For example, in the FAD-fluorobenzene complex, the presence of fluorobenzene as a neighboring molecule does not quench the double proton transfer in the FAD but decreases its tunneling splitting to 267.608(1) MHz.[2] In the FAD-fluorobenzaldehyde complex, the protons transfer does not occur via tunneling, but produces two non-equivalent isomers. Our spectra show that the isotopic substitution at different atomic positions have different influences on the tunneling process. The experiments were carried out by using the CP-FTMW spectrometer in Hamburg and the new-build one in Shanghai.
[1] Angew. Chem. Int. Ed. 2019, 58, 859 –865. [2] Angew. Chem. Int. Ed. 2021, 60, 25674 –25679.

Intermission

FB06 10:57 – 11:12

BRIDGING THE GAP: ROTATIONAL STUDY OF H_2 IN COMPLEXES WITH SMALL AROMATIC MOLECULES

<u>ROBIN DOHMEN</u>, *Institute of Physical Chemistry, Georg-August-Universität Göttingen, Göttingen, Germany*; MELANIE SCHNELL, PABLO PINACHO, *FS-SMP, Deutsches Elektronen-Synchrotron (DESY), Hamburg, Germany*; DANIEL A. OBENCHAIN, *Institute of Physical Chemistry, Georg-August-Universität Göttingen, Göttingen, Germany.*

Molecular hydrogen plays a key role in our efforts to shift our energy production to renewable resources. Hydrogen is an important energy storage molecule which in the future may replace our fossilized fuels as a transportable energy source. To appropriately model hydrogen storage materials, an understanding of the fundamental binding to organic systems is required. In previous works only a few inorganic and metallic complexes with hydrogen have be investigated by rotational spectroscopy.[a,b] This work aims to bridge the gap to large covalent organic frameworks (COF) by focusing on the microwave structure of hydrogen heterodimers with small aromatic ring systems.[c]

In this work the binding sites of hydrogen to halogen benzaldehydes which serve as mimics COF monomers, specifically boronic ester based COFs, are studied. These volatile systems possess a large dipole moment and provide a method of increasing the complexity of the system by the introduction of quadrupolar nuceli to finally look at small boronic esters in hydrogen complexes. Of particular interest are the differences observed for the rotational spectrum of *ortho-* and *para-* hydrogen and its structural impact investigated by isotopic substitution. The significant differences between these two species demonstrate there are significant differences in binding strength of o-H_2 and p-H_2 which are experimentally observable. Broadband rotational spectra are presented, are supplemented with cavity Fourier transform microwave spectroscopy data to resolve the additional hyperfine splitting of o-H_2 ($j = 1$). These experimental results can be directly compared to a number of quantum chemical predictions to provide a foundation for the simulation of large scale covalent organic frameworks.

---
[a] Jäger, W. et al., *J. Chem. Phys.*, **127** 054305, 2007, DOI: 10.1063/1.2756534
[b] Obenchain, D., Frank, H., Pickett, H., Novik, S., *J. Chem. Phys.*, **146** 204302, 2017, DOI:10.1063/1.4983042
[c] Geng, K., He, T., Liu, R. et al., *Chem. Rev.*, **120** 8814, 2020, DOI: 10.1021/acs.chemrev.9b00550

FB07   11:15 – 11:30

STRONG ORTHO/PARA EFFECTS IN THE VIBRATIONAL SPECTRA OF Cl-H2 and CN-H2

FRANZISKA DAHLMANN, *Institute for Ion Physics and Applied Physics, University of Innsbruck, Innsbruck, Austria*; PAVOL JUSKO, , *Max Planck Institute for Extraterrestrial Physics, Munich, Germany*; MIGUEL LARA-MORENO, *Institut des Sciences Moléculaires, Universté de Bordeaux, Bordaux, Hauts-de-Seine, France*; CHRISTINE LOCHMANN, *Institute for Ion Physics and Applied Physics, University of Innsbruck, Innsbruck, Austria*; ARAVINDH NIVAS MARIMUTHU, *FELIX Laboratory, Radboud University, Nijmegen, The Netherlands*; PHILIPPE HALVICK, *ISM, Université de Bordeaux, Bordeaux, France*; ROBERT WILD, TIM MICHAELSEN, *Institute for Ion Physics and Applied Physics, University of Innsbruck, Innsbruck, Austria*; STEPHAN SCHLEMMER, *I. Physikalisches Institut, University of Cologne, Cologne, Germany*; THIERRY STOECKLIN, *Institut des Sciences Moléculaires, Universté de Bordeaux, Bordaux, Hauts-de-Seine, France*; SANDRA BRÜNKEN, *FELIX Laboratory, Radboud University, Nijmegen, The Netherlands*; ROLAND WESTER, *Institute for Ion Physics and Applied Physics, University of Innsbruck, Innsbruck, Austria*.

The vibrational predissociation spectra of Cl^-H_2 and CN^-H_2 are measured in regions between 450 and 3000 cm^{-1} in an ion trap at different temperatures using the FELIX infrared free electron lasers. Strong differences between the vibrational spectra of the two *para* and *ortho* nuclear spin isomers X-(*para*-H_2) or X-(*ortho*-H_2), with X = Cl^- or CN^-, are detected [1,2]. Above a certain temperature, the removal of the *para* nuclear spin isomer by ligand exchange to the *ortho* isomer is suppressed efficiently. Not only do the transition frequencies agree well with calculated spectra using an accurate quantum approach [3], also the line profile matches with the calculated bands. When comparing the absolute frequency positions of the measured and calculated vibrational bands one finds a redshift of about 5cm^{-1} for the strongest band.

[1] F. Dahlmann, P. Jusko, M. Lara-Moreno et al., Mol. Phys., submitted
[2] F. Dahlmann, C. Lochmann, A. N. Marimuthu et al., J. Chem. Phys. Comm. 155, 241101 (2021)
[3] M. Lara-Moreno, P. Halvick, and T. Stoecklin, Phys. Chem. Chem. Phys. 22, 25552–25559 (2020)

FB08   11:33 – 11:48

ACCURATE EXPERIMENTAL VALIDATION OF AB INITIO QUANTUM SCATTERING CALCULATIONS USING THE SPECTRA OF He-PERTURBED H_2

MICHAŁ SŁOWIŃSKI, HUBERT JÓŹWIAK, MACIEJ GRZEGORZ GANCEWSKI, KAMIL STANKIEWICZ, NIKODEM STOLARCZYK, PIOTR ŻUCHOWSKI, ROMAN CIURYŁO, PIOTR WCISLO, *Institute of Physics, Faculty of Physics, Astronomy and Informatics, Nicolaus Copernicus University, Torun, Poland*; YAN TAN, JIN WANG, AN-WEN LIU, SHUI-MING HU, *Hefei National Laboratory for Physical Science at Microscale, University of Science and Technology of China, Hefei, China*; SAMIR KASSI, ALAIN CAMPARGUE, *UMR5588 LIPhy, Université Grenoble Alpes/CNRS, Saint Martin d'Hères, France*; KONRAD PATKOWSKI, *Chemistry and Biochemistry, Auburn University, Auburn, AL, USA*; FRANCK THIBAULT, *Institute of Physics of Rennes, Univ. Rennes, CNRS, Rennes, France*.

Due to its simplicity, molecular hydrogen perturbed by helium atom constitutes a great benchmark system for tests of *ab initio* quantum scattering calculations as a method of precise description of collisional effects in ultra-accurate experimental spectra. Here we present our recent cavity-enhanced measurements of H_2 lines perturbed by He. Our results exhibit an unprecedented subpercent agreement with fully quantum *ab initio* calculations. We investigate collisional line-shape effects that are present in highly accurate experimental spectra of the 3-0 S(1) and 2-0 Q(1) lines. We clearly distinguish the influence of six different collisional effects (i.e.: collisional broadening and shift, their speed dependences and the complex Dicke effect) on the shapes of H_2 lines. We demonstrate that if any of the six contributions is neglected, then the experiment-theory comparison deteriorates at least several times. We also analyze the influence of the centrifugal distortion on our *ab initio* calculations and we demonstrate that the inclusion of this effect slightly improves the agreement with the experimental spectra.

In addition, we describe the theoretical calculations that were performed to obtain the subpercent agreement with experiment. In the analysis described here, we employed the state-of-the-art statistical model of the collision-perturbed shape of molecular lines. We obtained all the parameters of this model from quantum scattering calculations, and the dynamical calculations were performed on the most accurate potential energy surface (PES) to date.

FB09

INVESTIGATION OF COLLISIONAL EFFECTS IN MOLECULAR SPECTRA - COMPREHENSIVE DATASET OF LINE-SHAPE PARAMETERS FROM AB INITIO CALCULATIONS FOR He-PERTURBED HD

KAMIL STANKIEWICZ, HUBERT JÓŹWIAK, NIKODEM STOLARCZYK, MACIEJ GRZEGORZ GANCEWSKI, PIOTR WCISLO, *Institute of Physics, Faculty of Physics, Astronomy and Informatics, Nicolaus Copernicus University, Torun, Poland*; FRANCK THIBAULT, *Institute of Physics of Rennes, Univ. Rennes, CNRS, Rennes, France.*

The abundance of molecular hydrogen and atomic helium in the universe makes them an important system to study in various fields. A mixture of molecular hydrogen and helium is the main component of the atmospheres of gas giants in the Solar System and is predicted to be a dominant constituent of the atmospheres of some types of exoplanets. The hydrogen molecule is also the simplest molecule, the structure of which can be calculated from first principles, which makes it well suited for accurate tests of *ab initio* calculations. In particular HD molecule, despite its lower abundance than H_2 isotopologue is noticeable in spectroscopic studies due to the presence of its dipole moment. Studies show that in some cases the uncertainty of astronomical observations (f.e. measuring the D/H ratios) of hydrogen molecule spectra is dominated by the uncertainties of collisional parameters, including pressure broadening and pressure shift coefficients.

We utilize the methodology of populating line-by-line spectroscopic databases with beyond-Voigt line-shape parameters [a], which is based on *ab initio* quantum scattering calculations and was first applied to the He-perturbed H_2. We report a comprehensive dataset of beyond-Voigt line-shape parameters (pressure broadening and shift coefficients, their speed-dependences, and the complex Dicke parameters) for all electric dipole and quadrupole transitions within the ground electronic state in He-perturbed HD that are present in HITRAN (11 575 lines) at temperatures spanning from 20 to 1000 K. We parametrize the temperature dependence of the line-shape parameters with double-power-law representation (DPL), recommended for the HITRAN database. In addition to the presentation of the calculations, we will discuss our latest experimental determination of collisional line-shape parameters for He-perturbed H_2 and its comparison with theoretical results.

---

[a] P. Wcislo et al., J Quant Spectrosc Radiat Transf 2021;260:107477. doi: 10.1016/j.jqsrt.2020.107477

FB10

PRECISION SPECTROSCOPY OF HD

QIAN-HAO LIU, CUNFENG CHENG, SHUI-MING HU, *Department of Chemical Physics, University of Science and Technology of China, Hefei, China.*

Precision spectral measurement of simple molecules such as H_2 and their isotopes is one of the important research fields of spectroscopy. Combined with accurate calculations, allows us to test the fundamental quantum chemistry theory and to determine the fundamental physical constants such as the proton-to-electron mass ratio. Here we present the Doppler-free spectroscopy measurements of first overtone transition of HD at a temperature as low as 10K, measured the saturated absorption spectrum of the first overtone transition of HD and observed the Doppler free spectral of R_0 (2-0) for the first time. The line profile is different from the saturated absorption spectrum. We analyzed the line profile and it is expected to determine the transition frequency with 11 digits.

FC. Atmospheric science
Friday, June 24, 2022 – 8:30 AM
Room: B102 Chemical and Life Sciences

Chair: Steven Federman, University of Toledo, Toledo, OH, USA

FC01   8:30 – 8:45

ROTATIONAL STUDY OF ATMOSPHERIC VOCS USING THE NEW CP-FTMW SPECTROMETER OF LILLE

<u>ELIAS M. NEEMAN</u>, NOUREDDIN OSSEIRAN, MANUEL GOUBET, PASCAL DRÉAN, THERESE R. HUET, *UMR 8523 - PhLAM - Physique des Lasers Atomes et Molécules, University of Lille, CNRS, F-59000 Lille, France.*

The introduction of the CP-FTMW technique by Pate and co-workers has revolutionized the rotational spectroscopy field providing rapid acquisition of broadband spectra.[a] The design of a newly constructed chirped-pulse Fourier transform microwave spectrometer CP-FTMW covering the range of 6-18 GHz will be presented. In particular, the chirped pulse (6-18 GHz, 4 μs) is generated by a fast-arbitrary waveform generator (AWG, Keysight M8195A 65 GSa/s). Free Induction Decays (FID) are detected and collected on a recent generation of a fast oscilloscope (Keysight DSOZ634A 160 GSa/s). The high speed of the oscilloscope allows to achieve a high spectral resolution (FWHM better than 40 kHz) by recording the FID during 80 μs. Up to three pulsed nozzles can be used simultaneously.[b] The CP-FTMW spectrometer is currently used to study volatile organic molecules of atmospheric interest. The results of this work will be discussed in detail.

Hervé Damart and Gauthier Dekyndt are gratefully acknowledged for their technical assistance.

The present work was funded by the ANR Labex CaPPA, by the Regional Council Hauts-de-France, by the European Funds for Regional Economic Development, and by the CPER CLIMIBIO and CPER P4S.

---

[a] Brown, G. G.; Dian, B. C.; Douglass, K. O.; Geyer, S. M.; Shipman, S. T.; Pate, B. H. Rev. Sci. Instrum. 2008, 79 (5), 053103

[b] Seifert, N. A.; Steber, A. L.; Neill, J. L.; Pérez, C.; Zaleski, D. P.; Pate, B. H.; Lesarri, A. Phys. Chem. Chem. Phys. 2013, 15 (27), 11468–11477

FC02   8:48 – 9:03

THE WATER VAPOUR SELF- AND FOREIGN CONTINUUM ABSORPTION AT ROOM TEMPERATURE IN THE 1.25 μm window

<u>ALEKSANDRA KOROLEVA</u>, SAMIR KASSI, DIDIER MONDELAIN, ALAIN CAMPARGUE, *UMR5588 LIPhy, Université Grenoble Alpes/CNRS, Saint Martin d'Hères, France.*

The water vapour self- and foreign-continuum are newly measured at room temperature in the high energy edge of the 1.25 cm^{-1} window by using highly stable and sensitive cavity ring-down spectroscopy (CRDS).

Self-continuum cross-sections, C_S, are derived between 8290 and 8620 cm^{-1} at 29 selected spectral points by using pressure ramps (up to 15 Torr) of pure water vapour. Purely quadratic pressure dependence is obtained for the absorption coefficient at each measurement point. Although the spectral measurement points were chosen to minimize the contribution of resonance line absorption, the latter represents between 30 and 70 % of the measured absorption in the studied region.

The self-continuum measurements are found consistent with a previous study of the low-frequency edge of the 1.25 cm^{-1} window (Campargue et al. J Geophys Res Atmos 2016;121:13,180 – 13,203. doi:10.1002/2016JD025531). The frequency dependence of the retrieved C_S values shows an overall good agreement with the MT_CKD values. Nevertheless, an additional broad absorption feature is observed with a centre near 8455 cm^{-1}. It is tentatively interpreted as a possible impact of the uncertainties on the resonance line contribution on the derived C_S values or as possible evidence of a band of the bound dimers, $(H_2O)_2$

Foreign-continuum cross-sections, C_f, are derived for humidified nitrogen, humidified oxygen and humidified air between 8120 and 8500 cm^{-1} by using pressure ramps (up to 750 Torr with 10000 ppm of H_2O) at 5 selected spectral points for each gas mixture. Although data treatment is in progress, the H_2O-air and H_2O-N_2 C_f cross-section values seem to be comparable while the H_2O-O_2 C_f value appears to be significantly smaller. A satisfactory agreement of the retrieved C_f for H_2O-air mixture with the MT_CKD model is demonstrated. To the best of our knowledge, it is the first H_2O-air, H_2O-N_2, H_2O-O_2 foreign-continuum study in this frequency range.

FC03 9:06 – 9:21
WILDFIRE SMOKE DESTROYS STRATOSPHERIC OZONE

PETER F. BERNATH, *Department of Chemistry and Biochemistry, Old Dominion University, Norfolk, VA, USA*; CHRIS BOONE, JEFF CROUSE, *Department of Chemistry, University of Waterloo, Waterloo, ON, Canada.*

Large wildfires inject smoke and biomass burning products into the midlatitude stratosphere where they destroy ozone, which protects us from ultraviolet radiation. The infrared spectrometer on the Atmospheric Chemistry Experiment (ACE) satellite has measured the spectra of smoke particles from the Black Summer Australian fires in late 2019 /early 2020, demonstrating that they contain oxygenated organic functional groups and water adsorption on the surfaces. The injected smoke particles produce unexpected and extreme perturbations in stratospheric gases beyond any seen in the previous 15 years of measurements: increases in formaldehyde, chlorine nitrate, chlorine monoxide and hypochlorous acid, and decreases in ozone, nitrogen dioxide and hydrochloric acid. These perturbations in stratospheric composition have the potential to affect ozone chemistry in unexpected ways.

FC04 9:24 – 9:39
STRATOSPHERIC AEROSOL COMPOSITION OBSERVED BY THE ATMOSPHERIC CHEMISTRY EXPERIMENT FOLLOWING THE 2019 RAIKOKE ERUPTION

CHRIS BOONE, *Department of Chemistry, University of Waterloo, Waterloo, ON, Canada*; PETER F. BERNATH, *Department of Chemistry and Biochemistry, Old Dominion University, Norfolk, VA, USA*; KEITH LABELLE, *Department of Physics, Old Dominon University, Norfolk, VA, USA*; JEFF CROUSE, *Department of Chemistry, University of Waterloo, Waterloo, ON, Canada.*

Following the eruption of the Raikoke volcano in 2019, infrared spectra from the Atmospheric Chemistry Experiment satellite[1] were used to evaluate the composition of stratospheric aerosols in the Northern Hemisphere. The layer of aerosols observed after the eruption ranged from 9 to 20 km in altitude and persisted in the stratosphere for several months. This layer was composed nearly entirely of sulfate aerosols, droplets of a mixture of sulfuric acid and water. To determine the aerosol composition, the spectra were modeled using extinction values calculated with Mie scattering code and sulfuric acid optical constants. Contrary to previous reports, there is no evidence of stratospheric smoke being present in the Arctic region.

[1] P. F. Bernath. The Atmospheric Chemistry Experiment (ACE). JQSRT 2017;186:3-16. https://doi.org/10.1016/j.jqsrt.2016.04.006.

FC05 9:42 – 9:57
ATLAS OF ACE SPECTRA OF CLOUDS AND AEROSOLS

JASON J SORENSEN, PETER F. BERNATH, *Department of Chemistry and Biochemistry, Old Dominion University, Norfolk, VA, USA*; MIKE LECOURS, CHRIS BOONE, *Department of Chemistry, University of Waterloo, Waterloo, ON, Canada*; RYAN JOHNSON, *Physics Department, Old Dominion University, Norfolk, VA, USA*; KEITH LABELLE, *Department of Physics, Old Dominon University, Norfolk, VA, USA.*

Clouds and aerosols play a vital role in the Earth's climate. Detecting polar mesospheric clouds, polar stratospheric clouds and aerosols is useful for monitoring climate change and atmospheric chemistry. ACE satellite data[1] is used to provide an infrared spectral atlas of polar mesospheric clouds, three types of polar stratospheric clouds (nitric acid trihydrate, sulfuric/nitric acid ternary solutions, and ice), cirrus clouds, smoke from fires, and sulfate aerosols. Nearly all example spectra have been modeled with either Mie scattering or T-matrix codes using the appropriate optical constants.

[1] P. F. Bernath. The Atmospheric Chemistry Experiment (ACE). JQSRT 2017;186:3-16. https://doi.org/10.1016/j.jqsrt.2016.04.006.

FC06 10:00–10:15

LOW-PRESSURE YIELDS OF STABILIZED CRIEGEE INTERMEDIATES PRODUCED FROM OZONOLYSIS OF A SERIES OF ALKENES

LEI YANG, MIXTLI CAMPOS-PINEDA, *Department of Chemistry, University of California, Riverside, CA, USA*; JINGSONG ZHANG, *Department of Chemistry and Air Pollution Research Center, University of California, Riverside, CA, USA.*

Ozonolysis of alkenes is an important oxidation pathway of alkenes in the troposphere because it is involved in the production of organic aerosol and OH radicals. The mechanism of ozonolysis of alkenes involves the formation of a primary ozonide (POZ), which then decomposes into a carbonyl and a high-energy carbonyl oxide (Criegee intermediate). Criegee intermediates are produced with a broad internal energy distribution. High energy Criegee intermediates decompose into atmospherically important compounds (e.g. vinoxy, OH radical). Stabilized Criegee intermediates (sCIs) undergo reactions to produce secondary ozonides and organic aerosols.

Cavity ring-down spectroscopy (CRDS) was utilized in combination with chemical titration with sulfur dioxide (SO_2) to quantify sCIs. The reaction is carried out under various flow and low-pressure conditions. Reference cross-sections of products and reactants are fitted with spectral features to obtain product number densities.

The yields of sCIs were measured at different low pressures and the nascent yields were determined by extrapolation to zero pressure. Endocyclic alkenes (cyclopentene and cyclohexene) show no sCI production at the pressures studied. However, acyclic alkenes show pressure-dependent sCI yields. Formaldehyde oxide (CH_2OO) from the alkenes studied (propene, 1-butene and isoprene) has a high nascent yield due to its relatively high energy barrier for dissociation. Cis-2-butene produces higher nascent sCI than trans-2-butene, possibly due to different syn- and anti-CI branching ratios, or different POZ conformations. There is an indication that alkenes larger than 2,3-dimethyl-2-butene would have higher nascent sCI yields. The information on low-pressure yields from the current studies can be used as a benchmark for theoretical calculations.

Intermission

FC07 10:57–11:12

REACTION MECHANISM AND KINETICS OF THE GAS PHASE REACTIONS OF METHANE SULFONAMIDE WITH Cl RADICALS AND THE FATE OF $CH_2S(=O)_2NH_2$ RADICAL[a]

PARANDAMAN ARATHALA, RABI A. MUSAH, *Department of Chemistry, University at Albany—State University of New York, Albany, NY, USA.*

Methane sulfonamide ($CH_3S(=O)_2NH_2$, MSAM) is an important trace compound detected for the first time in ambient air over the Red Sea and the Gulf of Aden.[b,c] The average mixing ratios of this compound were found to be in the range of 20 – 50 ppt with a maximum value of 60 ppt.[b,c] The energetics and rate coefficients for its reactions with Cl radical and in presence of atmospheric oxygen ($^3O_2$) to form various products have not been reported. In the present work, we investigated the atmospheric oxidation mechanism and energetics of the reaction of MSAM with Cl radicals using high level quantum chemistry calculations. The MSAM + Cl radical reaction mainly proceeds by H-abstraction paths. Abstraction of H-atom from the methyl group of MSAM by Cl radical to form $CH_2S(=O)_2NH_2$ radical + HCl products was found to be dominant compared to other possible paths. The barrier height for this reaction was found to be 4.8 kcal mol^{-1} above the energy of the starting reactants at the CCSD(T)/aug-cc-pV(T+d)Z//M06-2X/aug-cc-pV(T+d)Z level. The rate coefficients were calculated for all possible H-atom abstraction paths associated with the MSAM + Cl radical using canonical variational transition state theory (CVT) with a small curvature tunneling (SCT) approximation in the temperatures between 200 and 300 K. The rate coefficient data, atmospheric lifetime of MSAM, branching ratios and thermodynamic parameters associated with the MSAM + Cl radical reaction are discussed. In addition, the atmospheric fate of the major product (i.e., the $CH_2S(=O)_2NH_2$ radical) with respect to its interaction with $^3O_2$ to form the RO_2 radical adduct (R = -$CH_2S(=O)_2NH_2$) using the same level of theory was also investigated. The formed RO_2 radical adduct proceeds through various multichannel pathways in the presence of HO_2 radical to form several greenhouse gases and environmental pollutants including SO_2, CO_2, CO, HC(O)OH and HNO_3 as final products.

---

[a] The authors are grateful to NSF (grant numbers 1310350 and 1710221) for support of this work.
[b] Edtbauer, A. et al. Atmos. Chem. Phys. 2020, 20, 6081.
[c] Berasategui, M. et al. Atmos. Chem. Phys. 2020, 20, 2695.

FC08   11:15 – 11:30

FIRST ANALYSIS OF THE ν_1 BAND OF HNO$_3$ AT 3551.766 CM^{-1}

<u>AGNES PERRIN</u>, *Laboratoire de Meteorologie Dynamique, Ecole Polytechnique, University Paris Saclay and CNRS, Paris, France*; LAURENT MANCERON, *Synchrotron SOLEIL, CNRS-MONARIS UMR 8233 and Beamline AILES, Saint Aubin, France*; RAYMOND ARMANTE, *Ecole Polytechnique, CNRS / Laboratoire de Météorologie Dunamique, 91128 Palaiseau, France*; P. ROY, *AILES beam line, Synchrotron Soleil, Gif-sur-Yvette, France*; F. KWABIA TCHANA, *CNRS - Université de Paris - Université Paris Est Créteil, LISA, Créteil, France*; GEOFFREY C. TOON, *Jet Propulsion Laboratory, California Institute of Technology, Pasadena, CA, USA.*

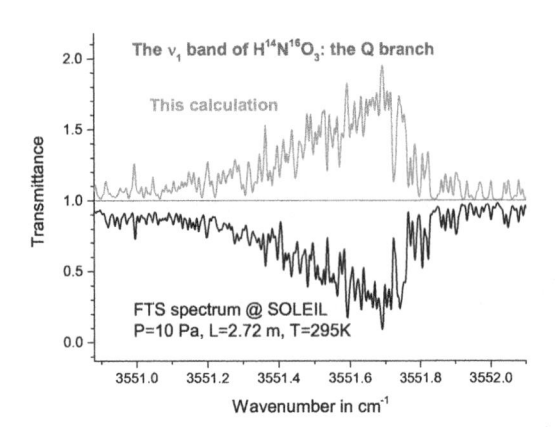

We present the first (preliminary) investigation of the ν_1 band (OH stretching mode) of Nitric acid (HNO$_3$) centered at 3551.766 cm^{-1} using high resolution Fourier transform spectra. These spectra were recorded in the 2.5 μm to 3.23 μm spectral regions on the spectrometer located on the AILES beamline of the SOLEIL synchrotron. Because of the large value of the Doppler linewidth (about 0.003 cm^{-1}) in the 2.8 μm region at 220 K or 296 K), the analysis was very complex and often uncertain and dubious. Furthermore, the ν_1 band is severely affected by numerous perturbations. Among these ones, unexpected line splittings were observed during all the analyses. Finally we have generated a preliminary list of "reasonable" line positions and intensities for the ν_1 band and of the $\nu_1+\nu_9-\nu_9$ bands and $\nu_1+\nu_7-\nu_7$ hot bands.

FC09   11:33 – 11:48

MILLIMETER-WAVE SPECTROSCOPY OF METHYLFURAN ISOMERS: LOCAL vs GLOBAL TREATMENT OF THE INTERNAL ROTATION

<u>JONAS BRUCKHUISEN</u>, *Laboratoire de Physico-Chimie de l'Atmosphère, Université du Littoral Côte d'Opale, Dunkerque, France*; SATHAPANA CHAWANANON, PIERRE ASSELIN, *CNRS, De la Molécule aux Nano-Objets: Réactivité, Interactions, Spectroscopies, MONARIS, Sorbonne Université, PARIS, France*; ISABELLE KLEINER, *Université Paris-Est Créteil et Université de Paris, Laboratoire Interuniversitaire des systèmes atmosphériques (LISA), CNRS UMR7583, Creteil, France*; ANTHONY ROUCOU, GUILLAUME DHONT, COLWYN BRACQUART, ARNAUD CUISSET, *Laboratoire de Physico-Chimie de l'Atmosphère, Université du Littoral Côte d'Opale, Dunkerque, France.*

Methylfurans (MF) are methylated aromatic heterocyclic volatile organic compounds (VOCs) and primary or secondary pollutants in the atmosphere due to their capability to form atmospheric particles such as secondary organic aerosols (SOAs).[1] MFs are produced by cracking biomass such as wood combustion and the pyrolysis of biomass, lignin and cellulose.[2] Therefore there is a fundamental interest to monitor these molecules in the gas phase. The high resolution spectroscopic studies of methylated furan compounds, except 2-MF[3], are generally limited to pure rotational spectroscopy in the ground state. This might be explained by the difficulties arisen from the internal rotation with a medium barrier and the complexity of the vibrationally excited state rotational spectra. As Finneran et al. for 2-MF, we faced the same difficulties for 3-MF to treat the first torsional state ($\nu_t = 1$) using a local approach (XIAM[4]) and therefore the global treatment, including all torsional levels given by the BELGI code[5], was used. This gave us access to the V_6 term characterising the anharmonicity of the potential, together with some higher order perturbation and coupling terms. Carrying out a BELGI global fit of $\nu_t = 0$ and $\nu_t = 1$ states using our new assignment for 3-MF and the assigned transitions of Finneran et al. for 2-MF enabled us to compare the molecular parameters of these two isomers.

[1] X. Jiang, *Atmos. Chem. Phys.* **2019**, 19, 13591-13609.; [2] M. Perzon, *Biomass and Bioenergy.* **2010**, 34, 828-837.; [3] I.A. Finneran, *J. Mol. Spectrosc.* **2012**, 280, 27-33.; [4] H. Hartwig and H. Dreizler, *Z. Naturforsch.*, **1996** 51a, 923; [5] I. Kleiner, *J. Mol. Spectrosc.*, **2010**, 260(1), 1-18.

FC10   11:51 – 12:06

AB INITIO STUDY OF THE EXCITED STATES OF O_2

<u>GAP-SUE KIM</u>, *Dharma College, Dongguk University, Seoul, Korea*; WILFRID SOMOGYI, SERGEI N. YURCHENKO, *Department of Physics and Astronomy, University College London, London, UK*.

O_2 is important for spectroscopic applications in the IR, Visible and UV regions. In this work eight lowest electronic states were studied using the CASSCF and MRCI methods and the AV5Z basis sets with the D_2h point group symmetry, namely $X\,^3\Sigma_g^-$, $A\,^3\Sigma_u^+$, $A'\,^3\Delta_u$, $a\,^1\Delta_g$, $b\,^1\Sigma_g^+$, $c\,^1\Sigma_u^-$ (bound), $C\,^3\Pi_g$, $d\,^1\Pi_g$ (unbound). Potential energy curves (PECs) for 8 electronic states and spin-orbit coupling, electronic angular moment and transition quadrupole moment curves for the five states $X\,^3\Sigma_g^-$, $a\,^1\Delta_g$, $b\,^1\Sigma_g^+$, $d\,^1\Pi_g$ and $C\,^3\Pi_g$, were computed and used to predict rovibronic spectra and lifetimes of O_2. Our aim is to construct an accurate ro-vibronic molecular line list for O_2. This will require an empirical refinement of the *ab initio* curves and will be considered in our future work.

FC11   12:09 – 12:24

INFRARED SPECTROSCOPIC AND QUANTUM CHEMICAL EXPLORATION OF AMMONIUM IODATE CLUSTERS

<u>NICOLINE C. FREDERIKS</u>, *Chemistry, Stony Brook University, Stony Brook, NY, USA*; DANIKA LEE HEANEY, *Department of Chemistry, Wellesley College, Wellesley, MA, USA*; JOHN J. KREINBIHL, *Department of Chemistry, Stony Brook University, Stony Brook, NY, USA*; CHRISTOPHER J. JOHNSON, *Chemistry, Stony Brook University, Stony Brook, NY, USA*.

New particle formation (NPF) comprises a substantial part of secondary aerosol particle formation in the atmosphere, and these particles play an important role in the radiative forcing balance governing climate change. Significant uncertainties in current global climate models persist in part due to the uncertainty surrounding NPF growth mechanisms. Establishing the surface structure and growth mechanisms of early-stage NPF clusters is necessary to develop accurate descriptions of particle formation and growth rates that can be included in climate models. Clusters containing ammonium, bisulfate, and water have previously been studied via mass spectrometry coupled with infrared spectroscopy as well as via quantum chemical calculations which provided structural and bonding information as well as potential isomer stability. Here we focus on an emerging class of clusters made of ammonium and iodate, which may be important for particle formation in coastal and polar regions. Cationic clusters containing zero, one, or two ammonia, iodic acid, and diiodide pentoxide molecules are the focus of this study. Ammonia appears to stabilize the clusters and promote the formation of larger iodine oxides with presumably lower vapor pressure, which would be expected to lead to higher stability and faster growth. Halogen bonding competes with hydrogen bonding in determining the minimum energy structures of these clusters. These studies are key benchmarks for computational efforts to model these clusters for their inclusion in larger-scale modeling efforts.

FD. Clusters/Complexes

Friday, June 24, 2022 – 8:30 AM

Room: 217 Noyes Laboratory

Chair: Joseph Fournier, Washington University in St. Louis, St. Louis, MO, USA

FD01   8:30 – 8:45

CHARACTERIZATION OF ALCOHOL:WATER TETRAMERS AND PENTAMERS VIA CHIRPED PULSE FOURIER-TRANSFORM MICROWAVE SPECTROSCOPY

S E DUTTON, GEOFFREY BLAKE, *Division of Chemistry and Chemical Engineering, California Institute of Technology, Pasadena, CA, USA.*

In this presentation, the identification and characterization of alcohol and water tetramers and pentamers using Chirped Pulse Fourier-transform Microwave (CP-FTMW) spectroscopy is described. This talk will address calculating candidate cluster structures using ab initio techniques, fitting the observed lines to obtain experimentally derived rotational constants, and analyzing the splitting of these rotational states due to the internal rotation of methyl groups present in the clusters of interest. Continued work on the characterization of alcohol:water mixing will be discussed, as will other future targets of interest for this instrument.

FD02   8:48 – 9:03

INTERPLAY OF INTERMOLECULAR INTERACTIONS: COMPLEXES OF 2-DECALONE WITH WATER, BENZENE, AND PHENOL

SWANTJE V. M. CALIEBE, PABLO PINACHO, MELANIE SCHNELL, *FS-SMP, Deutsches Elektronen-Synchrotron (DESY), Hamburg, Germany.*

Here we report the study on complexes between 2-decalone ($C_{10}H_{16}O$) and water, benzene, and phenol, respectively. The goal was to compare the interactions between the complex partners and the contributions of electrostatic and dispersion forces and which of them dominates when both forces are present. For that, a small hydrogen bond donor, water, was selected. Benzene is a good example for forming dispersion interactions, while in phenol both a phenyl ring and a hydrogen bond donor group are present and there could be competition between both forces. The complexes were studied in the gas phase in a cold and isolated environment generated by a supersonic expansion. The spectra were recorded using chirped-pulse Fourier transform microwave (CP-FTMW) spectroscopy in the 2-8 GHz frequency region. The sample consists of cis and trans 2-decalone, and complexes with both isomers were detected. In total five water complexes were identified with dominant electrostatic interactions between the complex partners. Three complexes with benzene were assigned showing mostly dispersion interactions. Another three complexes were identified with phenol. The analysis revealed that they have a higher percentage of electrostatic than dispersion forces and display a preference for a hydrogen bond when in competition with dispersion interactions.

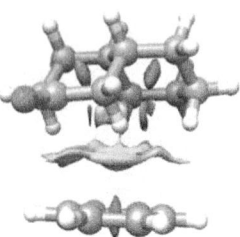

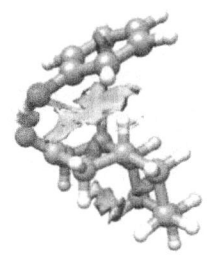

FD03 9:06–9:21

MOLECULAR STRUCTURES OF DIFLUOROBENZALDEHYDES AND THEIR HYDRATED COMPLEXES CHARACTERIZED BY CP-FTMW SPECTROSCOPY

DINGDING LV, WEIXING LI, XIAOLONG LI, GUANJUN WANG, MINGFEI ZHOU, *Fudan University, Department of Chemistry, Shanghai, China.*

Difluorobenzaldehydes are used as the starting substrate for the synthesis of high-efficiency pesticides and pharmaceutical bioactive materials. The rotational spectra of difluorobenzaldehydes and of their hydrated complexes are measured by using a new-build 2–8 GHz chirped-pulse Fourier transform microwave (CP-FTMW) spectroscopy at Fudan University. Their precise structures have been determined from the rotational constants of the parent species combined with that of the 13C, 18O and deuterated isotopologues. These results can benchmark theoretical methods for the structural optimization of weakly bound complexes. The effect of halogen substituents on intermolecular interactions is also discussed.

FD04 9:24–9:39

ANALYSIS OF THE MICROWAVE SPECTRUM, STRUCTURE AND INTERNAL ROTATION OF THE CH_3 GROUP IN N-METHYLIMIDAZOLE…H_2O AND 2-METHYLIMIDAZOLE…H_2O COMPLEXES

CHARLOTTE NICOLE CUMMINGS, *School of Chemistry, Newcastle University, Newcastle-upon-Tyne, United Kingdom*; EVA GOUGOULA, *Photon Science - Spectroscopy of Molecular Processes, Deutsches Elektronen-Synchrotron DESY, Hamburg, Germany*; CHRIS MEDCRAFT, *School of Chemistry, UNSW, Sydney, NSW, Australia*; JULIANE HEITKÄMPER, *Institute of Physical Chemistry, Karlsruhe Institute of Technology, Karlsruhe, Germany*; NICK WALKER, *School of Natural and Environmental Sciences, Newcastle University, Newcastle-upon-Tyne, UK.*

The broadband rotational spectra of N-methylimidazole…H_2O and 2-methylimidazole…H_2O have been recorded by Chirped Pulse Fourier Transform Microwave (CP-FTMW) spectroscopy in the frequency range 6.5-18.5 GHz. Each complex was generated by the co-expansion of the methylimidazole isomer and water in an argon backing gas. The spectra of five isotopologues of each complex have been assigned, allowing rotational constants (A_0, B_0 and C_0), centrifugal distortion constants (D_J and D_{JK}), nuclear quadrupole coupling constants (χ_{aa} and χ_{bb-cc}) and internal rotation parameters (V_3, $\angle(i, b)$) to be determined. In both N-methylimidazole…H_2O and 2-methylimidazole…H_2O, a hydrogen bond forms between H_2O acting as a hydrogen bond donor and the pyridinic nitrogen of the methylimidazole ring which is the hydrogen bond acceptor. In addition, there is a weak electrostatic interaction between the oxygen atom of H_2O and the hydrogen or CH_3 group attached to the C2 carbon of the methylimidazole ring. The (V_3) barrier to internal rotation of the CH_3 group has been determined for each complex. For N-methylimidazole…H_2O, the V_3 barrier is essentially unchanged from the monomer. For 2-methylimidazole…H_2O, there is a large increase in the barrier height (relative to the V_3 of CH_3 in the 2-methylimdizole monomer) which results from the interaction between the oxygen atom of H_2O and the CH_3 group.

FD05   9:42–9:57

GEOMETRIES AND CONFORMATIONAL CONVERSION OF THE BINARY 3,3,3-TRIFLUOROPROPANOL CONFORMERS: ROTATIONAL SPECTRA AND DFT CALCULATIONS

<u>ALEX NEILSON MORT</u>, FAN XIE, YUNJIE XU, *Department of Chemistry, University of Alberta, Edmonton, AB, Canada.*

Fluorinated alcohols have been widely used as co-solvents to study folding and unfolding behaviors of proteins and peptides. The detailed mechanism by which this happens is yet to be established. Recent molecular dynamics simulations suggested that clusters of the fluoroalcohol play an important role in the mechanism. In the current study, we applied jet-cooled chirped pulse Fourier transform microwave spectroscopy to probe structure and dynamics of 3,3,3-trifluoropropanol (TFP)[1] and its dimer. In comparison to 2,2,2-trifluoroethanol,[2] TFP is the smallest trifluoroalcohol molecule which exhibits folded conformations in its monomer form, thus serving as a prototype system for structural diversity associated with folding. The possible structural candidates of the TFP dimer were explored by using CREST, a recently developed conformational searching tool and nearly 70 stable binary conformers were identified. Rotational spectra of three low energy binary TFP conformers were assigned and their carriers identified. To help explain the observation of the binary conformers, a combined kinetic and thermodynamic conformational distribution model was developed to explain the non-observation of some lower energy conformations and to provide quantitatively explanation for the experimental conformational abundances. The study of the conformations of TFP and its dimer is a first and important step in understanding how TFP aggregates in bulk.

1. Marstokk, K.-M.; Møllendal, H.; Klika, K. D.; Fülöp, F.; Sillanpää, R.; Mattinen, J.; Senning, A.; Yao, X.-K.; Wang, H.-G.; Tuchagues, J.-P.; Ögren, M. Acta Chem. Scand. 1999, 53, 202; Heger, M.; Otto, K. E.; Mata, R. A.; Suhm, M. Phys. Chem. Chem. Phys. 2015, 17, 9899.

2. Xu, L.; Fraser, G. T.; Lovas, F. J.; Suenram, R. D.; Gillies, C. W.; Warner, H. E.; Gillies, J. Z. J. Chem. Phys. 1995, 103, 9541; Thomas, J.; Xu, Y. J. Phys. Chem. Lett. 2014, 5, 1850; Thomas, J.; Seifert, N. A.; Jäger, W.; Xu, Y. Angew. Chem. Int. Ed. 2017, 56, 6289.

Intermission

FD06   10:39–10:54

MICROWAVE SPECTROSCOPY OF TERPENOIDS NON-COVALENTLY BONDED TO HYDROGEN SULFIDE

<u>NOUREDDIN OSSEIRAN</u>, ELIAS M. NEEMAN, MANUEL GOUBET, PASCAL DRÉAN, THERESE R. HUET, *UMR 8523 - PhLAM - Physique des Lasers Atomes et Molécules, University of Lille, CNRS, F-59000 Lille, France.*

Biogenic volatile organic compounds (BVOCs) are a class of molecules that have a noticeable effect on atmospheric chemical and physical processes. They are emitted naturally into the atmosphere mainly by plants and forests. An interesting family of this class is the monoterpenes ($C_{10}H_{16}$) and terpenoids (oxygenated terpenes) which are unsaturated hydrocarbons that are formed by the combination of two isoprene units (C_5H_8). These molecules are known to contribute to Secondary Organic Aerosol (SOA) and tropospheric ozone formation,[a,b] mainly through oxidation pathways. In addition, these molecules can form Hydrogen-bonded complexes with surrounding atmospheric molecules. The synergic combination of quantum chemical calculations and Fourier transform microwave spectroscopy (FTMW) in jet-cooled conditions, is a powerful tool to study the gas phase micro-solvation of atmospheric relevant molecules. Many hydrated complexes were studied using this approach in our group.[c,d] We present herein a new approach, which employs the same theoretical-experimental approach to characterize complexes of terpenoids, i.e., alcohols and ketones, with H_2S, an atmospheric trace gas. The observed complexes are compared to their analog hydrates.

The present work was funded by the ANR Labex CaPPA, by the Regional Council Hauts-de-France, by the European Funds for Regional Economic Development, and by the CPER CLIMIBIO.

[a] D. Kotzias, J. L. Hjorth, H. Skov, Toxicol Environ Chem 1989, 20–21, 95–99
[b] T. Hoffmann, J. R. Odum, F. Bowman, D. Collins, D. Klockow, R. C. Flagan, J. H. Seinfeld, J. Atmos. Chem. 1997, 26, 189–222
[c] E. M. Neeman, J. R. Avilés Moreno and T. R. Huet, Phys. Chem. Chem. Phys. 2021, 23, 18137-18144
[d] E. M. Neeman, N. Osseiran and T. R. Huet, J. Chem. Phys. 2022, doi.org/10.1063/5.0084562

FD07   10:57 – 11:12

STRUCTURE AND NON-COVALENT INTERACTIONS OF THE BENZOFURAN-DIETHYL DISULFIDE COMPLEX CHARACTERIZED BY ROTATIONAL SPECTROSCOPY

YUAGO XU, *School of Chemistry and Chemical Engineering, Chongqing University, Chongqing, China*; WENQIN LI, RIZALINA TAMA SARAGI, ALBERTO LESARRI, *Departamento de Química Física y Química Inorgánica, Universidad de Valladolid, Valladolid, Spain*; GANG FENG, *School of Chemistry and Chemical Engineering, Chongqing University, Chongqing, China*.

The complex of benzofuran and diethyl disulfide has been investigated using Fourier transform microwave spectroscopy complemented by theoretical calculations. Two isomers have been observed, in which diethyl disulfide configures as gauche-gauche-gauche conformation sitting on the face of the benzofuran ring. The lone pair electrons of the sulfur atom points to the π-electron cloud of the benzofuran with a distance of about 3.6 Å, thus indicating a direct interaction between S and aromatic ring. NCIplot analysis suggests both observed isomers are stabilized by cooperative S$\cdots\pi$, CH$\cdots\pi$, and CH$\cdots$O weak intermolecular interactions with total interaction energies of about 26 kJmol^{-1} and is dominated by dispersion. Detailed spectroscopic and computational results will be presented.

FD08   11:15 – 11:30

MODELING CO_2 MICROSOLVATION: MICROWAVE SPECTROSCOPIC STUDIES OF DIFLUOROETHYLENE (DFE)/CO_2 CLUSTERS, $(DFE)_1(CO_2)_x$, FOR A TRIMER, TETRAMER, AND PENTAMER

HANNAH FINO, TULANA ARIYARATNE, PRASHANSA KANNANGARA, REBECCA A. PEEBLES, SEAN A. PEEBLES, *Department of Chemistry, Eastern Illinois University, Charleston, IL, USA*; CHANNING WEST, BROOKS PATE, *Department of Chemistry, The University of Virginia, Charlottesville, VA, USA*.

Microwave spectroscopy allows for analysis of weakly-bound clusters in a mixture of difluoroethylene (DFE) and CO_2. The present study probes variations in interactions and orientations of DFE and CO_2 within weakly-bound clusters as cluster size increases. Four chirped-pulse FTMW spectra of DFE/CO_2 mixtures were obtained from 2-8 GHz, where the concentration of CO_2 was varied from 1% to 4%, with a constant DFE concentration of 1%. This experimental design allowed variation in intensity to be observed based on the variation of CO_2 concentration, where the pattern of intensity variation was used to identify transitions belonging to a particular cluster. In addition, patterns of intensity variation provided information about the size and DFE:CO_2 ratio of the cluster. Using these methods based on intensity variation analysis,[a] three separate sets of transitions, each with unique intensity variation patterns, were extracted from the original raw spectra. Cluster composition was hypothesized based on further evidence from the intensity variation analyses, leading to compositions of $(DFE)_1(CO_2)_2$, $(DFE)_1(CO_2)_3$, and $(DFE)_1(CO_2)_4$. Fitted rotational constants for the spectra were compared to the results of ab initio calculations, which further supported hypothesized cluster compositions for the trimer, tetramer and pentamer. These results indicate that instead of forming a solvation shell around DFE, CO_2 molecules appear preferably to interact with other CO_2 molecules to form arrangements more closely resembling pure CO_2 clusters, with DFE on the outside of the cluster.

---

[a] H. Fino, R.A. Peebles, S.A. Peebles, C. West, B. Pate, International Symposium on Molecular Spectroscopy (Virtual), Talk FH12, June 25, 2021; R.A. Peebles, S.A. Peebles, P. Kannangara, H. Fino, International Symposium on Molecular Spectroscopy (Virtual), Talk FH13, June 25, 2021

FD09   11:33 – 11:48

REINVESTIGATION OF THE MICROWAVE SPECTRUM OF THE O_2-H_2O VAN DER WAALS COMPLEX

W. H. RICE IV, *Chemistry, Missouri University of Science and Technology, Rolla, MO, USA*; CAITLYN SAIZ, AMANDA DUERDEN, FRANK E MARSHALL, G. S. GRUBBS II, *Department of Chemistry, Missouri University of Science and Technology, Rolla, MO, USA*.

Further spectral data of the O_2-H_2O van der Waals complex was obtained, expanding the range of transition lines for structural determination. Previous work was done in the 14-29 GHz range[a]. Transitions have been measured as low as 11 GHz using a chirp pulse FTMW spectrometer. Working fits inclusive of these newfound transitions will be presented. Furthermore, current work with higher resolution cavity FTMW data utilizing Helmholtz coils on the complex will be discussed.

---

[a] Y. Kasai, E. Dupuy, R. Saito, K. Hashimoto, A. Sabu, S. Kondo, Y. Sumiyoshi, and Y. Endo. Atmos. Chem. Phys., 11, 8607-8612, 2011

FD10 11:51–12:06

MICROSOLVATION COMPLEXES OF α-METHOXY PHENYLACETIC ACID STUDIED BY MICROWAVE SPECTROSCOPY

<u>HIMANSHI SINGH</u>, PABLO PINACHO, MELANIE SCHNELL, *FS-SMP, Deutsches Elektronen-Synchrotron (DESY), Hamburg, Germany.*

Mandelic acid and its derivatives are useful as chiral synthons in the chemical and pharmaceutical industry because of their versatility. Their wide use in organic reactions makes them an important case to study their solute-solvent interactions. α-methoxy phenylacetic acid (AMPA), a methoxy-derived mandelic acid, can serve as a model to characterize the non-covalent interactions of such chiral solute with different solvents. The different functional groups in this chiral acid provide flexibility to the molecule, that conformational flexibility has been presented previously. Furthermore, the presence of a carboxylic acid and a methoxy group in AMPA provides good binding sites for solute-solvent interactions and thus serves as a good model system.

In this work, we investigate the microsolvation of AMPA in three different solvents using chirped-pulse Fourier transform microwave (CP-FTMW) spectroscopy. This technique coupled with the supersonic expansion reveals accurate structures of weakly bound complexes isolated in the gas phase. We chose three solvents that offer different functional groups and thus model more types of solute-solvent interactions. The three solvents were water, a small hydrogen bond donor partner, DMSO with a sulfoxide group, and phenol with a phenyl ring and a hydroxyl group. The preferred intermolecular interactions and the structural changes in complexes with three different solvents will be discussed.

FE. Lineshapes, collisional effects
Friday, June 24, 2022 – 8:30 AM
Room: 1024 Chemistry Annex

Chair: Wei Lin, The University of Texas Rio Grande Valley, Brownsville, TX, USA

FE01 8:30 – 8:45

A QUANTUM CASCADE LASER DUAL-COMB SPECTROMETER IN STEP-SWEEP MODE FOR HIGH-RESOLUTION MOLECULAR SPECTROSCOPY

MARKUS MANGOLD, PITT ALLMENDINGER, JAKOB HAYDEN, ANDREAS HUGI, *IRsweep AG, IRsweep AG, Stäfa, Switzerland*; OLIVIER BROWET, JEAN CLÉMENT, BASTIEN VISPOEL, MURIEL LEPÈRE, *Institute of Life, Earth and Environment (ILEE), Université de Namur, Namur, Belgium.*

To meet the challenges of high-resolution molecular spectroscopy, increasingly sophisticated spectroscopic techniques were developed. For a long time FTIR and laser-based spectroscopies were used for these studies. The recent development of dual-comb spectroscopy at high-resolution makes this technique a powerful tool for gas phase studies. We report on the use and characterization of the IRis-F1, a tabletop mid-infrared dual-comb spectrometer, in the newly developed step-sweep mode. The resolution of the wavenumber axis is increased by step-wise tuning (interleaving) and accurate measurement of the laser center wavelength and repetition frequency. Doppler limited measurements of N_2O and CH_4 reveal a wavenumber accuracy of 10^{-4} cm^{-1} on the complete covered range of 50 cm^{-1}. Measured half-widths of absorption lines show no systematic broadening, indicating a negligible instrument response function. Finally, measurements of nitrogen pressure broadening coefficients in the ν_4 band of methane show that the dual-comb spectrometer in step-sweep mode is well adapted for measurements of precision spectroscopic data, in particular line shape parameters.

FE02 8:48 – 9:03

A SPECTROSCOPIC PRESSURE SENSOR TARGETING ATOMIC POTASSIUM FOR HYPERSONIC FACILITIES

TAL SCHWARTZ, JOSHUA A VANDERVORT, SEAN CLEES, CHRISTOPHER L STRAND, RONALD K HANSON, *Mechanical Engineering, Stanford University, Stanford, CA, USA.*

We apply laser absorption spectroscopy to design a diagnostic measuring bulk gas pressure from collisionally-broadened absorption lineshapes. This diagnostic targets atomic potassium with a measurement rate of 200 kHz. The diagnostic is intended to operate in hypersonic ground-based facilities, where atomic potassium is nascent in the freestream flow and where microsecond temporal resolution is often crucial.

Recent studies have found atomic potassium in trace amounts in the freestream of hypersonic ground-based facilities, making it an attractive spectroscopic target. Potassium also has convenient spectroscopic transitions in the near-infrared – the D-line transitions ($^2S_{1/2} \rightarrow {}^2P_{1/2}$ at 770.1 nm and $^2S_{1/2} \rightarrow {}^2P_{3/2}$ at 766.7 nm), which absorb strongly and are easily accessible with low-cost commercial lasers and optics.

This line-of-sight laser-based diagnostic infers bulk gas pressure from the spectroscopic lineshape of the potassium D_2 transition, specifically the collisional linewidth parameter $\Delta\nu_C$. We apply empirical correlations to extract pressures from a Voigt fit of these lineshapes. These correlations depend on gas composition and temperature, which must be known. Lineshape parameters must also be corrected to account for power broadening effects, and hyperfine splitting is considered at low pressures.

For verification, the diagnostic is deployed in a shock tube to generate the temperatures, pressures, and timescales relevant to freestream flows in hypersonic ground-based facilities. Since atomic potassium is not present in sufficient quantity for measurement in our shock tube, we implement a novel technique to uniformly seed potassium into the shock-heated gas. We achieve excellent signal-to-noise ratios and measure pressures in good agreement with expected values between 0.25-2 atmospheres.

FE03 9:06 – 9:21
LEAST SQUARES FIT OF LINE PROFILES IN TRANSMITTANCE AND ABSORBANCE SPECTRA WITH DETECTOR OR SOURCE NOISE

HIROYUKI SASADA, *National Metrology Institute of Japan (NMIJ), Ntional Institute of Advanced Industrial Science and Technology (AIST), Tsukuba, Japan.*

When an observed profile of a spectral line is analyzed using an equally weighted least squares method, the noise property of the spectrum determines whether transmittance or absorbance spectrum is appropriate for the analysis. To verify this, we simulate transmittance spectra (TS) of Lorentz profiles with three simulation parameters of absorption strength, center frequency, and width and add either detector noise (DN) or source noise (SN) to the simulated TS. The TSs with DN or SN and absorbance spectra (AS), negative logarithms of them, are fitted to the Lorentz profile using least squares methods. Equally weighted fits of TS with DN and AS with SN, as statistic mathematics predicts, reproduce the noise magnitude and the parameters well and give the expected uncertainties close to the standard deviations of a thousand simulated spectra regardless of the absorption intensity and the noise magnitude. In contrast, equally weighted fits of TS with SN and AS with DN reproduce the simulation parameters but not the noise magnitude and do not predict the uncertainties of the parameters. Properly weighted fits of TS with SN and AS with DN reproduce the noise magnitude and give the expected uncertainties like those given from equally weighted fits of AS with SN and TS with DN but do not always reproduce the absorption strength and width.

FE04 9:24 – 9:39
MEASUREMENT OF COLLISIONAL SELF-BROADENING AT LOW-TEMPERATURES USING SUB-DOPPLER SPECTROSCOPY

BRIAN DROUIN, DEACON J NEMCHICK, TIMOTHY J. CRAWFORD, PAUL VON ALLMEN, DARIUSZ LIS, *Jet Propulsion Laboratory, California Institute of Technology, Pasadena, CA, USA.*

Collisional energy transfer in volatized exospheric materials dominates the uncertainty of comet models that trace comae composition back to surface composition. Methods for ab initio and semi-empirical calculation of quantum-state dependent collisional efficiencies are typically benchmarked to pressure broadening experiments when available. Here we detail experimental efforts to determine collisional efficiencies for selected transitions of water at temperatures demonstrative of the comet environment and well below the water condensation temperature. The method utilizes a collisional cooling cell with water injected into a bath gas at the target temperature. THz radiation is passed twice through the cooled gas to record a transmission spectrum exhibiting the Lamb dip effect. The sub-Doppler feature is subject to collisional broadening at pressures commensurate with the partial pressure of water in the system. Data analysis involves simultaneous extraction of intensity and pressure broadening information. The method, results and comparisons to calculated values will be discussed.

FE05   9:42 – 9:57

APPLICATION OF THEORETICAL CONSTRAINTS TO MODEL THE MEASURED TEMPERATURE AND WAVELENGTH DEPENDENCE OF COLLISION-INDUCED ABSORPTION IN THE 0.76 μm AND 1.27 μm O_2 BANDS

<u>ERIN M. ADKINS</u>, *Material Measurement Laboratory, National Institute of Standards and Technology, Gaithersburg, MD, USA*; HELENE FLEURBAEY, *UMR5588 LIPhy, Université Grenoble Alpes/CNRS, Saint Martin d'Hères, France*; TIJS KARMAN, *Institute for Molecules and Materials (IMM), Radboud University Nijmegen, Nijmegen, Netherlands*; DAVID A. LONG, *Material Measurement Laboratory, National Institute of Standards and Technology, Gaithersburg, MD, USA*; ALAIN CAMPARGUE, DIDIER MONDELAIN, *UMR5588 LIPhy, Université Grenoble Alpes/CNRS, Saint Martin d'Hères, France*; JOSEPH T. HODGES, *Material Measurement Laboratory, National Institute of Standards and Technology, Gaithersburg, MD, USA*.

Understanding collision-induced absorption (CIA) is a critical component to improving the O_2 spectroscopy for remote sensing applications. Traditionally in experimental spectra, CIA is defined as the remaining absorption after accounting for the baseline, Rayleigh scattering, and resonant absorption. This approach can present difficulties in systems, like the O_2 A-Band at 0.76 μm, where the CIA is relatively weak and is highly correlated with the line-mixing model. Theoretical constraints on the magnitude and shape of the CIA could aid in decoupling the resonant and broadband features ultimately leading to an improved spectroscopic model. The CIA model reported by Karman et al. [1] provides a theoretical basis for the CIA in the 1.27 μm and 0.76 μm O_2 bands [1]. In this work, we evaluate the theoretical model using cavity ring-down spectroscopy measurements collected at multiple temperatures in both the 1.27 μm [2-4] and 0.76 μm O_2 bands. In addition to a qualitative comparison between experiment and theory, this work explores parameterization of the CIA model reported by Karman et al. [1] for future inclusion in integrated multi-spectrum analyses incorporating advanced line shape models, line-mixing, and CIA.

[1] Karman T, et al. Nature Chemistry. 2018;10:549-54.
[2] Kassi S, et al. Journal of Geophysical Research: Atmospheres. 2021;126.
[3] Mondelain D, et al. Journal of Geophysical Research: Atmospheres. 2019;124:414-23.
[4] Fleurbaey H, et al. Journal of Quantitative Spectroscopy and Radiative Transfer. 2021;270.

FE06   10:00 – 10:15

CHARACTERIZATION OF THE H_2O+CO_2 CONTINUUM ABSORPTION WITHIN THE INFRARED TRANSPARENCY WINDOWS FOR PLANETARY APPLICATIONS

<u>HELENE FLEURBAEY</u>, DIDIER MONDELAIN, *UMR5588 LIPhy, Université Grenoble Alpes/CNRS, Saint Martin d'Hères, France*; JEAN-MICHEL HARTMANN, WISSAM FAKHARDJI, *Ecole Polytechnique, CNRS / Laboratoire de Météorologie Dunamique, 91128 Palaiseau, France*; ALAIN CAMPARGUE, *UMR5588 LIPhy, Université Grenoble Alpes/CNRS, Saint Martin d'Hères, France*.

Accurate knowledge of the absorption by a gas mixture of CO_2 and water is crucial for planetary sciences, as it allows for better modeling the atmospheres of rocky planets, e.g. improving our understanding of the early climate of Mars or why Venus and the Earth have evolved so differently. In addition to local monomer lines proportional to the density of each species, the absorption spectrum of such a gas mixture includes binary absorption features varying smoothly with frequency: self-continuum absorption proportional to the squared density, and "crossed" absorption involving both species and scaling as the density product $\rho_{CO_2}\rho_{H_2O}$. We used highly sensitive spectroscopy techniques (CRDS and OFCEAS) to measure the absorption by H_2O+CO_2 gas mixtures in several spectral regions situated in transparency windows where the monomer absorption of both species is weak (1.5-1.53 μm, 1.68-1.75 μm, 2.06 μm, 2.2-2.35 μm, 3.5 μm). For both water and CO_2, the monomer lines, modeled using HITRAN parameters, and the self-continuum absorption, calculated from literature values or measured in dedicated experiments, were subtracted from the measured absorption. The obtained "crossed absorption" coefficients are compared to the only available empirical model based on far wings of line shape profiles scaled by χ-factors.[a] An additional absorption peak centered at about 6000 cm^{-1} was attributed to a collision-induced simultaneous transition of H_2O and CO_2 through the ν_1 and ν_3 modes, respectively. The assignment was confirmed using humidified $^{13}CO_2$, where a similar band was observed about 68 cm^{-1} away corresponding to the isotopic spectral shift of the ν_3 band of CO_2. Classical molecular dynamics simulations (CMDS) of the considered collision-induced absorption were conducted and are found in good agreement with the experiment.[b]

---

[a] Fleurbaey H, Campargue A, Carreira Mendès Da Silva Y, Grilli R, Kassi S, Mondelain D. J Quant Spectrosc Radiat Transf 108119 (2022)
[b] Fleurbaey H, Mondelain D, Fakhardji W, Hartmann J-M, Campargue A. Submitted to J Quant Spectrosc Radiat Transf

Intermission

FE08 11:15 – 11:30

LINE MIXING STUDY OF CARBON MONOXIDE BROADENED BY NITROGEN, HELIUM, AND HYDROGEN

<u>WEY-WEY SU</u>, YIMING DING, CHRISTOPHER L STRAND, RONALD K HANSON, *Mechanical Engineering, Stanford University, Stanford, CA, USA.*

Upcoming exoplanet infrared imaging will likely include carbon monoxide (CO) absorption from deeper, higher-pressure regions of larger Jupiter-like exoplanets, with compositions of majority hydrogen (H_2) and helium (He). However, there have been limited experimental CO spectroscopy studies in H_2 and He at elevated pressure conditions. We present quantitative, broadband absorbance measurements of the fundamental ro-vibrational band of CO between 1965 and 2235 cm^{-1}, in bath gases of nitrogen (N_2), He, and H_2. Then, we demonstrate a modeling approach that accurately reflects the effects of line mixing that we observe in the results, utilizing the modified exponential gap (MEG) law with a fitted inter-branch factor. The room-temperature static cell measurements were taken using a narrow-linewidth, broad-scan external-cavity quantum-cascade laser at pressures of 15–35 atm. For CO in H_2 and He, minor adjustments to the MEG Law were necessary to reproduce the weaker J''-dependence of the broadening coefficients relative to that of CO in N_2. The resulting MEG line mixing model shows improved agreement with the measured spectra across different pressures and broadening partners. Further reduction of the residuals to within approximately 1% (CO/H_2, 35 atm) is shown through the fitting of MEG coefficients directly to measured spectra, resulting in relatively small adjustments to each of the coefficients.

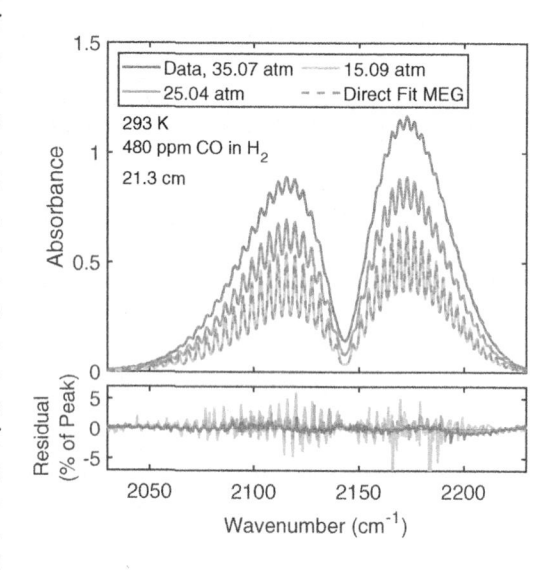

FE09 11:33 – 11:48

FT-IR MEASUREMENTS OF CROSSSECTIONS FOR TRANS-2-BUTENE IN THE 7-15 μM REGION AT 160-297 K FOR TITAN'S ATMOSPHERE

BRENDAN STEFFENS, *Space Sciences, Florida Institute of Technology, Melbourne, FL, USA*; <u>KEEYOON SUNG</u>, MICHAEL MALASKA, ROSALY M LOPES, *Jet Propulsion Laboratory, California Institute of Technology, Pasadena, CA, USA*; CONOR A NIXON, *Planetary Systems Laboratory, NASA Goddard Space Flight Center, Baltimore, MD, USA.*

We present temperature-dependent cross sections for *trans*-2-Butene (*trans*-2-C_4H_8: CH_3-CH=CH-CH_3) in the 7 - 15 μm region in support of remote sensing of Titan's stratosphere. It is one of many C_4-hydrocarbons predicted to be in detectable abundances in Titan's atmosphere by photochemical models, but no high-resolution spectroscopy is available in the public databases in the mid-infrared region, let alone at cold temperatures appropriate for Titan.

We collected 28 pure and N_2-mixture spectra and their corresponding background spectra at temperatures between 160-297 K using a Fourier transform spectrometer (Bruker IFS-125HR) at the Jet Propulsion Laboratory at spectral resolutions between 0.0039 and 0.062 cm^{-1}, depending on sample pressures in consideration of line shape resolving power. We obtained transmission spectra by ratioing the sample spectra to their empty-cell spectra, from which several fundamental modes of vibration were identified and updated in comparison to their band centers reported in the literature. We defined two distinct spectral regions, each of which contains multiple vibrational bands and hot band features and we measured the temperature-dependent cross sections, and report their integrated cross sections as well. We performed a separate linearity test between the sample absorbance and optical burden for the spectra obtained at various sample pressures. No significant dependence on temperature was observed in the integrated cross sections, which validated our measurements and methodology. Our measured cross sections will provide critical laboratory input toward a search for *trans*-2-Butene in Titan stratosphere that may be captured in the Cassini/CIRS spectra. To facilitate this, we will report our final results to the public databases, such as HITRAN and GEISA.[a]

---
[a]Government support acknowledged.

FE10   11:51 – 12:06

POTASSIUM LINESHAPE STUDY WITH COLLISIONAL PARTNERS OF NITROGEN, HELIUM, AND HYDROGEN

JOSHUA A VANDERVORT, YIMING DING, *Mechanical Engineering, Stanford University, Stanford, CA, USA*; RICHARD S FREEDMAN, *Carl Sagan Center, SETI Institute, Moutain View, CA, USA*; MARK S MARLEY, *Department of Planetary Science, Lunar and Planetary Laboratory, University of Arizona, Tucson, AZ, USA*; CHRISTOPHER L STRAND, RONALD K HANSON, *Mechanical Engineering, Stanford University, Stanford, CA, USA*.

Potassium can be used as a convenient tracer species in combustion and hypersonic test facilities and is naturally present in trace amounts in the atmospheres of brown dwarfs, where the resonance doublet is highly detectable. Currently, there are no experimental data of potassium lineshape parameters at temperatures over 500 K and model predictions vary widely above 1000 K. We present measurements of collisional broadening and pressure shift parameters for the potassium D-lines, near 770 nm, with collisional partners of N_2, He, and H_2. Atomic potassium is generated in a shock tube by shock heating KCl salts at temperatures between 1100-1900 K, and line parameters are measured using rapid-scanning tunable diode laser absorption spectroscopy. The lineshape measurements were modeled as Voigt profiles and a fitting algorithm determined pressure shift and collisional full-width-at-half-maximum. The collisional broadening and pressure shift coefficients are given as temperature-dependent power-law relations for the partners of interest. The helium and hydrogen results agree with lower temperature experimental data, within 15-20%, and high-temperature theoretical predictions, within 10-30%. The nitrogen results, however, have larger discrepancies with existing data and simplified impact theory predictions. This may suggest the need for a more detailed model for the nitrogen collisional broadening of potassium. The presented correlations may be useful for the development of potassium-based sensing methods with application to combustion, hypersonics, and astrophysics.

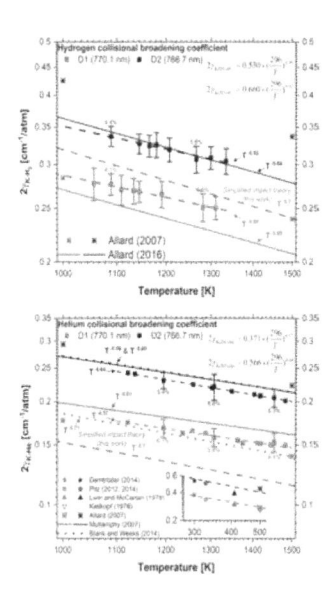

FE11   12:09 – 12:24

FILLING A CRITICAL GAP IN THE PRESSURE-BROADENING DATA NEEDED FOR MODELING SUPER-EARTHS AND NEPTUNIAN ATMOSPHERES

EHSAN GHARIB-NEZHAD, *Space Science Division, NASA Ames Research Center, Moffett Field, CA, USA*; NATASHA E BATALHA, *Space Science and Astrobiology Division, NASA Ames Research Center, Moffett Field, CA, USA*; ROBERT R. GAMACHE, *Department of Environmental, Earth, and Atmospheric Sciences, University of Massachusetts, Lowell, MA, USA*; RICHARD S FREEDMAN, *Carl Sagan Center, SETI Institute, Moutain View, CA, USA*.

One of the key findings regarding exoplanet science is that majority of the detected close-in planets from Kepler fall within the super-Earth/sub-Neptune regime 1–3.5 Earth Radii. Planet formation models of these systems suggest broad compositional diversity in this radius regime, with a high likelihood for large atmospheric metal content 100-1000xSolar. Our ability to unlock the mysteries of this new class of planet hinges on our ability to link the spectral observations to theoretical models, and then our ability to link those models to fundamental molecular and atomic opacities. However, there is a critical lack of data that is required to compute opacities and the subsequent theoretical atmosphere for high-metallicity atmospheres. This is because high-metallicity atmospheres are expected to contain larger fractional quantities of H_2O, CO, CO_2, and CH_4, relative to H_2-dominated systems that have been the focus of the majority of previous observing campaigns. Therefore, they require fundamentally different pressure-broadening parameters that are currently lacking. Nevertheless, ignoring the impact of these parameters will lead to errors in the calculation of the planet's energy budget, as well as errors in the ultimate atmospheric spectra. We will present an overview of our team's efforts to fill this gap by computing the theoretical broadening coefficients relevant to the super-Earth to sub-Neptune temperature range. The importance of these results will be discussed and their impact on exoplanet radiative transfer modeling of objects from space-based telescopes will be discussed.

FF. Spectroscopy as an analytical tool

Friday, June 24, 2022 – 8:30 AM

Room: 124 Burrill Hall

Chair: R. A. Motiyenko, Université de Lille, Villeneuve d'Ascq, France

FF01   8:30 – 8:45

FLUORESCENCE EXCITATION, EMISSION, AND SYNCHRONOUS SPECTRA AT LOW TEMPERATURES

CARLOS MANZANARES, SURESH SUNUWAR, *Department of Chemistry and Biochemistry, Baylor University, Waco, TX, USA.*

Computer deconvolution of experimental excitation and emission fluorescence bands is presented and used to generate synchronous spectra. The computer simulation successfully predicts the number of synchronous fluorescence (SF) bands, band shapes, and band maximum wavelengths for any constant wavelength difference ($\Delta\lambda$). To test the simulation, emission, excitation, and synchronous spectra were obtained for anthracene in n-hexane. Excellent agreement is obtained reproducing and finding the origin of the experimental SF bands for values of $\Delta\lambda$ between 2 and 100. The excitation, emission, and synchronous ($\Delta\lambda=10$) spectra of toluene, aniline, naphthalene, acenaphthene, pyrene, and anthracene are obtained. The synchronous spectrum ($\Delta\lambda=10$) of the same mixture is presented and assigned based on the synchronous bands of the individual compounds. The synchronous fluorescence technique and the computer simulation method are proposed to complement other techniques in the analysis of fluorescent samples from comets, as well as in missions to planets and satellites of the solar system. With our experimental set-up we will be able to obtain spectra for temperatures between 77 K and 298 K. Our laboratory is currently obtaining excitation, emission, and synchronous spectra of PAHs at temperatures that could be found on the surface of Titan and Mars.

FF02   8:48 – 9:03

NEAR INFRARED SPECTROSCOPY AS EFFICIENT ANALYTICAL TOOL IN PLASTIC ADDITIVES INDUSTRY.

EMANUELE PIZZANO, ASSIMO MARIS, *Dipartimento di Chimica G. Ciamician, Università di Bologna, Bologna, Italy*; MARZIA MAZZACURATI, *Analytical service, BASF Italia S.p.A., Pontecchio Marconi, Italy.*

Near Infrared spectroscopy (NIRs) is a potent tool for the analysis of several materials. It finds vast applications due its versability and finds applications in many fields such as pharmaceutical industry, food science, environmental, bio-applications and medical. In this work we report several applications in plastic additives industry. The determination of specific analytes in this kind of products is challenging without expensive instrumentations or difficult sample preparation. The NIR technique instead, with the application of chemometric approach, permits the quantitative analysis in complex matrix with simple, fast, and cheap procedures. To clarify the structure of the dataset spectra employed in the calibration curve, and so the nature of the bands involved, the calculated NIR spectrum of model compound is also reported and compared to its experimental gas phase counterpart.

FF03 9:06 – 9:21

ANALYSIS OF TINNEVELLY SENNA LEAVES HERBAL MEDICINE USING LASER-INDUCED BREAKDOWN SPECTROSCOPY AND ITS ANTI-CANCEROUS & ANTIBACTERIAL EFFICACY STUDIES

MOHAMMED A GONDAL, *Department of Physics, King Fahd University of Petroleum and Minerals, Dhahran, Saudi Arabia*; R. K. ALDAKHEEL, M A. ALMESSIERE, *Physics, Imam Abdulrahman Bin Faisal University, Dammam, Saudi Arabia.*

Tinnevelly Senna is a herbal plant whose leaves are being applied to cure many diseases in developing countries due to containing many bioactive compounds such as sennosides, phenols, and flavonoids. The conventional methods to determine the main contents of such Senna leaves are lengthy, cost-effective, require hazardous chemical solvents and reagents. In this work an elegant technique like LIBS was applied as a qualitative and quantitative method for Senna leaves sample's elemental analysis and their biological activities were measured by evaluating anti-cancer and anti-bacterial analysis. The quantitative analysis of Senna leaves was conducted using calibration-free LIBS) algorithm indicating the concentration of many nutrient elements, and the LIBS results were counter verified by using the standard analytical ICP-OES technique. The bactericidal efficacy of the Senna leaves was also studied against Staphylococcus aureus (S. aureus) by AWD assays and morphogenesis by scanning electron microscopy (SEM) and the anticancer activity was also investigated where different concentrations of Senna leaves extract were tested on cancer cells (HCT-116 and HeLa) and normal cells (HEK-293) using the cell metabolic activity MTT assay and Propidium iodide (PI) staining. We also estimated the inhibitory concentration (IC50) value for the various extracts' concentrations. The bactericidal efficacy of the Senna leaves extract showed significant inhibition against Gram-positive bacterium. Both MTT and PI analysis showed that Senna leaves extract induced profound inhibition on HCT-116 growth and proliferation. Additionally, Senna leaves extract did not exert an inhibitory influence on normal (HEK-293), which is non-cancerous cells. The extract specifically targets the cancerous cells is highly beneficial for the development of future safe anticancer and antibacterial drugs using these extracts.

FF04 9:24 – 9:39

IDENTIFICATION OF CHLOROBENZENE IN MIXTURES WITH THE SUGGESTED PRECURSORS BENZENE, BENZOIC ACID, PHTHALIC ACID, AND MELLITIC ACID IN MARS SAMPLES

SURESH SUNUWAR, CARLOS MANZANARES, *Department of Chemistry and Biochemistry, Baylor University, Waco, TX, USA.*

The discovery of chlorobenzene detected in a soil sample obtained in Mars has been controversial. The original sample was subjected to pyrolysis before the analysis with the gas chromatography-mass spectrometry (GC-MS) of the Sample Analysis at Mars (SAM) instrument on the Curiosity rover. It is believed that chlorobenzene was a product of other organic molecules reacting with chlorates of the Martian soil. In this paper, synchronous fluorescence spectroscopy is suggested for analysis of Mars samples in future missions. Synchronous fluorescence spectroscopy is a variation of the fluorescence technique where the excitation and emission scans are detected simultaneously with a predetermined wavelength difference ($\Delta\lambda$) between the two and multiplied. Depending on the $\Delta\lambda$ chosen, the resulting signal could produce a narrow single fluorescence band with a peak wavelength that is characteristic of the compound. To demonstrate the utility of this technique for Mars samples and in general for planetary and astrochemical applications, we present laboratory results with the characteristic synchronous peaks of chlorobenzene, benzene, benzoic acid, phenol, phthalic acid, and mellitic acid in solutions of n-hexane or water. Finally, we demonstrate a successful application of the technique using a mixture of chlorobenzene in the presence of the likely organic precursors that have been suggested for the Cumberland drill sample on Mars. The application of SFS for solid samples of Mars analog soils is also discussed for future experiments.

FF05 9:42 – 9:57

SYNCHROTRON-BASED ATTENUATED TOTAL REFLECTION INFRARED SPECTROSCOPY OF ARTIFICIAL GASOLINE BLEND

JOSHUA G SMITH, SYLVESTRE TWAGIRAYEZU, *Chemistry and Biochemistry, Lamar University, Beaumont, TX, USA*; BRANT E. BILLINGHURST, JIANBAO ZHAO, *EFD, Canadian Light Source Inc., Saskatoon, Saskatchewan, Canada.*

Attenuated Total Reflection (ATR) Infrared spectra(IR) of artificially-prepared gasoline blends have been recorded in the 600-4000 cm^{-1} region, using the Far-Infrared Beamline at Canadian Light Source. The observed spectra reveal rich but distinct vibrational signatures of the ethanol and gasoline blend. The analysis of C-C and CO stretch bands indicates significant vibrational shifts due to the changes of force constants as the hydrocarbon content increases. The present data provide vibrational centers useful for the characterization of ethanol in the presence of hydrocarbon matrices. The validity of ATR-IR for ethanol determination in gasoline mixture has been examined by measuring the ATR-IR signal response of artificial gasoline blend over a wide range of ethanol content(0 - 100%). The obtained linear correlations allowed the determination of recovery percentage(95-100%)and thus confirming the accuracy of ATR-IR method.

Intermission

FF06 10:39 – 10:54

PYROLYSIS REACTIONS OF OXOLAN-3-ONE STUDIED VIA MATRIX-ISOLATION FTIR

HEATHER LEGG, KATHRYN NARKIN, KHALED ALEY EL-SHAZLY, ELIZABETH RENEE SPARKS, *Department of Chemistry, Marshall University, Huntington, WV, USA*; XINLI SONG, *Wuhan Institute of Physics and Mathematics, Chinese Academy of Sciences, Wuhan, China*; CAROL PARISH, *Chemistry, University of Richmond, Richmond, VA, USA*; LAURA R. McCUNN, *Department of Chemistry, Marshall University, Huntington, WV, USA.*

Oxolan-3-one is a cyclic, oxygenated hydrocarbon that occurs frequently in the pyrolysis of many forms of biomass and is thus an important intermediate in the production of biofuels. In order to identify thermal decomposition products of oxolan-3-one, an approximately 0.4% mixture in argon was subject to pyrolysis in a resistively heated SiC microtubular reactor at 800-1400 K. Matrix-isolation FTIR spectroscopy was used to identify pyrolysis products. The products observed include ethylene, carbon monoxide, formaldehyde, ketene, acetylene, and propyne. A comprehensive computational study of the unimolecular decomposition mechanism shows reactions consistent with these products and suggests the appearance of hydroxyketene in the mechanism. Efforts were undertaken to pyrolytically generate and characterize hydroxyketene via matrix-isolation FTIR to confirm the assignment. The experimental and computational results combined provide clues to the overall mechanism of thermal decomposition of oxolan-3-one and are important in relating the molecule's structure to the mechanism.

FF07 10:57 – 11:12

ANALYSIS OF THE METHANE CH STRETCH OVERTONE USING INFRARED HIGH RESOLUTION COHERENT TWO DIMENSIONAL SPECTROSCOPY

DeAUNNA A DANIELS, *Chemistry, Spelman College, Atlanta, GA, USA*; THRESA WELLS, PETER CHEN, *Department of Chemistry, Spelman College, Atlanta, GA, USA.*

Methane is an important and heavily studied molecule because of its significance in astronomy, energy, and climate change. Studies of methane as a model are also important because it is the simplest hydrocarbon. For many molecules, the fundamental vibrational modes are well understood, but overtones and combination bands are often difficult to accurately identify. At higher frequencies there is significant congestion due to combination bands and overtones overlapping, making it difficult to determine which modes are responsible for each line. We have used a newly developed technique called IR HRC2DS to investigate the overtone region of CH stretches in methane. This technique uses a broadband source with wavelengths spanning the CH overtone region (5950-7000cm-1) and a tunable source scanning the CH fundamental (2900-3100cm-1). Coupling these two modes gives doubly resonant features which could allow us to confirm several frequencies from the CH overtones of methane, and to calculate the Coriolis constants for these overtones.

FF08 11:15 – 11:30

STIMULATED RAMAN SCATTERING IN KXe: A NOVEL SPECTROSCOPIC TOOL

<u>KAVITA V. DESAI</u>, *Electrical and Computer Engineering, University of Illinois, Urbana, IL, USA*; ANDREY E. MIRONOV, J. GARY EDEN, *Department of Electrical and Computer Engineering, University of Illinois at Urbana-Champaign, Urbana, IL, USA*.

Stimulated Raman Scattering (SRS) has been observed for the first time in any alkali-rare gas diatomic molecule, and the observed spectra provide a powerful tool for elucidating interatomic spectra. Specifically, laser pump-probe experiments in which the K vapor/Xe mixtures are excited with a narrowband dye laser radiation near the K D_2 line yields strong amplification of a probe pulse located 50-55 cm^{-1} to the red of the K D_1 line, a difference that is close, but not equal to the $4^2P_{3/2}$-$4^2P_{1/2}$ spin-orbit splitting of K. As shown by the representative data in the figure, sweeping the pump wavelength to the red, results in the SRS gain spectra spectrum (shown by the probe amplification spectra), tracking the movement of the pump. We interpret these data in terms of a molecular SRS process in which the Raman shift is associated with the KXe $B^2\Sigma^+_{1/2}$, $A^2\Pi_{3/2}$, $A^2\Pi_{1/2}$-$X^2\Sigma^+_{1/2}$ difference potentials at differing values of the internuclear R. Another unique aspect of this aspect of this process is that the Raman process originates with the K-Xe collision pairs in the thermal continuum of the ground state. Consequently, $B^2\Sigma^+_{1/2}$, $A^2\Pi_{3/2}$, $A^2\Pi_{1/2}$ interatomic potentials at large R can be determined by comparing experiment with calculations of $B^2\Sigma^+_{1/2}$, $A^2\Pi_{3/2}$, $A^2\Pi_{1/2}$-$X^2\Sigma^+_{1/2}$ Frank-Condon integrals and quasistatic line-broadening theory.

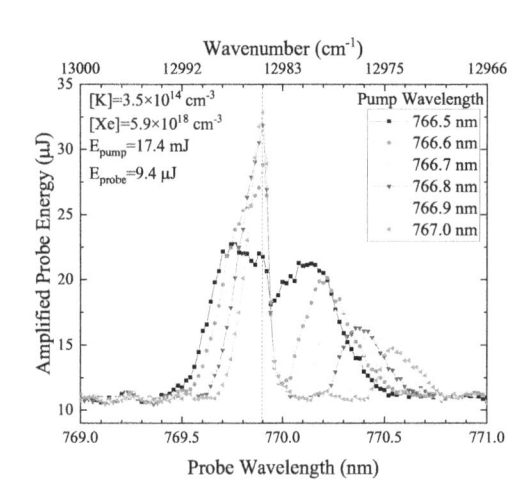

FF09 11:33 – 11:48

SATURATED ABSORPTION SPECTROSCOPY AND TWO-PHOTON CAVITY RING-DOWN ABSORPTION SPECTROSCOPY FOR TRACE GAS DETECTION OF NITROUS OXIDE

<u>MADELINE MEMOVICH</u>, *Department of Chemistry, University of Virginia, Charlottesville, VA, USA*; KEVIN LEHMANN, *Department of Chemistry and Physics, The University of Virginia, Charlottesville, VA, USA*.

Like Carbon Dioxide (CO_2), Nitrous Oxide (N_2O) behaves as a long-lived greenhouse gas. Increases in atmospheric concentrations of N_2O due to anthropomorphic sources have contributed to stratospheric ozone depletion and climate change. For these reasons it is imperative to formulate effective techniques for trace N_2O detection. Spectral line resolution and detection sensitivity are crucial for efficient trace gas quantification. One technique which enables the precise determination of the transition frequency between the ground and excited states of an analyte is saturated absorption spectroscopy (SAS). In SAS, counter-propagating beams of the same frequency produce Doppler-free peaks in absorption spectra. Each beam produces opposite Doppler shifts, therefore only atoms/molecules traveling with nearly zero-velocity along the axis of beam propagation couple with both beams, leading to Doppler-free spectral-hole burning. Additionally, cavity enhanced spectroscopic methods, such as the revolutionary cavity ring-down spectroscopy (CRDS), employ the use of a high finesse optical cavity, wherein light is trapped and the concentration of the analyte is determined by the rate of decay of the cavity light. Due to the high intensity of the light inside the optical cavity, this technique is remarkably sensitive, even for the detection of weakly absorbing transitions. However, the high density of one-photon transitions can often lead to spectral overlap and resolution loss. On the other hand, near-resonance two-level transitions, like those found in N_2O, result in low density spectra. Here we present a novel approach of gaseous N_2O detection by SAS and two-photon CRDS of the P(18) and Q(18) ro-vibrational transitions.

FF10   *Post-Deadline Abstract*   11:51 – 12:06

PROBING PLASMON-INDUCED TEMPERATURES IN FLUOROPHORE-PLASMONIC SYSTEMS USING RAMAN THERMOMETRY.

<u>GERRIT CHRISTENSON</u>, ZIWEI YU, RENEE R. FRONTIERA, *Department of Chemistry, University of Minnesota - Twin Cities, Minneapolis, Minnesota, United States*.

Plasmonic materials have increasingly grown in interest in chemical sensing, optoelectronics, and photocatalysis. Plasmonic media interact strongly with light, focusing and enhancing electromagnetic radiation to nanoscale volumes, not seen with typical propagation of electromagnetic radiation. Although plasmonic materials have countless desirable properties, we still struggle to form a fundamental understanding of energy and charge transfer at plasmonic interfaces.

We specifically desire to quantify energy transfer in plasmonic-molecular systems in this work. We utilize continuous wave, surface-enhanced anti-Stokes and Stokes Raman spectroscopy to probe the vibrational energy transfer. Further, we employ a Boltzmann distribution analysis to quantify our results, to correlate the anti-Stokes to Stokes scattering ratio of Raman-active vibrational modes to their corresponding temperatures. Specifically, we examine the temperatures of plasmonic-fluorophore systems, where molecules can undergo electronic transitions, which specifically follow an unforeseen mechanism. In comparison to room temperature population densities, we observe a 100K decrease in the temperature of various fluorophore molecules under resonant steady-state excitation. In contrast, under non-resonant excitation, we see an increase in temperature up to 200K. This resonant plasmonic cooling effect occurs regardless of vibrational mode selection and solvating environment. Our work provides new insight into plasmonic-molecular interactions and an initial investigation of this occurrence.

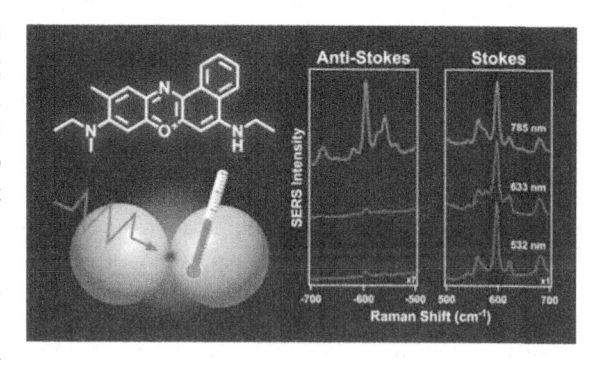

FF11   12:09 – 12:24

SPECTROSCOPY AND THE ETIOLOGY OF CATARACT AND DRY EYE

<u>DOUGLAS BORCHMAN</u>, *Ophthalmology and Visual Sciences, University of Louisville, Louisville, KY, USA*.

NMR and Infrared spectroscopies were instrumental in determining the relationships between lens and tear lipid composition, conformation and function. The major lipid of the human lens is dihydrosphingomylein, discovered by NMR spectroscopy and found in quantity only in the lens. The lens contains a cholesterol to phospholipid molar ratio as high as 10:1. Lens lipids contribute to maintaining lens clarity, and alterations in lens lipid composition due to age are likely to contribute to cataract. Lens lipid composition reflects adaptations to the unique characteristics of the lens: no turnover of lens lipids or proteins and contains almost no intracellular organelles. Long-lived species such as humans and the bowhead whale exhibits lens lipid adaptations that confer resistance to oxidation, and thereby allowing the lens to stay clear for a relatively longer time than is the case in many other species. With cataract, light scattering increases due to the increase in the lipid order of lens membranes measured using infrared spectroscopy. It is plausible that the increase in lipid-lipid interactions may contribute to myopia by causing greater compaction and overall stiffness of the lens. The TFLL is a thin, 100 nm layer of lipid on the surface of tears covering the cornea that contributes to tear film stability. NMR spectroscopy found that the major lipids of the TFLL are wax esters and cholesterol esters. The hydrocarbon chains associated with the esters are longer than those found anywhere in the body, as long as 32 carbons, and many are branched. More ordered lipid with dry eye, measured using FTIR, could inhibit the flow of meibum from the meibomian glands and contribute to the formation of a discontinuous patchy TFLL, which in turn results in deteriorated spreading, and decreased surface elasticity. One may also speculate that more ordered lipid results in the attenuated capability to restore tear film lipid layer structure between blinks.

FG. Astronomy

Friday, June 24, 2022 – 8:30 AM

Room: 274 Medical Sciences Building

Chair: Anthony Remijan, NRAO, Charlottesville, VA, USA

FG01   8:30 – 8:45

ROTATIONAL SPECTROSCOPY AS A TOOL FOR STRUCTURE-SPECIFIC IDENTIFICATION OF PRODUCTS OF UV-PHOTOLYZED COSMIC ICE ANALOGUES

OLIVIA H. WILKINS, KATARINA YOCUM, *NASA Postdoctoral Program Fellow, NASA Goddard Space Flight Center, Greenbelt, MD, USA*; STEFANIE N MILAM, PERRY A. GERAKINES, *Astrochemistry, NASA Goddard Space Flight Center, Greenbelt, MD, USA*; WILL E. THOMPSON, GUSTAVO A. CRUZ-DIAZ, *Department of Chemistry, University of Wisconsin-Madison, Madison, WI, USA*; SUSANNA L. WIDICUS WEAVER, *Chemistry and Astronomy, University of Wisconsin-Madison, Madison, WI, USA*.

Cosmic ice analogue experiments are an important aspect of astrochemistry because they help researchers construct the chemical pathways leading to molecules found in young stellar objects, comets, and meteorites. Decades of cosmic ice experiments have demonstrated the formation of various organics and how ice composition is affected by UV photons and temperature. The ice chemistry can be challenging to elucidate, and structure-specific techniques are required to uniquely identify products. We present the Sublimation Laboratory Ice Millimeter/submillimeter Experiment (SubLIME), which uses rotational spectroscopy to complement previous laboratory ice studies. Using this technique, we can detect a wide range of products, including structural and conformational isomers, of UV-photolyzed ice samples from a single spectrum. Furthermore, this technique can be used to model the observational spectra of pre- and protostellar cores and cometary comae. We will present the SubLIME setup and new spectroscopic results of sublimated UV-photolyzed ice samples containing water (H_2O) and carbon monoxide (CO).

FG02   8:48 – 9:03

RATIO OF OTHO/PARA-FORMALDEHYDE SUBLIMATED FROM ENERGETICALLY PROCESSED INTERSTELLAR ICE ANALOGS

KATARINA YOCUM, OLIVIA H. WILKINS, *NASA Postdoctoral Program Fellow, NASA Goddard Space Flight Center, Greenbelt, MD, USA*; STEFANIE N MILAM, PERRY A. GERAKINES, *Astrochemistry, NASA Goddard Space Flight Center, Greenbelt, MD, USA*.

The ortho-to-para ratios (OPRs) of interstellar molecules with symmetric hydrogen nuclei are thought to provide information about their thermal and chemical history. The OPR of formaldehyde (H_2CO) is sometimes used to predict whether this compound formed on a cold interstellar grain or in the gas phase at warmer temperatures, but the full meaning of the OPR detected in interstellar space is still a topic of debate. This work aims to unravel more information about the OPR of H_2CO formed on icy interstellar grains through laboratory experiments. In these experiments, the OPR of H_2CO is measured using submillimeter spectroscopy after low-temperature formation by ultraviolet photolysis of interstellar ice analog samples containing water (H_2O), carbon monoxide (CO), and/or methanol (CH_3OH). The experimental approach and preliminary results will be discussed.

FG03 9:06 – 9:21

THE SEARCH FOR COMPLEX ORGANIC MOLECULES DESORBING FROM INTERSTELLAR ICE ANALOGS: PRESENTING SubLIME2

GUSTAVO A. CRUZ-DIAZ, WILL E. THOMPSON, *Department of Chemistry, University of Wisconsin-Madison, Madison, WI, USA*; COLLETTE C SARVER, CATHERINE E WALKER, *Chemistry, UW-Madison, Madison, WI, USA*; PERRY A. GERAKINES, STEFANIE N MILAM, *Astrochemistry, NASA Goddard Space Flight Center, Greenbelt, MD, USA*; SUSANNA L. WIDICUS WEAVER, *Chemistry and Astronomy, University of Wisconsin-Madison, Madison, WI, USA.*

Dark and cold regions in space, including regions like prestellar cores and protoplanetary disks, have been shown to harbor high densities of complex organic molecules. Many organic molecules can form in interstellar ices and be deposited into the gas phase via heating, shocks, or other desorption mechanisms. Nonetheless, the expectation is that the density of large organics in cold, dark regions should be low because the molecules readily freeze out onto ices during collisions. Therefore, there is a debate about how molecules like methanol can be detected in the gas phase in regions where they should be depleted on the surface of dust particles. We have developed a new experimental technique, Sublimation Laboratory Ice Millimeter/submillimeter Experiment (SubLIME), to study these processes. We will present the latest experimental findings using SubLIME2, the newest ultra-high vacuum setup focused on detecting complex organics from interstellar ice analogs studied at cryogenic temperatures. With these experiments, we perform FTIR spectroscopy in the mid-IR to monitor solid-phase molecules, mass spectrometry to detect the molecules in the gas phase, and millimeter/submillimeter rotational spectroscopy from 100 to 1000 GHz to look for complex molecules desorbing from the solid to the gas phase. Here we will report on our recent experiments to study photolysis and photodesorption of simple ices containing water, methanol, and carbon monoxide.

FG04 9:24 – 9:39

ICE-SURFACE CHEMISTRY OF MgNC AND OTHER METAL-CONTAINING COMPOUNDS

DAVID E. WOON, *Department of Chemistry, University of Illinois at Urbana-Champaign, Urbana, IL, USA.*

Density function theory calculations in $17H_2O$ and $24H_2O$ clusters were used to study the deposition and subsequent chemistry of MgNC, the first metal-containing molecule identified in interstellar space. MgNC is a reactive radical with a mixture of covalent and ionic bonding between the Mg and NC. We found that H can react facilely with adsorbed MgNC to form HMgNC, a known astromolecule; there is sufficient energy to eject HMgNC into the gas phase. Acetylene (HCCH) and hydrogen cyanide (HCN) reactions with adsorbed MgNC were also characterized. While there are barriers to forming complexes in both cases, they appear to be submerged below the reactant asymptote. Among the outcomes of these reactions are the formation of the vinyl radical (C_2H_3) from HCCH and the methaniminyl radical (H_2CN) from HCN. Deposition of compounds containing Na and Al will also be summarized.

FG05   9:42–9:57

SPECTROSCOPY AND ASTROCHEMISTRY OF THE CN-TAGGED CYCLIC HYDROCARBONS CYANOCYCLOPENTADIENE AND CYANOINDENE

BRYAN CHANGALA, *Atomic and Molecular Physics, Harvard-Smithsonian Center for Astrophysics, Cambridge, MA, USA*; KELVIN LEE, *Accelerated Computing Systems and Graphics, Intel Corporation, Hillsboro, OR, USA*; RYAN A LOOMIS, *NAASC, National Radio Astronomy Observatory, Charlottesville, VA, USA*; ANDREW M BURKHARDT, *Department of Physics, Wellesley College, Wellesley, MA, USA*; CI XUE, *Department of Chemistry, MIT, Cambridge, MA, USA*; ILSA ROSE COOKE, *Department of Chemistry, University of British Columbia, Vancouver, BC, Canada*; MARTIN CORDINER, STEVEN B CHARNLEY, *Astrochemistry, NASA Goddard Space Flight Center, Greenbelt, MD, USA*; MICHAEL C McCARTHY, *Atomic and Molecular Physics, Harvard-Smithsonian Center for Astrophysics, Cambridge, MA, USA*; BRETT A. McGUIRE, *Department of Chemistry, Massachusetts Institute of Technology, Cambridge, MA, USA*.

The weak, often vanishing, dipole moments of polycyclic aromatic hydrocarbons pose a challenge to exploring their interstellar chemistry through radio astronomy. Funtionalization of a pure hydrocarbon with a highly polar nitrile (−CN) group yields a useful proxy, so long as the spectroscopy and chemistry of such CN-tagged molecules are well understood. In this talk, we present recent laboratory measurements of the CN-substituted cyclic hydrocarbons cyanocyclopentadiene, C_5H_5CN, and cyanoindene, C_9H_7CN, produced in a discharge expansion source and probed by cavity-enhanced Fourier transform microwave spectroscopy. We discuss the role that resonantly stabilized radical intermediates play in the likely formation chemistry of these species and the astrochemical implications of their abundances in the cold, dense molecular cloud TMC-1.

Intermission

FG06   10:39–10:54

BROADBAND ROTATIONAL SPECTROSCOPY OF 2,4,6-CYCLOHEPTATRIENE-1-CARBONITRILE: A POTENTIAL INTERSTELLAR MOLECULE

LAURA PILLE, GAYATRI BATRA, *FS-SMP, Deutsches Elektronen-Synchrotron (DESY), Hamburg, Germany*; BENJAMIN E ARENAS, *Department of Chemistry, Durham University, Durham, United Kingdom*; DONATELLA LORU, MELANIE SCHNELL, *FS-SMP, Deutsches Elektronen-Synchrotron (DESY), Hamburg, Germany*.

The recent astronomical observations of the simplest aromatic nitrile benzonitrile, c-C_6H_5CN, followed by a five-membered [1], [2] and a bicyclic [3] CN functionalized ring in TMC-1 have opened up a new field of complex organic molecules (COMs) in space. These new findings provided an impetus for the laboratory rotational spectroscopy studies of larger -CN functionalized rings. One such example is 2,4,6-cycloheptatriene-1-carbonitrile (2,4,6-CHT-1-CN), a seven-membered ring with a -CN group attached to the sp^3-hybridized carbon atom. With a permanent electric dipole moment of 4.3 D and a low boiling point, the molecule is an excellent candidate for laboratory rotational spectroscopy.

Experiments were performed in the 18-26 GHz and 75-110 GHz frequency ranges in a supersonic expansion setup and a room temperature flow cell setup, respectively. The measurements across the 18-110 GHz region enabled the identification and assignment of the vibronic ground state, singly substituted rare-atom isotopologues, and vibrationally excited states. In this work, we report the precise determination of the rotational constants, quartic centrifugal distortion constants, as well as nitrogen nuclear quadrupole coupling constants for the vibronic ground state. The rotational spectroscopy study of 2,4,6-CHT-1-CN presented here forms the basis for future astronomical detection of this molecule.

[1] M. C. McCarthy et al., "Interstellar detection of the highly polar five-membered ring cyanocyclopentadiene," Nat Astron, vol. 5, no. 2, pp. 176–180, Feb. 2021, doi: 10.1038/s41550-020-01213-y.

[2] K. L. K. Lee et al., "Interstellar Detection of 2-cyanocyclopentadiene, C5H5CN, a Second Five-membered Ring toward TMC-1," ApJL, vol. 910, no. 1, p. L2, Mar. 2021, doi: 10.3847/2041-8213/abe764.

[3] B. A. McGuire et al., "Detection of two interstellar polycyclic aromatic hydrocarbons via spectral matched filtering," Science, vol. 371, no. 6535, pp. 1265–1269, Mar. 2021, doi: 10.1126/science.abb7535.

FG07 10:57 – 11:12

THE SOLEIL VIEW ON PROTOTYPICAL ORGANIC NITRILES: THE ^{13}C SPECIES OF ETHYL CYANIDE

<u>CHRISTIAN ENDRES</u>, *The Center for Astrochemical Studies, Max-Planck-Institut für extraterrestrische Physik, Garching, Germany*; MARIE-ALINE MARTIN-DRUMEL, OLIVIER PIRALI, *Institut des Sciences Moléculaires d'Orsay, Université Paris Saclay, CNRS, Orsay, France*; J.-C. GUILLEMIN, *UMR 6226 CNRS - ENSCR, Institut des Sciences Chimiques de Rennes, Rennes, France*; OLIVER ZINGSHEIM, LUIS BONAH, *I. Physikalisches Institut, Universität zu Köln, Köln, Germany*; MICHAEL C McCARTHY, *Center for Astrophysics, Harvard & Smithsonian, Cambridge, MA, USA*; PAOLA CASELLI, *The Center for Astrochemical Studies, Max-Planck-Institut für extraterrestrische Physik, Garching, Germany*; STEPHAN SCHLEMMER, SVEN THORWIRTH, *I. Physikalisches Institut, Universität zu Köln, Köln, Germany*.

Vibrational spectra of the three singly substituted ^{13}C isotopic species of ethyl cyanide, aka propionitrile (CH$_3$CH$_2$CN), have been studied at high spectral resolution at the synchrotron facility SOLEIL using Fourier-transform far-infrared spectroscopy. The measurements, recorded up to 700 cm^{-1}, cover the fundamental modes of the CCN in-plane bending ν_{13}, the methyl torsion ν_{21}, the CCN out-of-plane bending ν_{20} as well as the CCC in-plane bending ν_{12}. A first spectroscopic analysis has been performed using the *Automated Spectral Assignment Procedure* (ASAP)[a] to derive accurate excited-state rotational level energies with a focus on the ν_{20} and the ν_{12} vibrational modes.

---

[a]M. A. Martin-Drumel, C. P. Endres, O. Zingsheim, T. Salomon, J. van Wijngaarden, O. Pirali, S. Gruet, F. Lewen, S. Schlemmer, M. C. McCarthy, and S. Thorwirth 2015, J. Mol. Spectrosc. 315, 72

FG08 11:15 – 11:30

PROTONATED ETHYL CYANIDE: QUANTUM CHEMISTRY AND ROTATIONAL SPECTROSCOPY

<u>HARSHAL GUPTA</u>, *Division of Astronomical Sciences, National Science Foundation, Alexandria, VA, USA*; KELVIN LEE, *Accelerated Computing Systems and Graphics, Intel Corporation, Hillsboro, OR, USA*; SVEN THORWIRTH, OSKAR ASVANY, STEPHAN SCHLEMMER, *I. Physikalisches Institut, Universität zu Köln, Köln, Germany*; MICHAEL C McCARTHY, *Center for Astrophysics, Harvard & Smithsonian, Cambridge, MA, USA*.

Protonated ethyl cyanide, CH$_3$CH$_2$CNH$^+$, a likely intermediate in interstellar clouds and in the planetary atmosphere of Titan, has been detected at high spectral resolution by means of Fourier transform microwave spectroscopy at centimeter wavelengths. From 13 a-type rotational transitions between 8 and 44 GHz, the three rotational constants have been determined to better than 0.05%, and two of the leading centrifugal distortion terms to a few percent. Since nitrogen hyperfine structure in the lower rotational transitions is highly compact, only the quadrupole coupling tensor element along the a-inertial axis χ_{aa}(N) could be determined. The agreement between the experimental rotational constants and those calculated theoretically is very good, of order 0.2%, a clear indication that the CCSD(T) level of theory provides an accurate treatment of the electronic structure. By scaling to isoelectronic butyne, even better agreement between the two is achieved ($\ll 0.1\%$). The similarity of the eQq(N) values derived along the C–N bond axis for both protonated vinyl cyanide and protonated ethyl cyanide along with the very small magnitudes of these constants implies a quadruply-bound nitrogen atom and an H$-$N$^+\equiv$C$-$R type structure that is affected little by protonation. Closely spaced torsional doublets in one $K_a = 0$ line and three $K_a = +1$ lines allow an estimate of the threefold barrier to internal rotation of $V_3 = 2.50 \pm 0.09$ kcal mol^{-1}, which is within 4% of that calculated theoretically. Ethyl cyanide has a high proton affinity and is abundant in rich astronomical molecular sources, implying its protonated variant is a good candidate for astronomical detection, particularly since this species is calculated to possess a sizable dipole moment along the a-inertial axis (2.91 D).

FG09   11:33–11:48

LABORATORY SPECTROSCOPY OF $A^2\Sigma^+$–$X^2\Pi_{3/2}$ ELECTRONIC TRANSITION OF ICN$^+$ TO ESTIMATE PROFILES OF INTERSTELLAR ABSORPTION LINES BY HALOGEN CYANIDE CATIONS

TAKUMI ITO, MITSUNORI ARAKI, SHOMA HOSHINO, KOICHI TSUKIYAMA, *Faculty of Science Division I, Tokyo University of Science, Shinjuku-ku, Tokyo, Japan.*

Diffuse interstellar bands (DIBs) are optical absorption lines by electronic transitions of interstellar molecules in diffuse clouds. Almost all bands are not identified yet, except for C_{60}^+. As a hint of DIB carriers, the presence of C_{60}^+ infers that molecules in diffuse clouds are ionized. Additionally, the molecules would frequently contain a cyano group and more or less include a halogen atom. Hence, halogen cyanide cations are good carrier candidates. To identify origin molecules of DIBs, laboratory data of band profiles of electronic transitions are essential as well as those of their wavelengths. Generally, a band profile is determined by a structural change of an electronic transition. In this work, the high-resolution spectrum of the $A^2\Sigma^+$–$X^2\Pi_{3/2}$ electronic transition for ICN$^+$, which is one of the halogen cyanide cations, was observed for the first time by cavity ringdown spectroscopy. The rotational constants were determined to be 0.10700(12) and 0.11002(12) cm^{-1} for the $A^2\Sigma^+$ and $X^2\Pi_{3/2}$ states, respectively. Therefore, the rotational constant ratio $\beta = (B' - B'')/B''$ was derived to be -2.7 %. This small β suggests that the profiles of the absorption bands of the halogen cyanide cations have symmetric structures irrespective of diffuse-cloud temperature. This information allows us to search the halogen cyanide cations in space.

FG10   11:51–12:06

JET-COOLED MID-INFRARED LASER SPECTROSCOPY OF CENTROSYMMETRIC TWO-RING PAHS

PIERRE ASSELIN, SATHAPANA CHAWANANON, *CNRS, De la Molécule aux Nano-Objets: Réactivité, Interactions, Spectroscopies, MONARIS, Sorbonne Université, PARIS, France*; MANUEL GOUBET, *UMR 8523 - PhLAM - Physique des Lasers Atomes et Molécules, University of Lille, CNRS, F-59000 Lille, France*; OLIVIER PIRALI, *Institut des Sciences Moléculaires d'Orsay, Université Paris Saclay, CNRS, Orsay, France.*

The recent detection of cyano naphthalenes within TMC-1 using radioastronomy[a] provided the first unambiguous confirmation of the interstellar PAH's hypothesis. In the mid-infrared (IR) domain, the launch of the James Webb Space Telescope opens exciting perspectives to collect information about polycyclic aromatic compounds. In this context, high resolution (HR) IR studies' enabling to resolve the rotational structure of vibrational bands of large aromatic species mainly used synchrotron-based Fourier Transform (FT) spectroscopy coupled to room temperature long path cells but the spectral analysis of such recordings remains very challenging. Nowadays, very few set-ups combining HR IR spectroscopy to the supersonic jet technique were developed to target low volatile PAH compounds[b].

A tunable mid-IR quantum cascade laser spectrometer coupled to a pulsed supersonic jet (SPIRALES set-up) recently implemented allows to record the rotationally resolved spectra of large molecules at low temperatures. We report the jet-cooled rovibrational IR study of three centrosymmetric two-ring PAH molecules: naphthalene, 1,5-naphthyridine and biphenyl in both regions of in plane ring C-H bending and C-C ring stretching vibrations, enabling to extract reliable spectroscopic parameters both in ground and excited vibrational states. Comparison between experiment and quantum chemistry calculations give confidence in the predictive power of corrected calculated rotational parameters. Last, experimental inertial defects of naphthalene and 1,5-naphthyridine complemented by similar two-ring and larger species agree well with an extended Oka's empirical formula developed for estimating the inertial defects of aromatic ring compounds.

---

[a] B.A. Mc Guire, R.A. Loomis, A. M. Burkhardt, K.L. K. Lee, C. N. Shingledecker, S. B. Charnley, I. R. Cooke, M. A. Cordiner, E. Herbst, S. Kalenskii, M. A. Siebert, E. R. Willis, C. Xue, A. J. Remijan, and M. C. Mc Carthy, Science, 371, 1265 (2021)

[b] B. E. Brumfield, J. T. Stewart and B. J. McCall, J. Phys. Chem. Lett 3, 1985 (2012) O. Pirali, M. Goubet, T. Huet, R. Georges, P. Soulard, P. Asselin, J. Courbe, P. Roy and M. Vervloet, PCCP. 15, 10141 (2013)

FG11

HIGH-RESOLUTION INFRARED SPECTRUM OF THE DIATOMIC VANADIUM OXIDE

<u>EILEEN DÖRING</u>, LUISA BLUM, *Institute of Physics, University of Kassel, Kassel, Germany*; ALEXANDER A. BREIER, THOMAS GIESEN, *Institute of Physics, University Kassel, Kassel, Germany*; GUIDO W. FUCHS, *Institute of Physics, University of Kassel, Kassel, Germany*.

Small molecules made of refractory materials are thought to play an important role in the dust formation processes around late-type stars. Likewise, they take part in the opacity process of variable late-type stars, as has been shown for the molecule TiO.[a] Because of similar formation conditions, the diatomic molecule vanadium oxide (VO) is thought to occur in similar locations around stars as TiO.[b] VO has already been detected in the near-infrared region in the envelope of the red hypergiant VY CMa[c], but due to the lack of high-resolution laboratory spectra, no astrophysical search of VO in the mid-IR region has been performed. In this work, we report the ro-vibrational absorption spectrum of $X^4\Sigma^-$ VO, including its hyperfine structure. In our experiment we used a frequency modulated quantum cascade laser in combination with Herriott-type multipass optics. The molecules were produced by laser ablation of a vanadium rod and an N_2O/He buffer gas, which was subsequently adiabatically expanded into a vacuum chamber. The rotationally cooled spectrum was analyzed using the pgopher software and the molecular constants were determined. The experimental data as well as line predictions will enable a dedicated search for this molecule in space at mid-IR wavelengths.

---

[a] M.J. Reid & J.E. Goldston, The Astrophysical Journal **568**, 931 (2002)
[b] L.K. McKemmish *et al.*, Monthly Notices of the Royal Astronomical Society **463**, 771 (2016)
[c] J. Bernal *et al.*, 74th International Symposium on Molecular Spectroscopy (2019)

AUTHOR INDEX

A

Aardema, Megan – WH03
Abdelkader Khedaoui, Omar – TN05, FA02, FA03
Abhari, Zain – WJ02
Abma, Grite L. – MH02, TA06
Abualsaud, Nawaf – RH07
Adam, Allan G. – WC01, RK04
Adil, Mohammad – RH07, RH10
Adkins, Erin M. – WB06, FE05
Aegurla, Balakrishna – TF10
Aerts, Antoine – MH09
Afonine, Pavel V – MI10
Aguado, Raúl – MI02, RL01
Ahad, Safa – TM06
Ahmad, Taha – TE03
Al ibrahim, Emad – WK02
Al-Jabiri, Mohamad H. – TF11, WM08, WM09
Albert, Sieghard – TE01
Alcaraz, Christian – WL09
Aldakheel, R. K. – FF03
Alekseev, E. A. – WN05
Alessandrini, Silvia – TD04, TD05, TI01, RN06
Alexandrova, Anastassia – MM04
Alhmoud, Dieaa H – TL04
Alkorta, Ibon – MI01
Allen, Heather C. – WK06, WK07
Allison, Thomas K – TH07
Allmendinger, Pitt – FE01
Almessiere, M A. – FF03
Alonso, Elena R. – MI02, MI05, MI07, MI08, WL03, WL04, WL06, RL04, RL09
Alonso, José L. – MI02, MI05, MI07, MI08, WL04, WL06, WN11, RL01, RL04, RL09
Alonso, Maria – RJ08
Alsulami, Ahmed Ayidh – RH07
Amberger, Brent K. – RM03, RM11
Anderson, David T. – RI10, FA09
Annis, Jezrielle R. – WK04
Antwi, Ernest – WH02
Araki, Mitsunori – TG05, FG09
Arathala, Parandaman – FC07
Arenas, Benjamin E – FG06
Ariyaratne, Tulana – FD08
armante, raymond – FC08
Arunan, Elangannan – WI11, FA07
Ash, Ryan T – WC08, WJ02
Asiamah, Maameyaa – WM01
Asmis, Knut R. – MH05

Asselin, Pierre – WF02, RI05, FC09, FG10
Asvany, Oskar – WG03, WG05, WG07, RL10, FG08
Athanasakis-Kaklamanakis, Michail – RM08
Au, Kendrew – WF03
Au, Mia – RM08
Augenbraun, Benjamin – MM04

B

Baba, Masaaki – MJ07, MM05, TL06, WF10, RL05, RL12
Babin, Mark C – MH07
Bagheri, Mahmood – WJ07, WJ08
Bailey, D. Michelle – TH05
Baker, Robert – TA02
Bales, Kristin N – RK07, RK08
Bandaranayake, Savini Sandunika – TA02
Baraban, Joshua H – TH06
Barbatti, Mario – RH03
Barclay, A. J. – WD06, WE10, RI09
Barnum, Timothy J – ML06, RH05
Barone, Vincenzo – TD04, RH04, FB01
Barrientos, Carmen – WN11
Bashiri, Termeh – TJ10
Basnayake, Gihan – MH04, TA08
Bast, Marcel – WG03
Basterretxea, Francisco J. – WL03
Batalha, Natasha E – FE11
Batchelor, Anna G – MJ11
Batra, Gayatri – TD03, FG06
Bauerle, Lauren – TA07, WL10
Beglaryan, Babken – ML01
Béguier, Serge – RN03
Behera, Bedabyas – WC09
Bejaoui, Salma – RN11
Belloche, Arnaud – WF11, WN07, WN11
Belmont, Kaitlyn – WL02
Belosevic, Ivana – RM08
Berezhnoy, Alexey A. – ML02
Berger, Robert – RM08
Berggötz, Freya E. L. – TE08
Bergmann, Uwe – WJ02
Bernal, Jacob – RN05
Bernath, Peter F. – TB05, TC09, TC12, TF02, FC03, FC04, FC05
Bersson, Jonathan Swift – TI02
Bhargava, Rohit – WE03, WE08
Bhattacharya, Susmita – RI07
Bhutani, Garima – TH02

Bi, Hongshan – TK06
Biczysko, Malgorzata – MI10, TI03
Bielska, Katarzyna – WB06
Biennier, Ludovic – WI11, RI05
Bieske, Evan – TJ01, WA04
Billinghurst, Brant E. – WF08, RL06, RM03, RM11, FF05
Bistoni, Giovanni – WB04
Bizzocchi, Luca – TD04, TD05, WG11, RH04, RN06
Bjorkman, Kristen K. – MK04
Blake, Geoffrey – FB03, FD01
Blake, Thomas A. – TN03
Blanco, Susana – MI01, TE02, TM04
Bloino, Julien – FB01
Blum, Luisa – FG11
Bödecker, Maragrethe – RI01
Boeije, Y. – RH03
Bogomolov, Alexandr – WD05
Bonah, Luis – WF11, RJ07, FG07
Boone, Chris – FC03, FC04, FC05
Borchman, Douglas – FF11
Borden, David W. – TE03
Bormotova, Ekaterina A. – ML02, TB10
Borrego-Varillas, Rocio – TH08
Boudon, Vincent – TC01
Boutureira, Omar – WL03
Bowesman, Charles A – TL07
Boyer, Mark A. – MJ01, MJ02
Bracquart, Colwyn – FC09
Brady, Ryan – TC08
Breier, Alexander A. – RM08, FG11
Brieuc, Fabien – RL10
Brinson, Alex – RM08
Brogan, Crystal L. – MN04, RN02
Bross, David H. – MJ04
Brothers, Michael C – WE09
Browet, Olivier – FE01
Bruckhuisen, Jonas – WB07, FC09
Brünken, Sandra – WA05, WB08, RI03, FB07
Brunson, Jonah – ML04
Buma, Wybren Jan – WA05, RH02, RH03
Bunn, Hayley – TD06, TD07, WB03, WN09
Buntine, Jack T – TJ01, WA04
Burchesky, Sean – MM04
Burevschi, Ecaterina – WM03
Burke, John H – TA03
Burkhardt, Andrew M – FG05
Bush, Rachel E. – WH02
Bush, Sarah A. – WH02

C

Cacciani, Patrice – RN03
Cai, Jia-Rong – TN09
Calabrese, Camilla – WB04, WL03
Caliebe, Swantje V. M. – FD02
Callahan, Charlie Scott – TL09
Cameron, William D – TC09
Caminati, Walther – MA05, FB01, FB05
Campargue, Alain – WF09, RN03, FB08, FC02, FE05, FE06
Campbell, Wesley – MM04
Campos-Pineda, Mixtli – FC06
Canedy, Chadwick L – WJ07, WJ08
Caracciolo, Adriana – WH02
Caram, Justin – MM04
Carder, Joshua – MN02
Cardon, Joseph M. – TC11
Carlson, Colton – TM03
Carney, Annabelle N – WD07
Caron, Nicholas – WC01
Carrigan-Broda, Theodore Jacob – WL08
Carrillo, Michael J. – MI03, TD09
Carroll, Brandon – TD10, TD11, FA05
Carty, Brayden – WL05
Caselli, Paola – WN02, FG07
Catikkas, Berna – WA07, RH01
Cavaletto, Stefano M. – TA04
Ceponkus, Justinas – WL08
Čermák, Peter – RN03
Cerullo, Giulio – TH08
Chakraborty, Shubhadip – WI11, RI05
Chan, Ya-Chu – MK04, TN01
Chandra, S – FA08
Chandrasekaran, Vijayanand – WI11
Chang, M.-C. Frank – RJ08
Chang, Peter – WJ09
Changala, Bryan – MI06, MJ04, TD10, TH06, RL07, FA05, FG05
Charnley, Steven B – FG05
Chatterjee, Kuntal – WD08
Chatterjee, Satadru – ML09
CHAWANANON, SATHAPANA – FC09, FG10
Chekmarev, Sergei F. – FA10
Chen, Junha – FB01
Chen, Liangyi – TG07
Chen, Peter – WG08, WI03
Chen, Peter – WJ01, FF07
Chen, Tianxiang – TL01
Chen, TzuLing – WJ07, WJ08
Chen, Ziqiu – WF08
Chenard, Geoffrey M. – RK04
Cheng, Cunfeng – FB10
Cheng, Lan – MJ08, TB01, TB04, TB11, TL01
Chernov, Vladislav E. – ML02
Chick Jarrold, Caroline – WD03, WD04
Chitarra, Olivia – TD02, TN02
Chollet, Etienne – FA06
Chrayteh, Mhamad – WF04, WM03, RJ09
Christenson, Gerrit – FF10
Chrysalidis, Katherina – RM08
Chung, Chen-An – TN09
Ciavardini, Alessandra – TF03
Cich, Matthew J. – WJ06
Cisneros-González, Miriam E. – TL08
Ciurylo, Roman – TI05, WB06, FB08
Clark, Keith T. – TJ06
Clees, Sean – FE02
Clément, Jean – FE01
Clendening, Reese – WC08
Clouthier, Dennis – TC11
Coburn, Sean – TL09
Cocinero, Emilio J. – WL03
Cocolios, Thomas – RM08
Cole-Filipiak, Neil C. – TA05
Colley, Jason E. – TJ03, WG06, WH01
Constantin, Florin Lucian – ML11
Conti, Irene – TH08
Conway, Eamon K – TC10, WI10
Cooke, Ilsa Rose – TN05, FA02, FA03, FG05
Cooke, S. A. – TN03, WF07
Cooper, Ken – RJ02
Cooper, Nicholas D. – TH01
Cordiner, Martin – FG05
Coreno, Marcello – TF03
Corzana, Francisco – WL03
Cosleou, Jean – RN03
Coudert, L. H. – WF09, WN02, FB04
Cox, Erin Guilfoil – MN04
Cox, Sam – MK06
Coy, Stephen L – ML06, RH05
Cozijn, Frank M.J. – ML07
Crabtree, Kyle N. – TK05, TN04, RN10
Crandall, Parker B. – RN09
Crawford, Timothy J. – FE04
Crim, Fleming – TO02
Crouse, Jeff – RM10, FC03, FC04
Crowther, Parker – RK02
Crozet, Patrick – RK05
Crutcher, Richard – MN04
Cruz-Diaz, Gustavo A. – FG01, FG03
Császár, Attila – RL10
Cuisset, Arnaud – WB07, WF04, RJ09, FB04, FC09
Cummings, Charlotte Nicole – WM02, FD04
Cvitaš, Marko – TF11
Cygan, Agata – TI05, WB06

D

Dahlmann, Franziska – FB07
Daniels, DeAunna A – WJ01, FF07
Das, Arijit – FA07
Dass, Amal – ML09
Datar, Avdhoot – TL02, TL03
Daunt, Stephen J. – RL06
Davis, John Patrick – WA06
Davis, Michael J. – WK03
De, Arijit K – TH02
Dean, Jessika L.S. – TH04
Debrah, Duke A. – MH03, TA08
Degroote, Ruben – RM08
Dehghany, M. – WM10
Delcamp, Jared – ML08, ML09
Dengler, Robert – RJ02
Derbidge, Jordan – TJ06
Desai, Kavita V. – FF08
DeWitt, Martin – MH07
Dewyer, Amanda – WF03
Dey, Diptesh – TA09
Dhamija, Shaina – TH02
Dhont, Guillaume – WB07, FC09
Dias, Nureshan – WJ04, FA01
Dickerson, Claire E – MM04
Diddams, Scott – WJ09
Ding, Yiming – RJ01, FE08, FE10
Diouf, Meissa – ML07
Djuricanin, Pavle – TJ09, TJ10
Dmitriev, Yurij – TN08
Dodangodage, Randika – TB05
Dodson, Leah G – TG04, WL11, RJ04, RJ05
Dohmen, Robin – FB06
Dopfer, Otto – TJ02, TJ04, WG01, WG02, RN09
Doran, Ioana – MJ09
Dore, Luca – TD04, TD05, WG11
Döring, Eileen – MN07, TG02, FG11
Dorman, P. Matisha – MI06, TF05
Dorne, Anais – RM08
Dorovskaya, Olga – WN05
Doyle, John M. – MM04
Dréan, Pascal – WF04, WM03, FC01, FD06
Drissi, Myriam – TN05, FA02, FA03
Drouin, Brian – RJ02, RJ08, FE04
Duerden, Amanda – MI02, WL05, FD09
Duncan, Michael A – MJ11, TJ03, WG06, WH01, WH11
Dutton, S E – FB03, FD01

Dykstra, Conner – TJ07
Dynak, nathan John – WH01

E

Ebert, Volker – WB06
Eckhardt, André K. – MM08
Eden, J. Gary – RJ10, FF08
Edington, Sean Coleman – TG08, TI07, WE06
Edlin, Matthew L – WJ04
Egbert, Scott C – WJ09
Eichmann, Ulli – MJ10
El-Abd, Samer – RN02
El-Shazly, Khaled Aley – TG03, FF06
Eliason, Todd – TH01
Elkhazraji, Ali – RH07
Elmaleh, Coralie – RJ09
Emmenegger, Lukas – WJ11
Enders, Abigail A – WK06, WK07
Endo, Yasuki – WLUN
Endres, Christian – WN02, FG07
Enomoto, Katsunari – MM05
Eraković, Mihael – TF11
Erukala, Swetha – TG11
Erwin, Justin – TL08
Esposito, Vincent J. – WC05, WH02
Esselman, Brian J. – MI06, TD01, TD07, TF05, TF06, TJ08, WB01, WB03, RL07, RM03, RM10, RM11
Evangelisti, Luca – MA05, TF03, WB04

F

Fábri, Csaba – RL10
Fagan, Jonathan Wood – TG10
Faist, Jérôme – WJ11
Fakhardji, Wissam – FE06
Falls, Christopher – TN03
Fan, Jiayun – RH02
Farooq, Aamir – WK02, RH07, RH10
Fatehi, Shervin – MI03
Fatima, Mariyam – WF11, WM04, WN08
Faure, Alexandre – RN07
Federman, Steven – RN10
Feinberg, Alexandra J – TG11
Feller, David – MJ04
Feng, Gang – WB02, WM02, FD07
Ferrer Asensio, Judit – WN02
Ferres, Lynn – MA05
Field, Robert W – ML06, WC02, RA03, RH05, RM02
Finazzi, Laura – RH02

Finney, Jacob M – MJ06
Fino, Hannah – FD08
Fischer, Taija L. – RI01
Flanagan, Kieran – RM08
Fleisher, Adam J. – TH05
Fleurbaey, Helene – FE05, FE06
Foley, Casey Daniel – FA06
Foltynowicz, Aleksandra – TC01
Foote, David B. – WJ06
Foreman, Madison M. – MM06, WG10, RK03
Förstel, Marko – TJ02, TJ04, WG01, WG02, RN09
Fortenberry, Ryan C. – RI06
Fournier, Joseph – MA03, TG07, TH04
Franchoo, Serge – RM08
Francisco, Joseph S – WC05, FB02
Franke, Peter R. – WF07, WL07
Frederiks, Nicoline C. – FC11
Freedman, Richard S – TC02, FE10, FE11
French, Ethan – TK06, WK05
Frez, Clifford – WJ07, WJ08
Friskey, Jacqueline M. – WC05
Frontiera, Renee R. – FF10
Fuchs, Guido W. – MN07, TG02, TG06, FG11
Furukawa, Hoga – TD01

G

Gajapathy, Harshad – TA02
Gamache, Robert R. – FE11
Gancewski, Maciej Grzegorz – FB08, FB09
Garand, Etienne – WI07, WJ03, WM06, RK01
Garavelli, Marco – TH08
Garcia Ruiz, Ronald Fernando – RM08
Garrod, Robin T. – WN11
Gartner, Travis A – WE10
Gaul, Konstantin – RM08
Gavin-Hanner, Coire F – MJ02
Geldhof, Sarina – RM08
Génévriez, Matthieu – MJ10, WG04
Genossar, Nadav – TH06
Gentile, Marziogiuseppe – TH08
Georges, Robert – WF02, WI11, RI05
Gerakines, Perry A. – FG01, FG02, FG03
Gergess, Chris – WM10
Gerin, Maryvonne – MN11
Germann, Matthias – TC01
Gerosolina, Anna Kay – TM09, TN06
Gharib-Nezhad, Ehsan – FE11

GHOSAL, SUBHAS – TI04
Gianella, Michele – WJ11
Giese, Morgan – TM09
Giesen, Thomas – MN07, TG02, RM08, FG11
Giles, Rohini S – MN07
Giri, Binod – RH07, RH10
Glorieux, Robin – WD05, WD10
Gluszek, Aleksander – TC01
Gold, Katherine R. – MN10
Goldsmith, Randall – WA01
Gómez-Bombarelli, Rafael – MK03
Gomez-Pech, Cecilia – WB07
Gondal, Mohammed A – FF03
Gonzalez, Fernando – TE02
Gonzalez, Zayra Leticia – RL02
Gorbachev, Vladimir – WG08, WI03
Gordon, Iouli E – TC10, WI10
Gordon, Robert J – RM02
Gorza, Simon Pierre – MH09
Gou, Qian – FB01
Goubet, Manuel – WB07, WF02, WF04, RI05, FB04, FC01, FD06, FG10
Gougoula, Eva – TD03, WF01, WM02, FA07, FD04
Grabow, Jens-Uwe – FB01
Greathouse, Thomas K – MN07
Grechishnikova, Galina – TM06
Green, William H. – MK03
Greenman, Kevin P. – MK03
Greis, Kim – TG09, WG09
Grellmann, Max – MH05
Groenenboom, Gerrit – RI03
Groner, Peter – TF01, WF07
Grubbs II, G. S. – MI02, MI03, WL05, RL02, RL03, FD09
Gruebele, Martin – MH10, TL10
Grzywacz, Robert – RL06
Guan, Hui – MK07
Gudivada, Saisrinivas – TL03
Guerrero, Sebastian – MM07
Guillaume, Theo – TN05, FA02, FA03
Guillemin, J.-C. – TD04, TD05, WN01, WN04, WN07, WN10, RJ07, FG07
Guirgis, Gamil A – MI02, WL08
Guislain, Bradley – WC01
Gulaczyk, Iwona – RI08
Guo, Hua – MH07
Gupta, Divita – TN05, FA02, FA03
Gupta, Harshal – MN11, FG08
Gurusinghe, Ranil – WJ04, FA01

H

Haider, Md. Ali – WM04

Haimberger, Chris – WJ06
Halvick, Philippe – FB07
Hammer, Nathan I – ML08, ML09, WC06, RI06
Han, Bowen – MK02
Han, Jiande – MM01, MM02
Hansen, Anne S – WH04
Hansen, Nils – WF03
Hanson, Ronald K – RJ01, FE02, FE08, FE10
Hargreaves, Robert J. – TC10
Harms, Jack C – RK07, RK08
Harrison, Rachel E. – MN04
Hartmann, Jean-Michel – FE06
Hauser, Andreas W. – WI01
Havenith, Martina – WD08
Hayden, Jakob – FE01
Hays, Brian M – TN05, WD05, WD10, FA02, FA03
Hazrah, Arsh Singh – WM08, WM09
Heald, Lauren F – MH06
Heaney, Danika Lee – FC11
Hearne, Thomas Sandow – TD02, TN02
Heaven, Michael – MM01, MM02, WC07, WD02, RK10
Heiniger, Adam – WJ06
Heitkämper, Juliane – FD04
Herbst, Eric – MN02
Herburger, Holger – WJ05
Herman, Michel – WD05, WD10
Herman, Tyler J – RK02
Hermanns, Marius – RJ06
Herreras, Diego – RL09
Heyne, Bettina – WF11, RJ06
Hickman, Daniel Vincent – WL08
Hindle, Francis – RJ09
Hiramoto, Ayami – MM05
Hirano, Tsuneo – MJ07, TL06
Hjältén, Adrian – TC01
Ho, Ruo-Jing – WE08
Hockey, Emily K – TG04, RJ04, RJ05
Hodges, Joseph T. – TH05, WB06, FE05
Hoffman, Caitlin – TE03
Hoghooghi, Nazanin – WJ09
Holland, Torrey E. – WE02
Hollenstein, Urs – WJ05
Hölsch, Nicolas – MJ09
Hong, Seohyun (Cece) – WM05
Hopkins, Scott – TL07
Hoppen, Dirk – WN08
Horke, Daniel – MH02, TA06
Horowitz, Jonah R. – TE06
Hoshino, Shoma – TG05, FG09
Hotz, Gabriel A – RK07
Howard, Thomas – TG04, RJ04

Hruska, Emily B – TA02
Hsiao, Sheng-Chang – WH05, WH06
Hsieh, Pei-Hsuan – WE03
Hsu, Yen-Chu – WH05, WH06
Hu, Shui-Ming – WI10, FB08, FB10
Huang, Libai – TM06
Huang, Xinchuan – TC02, TC03, TC04, TC05, TC10
Huchmala, Rachel M. – TF08
Hudson, Eric – MM04
Hudzikowski, Arkadiusz – TC01
Huet, Therese R. – FC01, FD06
Hugi, Andreas – FE01
Huis in't Veld, Frank – WB08
Huizenga, Caleb D – WD03
Hull, Alexander W – ML06
Humphreys, Roberta M. – MN09
Hunter, Todd R. – RN02, RN07
Hurlbut, Walter – WJ06

I

Ilyushin, V. – WF02, WN05
Insausti, Aran – MI07, TF11, WL03, WM09
Isaev, Timur A. – RM08
Isborn, Christine M – MK02
Isert, Joshua E. – MI03, WL05, RL02
Ishikawa, Haruki – WA09
Islam, Md Touhidul – RL11
Ito, Takumi – FG09
Iwakuni, Kana – MM05

J

Jackson, William M. – RN10
Jacob, Lorrie S. D. – WH09
Jacovella, Ugo – WL09
Jaffe, Noah B – WD02
Jäger, Wolfgang – TF11, WM08, WM09
Jaiswal, Vishal K. – TH08
Jakob, Jan – TG02
Jamil, Md Abrar – ML10
Janik, Ireneusz – ML05, RI07
Jaron, Agnieszka – TA07, WL10
Jarugula, Sreevani – MN06
Jayachandran, Ajay – TH02
Jayaram, V – WI11
Jeffries, William R. – WD01
Jeong, Changseop – TE10
Jiang, Jun – RA03, RJ03
Jiang, Ningjing – TD04, TD05
Jiménez-Serra, Izaskun – WN11
Jin, Jiaye – MH05
Johansen, Sommer L. – WC11

Johnson, Christopher J. – TG10, FC11
Johnson, Mark – MA01, TG08, TG09, TI07, WE06, WG09
Johnson, Ryan – TC12, FC05
Jones, Ian – TI02
Jones, Walker M. – TH01
Jorgensen, Jes – WN07
Joshi, Prasad Ramesh – TN07
Jóźwiak, Hubert – TI05, FB08, FB09
Ju, Chengwei – MK07, TK06
Juárez, Gabriela – MI05, WL04, RL04
Jusko, Pavol – FB07

K

Kabaciński, Piotr – TH08
Kable, Scott – WH09
Kaiser, Ralf Ingo – MM08
Kang, Lu – TN03
Kania, Patrik – WN10, RM03, RM11
Kannangara, Prashansa – FD08
Kappes, Manfred M – WL11
Karman, Tijs – FE05
Karsili, Tolga N. V. – WH02
Karunanithy, Robinson – WE02
Kasahara, Shunji – WF10, RL05
Kassal, Ivan – RH09
Kassi, Samir – FB08, FC02
Kawagoe, Thomas T. – TJ06
Kawashima, Yoshiyuki – TD08, WL01
Kellar, Douglas J. – WH01
Keppler, Karen – TE01
Khatri, Jai – WD08
Khemissi, Safa – FB02
Khiabani, Neda – RJ08
Khrapunova, Aryna – TF07, TG01
Kidwell, Nathanael M. – WA03, WA06
Kilburn, Josie L. – MJ04
Kim, Doyeon – RM10
Kim, Gap-Sue – TC06, TC08, FC10
Kim, Nam Joon – TE10
Kim, Navie – TE03
Kim, Steve S – WE09
Kisiel, Zbigniew – RM03, RM11
Kisuryna, Darya – TF07, TG01, RJ04
Kleimeier, N. Fabian – MM08
Kleiner, Isabelle – WF01, WF02, FB02, FC09
Klippenstein, Stephen J. – WH04
Knappenberger, Jr., Kenneth L. – WD01
Knight, Caitlin – TE07
Kobayashi, Kaori – TD01, RK06
Kockaert, Pascal – MH09
Koelemay, Lilia – MN05
Kolesniková, Lucie – MI07, WL06,

WN10, WN11
Komagata, Kenichi – WJ11
Konar, Arkaprabha – TH09
Koroleva, Aleksandra – FC02
Koszorus, Agota – RM08
Koucký, Jan – WN10
Kougias, Samuel M. – TJ08, WB03, RL07
Koumarianou, Greta – TE04, TE05, RM07, RM09, FA04
Kowzan, Grzegorz – TH07, TI05
Koziol, Kenneth J. – FB02
Kreglewski, Marek – RI08
Kreinbihl, John J. – FC11
Kreis, Carla – WG04
Kruse, Holger – MI10
Kruse, Nicholas A. – WC06
Krzempek, Karol – TC01
Kubasik, Matthew A. – FA06
Kujanpaa, Sonja – RM08
Kukolich, Stephen G. – MI03
Kulik, Heather J – TK04
Kuma, Susumu – MM05
Kuwahata, Kazuaki – MJ07
Kuze, Nobuhiko – TD08, WL01
Kwabia Tchana, F. – WF02, FC08
Kyuberis, Aleksandra A. – WB06

L

LaBelle, Keith – FC04, FC05
Labutin, Timur A. – ML01, ML02
Lacy, John H. – MN07
Lalanne, Louis – RM08
Lamas, Iker – MH08
Lambert, Ethan Chase – RI06
Lang, Jinxin – WJ04
Lao, Guanming – MM04
Lara-Moreno, Miguel – FB07
Lasner, Zack – MM04
Lattanzi, Valerio – WG11, WN02
Lau, Jascha – MH07
Lauzin, Clément – TL08, WD05, WD10
Lecours, Mike – FC05
Lee, Danny J – RL07
Lee, Kelvin – MN02, MN11, TK05, WH09, RN02, FG05, FG08
Lee, Suk Kyoung – MH03, TA08
Lee, Timothy J. – TC02, TC03, TC04, TC05
Lee, Yuan-Pern – TN07, TN09, WC09
Lees, Ronald M. – WN05
Legg, Heather – TG03, FF06
Lehmann, Kevin – FF09
Lei, Jianting – RM06
Leinwand, Leslie A. – MK04

Lemmens, Alexander Karel – WA05, RH02
León, Iker – MI02, MI05, MI07, MI08, WL04, WL06, RL01, RL04, RL09
Leone, Stephen R. – TA01
Leopold, Kenneth R. – TM02, WC10, WL02
Lepère, Muriel – FE01
Lesarri, Alberto – FD07
Lester, Marsha – WH02, WH04
Leung, Helen O. – TE03, TE06, TE07, WM05
Levine, Benjamin G – TH07
Lewen, Frank – WF11, WN03, WN05, RJ07
Li, Gang – WB06
Li, Guojie – TE09
Li, Minghe – WI08
Li, Weixing – MM09, WB04, FB05, FD03
Li, Wen – MH03, TA08
Li, Wenqin – FD07
Li, Xiaolong – MM09, FD03
LI, Yan – WE07, WJ10
Li, Zhi-Yun – MN04
Liang, Qizhong – MK04
Liang, Yue – WF08
Liévin, Jacques – TB05, TC12
Lin, Ming-Fu – TA10
Lin, Wei – MI03, RL02
Lin, Zhe – MJ08
Lin, Zhou – MK07, TB06, TK06, TL04, WK05, RH11
Linton, Colan – RK04
Lique, François – RH04
Lis, Dariusz – MN01, FE04
Lisak, Daniel – TI05, WB06
Liu, An-Wen – FB08
Liu, Bowen – WF08
Liu, Chang – TJ01, WA04
Liu, Jinjun – TB08, TB09, TI02, RL11, RM01
Liu, Qian-Hao – FB10
Liu, Tianlin – WH02
Liu, Xunchen – ML03
Lochmann, Christine – FB07
Lodi, Lorenzo – WB06
Loison, J.-C. – TN02
Londo, Stephen – TA02
Long, David A. – WJ06, FE05
Longarte, Asier – MH08
Loomis, Ryan A – FG05
Looney, Leslie – MN04
Lopes, Rosaly M – FE09
Lopez, Juan Carlos – MI01, TE02, TM04

López-Puertas, Manuel – TL08
Loru, Donatella – TD03, WM03, WM07, FG06
Love, Nathan – TM02, WC10, WL02
Lu, Fenris – TK02, TK03
Lu, Minjian – WE07, WJ10
Luber, Sandra – RA04
Luková, Kateřina – WN10
Luo, Pei-Ling – TN10
Lv, Dingding – MM09, FB05, FD03

M

Ma, Jiarui – WM09
Ma, Xinwen – TB02, WI04, RM06
Macario, Alberto – TE02, FA02, FA03
MacDonell, Ryan J – RH09
Macyte, Jogile – WL08
MAHAPATRA, NANDALAL – FA08
Mahoney, Kyle – TJ10
Malaska, Michael – FE09
Malevich, Alex – TF07, TG01
Malme, Justin Thomas – WC08
Manca Tanner, Carine – TE01
Manceron, Laurent – FC08
Mangold, Markus – FE01
Manzanares, Carlos – FF01, FF04
Marangoni, Marco – RH07
Marasinghe, Dinesh – TD09, WF05
Marchetti, Barbara – WH02
Margulès, L. – WF07, WN01, WN04, WN07, RN01
Marimuthu, Aravindh Nivas – WB08, RI03, FB07
Marin, Timothy W – ML05
Maris, Assimo – MA05, TF03, WB04, FF02
Markland, Thomas E – MK01
Marks, Joshua H – MJ11, MM08
Markus, Charles R. – WG07, WJ07, WJ08
Marley, Mark S – FE10
Marlton, Samuel Jack Palmer – TJ01, WA04
Marshall, Frank E – FD09
Marshall, Mark D. – TE03, TE06, TE07, WM05
Martin-Drumel, Marie-Aline – TD02, TN02, FG07
Martín-Pintado, Jesús – WN11
Marx, Dominik – RL10
Maslowski, Piotr – TI05
Mason, Daniel – TM03
Mata, Ricardo A – RI01
Mata, Santiago – MI02, MI05, MI08, WL04, WL06
Mato, Sergio – MI08, RL01

Matsushima, Fusakazu – RK06
Matthews, Devin A. – TL02, TL03, WI05
Maul, Christof – WN05
Mazzacurati, Marzia – FF02
McBane, George – WH03
McCarthy, Michael C – MI06, MN11, TD10, TD11, WG11, RL07, FA05, FG05, FG07, FG08
McCartt, A. Daniel – RJ03
McCaslin, Laura M – TA05
McCoy, Anne B – MJ01, MJ02, MJ06, TF08, TK02, TK03
McCunn, Laura R. – TG03, FF06
McFadden, Thomas M. C. – MI02
McGuire, Brett A. – MA04, MN02, RN02, RN07, FG05
McKellar, A.R.W. – WD06, WM10, RI09
McKemmish, Laura K – RI04, RI11, RN08
McKinnon, Alexandra – TJ09, TJ10
McMahon, Robert J. – MI06, TD01, TF05, TF06, TJ08, WB03, RL07, RM03, RM10, RM11
Medcraft, Chris – FD04
Medvedev, Ivan – WE09
Mehmood, Arshad – TH07
Meijer, Gerard – MM03
Melandri, Sonia – MA05, TF03, WB04
Melin, Timothé R. L. – WC04
Mellau, Georg Ch. – WF09
Melli, Alessio – TD04
Melosso, Mattia – TD04, TD05, TI01, WG11, RH04, RN06
Memovich, Madeline – FF09
Menges, Fabian – TG08
Menten, Karl M. – WN11
Merkt, Frédéric – MJ09, WG04, WJ05
Merriles, Dakota M. – TJ05
Messinger, Joseph P. – TG08, TG09, WG09
Meyer, Jerry R – WJ07, WJ08
Meyer, Katharina A. E. – TI08, WM06, RI02
Mhanna, Mhanna – RH07
Michaelian, K. H. – WM10
Michaelsen, Tim – FB07
Mickein, Emil – TJ04, WG01, WG02
Mikhailenko, Semen – WF09
Milam, Stefanie N – FG01, FG02, FG03
Millar, Thomas J. – MN08
Miller, Dane – WD09
Miller, Terry A. – TB08, TB09, TI02, WLUN

Miloglyadova, Larisa – WI03
Mironov, Andrey E. – FF08
Mishra, Piyush – ML06
Misono, Masatoshi – RL05
Mitev, Georgi B – TC07
Mitra, Debayan – MM04
Miyamoto, Yuki – MM05
Mizuse, Kenta – TM01, WA09
Moazzen-Ahmadi, Nasser – WD05, WD06, WE10, WM10, RI09
Mogauro, Kenneth C – WD07
Mohamed, Ahmed – TI07, WE06
Momjian, Emmanuel – RN07
Momose, Takamasa – TJ09, TJ10
Mondelain, Didier – FC02, FE05, FE06
Montero, Raúl – MH08
Montoya-Castillo, Andres – MK05
Moon, Nicole – MI02, MI03, WL05, RL02, RL03
Moonkaen, Pattarapon – TK03
Moore, Brendan – TJ09, TJ10
Moore, Colton – TD06
Morales Hernandez, Hanna – TG10
Moriarty, Nigel W – MI10
Morin, Julien – RK05
Moriwaki, Yoshiki – RK06
Morse, Michael D. – TJ05, TJ06
Mort, Alex Neilson – FD05
Morville, Jérôme – RK05
Moss, Olivia – TG09, WG09
Motiyenko, R. A. – WF07, WN01, WN04, WN07, RN01
Mouret, Gaël – RJ09
Muddasser, Ibrahim – RI10, FA09
Mukamel, Shaul – TA04
Mulas, Giacomo – RI05
Müller, Holger S. P. – WF11, WN03, WN05, WN08, WN11, RJ07
Murugachandran, S. Indira – WM07
Musah, Rabi A. – FC07

N

Nagashima, Umpei – MJ07, TL06
Nahvi, Nima-Noah – TJ02
Najjari, Bennaceur – RM06
Nakajima, Kosuke – WF10, RL05
Nakatani, Riouhei – WN06
Nakayama, Naofumi – RL12
Nakhate, Sanjay G. – WC02
Narkin, Kathryn – TG03, FF06
Nascimento, Daniel R. – TB07, TI06
Nauta, Klaas – WH09, RA03
Ndaleh, David D.N. – ML08, ML09
Neeman, Elias M. – FC01, FD06

Negri, Fabrizia – TF03
Neill, Justin L. – ML10
Nejad, Arman – TI08, TI09, RI02
Nemchick, Deacon J – RJ02, RJ08, FE04
Nenov, Artur – TH08
Nesbitt, David – TN01
Nesbitt, David J. – MK04
Neumark, Daniel – MH07
Newby, Josh – WD07
Neyens, Gerda – RM08
Nguyen, Ha Vinh Lam – MA05, TN03, WF01, FB02
Ni, Kang-Kuen – MA02
Nichols, Miranda – RM08
Nickson, Kathleen Ann – WM06, RK01
Nielson, Christopher – TJ05
Nishimiya, Nobuo – RL08
Nishiyama, Akiko – TI05
Nixon, Conor A – FE09
Nole, Ananda Q. – RJ08
Nomura, Katsuki – RL08
North, Nicole – WK06, WK07
North, Sasha C. – WC04
North, Simon – WH03
Novick, Stewart E. – TN03

O

O'Brien, James J – RK07, RK08
O'Brien, Leah C – RK07, RK08
Obenchain, Daniel A. – FB06
Ober, Douglas – WJ07, WJ08
Ohno, Yuki – WN06
Ohshima, Yasuhiro – TM01
Oka, Takeshi – WLUN, RN04
Okumura, Mitchio – WJ07, WJ08
Olejniczak, Malgorzata – WB07
Orito, Masataka – WA09
Orr, Dylan S. – TJ03, WG06
Orr, Vanessa L. – RM03, RM11
Orunesajo, Emmanuel Ayorinde – MH04
OSSEIRAN, Noureddin – FC01, FD06
Owen, Andrew N. – RM03, RM11
Oyama, Takahiro – TG05, WN06
Ozawa, Ryoto – TD08
Ozeki, Hiroyuki – RK06
Ozeki, Masayoshi – WA09

P

Pak, Sarah – TB07
Palko, Jessica – TG04, RJ04
Paoloni, Lorenzo – MJ05

Parish, Carol – FF06
Parker, Roy – MK04
Pasquale, SELLITTO – WF02
Pate, Brooks – FD08
Patkowski, Konrad – FB08
Patterson, David – TE04, TE05, RM07, RM09, FA04
Paul, Anam C. – TB09
Payne, Taylor – WE01
Pazhani, Aassik – MN04
Pazyuk, Elena Alexandrovna – WI09
Peebles, Rebecca A. – FD08
Peebles, Sean A. – FD08
Peña, Isabel – WM07
Perez, Cristobal – TE08
Perez, Evan H – TG08, TG09, WG09
Perrett, Holly – RM08
Perri, Armando N. – RI11
Perrin, Agnes – FC08
Persinger, Thomas D. – MM01, MM02
Peterß, Fabian – TG06
Pezzella, Marco – WH08
Phal, Yamuna Dilip – WE08
Pietropolli Charmet, Andrea – WD06, WM11
pilarisetty, tarakeshwar – WD09
Pille, Laura – FG06
Pinacho, Pablo – FB06, FD02, FD10
Pirali, Olivier – TD02, TN02, WF02, RI05, FG07, FG10
Pitsevich, George – TF07, TG01
Pizzano, Emanuele – FF02
Platakyte, Rasa – WL08
Plunkett, Adele – MN03
Poirier, Bill – RH08
Pollow, Kai – TJ02, TJ04, WG01, WG02
Polyansky, Oleg L. – WB06
POONIA, TAMANNA – TF04
Popov, Andrey – ML01, ML02
Porohovoi, R. – WN05
Pototschnig, Johann V. – WI01
Pradhan, Omkar – RJ02
Pringle, Wallace C. – TN03
Prozument, Kirill – WH07, WK03
Puzzarini, Cristina – TD04, TD05, TI01, RH04, RN06, FB01

Q

Qian, Yujie – WH04
Qin, Yuan – WH10
Quack, Martin – TE01

R

Radloff, Robert G. – RN09
Rakovský, Jozef – RN03
Ramanathan, Nagarajan – FA08
Ramasesha, Krupa – TA05
Ranathunga, Yasashri Ranganath – MH03, MH04
Rao, G. Ramana – TF10
Rao, Mihika – MN03
Rap, Daniel – WA05
Raston, Paul – WM01
Razumtcev, Aleksandr – WE04, WI08
Rebelsky, Jonathan – TM09, TN06, WF06
Reber, Melanie A.R. – TH01
Reboli, Thomas – RJ10
Redlich, Britta – WB08, RI03
Redondo, Pilar – WN11
Reed, Zachary – WB06
Reilly, Jordan – RM08
Remijan, Anthony – MN03, MN08, RN07
Ren, Tong – WC08
Reppert, Mike Earl – TM06
Reyna, Katarina – MM07
Reynolds, Aaron J – TM02
Rice IV, W. H. – FD09
Richard, Cyril – TC01
Richards, Anita M – MN09
Richmond, Geraldine – TO01
Rieker, Gregory B – TL09, WJ09
Rijs, Anouk – WA05
Ritchey, Adam – RN10
Rittgers, Brandon M. – WH01, WH11
Rivilla, Victor Manuel – WN11
Robert, Séverine – TL08
Rodriguez, Arianna – WC07, RK10
Rodriguez, Diego – RL02
Rodríguez-Almeida, Lucas – WN11
Rodriquez Monje, Raquel – RJ02
Rodziewicz, Pawel – WL08
Roenitz, Kevin – TM09
Roesch, Gina – WJ03
Romanov, I. – RH03
Romanzin, Claire – WL09
Ross, Amanda J. – TC11, RK05
Rossi, Corentin – WL09
Rossi, Thomas – TJ07
Rothe, Sebastian – RM08
Rothman, Laurence S. – TC10
Rotteger, Chase H – TM07, WD09
Roucou, Anthony – WF04, FB04, FC09
Roy, P. – FC08
ROY, TARUN – TI04
Roy, Tarun Kumar – WD08

Rullán Buxó, Anna Gabriella del Rosario – TG08, TG09, WG09
Ruscic, Branko – MJ04

S

S. Almeida, Nuno M. – WC03, WC04
Sa'adeh, Hanan – TF03
Sablinskas, Valdas – WL08
Sagan, Cole R – WI07
Sahoo, Nitai Prasad – MI01
Saiz, Caitlyn – FD09
Sakai, Nami – WN06
sakai, takeshi – WN06
Salama, Farid – RN11
Salazar, Karla V. – MI03, RL02
Salomon, Thomas – WG05, WG07
Salumbides, Edcel John – ML07
Salvitti, Giovanna – TF03
Sander, Wolfram – MM10
Santis, Garrett D – RM05
Sanz, M. Eugenia – WB05, WM03, WM07
Sanz-Novo, Miguel – MI02, WL04, WN11, RL04
Sapeshka, Uladzimir – TF07, TG01
Saragi, Rizalina Tama – FD07
Sarka, János – RH08
Sartakov, Boris – MM03
Sarver, Collette C – FG03
Sasada, Hiroyuki – FE03
Sato, Hikaru – WA09
Sato, Takeru – TG05
Sato, Urara – TM01
Satterthwaite, Lincoln – TE04, TE05, RM07, RM09, FA04
Saxena, Shefali – WB05
Sayres, Scott G – MH06, TM07, TM08, WD09
Schewe, Christian – MM03
Schleif, Tim – TG09, WG09
Schlemmer, Stephan – WF11, WG03, WG05, WG07, WN03, WN05, WN08, RJ06, RJ07, RL10, FB07, FG07, FG08
Schlesag, Marcel – TG02
Schmid, Philipp C – WG05
Schmidt, Deborah – MN10
Schmidt, Timothy – WH09, RA03
Schmitz, Joel R – WC07, RK10
Schneider, Erik K. – WL11
Schnell, Melanie – TD03, TE08, WM04, FB05, FB06, FD02, FD10, FG06
Schrader, Paul – TA05
Schran, Christoph – RL10
Schuler, Natalie A. – MI06

Schultz, Chase P – TD06, WF06, WN09
Schultz, Zachary – WE01, WE05, WE11
Schultze, Martin – TA02
Schwaab, Gerhard – WD08
Schwartz, Tal – FE02
Schweer, Sophie M. – RI01
SCHWELL, Martin – WF01, FB02
Schwenke, David – TC02, TC03, TC04, TC05
Scolati, Haley N. – MN02
Sedo, Galen – WL05
Seifert, Johannes – MM03
Seifert, Nathan A. – MI02, TM03, WH07, WK03
Seys, Alexander – TN03
Shaik, Abdul Kalam – ML08, ML09
Shakfa, Mohammad Khaled – RH07
Shao, Kuanliang – ML04
Sharma, Ketan – TB08, TB09, TI02
Shen, Yili – MK07, TK06
Sheps, Leonid – WC11
Shi, Liang – MK02
Shimizu, Akira – WF10, RL05
Shipman, Steven – TD07, TK01, TM09, WF06
Shoup, Deben – WE05
Sibert, Edwin – MH10, TF02, TI09, RA02
Siebert, Mark A. – MN08
Silander, Isak – TC01
Siles, Jose – RJ02
Silfies, Myles C – TH07
Simkó, Irén – RL10
Simon, Fabien – RJ09
Simons, Megan – WI05
Simpson, Garth – WE04, WI08
Sims, Ian R. – TN05, FA02, FA03
Singh, Amandeep – TG11
Singh, Ambesh Pratik – MN09
Singh, Himanshi – TE08, WM04, FD10
Singh, Vipin Bahadur – TF09
Sinjari, Aland – TI04
Sivakumar, P – WE02
Slaughter, Daniel S. – TL05
Smith, Cameron L – ML08
Smith, Houston H. – TF06, RL07, RM03, RM11
Smith, Joshua G – FF05
Smith, Tony – TC11
Soboń, Grzegorz – TC01
Somani, Ankit – MM10
Somogyi, Wilfrid – TC06, TC08, FC10
Song, Hongwei – MH07

Song, Xinli – FF06
Song, Yu – WH10
Sorensen, Daniel – TE04, RM07, RM09
Sorensen, Jason J – FC05
Soulard, Pascale – WF02, RI05
Spaniol, Jean-Thibaut – TN02
Sparks, Elizabeth Renee – TG03, FF06
Speare, Lindsey Ann – TD09
Spezzano, Silvia – WN02
Srishailam, K – TF10
Srivastava, Amit – TM06
Stahl, Pascal – TG02
Stahl, Wolfgang – MA05
Stankiewicz, Kamil – TI05, FB08, FB09
Stanton, John F. – MI01, MI06, MJ03, MJ04, TI02, TN06, WB03, WD02, WL07, RH05
Steenbakkers, Kim – RI03
Steffens, Brendan – FE09
Steimle, Timothy – MM02, WC07, RK10
Stephens, Ian – MN04
Sterczewski, Lukasz A. – WJ07, WJ08
Stewart, David Archie – WD02
Stewart, Gabriel A. – MH03, MH04, TA08
Stewart, Jacob – MM07
Stocka, Joanna – WL08
Stoecklin, Thierry – FB07
Stohner, Jürgen – TE01
Stolarczyk, Nikodem – TI05, FB08, FB09
Stolyarov, Andrey – ML02, TB10, WI09
Strand, Christopher L – RJ01, FE02, FE08, FE10
Strom, Aaron I. – RI10
Studemund, Taarna – TJ02, TJ04, WG01, WG02
Su, Jung-Hsuan – TN09
Su, Wey-Wey – RJ01, FE08
Südmeyer, Thomas – WJ11
Suhm, Martin A. – TI09, RI01, RI02
Suits, Arthur – WJ04, FA01
Sumi, Tatsuki – RK06
Sun, Ge – WH10
Sun, Wenhao – TE08
Sundararajan, K – FA08
Sung, Keeyoon – FE09
Sunuwar, Suresh – FF01, FF04
Sutton, Shaun – TM07, WD09
Suzuki, Masao – RL08
Suzuki, Shota – RK06
Syme, Anna-Maree – RN08
Słowiński, Michał – TI05, FB08

T

Tabor, Daniel P. – WK04
Tachikawa, Masanori – MJ07
Takahashi, Kaito – WC09
Takahashi, Yuiki – MM05
Tamanai, Akemi – WN06
Tamassia, Filippo – WG11
Tamppari, Leslie – RJ02
Tan, Liang Z. – TL05
Tan, Y. – WI10
Tan, Yan – FB08
Tanaka, Hikaru – MJ07
Tang, Adrian – RJ08
Taniguchi, Rin – WF10
Teague, Richard – MN04
Telfah, Hamzeh – TB09, RL11
Telles do Casal, Mariana – RH03
Tennyson, Jonathan – TC07, TC08, TL07, WB06, WH08
Terashkevich, Vera – WI09
Thibault, Franck – TI05, FB08, FB09
Thimmakondu, Venkatesan S. – TI04, WB09
Thissen, Roland – WL09
Thompson, Will E. – MN01, FG01, FG03
Thorpe, James H. – MJ04
Thorwirth, Sven – WB08, WG03, WG05, RJ07, FG07, FG08
Thurston, Richard – TL05
Tian, Aaron – TK06
Tian, Yi – ML04
Tieu, Erick – TJ06
Tikhonov, Denis – FB05
Tobaru, Reo – MM05
Tobata, Yuya – TM01
Toh, Shin Yi – TJ10
Tokaryk, Dennis W. – WC01, RK04, RM10
Toldo, Josene Maria – RH03
Tomchak, Kimberly H. – TJ05, TJ06
Tonolo, Francesca – RH04
Toon, Geoffrey C. – FC08
Toscano, Jutta – MK04
Townsend, Dave – MH01
Trabelsi, Tarek – WC05, FB02
Tross, Jan – TA05
Truppe, Stefan – MM03
Tsukiyama, Koichi – TG05, FG09
Tsybizova, Alexandra – WG08, WI03
Tubergen, Michael – TD09, WF05
Turner, Andrew Martin – MM08
Twagirayezu, Sylvestre – ML10, FF05
Tyree, Daniel J – WE09

U

Ubachs, Wim – ML07
Udagawa, Taro – MJ07
Udrescu, Silviu-Marian – RM08
Uhlíková, Tereza – WN10
Urban, Stepan – WN10, RM03, RM11
Usabiaga, Imanol – WB04

V

Vaeck, Nathalie – MH09
Vaish, Shivangi – WD03, WD04
Valle, Juan Carlos – WN11
Vallet, Valérie – WB07
Van de Sande, Marie – MN08
van den Borne, Bran – RM08
van der Veen, Renske – TH03, TJ07
Van Voorhis, Troy – RA03
van Wijngaarden, Jennifer – TF04
Vandaele, Ann Carine – TL08
Vander Auwera, Jean – MH09, RN03
Vandervort, Joshua A – FE02, FE10
Vanfleteren, Thomas – WD05
Vansco, Michael F. – WH02
Vávra, Karel – TG02, WN10, RM03, RM11
Venkatram Reddy, Byru – TF10
Verde, Andres – MI01, TM04
Vereijken, Arne – TG02
Verhoeven, Sophie – WG01
Vernon, Adam – RM08
Vilesov, Andrey – TG11
Vispoel, Bastien – FE01
Vlahos, Korina – TG04, RJ05
Vo, Binh Nguyet – MM07
Vogel, Simon – WJ11
Von Allmen, Paul – FE04
Votava, Ondřej – RN03
Vura-Weis, Josh – TA03, TH03, TJ07, WC08
Vurgaftman, Igor – WJ07, WJ08

W

Walker, Catherine E – FG03
Walker, Nick – WF01, WM02, FA07, FD04
Waller, Mark P – MI10
Wallick, Rachel – TH03
Walter, Nicole – MM03
Wang, Guanghan – WH02
Wang, Guanjun – FB05, FD03
Wang, Hao – FB01
Wang, Irene – TE05
Wang, Jia – MM08
Wang, Jin – FB08
Wang, Juan – FB01
Wang, Junpeng – RH11
Wang, Lai-Sheng – WA02, WI02
Wang, LiHan – WI06
Wang, Na – RM06
Wang, Shengkai – RH06
Wang, Zhen – WB02
Ward, Timothy B – MJ11
Watanabe, Yoshimasa – WN06
Watkins, Davita – ML08
Watkins, Patrick – TJ01, WA04
Wcislo, Piotr – TI05, FB08, FB09
Weaver, Emily M – WD07
Weber, J. Mathias – MM06, WG10, WL11, RK03
Weber, Thorsten – TL05
Wehres, Nadine – RJ06
Wei, Haoyun – WE07, WJ10
Weis, Patrick – WL11
Welch, Bradley – WC03
Wells, Thresa – WJ01, FF07
Welsh, Blair – TN04, WF03
Werba, Olivia – WH02
Wessolek, Julius – RM08
West, Channing – FD08
Wester, Roland – FB07
Westerfield, J. H. – TN04
Western, Colin – RL06
White, Andrew – MK06, WK01
Widicus Weaver, Susanna L. – MN01, TD06, TD07, TM09, TN06, WB03, WF06, WN09, FG01, FG03
Wijesinghe, Kalpani Hirunika – ML09
Wild, Robert – FB07
Wilkins, Olivia H. – FG01, FG02
Wilkins, Shane – RM08
Williams, Ashley E. – RI06
Wilson, Angela K. – WC03, WC04
Wirth, Vincent – WJ05
Witsch, Daniel – MN07
Wojtewicz, Szymon – TI05
Wolynes, Peter Guy – TL10
Wong, Ying-Tung Angel – TJ10
Wood, Samuel A. – TJ08, RM03, RM11
Woods, Nyla S – RK07
Woods, R. Claude – MI06, TD01, TF05, TF06, TJ08, WB03, RL07, RM03, RM10, RM11
Woon, David E. – FG04
Worth, Graham – TA09
Wright, Andi – TD07
Wright, Catherine – TL02
Wright, Connor J. – TM09, TN06
Wu, Chung-Tse Michael – RJ08

X

Xantheas, Sotiris – RM05
XIE, FAN – FD05
Xu, Yanting – MI10
Xu, Yuago – WB02, WM02, FD07
Xu, Yunjie – TE09, TM03, WM09, FD05
Xu, Zhongxing – RN10
Xue, Ci – RN07, FG05

Y

Yadav, Swatantra Kumar – FA11
Yaddehige, Mahesh Loku – ML08
Yáñez, Manuel – MI01
Yang, Haifeng – MN04
Yang, Jie – TB02, WI04
Yang, Lei – FC06
Yang, Q.-Y. – WI10
Yang, Qian – TM03
Yang, Xiaofei – RM08
Ye, Hexu – TI01
Ye, Hong-Zhou – RA03
Ye, Jun – MK04
Yi, Jun – MK07, TB06, RH11
Yocum, Katarina – FG01, FG02
Yokie, Eric – TH09
Yong, Haiwang – TA04
yu, xuan – RM06
Yu, Yao – TB02, WI04
Yu, Ziwei – FF10
Yuan, Daofu – WA02, WI02
Yukiya, Tokio – RL08
Yurchenko, Sergei N. – TC06, TC07, TC08, TL07, WH08, WI11, FC10

Z

Zaborowski, Mikolaj – TI05
Zagorec-Marks, Wyatt – WL11, RK03
Zakuskin, Aleksandr – ML01, ML02
Zapata Trujillo, Juan C. – RI04
Zaytsev, Sergey – ML02
Zdanovskaia, Maria – MI06, TD01, TF06
Zega, Thomas J. – RN05
Zehnacker-Rentien, Anne – MA06, RI01
Zeng, Mei Fei – TJ10
Zeng, Shaoshan – WN06
Zhang, Angie – WF03
Zhang, Chaoqun – MJ08, TB01, TB04, TB11, TL01

Zhang, Chenghao – MH10, TL10
Zhang, Jingsong – ML04, WH10, FC06
Zhang, Lei – TB02, WI04
Zhang, Shaofeng – RM06
Zhang, Yue-Rou – WA02, WI02
Zhang, Yujia – WE07, WJ10
Zhao, Jianbao – RL06, FF05
Zheng, Xianfeng – WH10
Zheng, Xuechen – MJ08, TB01, TB11
Zheng, Yang – FB01
Zhou, Mingfei – MM09, FB05, FD03
Zhou, Zunwu – MI03
Zhu, Guo-Zhu – MM04
Zhu, Ying – TB06
Zingsheim, Oliver – WF11, WN08, RJ07, FG07
Ziurys, Lucy M. – MN05, MN09, MN10, RA01, RK02, RN05
Zobov, Nikolay F. – WB06
Zoltowski, Chelsea M. – WE11
Zou, Luyao – WN01, WN04, WN07
Zou, Wenli – RK07
Żuchowski, Piotr – FB08
Zulch, Carsten – RM08
Zwier, Timothy S. – TN04, WF03, FA06

THANKS TO OUR 2022 SPONSORS!

Coblentz Society

Fostering the understanding and application of vibrational spectroscopy since 1954

The Coblentz Society, founded in 1954, is a non-profit organization of scientists interested in fostering the understanding and application of vibrational spectroscopy within the fields of Chemistry, Physics, and Biology. Vibrational spectroscopy includes infrared (IR), near-infrared (NIR), and Raman spectroscopies along with their associated sampling techniques, instrumentation, and data processing. The Coblentz Society is a technical affiliate of the Society for Applied Spectroscopy (SAS).

As part of fulfilling our mission, the Society presents several awards to recognize the efforts of professional spectroscopists who have made significant contributions in vibrational spectroscopy. These Awards are presented at conferences where The Coblentz Society is an active participant - Pittcon, ISMS, SciX, and EAS. The Society is a member organization of the Federation of Analytical and Spectroscopy Societies (FACSS).

By encouraging the visibility and recognition of quality science, the Society hopes to highlight solutions and chart new opportunities in vibrational spectroscopy.

Mentoring *(www.coblentz.org/mentor-program)*

Everyone needs mentors – people who guide us by advising, questioning, doubting, or supporting us as we progress through life. Mentoring is for everyone at all stages of their career; we are happy to advise anyone whose interest is in the interaction of light with matter. One way in which the Society promotes mentoring is through our speed mentoring program. Speed Mentoring is a fun, fast-paced session that enables a structured interaction between young spectroscopists and chemists and a dozen or more spectroscopists and chemists from various industries, academia, and government labs.

www.coblentz.org

Awards (www.coblentz.org/awards)

THE COBLENTZ AWARD
The Society's original award (first awarded in 1964) presented to an outstanding molecular spectroscopist under the age of 40

THE CRAVER AWARD
Recognizing the efforts of young professional spectroscopists for significant contributions in applied analytical vibrational spectroscopy

THE WILLIAMS-WRIGHT AWARD
Presented to an industrial spectroscopist who has made significant contributions to vibrational spectroscopy while working in industry

THE LIPPINCOTT AWARD
Presented to scientists who have made significant contributions to vibrational spectroscopy as judged by their influence on other scientists. Co-sponsored by the Coblentz Society, SAS, and Optica.

THE WILLIAM G. FATELEY & STUDENT AWARDS
Encouraging young scientists to pursue studies in vibrational spectroscopy

Grants & Scholarships (www.coblentz.org/awards/grantsandscholarships)

TRAVEL & CHILDCARE GRANTS
These grants assist in defraying the costs of travel and childcare to one of the conferences where the Coblentz Society is an active participant, including: Pittcon, SciX, EAS, ICAVS, ICORS, and ISMS.

SCHOLARSHIPS
Scholarships help defray part of the tuition costs for courses offered by **Infrared & Raman Courses, Inc.** These courses are Coblentz-affiliated activities and have been presented annually for over 50 years, historically at MIT and Bowdoin College. The aim of the courses is to provide a rigorous foundation for interpretation of vibrational spectra.

www.coblentz.org

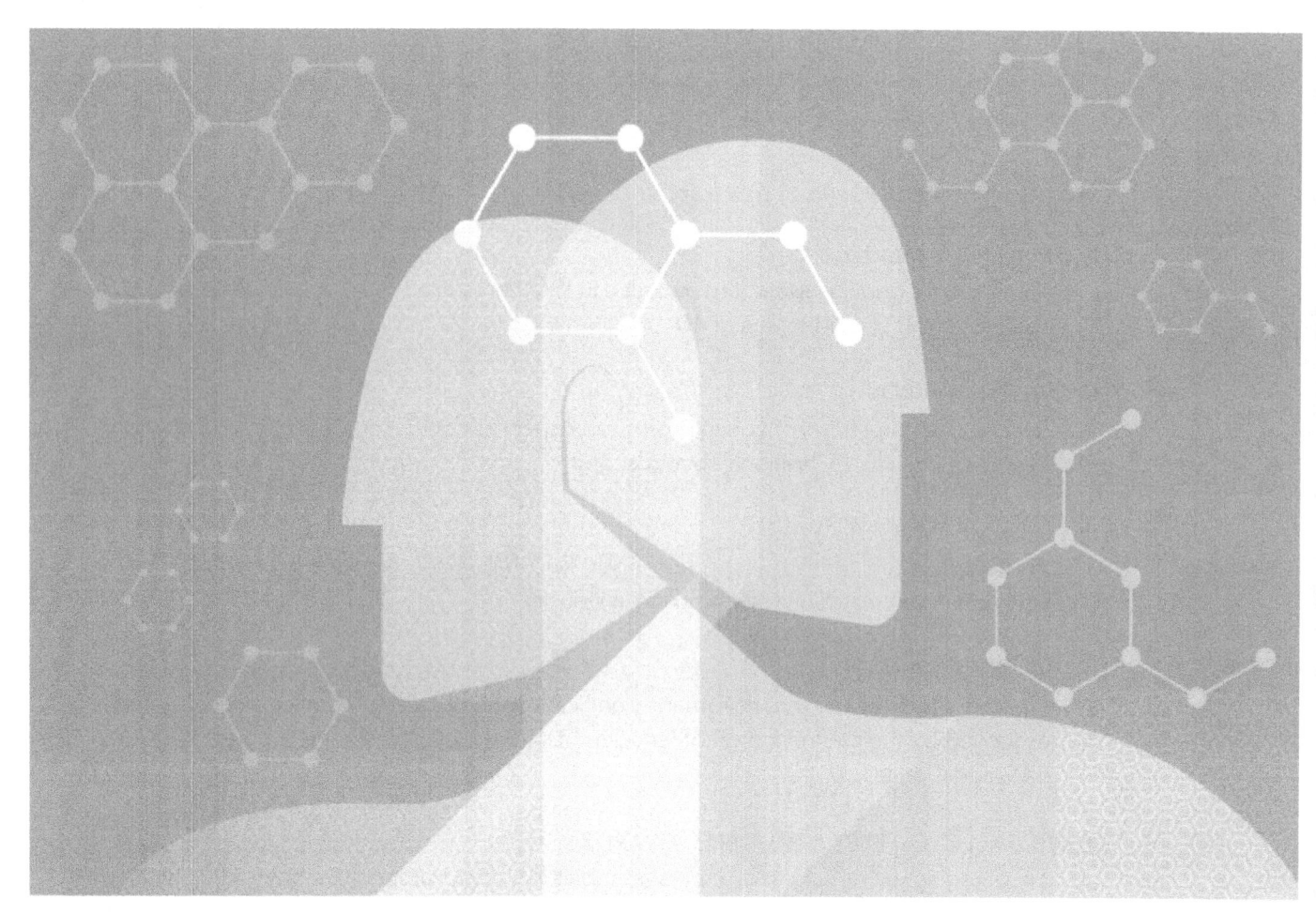

"Information is not knowledge"
ALBERT EINSTEIN

Knowledge is what, at any given moment in human history, passes for Truth. It is our best understanding of the way things are. It is the sum total and highest expression of search and discovery, of all our intellectual strivings.

Elsevier is first and foremost, a knowledge brand. It transforms data and information - the raw materials and building blocks of knowledge - into a vital, organic system of ideas that produces solutions to critical human challenges. It achieves this by combining information with digital tools, platforms, and analytics that dynamically 'activate' it, to create knowledge that is both empowered and empowering - placing them in the hands of authors, educators, scientists, researchers, clinicians, professionals, and students.

By placing knowledge into the hands of our clients and end-users, Elsevier enables them to be more efficient, effective, and productive at what they do. It makes them more collaborative and competitive. It allows them to perform important endeavors at a higher pitch, to realize the ideal, and to expand our sense of the possible.

Elsevier empowers knowledge, which empowers those who use it. elsevier.com

ELSEVIER

Volume 385, March 2022

ISSN 0022-2852

ELSEVIER

Journal of MOLECULAR SPECTROSCOPY

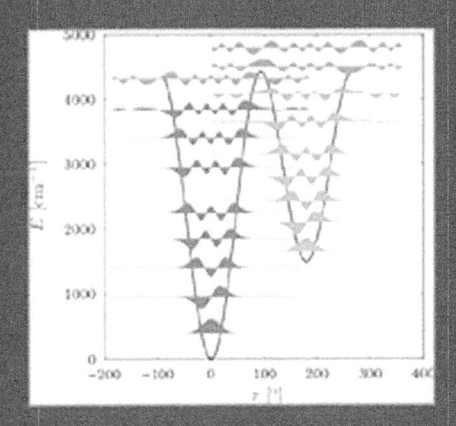

Cover Art: Variational vibrational states of HCOOH (Alberto Martín Santa Daría, Gustavo Avila, Edit Mátyus 385 (2022) 111617).

Editors-in-Chief
Michael Heaven

online at www.sciencedirect.com
ScienceDirect

Ideal vacuum cube

SEALING TECHNOLOGY
TAPER SEAL
PATENT No.
US 9,969,527 B2

We offer a unique patented modular vacuum chamber solution for your process. Each side of the aluminum vacuum chamber frame geometry accepts one of many vacuum chamber wall options, allowing a myriad of feedthrough, vacuum port, or window possibilities. An optical breadboard on the vacuum side facilitates fastening hardware. Prototyping processes or running different high vacuum experiments is no longer limited by expensive, application-specific welded vacuum chambers.

- 6x6x12
- 6x12x12
- 6x12x12
- 6x6x6
- 6x6x12
- 6x6x12
- 12x12x12
- 24x24x24

Ideal vacuum cube
MILLED CHAMBERS
MADE IN USA

Ideal Vacuum Products LLC | idealvac.com | 505.872.0037

Ideal vacuum WELDED VACUUM CHAMBERS

Ideal Vacuum manufactures welded aluminum and stainless steel vacuum chambers for most high-vacuum applications. Each welded vacuum chamber is available with preconfigured flange options and is sold with your choice of vacuum chamber door material. Ideal Vacuum will also quickly and efficiently customize any vacuum chamber to your exact specifications.

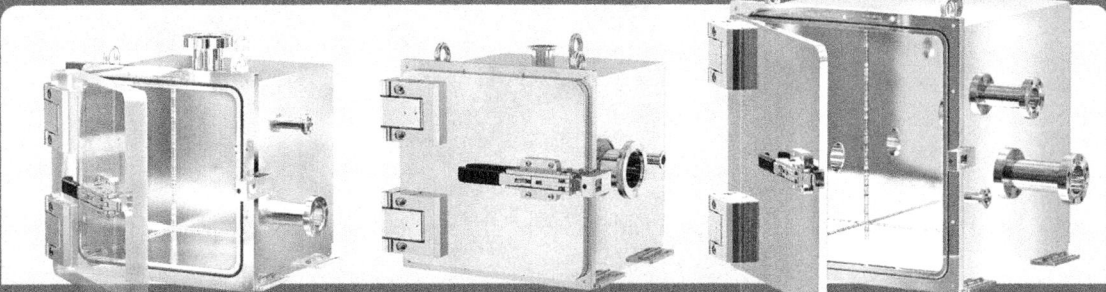

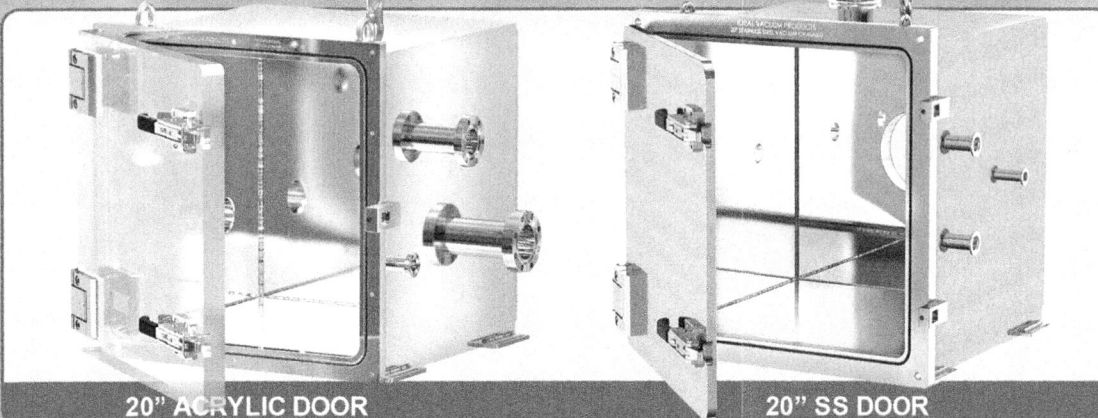

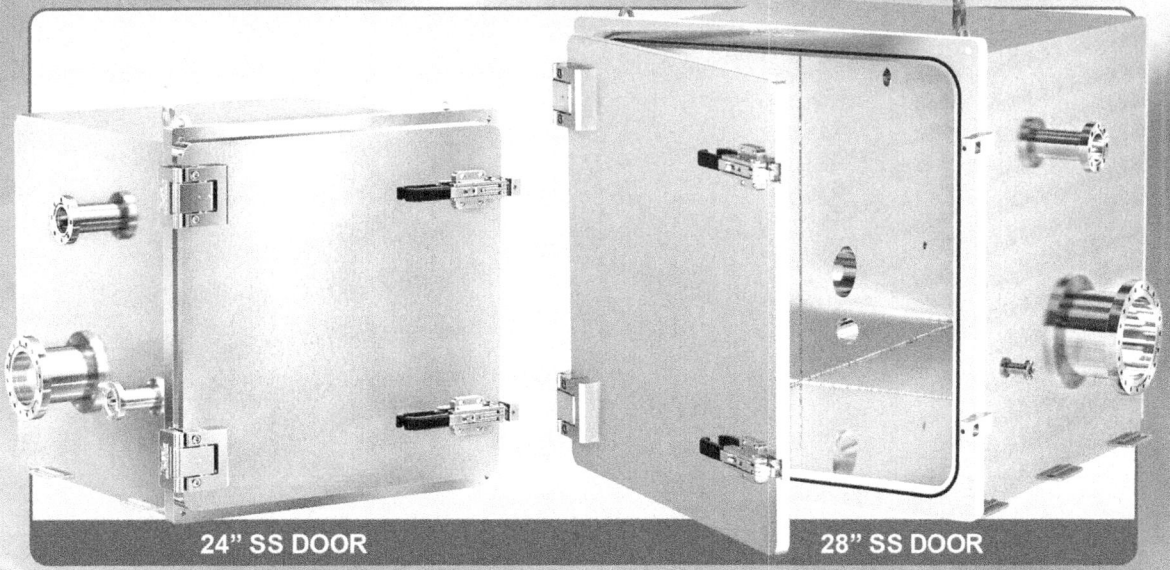

MADE IN USA

- 12" ACRYLIC DOOR
- 12" SS DOOR
- 16" SS DOOR
- 20" ACRYLIC DOOR
- 20" SS DOOR
- 24" SS DOOR
- 28" SS DOOR

Ideal Vacuum Products LLC | idealvac.com | 505.872.0037

Plays well with others.*

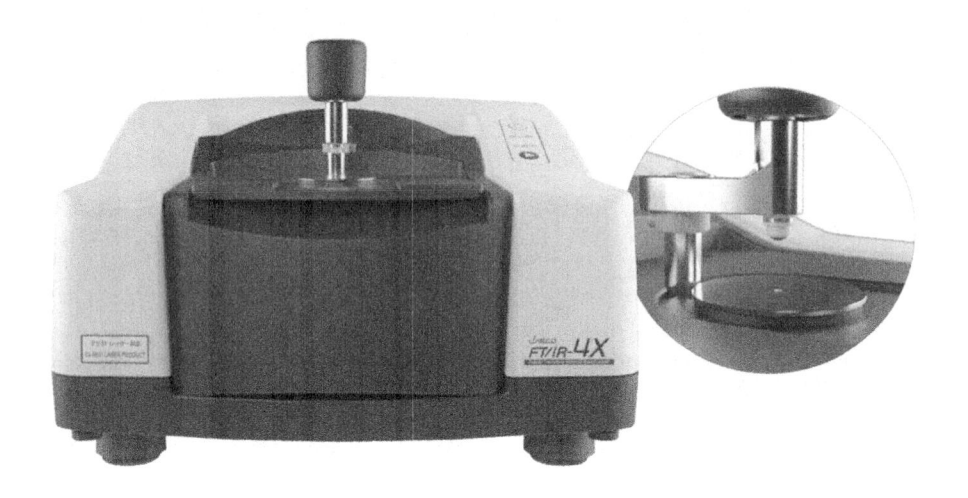

JASCO developed the first infrared spectrophotometer, the DS-101, in 1954. Since then, we have developed a long line of innovative products that has led us to the new compact FT/IR-4X and a 30% reduction in power consumption. The 4X has functionality and expandability only seen in research grade instruments.

Full-sized sampling accessories:

- Transmission
- ATR
- Diffuse Reflectance
- Gas
- Microscopy

Choice of ranges:

Standard 7,800 - 350 cm^{-1}

Near to Mid IR 11,500 - 375 cm^{-1}

Mid to Far IR 6,000 - 220 cm^{-1}

Mid to Far IR 6,000 - 50 cm^{-1}

FT/IR-4X

www.jascoinc.com

*Other:

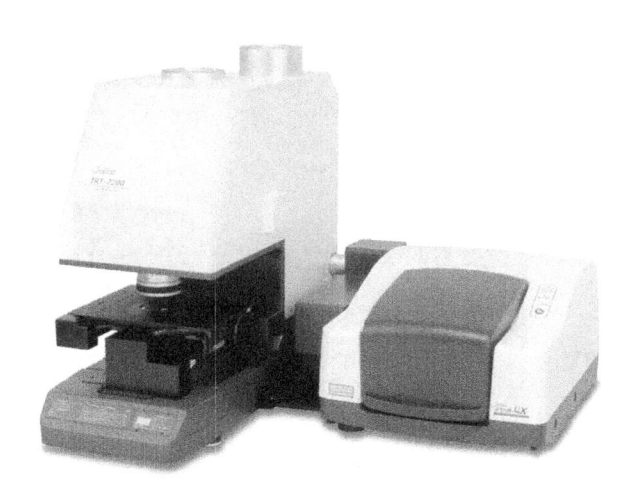

FT/IR-4X spectrometer & IRT-5200 IR microscope with unique JASCO technology.

IQ Mapping™
Versatile ATR mapping with IR microscopy. IQ Mapping allows the ATR to image an area without raising and lowering the objective form the sample. Great for soft materials that deform under pressure or for gel and liquid samples than can easily move.

ClearView™
Use this ATR to view and identify the exact measurement point, then observe the contact position as the sample comes into contact with the crystal. Can be used with germanium, diamond and zinc sulfide prism crystals. Combined with the pressure stage control for exact and repeatable pressure.

Spectra Manager™ Suite
Complete imaging software, easy to use, powerful and flexible, easily chemically map samples with multiple components using false-color imaging.

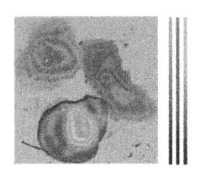

JASCO

North American ALMA Regional Center (NA ARC)

The North American scientific community access to the **Atacama Large Millimeter/submillimeter Array (ALMA)**

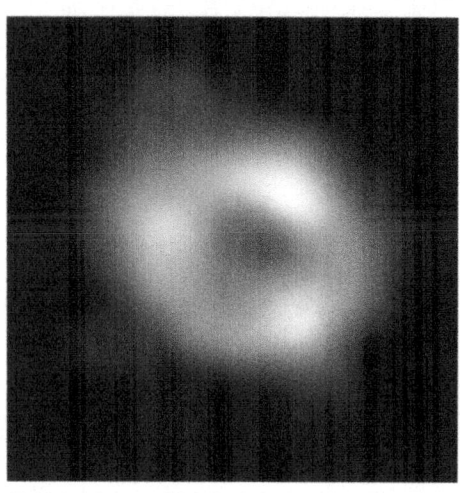

Headquartered at the **National Radio Astronomy Observatory (NRAO)** in Charlottesville, Virginia

The first direct image of Sagittarius A*, the black hole at the center of the Milky Way. Credit: Event Horizon Telescope Collaboration/National Science Foundation

Outreach services to everyone interested in ALMA science:

Data Reduction and Expert Analysis Assistance: Travel and lodging support to visit the NA ARC for investigators of successful ALMA programs, archival researchers, and users needing help preparing the technical aspects of future ALMA proposals.

Data Reduction Parties: 10-12 ALMA users visit the NA ARC for a three-day intensive data reduction training.

Summer Student Program: Introducing undergraduate/graduate students to innovative research.

Student Observing Support: Funds graduate students working on eligible ALMA proposals.

Graduate Pre-Doctoral Program: Conduct the last 2 years of thesis research under the supervision of an NRAO scientist funded by NRAO.

ALMA Ambassador Postdoctoral Fellows Program: Provides training and $10,000 research grant to postdoctoral researchers interested in expanding their ALMA/interferomerty expertise and sharing that knowledge with their home institutions through ALMA proposal writing workshops.

To learn more about the NA ARC and ALMA, visit:
science.nrao.edu/facilities/alma

National Radio Astronomy Observatory (NRAO)

Founded in 1956, the NRAO provides state-of-the-art radio telescope facilities for use by the international scientific community. NRAO telescopes are open to all astronomers regardless of institutional or national affiliation. Observing time on NRAO telescopes is available on a competitive basis to qualified scientists after evaluation of research proposals on the basis of scientific merit, the capability of the instruments to do the work, and the availability of the telescope during the requested time.

science.nrao.edu

NRAO is a facility of the National Science Foundation operated under cooperative agreement by Associated Universities, Inc.

stretch.
Fully-automated tuning at high resolution

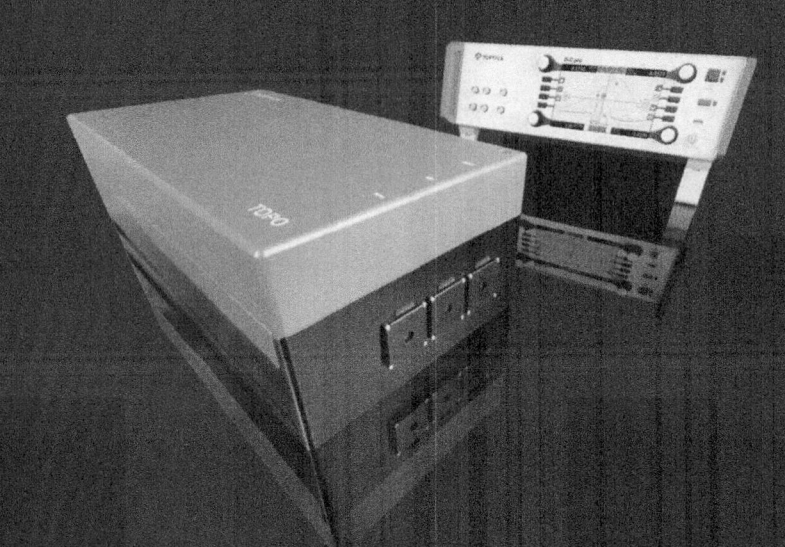

2500 – 6900 cm⁻¹
CW optical parametric oscillator

CW optical parametric oscillator for continuous molecular spectroscopy of "stretch" vibrations...

- Narrow linewidth: 2 MHz (1·10⁻⁴ cm⁻¹)
- Hands-free motorized tuning
- 1.45 .. 4.00 µm

TOPTICA

learn more...

www.toptica.com/TOPO

◎ TOPTICA

STRETCH your lab capabilities with the TOPO

TOPTICA's TOPO, a continuous-wave tunable optical parametric oscillator, provides continuous high-resolution tuning between 2500 - 4500 cm^{-1}. It is the ideal tool for tunable laser absorption spectroscopy of molecular stretch vibrations, and we have recently demonstrated advanced capabilities like frequency modulation spectroscopy, cavity-enhanced spectroscopy, and even dual comb spectroscopy from the TOPO.

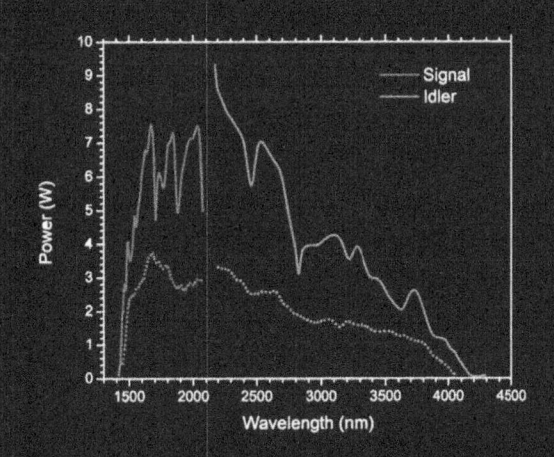

Join our Lunch-and-Learn:
Tuesday, June 21 • 12:30pm

Register at:
go.illinois.edu/ISMS_Toptica_LnL

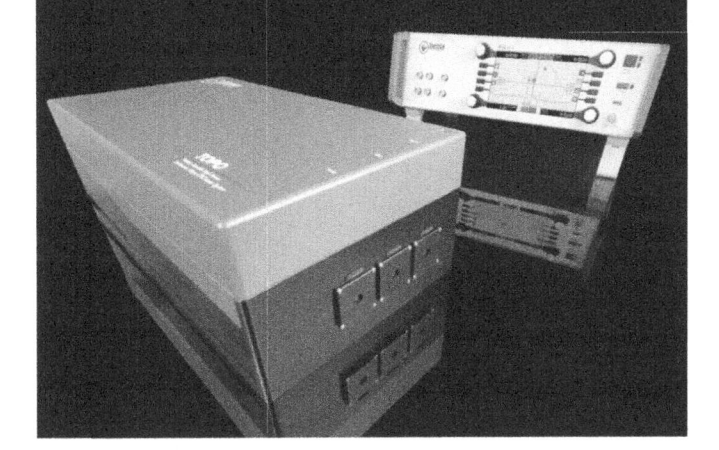

Lunch-N-Learn
Chiral Molecular Spectroscopy
Monday, June 20, 2022
12:40 – 1:35 pm, 157 Noyes Lab

Chiral molecular spectroscopy is best known through circular dichroism, namely the study of higher order protein structures. However, the usefulness of circular dichroism can be expanded to study other molecular systems such as metal mediated organic complexes. JASCO has been an innovator in CD (the differential *absorption* of circularly polarized light), and has also lead the field of an equally difficult measurement: circularly polarized luminescence or CPL (the differential *emission* of circularly polarized light). CPL is particularly useful for emerging technologies such as biosensors, optical devices and displays (like organic LEDs known as OLEDS).

The JASCO Molecular Spectroscopy team would like to invite you to join us for a Lunch-n-Learn session on Chiral Spectroscopy. Dr. Forrest Kohl will explain Circular Dichroism and CPL methods, reviewing theory and measurement. A survey of applications for both methods will be presented, ranging from biomolecules to metal complexes. Come and see if CD and CPL can provide insights on your samples!

Please register online with your name, email, and department using this link: https://go.illinois.edu/ISMS_JASCO_LnL

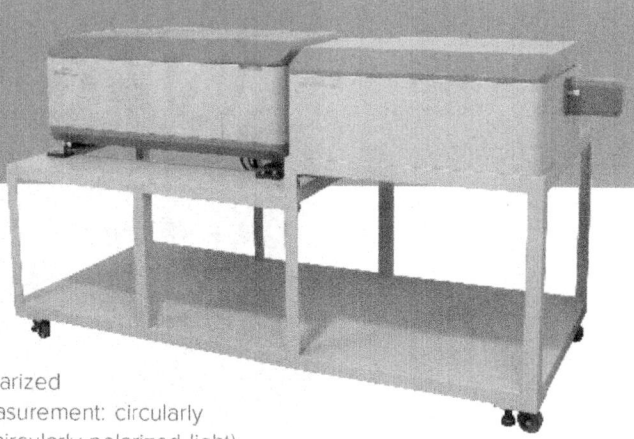

JASCO

Sherry L. Hemmingsen, Ph.D.
Product Specialist
Molecular Spectroscopy
shemmingsen@jascoinc.com
Cell: 410-924-8353

Forrest R. Kohl, Ph.D.
Spectroscopy Applications Scientist
fkohl@jascoinc.com

www.**jasco**inc.com

ISMS MEETING VENUE INFORMATION

All contributed talks will be held in the Chemistry complex (and immediately adjoining buildings). The plenary talks will be held across the quad (about 600') in Foellinger Auditorium.

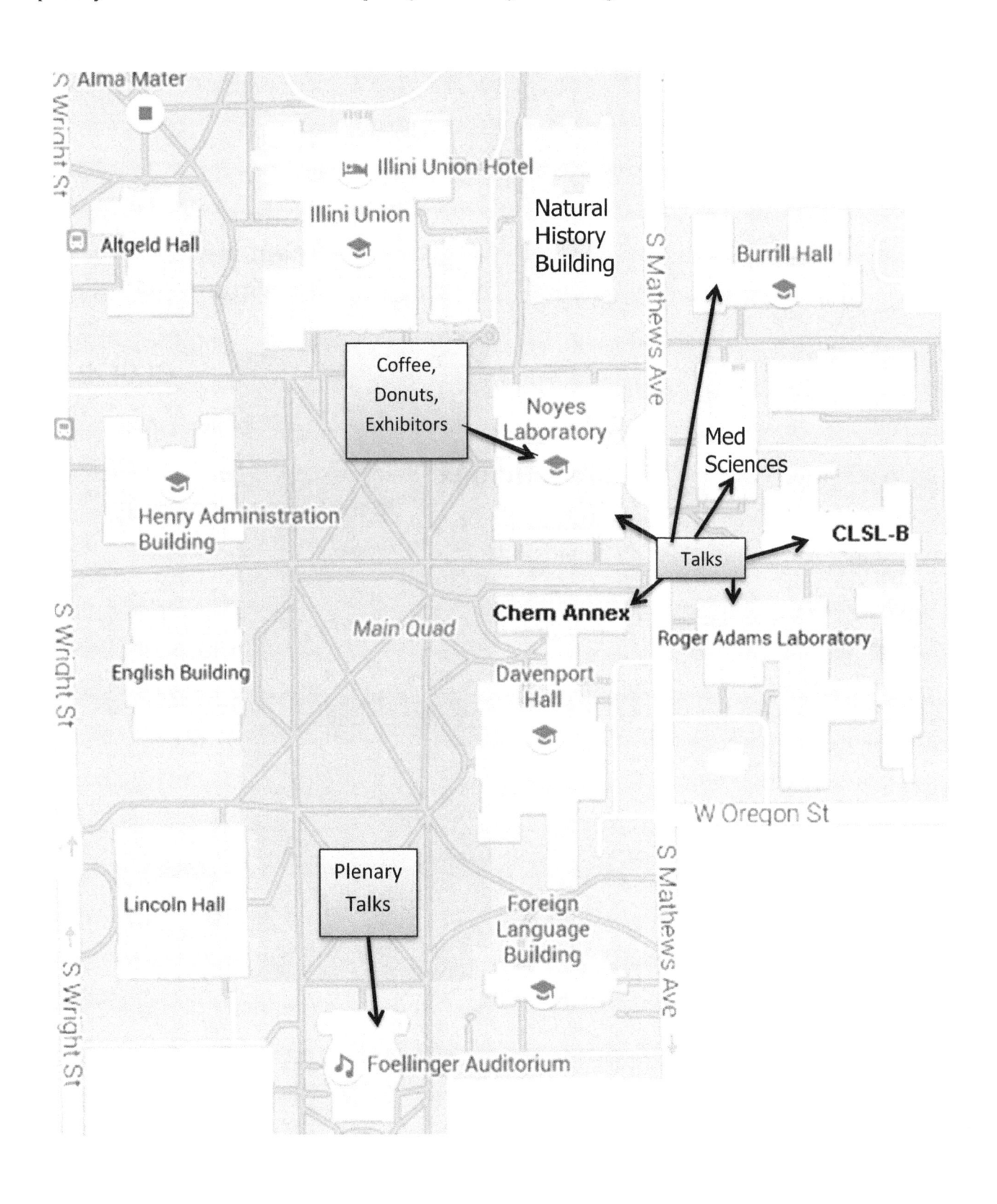

ACCESSIBLE ENTRANCES

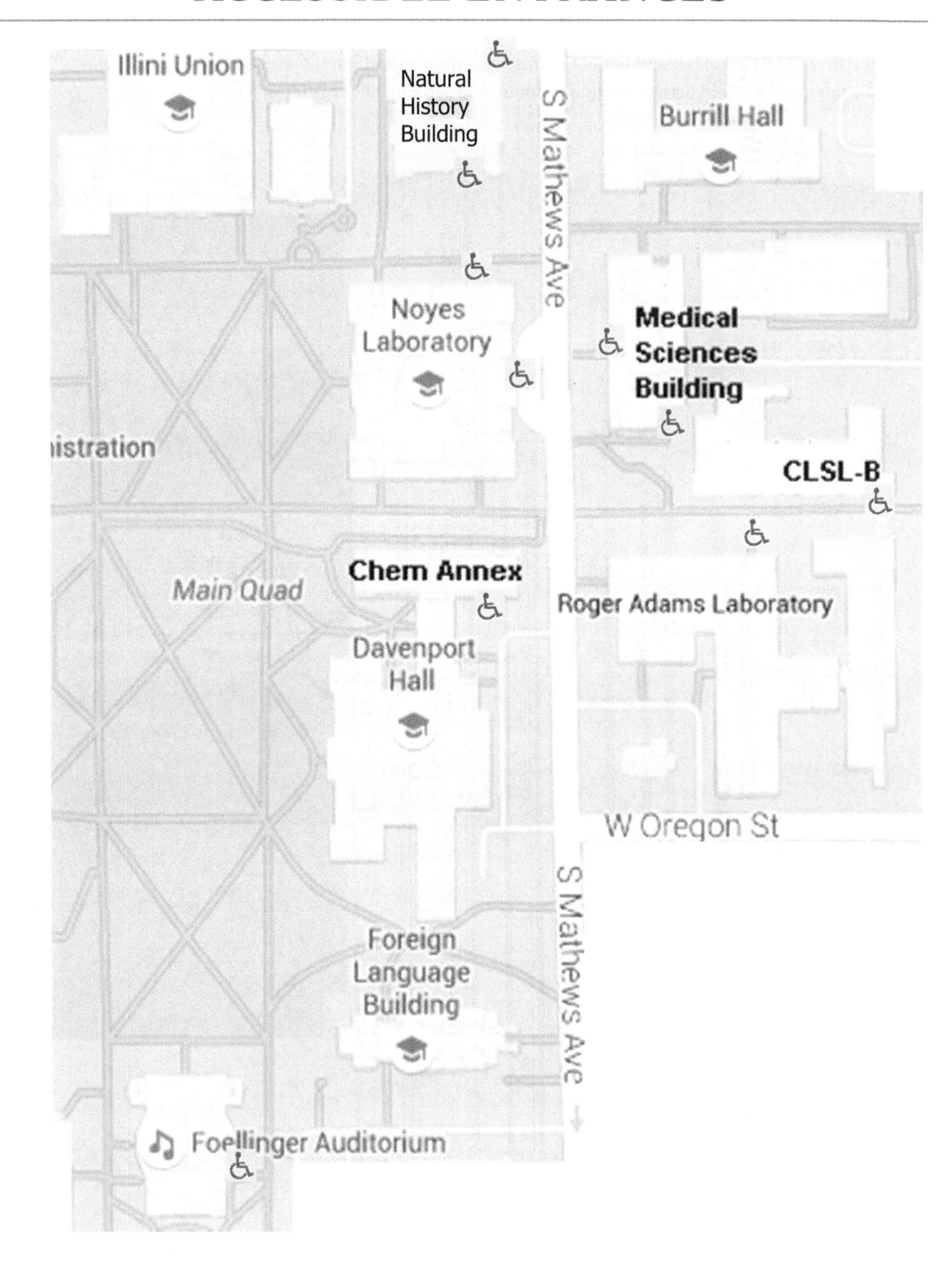

NOYES LABORATORY (NL)

Noyes Laboratory houses our Registration and Exhibitor/Refreshment Rooms (Chemistry Library), the Computer Lab (151), and two lecture halls (NL 100 and 217).

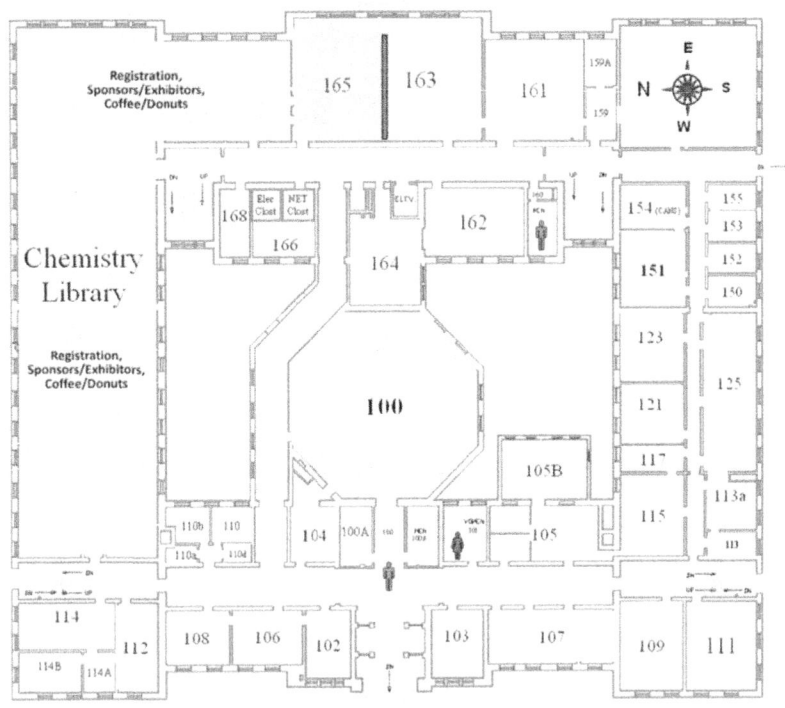

Noyes Laboratory - 1st Floor

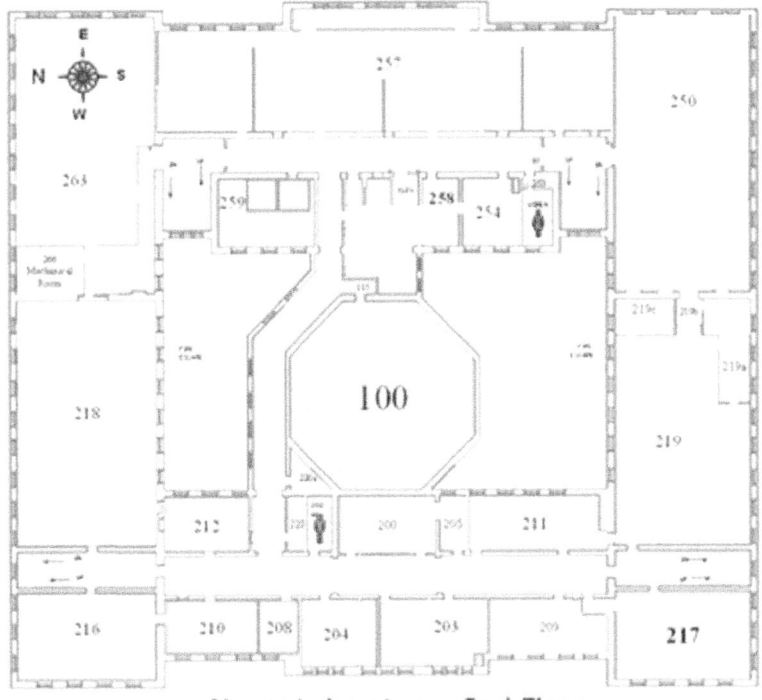

Noyes Laboratory - 2nd Floor

CHEMISTRY ANNEX (CA)

Chemistry Annex is immediately to the south of Noyes Laboratory across a pedestrian walkway. It has one lecture hall (CA 1024)

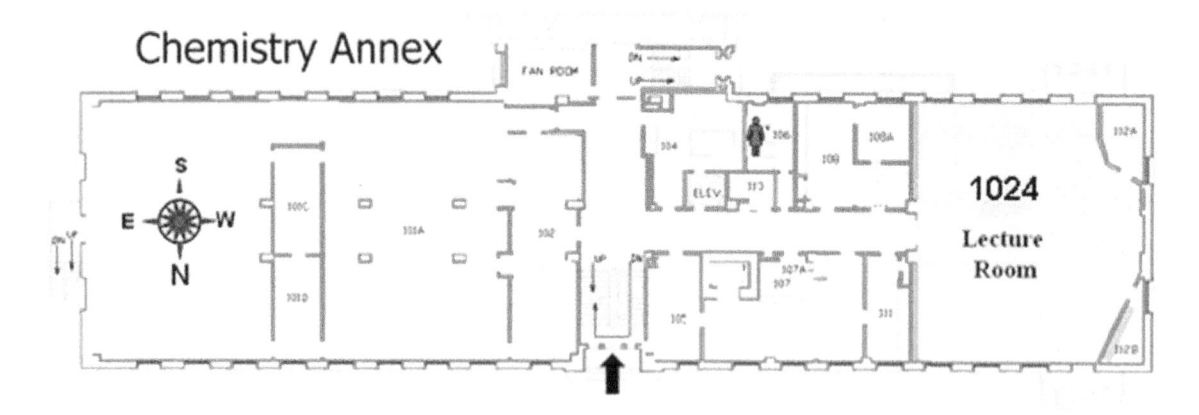

ROGER ADAMS LABORATORY (RAL)

Roger Adams Laboratory is across the street to the east of Chemistry Annex. It has one lecture hall (RAL 116). Please note that in Roger Adams Lab, the ground level is called "Ground" and the First Floor is equivalent to the Second Floor in the other buildings.

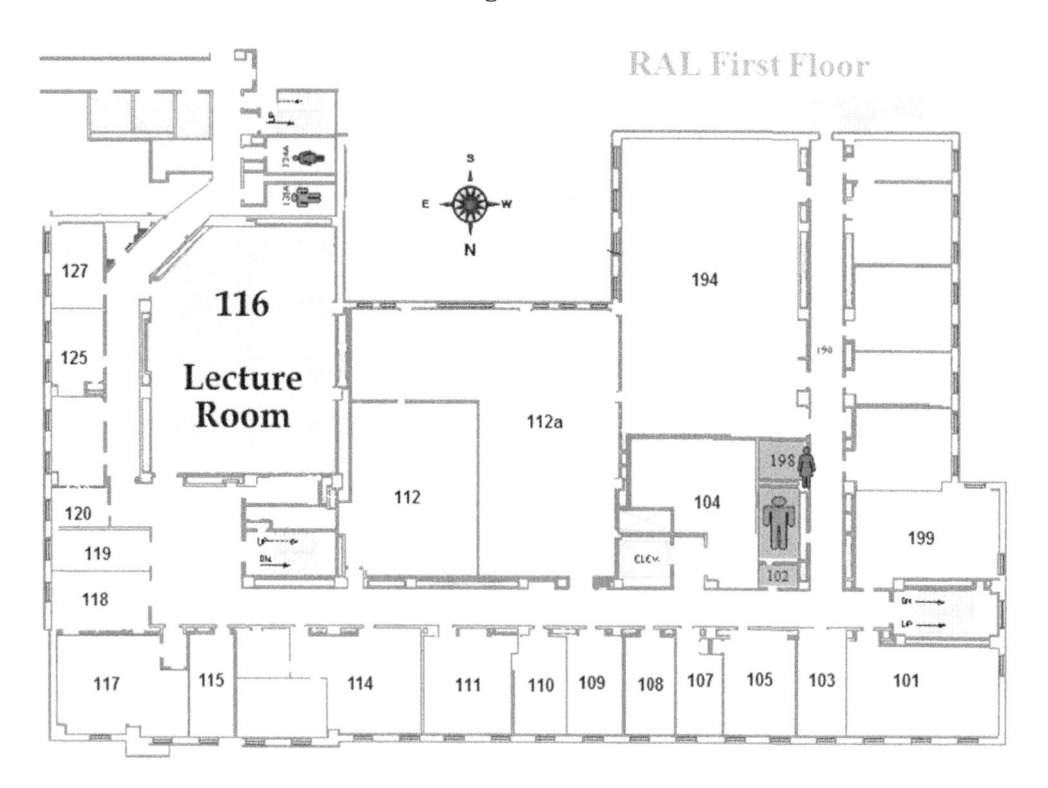

CHEMICAL AND LIFE SCIENCES (CLSL)

CLSL is a multi-wing building located across the street to the east of Noyes Laboratory. The lecture hall (CLSL B102) is in the B wing across the pedestrian walkway to the northeast of Roger Adams.

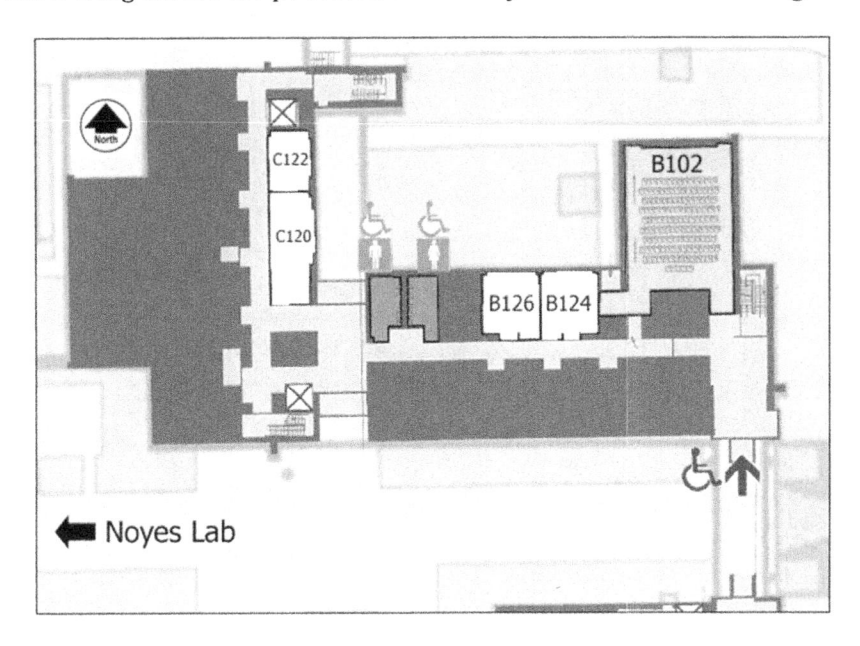

MEDICAL SCIENCES BUILDING (MSB)

Medical Sciences is across the pedestrian walkway to the north of RAL. It has one lecture hall (274).

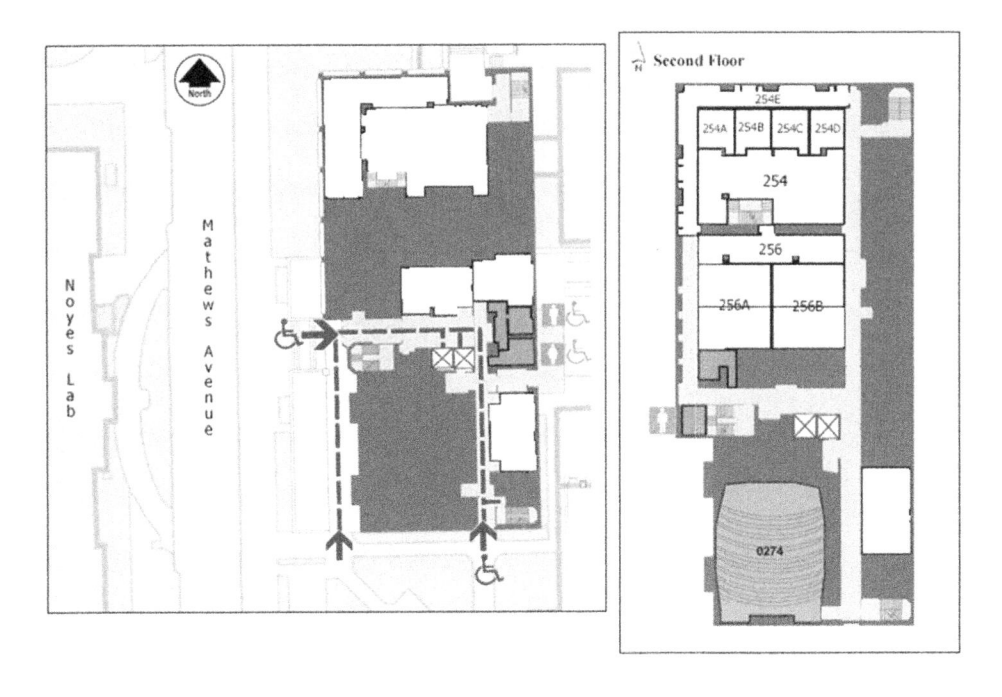

BURRILL HALL

Burrill Hall is due north of Medical Sciences. It has one lecture hall (124).

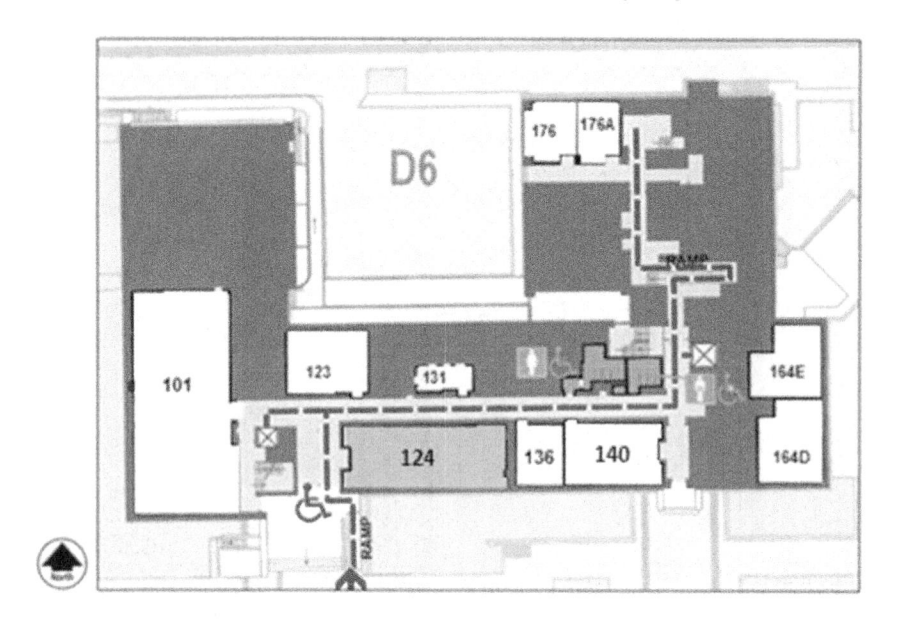

Foellinger Auditorium (Plenary and Intermission)

Foellinger Auditorium is located at the south end of the Quad. The main doors on the north (quad) side will open at 8:10 AM (the side ADA/wheelchair door will be open around 8:00 AM). There is seating on the main level and the upper balcony. There is no elevator in the building.

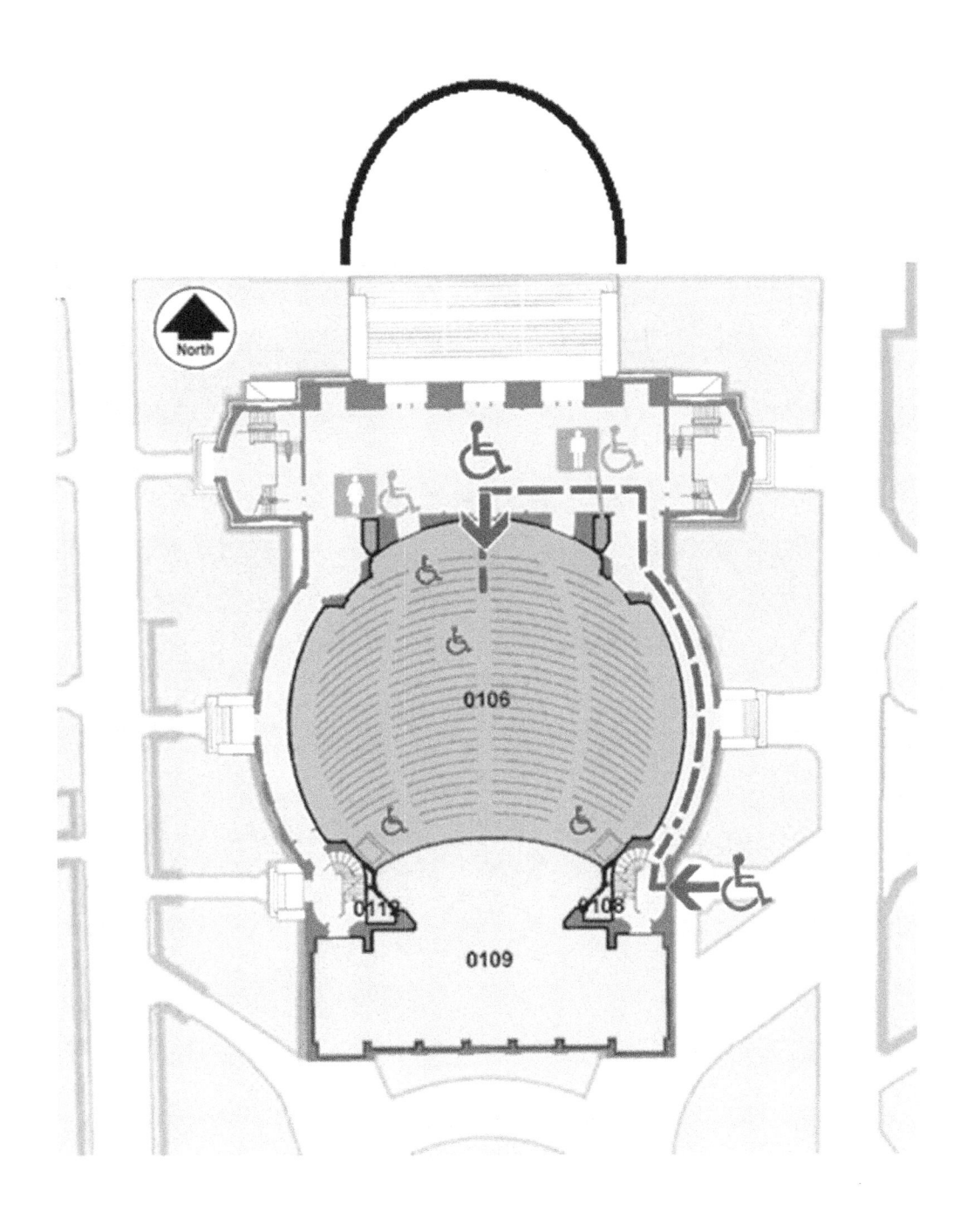

PARKING (E14) TO BOUSFIELD DORM

If you purchase a parking permit and are staying at the dorm, you will park in lot E14 (any spot). E14 is nearly due south of Bousfield Hall Dorm.

Parking enforcement begins at 6:00 AM on Monday, so you will need to have your car in lot E14 with your permit displayed before then. There are many parking meters on E. Peabody Drive (and in the lot across from Bousfield) if you wish to park closer for short periods (25 cents/15 minutes – generally between 6 AM and 6 PM, but check the meter because some go until 9 PM).

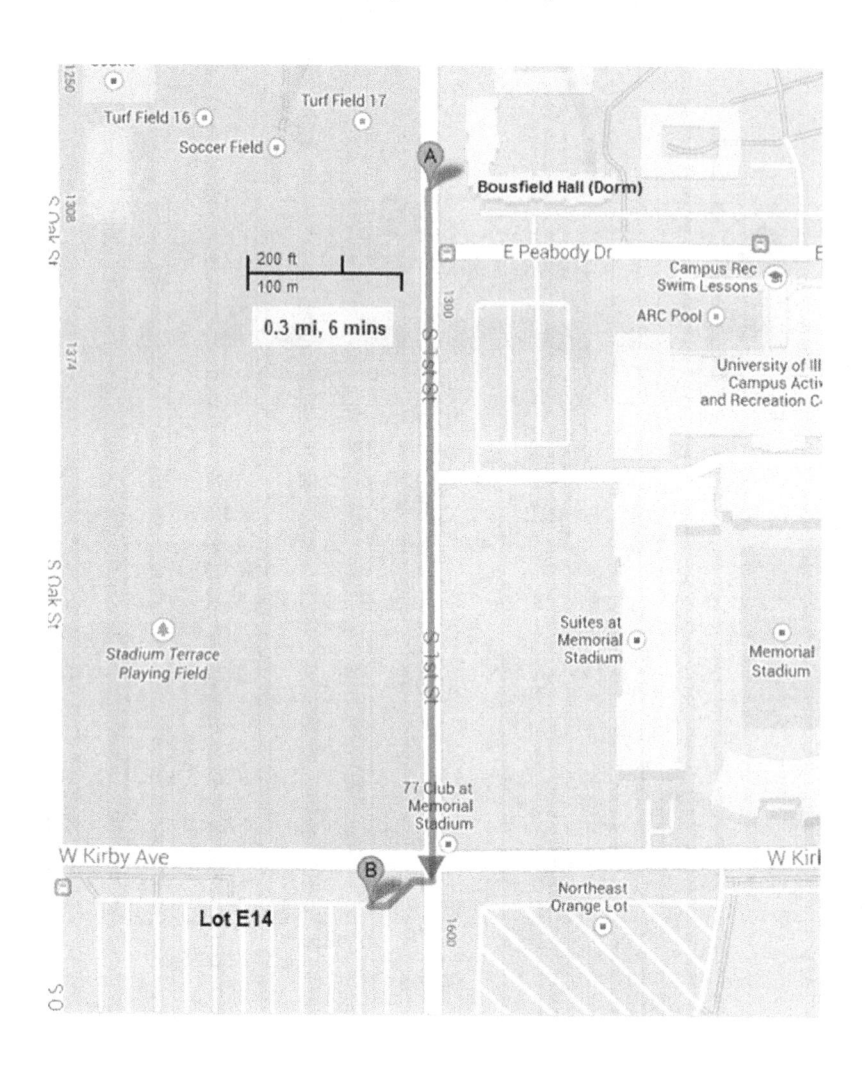

BOUSFIELD/WASSAJA DORM to MEETING VENUE (walking)

Bousfield & Wassaja Halls are just under a mile (15-20 minute walk) from the main symposium buildings

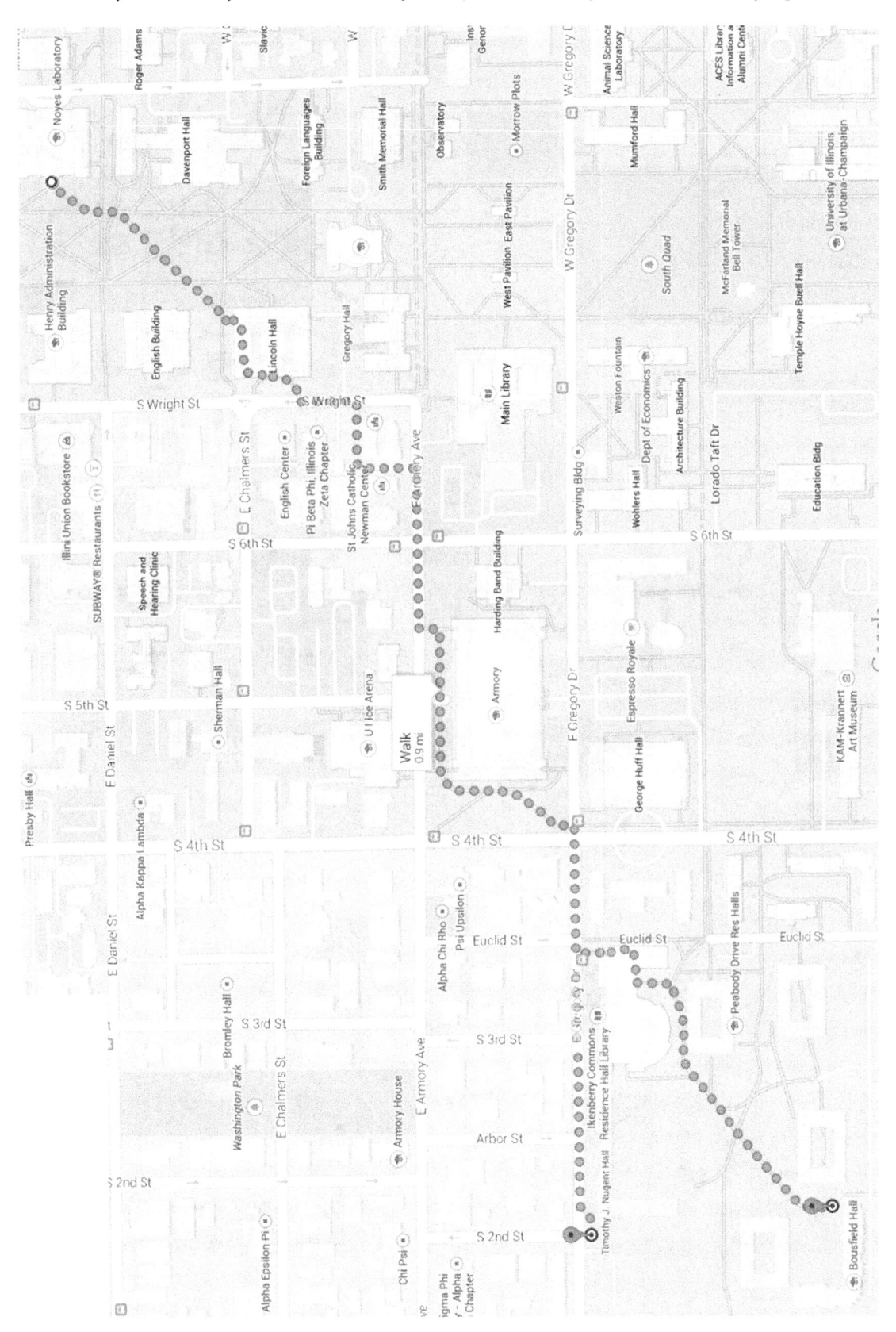

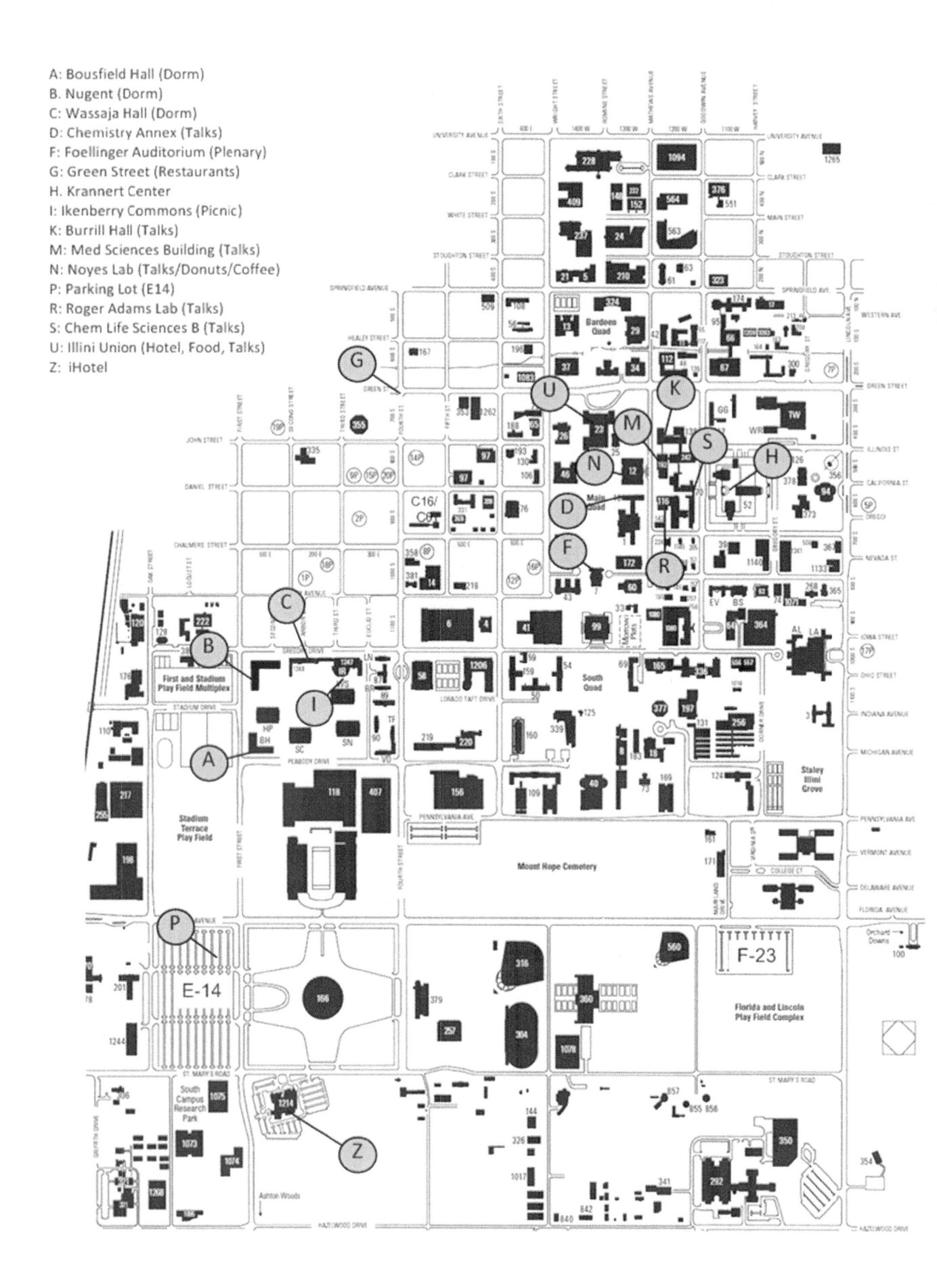

A: Bousfield Hall (Dorm)
B: Nugent (Dorm)
C: Wassaja Hall (Dorm)
D: Chemistry Annex (Talks)
F: Foellinger Auditorium (Plenary)
G: Green Street (Restaurants)
H: Krannert Center
I: Ikenberry Commons (Picnic)
K: Burrill Hall (Talks)
M: Med Sciences Building (Talks)
N: Noyes Lab (Talks/Donuts/Coffee)
P: Parking Lot (E14)
R: Roger Adams Lab (Talks)
S: Chem Life Sciences B (Talks)
U: Illini Union (Hotel, Food, Talks)
Z: iHotel

BOUSFIELD/WASSAJA DORM to MEETING VENUE (bus)

There is convenient and free bus service between Bousfield/Wassaja Dorms and 1 block from the meeting venue. The Yellow Line picks up on the corner of First and Peabody (Bousfield), and also on Gregory Drive (Wassaja) in front of Ikenberry Commons, drops off at the Krannert Center (across the street from CLSL-B. Return locations are the same but across the street. The Yellow Line will also take you to downtown Champaign, but you will need to pay for your return (only iStops are free). Approximately every 10 minutes during the day.

PLEASE NOTE NEW DROP-OFF LOCATION AT KRANNERT CENTER DUE TO WRIGHT STREET CLOSURE!

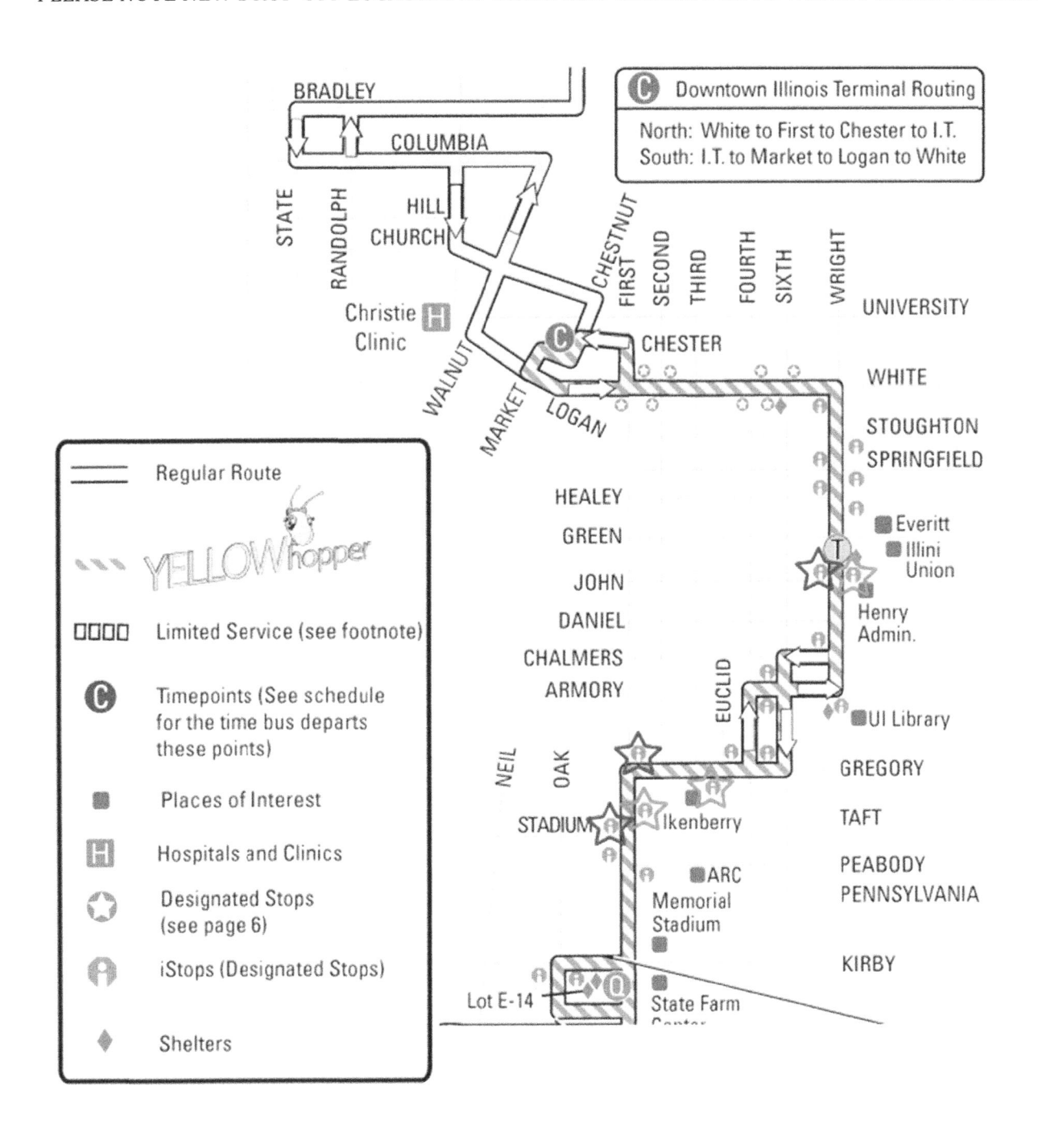

Downtown Illinois Terminal Routing
North: White to First to Chester to I.T.
South: I.T. to Market to Logan to White

Legend:
- Regular Route
- YELLOWhopper
- Limited Service (see footnote)
- C Timepoints (See schedule for the time bus departs these points)
- Places of Interest
- H Hospitals and Clinics
- Designated Stops (see page 6)
- iStops (Designated Stops)
- Shelters

The Gold Line picks up on the corner of First and Peabody, and also on Gregory Drive in front of Ikenberry Commons and drops off at the Krannert Center (across the street from CLSL-B). Return locations are across the street. Runs every ~10 minutes during the day (offset from the Yellow Line by 5 minutes).

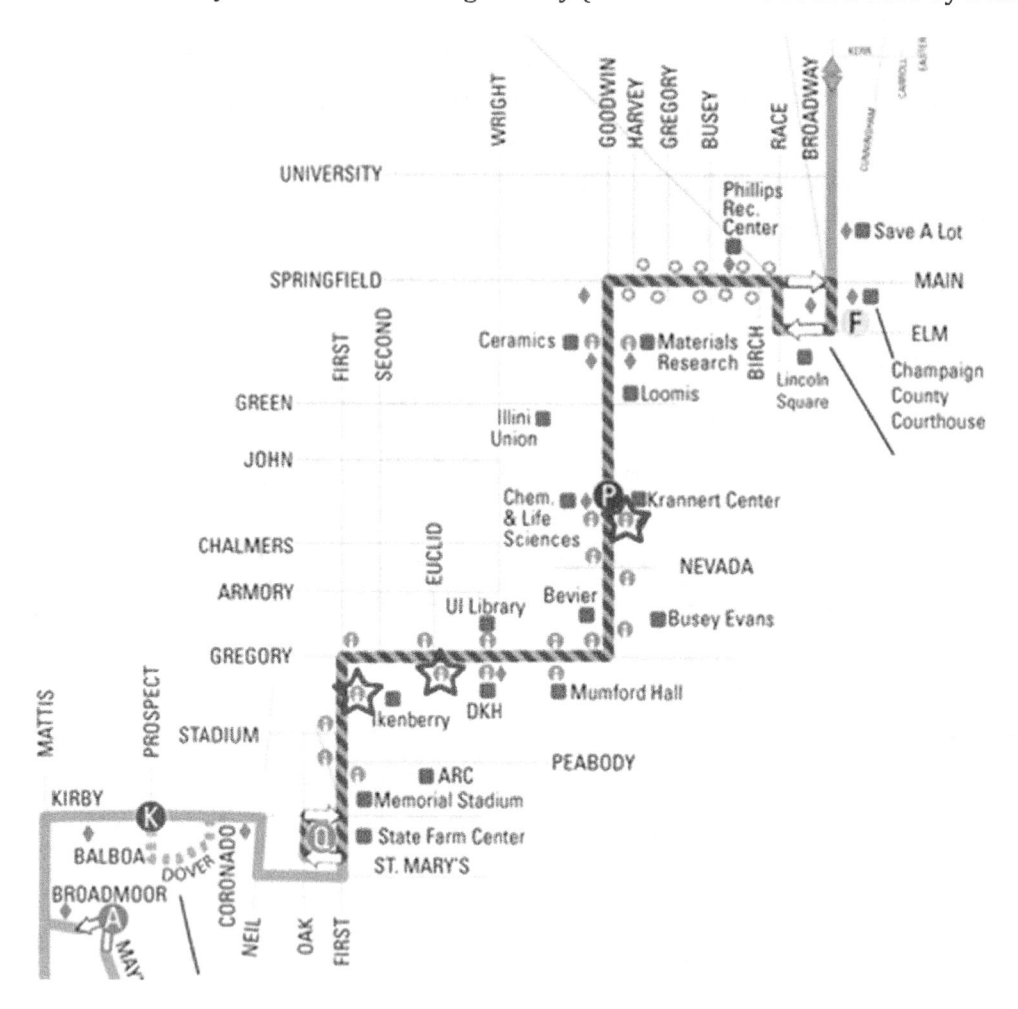

Bus Stops (Yellow Line = Left Down Arrow, Gold Line = Right Up Arrow, Foellinger Auditorium (Plenary) and Noyes Lab = Stars)

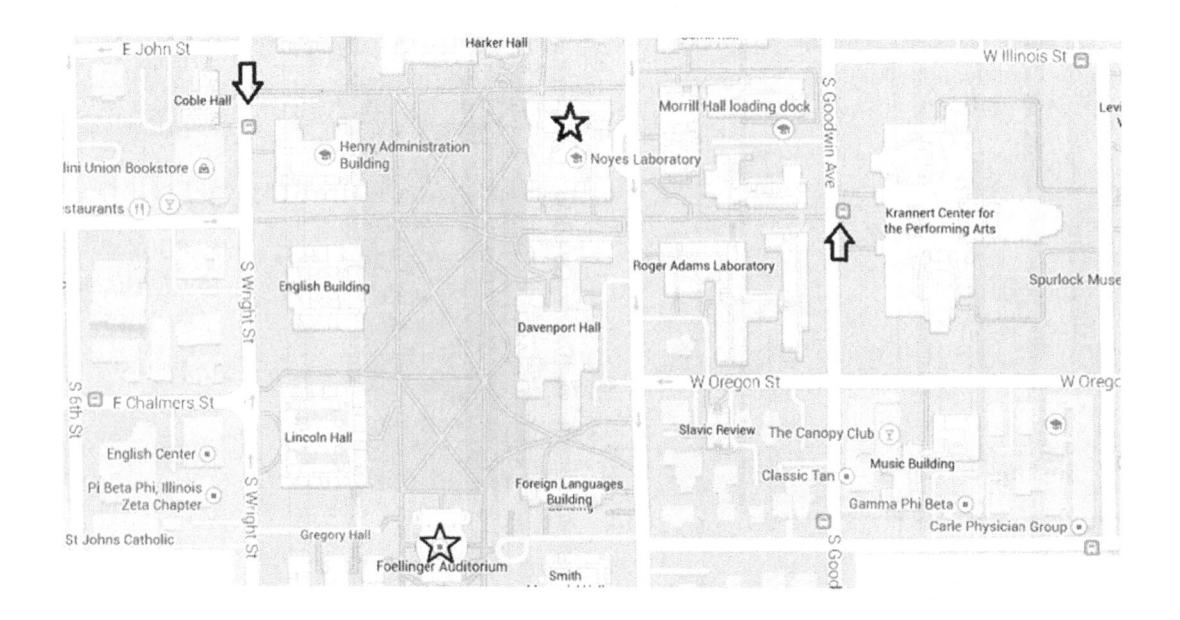

NOTES

NOTES

NOTES

NOTES

Made in United States
North Haven, CT
24 October 2022